The Accidental Public Servant

The Accidental Public Servant

Nasir Ahmad El-Rufai

Safari Books Ltd
Ibadan

Published by
Safari Books Ltd
Ile Ori Detu
1, Shell Close
Onireke, Ibadan.
Email: safarinigeria@gmail.com

© Nasir Ahmad El-Rufai

Publisher: Chief Joop Berkhout, OON
Deputy Publisher: George Berkhout

Advisor: Ismail Abubakar Tsiga
Editors: Dele Olojede
                       Muyiwa Adekeye
                       'Seni Pinheiro

Cover Design: Mike Adetona
                       Emmanuel Osanaiye

First published 2013
Reprinted: February 2013

All rights reserved. This book is copyright and so no part of it may be reproduced, stored in a retrieval system, or transmitted, in any form or by any means, electronic, mechanical, electrostatic, magnetic tape, photocopying, recording or otherwise, without the prior written permission of the author.

ISBN: 978-978-8431-30-5   Cased
ISBN: 978-978-8431-31-2   Paperback

Dedication

To the loving memory of Yasmin El-Rufai

1986-2011

Contents

Dedication	*v*
Photo Sections	*ix*
List of Abbreviations and Acronyms	*xi*
Foreword	*xvii*
Acknowledgements	*xxi*
Introduction	*xxvii*
Prologue	*xxxv*
Chapter One: Humble Origins	1
Chapter Two: The Calm Before the Storm	33
Chapter Three: From Abacha to Obasanjo – A Series of Accidents	51
Chapter Four: Taking Charge of Privatisation and Policy Reform	73
Chapter Five: "You Will See the Meaning of Power"	89
Chapter Six: The Enemy of My Enemy is My Friend – Unless the Friend is El-Rufai	131
Chapter Seven: The Economic Team – Key Players	155
Chapter Eight: Abuja – The Economic Reform Laboratory	197
Chapter Nine: Land Reforms	239
Chapter Ten: Sale of Government Houses in Abuja	263
Chapter Eleven: Restoring the Abuja Master Plan	277
Chapter Twelve: A Large Construction Site	301
Chapter Thirteen: Reforming the Public Service	313

Chapter Fourteen:	Covert Battles	329
Chapter Fifteen:	From Bad to Worse	355
Chapter Sixteen:	Exile	385
Chapter Seventeen:	Five Years of Invaluable Experience	415

Epilogue		481
Afterword		491
Endnotes		493
Appendix 1	Correspondence on Mambilla House	533
Appendix 2	Ahmad Rufai's application for employment	536
Appendix 3	Reimbursable pay to two Special Assistants	538
Appendix 4	Weekly Briefing on Privatizations	540
Appendix 5	FCT Senate Hearings Correspondence	543
Appendix 6	Functus Officio documents - FEC	556
Appendix 7	"Land Grab" details	562
Appendix 8	FCT Executive Committee Attendance	571
Appendix 9	Official Gazette	575
Appendix 10	Justice Bashir Sambo Correspondence	580
Appendix 11	Obasanjo's apology letter to the Senate	606
Appendix 12	Withdrawal of Consular Assistance	607
Appendix 13	Musa Yar'Adua letter to Ahmad Rufai	609
Appendix 14	Charles Okah's prison letter	611
Index		615

Photo Sections

Section I

Section II

Section III

List of Abbreviations and Acronyms

3G	Good Governance Group
AAV	Abuja Automotive Village
ABU	Ahmadu Bello University
AC	Action Congress
ACN	Action Congress of Nigeria
AD	Alliance for Democracy
ADC	Aide de Camp
ADP	Agricultural Development Project
AEA	Abuja Enterprise Agency
AGIS	Abuja Geographic Information Systems
AICL	Abuja Investment Company Ltd.
AIPDC	Abuja Investment and Property Development Company Ltd.
AIT	African Independent Television
AMAC	Abuja Municipal Area Council
AMMA	Abuja Metropolitan Management Agency
AMP	Advanced Management Programme
ANPP	All Nigeria Peoples' Party
AP	African Petroleum Plc
APGA	All Progressives Grand Alliance

APP	All Peoples' Party
ATV	Abuja Technology Village
AUST	African University of Science and Technology
BASA	Bilateral Air Services Agreement
BOBA	Barewa College Old Boys' Association
BP	British Petroleum
BPE	Bureau of Public Enterprises
BPSR	Bureau of Public Service Reforms
C of O	Certificate of Occupancy
CAC	Corporate Affairs Commission
CAN	Christian Association of Nigeria
CBN	Central Bank of Nigeria
CCECC	China Civil Engineering Construction Company Ltd
CCT	Code of Conduct Tribunal
CDMA	Code Division Multiple Access
CPC	Congress for Progressive Change
CPS	Career Public Servants
CRC	Current Replacement Cost
CSO	Chief Security Officer
DFID	Department for Overseas Development (now UK Aid)
DG	Director-General
DPP	Democratic Peoples Party
ECA	Excess Crude Account
EFCC	Economic and Financial Crimes Commission
EIU	Economist Intelligence Unit
EMIS	Education Management Information System

EOI	Expression of Interest
EPCC	Economic Policy Coordinating Committee
EPSR	Electric Power Sector Reform
ES	Executive Secretary
ESP	Education Sector Plan
FACA	FCT Action Committee on AIDS
FBI	Federal Bureau of Investigations
FCC	Federal Capital City (official name of Abuja City)
FCDA	Federal Capital Development Authority
FCSC	Federal Civil Service Commission
FCT	Federal Capital Territory
FCT EXCO	FCT Executive Committee
FCTA	Federal Capital Territory Administration
FEC	Federal Executive Council
FEEDS	FCT Economic Empowerment and Development Strategy
FGN	Federal Government of Nigeria
FIRS	Federal Inland Revenue Service
FIU	Financial Intelligence Unit of the EFCC
FMBN	Federal Mortgage Bank of Nigeria
FT	Financial Times of London
G-53	Group of 53 Concerned Citizens of Nigeria (precursor to SNG)
GMB	General Muhammadu Buhari
GSM	Global System for Mobile Communications
HBS	Harvard Business School
HIPC	Highly Indebted Poor Countries
HKS	Harvard Kennedy School of Government

HSE	Health, Safety and Environment
IBB	Ibrahim Badamasi Babangida
ICPC	Independent Corrupt Practices Commission
IFC	International Finance Corporation
IMF	International Monetary Fund
INEC	Independent National Electoral Commission
IOCs	International Oil Companies
IPA	International Planning Associates
IPPIS	Integrated Payroll and Personnel Information System
IQS	Institute of Quantity Surveyors
JBN	Julius Berger Nigeria Plc
LP	Labour Party
LSE	London School of Economics
MDAs	Ministries, Departments and Agencies of Government
MFA	Ministry of Foreign Affairs
MFCT	Ministry of Federal Capital Territory
NAFDAC	National Agency for Food and Drugs Administration and Control
NASS	National Assembly of the Federal Republic of Nigeria
NCP	National Council on Privatisation
NC	National Conference
NECO	National Examinations Council
NEEDS	National Economic Empowerment and Development Strategy
NIA	National Intelligence Agency
NIQS	Nigerian Institute of Quantity Surveyors

NITEL	Nigeria Telecommunications Limited
NNPC	Nigerian National Petroleum Corporation
NOLCHEM	National Oil and Chemical Marketing Plc
NPRC	National Political Reform Conference
NSA	National Security Adviser
NYSC	National Youth Service Corps
OHCSF	Office of the Head of the Civil Service of the Federation
OLPC	One Laptop Per Child
OMV	Open Market Value
OPM	Owner-President Management Programme
PDP	Peoples Democratic Party
PIMCO	Programme Implementation and Monitoring Committee
POH	Political Office Holders
PP	Private Practice
PPA	Power Purchase Agreement
PPP	Public Private Partnership
PSRT	Public Service Reform Team
PSTF	Petroleum (Special) Trust Fund (sometimes abbreviated as PTF)
PTDF	Petroleum Technology Development Fund
QS	Quantity Surveying (or Surveyor)
R of O	Right of Occupancy
RICS	Royal Institution of Chartered Surveyors
SAN	Senior Advocate of Nigeria
SAP	Structural Adjustment Programme
SDMP	Social Democratic Mega Party
SGF	Secretary to the Government of the Federation

SLGP	State and Local Governments Programme of UK DFID
SMEDAN	Small and Medium Scale Enterprises Development Agency of Nigeria
SNG	Save Nigeria Group
SSCE	Senior Secondary Certificate Examination
SSS	State Security Service
STDA	Satellite Towns Development Agency
TCPC	Technical Committee on Privatisation and Commercialisation
UAE	United Arab Emirates
UK	United Kingdom
UN	United Nations
US	United States
USA	United States of America
USAID	United States Agency for International Development
VAT	Value Added Tax
VP	Vice President
WASC	West African School Certificate

Foreword

I first heard about Mallam Nasir El-Rufai from a distance through the press early in 2000. It was not until our mutual friend, Sarah Omakwu, Senior Pastor, Family Worship Centre, Abuja, gave me a firsthand account of the good job he was doing as the then Minister for the Federal Capital Territory in 2005, that I began to pay any attention to him as a public servant.

It was even much later, in early 2010 that our paths crossed for the first time in Dubai. So, it came as a surprise, albeit a pleasant one, when he asked me to write this foreword to his maiden book – The Accidental Public Servant. It is a pleasant surprise because it is a manifestation of the truism of the adage that in any meaningful human relationship, it is not just how long but also how well that matters. For, since our first meeting almost three years ago, there has been no one week that we did not speak; just as there has been no one month that we did not meet at least once. The relationship has become so close such that he stays with my family when in Lagos as I spend time with his when in Abuja. Thus, I have gotten to know the real man – Nasir El-Rufai as a very dear friend and brother.

It is character that maketh the man! In getting to know Nasir, I have gotten to know an exceedingly courageous, inherently honest, highly intelligent, extremely loyal, humble and, above all, a God fearing man. He is a rare gem in our nation and in our time. These personality traits provide the underpinning for the friendship we have enjoyed as I do not make friends easily. They also constitute the rationale for his decisions and actions throughout his nine-year stint in public service. After all, it is virtually impossible to separate the man from his deeds, just as the Scriptures I live my life by says: "a man shall be judged by his deeds" (Romans 2:6).

Thus, this book is a must read for anyone that wants to know Nasir well, up close and personal, without the benefit of the close day to day relationship I have enjoyed with him. Even to those who know him as a friend or an acquaintance, the book is also highly recommended; if only to fully understand the rationale behind the seemingly controversial decisions he took whilst in office. Above all, students, academics, historians, administrators, managers, politicians, public servants and the general public at large would benefit immensely from learning a thing or two about how to protect the greater public good rather than the narrow personal interest.

The book is as lucid as it is most revealing. The rare but necessary prerequisites for a successful career in public service by way of decency, integrity and hard work are implicit throughout the book; right from the Prologue on the "Third Term" debacle – a scintillating insider revelation that put paid to the notion of plausible deniability, through 'Humble Origins' in Chapter One, to the explicit reference in Covert Battles in Chapter Fourteen.

In this book, Nasir enumerates four cardinal points which governed his orientation and disposition as a public servant. First is a detribalised, religiously neutral, humanistic view of the Nigerian person - whether good or bad; next, is an acknowledgment of the intrinsic strategic rationality that is inherent to human thinking and conduct which gauges interests and intentions in the light of enlightened self-interest in order to negotiate fair and favourable outcomes. The third idea is the belief in the conditioned reflexive response to sanctions and incentives as a basic tool for shaping human conduct irrespective of race, gender or age; and finally the poignant awareness of the stark disparity in Nigeria, between publicly-owned/managed enterprises/institutions and privately owned/run organizations particularly in terms of system efficiency and quality of human resources. In his own words:

> "This is essentially what was wired into my brain well before I was appointed to head the BPE. These four guiding principles played roles in defining our hiring practices, in the pursuit of restructuring the BPE, and in the design and aggressive implementation of the privatisation and commercialization programme from 1999 to 2003. I do not think it is any coincidence that by the end of my nearly four

years there, people across the political spectrum considered the Bureau of Public Enterprises to be one of the most respectable public institutions in the country, a big change from what it had become towards the end of 1999 – a dysfunctional and low-morale institution with more deputy directors than real staff."

The foregoing is in essence the story of The Accidental Public Servant and of Mallam Nasir El-Rufai. I hope you enjoy reading it and find it informative and insightful as I have. Our nation is in dire need of more capable, competent and decent public servants like Nasir; to make the country better and greater during our lifetime. This is my calling and what I have dedicated the remainder of my life to achieve. Please join us in making the goal a reality.

Tunde Bakare
Lagos,
Nigeria. 2012

Acknowledgements

As an avid reader and a lover of books, I have always had a healthy dose of respect for authors. This respect has increased dramatically as I navigated through more than three years of writing this book, starting with an outline in Aspen, Colorado in July 2009. I did not realize how difficult it is to write even a story in which one is intimately involved. I can only imagine how much tougher it is to write accounts in which one is not a principal actor. I therefore owe debts of gratitude to many people who played various roles in getting this book written, and supporting me while I tried putting it together. The sheer number of helpers means it is impractical to name them all, but I owe a special debt of gratitude to the following people:

My immediate family, particularly my late father, Mallam Ahmad Rufai Muhammad and my mother Fatima Umma El-Rufai laid all the foundations. My father's last wish was an admonition to me to take reading, learning and education as a serious, lifetime duty. My mother reminded me of this constantly and brought me up strictly to know the difference between right and wrong, and avoid wrongdoing that would tarnish our family name. My uncle, the late Alhaji Hamza Gidado, my cousin, Mallam Yahaya Hamza, and his kind-hearted wife, Guggo Zuwaira, continued this traditional upbringing that defined my worldview. I remain eternally grateful to them.

My brothers AVM Ali Rufai and Bashir El-Rufai, and my spouses Hadiza, Asia and Ummi, are not only important parts of my story in public service and after, but their collective sacrifices and unstinting devotion and love provided the crucial ingredients that I needed to write the book. My lovely children were equally self-sacrificial and unconditionally devoted. I am grateful to them all.

The period of writing this book was partly spent in exile. My brother and mentor, Bashir El-Rufai has always been singularly there for me. He encouraged this project actively, made exile less unbearable by accommodating me for a period in his home in Sharjah, near Dubai, and always supported me financially through my most difficult times. I remain grateful to him and his wonderful family.

My first wife Hadiza had to not only bear the burden of direct attacks by the Yar'Adua government, but also keep our family together by providing the extra support that my elder children needed to pass through those challenging times. I was lucky to have the Isma sisters as in-laws: Fatima Abdullahi, Furera Jumare, Maryam Muazu and Rabi Isma, that helped Hadiza to remain stable and grounded during the persecution period. Maryam also looked after one of our sons who lived with her for two years while attending elementary school in Maryland. I remain grateful for their continuous support.

With my second wife Asia and our younger children mostly in Nigeria during my exile, it wasn't any easier for them either. The love and support of Asia's family enabled me to have the peace of mind to write this story. I am grateful to Hajiya Hafsatu Garba Saeed (Maman Gusau), Kadaria Ahmed, Faika Ahmed and Zainab Marshall for the support given to Asia and my children.

My third wife Ummi Haliru not only encouraged me with her genuine care and support; but with her eagle eyes, reviewed the earlier and concluding drafts of this book, modifying language and raising observations about context and events that vastly improved the content and narration of the story. I am particularly grateful to her and her family for their affection and belief in me during those challenging years.

Issam Darwish is a person of rare kindness, and not surprisingly a close friend of my brother Bashir. Issam provided the apartment in Dubai from which most of this book was researched, written and re-written over the three year period. I am very grateful to him. Omar Ibrahim El-Beloushi was my sponsor and business partner in Dubai in those difficult days, and I remain appreciative of his support and encouragement.

My ever-reliable brother Idris Othman, my Nigerian lawyers Bamidele Aturu, Abdul-Hakeem Mustapha, Kanu Agabi, and Akin Olujimi, collaboratively defended my name and reputation in Nigeria during my exile and continued when I returned home. Without the support and encouragement of these friends and distinguished professionals, I might have given up on the project even before starting.

Writing does not come naturally to me, as I am more comfortable with numbers than words. Ulysses De La Torre and James Kimer helped get me started by recording the series of stories, interviews and answers to questions derived from my Aspen outline that constituted the primary foundation for this book. My lawyers abroad, Jared Genser and Bob Amsterdam, and the Washington publicist Riva Levinson, coaxed me out of bouts of lethargy to keep writing, even when under incessant attack by the Yar'Adua-Jonathan administration.

I am forever thankful to God for a few friends that have been pillars of support both in and out of public office. This circle of friends, brothers and sisters, particularly Idris Othman, Tijjani Abdullahi, Dr. Angela Onwuanibe, Husaini Dikko, Balarabe Abbas Lawal, Sagir Hamidu, Alhaji Aminu Saleh, Alhaji Ahmadu Chanchangi, Pastor Sarah Omakwu, Kabir Shuaibu, Dr. Goke Adegoroye, Osita Chidoka, Tanimu Yakubu, and Oby and Chinedu Ezekwesili took turns keeping an eye on me and my family members. I am grateful to them and their families for the love and care, without which this book would not have been written.

Idris Othman, Uba Sani, Husaini Dikko,
Hakeem Belo-Osagie and Jimi Lawal supported me materially and emotionally during these most difficult and challenging years. They were all unquestioning in their loyalty and belief in me even when I began to doubt my ability to withstand the viciousness and vindictiveness of the Nigerian government. Tijjani and Jimi also read and re-read several drafts of the book, contributed to the editing and reminded me of many forgotten events that took place in the BPE and FCT that ended up enriching the book.

Pastor Tunde Bakare, *egbon mi atata*, deserves special mention because he became another elder brother virtually from the first moment we met in March 2010. He has been a source of strength, inspiration, and spiritual and material support since then, while also leading me into activism with the Save Nigeria Group and into opposition politics with the Congress for Progressive Change. I am grateful that he became an integral part of my life in many ways, and for writing the foreword to this book.

Dele Olojede and I met face to face for the first time at an Aspen Institute seminar in 2006, and bonded instantly. More than anyone, Dele encouraged me to write pieces for his magnificent newspaper, NEXT, and also this story as a necessary public service. Dele also helped read and re-read the earliest drafts, undertaking extensive editing of the drafts, making suggestions to improve clarity and consistency that is the hallmark that earned him a Pulitzer Prize in Journalism. Whenever I got discouraged about writing, Dele was there to remind me that my story needs telling to make our country a better place. I am not sure of this, but I sure hope Dele is right that this book helps in a small way to make our public service and politics even a little better. He also graciously accepted my request to write the afterword for the book. My heartfelt appreciation goes to this true friend, brilliant writer and passionate patriot.

Peter Akagu Jones has been my assistant and personal administrator before, during and after my public service years. He kept my diaries, correspondence and the official files, and meticulous notes of conversations and meetings. Without Peter's patience, intelligence and dedication, the level of detail and accuracy required for this book would never have been attainable. In his absence, Umar Farouk Saleh took over many of these roles with ease. My close circle of family and friends including Mohammed Salihu, Japheth Omojuwa, Mohammed Bello El-Rufai, Tijjani Abdullahi, Hadiza Bala Usman, Amina Othman, James Bura Mamza, Roz Ben-Okagbue, Dr. Omano Edigheji, Salisu Suleiman and Ajayi Olatunji Olowo all helped review earlier drafts and gave me their frank and varied perspectives which led to extensive rewriting and changes to the script. I am grateful to all of them.

Embarking on a project such as writing about experiences in government is risky. Even those involved may end up disowning or denying one's version of events. Asue Ighodalo, Husaini Dikko, Nuhu Ribadu, Oby Ezekwesili, Dele Olojede and Muyiwa Adekeye gave extensive and often conflicting points of view on the effort which resulted in this book being written. Some encouraged me to write while others were far more cautious. I am grateful to all of them, but in the end take full responsibility for the decision to go ahead with the story as well as any errors contained in the book.

My faithful and remarkable media adviser Muyiwa Adekeye deserves special mention. He not only kept me out of trouble in the public space many times, but suggested many exclusions and inclusions for this story. He also gave insights into what public expectations are regarding a book of this nature, read the script several times and made excellent improvements. I am particularly grateful to him.

Many friends and white knights in the media and public commentariats were helpful in various ways throughout my tenure and the interesting years after I left office. I am particularly grateful to Dele Olojede, Kadaria Ahmed, Kayode Akintemi, Musikilu Mojeed, Omoyele Sowore, Dr. Pius Adesanmi, Philip Adekunle, Idang Alibi, Sam Nda Isaiah, Sam Amuka-Pemu, Gbenga Adefaye, Nduka Obaigbena, Segun Adeniyi, Kayode Komolafe, Ijeoma Nwogwugwu, Constance Ikokwu, Emeka Izeze, Martins Oloja, Emmanuel Asiwe and Yomi Odunuga for their support at all times.

The early ideas of writing about my years in the FCT came from one of my special assistants in the FCT Administration, Amina Salihu, and two journalists, Shamsudeen Adeiza and Tunji Ajibade. Shamsudeen went ahead to write and publish his work that will soon be ready for presentation, along with another book on my years in FCT, by Tunji Ajibade. The passion of these two author-journalists pushed me to try writing my own version of events not only to cover the FCT years but partly to include some of the BPE years. I want to thank them for the inspiration and encouragement to write this book, and their willingness to delay presentation of their works until this book is completed.

My first literary attempt would have ended up as another incomplete project but for the intervention of Chief Joop Berkhout and his energetic young son, George Berkhout. The two publishing partners pushed and encouraged me to complete a rough draft and then handed that over to two outstanding professionals who polished and rendered my modest effort into a readable material. Professor Ismaila Abubakar Tsiga was my senior in Barewa College and FCT colleague who offered to help do an initial review of the draft. His experience as an author, public servant and teacher substantially improved the context and content of the book. This was further sharpened and made clearer by the awesome editing skills of Safari Book's editorial manager, Seni Pinheiro. Dele Olojede then undertook another review and editing of the improved work. If this book turns out to be readable and sensible, it is the result of the surgery done by Professor Tsiga, Seni Pinheiro, and Dele Olojede, even if all the errors remain mine. I thank them for trying to make a writer out of the applied mathematician that I think I am!

Nasir Ahmad El-Rufai
Abuja, Nigeria
October 2012

Introduction

"The Accidental Public Servant" was not the original title for this book. The phrase was used by a Harvard Kennedy School publicist who interviewed me as part of the 50th Anniversary of the Mason Fellows Programme and I liked it. I thought it a fitting description of someone who never purposefully set out to be a public servant, but rather fell into it through a series of accidents – strokes of luck met with fortuitous preparedness – that landed me in the stormy waters of Nigerian politics and governance. Nearly nine years after the first accident, I left public service as a well-known minister and loyalist of President Olusegun Obasanjo and since May 2007, I have gone through a roller coaster period of surviving attacks on my person and family, sustained smear campaigns, death threats, persecution at home and abroad through withdrawal of my Nigerian citizenship, malicious prosecution and involuntary exile, on the one hand. On the other hand, I have received awards and recognitions for my service, particularly for bringing order into the chaos that was Abuja, our nation's capital. All these constitute major departures from what I thought was my life plan.

As a child, when I first conceived of the idea of what I might want to be when I grow up, my role model at the time was the single native authority policeman in my village of Daudawa, in Katsina state. What called my attention to him was the uniform. The first time I ever saw a thief was when the policeman, passing through the village, single-handedly apprehended him as he was breaking into people's houses to steal their belongings. My admiration for his valour made me fall in love with the job and the uniform. Then at about the age of six I was circumcised and I met the village doctor. He was not actually a doctor, but a paramedic, yet he looked so clean and professional in his crisp, clean and starched white uniform, and was so kind, that I believed I had to be a doctor when I grew up. As I grew a little older, I realized that the agricultural officer who was the head of the local agricultural settlement and who lived in the Daudawa Government Reservation Area (GRA) was not only my father's boss, but the most important man in town, so then I wanted to be an agricultural officer, and then at the outbreak of the civil war that saw two of my brothers join the army, and another the air force, I thought of joining the armed forces. This series of aspirations and adjustments remained a regular feature of my youth, and I guess, is typical of most people of my generation. What I did not realize then was that it would be assignments, never sought for, rather than ambition that would define my private and public life.

There were other public service and government figures featuring somewhat prominently in my upbringing, but what loomed even larger was the fact of growing up poor. We were many children under my father's roof in Daudawa – eight siblings growing up together and six other siblings that had grown up and gone on to establish their own families. The first time I got a 'hand-me-down' pair of shoes was when I was six years old. I got my own first pair of new shoes when I was eight. Until today, I feel more comfortable barefooted than in socks and shoes!

As a result of these privations, I was driven to achieve financial independence as quickly as I could. In an environment of poverty, one learns quickly that financial independence is essential to preserving one's dignity. Another seminal event from that period of my life was the death of my father, which also occurred when I was about eight years old. His final words to me were about the importance of education, specifically that my success in life would be determined by how seriously I pursued knowledge. So I worked hard and took my studies seriously because I was led by my father to believe that it would be the key to preserving one's dignity and self-respect.

On the way to achieving that goal, a path that initially led me into the private sector as a consulting quantity surveyor, a funny thing happened. I realized that in order for the private sector to flourish, the public sector needed a certain minimum level of functionality. What made this thinking novel to me was that for the longest time, like others aspiring to middle-class status in Nigeria, I thought that if I just made enough money, I could buy all the things I needed. If the public electricity supply was inefficient, I would just buy a diesel-powered generator. If the public water supply was not working, I would simply construct my own household borehole and install a water treatment plant. However, there came a point when I realized that even if one had those, one cannot build one's own gasoline refinery. When one woke up one morning, as we did in 1996, to find that all of a sudden there was no gasoline for the electric generator and the cars – and this, in a country that was the ninth largest exporter of crude oil in the world – a whole new level of thinking became inevitable. To provide social services: security of life and property, decent schools, health facilities, and even a financial system - required collective action, some level of collaboration between individuals. To provide or enable the creation of functional infrastructure – like transportation, communications and electricity networks, for example – a strong and effective public service was essential.

Twice before getting to that point, I had declined invitations in 1989 and 1991 to work in the public service of my state of residence - Kaduna. Once I came to this point of realization however, I made up my mind that if I got another opportunity to work in the public sector, I would not only accept, but would do nothing but my very best. As it turned out, the very attributes that drove me to be financially independent early in life — my dedication to ongoing study and education, and honesty not just in dealing with others but also with myself — were the selfsame attributes that ultimately earned me the invitation to public service at the national level.

Certain people hold the opinion that I am feisty, argumentative and antagonistic – they formed those views about my personality based on media reports. Contrary to these perceptions however, it is neither intentional nor deliberate. I just believe in being honest with myself and with others and in speaking my mind frankly and preserving my dignity. In a society that now prizes sycophancy, hierarchy and tradition at the cost of courtesy, frankness and pragmatism, perhaps such characteristics are anomalous. Frankly however, I do not know any other way of being.

I have felt the calling to write this book for a few different reasons, all of near-equal importance. One is to make the case that public service is important – a necessary thing for every well-meaning Nigerian to consider in order to set our nation on the right track, so that it may attain the potential we all know it is capable of realizing. For developing countries like Nigeria, where institutions are weak and the capacity for people to help themselves is limited, a responsive public service is vital – it gives honest people the minimum base for them to lift themselves up by their bootstraps. There are certain things that an individual cannot achieve single-handedly; hence the mission of the public servant is really to solve collective, public problems.

Another reason I am writing this book is to convey a message to those already aspiring to a career in public service. To them I say: be prepared to be tested in ways impossible for you to foresee. What is practicable in one situation will not be possible in another situation, but there will be no shortage of voices surrounding you aiming to distract or persuade you from that fact. Although no reasonable person would disagree with the idea that the public sector can do with better management, more efficient processes and more transparent procurement of goods and services, quantifying the success or failure of any given initiative is by nature far more difficult in this sector than its application in the private sector.

A third reason I am writing this is a message for those that have opted out – the Nigerian Diaspora. My message to those of you in this category is very simple: The Nigerian public service needs you, but you can only succeed under certain conditions. Specifically, we need you to come home when you are financially independent and can stomach the pay cut that you will face when entering public service. You should make no mistake about it – you must come home at some point. We cannot improve as a nation without attracting our best and brightest human resources to the public sector. As things stand currently, we have surrendered the bulk of our political space to the dishonourable, the incompetent and worse, to the criminally-minded. This is the basic problem of Nigeria. The brightest Nigerians are either abroad, or at home in academia, in the military or the private sector - particularly in the telecommunications, oil and gas or financial services industries.

From
Muni S. Ali
08187376164

To

Kojima magsem

Room 748

This is an undeniable fact; the dregs of our society dominate the politics and have created a negative image that makes talented people spurn helping the country. So to those in the Diaspora who have achieved financial independence through merit and hard work, I say this: good for you, earn what you deserve which appears impossible to earn at home. Nonetheless, unless at some point you make the rational decision to come back and get your hands dirty with politics or public service, Nigeria will never work in our lifetimes.

This book is also an appeal to persons that have held public office to document their experiences and tell their sides of the story. I have made such appeals repeatedly to two persons in particular - Mallam Adamu Ciroma and Professor Jerry Gana. These exceptional individuals have served in three or four different administrations. Their public service record and personal stories would have helped first timers like me when sworn in as a Minister of the Government of the Federation on July 16, 2003. Alas, they had not, and still have not. While continuing to nag them to write, I hope this story will nudge them (and others) a little in the direction of documenting their rich and varied experiences. Another prominent Nigerian whose grass to grace story, complete with gubernatorial, ministerial, and presidential experiences, plus field experience in civil war, needs telling is General Muhammadu Buhari. His life story, snippets of which he has shared with me and Pastor Tunde Bakare at various points will paint the picture of a nation whose leaders at one time, professed, pursued and practised social justice. How we got to where we now are as a country will be apparent from Buhari's memoir, and I am gratified that our collective nudging has finally got him working on one.

Finally, I am writing this book to put on record my version of events, in my voice and in my own hand. Whether you are already familiar with the broad outlines of my story, or you are hearing my name for the first time, please read this with the following facts in mind: in the intervening two years between the time Umaru Yar'Adua emerged as the president of Nigeria and the onset of writing this book, I have suffered a lot of harassment. My house in Abuja has been invaded once by security agencies with my family imprisoned for hours.[1] Warrants have been obtained thrice to search my house for suspected "subversive materials."[2]

I have been serially investigated by various committees of the National Assembly[3] and by virtually every regulatory and law enforcement agency in Nigeria.[4] I have been accused of phantom crimes and declared a wanted man by the Yar'Adua administration with empty but media-grabbing threats of arrest by the Interpol,[5] extradition[6] and so on. Yet the same government ordered all Nigerian diplomatic missions not to renew my passport when I completed my studies and announced plans to return home!

In the face of politically motivated persecution of my person, friends and family, I have protested and maintained my innocence of all the allegations and consistently issued statements to explain my own side of the story. I have filed several lawsuits against the federal government and its agencies,[7] companies and individuals[8] that have attempted to impugn my integrity and mounted a vigorous defence against the single criminal case the Nigerian government has launched against me.[9] These are all ongoing developments and remain open questions as I write this story. At my age and in my political circumstance, writing a book that attempts to open the black box of politics and governance in Nigeria is a very risky endeavour. Deciding what experiences to reveal and what to leave out, exposing oneself to risks of being accused of having an agenda even when there is none, and avoiding early and premature judgments continue to be issues at every point of writing. There is also the greater risk of what I have written being used as evidence of some undesirable tendency of mine.

My many friends and family members played important roles in guiding me in my attempts to resolve some of these conflicts. I take solace in this regard in the words of Nelson Mandela to the effect that only a fool refuses to change his mind when confronted with new facts and better information. My life is still evolving, and I am still learning, so no views expressed here are as sacrosanct as a religious text. I am open to change as I learn more. I am still grateful to my friends for helping me to understand better some of these tricky matters.

My life and personal history are of little interest except insofar as certain events and experiences have shaped my preparation for public service. My years in government – about nine in all, and the aftermath – are too short to present more than a snapshot of the challenges of being in public service and politics in a developing country like Nigeria. So this is neither a full-scale autobiography nor a memoir because I think it is premature at my age, and I have achieved too little to write either an autobiography or a memoir. This is simply a story of my years in government and after; the autobiographical style and context just lay the foundation for why I think the way I think and why I took the actions I took when I was in public service.

What I found in my public service career was sobering, to say the least. I would not say my experiences made me more hopeful, or more cynical; and while I found some aspects of public service a pleasant surprise, there were certainly others that I consider a big disappointment. For instance, the aftermath of my years in government, during which I experienced betrayal by some friends and relations, the concoction of falsehoods against me and my loyal friends, the smear and persecution, and the widespread suspicion that once a minister even for a day, one must have looted public funds are both typical and painful experiences, but part of the price one pays in order to make one's nation function even slightly better. Ultimately, the experience is hardly different from the normal pattern in human life: the dissonance between what one anticipates and what one actually finds – no matter how much one studies something, reads about it, thinks about it, hears about it - is no substitute for one to actually do and experience it directly. This is the crux of the story I intend to narrate here.

In narrating this story, I have tried my best to be accurate and factual, and in describing persons and events with minimal judgment and use of adjectives. I have just one motive in mind - to tell the story of my public service years to prepare the younger generation for the sorts of challenges they may face. As a human being, I am bound to have erred or recollected events differently. I apologize in advance to those that would beg to differ with my version of events, and suggest they should write theirs. That is the only way more and more people would understand our government and governance, for the better, too.

Nasir Ahmad El-Rufai
Abuja,
November, 2012

Prologue:

The Beginning of the End

"No third term – no Nigeria."
– President Olusegun Obasanjo,
February 2006

There it was – confirmation from the man himself of what I, not to mention the rest of the country, had suspected for months. The words hung in the night time air as I contemplated how to respond. I knew immediately what I was thinking though. I was thinking that he was wrong and that this sort of manoeuvring was not at all what I signed up for when I first agreed to join the Obasanjo Administration in 1999. Hearing President Obasanjo saying these words did not surprise me as much as it disappointed me. For it was obvious to anyone who was even remotely paying attention at that point in early 2006, that there was some sort of effort underway to secure him a third presidential term. What had up until that point remained elusive was any clear confirmation that the man himself had thought about it, wanted it, or was even aware of it. There, that evening, in the lush gardens outside the main residence but within the sprawling estate known as the Presidential Villa, with a single phrase, the president had emerged from behind the shadows of plausible deniability.

I do not remember where or when I first became aware of the actual phrase, 'plausible deniability', but the gist of it, that some powerful person might arrange for some act to be undertaken on their behalf via a third party in order to avoid any connection with the said act, had by 2006 become an Obasanjo trademark. With the benefit of hindsight and the roller coaster ride that was my relationship with the former president, it is difficult for me to pinpoint exactly when things began to go wrong, but I think it was in early 2005 when we on the economic reform team began to hear rumours of a plan for a third presidential term. As was usual for me, after hearing various versions of it a couple of times, I spoke about it with my closest working colleagues at the time, Finance Minister Ngozi Okonjo-Iweala, Economic and Financial Crimes Commission (EFCC) Chairman Nuhu Ribadu and Special Assistant to the President on Budget Monitoring Oby Ezekwesili. They said they were hearing similar rumours. Abuja is a city of rumours, so we let it pass. However, by February 2005, when the list of all government nominees to the National Political Reform Conference was made public, we thought that we should ask the President to confirm or deny the rumours. So as is usual with me, I went to President Obasanjo for the second time in two weeks to raise the subject.

"Mr. President we have been hearing stories about this tenure extension. Is it something in contemplation?" I asked him. His first response I thought odd, but it was only just the beginning.

"Look at me very well, Minister," he said. "Do you think I am looking for a job? I came out of prison, I was on my farm, I was begged to come and do this job. Now that we are about to finish this job, do you honestly think I would be looking for another job?"

"Well, are you looking for another job, Mr. President?" I asked.

"Certainly not," he said. "I am looking forward to May 29, 2007, I will go back to my farm and that is it."

"So there is no plan for any constitutional amendment on term limits, Mr. President?"

"Certainly not."

I left the president's office with a sense of relief after this conversation. I believed him because he was quite definite about it. In fact, he was a little bit irritated about my questions. To be fair to President Obasanjo, up until what came to be known to us as the 'Third Term' debacle, he was a man of his words that did not entertain rumours and gossip about such serious national issues. If one said something accusatory or unfair about another official to Obasanjo, it was typical of him to call the person immediately, put one and the person on speaker phone and demand that one repeat what one just said so that the person would have a chance to defend his honour! With that likelihood, one learnt never to tell Obasanjo something that one could not defend easily with facts and figures in the possible presence of the persons mentioned in the 'rumour'.

The rumours continued throughout most of 2005. Because a few of us in the economic reform team – Ngozi, Oby, Nuhu, and I – were considered very close to Obasanjo, many assumed us to be in the know about it. We were visibly implementing an economic reform programme that was on track: the Nigerian economy was booming, accumulating huge foreign reserves and a big savings account from excess oil revenues. However, for many outside our inner circle, these achievements were the justification for the third term project.

Indeed, I had a brief chat with a chieftain of one of the opposition political parties, the ANPP, while waiting for a flight from Lagos to Abuja in October 2010 during which he blamed the economic team for the failed third term attempt. He heard that we authored a memo to Obasanjo making a case for tenure elongation. Others take speeches Chukwuma Soludo and I made at the Murtala Mohammed Memorial Lecture in February 2007 about the Asian Tigers 'political continuity' as basis of attributing ideas of many years of PDP rule to us and other economic team members. All of these are innocent misrepresentations and completely untrue as far as I know.

The truth of the matter was that the third term project was believed by many of us in the administration, to have been initiated by Lagos businessmen who were looking to keep the economy undisturbed by a transfer of power. Since this economic boom all happened on Obasanjo's watch, according to the assumption, these Lagos businessmen wanted Obasanjo to have an extra four years. It was also around that time that some of our seminal macroeconomic achievements were realized. Among them, we got our $30 billion of Paris Club debt written off, and with the money saved government contracted to build seven new power stations using gas in the Niger Delta and South-West, and a brand new, modern national railway system. We also streamlined the management of the seaports for private sector use so that it would be easier to import and export. Many huge steps were being taken all in the same year and I think the business community saw that as a clear signal that if we fixed power and transportation, the biggest bottlenecks to business in Nigeria would be removed.

Who these Lagos businessmen were that were behind this idea remained unconfirmed, but several names were mentioned eventually and these repeatedly made the rounds in many circles in Abuja. Festus Odimegwu, the then chief executive officer of Nigerian Breweries, and Ndi Okereke Onyiuke, the head of the Stock Exchange, were alleged to have started it. They were reportedly supported by Nigeria's foremost industrialist and richest man Aliko Dangote, Tony Elumelu of the United Bank for Africa, Cecilia Ibru of Oceanic Bank and Jim Ovia of Zenith Bank. The logic behind the rumours is that the companies these people represented benefited on an unprecedented scale under our tenure and a third Obasanjo term surely would have enabled them to consolidate their gains and live happily ever after! Whether these rumours were true or not, fair or unfair, the presumption that these individuals and organizations benefited from the Obasanjo administration in the past, and stood to benefit if it remained in office, made virtually everyone in government declare them the prime movers of the tenure extension plan. I sounded out a few of them that I was in touch with and all denied knowledge of any such plot - just like Obasanjo!

The rumours, of course, increased. Unsatisfied, I decided to try again, and this time I approached Obasanjo's Chief of Staff, General Abdullahi Mohammed, who was also a mentor of sorts and had been close to Obasanjo for more than 40 years and asked him what he knew. His response was that he had certainly heard the rumours, had asked Obasanjo the same question and Obasanjo had denied everything. To me, this was very interesting, because if Obasanjo denied the existence of the third term project to his chief of staff it meant that either Obasanjo was not behind the project or the chief of staff was not trusted enough. The prospect of the chief of staff lying was, in my view, not a possibility – he was one of the few people I believed had integrity in public service in Nigeria at that time (and up till the time I am writing this). If he had known of such an effort, he would have admitted to me, but request that I should not share the knowledge with anyone. So I decided to believe Obasanjo was not behind the tenure elongation idea and that this was a private initiative of other politicians and businessmen trying to feather their nests.

Yet the rumours persisted. So early in September 2005, I went back to Obasanjo again and he had the same attitude – 'I do not need a job' – but this time he added a rider: "It is not my job to amend any constitution; it is the prerogative of the National Assembly. If the National Assembly chooses to amend the Constitution, I cannot stop them. I can veto it but they can override the veto."

Later in the year, some time after these series of conversations with Obasanjo, the ruling Peoples Democratic Party (PDP) published a document dated December 2005 titled "Declaration of Principles concerning amendments to the Nigerian Constitution" restating the views expressed to me earlier by Obasanjo as the official party position. This publication confirmed that the party leaders - Dr. Ahmadu Ali (Chairman), Ojo Maduekwe (National Secretary), Tony Anenih (Chairman, Board of Trustees), Bode George (National Vice Chairman, South-West) and Dr. Bello Halliru Mohammed (National Vice Chairman, North-West) strongly supported the 'constitutional amendments' – the phrase that later became the respectable-sounding pseudonym for the tenure elongation project.

The Benefit of Hindsight

After thinking about this addition of the rider by Obasanjo and sharing it with a few people, we concluded that indeed there was a project underway for a third term in office, but Obasanjo obviously did not want it to be public at that point. It was at that point that I remembered an event earlier in the year whose significance did not occur to me at the time it happened. In January 2005, the Economist Intelligence Unit (EIU) held its first roundtable with the government of Nigeria. The roundtable organizers approached us, the economic team, to collaborate, with me, as the FCT Minister, playing the prominent role of chief host. President

Obasanjo came and delivered a speech, as did I, along with some other cabinet ministers and business leaders.

The event wound up being a great success and in the end, the Economist's senior economist covering Nigeria, David Cowan, came to my house for dinner before leaving. He thanked me for my efforts in getting the roundtable organized, and said, "You know, our projections in The Economist's Intelligence Unit show that if Nigeria continues on its current trajectory, by the middle of 2007 when you guys hand over power, Nigeria will have about $40 billion of reserves and nearly $20 billion in your excess crude account (ECA)." At the time we had about $10 billion in the ECA. "Really?" I replied. "The numbers are going to be that big?"

"Well, that was our projection," he said. "And we are often right."

"Wow. That will be wonderful. So we will be leaving a nice legacy for the next administration."

He continued, "But you know something? I am an economist. I run these numbers, I conduct these scenarios and I see this. But you know someone else that knows? Your potential successors. They can smell the money. They know that the way you are going, by the middle of 2007, there will be a large amount of money in the bank. They are not economists, they do not know the numbers, but like dogs with raw meat, they can smell it."

"What are you telling me?" I asked.

"If your boss has not done so already, you guys have to start thinking about who is going to succeed you. Because the guys that want to steal already know there is a huge bank account in the future and they will start planning now. I have not seen anything indicative of a succession plan. You tell Obasanjo to start planning. Ok?"

When I asked him to share some of these figures with me, he said they were not yet authorized for publication.

"I cannot give you the numbers; I can't give you the projections. But I can tell you, this is what we see."

"Please tell the minister of finance, share this with her." I said.

"No. I am not telling the minister of finance. I am telling you."

"Why me?"

"Because throughout the roundtable, I observed that you have a different level of relationship with Obasanjo than Ngozi has."

I did not understand what he meant and I did not care initially. I promised him I would share it with the president. As soon as he was gone, I called President Obasanjo and arranged to meet him. He was at his farm in Otta for the New Year holidays.

When I arrived to discuss this issue, the president had a number of other officials and governors in the room for various meetings. Given the sensitivity of my news, I requested to speak to him alone, so he finished his consultations with everyone else and once it was just the two of us, I told him everything I had learned from the EIU economist. Almost the moment I began sharing this knowledge, President Obasanjo left the settee and sat down on the floor cross-legged, compelling me to do the same. So there we sat, secretively, like two little boys plotting to eat some candy we should not. You see, that gesture, which was involuntary – he did not realize he did it – leaving his chair to sit on the floor, said a lot about how important he considered the subject matter. Any time you are being conspiratorial with Obasanjo or something like that he wants to sit on the floor and bring you closer so that nobody else can hear. I think it has something to do with his military training and the suspicion that such rooms may be wiretapped for voice recordings. We sat there talking in hushed tones, only the two of us, in this huge living room. When I was finished, he thanked me for sharing this information with him.

"Did you know about this, Mr. President?" I asked.

"Not really." He paused, and then asked, "So what are we going to do?"

"Mr. President, I am just a messenger. My job is to give you the information. You are the president; it is up to you to figure out what to do with it."

"No Nasir, this is a problem for the country. What are we going to do? None of my prospective successors will make good use of this."

"Well who are those seriously interested in succeeding you?"

"(Vice President) Atiku is obviously interested, but you know I will never hand this over to him. Babangida is interested and you know very well what he will do with these levels of financial resources, he already showed his hand the last time he had the chance."

"But Mr. President, the point that the EIU economist was making is that the guys interested in succeeding you can already smell the money, so what are YOU going to do?"

"I do not know but we have to do something - Something drastic."

"Drastic?"

"Yes."

I remember that word – drastic, and he had started using the pronoun 'we', not 'I'. I left Ota for Abuja the same day in a pensive mood, thinking that the country was again at the crossroads. The leader we chose in 2007 would either make or mar the legacy of reforms we would leave behind, and invest or mismanage the accidental monetary windfall by way of reserves and excess crude oil earnings that had begun to build up by then. I prayed that Obasanjo and his political advisors would make the right choices and did not even direct my mind to the possibility that Obasanjo would want to stay on beyond 2007! Unknown to me, things would move in quick succession from that day of innocence to the emergence of the third term intrigues within weeks. It is an indication of my political naivety that I did not get it nor link the two issues until much later.

He Gets It Who Wants It Not

Shortly after that, President Obasanjo called me and said he had decided, because of persistent calls for a national conference[10] to discuss the future of the country, to convene a national political conference in Abuja. One of the mandates of the conference was to recommend which constitutional amendments are needed to make our democracy work better. Representatives from each state were to attend the conference and I was to nominate two persons from the Federal Capital Territory (FCT) to participate. We nominated retired General A. B. Mamman from Abaji to represent the original inhabitants of the FCT and Reverend Okoye, the chairman of the local chapter of Christian Association of Nigeria (CAN) and a pillar of the Igbo Community in Abuja, to represent everyone else. Later, one-time Abuja Municipal Area Council (AMAC) chairman Princess Esther Audu was nominated by President Obasanjo to represent special interests.

When I went to the president with the list and bio data of the FCT nominees, I decided to take the opportunity to ask Obasanjo for the first time about the rumours that had begun to circulate then, of a third term project. I got straight to the point.

"Mr. President – third term, has this conference got anything to do with the rumours of such a plan?" I asked.

"There is nothing like a third term being discussed at the conference. You will receive the conference agenda soon and see that the rumour is unfounded." I believed him and left convinced that the whole 'third term' rumour had no basis. I did not connect the rumour with the conversation we had in Ota a few weeks earlier, but the rumours did not go away.

At a point after the conference commenced in earnest, we became increasingly concerned that there was a 'third term agenda' even if the president was unaware of or sitting on the fence about it. We felt this strongly even though Obasanjo continued to completely deny it. I came to the conclusion that we were kept out of it because Obasanjo's political team either did not trust us, or thought we would not buy into such a major constitutional manipulation. I reflected deeply about the whole situation for some time and decided to confront Obasanjo for the last time and offer some advice. I met him in his office and asked again about 'third term' and got his standard, qualified denial of any such thing. I then offered what I considered to be my advice in the midst of the denials.

"Just listen to me. Please, Mr. President, do not interrupt me, sir. Let me speak first and then you can respond." He agreed. I continued, "We are hearing too many stories about this to believe that there is nothing like that. There is something. You have told me that the National Assembly can amend the constitution that is true, they can. You have convened a conference to recommend, among other issues, what parts of the constitution should be amended. After adding up the rumours to what you have said to me, and to what you have just done, I have come to the clear conclusion that there is a third term project. Now, I may be wrong, or I may be right. But Mr. President, let me give you my own piece of advice. I have studied you as a person; I have studied your life. I have come to the conclusion that the only things that you ever get in your life are those that you did not ask for, struggle for or fight to have."

I paused to let him digest this. He remained silent but exhibited some discomfiture. I went on, "Let me repeat sir. Throughout your life and your career, both professional and political, any time you made a move to get something you wanted, or took any active steps to get anything, you did not get it. The only time you got anything is when you sat back and let the desired thing come to you. That is your life pattern. I believe in that. I believe very much that everyone has something about him such that God blesses him in a particular way. There are people that can only get something when they work hard for it. Then there are those who just get it on a platter. If one does not understand what kind one is, and remain consistent, one would get it wrong often. In summary, what I am saying is this, Mr. President: if you want a third term, do not do anything to try to get it. Then you will probably get it, even though I think it is not a good idea. But if there is nothing like third term, or if I am wrong in my conclusions, then forgive me, and we have nothing to worry about."

Obasanjo looked at me, unwavering. "Are you finished?" he asked.

"I am done."

"Thank you."

"That is all?"

"Yes, that is all. Now get out of my office."

The National Political Reform Conference (NPRC) sat between February and July 2005. We got our Paris Club debt relief at the end of June 2005, and President Obasanjo presented the Report of the NPRC to the National Assembly on 26th July 2005, and its report and proceedings are matters of public record. However, I can say that the conference was not a complete exercise in futility in that certain important things were achieved. However, from the standpoint of achieving what the third term protagonists may have desired to say things did not quite go the way they wanted would be an understatement. None of the agreements and recommendations of the conference included or even touched upon flexibility regarding term limits. Instead, a movement even began to spring up promoting a single six-year term in lieu of two four-year terms for the office of the president. This, of course, did not stop allegations that Obasanjo encouraged a variety of gambits toward his aim: put one ethnic group against another, one religion against another, one gender against another, one northern group against one southern group, one northern group of one religion against another northern group of another faith, get the Niger Delta representatives to say they wanted 50% of oil revenues – all kinds of rumoured shenanigans. At the end of the day the national political conference was a giant waste of time and over N900 million, as far as presidential term limits were concerned.

Platter of Gold

I firmly stand by what I said to him that day with regard to life patterns and I believe that events since then have only proven my thesis correct. Obasanjo did not understand that any time he desired political or career advancement, anytime he took any step toward achieving any position, he never got it. If one reads Obasanjo's various biographies carefully, as I have several times, one will understand that pattern about his life. The only reason he became head of state the first time around was when his boss was killed. The only reason he became president the second time, when Chief Abiola died, was because someone from the southwest was needed as president to assuage the grievance arising from the annulment of the June 12 election which the deceased Abiola had won, and people like Generals Ibrahim Babangida and Aliyu Gusau came to him, drafted him, organized everything and handed it to him for what many people alleged was in pursuit of their interest and long-term survival. Obasanjo did not spend one penny to be president. It was all done for him by others and handed to him on a platter.

When he aspired to be Secretary-General of the United Nations in 1985, and even began learning French so that he would be bilingual, he lost to Boutrous-Ghali, despite being a far better candidate and having a much more formidable international profile than Boutros-Ghali. Any time Obasanjo made a move to want something; he did not get it, simple! When we had a political crisis in 1993 and Obasanjo desired to head the interim national government, he lost out to the less prominent Chief Ernest Shonekan the moment he made a couple of moves. This is how Obasanjo is, and I am not sure he thought that about his life until I laid it out to him. I am not even sure he ever took me seriously on that subject.

Still, he could not restrain himself and let things ride even if he believed what I thought about his life pattern.

Third Term's not a Charm

One day in late October 2005, an Ahmadu Bello University (ABU) alumnus and friend who chaired the board of a federal parastatal and was very close to Obasanjo, called to say we needed to talk. I invited him over for dinner, and following the meal we went into my study to discuss the issue that had simmered below the surface during dinner.

"I want to talk to you about the third term project," he said. This was the first semi-official acknowledgement that a third term effort was, indeed, underway and despite all my suspicion, I was still taken aback to finally hear it confirmed. This friend, along with Andy Uba, had by then emerged as Obasanjo's closest allies and confidants and if there was anyone who would know about a third term effort, it would definitely be my one dinner guest that evening.

"So there is a third term project?" I asked.

He laughed. "Of course there is. You are too well-informed to tell me you do not know that."

"Well, you know, I am not sure what to believe. I have had three attempts at conversation with Obasanjo about this subject and each time he denied it."

"Yes, he told me. That is why I came to confirm that there is a third term project. We are working very hard on it and we need you on board." While initially taken aback at the confirmation, I was not entirely surprised at this revelation, because by then, we had all concluded that there was such a project, but we were simply not trusted to be part of it.

"Well, you know me. Before I get involved in anything, I need all the details. I have to know the whole truth, everything. Tell me why it is being contemplated and what the end-game is. Who is involved in planning and execution, who are those providing the money, everything. When you do all of that, I will make an assessment of what is in Nigeria's best interest first, using my conscience as a guide. When so briefed and given some time to evaluate and reflect, I will decide on a position."

"Well, what are your initial thoughts, gut reaction?" he asked.

"I think it is misguided. I believe it will fail in the legislature. But I do not have all the facts. If you give me all the information and rationale for it, I may be in a position to reconsider. New information may lead to modification in position."

He nodded, adding "Ok. I am going to Lagos for a couple of days to attend an event and when I return by God's grace, I will give you a call so we continue our discussion. I promise I will share all I know." He then suggested that the patronage - like land allocations and employment opportunities - available in the FCT Administration would help in securing the support of several constituencies – members of the legislature, traditional rulers, and leading politicians, particularly from the north. I suspected he was sent to me by Obasanjo, but never asked for confirmation. Obasanjo never felt he could talk to me directly about many of these dodgy matters because he was uncertain how I would react.

My friend continued, "We need you to bring the economic team on board and behind this project." I was not the head of the economic team. Ngozi was, but I believe he chose to confide in me perhaps because we had a friendship dating back to our university days in the late 1970s. I agreed to meet him again in a couple of days and he left. That was the last time I ever saw him. On the flight back from Lagos, the Bellview Airlines plane conveying him and 113 other passengers and crew crashed shortly after take-off from Lagos on October 22nd, 2005. It was a double tragedy for the nation as the First Lady, Mrs Stella Obasanjo died in Spain the next morning. We confirmed the plane crash and the deaths the morning of October 23rd. Obasanjo was devastated, and we all mourned the loss of close friends and compatriots, including the last permanent secretary I worked with at the FCT, Deji Omotade.[11]

The next thing I did after some weeks of mourning was to go back to Obasanjo. "Mr. President, about third term – I am now convinced there is a third term project." "You are convinced, that is fine. I have told you that if the National Assembly wishes to amend the Constitution, it is not my business," he said. "Yes, I know."

I suspect that he expected me to mention the conversation with my deceased friend, but I declined to do that. Instead I asked, "Have you discussed this issue with your predecessors in office, the former presidents? You know, it is perhaps understandable why you would want to remain in office because you probably believe you have many important programmes and projects to complete. I think the former presidents will probably relate to that and understand it too. If you discussed it with them, maybe they will openly support such constitutional amendments you have in mind." He once again denied the existence of any effort to extend presidential term limits, claimed he had not considered this, and brushed it off.[12]

The core leadership of the economic team – that is Ngozi, Oby, Nuhu and I – met several times during this extended period of intense speculation to discuss the alleged third term effort and were just getting nowhere. Nuhu, as EFCC chairman, was briefing us that the EFCC's Financial Intelligence Unit (FIU) noticed a lot of money flowing around from state governments to certain accounts in Abuja, but he gave us no details as to who it was going to. We all suspected that Andy Uba was likely to be the treasurer of the Third Term effort, but said nothing. Meanwhile, we all lived and worked in Abuja, I administering the federal capital territory, watching the suspected Third Term organizers come and go every day, and nobody said a thing to any one of us. Then one Wednesday, Ngozi informed me that Obasanjo had finally talked to her about 'third term' and confirmed that the administration would pursue the rumoured constitutional amendments. His reason, according to her, was that he had in his mind who should be his successors, but they were not ready yet. He hinted that we – the technocrats that were members of the economic team – should be his 'natural successors'. However, he "needed time to prepare" the team and "lobby" the politicians to accept technocrats like her in top-level political leadership. He explained that his plan was that if elected for a third time, he would pick one member of our group as running mate in place of his estranged Vice-President Atiku Abubakar and then groom that person to take over from him. This was the line he pursued and the tacit impression he gave Ngozi, who appeared persuaded of the logic of this storyline. I did not buy it for a minute and told her so.

We subsequently learned he had told versions of this story to other people whose support he needed in the Third Term Project. For instance, he hinted to the then Speaker of the House of

Representatives, Aminu Bello Masari, that if he supported the third term project, Obasanjo would pick him as his running mate and prepare him to be the next president. Surely the Speaker could not have been the only one Obasanjo made this pitch to.

Ngozi's pragmatic political mindset came out clearly at this point. Her attitude was that as far as she was concerned, this third term project was a done deal, it would happen, so we should just accept it as a fact that "these unprincipled politicians will be bribed and will vote overwhelmingly for the amendment. It is not necessarily a bad thing because we will continue to do our work and make the country's economy better until the time is right."

She furthermore showed me a document authored by a private think tank for Obasanjo which analysed 'the options before the president' at the time. This think tank was a group Obasanjo established to study the political scenarios for 2007, and they came up with three options. One option was obviously leaving office and handing over power to a northerner, as expected. The zoning provisions in the PDP constitution made handing power to a "southerner" nearly out of the question, but the document argued that "northerners" had ruled Nigeria for a disproportionate period of time since independence, and had always messed up the country's economy and governance when in leadership positions. The document therefore identified this option as the least preferred.

The document was silent on the historical fact that the perception of most Nigerians old enough to know are that the Tafawa Balewa, Yakubu Gowon, Murtala Mohammed and Muhammadu Buhari governments were the least corrupt, most inclusive and ranked higher in good governance than all other military or civilian administrations we have had. All four administrations were headed by "Northerners". In addition, the fact that every successive federal administration always had an ample mix of 'northerners' and 'southerners' in top-level positions is often conveniently forgotten. This kind of selective amnesia and ethnic irredentism have remained major tools of division deployed by the Nigerian power elite for personal political gain. The 'transition strategy' document went further to present other options.

The next option was to identify a person from the Niger Delta to hand over power to. A person from the Niger Delta would be from the south, which would be in technical violation of the zoning arrangement entrenched in the PDP constitution, but the justification of "fairness and justice" argument made was that no one from the Niger Delta had ever been president of Nigeria, even though that region has been the cash cow of the federation since the mid-1970s. The argument was that the zoning arrangement in the PDP should be set aside as an unconstitutional contraption, and Obasanjo should identify someone from the Niger Delta to hand power to no matter what it takes. Clearly, the person to emerge would have been Obasanjo's favourite politician - Governor Peter Odili of Rivers State. This was the second preferred (reserve) option.

The best option, according to this document, was to amend the nation's Constitution for Obasanjo to have one more term to put all the foundations of the "modern Nigerian state" in place, before taking the risk of leaving office. The group was silent on who that person was, or from what part of the country the post-third term president would be. This was the document Obasanjo gave to Ngozi one early Wednesday morning to read and return to him, and she shared it with me during the course of our cabinet meeting. I should have taken a copy of it, but I did not need to. I was certain about what the real agenda was and was firm in my personal decision about what needed to be done.

Ngozi took the existence of this document as proof that the Third Term effort was a fait accompli since its protagonists had clearly put a lot of thought into it and had the resources to buy off the legislature to ensure its enactment. The divisive foundations of the document were not of concern to Ngozi, perhaps because many "Southerners" believe the convenient lie that there was ever a purely-Northern administration. The inconvenient truth is that except for the Buhari-Idiagbon junta, every administration headed by a Northerner had a Southerner as number two, with the positions of secretary to the government, ministers of finance, defence and petroleum equally shared between the two regions. With the exception of the Gowon regime which, with Admiral Akinwale-Wey as deputy, had two Christians at the helm, and the Buhari junta with two Muslims on top, every federal government had the two major religions equally represented at the two top spots.

Indeed in 1993, Nigerians freely voted for the Muslim-Muslim ticket of Abiola and Kingibe, defeating the 'balanced' Tofa-Ugoh ticket, and destroying the untenable assumption that ordinarily, Nigerians voted along largely ethnic or religious lines! The reality for me has always been as clear as tropical sunshine - the Nigerian political elite - military and civilian, Northerners and Southerners - consistently collaborated to short-change our nation and majority of the people all the time without regard to any ethnicity or religion. The mythical ethnic, regional and religious divisions only come into play when they seek to outwit one another for the top job or a bigger slice of the political and economic pie! I have never and will never buy this crappy, worn-out line. I have lived in Nigeria all my life, have observed its sociology, politics and economics and will never be fooled by these outwardly-antagonistic regional, religious and ethnic bigots who one day are sworn enemies, only to become cooperating-looters the next day! Ngozi was relatively new to Nigeria's politics, retained hang-ups about her civil war experience, and may therefore interpret the situation differently. I felt I had a duty to ensure that she was not fooled.

Over lunch at Chopsticks Restaurant, after concluding the cabinet meeting, I disagreed with her position and was quite blunt in the conclusions I drew. "Ngozi, it is not going to happen," was my response. "A constitutional amendment requires two-thirds of the members of the legislature voting in support – that means 67 per cent of the membership and 57 per cent of the legislature consists of membership from the north. The bulk of the 'northern' legislators will never vote to give Obasanjo a third term because political power and its perceived benefits will be seen to elude that part of the country for another four years or longer. Why should they? Even if they are paid huge amounts of money to vote in support of such a scheme, none of them could go back to their constituencies and explain that they gave a 'southerner' another four years in office. It is not a question of whether those legislators will then be re-elected or not – they could be physically attacked and their properties destroyed. It will not just be cases of political suicide; it will be actual suicide for those that support this in many parts of the country. Some of them living in politically-charged places like Ondo and Kano could have their houses burned and their entire families ostracized. That would be the feeling in the north and many parts of Obasanjo's south-west home base. In the north, I am more certain because I speak to ordinary people and they talk to me, I know the feeling. This 'third term' thing is just not going to happen."

I explained further that in the unlikely event that all the legislators from the north accepted the monies that would be offered to them, supported the move, stayed in Abuja and gave up ever going home, for the constitutional amendment to take effect, 24 out of 36 states' assemblies then also must vote to support it. There are 19 states in the north and 17 in the south. So in addition, assuming that all the southern state legislatures approved it, which I doubted – it still needed seven more states in the north. I did not see how seven state assemblies in the north would support this third term thing. It was just not possible. The state assemblies' buildings and their members would stand the risk of being physically attacked by angry mobs on the day they voted to support it.

"We Have Three Choices"

The defiant feelings on the third term project were not peculiar to or just prevalent in the north. In every part of Nigeria, particularly within the media and civil society organizations, the opposition to Obasanjo's tenure extension plans was vehement, even violent. Nigerians of every political, religious and ethnic persuasion were dead set against it and very angry at even the thought of it.

"It is not going to happen, so do not even think about it," I repeated. "So what do we do?" asked Ngozi. "Well, we have three choices. We could decide to support it. I told you it would fail. We'll have a burden (of public betrayal) to carry for the rest of our lives. Or we could come out publicly and announce that we are convinced there is a third term project, we were not a part of it and for this reason, we were resigning together. We could do that. We will acquire a lot of national and global credibility in the end, because I am sure this third term scheme will fail. But then the work you said we are doing for our country may suffer and what we are doing is for the country, not for Obasanjo or anybody else, and we still have some work to do – the Paris Club debt relief deal is yet to be signed and sealed, and London Club is still a long way from closure."

This was in late 2005. I continued, "Or we could take a third option – 'siddon look'. Remain in government, keep out of the radar, pretend neutrality towards the third term project, or even perhaps indicate benign support privately to Obasanjo, though we must not be actively engaged in anything to do with it. We could then use as much information as we can obtain as insiders or bystanders as the case may be, to work with those that are working openly to unravel it. This option enables us to keep our jobs, preserve the implementation of our economic reform programme and to some extent, we can also help the president, because there will be life after the collapse of the third term project and it is important for him to be at least credible enough to select a decent successor. In my considered view, that last option was the least controversial, enabling us to promote good and help the defeat of evil in our administration, which was therefore our best choice. We agreed to stop saying even in private conversation that we were against third term. We chose not to comment on what they were doing, but never support them even in private conversations. I summarized the next steps for our group:

"We should never do anything to help them – the third term plan is morally wrong, legally indefensible and publicly unpopular. But we must position ourselves in such a way that we are trusted enough to have some information about what the protagonists are up to, yet not be engaged so that we can pass on that information to the opposition groups that will be organizing to fight it openly and frontally." I was confident there would be such groups in the legislature, civil society and the media for us to engage with in the near future.

In the end, Ngozi and the rest of the core team were persuaded and that was what we decided to do. We all focused on our jobs, maintained low profiles and kept our mouths shut for the time being. Of course, we were not the only faction in the government against the idea of a third term, and in due course we wound up collaborating with opposition political parties and the leadership of the National Assembly to ensure that the effort was in the end dramatically defeated. That story is much longer and I will return to it later in this book, but suffice it to say here that by the time we had enough evidence from the opposition that they were set to defeat the third term amendment vote in the National Assembly, we took our evidence as a group to the president's chief of staff. On that Wednesday evening, on the 10th of May, 2006,

Ngozi led us - Oby, Nuhu, Dr. Aliyu Modibbo, (who became FCT minister after I left office in 2007) and I, to see General Abdullahi Mohammed in his official home in Asokoro District of Abuja.

"Third term – Obasanjo is still denying the existence of a third term project," we said to him.

"Yes, but you all know there is," he replied. At that point, the merits of a constitutional amendment were already being debated in the legislature. We told the chief of staff that the entire bill was certain to be defeated and in our view the president should get the National Assembly to withdraw this term limit amendment from the debate and let him preserve some semblance of his stature and honour. Otherwise, by the time it is defeated after protracted acrimony and division even within the ruling party, he would be weakened as president that he would lack the moral authority to influence the choice of a successor. The political ball would effectively be out of his hands. We were concerned about that because we believed then that Obasanjo would always make certain decisions and choices affecting the country based on overriding national interest. In spite of the misjudgement evident in the third term debacle, we still trusted his judgment on succession.

We suggested to the chief of staff that he should lead us to go and confront Obasanjo and persuade him that this constitutional amendment business had to stop. The chief of staff listened carefully, sympathized with us, but did not want to do it that way though. "Give me the documentation you have and I will talk to the president myself. I would not want to go with you because he has consistently denied to me that there was a third term, so how can I lead you guys to go and confront him on third term? Let me go and see him, just two old soldiers talking." Till today, the chief of staff never told anyone of us how the conversation with Obasanjo went that night, as he never got back to us on what transpired. Subsequent events made that unnecessary.

The following morning Obasanjo called Oby and Ngozi aside directly and dressed them down. They had gone to worship, as usual, at the morning church service at the State House chapel. "You are of weak faith and do not believe we can build a modern Nigeria. We are going to achieve what you do not think is possible", was his refrain, still confident that his third term was going to happen. I got my own call later in the day.

"I hear that you are now the leader of the coup plotters," he said.

"Coup plotters, Mr President?"

"Yes, you went to see the chief of staff."

"Yes Mr President, we went to see chief of staff to save the government which you head."

"Save the government! Save me from what?"

"Save us all - the administration from humiliation and defeat. This constitutional amendment thing is not going anywhere, sir, it is better to get out of it than wait for it to be thrown out. It will be a blemish on our administration." He was travelling out of the country that day.

"When I come back, you and I are going to sit down and you will see that you are wrong."

Clearly, he still had the delusion that the amendment would succeed. Two days after our nocturnal visit to Obasanjo's chief of staff, it made the front page of Leadership newspaper, a leading anti-Third Term paper of the time. The story filed by Chuks Ohuegbe was headlined - "Economic Team threatens to resign" (Leadership #143, Friday, 12th May 2006). We were all shocked at how the story got out. Leadership's publisher Sam Nda Isaiah, my good friend, subsequently told me that Chuks never revealed his source to him, but was certain of its reliability. I still wonder who amongst us leaked details of our top-secret visit.

As we all know now, the amendments failed in the Senate on Tuesday, May 16, 2006 while Obasanjo was away,[13] so there was nothing more to discuss on his return. It was a very challenging period for us all and quite a distraction from the work we were all trying to do. Furthermore, because we had shown our hands, particularly in my own case (and Oby) in direct conversations with Obasanjo much more than with other people, Obasanjo knew exactly what we thought about the adventure. As a result, I think this affected our relationship for the rest of our tenure, and to this day I know it is probably something he holds against us but cannot even mention it.

He would feel that because he was like a father to us all, consistently stood by us, and was so good to us, we should have just unquestionably signed on to the Third Term project. I guess that is how old soldiers think. This is what I now understand to be his definition of loyalty – loyalty means – 'follow me blindly, without regard to national interest or questions of constitutional order.' I have come to realize that many leaders think and act like that. Loyalty is personal, not national. I do not agree with this interpretation.

Taking the Good with the Bad

'No third term – no Nigeria.'

This phrase – Nuhu and at least one other person still serving in the federal government had heard similar words too in separate conversations with Obasanjo. In retrospect now, it seems a grandiose statement, outlandish, crude, arrogant, and primitive even. For in the end, there was no third term and yet, here we are. We have never had this uninterrupted length of time in our history as a democracy – Nigeria is over 50 years old but the last 13 years have been our longest stretch as a democracy. Among the many things that we learned from the failed third term effort, one of the most significant to me is that democracy was to some degree working in Nigeria. If we had continued along these lines with a few adjustments here and there, things would have got better, even with all the problems we have had. But looking at the last 13 years and the opportunities we have had, I am not sure if we have made the best use of our resources

The fact that Obasanjo did not even explore the idea of grooming a suitable successor speaks of the depths of his delusion. We later learnt that the mere suggestion to have a Plan B, in case of failure by the Third Term protagonists, to him amounted to insubordination, because as a general planning for battle, he intended to win! No one amongst some of us dared broach the subject of succession with him for fear of being accused of inordinate ambition, even after the Third Term project collapsed. Whether his handpicked successor should have been any member of the economic team, a state governor, national legislator, businessperson or someone else was hardly the point; out of a country of 140 million people then, surely there must have been someone or two suitable to groom, for the nation to choose from. Obasanjo deprived the ordinary Nigerian of that luxury of making a real choice, even one so severely limited.

In the end, President Obasanjo was our boss, remained a leader that had done a lot for us, our careers and Nigeria. This is why we were so disappointed by his bid for a third term. Personally, I took an oath of office which required my loyalty to the Federal Republic of Nigeria, the law and the Constitution. I think my loyalty ends where any assault on the national interest, our constitution and our laws begins. I cannot, out of loyalty to a friend or even to a mentor, break the law or violate the constitution or do something that in my assessment could be wrong, illegal and against Nigeria's overall interest. The Third Term project fell within that class of situations.

Honestly, what is the difference between an Obasanjo third term and a sit-tight Mugabe? Technically speaking, the difference is three terms versus five. However, you never know what happens when you open the door too wide. This to me is the tragedy of Obasanjo's legacy, the contrast between the derision with which he was held immediately after leaving office partly as a result of attempting to get a third term, with the man who first won international acclaim for being the first military ruler in Africa to voluntarily cede power to a democratic process.

Many would like to think that had they been in Obasanjo's shoes, they would have been more reasonable but the truth of it is that they do not know for sure. One does not know what it is like to serve as president for two terms in a country like Nigeria; to anyone else who likewise has never had that experience and yet is quick to disparage Obasanjo; I would say simply that you cannot judge a man until you walk in his shoes.

So I stop short of judging Obasanjo – believe it or not, I still consider him an elder and a mentor, albeit a complicated one – but we all remain disappointed at the blemish our administration got by the pursuit of the tenure extension, and the consequences of what has turned out to be poor outcomes resulting from his personal choice of successors. The very notion of thinking that no third term means the end of Nigeria seems to suggest that he considered himself more important than Nigeria. It was a breath-taking realization: all his decisions and actions since that fateful evening indicated to me that he believed that Nigeria was a creation of nature for him to use at will, that wherever and whenever the narrow interest of Obasanjo and the broad interests of Nigeria conflicted, Obasanjo's preferences must trump Nigeria's interest. One still does not know how he arrived at that conclusion, but it was quite clear to me that this was what he had come to believe, and perhaps what he still thinks.

To me, if one chooses or agrees to be part of a group, whether that group is a family, a team, a company or a country, one's primary loyalty ultimately should be to the group. Apart from obedience to God, my primary loyalty is to Nigeria before anyone and anything else. When I joined the public service, I took an oath of office to be loyal to the Federal Republic of Nigeria and its Constitution and there was never anything in the oath of offices I held that required any personal loyalty to any person, the president included. I believe in this doctrine and I have practised it in my relationships with groups that I work with, so to me, it is a no-brainer choosing which way to go at any point of conflict. However, my guess is that for many people like Obasanjo, loyalty means you do everything that they want or demand; that you are on their side all the time with little regard to other objective values. Accordingly, Obasanjo and his capricious views and opinions are the benchmarks of one's patriotism. The constitution and the law are the secondary, not the primary standards. I do not agree with this view and I never will. Whenever I felt this was at issue, I disagreed with him, sometimes openly in cabinet and other meetings, and most other times, behind closed doors.

In spite of all these deficits, President Obasanjo is an intelligent, hardworking, dedicated and competent leader. I consider my experiences working with him, one of the pinnacles of my public service career, to be instructive of not just the political realities of Nigeria, but also of the meaning of loyalty, of democracy, of development, of success, of failure, and last but not least, the dynamics of working in public service in Nigeria today. As I think back to my experiences prior to entering public service, I can see that really the lessons I learned early on came to bear consistently and constantly since joining the Obasanjo Administration. Only God knows where my experiences and knowledge will lead me next, but I am confident that wherever that is, the principles imbibed and the lessons learnt from the beginning of my life to date will continue to help me serve Nigeria in the public and private realms, with the aim of helping the country realize its full potential.

The Third Term period was one in which the trajectory of our administration changed for the worse. Corruption at the highest level became more overt, impunity escalated, compromise with unscrupulous politicians became the order of the day, and the nation's governance took a turn for the worse in many areas culminating in Obasanjo's choice of successors that have led to the current economic and political crises that Nigeria has been thrown into. How we will get out from the long shadows cast by Obasanjo's decisions and actions during this period remains an open-ended issue even as I write this.

However, these thoughts were not in contemplation during the period of navigating through the third term debacle. On reflection, it seemed to me that the previous forty years or so of my life amounted to little more than preparation for the challenges and triumphs I experienced in public service. Let us examine how this happened – starting from my humble beginnings.

Chapter One

Humble Origins

"Genetic inheritance determines a child's abilities and weaknesses. But those who raise a child call forth from that matrix the traits and talents they consider important."

– Emilie Buchwald

Some people become aware at a very early age what their calling is in life. For better or worse, I was never one of those people. When I look back now, though, it strikes me that my awareness of public service occurred at a fairly young age, even if I never really considered it significant as an event in and of itself until I began to write this book.

In general, there was always discussion about government when I was growing up (particularly in the houses I was brought up), because those who brought me up (my father, uncle and cousin) were all public servants. The twin topics of government and public service were therefore consistently present in our household discussions. In the time and place I was born – Daudawa village in Katsina State around 1960[14] – peoples' expectations of life were quite modest.

Virtually every boy (but excluding most girls, including all my sisters) in the village went to primary school but only three or four out of the whole graduating class of about 30 pupils each year would pass the National Common Entrance Examination to go to a high school - which at the time would be a government college, a provincial secondary school, craft school or teachers' training college in that order of preference. Everyone else went to the ministry of agriculture to learn to drive a tractor. Many did not even get that kind of job; they just remained in the village and joined their parents as farm hands, farmers or traders. The highest ambition anyone had in the village at the time was to be the agricultural officer, the most senior government official in Daudawa. Needless to say, it was outside the realm of possibility for most people from my village to ever see the regional capital, Kaduna or Lagos which was the nation's capital, to say nothing of England, the United States or anywhere else. Only a handful in the village had gone to Saudi Arabia for Hajj. My father died without ever being able to afford the trip to perform the Hajj or Umra pilgrimage.

Life then was very simple. We had little crime in the village. There was some inequality, but everyone was generally poor. The village head was better off than most. There were a couple of traders, - the merchants who had shops and sold groceries and things like that - those were the 'rich' people. Then we had the judges and the mallams, the advisers to the ruling class, and then we had the peasants or 'the talakawa' in Hausa parlance.

My father worked for the ministry of agriculture of the northern region at the time. After retiring from the ministry, he acquired a farm in Daudawa and went into full-time subsistence farming, not a huge farm, but a modest sized one, enough to grow the food we needed as a family. He lived in Daudawa with two of his wives, including my mother, his third wife. The oldest wife, whom he visited every month after collecting his monthly pension of three Nigerian pounds, lived in Zaria.

So I suppose my father would have been considered one of the mallams, putting us somewhere in the middle ranks. of a largely impoverished community. Everyone was generally poor, so relatively speaking, nobody felt noticeably different, though it was around that time that the emergence of a middle class was beginning to be defined by those who had Western education ("Yan Boko").

There was the Government Reservation Area (GRA) where senior civil servants of the ministry of agriculture lived, and then the rest of the village where everyone else resided. We lived in the village because our father was on the junior staff of the ministry. The village had no electricity, no running water and no paved roads. I think it was about 1967 or 1968 when the first television set got to the village, running on a generator, I suppose – I was about seven or eight years old at the time. There was a telephone system in the GRA part of the village, which connected the agriculture ministry and the GRA to the rest of the country because Daudawa was a major agricultural settlement at the time. An annual agricultural show - a trade fair of sorts took place there every harvesting season. The village was also a major cotton buying and processing centre, so a telephone network was necessary to facilitate these.

Out of this simple life and upbringing, I was fortunate not only to acquire a decent educational foundation in a supportive family environment and survive diseases like measles and tuberculosis that killed several infants around the same time, but to have had the opportunity to cross paths with remarkable individuals that became early role models, whose inspiration continues to impact upon me today.

My Father, Ahmad Rufai Muhammad

I still remember the day my father died. It was the 9th of May 1968 in Zaria. I did not realise it at the time, but two immediate consequences of his death would not only define the rest of my upbringing but also continue to influence my personality and decisions for many years afterward, even as I write this. One immediate consequence was the role of education; the other was a shift in my attitude toward adversity and in particular how I responded to antagonism directed against me. The latter took more time to develop and I will discuss it in due course; the former came straight from my father's deathbed.

My father was a self-educated man. He never really went to school, but he taught himself to read and write, and to speak English. He gained entry into the agriculture ministry by writing an application in Hausa dated November 1, 1928 to the local agricultural officer at the time, a white man, asking for a job as a vet assistant.[15] The man called upon my father, interviewed him, asked him which school he went to, and when my father replied that he never went to school, the man asked him who wrote the application. My father responded that he wrote it himself, and the man then asked my father to rewrite the application again on the spot. The white man was so impressed that he hired my father right there and then. This was in Samaru, Zaria, where he worked until the early 1940s. From Zaria, my father transferred to Kasarawa near Sokoto. It was while working at the agriculture ministry in Kasarawa that he met, courted and married my mother, whose maiden name was Fatima (Umma) Ibrahim. She is now about 79 years of age and in good health, Alhamdulillah, Thanks be to God. He finally ended up in the ministry of agriculture in Daudawa, and retired to live there on his three-pounds-a-month pension and a small farm where we grew mostly food crops – corn, millet and grains that we consumed in the household.

After he retired, - I was about five then, I was told - he took up full-time what he had already been doing part-time for some years, which was serving as a sort of teacher-imam-cleric in the village. He received the grounding for this role from his father, Muhammadu Kwasau who was such a famous cleric in Zaria, that the Emir offered the hand of his daughter in marriage to him. My father became the imam of the neighbourhood mosque and was probably the leading Islamic scholar in our village after he retired from the agriculture ministry. Every evening, people would come for him to recite, translate and interpret the Qur'an and other Islamic books for them.

Sometime during 1967 he fell ill, a state which lasted many months up until his death in 1968. He was hospitalized in the Zaria General Hospital (now ABUTH) with what I later learnt was terminal cancer. I do not recall which cancer or details of the treatment, but there came a point when the hospital discharged him with the comment that there was nothing more they could do. He was taken back to our family home in Zaria and we all came from Daudawa to stay with him – I therefore dropped out of school for some four months – until he died.

That day our father died, it was as if he had the premonition. He called each of his children present into his room for a two to three minute conversation, one-on-one. While waiting my turn to see him, one of my sisters came out of his room crying. I asked her why she was crying and she said, "Well, the way our dad spoke was as if he is going to die soon."

Being so young at the time, I had only some conception of what death meant, but not enough to fully appreciate what she was saying. But soon it was my turn to enter his room in the darkness, and approach his bedside for what would be my last conversation with my father. With clear sense of effort and focus, he turned to me and said, "You know, you are a very good boy, a clever boy. One thing you must do all your life, is to take your schooling seriously. Education is the key to your success. So whatever you do, make sure you take school seriously."

I promised that I would do exactly as he instructed, and that was all. That was his advice to me. I left his bedside to rejoin my confused and frightened siblings outside, and two hours later, he was dead. We wept at his loss and he was buried the same evening as required by Islamic law and custom. My mother, the third wife, who had the youngest children, was more worried than most about being a young widow with no education, skills, savings account or any pension to fall back on.

In accordance with the Islamic law of inheritance, our father's estate was valued and distributed amongst his three wives and fifteen children. My share consisted of more than a dozen Islamic books and the sum of eleven shillings and three pence, which was slightly more than half of one pound. These were handed over to my uncle, Alhaji Hamza Gidado, who adopted me on my father's death, which meant that I had to move to Kawo, then a suburb of Kaduna, to live with him under the care of his second wife, Hajiya Dije, who had no biological children of her own. From that point on, I saw my mother perhaps once a year, when I visited her in Daudawa (and later, Funtua) during the long vacation. Foremost on my mind then was how to fulfil my promise to my deceased father to take my education seriously always, while adjusting to my new, strange and uncertain environment.

My Elder Brother, Bashir Ahmad El-Rufai

Like most young people with older siblings, my very first role model is and remains my immediate elder brother, Bashir El-Rufai. Bashir not only taught me to read and write before I was formally enrolled in school, but has remained a mentor, an adviser and guiding light of my life. At virtually every turning point in my life, whether it was education, career, and family matters, Bashir has been prominent and my biggest advocate and defender. A brilliant marketer and the most kind-hearted man I know, Bashir is more responsible than anyone in directing my innate abilities in the right path, and shaping my varied forays into business, telecommunications, public service and politics. He will feature prominently in this story because he has remained a substantial and consistent counsellor in my life.

It was from observing and discussing with Bashir that I learnt some patience, fidelity to family and loyalty to friends. Bashir taught me the importance of keeping one's friends through thick and thin and standing up for them. Unlike most people, Bashir's circle of friends has remained with him from childhood, and even when he was more successful than some of them, he never changed towards them. Generous to a fault, populist and altruistic, Bashir is the kind of person ideal for public service and politics. That he was prematurely and compulsorily retired from NITEL by the Abacha regime at the prime of his career was indicative of what was wrong with our type of military rule and the poisonous politics it bequeathed to our nation. Bashir remains a success in the private sector, establishing Intercellular Nigeria Limited which was acquired by Sudan Telecom in 2006, and sits on the boards of several telecommunications and financial services companies.

Sir Ahmadu Bello, the Sardauna of Sokoto

When Sir Ahmadu Bello came to visit Daudawa for the annual agricultural show around the end of 1964 or the start of 1965, it was a rather big deal, given the very basic conditions in which we lived. Ahmadu Bello was the premier of the northern region and it was the first time in my memory we had the premier in the village. In my childish mind the premier was like the king of the region, considered a political as well as spiritual leader.

Around the time that Ahmadu Bello visited our village, I remember asking my father why Ahmadu Bello was the premier, what that meant, what government was and what the relationship was between the government and our village head, among other questions. My father explained that government provided security, built the primary school I was about to begin attending, and provided the primary health care centre, or the dispensary, in which I was to be circumcised.

About a year after Ahmadu Bello's visit, the military coup of January 1966 took place and he was assassinated. My father was very depressed and there was a lot of weeping and sadness in our household because when Ahmadu Bello visited Daudawa, he along with Sarkin Maska Shehu, the District Head of Funtua, had a private audience with my father as well, so we considered ourselves part of the Sardauna's larger family. One of my sisters, Lanti, is married to Sani Gwandu, the eldest son of Alhaji Ahmadu Gwandu- one of Ahmadu Bello's close friends then, which linked us to the premier's extended circle of family and friends. Indeed, my sister still recalls the traumatic events of 15th January 1966, when armed soldiers stormed the residence of Alhaji Ahmadu Gwandu looking to arrest (and perhaps assassinate) him after killing the premier. Both Ahmadu Gwandu and his son had to be secreted away to safety by their neighbours.

Ahmadu Bello's assassination brought my first awareness of the lengths that people went to over disagreements in the political realm. Shortly after that came the counter-coup of July 1966, rioting and killings largely targeting south-easterners who were blamed for the assassination of northern and south-western military and political leaders. These mistakes, misfortunes and mishaps eventually led to the Nigerian civil war that lasted till January 1970 and cost millions of Nigerian lives. I was not yet in school at the time, and even years later, we were not taught any civics in primary school, but I still came to understand a bit of what government meant, for better or for worse, during that turbulent period.

Ahmadu Bello was a selfless, fair and inclusive leader. He was a visionary, focused on the development of the region he administered. He saw the north larger than his immediate Hausa-Fulani-Muslim roots and tried to give all the ethnic minorities of the north and south a sense of belonging. Ahmadu Bello's fairness and integrity enabled the forging of personal friendships and political partnerships with many leaders of the ethnic minorities of the south like Harold Dappa-Biriye and Melford Okilo. Sadly, his political successors largely failed to sustain his visionary, just and inclusive leadership style and our nation as a whole and the North in particular have been the worse for it.

Sheikh Abubakar Mahmud Gumi

Another larger-than-life figure from those early years that impacted my views on public life was Sheikh Abubakar Mahmud Gumi. I never personally met him, but his presence in the public sphere was palpable even from my standpoint as a growing child. He was an Islamic cleric who was unique in that he was not afraid to express unpopular sentiments in those days. Among them: western education is not sinful, building schools was more important than building mosques, Muslims should join the military, own hotels, and invest in banks. Until Gumi came onto the scene, the traditional view of Islamic scholars was that because hotels sell alcohol and their existence would 'enable' fornication and adultery, a Muslim should not own any shares of a hotel company; because banks charge interest on loans, which is prohibited in Islam, Muslims should not own banks; because the only war Islam allowed as lawful is religious war, jihad, Muslims should not enlist in a secular army. Gumi started campaigning alone against these extremist tenets and interpretations for a long time.

Of course, Ahmadu Bello, who was a great-grandson of Sheikh Usman Danfodio, the great Islamic reformer and founder of the Sokoto caliphate, did not accept some of the extreme views held by the Islamic establishment at the time either. Under his leadership, the northern regional government established hotels[16] which sold alcohol, and the Bank of the North which charged interest on loans.[17] Even though Bello was under pressure to adopt strict Sharia law in the north, he refused. He adopted the penal code, which was applicable in the Sudan and Pakistan, with some variations, but his overarching attitude was that the north was an inclusive society of Muslims and Christians that must learn to coexist without either one imposing values on the other.

Ahmadu Bello was not a cleric, however, but a political leader, so he could afford that kind of flexibility in interpretation of Islamic doctrine. All other Islamic scholars at that time held the fundamentalist, traditional views of strict prohibition and it was Gumi that started a very public campaign, effectively saying, "If all Muslims do not own banks, then how will Muslims get loans for their businesses?" For him, it was a practical matter – the banking system depended on interest and Muslims must be part of it, they must invest. Similarly, if all hotels are owned by non-

Muslims, then Muslims may be discriminated against when they need accommodation. He even led by example when he encouraged at least two of his sons to join the army.[18]

Not only did Gumi have a very pragmatic interpretation of Islam, he undertook the first translation of the Qur'an into the Hausa language so more people could read the holy book for themselves rather than rely on clerics (mis)interpreting for them. He co-founded the leading Islamic organisation in Nigeria - the Jama'at Nasril Islam, and several schools including Sheikh Sabah College (renamed Sardauna Memorial College) in Kaduna. Sheikh Gumi died in 1992 and I firmly believe that if people like Gumi were alive in 1999 when the political Sharia movement[19] started, it would have gone nowhere. Gumi had the standing and stature of a respected and objective public voice to come out and call it precisely what it was: political posturing and nothing more. It would have died away faster than it finally did.

What impressed me most about Gumi at the time, and this was internalised in my attitude, was primarily his conviction plus courage, and also the fact that he had the clear-headedness to promote pragmatism above fundamentalist ideology and beliefs – something that I have done my best to embrace in my own career and platform in the public domain. He was a very courageous man to do what he did at the time as nearly all the voices in the Islamic establishment attacked him. Nevertheless, he always stood his ground, relied on the Qur'an and Sunna of the Holy Prophet Muhammad, and had read virtually every book written on Islamic jurisprudence, so he could successfully debate his opponents to a standstill. The seminal work on Sheikh Gumi, by Professor Ismaila Tsiga - "Where I Stand" (Spectrum Books) is recommended reading for all those wishing to know more about this visionary, complex, yet grossly misunderstood man.

"Can you read a newspaper?"

Fortunately, my father's request that I continue my education was a good fit for my personal disposition, as I had always found school easy and excelled as a student. My elder brother Bashir, who has continued to be a role model and mentor throughout my life, taught me the English alphabet, in our mother tongue, the Hausa language, starting when I was about five years old or so as there were no kindergarten or nursery schools in Daudawa. When Bashir returned from school and would leave his books to go out, I took his books and started looking at the pictures and copying what I saw. He very soon decided it was better to teach me himself for fear that I would ruin his books.

In January 1967, as was customary with all our father's male children, I was enrolled in class one of the Daudawa Primary School. It was the only school within a 10-kilometre radius, and since I already knew the alphabet and could read and write, I found it incredibly boring being taught the alphabet. Bashir was in class seven, the final year then.[20] We awoke early five days a week to pray, have a quick breakfast and trek about three kilometres to be at school by eight o'clock. At around two o'clock, we would trek back home in the hot sun just in time for late afternoon prayers.

I had just commenced Class Two when our father fell ill and I was out of school till he died. In addition to setting forth the path of my education, what my father's death also did was to bring to the fore my sense of vulnerability. I moved to Kaduna to be under the legal guardianship of an uncle I did not recall meeting before. I had only been to Kaduna once in my life before then, and my mother remained in Daudawa, so I had no real mother figure. There was a lot of anger in me and loneliness - a feeling of being all on my own, and despite the care and guidance that my uncle and his wife tried to provide, I still had the feeling for quite a while that there was no one there for me. It was a difficult adjustment in a young boy's life.

Somehow, this turbulence did not affect my studies negatively. In fact, in certain ways, it helped me focus on them. When I first came to Kaduna in June 1968, my uncle took me to what was to be my new school to register, Local Education Authority Primary School in Kawo. We were waiting in the office of the headmaster, Mr Julius O. Audu, and I saw that day's edition of The New Nigerian - the leading newspaper in the north at the time - on his desk. My uncle said it would be okay to read the paper but I should put it back as soon as the headmaster returned. I took the paper and became so engrossed in reading it that I did not notice the headmaster standing there watching me when he returned. My uncle explained that my biological father had just died, that he had assumed the role of being my father, and showed the headmaster the transfer certificate which indicated that I was in class two. He then asked my uncle my date of birth as this was not indicated in the certificate. My uncle replied after a little hesitation - 16th February, 1960. That was how I came to know my birth date, which some 40 plus years later, I found to be of doubtful veracity.

"You were reading my paper. Can you read a newspaper?" asked the headmaster. I said I could. So he asked me to read the headlines, which I then did. He then directed me to read the first paragraph, which I also did. Of course, my pronunciation was not perfect, but he was impressed with the extent to which I could read because the norm for students coming from a village school to a city school was to be held back a grade. "You are in class two. My students here do not read newspapers until they are in class five. So I am going to promote you to class four. If you do not make it, then I am going to bring you back to class three. We'll see how you do in your first term. If you are unable to be in the top 20 in the class" – we had a class of about 40 pupils – "I will have to downgrade you."

Joining a class in the middle of the academic year and two full years ahead of where I was supposed to be, became a major challenge. Happily, at the end of that term, I placed ninth, so I remained well above the level as per the agreement with the headmaster. By the end of Class 4, I placed fifth. When I was cured of my love for football after suffering a right arm fracture in a class game, I then spent most of my spare time reading everything I could find. Side by side with modern education, I attended and excelled in Islamic School five afternoons a week, where I studied the Qu'ran, grasped a bit of classical Arabic and learnt the basics of Islamic jurisprudence.

A Bully Meets his Match

While my study habits remained intact after my father's death, my agreeability did not. In addition to being without my birth parents in Kaduna, I was also without Bashir to look after me, and being one of the smaller students in my class, it was only a matter of time before class bullies came around to test me. I never fought with anyone before my father died. His death, coupled with moving to Kaduna and being in a new environment, with new parental guardians, new school and no elder brother signalled a major shift in how I related to my peers. The first time I fought with anybody I was actually blamed. What I realised very quickly was that since nobody was going to stand up for me, I had to do it on my own, and if I did not fight back I was just going to become the punching bag of the neighbourhood.

That attitude changed the way I reacted to anyone that attacked me. People had to know that if they fought me, I would fight back, and even if they beat me up, I would leave scratches on their faces or something even more permanent so that they would remember that even though they won, it came at a cost. To be sure, the bigger boys might always beat me up, but I also always made sure they walked away with some sort of mark to remember me by. I never thought twice about resisting every bully who had a go at me.

There was only one bully that I fought more than once, a boy in my school named Sunday, who eventually dropped out, joined the army and was rumoured to have died in the Nigerian civil war. I do not remember what started us fighting, but he was definitely bigger and stronger than I was and had no problem beating me up in that first encounter.

That first night at home nursing my bruises, the matter was probably over and done with to him, but for me, all I could think about was what should be done next. The following day, I watched him until we went for lunch break. He got his food and started eating. I took some sand in my hands and went and poured it on his food. This meant he had no lunch that day, so he beat me up in anger. The next day after that, I did the same thing – and the next day, and every day after that.

Each time I did that he would beat me up because he was bigger and stronger. However, after about two weeks, I noticed that he became paranoid. We would break for lunch and he would get his food and run over to the football field way out of my sight. Another thing I used to do to Sunday was wait until he would be sitting with his friends, relaxed, and I would walk up behind him and smack him on the head, and give him a nice surprise beating. He would then turn around to beat me up. But I had the element of surprise so I would always get in the first good slap and he could never relax. Eventually he reported me to our class teacher that I was fighting him all the time.

"But how can this small kid be fighting you?" asked the teacher.

"He is – he is harassing me," said Sunday.

Our teacher then took me aside and asked me what was going on.

"Sunday bullied me."

"When?"

"Two months ago," I said.

"Two months ago?!" exclaimed the teacher.

"Yes."

"Nasir, it was two months ago, it is over."

"It is not over. He bullied me. The account is not balanced. He beat me up."

After some failed attempts to get us to reconcile, the teacher took Sunday and I to the headmaster and said she did not know what to do about this, that this tiny boy – that was my nickname, tiny boy – has been harassing Sunday. The headmaster looked at us and said, "This is impossible." Sunday assured the headmaster that it was true and went on to tell the story. The headmaster then turned to me and asked what happened.

"He bullied me," I said.

"Did you bully him?" the headmaster asked Sunday.

"Yes we fought, sir," Sunday replied.

The headmaster directed Sunday to apologise to me, which he then dutifully did. The headmaster then turned to me.

"He has now said he is sorry. Go now and do not fight anymore."

"But sir, he beat me up several times. Sorry? That is it?"

"Yes! If I see you fighting on school premises, I will deal with you."

The moment we got out of school, off the premises, I started fighting Sunday again. This carried on for another month. Eventually, his father came to meet my uncle and explained what had been happening. My uncle then sent for me.

"Is this true – you have been fighting with this boy?"

"Yes."

"Why?"

"Because he bullied me."
"When?"
"Three months ago."
"Three months? You have been fighting for three months?"
"Yes, on and off."
"Ok, this has been settled now. They have come over. Sunday is sorry. His father has talked to me, so no more fighting. Do you understand?"
"I understand. But can I just slap him one last time?"

Since many of our school mates knew about this incident, nobody else fought with me afterwards, and the only bullies I had to contend with were around town. This incident taught me a tactic that I have since found endlessly useful in public life: standing up to bullies is a good way of buying permanent peace. As a child I knew that I was not very strong, I was not big, and I would likely lose, but if I can give the bully a hard enough time, he would not do it again. Permanent peace comes about as the result of a resolute and uncompromising effort to define your position on a matter – and that is the way things are.

Barewa College Days

Despite my early struggles against bullies, I graduated from elementary school at the top of my class, which meant that I could be expected to go to any high school of my choice. I was admitted to the Federal Government College in Sokoto, but Mallam Yahaya Hamza, who was my guardian then, felt that I was too fragile and of poor temperament to survive in a place as far away as Sokoto. My first choice of high school was Government College, Kaduna, because my best friend, Saidu Abdu Jae, was then in the second form. But Yahaya Hamza, then the North-Central State[21] Chief Education Officer for teacher training and primary schools, ensured my admission into the elite Barewa College in Zaria rather than my preferred first choice. I protested to him, but he insisted that he wanted me as far as possible from Kaduna because I was getting increasingly involved with the Tariqah sects and their interpretations of Islam which he felt could lead to fanaticism. He was specifically concerned about my admiration and close affinity to two Islamic teachers – Sheikhs Mamman Fagge and Umaru Sanda, both prominent Tijjaniyya clerics in Kaduna. I cried and cried but ended up going to Barewa. I remain grateful to him for this decision, which changed the rest of my life in fundamental ways. Our parents often know what is best for us as children even if we disagree.

The impact – my mourning, really – of my father's death I think finally began to fade away when I arrived at Barewa in January 1972. By that point, I had more or less accepted my uncle as my father figure, I was developing some other very close friendships and mentorships and Bashir was in university then at Ahmadu Bello University in Zaria, the same town where Barewa is located. So there was a bit of a support network, which made my life easier. The challenge I faced during my elementary school days in Kaduna of feeling there was no one close by that could stand up for me was already changing for the better when I got to Barewa.

A close friend of the Yahaya Hamza family, Mallam Bello Kofar Bai,[22] who was a senior education officer and former teacher like Yahaya Hamza, visited from Katsina. He thought that since I was a frail little 12-year old and much too small for my age, I needed care and protection, so he personally drove me to school. In line with our culture and tradition, he sought out a senior student he knew very well – Halilu Kofar Bai, who was a second year Sixth Form student and house captain of Nagwamatse House to be my guardian.

A couple of days after arriving, I reported to the Principal of Barewa College, a scary old British soldier and World War II veteran, Mr S. V. Baker. I was assigned to Class 1A and Mallam Smith House. I recall being assigned the same day along with Muntari Abdu Kaita to the same class, but he went to Lugard House. Halilu in turn handed me over to Sani Maikudi, a fourth form student also from Katsina, to be my guardian in Mallam Smith House. Sani was a wonderful and caring guardian. He kept my pocket money, collection of books and clothing, while providing guidance and mentoring in academic and related matters. I became closer to him than I was with my own siblings and our relationship deepened over the years as he became a brother, careers' guide, teacher, adviser and later professional partner in our very first quantity surveying consulting business. It was also through Sani that I met Umaru Musa Yar'Adua, his cousin and mentor, sometime in 1973.

Barewa was a parochial school of sorts in which the hierarchy was clear: the second year students could send first year students to buy cigarettes (the possession or smoking of which was even against the rules!) for them, to get them food from the dining hall, and generally could treat them any way they wanted because they were a year older in the college. That was the system. So I learned to be obedient to strange people, who were not my brothers or cousins or uncle, that I had just met in school. We did not have that in primary school, we would just come, take classes and go back home.

At Barewa College, we cleaned the toilets, washed the clothes of the seniors, ironed them, and bought their cigarettes. I still remember the first person to send me to buy cigarettes – he became the head of internal security in Nigeria in 2007, Afakirya Gadzama. I once reminded him of that, something he had since forgotten and he was slightly embarrassed because we became very good friends. We got closer while I was FCT minister and he a senior director at the headquarters of the state security service (SSS). Gadzama remained a guide and mentor throughout my four years as FCT Minister and I remain grateful for his generosity and belief in my innocence at the height of my persecution by the Yar'Adua administration. Afakirya Gadzama was unfortunately retired from service by President Goodluck Jonathan, along with several senior directors of the SSS to pave way for the appointment of Ita Ekpenyong as Director General. Gadzama is a thorough professional who spent his entire working life in intelligence, and is widely respected till today for his competence, dedication and integrity.

Early Relationships and Leadership Lessons

My four and a half years at Barewa remain the most significant in shaping my future life, friendships and person. I learned to be less angry, to manage my impatience, quick temper and moderate the tendency to speak my mind without thinking; I learned to be more respectful of hierarchies; I learned to be more tolerant of others and to obey, particularly rules I do not like or had no regard for; I learned about the various ethnic and religious persuasions that make up Nigeria because Barewa was very much a melting pot of the best and brightest from all over the country. I made some of my most enduring friendships and met virtually all my future business partners in Barewa College. I fell in love for the first time and suffered my first heartbreaks while there. I discovered my love for Chemistry and weakness in learning languages. Suffice it to say, my experience at Barewa was a period of great personal discovery and it shaped my life in very positive ways.

From our tutors, many of whom were British, Indian and Pakistani, we not only learnt academically but from our two British principals, S V Baker and E P T Crampton, we picked early lessons of leadership. Mr Crampton was a hands-on leader who never ceased to remind us that being students of Barewa College was both a privilege and a burden - of future public leadership. I still recall vividly the early morning assembly of July 30, 1975 when he announced that General Yakubu Gowon, a Barewa old boy, had been overthrown in a bloodless military coup. He thanked God that Gowon was alive and well in Kampala, and then went on to say that his replacement Murtala Mohammed is yet another Barewa old boy, mentioning his admission number and year of graduation. Both Murtala and Gowon were school prefects and were active in the College Cadet corps in their days. Gowon was college Head Boy in his final year. The assembly cheered.

Crampton reminded us that anyone of us could in the future be Nigeria's leader and we must therefore be of academic excellence and the best moral behaviour. It was both an exciting and sobering moment for many of us. Crampton retired to his hometown of Cambridge, England, with his Nigerian wife and four children. He died on Easter Monday in April 2011. I took time off to attend his funeral, along with another Barewa old boy, Rajneesh Narula who is a professor of industrial management, author of many books and UN consultant based in the UK. The family was touched by our attendance, and I was particularly humbled by what his son, George Audu Crampton wrote to me afterwards about their affections for Barewa College, experience living in Zaria, and his father's impressions of his students, which I excerpt below:

> "Zaria: what a wonderful, wonderful city, which is still indelibly part of The Cramptons' DNA. It was most definitely where my father had the most memorable time of his life. He was so proud of his

students' achievements, none more so than hearing of your accomplishments, as well as others from Barewa College. I once probed him several years ago on whom he felt were his best students when he taught in Northern Nigeria and he said of you that you were, and I paraphrase, "someone he knew would turn out to be a pillar of his community due to his formidable academic prowess". I hope I am not being impertinent when I write that you and so many others he knew as students first, and then friends later on, breathed so much life into him: he was at his element when he was with alumni or talking about them. He will be sorely missed."

My first real friend and mentor in Barewa College was Sani Maikudi, then in the fourth form. Sani is calm, very intelligent and austere in his lifestyle. He taught me to love reggae music of Bob Marley and U-Roy, introduced me to Dolly Parton's country music, to read the works of Walter Rodney, Karl Marx, William Shirer, Lobsang Rampa and James Hadley Chase - and first introduced me to his cousin, Umaru Musa Yar'Adua. Sani became a surrogate brother and role model. Indeed, his influence on my life was so large at the time that I decided to be a Quantity Surveyor mainly because Sani was studying to become one! I was so close to Sani and his family that I spent some of my holidays in his family home in Katsina. Through Sani I met and became friends with many people that would be prominent in my professional career, education and life: Mallam Mukhtar Bello, Walin Katsina, who as managing director of Allied Bank commissioned our young quantity surveying firm to handle its first high rise building project in Lagos, and other projects followed, Aminu Iro, Sani's cousin, who I persuaded to transfer from Katsina State public service and accept appointment as the head of the Abuja Road Traffic Service during my tenure in FCT, and others too numerous to mention. Sani remains till today, one of the most influential and respected people in my life and I will forever be grateful to him for his care, concern and guidance at critical phases of my life.

It was also in Barewa that I met Abba Bello Ingawa and Husaini Dikko who became not only close friends and brothers but business partners in the professional firm we established in 1982, with Sani Maikudi of course, as an equal, but part-time, outside partner. Abba is very intelligent, of a kind disposition always, conscientious, honest and focused. We were so close that we had a common wardrobe from University until the end of our bachelor days - we were physically almost the same height and size, eerily wear the same sizes of shirt, trousers and even underwear! We were roommates in University for two out of the three years we spent in the degree programme, and went on to share apartments until we both married in 1985! We planned our lives jointly and did everything together almost as twins, until our falling out as business partners in 1989.

Throughout my years in Barewa, I developed close friendships with several kind and wonderful people - Usman Muazu who became an accomplished pilot, but died very young of leukemia, Hassan Dikko, Husain's twin brother who became a university professor, Aminu Mahmood who became a senior immigration officer, Salahu Naibi Wali who is a successful public servant and politician based in Kano, Augustine Eno, an engineer with NEPA, Oka Kama Ama, an engineer who now lives in the UK with his Russian wife, Ibrahim Adamu Yakasai who is a gynaecologist, became an Abacha aide and is now active in Kano politics and Nnamdi Nwuba - a medical doctor who lives in the UK with his wife, Chiedu, a dentist. My keenest academic rival was an Indian boy - Matthew Stephen, who now practices paediatrics in Florida, USA. Many other classmates and friends too numerous to mention, went on to achieve greatness in their professional careers as doctors, lawyers, officers in the military and politics. Barewa was an establishment training ground so we did not have many activists and social critics, though one of our one-time Barewa teachers - Dr. Yusuf Bala Usman became the beacon of socialist ideology and progressive politics in Northern Nigeria. Years later, his brilliant and outspoken daughter, Hadiza, served her NYSC year in BPE, and subsequently got permanently employed. She was found to be such a competent and loyal staff that I ended up appointing her as one of my special assistants and close confidants when I moved to administer the FCT in 2003.

Early Career Thoughts

Many parents seem to think that if a child does well in the sciences, it necessarily means the child should become either a doctor or an engineer. So my educationist cousin, Mallam Yahaya Hamza, naturally believed that because I was already a good science student, I should study medicine at university and become a doctor or take a single honours' degree in chemistry or physics in the alternative. Personally, the moment I got to my teenage years, I never considered studying medicine because spending my working life in a hospital was not that appealing to me. Largely as a result of the influence of Sani Maikudi and Bashir El-Rufai, I toyed with the idea of studying either computer science or electrical engineering - largely due to the mathematics content. Abba thought we should study industrial chemistry or chemical engineering since we both loved and competed to be the best students in chemistry! I was under several influences, and as one can imagine, at that age, things can be pretty confusing.

My cousin studied physics at the University of Wisconsin at Madison and he felt I should pursue a single honours degree in physics or chemistry, go on to study for a doctorate and discover great things, or study medicine. I was not interested in doing any of that, and I told him so, which he was initially unhappy with. By the time Sani Maikudi decided to be a quantity surveyor and persuaded me that that was the way to go - high math content, large dose of humanities subjects, and early financial independence - I made up my mind. I informed my family that I wanted to be a quantity surveyor and my cousin was very disappointed I chose to do so.

Once I decided to study quantity surveying, my choice of university could not have been easier. Ahmadu Bello University, apart from being among the first generation of Nigerian universities, was also in Zaria, close to my family, and home to my brothers, Bashir and Sani Maikudi, was also the only university in the world at that time that offered a full honours degree in quantity surveying. So while my choice of school made my family happy, my choice of course of study did not. At some point, my cousin cut me off - withholding the pocket money he usually gave to all of us – to express his dissatisfaction about my career choice. Since I had received a full scholarship from the Kaduna state government anyway, I did not really need the money that badly, so I could understand his decision. Though we eventually made up and remained quite close, this disagreement was the source of some friction for a short while. He was simply upset with me because he thought I was wasting my talent. Quantity surveying has a lot of overlap with civil engineering but he did not think it was challenging enough for me. I was even offered a scholarship by the Kaduna Polytechnic to study mining engineering at the Camborne School of Mines in the UK and I declined.

The main point of this episode though is that while I listen to every piece of advice, once I made up my own mind, I was always ready to suffer a little bit to do what I believed in. I was not getting any extra money from my cousin for a period while in university and he was unhappy. Even after graduation he would have nothing to do with assisting me get a job, but that was not a huge issue then. I had three job offers to choose from just based on my resume and zero connections. Sometimes these tensions with relations happen, but they pass.

There is of course the argument that real education only happens outside the classroom, but I believe the foundation for anyone to take advantage of life outside the classroom is learned in school. Without that education from school, a person will not get the value added. Exposure and experience probably together account more for one's success in life than education does, but without education, the exposure and the experience would not only be quite limited but also be of limited utility. It would amount to little or nothing. One cannot have one without the other.

Lagos, once upon a time

My decision to study quantity surveying led to many experiences that I would not have otherwise had. The first significant one was that it led to my first ever trip to Lagos in December 1979, when I was about 20 years old. I had been elected the general secretary of the quantity surveying students' association and the university sponsored me to attend the national conference of the professional body of Nigerian quantity surveyors - the Nigerian Institute of Quantity Surveyors, (NIQS). Aside from being my first trip to Lagos, that trip represented a number of other firsts for me: it was the first time I travelled anywhere by air; it was the first time I saw a concrete cloverleaf interchange and 'flyover' bridge, because nothing like that existed in Kaduna; it was the first time I saw a really tall building – 'tall' being defined as above 12 storeys. The tallest building in Kaduna at the time was the NNDC Building - about ten storeys. It was the first time I saw curtain walling - glass totally covering the exterior of a building.

I spent two days in Lagos, just long enough to attend the conference and come back. That trip was also the first time I ever stayed in a hotel. Prior to this, all I ever did was to stay in a friend's home, my family's house or a dormitory. So when some of my wards studying abroad complain to me, "Oh Baba, when we return home from school, we travel economy, why aren't we travelling economy plus or business class on British Airways, like some of our friends?" – I just smile. I know they are tired of hearing me tell them that I did not own a new pair of shoes until I was eight years old and I did not get on an aeroplane until I was over 19 years of age, so they had better appreciate what they have. One time, one of them, one of my sons, said, "Baba, our father is richer than your father. Do not compare us with you. We wore our first shoes when we were eight days old. You wore your first shoes when you were eight years old."

In any event, my first impressions of Lagos remain quite vivid. Based on the stories I had heard, I was expecting Lagos to be hugely populated by lots of unfriendly and loud people, juxtaposed by a metropolis of skyscrapers like a Manhattan skyline or something like that. Honestly, given the lurid tales which circulated so ravenously in Zaria and Kaduna, I was led to believe that the city would be packed with young women wearing miniskirts and no bras, because that was how the villagers see Lagos, as if it were some huge nudist colony. Instead, the first thing I noticed about Lagos was that the airport where we landed – the domestic airport – was not like the airports I was used to seeing on television. There were no automated luggage claim conveyor belts, and instead the suitcases and bags were brought manually and placed on the floor. I had also heard about how horrible Lagos traffic was, how people spent so many hours of the day in traffic, even in 1979. But the traffic I encountered was not nearly as bad as I was expecting.

On my first night in the city, I asked my friend whom I had travelled with to take me to the Shrine where the legendary Fela

Kuti performed every night. We made our way out to the venue, despite our difficulties navigating the unfamiliar territory, and it turned out to be a most wonderful experience. We spent the first part of the evening watching the go-go dancers and revellers, and then Fela came out to perform at about 2 a.m., smoking marijuana on stage and doing his thing, criticising everything and insulting everyone – Fela was not happy with the government, he was not happy with anything, really. We finally got home at about five in the morning and I was floating from the experience at the Shrine. Realise, I had never smoked in my life, not even a cigarette, but I inhaled so much second-hand marijuana that night from the ambience that by the time I came back home I was really floating. That was my only experience with this kind of stuff.

However by the next morning, our first time seeing Lagos in the daylight, my attention returned to the main focus of my visit: studying the buildings and engineering structures – I was, after all, in the final year of my undergraduate programme in quantity surveying. So apart from the traffic situation, which I thought was not that bad, and the fact that people in Lagos were as normal as people in Kaduna – they dressed the same way, and contrary to the legend (and the near disappointment of my teenage mind) the women were not half-naked – what I was mostly thinking about was how much money the government spent in Lagos. By then, I could look at a building and put an approximate construction price on it, so looking at all those bridges and roads and buildings and pricing them in my mind absolutely fascinated me.

I was disappointed by what I saw in Lagos, quite frankly. I did not get to see the Bar Beach and other nice attractions; I did not visit Victoria Island and Ikoyi, which were the highbrow residential neighbourhoods at the time. I saw the not-so-good parts and I thought, if this is Lagos then it is nothing impressive. The one thing I came away with, and this has remained in my mind since then, was that Nigeria was pretty much the same everywhere. The upper class areas were all similar. Kaduna and Lagos were very similar; it was just a matter of scale. The people are the same. The buildings were the same. Lagos had overhead expressways and bridges, Kaduna did not then, though it does now. It was the same people. Any differences in social and economic levels were minimal if not artificial in my view. I also thought that Lagos was a bit of a basket case. It was just too disorganised to be capable of significant improvement.

Today, of course, Lagos is much bigger. At the time I visited it had about five million people, but now it has some 15 million, and it is expected to expand rapidly to the point of being a sprawling mega-city in a decade or less. The human problems have multiplied accordingly. Although the pressure on Lagos as the capital of Nigeria has been partly gone since 1991, the influx of people into Lagos continues because it is still the centre of commercial opportunities in Nigeria. Other than that, it has not changed much fundamentally. The governor of Lagos, Babatunde Raji Fashola, I think has done a good job in trying to bring some order to the city. He has created BRT lanes for bus rapid transit; he has organised traffic, is building more infrastructure; maintaining what was on ground and has relocated squatters. He was doing a lot of work similar to what we did in Abuja to mitigate the consequences of rapid urbanisation and uncontrolled expansion.

I was humbled when upon my return to Nigeria in May 2010, I visited Governor Fashola to thank him for sending a representative to Dubai to attend my fiftieth birthday dinner and congratulate him over the visible improvements recorded in his administration of Lagos State. He reminded me of my work in Abuja and the speech I gave about the compelling need to reduce the disorganisation in Lagos when I received the Silverbird Man of the Year award for 2006. He added that he was inspired by both in the discharge of his functions as Lagos State governor. Governor Raji Fashola's courageous efforts to make the megacity work better for more citizens deserve the commendation and support of all Lagosians and indeed every Nigerian.

The Lessons of National Youth Service

The second time I went to Lagos was about a year later, to report for my national youth service. I was posted to Ogun state, so I had to fly again to Lagos and then drive about two hours to Abeokuta, and then onto Aiyetoro for camping at the famous comprehensive high school there. Some of my ABU classmates at the NYSC camp included Aliyu Omar, Sabiu Baba and Mansur Mukhtar. Were it not for my national youth service, I can say without a doubt that I would not have gone and spent one year in the southwest, and I am very thankful for it because a lot of what I experienced during those 12 months have and will remain with me for the rest of my life. I picked up a bit of the Yoruba language, but have unfortunately lost most of it by now. I learned enough to chat up girls - the most important thing in the world to a 20 year old that I was at that time. I also got used to going to the market and buying groceries and then improving my cooking skills - for the first time I had to live mostly on my own and I had to learn to cook.

My streak of good luck continued when I found that on being posted to George Wimpey & Co. Ltd., two people appeared out of nowhere and made my life much easier. Moses Aigbogun was the accountant and Ahmed Alhassan was the storekeeper in the company. Moses lived alone as his family was in Jos, even though he was originally from the old Ondo State. For the whole of the youth service year, I stayed in Mr. Moses Aigbogun's three-bedroom flat in Lafenwa, and was a regular dinner guest in Ahmed's house in the same neighbourhood. His wife Lami was a patient and gracious hostess all through the year. These wonderful people and bosom friends confirm the possibilities of a diverse, yet peaceful and united Nigeria. Moses, a Christian from the south, Ahmed a Muslim from the north married to Lami, originally a Berom Christian from Jos, doing whatever it took to make the stay of a total stranger - a Hausa-Fulani youth serving in Abeokuta, pleasurable - and it was. I remain grateful to them. Moses has now retired to live in his village in Ekiti State while Ahmed moved back to Jos and remains active in construction of homes and so on. Sadly, Jos, a city that was the epitome of religious, ethnic and cultural inclusion, has become a cauldron of xenophobia, ethnic intolerance and religious crisis instigated by 'democratic' politics.

The most important thing I learned that year was the realisation that Nigerians are pretty much the same. I noticed that the levels of development that we had previously thought of the south - that it was very much ahead of the north - was not really correct. A few urban centres had developed but the rest of the country was pretty much the same, and faced the same challenges. There was no running water in most of Abeokuta at the time, and it was a state capital. In fact, Kaduna had more coverage of running water then than Abeokuta had. The roads were awful. Ordinary people faced the same challenges of how to educate their children, pay for healthcare, and feed their families. It really did not matter which part of Nigeria one came from, these were all the same bread and butter issues. Ethnicity and religion just did not factor in their daily lives - except when politics intruded through undeserving people seeking undue advantages - and this had a major impact on the way I increasingly saw the world, my country and its citizens.

All through my years in secondary school and university, I thought that the southerners did not quite like the northerners and that southerners were far more advanced in having the benefits of superior education and social services than northerners. The southerners I came across did nothing to dispel that view. They gave the impression that they were far more advanced and that we were the more backward people. Spending a year in Abeokuta really helped level the playing field in my eyes and I stopped looking at Nigeria through that lens of contrived and false division. I realised that our common humanity, development challenges and desire for a fairer and just society ought to unite us to pull in the same direction! That was when I realised that the national youth service really was effective in changing the way I thought. Before then, the only interaction I had with southerners was either in Barewa College or with the ones living in Kaduna, but they had been there forever so they were like everyone else – I did not see them as "typical" southerners, I saw them as northern southerners –the true Nigerians. Those in Ahmadu Bello University were no different in our eyes. Lagos, of course, was a bit more advanced in terms of infrastructure, nevertheless, in terms of physical progress, the country was about the same across board - the people, and their day-to-day issues and struggles were all about the same.

As mentioned earlier, for my national youth service, I was posted to a construction company called George Wimpey which was the largest construction company in the world at that time. Wimpey was building a dam to supply water and electricity to Abeokuta. It was during this national service year that I first made what to me, was serious money. In addition to what the government paid me for that year, I was also paid an extra allowance by the company, and was doing a lot of "PP - private practice", i.e. consulting work in my spare time. These were the oil boom days during the Iranian crisis, when the price of oil shot up to $40-a-barrel and a lot of money was accruing to Nigeria, so there was a lot of construction work going on and enhanced demand for the services of construction professionals like me. When I finally went back to Kaduna after my national youth service year, I had the equivalent of about $20,000 in the bank, a lot of money for a fresh university graduate at the time.

At Wimpey, I was assigned to the construction site of the Oyan River Dam as the assistant quantity surveyor on-site, which meant my job was to evaluate progress both in terms of time and finances, and then make payment claims to the client. I was working for the construction contractor, so we applied for payments monthly to the client to pay. There was a British quantity surveyor (QS) named Steve Parkin who was the man in charge and I worked under him; I did all the measurements, handled all the technical details, and he checked and signed off on it.

For my community service that year we built a bridge for a small village about ten kilometres away from Abeokuta. We were supplied with cement and steel rods and there was a civil engineer amongst our team, also posted to Wimpey, who designed the culvert while I calculated the quantities of cement and steel we needed. The government purchased them all and gave to us and we provided our professional expertise and labour free of charge. We built these culverts in about four locations in the village and they gave us a very good send-off with a big feast when we finished, expressing their gratitude.

The dam is still there. Unfortunately it never supplied any of the 10MW of electricity it was designed to, but is used solely for water and irrigation in the area. Wimpey eventually wound up and left Nigeria, but my boss there was invaluable in helping me prepare for my UK professional licensing exams during my service that year. He got me books; the company paid the exam fees, and gave me time off to prepare for the exams. In a typical year, between 200 to 300 people from Africa attempt the Institute of Quantity Surveyors (IQS) and Royal Institution of Chartered Surveyors' (RICS) professional competence examinations and only two or three pass, so it was like a one percent pass rate. The year I took it, 1981, I was actually the only person from Nigeria that passed.

That year was also the first time I visited President Obasanjo's hometown or more accurately, his village of Ibogun. He had at the time just retired from public office and returned to private life in Abeokuta. His first book, My Command, which told the story of the Nigerian civil war, had just been published. He described the role he played up to and including signing the instrument of surrender. One thing I remember about the release of that book was that he was attacked immediately by virtually everyone – all the guys involved in the war said he was not being truthful, that he did not play as prominent a role as he made it appear in the book, and some of his commanders and colleagues disowned his version of events. Reading about this furore, I naturally became curious because General Obasanjo had moved back to Abeokuta. Obviously I did not think of going to see him because I thought he would not see me anyway, but I decided to go to the village where he was born, just to visit, because there was something circulating about his village and how poor he was growing up.

His village had, I recall, some nine houses or huts – that was it, the entire size of the village. I remember thinking that if a person born in this village and by providence, hard work and some luck could become the president of Nigeria, well then social mobility and indeed anything was possible in this country. I concluded that Nigeria was not a country like the UK where leaders went through a certain or fairly predictable trajectory, either the royal family or Eton, then to Oxford, Cambridge, LSE, but rather more like the American Horatio Alger story. When I first came to work for President Obasanjo in 1999, I told him this story and he kept repeating it to everyone. He would say, "This short man visited my village and this is what he said......" and would relate the story I shared with him and my views on social mobility in our country.

More firsts from my national youth service year – I left Nigeria for the first time, to the Republic of Benin, with a friend of mine named Aliyu Omar; and that trip was the first and only time I ever took a shot of whisky. We left Abeokuta, we had some money and we went to Cotonou without making any hotel bookings. We just thought we could walk in there and get a room. So we went to the Sheraton in Cotonou and they said they were fully booked, but recommended we try a hotel 'around the corner,' which turned out to be about a kilometre. While we were walking to the other hotel, it started raining and by the time we arrived there, we were soaking wet and shivering cold. We got rooms in the hotel and settled in, but I was still shivering, so Aliyu suggested that we should take a shot of whisky each because it would warm us up.

"Where did you learn that?" I asked him. "Have you ever done this?"

"It is ok, have not you read James Hadley Chase novels?" he replied.

Everyone had read James Hadley Chase novels in those days. We were in a country where we could not buy any medicine over the counter, we could not do anything and I was shivering like a leaf. So we went down to the bar and asked for a shot of whisky each. They asked for our passports because we looked really young. When they confirmed we were over 18, we got our shots of whisky and I asked how to do it.

"You just, you know, take it in one gulp. One gulp – that is how it works," he said.

We did it. The first thing I noticed was that the ceiling began to spin and something really hot was burning through my gut. I looked over at Aliyu to complain and he, who had read about doing this in James Hadley Chase novels, had already collapsed - down on the floor. I got really scared. I remember thinking, what if this guy dies, what will I say to his mother? However, we eventually recovered and somehow managed to go up to our rooms and fall asleep. When we awoke the day after, needless to say, we had very bad headaches. That was the first and last time I ever took a sip of whisky or any spirit for that matter.

My overall impression of Benin was that it was just another African country, but far less developed than Nigeria. They did not have the asphalt-paved roads we had, but they did have stable electricity, which was novel. We spent three days in Benin and never saw the electricity go off even once. But they struck me as being like us in every way except that nobody spoke English, they spoke French and other languages, and this made me ruminate over what colonisation has done to make us believe and behave as if we were different people.

Toward the end of my national youth service year, I was introduced to a phenomenon that has reappeared over and over again in my professional life since then: corruption. I found that Wimpey was slightly over-invoicing the federal government. They were slightly padding the amount of work done and now that I am older and wiser I think that it was a whole arrangement in which everyone in the loop was benefiting financially. The Israeli consulting engineering firm, Tahal Consultants, needed to sign off on this, and they were one of the best firms in water engineering in the world. Because I did all the measurements, I realised that when I did my measurements and my boss signed off on it, the application for payment that went out was increased by a small percentage over and above what I actually measured.

I went to my boss and told him that the quantities in the final certificates of payment were a little higher than what we had been applying for and asked him what was going on. He brushed it off and told me not to worry about it. But I noticed over the three or four months that I had access to their files that this was something that was happening every month. When I added up the figures, I realised the federal government was paying a lot of money for work not done, and it amounted to hundreds of thousands of dollars every month. I went back to my boss.

"You know, we are not supposed to be doing this, as a company," I told him.

"Look, I do my bit and the project manager has the final say, you want to talk to anyone, go talk to the project manager," he said. "We are quantity surveyors, we are technicians, and we do not get involved in management and administrative decisions." This is similar to saying "we are technocrats, not politicians" so it is acceptable to let the wrongdoing to stand. I was not deterred.

So I asked to see the project manager, another British guy, named M.R. Askins. When I asked what was going on there, he was similarly dismissive.

"Well you know, there are some withholding taxes that are applicable that we have to add to the payments," he said. But I was not satisfied. When I reflect on this now, I realise that I have been a troublemaker all along – I sat down, documented these things and wrote a letter to the project manager demanding they come out and refund the money to the federal government or else I would make it public. The management's reaction was to write the national youth service headquarters asking that I be withdrawn from the company.

It did not quite work. I was neither recalled nor re-posted, but since the company did not want me I was free to do what I wanted for the weeks left of the national youth service. I moved to Lagos whereupon I gave all this information to a friend of mine who was a member of the House of Representatives, Honourable Bello Dauda Furo. I think he wrote Wimpey and threatened to initiate an investigation if the company did not come clean with the alleged over-measurement and excess payments. As it turned out, the chairman of Wimpey in Nigeria at the time was a very powerful Nigerian, from the same part of Nigeria as my friend in the House. The issues must have been discussed and somehow the matter was settled. Nothing came out of it, but I never went back to Wimpey and my last few weeks of national youth service turned out to be in animated suspension, during which I was active in my private consulting work. I still got my certificate of service without any problem, but got no commendations.

I was 21 at the time and I had developed this activist mentality that certain sort of behaviour is wrong and must be challenged. Now that I am older, I understand clearly what they were doing and part of the money was going to government officials, maybe some of it went to the consultants, but it was a whole structure of monthly payoffs. I did not know it then because no one taught us that in our quantity surveying curriculum, and I did not believe that people did that kind of stuff. Once I started practising as a QS consultant and started getting offers from people, I then fully realised what was going on with Wimpey and I was just too naïve at the time to understand it. Little did I know, the scheme I uncovered there was only the first of many that I would encounter both while working in the private sector and years later in public service – on a grander scale.

Chapter Two

The Calm Before the Storm

"What is a friend? A single soul dwelling in two bodies."
"Knowing yourself is the beginning of all wisdom."

– Aristotle

When I returned to Kaduna in August 1981, I had three job offers. One was to work for the French construction giant, Fougerolle on another hydroelectric dam project, the Jebba Dam; another was with a Kano-based professional quantity surveying firm that I had interned with while in university, then known as Murt-Lamy Associates; and the third was with the Kaduna-based, NNDC[23] affiliate, the New Nigeria Construction Company Ltd. Since Sani Maikudi and I were then planning to establish a construction company to build homes, factories and roads and such, I decided to take the job with the New Nigeria Construction Company and was assigned to a teaching hospital project site in nearby Zaria. In this job, I learned the risks of being involved in an office romance. The job of Site Quantity Surveyor with the New Nigeria Construction Company ended after six months due to a conflict with the financial controller of the company involving a mutual romantic interest. Essentially, we were both dating his secretary at the same time and for a while I was the only one in the company who did not know that. As a more senior officer he was in a position to target me, make my life miserable in several ways and he did. After six months of employment, I resigned and returned to Kaduna and began thinking of impromptu ways to start our own business.

While waiting to get the business started, I worked for various firms in an individual consultant capacity that enabled me visit the future capital, Abuja, for the very first time. We went on a project visit while I was on the team working with a planning consulting firm called Environment Seven from Chicago, USA. The firm came to Nigeria to prepare a master plan for one of the satellite towns of Abuja, a new town called Karu, in association with a Nigerian subsidiary, Environment Seven (E7) Nigeria Ltd., led by an architect and ABU alumnus, Ibrahim Mahmood. Others I met and worked with at the time include architects Greg Icha, Ahmed Dantata (deceased), and a town planner, Dr. Mohammed Sani Abdu – developing friendships that endured even after we all went our separate professional ways.

At that time, Abuja was basically just savannah, a few huts and trees here and there and nothing else. The airport had just been constructed and the express-road had been built from the airport to the city, and nothing more. The Hilton hotel was then under construction, the 'Shagari' presidential complex was being built, but nothing more. So we took the old Keffi Road, through what is now Millennium Park, and went to Karu and looked around with the American team and their Nigerian counterparts that were working on the master plan for the new town.

This was in 1982, six years after the decision was made to move the capital from Lagos to Abuja within a 25 year timeframe. Honestly, my first impression upon finally seeing the city site was that Abuja was a dream that would never happen in my lifetime, and that it was impossible for this jungle, this bush, to ever be the capital of Nigeria in the next 25 years. Fifty was the more likely scenario in my estimation. Even as late as in 1988, when my partners and I debated whether we should move the headquarters of our consulting business from Kaduna to Abuja, the pessimism about Abuja remained. Three out of four of us voted against relocating to Abuja because we did not believe it would ever turn out to be what it became by the mid-1990s. When I bought my first house that year, I had the option to buy or build in Abuja and I

The Calm Before the Storm 35

decided in favour of Kaduna, which was clearly, with the benefit of hindsight, perhaps the worst investment decision I ever made. If I had built that same house in Abuja, I could sell it today for over a billion naira, the equivalent of nearly ten million dollars. In Kaduna, I could not get more than a couple of hundred million naira or the equivalent of one or two million dollars today. The way Abuja grew and became a viable capital is nothing short of miraculous, really. It is one of the decisions that former President Ibrahim Babangida deserves all credit for taking, because his administration did it nearly single-handedly. He is without a doubt, not only largely responsible for building the future city's core infrastructure but also for accelerating Abuja's growth when he relocated the seat of government from Lagos in December 1991.

In any event, my private sector experience exposed me to many people very early in my life, so I gained a lot of experience in dealing with people. I learned to be more patient because as a construction consultant I had to be not only professional, but courteous to prospective clients to get appointed as consultant to certain projects. I registered a quantity surveying consulting firm in 1982 and started operating out of the bungalow which I shared with my closest friend at the time, Abba Bello Ingawa. Our very first income-earning job was the First Bank Sokoto Branch, which pre-contract functions we completed in late 1982, for a gross fee then of twelve thousand naira which was the equivalent of about $15,000. We then applied the proceeds to purchase our first Sharp photocopy machine and Olivetti electronic typewriter, and that was pretty much how we got started. Abba Bello's day job was working for Conital, an Italian construction company at the time, while assisting me during weekends. I worked full-time for our own QS consulting firm which after several metamorphoses became three firms, Design Cost Associates (Project Management), El-Rufai &Partners (Chartered Quantity Surveyors) and Proquest Consultants (Procurement Advisory). Since there were just about a dozen chartered quantity surveyors in Nigeria at the time, to use the prestigious and more distinctive "Chartered" appellation, the firm was required by the rules of the RICS to carry my name as the only person so qualified. Since then, many of our staff and partners have acquired the qualification and I have not been involved in the firms' day-to-day operations since 1998, but they have chosen to keep the name. So to sum up, eighteen months after graduating from university, and six months after completing national youth service, circumstances compelled me to be my own boss and a small business owner. Apart from national service, I had worked for someone else for all of six months, did not get to like that idea, and was forced by unplanned chain of events to start our own consulting business with initially dormant partners.

The Early Days of Private Practice

In short order, we had a lot of new business rolling in and with that, came a lot of money at a very young age. The first time we made our first million naira - the equivalent of more than a million dollars then - was around 1986, in our mid-twenties. What having money early showed me was that money was not particularly important to one's happiness. In the beginning we partied, bought things we have always wanted and gifts for relations and friends and it was fun, no doubt. During that period, many close friends began to change the way they interacted with us. They became more respectful and started deferring to me and Abba. Personally, after the initial euphoria, the deference got me worried and in one or two instances scared me. I began to feel increasingly isolated, lonely and unhappy. Suddenly, government economic policy changed that state of affairs.

We woke up one morning to learn that the naira had lost half of its value overnight. Nigeria was going through an IMF-type structural adjustment programme at the time that involved devaluing the currency every week in an auction and within a year we were nearly broke. In 1986, we had a million dollars or so each to our names; by the end of 1987, we were down to almost nothing, thanks to Babangida's economic programme – the structural adjustment programme (appropriately called SAP), and Nigeria has never been the same since then, and in the view of many people, mostly not for the better. So when we went nearly broke, our friends reverted to the normal relationship we were accustomed to. They stopped being too deferential and resumed treating us like buddies.

For me that was a huge lesson. I also realised that one did not need a lot of money to live a good life and that too much money can even distort the reality of one's relationships with people. In short, it sounds like a cliché, but it is true: money can be the root of all evil. If a man has a lot of money and sees a beautiful girl he likes, and he has a nice car and looks rich, he cannot be sure if she truly likes him when he asks her for a date because she is likely to say yes anyway. The same applies to a rich madam who drives along the street and sees a young man whom she likes – you can fill in the gap! So with this experience, I made up my mind that based on the legitimate income from my profession and the blessings of God, I could live a comfortable life without having to do anything dishonest. Seeking for anything more, dishonestly, would only damage one's humanity and affect a person's dignity, and was therefore not really worth it. This became etched in my mental architecture very early in my professional life.

I have also been privileged to meet several professionals in the course of my career that assisted me and nurtured my innate talents. Shehu Lawal Giwa was in many ways a quantity surveying pioneer. He graduated at the top of his class both at Barewa College and Ahmadu Bello University, and established a firm in the mid-1970s that enabled many young northerners to believe they could do the same and not starve in the process. Though he spent all his professional life in the private sector, he was the quintessential public servant, who drove from Kaduna to Zaria every Sunday to teach us Advanced Building Quantities for many, many years. It was this example that encouraged me to do the same for 17 years, at various times, teaching Cost Control, Professional Practice and Procedure, as well as Advanced Building Quantities to final year QS undergraduate students. I became an active member of our local professional body, the Nigerian Institute of Quantity Surveyors (NIQS) and got elected as Assistant General Secretary, and at some point the Vice Chairman of the Professional Examinations Board. I was privileged again to serve alongside distinguished professionals like Abdulkadir Kawu, the late Chief O W E Owete and Chief Ezugo Isiadinso. They encouraged me and assigned responsibilities that deepened and broadened my perspectives about the QS profession, public service and our unity in diversity as a country. I made acquaintances and developed close friendships with Godson Moneke, for many years the NIQS Executive Secretary and near contemporaries like Segun Ajanlekoko, Felix Okereke-Onyieri and Alex Nwosisi. Working with these people convinced me that

Nigeria's greatness is achievable if good people from every part of the nation come together to work as teams pulling in the same direction. I appreciate these fine people for their roles in contributing to the richness of my professional life. I remain grateful to God for these early blessings.

Our active participation in NIQS activities encouraged others around Kaduna to join. My partner, Husaini Dikko was a reluctant convert, but rose to be the president of the institute and currently heads the professional regulatory body, the QS Registration Board of Nigeria. We established state chapters in virtually every state of the federation and made the examination and professional entry paths more transparent. We also published our Nigerian Standard Method of Measurement, and encouraged QS participation in engineering as well as oil and gas projects. These experiences and exposure all came handy later in public service.

Marriage and Challenges of Family Life

I met my first wife, Hadiza Isma, one pleasant August evening at Queen Amina Hall of the Ahmadu Bello University, Zaria, in 1976. I knew the moment I saw her that she was the girl for me, but thought it best to hang around and wait for the right moment to make the move. We became friends and got closer over time, and supported each other through our various romantic experiments until about 1983 when we began dating for real. We got married in Kano on the 17th of August, 1985 and moved into our first home three months later – a rented three bedroom bungalow along Dawaki Road (now Isa Kaita Road) in Kaduna GRA. Shortly after the wedding, we sought to answer the question of where would we build our marital life together. We considered this question along with our choice of honeymoon destination: London.

The first time I had visited the UK was in 1982, after I qualified as a certified quantity surveyor. I took the qualifying examinations of the Institute of Quantity Surveyors of the UK in 1981 during my national youth service year and passed. I then had to go to the UK to fill out some forms and go through the formalities required to be qualified and recognised as an associate of the UK Institute of Quantity Surveyors (AIQS). Nigerians did not need a visa then to visit the UK. You got a six-month entry stamp at the airport! It was a quick visit to formalise my licensing and get properly admitted into the Quantity Surveying profession.

My next time back in the UK was in 1985 for our honeymoon. Hadiza had been to Europe and America long before me as she was from an affluent middle class family, and they were vacationing abroad while we were in secondary school and university. When we went for the honeymoon in 1985, I was also going to be interviewed for a job. Since we had both trained to be professionals in the construction industry – she as an architect and I as a quantity surveyor – we thought that given the economic situation Nigeria faced at the time, it might make sense to explore relocating to the UK to make a living there. In 1982, the Shagari civilian government declared austerity measures when oil prices collapsed. The elections in 1983 were a farce, and became violent with riots and post-election killings in Ondo State. Most Nigerians were not shocked when, on December 31st, 1983, the military took power once again, with Major-General Muhammadu Buhari emerging as Head of State. Buhari inherited a near-empty treasury and huge trade arrears accumulated during years of reckless spending. Cutbacks in capital spending were inevitable and the construction industry was the first to feel the recession. In 1984, Nigeria looked like a hopeless place to be for young construction professionals. The military had returned without mentioning a hand-over date, oil prices had collapsed and there were very few new construction projects happening anywhere. The only consolation was that the regime was essentially honest, imposed discipline and was intent on repaying our debts instead of submitting to an IMF-imposed austerity programme! As a young couple, we explored every option.

I sent my resume to the Property Services Agency, an agency of the central government in the UK, and was invited to be interviewed for a job as quantity surveyor. The agency ended up offering me the position, with a salary of 12,000 pounds per annum. After making enquiries as to how much money that really was in concrete terms, after deducting taxes and basic living expenses, we both decided that the job was not worth the sacrifice of leaving our country. There was no point emigrating if the most we could save was some 200 pounds a month – at the end of one year, we would have saved 2,400 British pounds, which was about the money we could save working hard in Nigeria over the course of some months, even with our depressed economy at that time. This was the one and only time that we seriously contemplated living abroad.

Three things I noticed from those first trips to the UK created lasting impressions. The first was, compared to what I was accustomed to, Londoners were not very friendly. Everybody tended to mind their own business too much. People did not greet each other, neighbours did not know each other, and that was very strange to me. Where I come from, you know the name of your neighbours, and you pop in to share drinks and meals during moments of sadness and joy. In the UK, people did not seem to know their neighbours and they did not seem to care. Even when people greeted, the accompanying smile seemed plastic.

The second thing I noticed was that everything was so expensive. With the salary I was offered by the UK Property Services Agency, which by strict conversion to Nigerian currency looked like a lot of money, most of it would go towards taxes, utility bills, groceries and mortgage payments. It dawned on me that in places like the UK, one could have a decent quality of life - the electricity works, water runs, the trains run, but it really is not possible to save much or accumulate wealth without doing something really different. Otherwise, one is destined to be middle class at best, and we were not prepared to just be that and have a good life. We had the ambitions of being something better.

The third observation was how well the public transportation system worked – and this really impressed me. The trains ran well, the bus system worked, the taxis were designed to take a lot of luggage and seat five passengers comfortably. I found that very impressive and wished we could have something like that in our country. However, I also thought London was not pretty. The buildings all looked the same, particularly the residential areas, which struck me as one massive low-income housing estate. In most of London, virtually all the buildings looked the same. Coming from Nigeria where each house stood on its own with its own grounds and fence, I was expecting something else, something better.

The appeal of the transportation system was really an outgrowth of a broader statement about Britain, which is that there is a general sense of order there. Everyone joined queues. Traffic rules were strictly observed, houses were numbered with odd numbers on one side of the street and even numbers on the other side. This order and predictability appealed to my mathematically-inclined mind a great deal, and I kept asking myself why we could not have this kind of voluntary orderliness and rule-compliance in Nigeria. I thought fleetingly at the time, that if they could do it, we must do it too.

On that trip, we stayed in Stratford, East London, E15, with a Nigerian friend of mine who worked for the BBC at the time. He still lives in that East London neighbourhood, and the last time Hadiza and I went to visit him, we thought that if we had decided to take that job with the Property Services Agency, we would probably live in the same neighbourhood. They had moved from the single-room apartment we knew into a spacious three bedroom apartment in another part of Stratford, and their lives looked about the same – decent, comfortable and stable. Their children have acquired a sound education and we could not help but speculate how different our life and that of our children would have been if we had made a similar choice.

Shortly after our UK trip, the Buhari military government was overthrown in a palace coup and Ibrahim Badamasi Babangida (IBB) took over as president. He delivered an inaugural speech that made everyone adopt a wait-and-see stance, with hopes that things would change for the better. He released political prisoners, promised to hand over power in 1990 and work out an arrangement with our creditors. The rest, as the saying goes, is history. However, some of the issues that confronted us then as a family, as construction professionals and as Nigerians at that time have still not gone away.

One of the biggest issues is that parenting remains as formidable a challenge as ever. Yasmin our first child, I think was conceived during our honeymoon in London, so I am not surprised that she liked it there. Yasmin died in her Lisson Grove flat in London on 26th November, 2011. She was buried a week later in Abuja, Nigeria. Yasmin's death was both sudden and heartbreaking. A sweet child who had grown into an intelligent, confident and altruistic young lady, Yasmin was the pillar of strength in our household and carer for all her siblings, including cousins older than her. My wife and I, along with every member of our family, will miss Yasmin dearly and for the rest of our lives. She had studied Economics at the University of Bath and completed an M.Sc in Political Economy of Late Development at LSE. Her sister, Ramla, who studied Economics and earned an M.A. in Development Economics from the University of East Anglia, Norwich, preferred a life in the UK - individual differences, I think rather than upbringing! My other children are Aziza who holds an M.Sc in Human Resources Management from the University of Surrey, UK,Zulkiflu who also studied Economics at Southern Illinois University at Carbondale, USA, Mohammed Bello who is pursuing a Masters' degree in public relations at Georgetown University and Hamza, an undergraduate engineering major at the University of Virginia. The younger ones are Bashir Jr., Ibrahim, Ahmad Jr., Bilqis and Mustapha.

Prior to her death, from the standpoint of where she wanted to make her life having completed her master's degree, and then studying law, Yasmin's choice was apparently Nigeria, as is her immediate brother, Mohammed Bello's. The very existence of this question is certainly a departure from the way life was when I was their age. Back then, the brightest students got into Nigerian universities and hardly ever went abroad. The exceptional cases were parents with a lot of money who could send their kids to Oxford, Cambridge or Imperial College in the UK. Hardly anyone sent children to America as American education was then considered inferior – the only children that went to the US for undergraduate studies were those that could not get admitted to Nigerian or UK universities.

Nigerian universities, for those old enough to remember, used to be quite good. For me, when I look back at my life, I find that a lot of the enduring friendships which contributed to my personal success had to do with the networks I built in high school and university. I really would have loved for my children to have gone through the same system, I would have loved for my boys to have gone to Barewa College, and the girls to St. Louis Girls' Secondary School in Kano, and for all of them to have gone to Ahmadu Bello University. Unfortunately, in the 1990s, the sense of order, academic freedom and the quality of education in our universities collapsed. We began to produce some graduates who could not construct two sentences in decent English, even though English is the language of academic instruction in Nigeria. So we were forced to make adjustments in our family spending priorities to send our children abroad just for them to get a decent quality of education. Sending them abroad is not only horrendously expensive but that also means depriving them of the local networks they would have built by going to the same schools as other Nigerians, with access to Nigerian alumni networks, which are potentially quite powerful. I got a lot of help in my life and career because I went to Barewa College. The Ahmadu Bello University alumni network is very wide and quite beneficial as well. My children have been deprived of access to these kinds of networks, which are important in business as well as politics.

A second issue with this scenario is the risk that one's children become excessively westernised and have great difficulty settling back into the society they came from to contribute to nation-building. We have seen many examples of our friends who stayed too long abroad during those formative years and they have never really quite come back to face the on-the-ground realities of Nigeria. Many, who returned, left Nigeria frustrated and went back to the UK and the US where they felt more at home!

So with all this said, it was quite a surprise to me to hear that two of my children - a daughter and a son, say they both wished to enter public service or run for public office here in Nigeria. I am quite serious when I say I have not attempted to influence them in any way on this question, but what I have said frequently to Nigerians abroad is that they should all come back home, but not right away.

How this applies to my own children is that I have told them that I would starve if necessary for them to have the best education they can anywhere in the world. No matter which school they get admitted to, I will pay for it all, even if it means selling the last shirt on my back. Not only will I pay the tuition, I will pay everything because I want them to be more comfortable than I have been. I do not care about my comfort – that is my gift to them. When I die, I will not leave a big bank account because that is not what I inherited from my parents. What I give to them is not only an education but a range of options so that each of them can choose what they want to do. It is their call to choose what they want to do, and if any one of them asks me for advice, I will advise them based on the circumstances of the moment. One question I did put to them recently, on the heels of my return from exile, was, "After the experience we went through as a family - the persecution, the sponsored smear campaigns in the news media targeted at me - do you still have the courage to go into public service in Nigeria?"

I found their responses quite surprising. Aziza has an entrepreneurial flair and would prefer starting her business as soon as she acquires some experience. My deceased daughter Yasmin's take on it was simply, "If we do not build on what you and the likes of Uncle Nuhu and Aunty Oby have started, where will the country be when we have your grand-children?" Her sister Ramla, did not see it quite that way, and would have preferred to quietly work and live in the UK. Bello is interested in politics: "You have made a name for us. It is our duty to take that name and leverage it. I could be the first El-Rufai to be in partisan politics for real, not like you, starting as a technocrat." His attitude is that since I have already paid the price, he intended to capitalise upon the name recognition and thereby build a political career. I am not sure what else to do here but to be as encouraging as I can and provide whatever they need to do whatever they wish to legitimately pursue.

As I have mentioned, my father died when I was eight, so my memories of him are few, but what I remember was that he was everything. If I had problems with anything or anyone, I ran to him. He was next to God. That was how I thought I should be as a father. Although I had my uncle and will remain eternally grateful for all he did for me, and I have had many people who played very important roles in my life but I did not have much of a father figure since my father died because no one can really take the place of one's father. In general I think a father should be there for his children, ensure they can get the best in life that he can afford and be protective of them without smothering them to a point that they become too dependent on him all their lives. Striking the balance between love and responsibility is incredibly tough, but I hope we have done that pretty well.

As if parenthood was not already tough as it is, the environment in which we bring up children now makes it even tougher. Technology, lots of television and the internet have made parenting really very difficult. The cost of bringing up children has also risen astronomically. If I were getting married for the first time, and I were to bring up children now, I would not have so many because it is a huge challenge and horrendously expensive to bring up children the way one would want these days. Frankly, considering the environment they grew up in, I am surprised that my children are all avid readers and most of the older ones are not really into television or video games. The world is changing which means parenting will have to change I suppose. Nevertheless, I am a little scared of the environment in which parents now must bring up children.

Hamza Zayyad

As I stated earlier, since my father died, I have had a handful of men who became role models. My elder brother Bashir was certainly one of them, as was my cousin Yahaya Hamza in Kaduna. With my marriage to Hadiza Isma came a third one - unwittingly, Dr. Hamza Zayyad, Wazirin Katsina.

Dr. Hamza Zayyad was Nigeria's first privatisation czar and at one point one of the most influential people in Nigeria. I got to know him and we got very close when Hadiza and I married because it happened that Dr. Zayyad was a very close friend of her late father's and was the one who stood in as her father during our wedding. We therefore became family members and he became very much my father-in-law. For this reason, we visited the Zayyad household regularly and he got to like me. I would go visit him virtually every Sunday and we would have lunch and just chat. He was a chartered accountant by training who spent most of his life in public service in finance functions and grew to be very influential. In his lifetime, there was virtually no one that Hamza Zayyad could not call in Nigeria and arrange an appointment with, from the president downwards. He had at different times telephoned at least four presidents of Nigeria in my presence. In his life time, I believe he knew everyone of substance in Nigeria.

I once asked him, "What is the secret? Should I go back to school and be a chartered accountant?" His response I have kept in mind through all the years since. "The first secret is Barewa College," he said. Like me, Zayyad was a Barewa old boy, as were four or five Nigerian heads of state. At the time that Zayyad attended Barewa, it was without a doubt the premier high school in the northern region. So the Barewa network was one secret. "The second" he continued, "is, developing people. In my career I developed people; I hired good people and trained them to be better. I trained many people, I made sure I educated more and more people; these people tend to grow in their careers and one can always draw satisfaction from that." Finally, he said, "Maintain your friendships."

He then explained to me that when he was head of the New Nigeria Development Company – the NNDC – and when he was the chief financial officer of Ahmadu Bello University, he made sure that all those that worked for him obtained degrees and professional qualifications that they did not previously have. He sent them to the best institutions like Harvard Business School, Massachusetts Institute of Technology (M.I.T.), and such other places for professional development and training. Many of those people eventually became successful in their private and public lives and they owed part of their success to him, so he could call anybody when needed. Even through my time at Barewa College, the old boys' network mostly worked that way – General Gowon was Zayyad's senior and head boy, Murtala Muhammad, I think was his classmate. So Hamza knew several Nigerian presidents, either through being classmates/schoolmates, or via the influential alumni association - the Barewa Old Boys' Association (BOBA). Fast forward to our generation, the Barewa tradition and networks were sustained - Umaru Yar'Adua was Sani Maikudi's cousin, who was in turn my guardian, so we were linked. Afakirya Gadzama was my house prefect, General Luka Yusuf was a Barewa Old Boy - President Umaru Yar'Adua appointed Gadzama head of SSS, and Luka to head the Nigerian Army!

Hamza Zayyad also assisted our consulting business in a significant way because whenever we came across any public or private institution undertaking a major construction project that we had no direct contacts with or did not know well enough to approach on our own, he would call and set up an appointment for us to go, market our services and make a presentation. We got a lot of work that way and our business grew with his kind assistance. So he was really a mentor in addition to being father-in-law and a role model.

It was also Hamza Zayyad who interested me in privatisation and encouraged me to enrol in a certificate course in privatisation with the Arthur D. Little School of Management. As the head of the TCPC and its successor, the BPE - the federal privatisation agency - he got me involved in the work he was doing and got me doing part time work in several committees of the agency. He asked me to join Mouftah Baba-Ahmed to be his second Special Assistant in 1992, but I was unable to accept due to my disdain for full-time public service. Nevertheless, my eventual appointment to head the BPE probably would not have happened – either from the perspective of my qualifications or knowledge – had it not been for Hamza Zayyad's mentorship. When he died in 2001, I thought it only appropriate to have the BPE building named after him, not only because he began the nation's privatisation journey, helped mentor me and several others in so many ways, but more importantly, from a public service standpoint, he had an awesome capacity to build strong public institutions almost from scratch. The NNDC was one such example – he built it up to be at one point, the largest conglomerate in Nigeria. He also built the BPE from scratch to be one of the best run public institutions in Nigeria. By the time I took it over from Bernard Verr less than a year after Zayyad's exit, it was the solid foundations that we inherited that made the job easier. However, before I was to take the reins of the BPE, there were still more lessons I had to learn in the private sector first.

El-Rufai & Partners

Without a doubt one of the most difficult decisions I have ever made in my professional life came with the restructuring of the ownership of El-Rufai & Partners in 1989, when I was faced with the prospect of giving up something I contributed to creating and in the process lost one of my best friends. Though I was first to be professionally licensed and I started the practice full-time, we all agreed to be equal partners with the tacit understanding that they would come on board when the workload expanded beyond what one or two professionals could handle. The partners were Abba Bello Ingawa, myself, Husaini Dikko and Sani Maikudi. All of us met and became friends in Barewa College. Sani was our senior, graduating in 1978, Husaini and I in 1980 and Abba in 1981.

Abba Bello Ingawa was my closest friend from our Barewa College days. I used to spend some of my holidays in his home town of Katsina, and he would spend some holidays with me in Kaduna. We were so close, we were more than just friends we were, simply put, brothers. In 1988, we landed a huge construction consulting job to provide QS services that would entail building six hundred and fifty political party offices covering every part of the country. We were about to be a national brand and we were going to get into a lot more money than we ever dreamt of. One day, without any hints at all, Abba shocked us all by giving us notice to wind up our firm. When I asked him what the problem was, his response was simply, "You are the problem."

Our firm had grown to be the largest quantity surveying and construction management consulting firm in Nigeria, a speedy ascent from its founding by one full-time person in 1982. We achieved such fast success, in my opinion, because we had a good mix of skills among the four of us. In fact, it was more than just a good mix; I thought we had a perfect partnership. Abba was calm and reserved, sometimes spoke with a stutter when excited, and initially, was reluctant to approach clients and to do the presentational and marketing ends of the business, with which the rest of us were more comfortable. He was at his best in the office running things - a sound operations and meticulous financial manager who organised internal resources and kept the accounts and books in balance. Husaini Dikko was street smart and very patient, excellent at following up on jobs and payments, getting new work and he did not get upset easily. Husaini could go to an office and wait from morning until night for a lowly clerk to sign a paper so that we could get paid. Abba and I did not have the patience to do that. The fourth, Sani Maikudi was older, more mature and better-connected, particularly in government circles where the people you know are often more important than mere technical competence. This mix of strengths enabled us to go from a start-up to being the largest quantity surveying firm in Nigeria in less than eight years.

There generally were very few disagreements about strategy and decision making until Abba shocked us that fateful morning in 1989 and decided things were not to his liking. The heart of the problem, we later realised, lay in the firm's name: El-Rufai

&Partners. As noted, the reason for the name was historical - that I was the first to pass the professional licensing exams and then stepped out of paid employment to establish the consulting firm. As the other partners joined in a full-time capacity and we grew more successful, people began to call it 'El-Rufai's firm' instead of what it truly was - El-Rufai and three equal partners. Just my name was becoming better known and over time, this apparently may have grated on Abba without the rest of us being aware of it.

On top of it all, at that point I was planning to leave the firm on a career sabbatical and had been offered a job with AT&T Network Systems International BV in the Netherlands. We called a partnership meeting to discuss my offer to withdraw from the firm instead of considering Abba's request to dissolve the partnership. I offered to resign, which everybody initially accepted. My partners then proposed we asked our statutory auditors, Dala Akpati & Co., to value the firm and that I should be paid one quarter of it in cash and kind, effectively liquidating my stake. My stance was that our friendships were too close for me to take money out of the firm, so I thought it better if they just kept my part and continued the business as three equal partners while I went and did something else with my life. I had developed an interest in telecommunications and management consulting and was willing to move on anyway, I added. What was the point in taking money out of the firm? We were like blood brothers. I said if they wanted to continue using my name on the notepaper and the firm's curriculum vitae, it was fine by me because I had no plans to practice quantity surveying anywhere else in the world so would never be a competitor. I suggested that if they chose to remove my name, that was fine too – I gave them every option but did not want any money or share of the business. This became a deal-breaker for Abba, who perhaps took my offer as an insult. In the end, the three of us paid off Abba in cash and some assets, and he left to start his own firm with some of our staff who elected to go with him.

This became the painful interruption of what had been a very long friendship and one of the toughest personal challenges I have ever had to confront. I named my second son Mohammed Bello, after Abba's deceased father – we were that close. To this day, thinking about the incident and aftermath still causes me some pain. We have seen each other from time to time since then, but never really got back to what we used to be. Among the many things I learned from that experience, was that a business partnership is not easy to sustain, especially with friends. In fact, being friends makes it even more difficult to manage. Equally as significant, I learned what can happen when ego and interests are not appropriately understood and managed. This lesson in particular was to recur several times in my public service experiences.

This same lesson was to influence my subsequent public and private sector career – the need for clear, de-personalised rules of engagement in any official relationship, regular and open communication, and consciously minimizing the frequency of business dealings with close friends and family members. El-Rufai & Partners continued to thrive in spite of this setback and I moved on to other engagements in telecommunications consulting sporadically over the next nine years. What never occurred to me at any point while I was acquiring exposure in areas as diverse as privatization and telecommunications was that the experiences would lead me to a memorable nine years in the public service of the government of the federation.

Chapter Three

From Abacha to Obasanjo – A Series of Accidents

> *"The punishment we suffer, if we refuse to take an interest in matters of government, is to live under the government of worse men."*
>
> *– Plato, 3000 BCE*

I still remember where I was the day General Sani Abacha died in 1998. I had relocated from Lagos back to Kaduna in February of that year and was trying to figure out how El-Rufai & Partners would remain afloat amidst spending cuts in public works with crude oil prices barely above $10 a barrel. I am not usually an early riser, but for some strange reason I was up at five that morning – the 8th of June, 1998 – and was in the office by six. I had taken my first cup of coffee when I got a call from a friend in Abuja informing me that General Abacha was rumoured to be dead.

The death of Abacha was quite critical an event in the history of Nigeria's democracy. For fifteen years between 1984 and 1998, Nigeria had been ruled by a series of increasingly malevolent military dictatorships, and the Abacha regime, which came into being in November of 1993, was considered among the worst by many commentators. Rumours of his ill-health and regular need for steroid injections were quite commonplace in those days, but he had such a larger-than-life persona that nobody quite thought the man could die anytime soon. His control of the political space was so firm that all five officially recognised political parties in Nigeria had adopted him as their presidential candidate for the October 1998 elections even though he was still in military uniform. That Abacha was mortal and could die simply never occurred to many Nigerians like the foreign minister in the Yar'Adua regime, Ojo Maduekwe, who suggested in March 1998during the infamous 'million-man-march to draft Abacha' that unless Abacha continued to rule the country, Nigeria would cease to exist as an entity. Yet he died soon after and here we are!

By nine o'clock that morning, we had firm confirmation that Abacha had indeed died from a sudden heart attack. The uncertainty surrounding his succession ended some fifteen hours later when Major-General Abdulsalami Abubakar was sworn in as Head of State and Commander-in-Chief of the Nigerian Armed Forces. By the following morning, Mallam Ibrahim Aliyu, then Chairman of Intercellular Nigeria Ltd., had called me on behalf of the new president to come to Abuja 'for two weeks' to help think through and design a social, economic and political transition programme for the Abdulsalami Administration. I went to Abuja on the 10th of June 1998, and unknown to me, was to remain there more or less permanently in various public service positions until about ten years later in June 2008.[24]

Intercellular Nigeria Limited was the fixed wireless telephone services company my brother Bashir and some of his colleagues and friends established in 1996 after being compulsorily retired by Abacha from Nitel, the defunct monopoly of the Nigerian telecommunications industry. Bashir invited Ibrahim Aliyu to be the chairman of the board because as an intelligent and well-respected technocrat, and former permanent secretary of the ministry of communications, he knew the telecommunications business, was wealthy and well-connected. Personally, I consider Ibrahim Aliyu to be one of the wisest and most capable persons I have had the pleasure to work with and learn from. General Abubakar happened to be an in-law of Ibrahim and requested him to put together a small team of trusted, apolitical experts to advise him on political and economic transition. Ibrahim suggested a six-person advisory committee, consisting of three northerners and three southerners. This was what came to be known as General Abubakar's personal think-tank - the Programme Implementation and Monitoring Committee, generally referred to as PIMCO. Alhaji Yesufu, an experienced permanent secretary represented the secretary to the government of the federation, Gidado Idris, on the committee.

I subsequently learnt from a mutual friend that Abubakar had remembered me because I had met him a couple of times in the course of my quantity surveying career and may have debated the role of the military in politics and governance. My guess is the new Head of State thought he needed some contrarian views to enrich his policy decisions, so he had two such people. Abdulsalami's bosom friend, Dr. Tunde Soleye - an intelligent, cynical and feisty medical doctor - would be my southern counterpart, and we went on to become very close friends. The other members of PIMCO were Ibrahim Aliyu (chairman), Brigadier-General Anthony Ukpo, Abubakar Gimba, Amah Iwuagwu, Dr. Ajuji Ahmed (a civil servant) was the secretary, Dantala Mohammed was our absentee protocol officer, and my assistant, Peter Akagu-Jones, was the assistant secretary who did most of the secretarial work. PIMCO at my urging brought Dr. Mansur Mukhtar from the World Bank to be our 'Chief Economist'. As an ad-hoc committee, we had no offices or staff as such. Our de facto secretariat was my suite at the Hilton Hotel - room 132 where I lived for nearly 11 months.

Our task at PIMCO was multifarious. In no particular order of importance, PIMCO ultimately had responsibility for drawing up an economic and political transition programme for the new administration; designing a plan to re-engage with the International Monetary Fund and other multilaterals; outlining the broad policy thrust of the 1999 federal budget; supervising the constitutional review and consultation process; drafting pieces of key legislation that eventually laid the foundations for Nigeria's Fourth Republic; supervising the planning and organisation of the elections and the handover of power to a democratically elected government; and advising General Abubakar on whom to appoint as ministers and the like.

Amah Iwuagwu and I worked and focused mostly on the economic programmes, leading the IMF negotiations, drafting the letter of intent, redesigning the privatisation programme and crafting the enabling legislation, doing some speech-writing, and vetting INEC's election budget, among other assignments. Abubakar Gimba was the lead presidential speechwriter. The one speech that I recall writing almost single-handedly was for the swearing-in of the thirty six state governors - or military administrators as they were called at the time. We all learnt a lot about how the federal government functioned under the military, and I was personally intrigued and educated throughout the period of being a presidential counsellor.

How people get appointed into senior positions in government

Among these many tasks, there were two major eye openers for me. One was learning how people get appointed to senior positions in government. Shortly after we were constituted as PIMCO, General Abdulsalami sent us a sheaf of papers with a list of people by name, ministry and state, with some names already assigned to ministries. He was assembling his cabinet and needed us to plug the names into the appropriate positions and all we had was a list of names, no curriculum vitae, no biographical profiles, nothing. We also had to identify which were the key ministries to ensure that each geopolitical zone had a minister in each of these key areas. We concluded that the key ministries were finance, works, petroleum, agriculture, education and defence. Interestingly foreign affairs, FCT, Transport and Power were considered 'second-tier'! What made a ministry 'key' I came to learn, was largely determined by history, politics and having a big enough budget such that were anyone in charge so inclined, he or she would find no shortage of patronage to take care of our rent-seeking elite!

In addition to the few names Abdulsalami personally wanted to appoint as ministers, he must have called his armed services heads – the chiefs of army staff, air staff, navy, chief of defence staff and the inspector-general of police and asked them for nominations for ministerial appointments. He then must have contacted all living former presidents, and such prominent Nigerians, informing them that he was forming his cabinet and asked them for 'recommendations'. Of course, in addition to all these 'influencers,' any other person who might have the president's ear - like his wife, close friends and associates may also have contributed names. By the time the list and accompanying information came to us in PIMCO, it was a rather long list and we were supposed to trim, choose, and make sense of it all.

One of the more memorable people whose emergence I thought was indicative of the accidental nature of how this process can unfold was Mallam Ismaila Usman, who became Abdulsalami Abubakar's finance minister. The way in which he became a minister was weird, particularly for a ministry as important as finance. The original name that came recommended for finance minister was Dr. Shamsuddeen Usman. In the course of the debate over key ministries and need for balance, the nomination was set aside in favour of someone from South-West, and a Minister of State from the North-West was required instead. I suggested Ismaila Usman, a person I had met only once when he was an Executive Director at First Bank in the early 1980s, and whose name was not on the original long list, but who was well-known then in the public space. What we all knew was that he was the deputy governor for international operations of the Central Bank of Nigeria (CBN) during Abacha's regime. He became better known and earned respect nationally when, according to the Abuja rumour mill, Abacha, through Paul Ogwuma the governor, instructed him to transfer some monies in tens of millions of dollars, to an account abroad and he allegedly told Ogwuma and Abacha to take a hike. Nobody disobeyed Abacha in those days, but Ismaila Usman was reported to have said he was not going to sign off on the transaction, because, it was highly irregular and contrary to the law.

Abacha allegedly suspended Ismaila Usman for his temerity and insubordination and he remained suspended until Abacha died. One of the first decisions that Abdulsalami took on assumption of office was to recall Ismaila and reinstate him to his CBN job, so suggesting his name up for the finance ministry seemed logical to all of us. Here is a decent guy, chartered and certified accountant, former CEO of banks and then deputy governor of the central bank – why not? Rasheed Gbadamosi, a one-time chairman of the NIDB (now Bank of Industry), who was well-known to Ibrahim Aliyu had been proposed as Finance Minister, with Ismaila Usman as minister of state. This was PIMCO's recommendation that went to the ruling junta. As it turned out, the junta's reconfiguration had Gbadamosi end up as minister of national planning, and Ismaila Usman became the finance minister. Apart from some minor changes, a lot of what we recommended was more or less upheld. To this day I do not think Ismaila fully knew how he got there or may have been told other versions, and we finally met in his capacity as finance minister, worked very well together on many issues like privatisation, and he became an elder brother and guide in many ways.

Professor Musa Yakubu, who eventually became internal affairs minister, was a similar sort of story – a distinguished academic appointed minister, apparently with no political godfather, no lobbying, nothing of any sort, but just a freak accident. The original debate that brought his name up was about who would be Abdulsalami's special adviser on legal matters. The legal adviser to Abacha was Professor Auwalu Yadudu, who was expected to be replaced. We discussed names for this position and one of the names that emerged on the shortlist was Musa Yakubu, then a law professor at Ahmadu Bello University. I remember that he was from Adamawa state, and the name came up as a possibility for legal adviser to replace Yadudu. When the shortlist of cabinet nominees went to the junta, the reconfiguration required a cabinet nominee that was not Fulani, but from one of the smaller ethnic groups, and General Abdulsalami wanted it within the next hour. PIMCO chair Ibrahim Aliyu made one phone call to confirm that Musa Yakubu was not Fulani and then gave his name to the head of state. That was how Musa Yakubu became the minister of internal affairs!

The percentage of the president's cabinet and senior government positions that are filled in the manner that found Ismaila Usman and Musa Yakubu in their positions does warrant some reflection. To begin with, this hardly needs saying, but I will do so anyway: there is neither rarely any merit attached nor any selection and review process, to appointing leadership particularly under military regimes. Typically, various names are contributed by the political elite, collected into a long list; someone or a small group reviews the list, prunes some out, sending the result to some committee to assign them to various ministries and the head of state makes some last minute reassignment of portfolios. In other words, Nigeria's governance outcomes really depend on a series of accidents rather than any meritocratic or rigorous process. When you have a good person in a high level job, it was most likely an accident – and my own story, if I am judged as any good, fits this mould as well. I will be the first to say that my own rise through public service was largely luck, being at the right place at the right time, being known by Ibrahim Aliyu as a frank, outspoken and feisty character, and perhaps simply being Bashir El-Rufai's geeky, studious kid brother.

I believe that we have failed to develop any process of identifying, training and rewarding leadership, of putting people who are potential leaders through a crucible to determine their preparedness and worth. Instead, people just emerge out of nowhere. Sometimes we get lucky, like with Ismaila Usman, who was not on anyone's shortlist but turned out to be a fantastic finance minister although the process from which he emerged at the point he did was mostly pure accident. As I observed earlier, Nigeria no longer has the likes of Oxford, Cambridge and LSE where the bulk of the British leadership is incubated, nor a Harvard, Princeton and Yale, where a large percentage of American's business and political leadership is groomed. This is why every Nigerian above the age 30 believes he or she can run for governor, senator or president. The final nails in the coffin of any meritocracy or track record of governance in Nigeria as basis for leadership selection were driven in when President Obasanjo chose Umaru Yar'Adua whose ill-health, among other challenges, was known already to constitute a serious impediment to the possibility of any inspired and energetic leadership. The view of many well-informed Nigerians is that Yar'Adua and his deputy, Goodluck Jonathan, emerged for no other discernible reasons than being 'weak' governors sympathetic to the 'Third Term' project and therefore hand-picked as payback. The subsequent electoral imposition of Goodluck Jonathan as president in 2011 via military occupation and rigging has been unhelpful in raising leadership quality. Jonathan went into a presidential contest without a campaign manifesto, boasting of no experience, merit and any track record of previous performance other than wearing no shoes to school and his "good luck"! I believe that we need to work on unwinding such scripts as the routes to leadership attainment in our country.

Determining a handover date

The other big eye opener for me was how literally a handful of people decided a date for Abdulsalami to hand power to the next democratically elected president. At the first meeting of PIMCO on the 10th of June, 1998, Abdulsalami made it clear that because the military had lost credibility from seemingly endless transitions, postponements and cancellations of elections, he wished to conclude the Abacha transition and hand over power on the first of January, 1999. Our initial response was that this sounded fine, but the junta still needed to consult more widely - to find out what majority of Nigerians thought on that and other related matters. By that point, Abacha's transition to democracy had advanced with elected state and national assembly members and we had the governorships and presidential elections left to hold when Abacha died. Abacha had created political parties which were more or less state organs all working toward endorsing him to be the sole candidate in the coming presidential election then scheduled for October, 1998[25].

Once that happened, it meant we had to start the transition process nearly afresh. Abolishing all parties and cancelling all previously scheduled elections necessarily meant a new programme would have to be designed from scratch. The new parties would need some time to form, hold congresses, primaries and convention, followed by national elections with enough room for any potential post-election litigation to take its course. Only then could power be handed over by the military junta.

Considering that based on this feedback, elections had to be postponed until February 1999, Abdulsalami's wish to be out of power by the first of January was obviously off the table. The initial date that was fixed for handing power was in mid-April, but our chairman Ibrahim Aliyu raised the point that two months may not be enough time for all the post-election litigation and adjudication process to be done before hand-over. More time may be needed because we knew that our elections tended to be contentious, and politicians therefore litigated a lot – candidates always go to election tribunals even when they have clearly lost an election, hoping a technicality will earn a cancellation and re-run. I was mandated to see the then Chief Justice of Nigeria, Justice Mohammed Lawal Uwais, to get an idea of how much time in the courts would be adequate after the elections for all post-election litigations to run their course. The experienced jurist did a step-by-step analysis of civil procedures likely to be complied with, and was of the opinion that the courts would need until the end of April to the middle of May to dispose of all election petitions from the proposed February election dates. When I took that back to PIMCO, we added four weeks from mid-May and we landed on Saturday, the 12th of June as the hand-over date. The first lady, Justice Fati Abubakar - a senior high court judge herself - weighed in on Justice Uwais' recommended time-line with her husband to get his quick buy-in to adopt what PIMCO suggested as the hand-over date.

Now, any student of Nigerian politics should know that the 12th of June is about as close to bad karma for the military regime as you can get - it was the date of the election which M.K.O. Abiola won and was later annulled by General Babangida. Abdulsalami recognised this date as well, so we moved two weeks backward to the 29th of May, which has remained our 'Democracy Day' and a national holiday ever since. Our colleague, Dr. Tunde Soleye, was not privy to this decision but had a different basis of objection to any handover date later than June 8. Tunde believed that any person that spends more than 12 months in Aso Villa goes mad literally and begins to try every scheme not to ever leave the office and residence of the president. He was determined to protect his friend Abdulsalami Abubakar from that affliction and therefore separately insisted that he must hand over before the anniversary of Abacha's death. Only time will prove Tunde's theory wrong because so far, it appears to hold true - with all occupants of the Villa from Babangida through Obasanjo to Yar'Adua, and even Jonathan - being rumoured (or in some cases, confirmed) to have had/have tenure extension plans!

The IMF Experience

It was not only the inner workings of the Nigerian government which opened my eyes; re-establishing a working relationship with the multilateral institutions and, in particular, the International Monetary Fund provided some unexpected insight into Nigeria's place in the world. At that point, the multilaterals had virtually left Nigeria and the club of British ex-colonies, the Commonwealth, had suspended Nigeria from its active roster of engaged membership. In short, Nigeria had become an international pariah.

PIMCO, along with Finance Minister Ismaila Usman, agreed that re-establishing ties with the IMF was desirable in sorting out our debts and obtaining grants-in-aid from international donors. The IMF team, led by Dr. Hiroyuki Hino, arrived from Washington, DC for the re-engagement negotiations. We debated and agreed the broad contents of key reforms that will be required to implement an IMF-Staff Monitored Programme (SMP), the outline for the letter of intent and the benchmarks the country needed to meet to earn some concessions on our external debt burden. The next day, some members of PIMCO went to meet with finance ministry staff to work on the letter and found an existing draft on the table, already written. I was impressed initially because I thought the finance ministry had drafted it overnight, but later found it was a 'suggestion' from the IMF. The letter of intent is supposed to be a letter written by the government, committing to specific reforms addressed to the Fund, but the draft on the table was what the IMF wanted us to write them. I do not know if the assumption was that we could not produce such a letter ourselves, but I have since learned that this was what they did everywhere at the time. This partly explained why most of the reform programmes 'agreed with' African countries have failed. Frequently, it is not a cooperative process, but imposed from the outside. Most of the time, the people signing the dotted lines do not care to fully understand what they are committing to so it is hard to fulfil it. There is no sense of ownership by the officials, the government and the country.

At that moment, I understood that the reason many African countries agreed to the 'conditionality', took this pre-fabricated letter, signed it, got the money and then refused to implement the reforms, was that often, they are not reforms from which any self-respecting government can legitimately derive any sense of ownership. I also appreciated why in the mid-1980s, a lot of the multilateral policies turned out to be destructive for Africa. These policies required many indebted African countries to balance their budgets, with the assumption being that budget deficits are bad, caused interest rates to rise, leading to inflation and a whole mess of other problems, so we all must first balance our budgets at all costs and nearly immediately. But what did it mean to balance the budget? It meant cutting expenditures on social services, firing teachers, reducing the numbers of health care staff, and raising the cost of medicines, education and other social services.

The result, at least in the 1980s, was that many of our children dropped out of school, maternal and infant mortality increased because parents could not afford suddenly higher medicine prices and household budgets had to adjust accordingly. The so-called 'Washington Consensus' has since been shown to fail. Balancing the budget, cutting social sector spending, devaluing the currency – these actions did not necessarily lead to economic growth, and to the extent they did, that growth came at a steep price, often without creating jobs or reducing poverty. The policies were not totally negative, though. Forcing African nations to be prudent and balance their budgets resulted in many governments learning to be more fiscally efficient. Compelling countries to deregulate and privatise certain public enterprises resulted in concentrated growth within some sectors, reduction of waste and corruption and improved quality of goods and services. So some things worked, but most of the policies failed because they did not account for context, or cared about the well-being of the ordinary citizens of the developing countries.

In the end, we made a lot of corrections, introduced some major changes to the draft the IMF provided and did not agree on many of the policies initially proposed. We did finalise a draft acceptable to the government and the IMF, and Ismaila Usman as minister of finance put his letterhead on it and sent it in. The IMF's sometimes heavy-handed tactics aside, I came out of the encounter with two very worthy results: I gained a valuable friend in Hiroyuki Hino, who played a vital role in helping the BPE thrive during our early days there; and I had a hands-on frame of reference for facing multilaterals when some years later we negotiated a credit to support the privatisation programme and later, the conditions precedent for the forgiveness of part of our Paris Club debt.

The IMF no longer does business the way we experienced it in the eighties and nineties, and the Washington Consensus has since been revised, expanded and largely discarded. Indeed, the biggest joke on the Washington Consensus is being played out in Washington, DC itself. With the economic meltdown in the USA in 2008 and the on-going Euro crisis that began in 2010, the IMF sadly failed to advise these highly-indebted countries to devalue their currencies, balance their budgets and cut social spending! Instead, the IMF was silent while reflationary spending, huge budget deficits and currency appreciation measures were taken by clearly bankrupt, but 'developed' nations and its substantial shareholders. These actions are the exact opposite of the mantra preached to Less Developed Countries in the 1980s! Many Africans see this double standard, and ask whether the policies of the eighties and nineties were intentionally designed to further impoverish them and their nations! Some have even implied that racism was at work when these policies were designed, but the 'shock therapy' reforms in Russia, arising from the advice of then Harvard (now Columbia) professor Jeffrey Sachs, gives the lie to all these racist conspiracy theories. I think the IMF just did not know better then, and hopefully, has since learnt a few lessons regarding its own infallibility.

Meeting Obasanjo, for the first time

The first time I met President Obasanjo, in the aftermath of the 1999 elections, hardly left the impression that we were destined to develop a working professional relationship, or that we would come to know each other as well as we have, or even that he would ever want anything to do with me. Quite the opposite appeared to be the case, in fact.

The setting was a briefing on the state of Nigeria's relations with the multilateral institutions in April 1999. As he was the president-elect, PIMCO was directed to brief him on what economic policy directions we had been working on and the vital components of the transition that should be expected. I was assigned by PIMCO chair Ibrahim Aliyu to lead this briefing, along with Amah Iwuagwu. The country director of the World Bank and the head of the IMF team from Washington, and their staff accompanied us, while Obasanjo was with Atiku Abubakar, numerous aides, staff and future cabinet ministers that I cannot now recall.

Obasanjo had once been head of state, so we knew a bit about him and I had read a lot about him as well. He was known for his sense of humour, but not necessarily as someone that came across at first blush, as clever, witty or intelligent. All of the Obasanjo jokes then were about how much of a bumpkin he was thought to be. But at that first face-to-face meeting, I was quite impressed with him. He came across as a smart and well-informed person and it was clear that he picked up new concepts and absorbed information quickly. However, I was a little disappointed in one respect: he seemed to be firmly rooted in the past. He thought Nigeria was exactly where he left it in 1979. When we explained to him that we had executed a staff-monitored programme with the IMF which committed the incoming administration to privatisation of public enterprises, reform of the public service and overhaul of the federal procurement system, he stopped us right on our tracks.

"I am not going to do any privatisation. Military rule destroyed all these public institutions by putting some bad people in charge. My government will fix these problems; I will make sure the parastatals work efficiently by appointing the right people to run all the public institutions." he said.

As I think the ensuing years have shown us, Obasanjo entered the first term of his second presidency with a pair of 20-year old blinders on his eyes. He felt that the post-Obasanjo civilian and military regimes were solely responsible for the malfunctioning of public utilities and the dysfunction in the civil service. This was not entirely inaccurate, but not the whole story. Intuitively, Obasanjo's gut feeling informed by his background, age and previous experiences is that only the government could be fair to everyone. He therefore wanted a significant government presence in economic activities as it had during his first outing as head of state in the mid-to-late 1970s. That first time, he actually doubled the role of the government and public enterprises in the economy from about 22 per cent of GDP[26] to 44 per cent within three years of taking charge.

During that April 1999 briefing, he very clearly failed to realise that in the twenty intervening years the civil service had become totally dysfunctional and public utilities were not working at all. The attitude that he could fix them all and that no privatisation or public sector reform would be needed was in my view a very simplistic approach to a very complex problem. I told him so very politely, which started an argument that left everyone's jaws on the floor, because nobody argued with General Obasanjo then. He came into the presidency with this high profile: a war hero and former general that signed the instrument of surrender of the Nigerian civil war, the only military head of state then to voluntarily hand over power in Nigeria. Nobody argued with him. Even my boss, General Abdulsalami, deferred to him because Obasanjo was a senior colonel at the time he joined the armed forces in 1969. This technically made Obasanjo his 'ex-boss' and he referred to him as such. Everyone deferred to Obasanjo and here I was openly disagreeing with him. He did not appear pleased with that.

That was the first time I met this African big man, and I honestly thought it would be my last time. When I was arguing with him, everybody just froze out of shock. We moved on to other topics, and then towards the end of the briefing, we began discussing the accomplishments of the Petroleum (Special) Trust Fund (PTF). The PTF was headed by General Muhammadu Buhari and was set up to fund the construction and maintenance of roads, water works, schools, hospitals and social infrastructure in the country directly from the proceeds of increase in the prices of petroleum products. Obasanjo again took the opportunity to give us a preview of his intentions.

"It (the PTF) is unconstitutional and as soon as the constitution takes effect, I am winding that up. We will not have any organisation existing as a parallel government." My response was an immediate, knee-jerk reaction to what I thought was another misconception.

"General Sir, I suggest that you should not wind up the PTF immediately, but should align its funding and operations with the constitution and democratic government." I replied. "What you said is true, its funding would be unconstitutional in a few weeks, but it is the only government agency doing any meaningful infrastructure and capital projects in the country."

"No – no. I don't think so. We will fix these other agencies to work too" he said.

He plainly thought he was a magician who could snap his fingers and make things work. I was afraid that things were not going to work quite the way he thought.

"Sir, this is the only agency re-building roads, fixing schools, water works and hospitals in the country. You should re-consider the decision to abruptly wind it up," I insisted. "Delay that action until you re-build the implementation capacity of the line ministries while slowing down the scope of activities of the fund."

"No, young man, I will not, and I know what I am talking about."

Again everybody froze. So, in a single 45-minute meeting, I argued with Obasanjo twice, and our debating took up nearly one third of the time. In a post-meeting attempt at damage control, I called Ibrahim Aliyu and General Abdulsalami Abubakar immediately after the meeting to report myself, and told them that I just disagreed and argued with Abdulsalami's boss - twice. Ibrahim Aliyu was unconcerned since he knew me better, but Abdulsalami was initially alarmed. When I explained the full discussion, he said, "Well I think you are right but Obasanjo does not like being argued with." With better understanding of Obasanjo in subsequent years, I realised that many people got that wrong about him - the Obasanjo I came to know loved being argued with, providing your contrary positions are driven by logic and objectivity rather than any hint of some narrow self-interest! In cabinet meetings between 2003 and 2007, Oby Ezekwesili and I disagreed and argued with Obasanjo on several occasions, and he loved us for it! The proof was that we served out our tenures while other more timorous souls got booted out!

I do not know if my confrontation with Obasanjo was courage as much as it was mostly just honesty. I believed that wrong decisions would be taken that could adversely affect the welfare of millions based on incorrect assumptions about the realities of the country. I was convinced I was right and he was wrong and that when he took over he would realise this about both privatisation and the PTF. It was clear to me that Obasanjo was living in the past, and a lot had happened (and changed) since 1979 that he had been unable to appreciate. I was set in the view that I was right and had no difficulty at all voicing my opinions. Regardless of the consequences, I was sure Obasanjo would never want to see my face again but thought someone needed to tell him what I said to him. I was therefore caught completely off-guard a few days later when a friend of my brother Bashir's called me on behalf of the president-elect.

"General Obasanjo wants to see you."

"Really? What about?" I asked.

"Well, he was asking people around him who knows how to

get hold of you. 'Does anyone know that light skinned Fulani boy, the small Fulani boy?' This is what he was asking everyone. I said I could get you."

He could not even remember my name, he just remembered me as the small light skinned Fulani boy. This friend of my brother's, Captain Shehu Iyal, told him that I was like a kid brother to him. I met with Obasanjo in his hotel suite then - room 546 at the Abuja Hilton, late in April 1999.When I entered his suite, he was wearing nothing except the hotel bathrobe – almost completely naked. He had just that dressing gown, with nothing under. I learned much later that he deliberately worked at giving people the impression that he was a bushman, but it was all just a disarming or provocative act. In any event, that day in his hotel room, the second time I met Obasanjo, he told me he was impressed by my arguments and grasp of the facts even though we differed ideologically and he disagreed with my suggestions.

"You know young man, I like you. You are a very clever man. I want you to work with me when I take over."

I was somewhat surprised to hear that and he went on to explain why.

"When I was military head of state, I had a group of five or six people who were young, sharp, dedicated and honest and I used them as sounding board of every major policy position that got to my desk.[27] Whenever I have a key policy decision to take, I handed the problem to them to debate and then they would come back to me with options, their conclusions and recommendations. They are all old now - some are deceased, but I will need a group like that to help me when I take over as president. So I am going to look for you then."

"Well thank you very much sir," I said. "It would be a pleasure to work with you, but I would like a real job."

"What do you mean, 'real job'? Working with me is not a real job?"

"Not an advisory job. I do not want to be advising people, even presidents, Sir – I have done it all my life. I want something that will enable me to put advice into practice."

"Ok, well you will have that too, it can be interesting. When I take over, I will look for you, I will find you." I thought that would be the end of it.

Some weeks later, Steven Oronsaye (who was still at the finance ministry then, but in regular touch with Obasanjo), asked me to come to Abuja to meet with Obasanjo[28]. Obasanjo informed me of his intention to proceed with winding up the Petroleum (Special) Trust Fund and suggested that I should join Dr. Haroun Adamu to work on that assignment. I declined politely, explaining that I did not believe it was the best decision in the circumstances, and did not meet my expectations of a real job and a 'positive contribution'. President Obasanjo was not very pleased with that response and threatened to announce my name as part of the PTF winding-up team. In the end he relented and let me off the hook. I left for Kaduna the following day.

Early in July, Steve called again on behalf of the president. Again, I went to Abuja to meet with Obasanjo, who informed me that he had decided to proceed with implementing the privatisation and commercialisation programme, but cautiously and in a phased manner. We debated phasing and came up with three implementation stages. Steve and I then drafted letters of instruction for the inauguration of the privatisation council to be headed by Vice-President Atiku Abubakar, and handed them in the next day.

A month later, President Obasanjo invited me again to the state house and asked whether I would like to be his Special Assistant on Budget Matters. I respectfully reminded him that I would prefer a real job - an executive position with responsibility instead of an advisory or assistantship role. As a construction consultant for many years, I advised people on how to spend their money and in PIMCO I was part of a team advising the head of state on economic and political programmes. I was all too familiar with the limitations of being an adviser. An adviser gives advice that may be accepted or rejected, but I do not believe that one gets things done by being an advisor or being an assistant at 39 years of age. I wanted the opportunity to get things done, to get my hands dirty, which is why I preferred an executive position. In any event, I thought that an assistant to the president on budget matters would put me squarely in the firing line between two senior cabinet members – the minister of finance, Adamu Ciroma, and the Chief Economic Adviser, Philip Asiodu, both struggling at the time for control of economic policy and the budget in the new dispensation. I was not sure that was the best place to be.

In the end I ended up joining the Obasanjo administration at the end of 1999 as the director-general of the Bureau of Public Enterprises, more commonly known as the BPE. In retrospect, it is hard for me to discuss how this happened without acknowledging the role that Vice-President Atiku Abubakar played in this – yet another in the series of accidents.

Earlier in 1999 and immediately after the briefing of the incoming administration, I took time off to the UK to attempt my LL.B. final part II exams at the University of London. While I was in London preparing, Amah Iwuagwu contacted me to consider presenting a paper on the proposed privatisation programme at a seminar on Nigeria. I reluctantly agreed, knowing this might mean deferring my exams to another future date, which I did not realise at the time, would be resumed some nine years later. As it happened, General Abdulsalami Abubakar had signed the enabling law for the privatisation programme the day before I presented my paper in London – on May 4, 1999[29]. Vice President-elect Atiku Abubakar was in the audience and he learnt for the first time during my presentation that he would be the chairman of the National Council on Privatisation in a few weeks. He approached me after the seminar introducing his aide, Abdullahi Nyako, and asked for a copy of the paper I had presented.

In short, the presentation in London not only announced the enactment of the privatisation decree, but argued that the enabling law that General Abdulsalami had signed made the implementation framework and the BPE itself more robust. As the programme called for the vice-president to lead the privatisation effort and considering that the vice-president-elect first learned of this from my presentation, he naturally recalled my presentation when the Obasanjo administration finally took office, and recommended that the president should appoint me to be the director general of the implementation agency – the BPE. I had by then renewed my employment contract with Motorola as business development manager in Africa with Bashir's Intercellular Nigeria Ltd., as its first customer. I was in Chicago when Dr. Usman Bugaje, then political adviser to Atiku Abubakar, called to inform me that the Vice President wished to see me as soon as possible. I wondered why since I had had no contact with the VP since the conference in London six months earlier. Usman confided that Atiku wanted me to head the BPE but required my consent before obtaining the final approval of the President. I thanked Usman and promised that I would think about it and then consult my family members and friends prior to returning to meet with Atiku.

It was fortuitous that I was in Chicago with two of my mentors – Mallam Ibrahim Aliyu and my brother Bashir to assist me in coming to a decision. Both agreed this was a great opportunity to make a real difference in our nation's political and economic landscape. Furthermore, it was not an advisory position, but an executive position, which is what I had always wanted. A few months earlier, in August 1999, I had married Asia Mohammed Ahmad as my second wife. I met her in 1996. Asia was running her law firm in Abuja when she went to the World Bank annual meetings in Washington, DC. We met on a KLM flight from Amsterdam to Lagos. Five hours of conversation was the beginning of a friendship that became a relationship and then marriage. I, therefore, needed the consent and support of my two spouses before accepting the assignment. Happily for me, both Hadiza and Asia were supportive, but my children, led by Yasmin, were not too enthusiastic and expressed reservations. I explained away their concerns which had to do with reluctance about relocation to Abuja and the perception of all public servants as corrupt.

I returned to Nigeria and made contact with Abdullahi Nyako, the principal secretary to the Vice President, to see Atiku. He said he would call back but never did. After two days of waiting in Abuja, I called Steve Oronsaye to arrange an audience with Obasanjo. I met him whereupon he confirmed that he had approved my appointment as DG of BPE if I would accept. I thanked him and he instructed me to "report immediately and get cracking." As I was about to leave the President's office, Atiku and his coterie of staff arrived; he was a little surprised to see me there, and requested that I should go to his office and wait. I had a short meeting with him in which he repeated his reasons for wanting me to lead BPE, Obasanjo's approval and directives to report immediately. I had no letter of appointment, no one asked for my resume and that was it. Atiku was not even aware that I had been waiting for two days to see him. The appointment was announced in the media (national radio and television) the same afternoon of the 7th of November 1999. The print media carried it the next day. I left for Kaduna immediately after meeting Obasanjo and Atiku, dozing all through the two-hour drive. My phone - the NITEL analogue cellular service "090", was switched off so the VP's media people that needed some biographical information about me could not reach me. They went ahead with the announcement based on information given by Dr. Usman Bugaje - who thought I was 43 years old and a lawyer by profession. Actually, I was then a law student and more like 39 years of age at the time! I left for Kaduna and reported for work back in Abuja two days later.

Entering the BPE

On the 9th of November 1999, I reported to the BPE to start what has turned out to be another eight exciting years in Abuja - of fast-paced change and growing up in various ways. My professional life until then had been spent entirely in the private sector, which gave me a perspective that career public servants lack. Specifically, the private sector has a single goal: to make profits for shareholders. A single goal makes it easier to focus, and because a private sector actor wants to make as much money as possible for partners and shareholders, the most efficient methods possible and the most cost effective operations tended to be used. I believed then, and still do now, that that approach can be applied to the public sector. Cost cutting, efficient management - these are things required in the public sector, even though the purpose of public sector organisations is usually not to turn profits, but to provide social goods and services whose benefits are more difficult to quantify in simple monetary terms.

This was the basic attitude I brought into the BPE. It did not always satisfy everyone, but then this is the nature of public service and indeed politics - there will always be someone who is ill-served by a decision. To the extent that my actions were or are ever governed by a political ideology, that ideology is pragmatism. Such is the legacy of spending my formative professional years in the private sector. For those who take exception to the way I practice pragmatism, I would respond by saying two things: first, I would encourage a close examination of the interests and loyalties held by my naysayers over the years – not only do they tend to differ significantly from my interests and loyalties, but in many cases also the interests and loyalties of the Nigerian people at large. Second, I do my best to keep my word, no matter how inconvenient. I do this as a matter of habit – it is how I was raised. Conveniently for me, this matters in politics more than anywhere else. Indeed, one could say the only true currency in politics is keeping one's word, because that is the basis upon which relationships are built and agreements are enforced.

Upon entering the BPE, I, like many other Nigerians, attributed our country's famous lacklustre progress to corruption. What I soon discovered was that corruption is really only a symptom of Nigeria's problems. The true culprit behind our country's lacklustre progress is actually much deeper and even more difficult to identify, but for the time being I refer to it as disastrous political leadership and bad decision making leading to a culture of impunity. I did not come around to this assessment of our country's malaise until I was actually in public service for some time. As I was entering BPE, my philosophical framework was simply that I knew that the public sector had to work at a basic minimum level in order for the private sector to flourish. I came to this realisation during the Abacha years and it was during his rule that I made up my mind that if I ever got the opportunity to work in the public sector, I would not only accept, but would do my very best.

Chapter Four

Taking Charge of Privatisation and Policy Reform

"Excellence is never an accident. It is always the result of high intention, sincere effort, and intelligent execution; it represents the wise choice of many alternatives – choice not chance, determines your destiny."

– Aristotle

As I stated earlier, I returned to Abuja on 9th November 1999 without a letter of employment or any formal introduction, to report at the BPE offices then located within the NDIC building. I was in the office by 8am, and it was virtually empty. None of the staff was at work except an assistant in the DG's office named Effiong. He welcomed me and asked who I wanted to see. I informed him that I wanted to see Mr Bernard Verr, the outgoing DG. He guided me to a visitor's seat and said Mr Verr will be in the office soon. Within the hour, Ibrahim Shehu Njiddah, then a Deputy Director and who knew me well from my previous interactions with the BPE, sauntered in, identified who I was and all hell broke loose. The directors then came over to say hello, and suggested I move to the DG's office. I declined and waited instead in Ibrahim's office until Mr Verr arrived an hour or so later.

The hand over was very brief. I was given the balances in all of BPE's accounts and a short inspirational speech not to be intimidated by the directors that were all older and more experienced than I was! Mr Verr said he was appointed DG at 39 years of age as well, so I had nothing to worry about. With that, he left and I never saw him until a couple of years later. Within days, a memo to pay his severance and terminal benefits was brought for my approval, which I gave immediately and it was settled the next day. Then the acting director of finance and administration, Mrs Modupe Abiodun-Wright, sought to take me through what were my entitlements as DG, and asked permission to book me into the Hilton Hotel immediately for the first 28 days at government expense which I was entitled to as a new senior government appointee. I declined since I had a home in Abuja where my bride, Asia, lived along Amazon Street in Maitama. I paid little attention to the levels of pay and allowances, as I knew they would not add up to much. I had already arranged with El-Rufai & Partners to pay me a quarterly supplemental to augment what I knew would be my low, government pay. I had to start looking for a house as my first wife, Hadiza, wished to relocate to Abuja. My second wife, Asia, never enjoyed a real honeymoon period, because another bride - the BPE - came into our lives less than three months after we got married!

The heads of departments - the directors - I think four in number at the time, now began briefing me in detail. In terms of privatisation activities, there had been none the previous five years under Abacha. The organisation had so many deputy directors (over 20 in number) mostly doing little or nothing. I found that all the staff of BPE originated from only 22 states of the federation, so 14 states and the FCT had no representation. While the BPE had some incredibly competent people at all levels, the quality of some of the more recent employees left much to be desired. More importantly, the most experienced staff had no idea how to do privatisation transactions involving core investor sales as they were largely familiar with listing shares on the Stock Exchange or sale of assets in liquidation situations. A lot of new hiring was needed, and intensive training for existing staff. I knew from day one that I would have to bring into the BPE many good people and from each state of the federation to satisfy the 'federal character' requirements of our sometimes cumbersome constitution. The BPE needed re-engineering, revamping and skills development. In a few days, I had to brief the Privatisation Council chaired by Vice President Atiku Abubakar on the plans for the implementation of Phase 1 of the programme.

I had attended a programme on practical approaches to privatisation at the Arthur D. Little School of Management in 1992, and had the privilege of serving as a member of a Study Group on Socio-Economic and Related Problems of Privatisation and Commercialisation in 1991. I had also served as Member and Secretary of two committees set up by the governors of the northern states to restructure the operations of the northern regional development finance company - the New Nigeria Development Company (NNDC), so none of the challenges in BPE was brand new or difficult to understand. The draft of the privatisation implementation programme was presented to me by the two directors, Salisu Liadi (privatisation) and Okpa-Obaji (commercialisation). It was a good plan on the whole, and I reworked it overnight, introduced the concept of at least one high-profile, 'flagship transaction' each year to measure our success. The national carrier, Nigeria Airways Ltd., had already been so identified for the 1999-2000 year, and the IFC, the private sector investment arm of the World Bank, had been enlisted as advisers a couple of weeks before my appointment. I proposed that NITEL be our flagship divestiture for 2001. The revised plan was presented to the NCP early in December 1999, and it was approved. Before then, I had to learn how to write and present government memoranda (memos), how they all ended with a summary and 'prayers' and BPE's unique style of presentation developed by my mentor, Hamza Zayyad. It was a great learning experience and I could see that the council was impressed with my first outing as DG. The next day, we had to brief the media and announce the kick-off of the second privatisation and commercialisation programme of the federal government of Nigeria.

Internally, we initiated the process to recruit more staff - entry level, senior and directorate grades. I approached several friends and ex-classmates to join the BPE as directors to help me. I approached Bature Shehu Garba, who held a Masters in Construction Management and had been a commissioner of water resources in my home state of Kaduna but he declined. So did Dr. Mansur Mukhtar, a first class economics graduate and our chief economist in PIMCO who was then working for the World Bank. Dr. John Ayuba, another first class marketing graduate then working with a commercial bank, also declined. Only Tijjani Mohammed Abdullahi, an accountant and banker, who was then deputy managing director of one of our leading merchant banks – First Interstate Merchant Bank - accepted to work with me. I think it is difficult for classmates to work under one another, but this was not apparent to me when I made the approach to several of them! Those that declined all had good reasons other than serving under their somewhat erratic former classmate! I believe strongly though, that the people you know best are those you went to school with or worked with in near-equal capacities, so in whatever position I found myself, I always tried bringing in some former schoolmates and classmates to help out, and many accepted and we worked beautifully with little or no tensions.

We hired Bashir Yusuf Ibrahim's New Paradigm Consultants to review BPE's structure, staff and training needs and make recommendations for improvement. On the basis of the final report of the consultants, we fired many of the directors and deputy directors, and began a transparent hiring process with an advertisement in the national newspapers inviting applications from people with first degrees or equivalent. We were looking to hire about 108 people but received over 3,000 qualified applications. The short-listed applicants sat a GMAT-type aptitude test and were hired on the basis of best three scores from each state. We did not hire anyone that failed the aptitude test. Some states, notably Bayelsa, Rivers, Zamfara and Yobe, had no qualified candidates, so we had to head-hunt for them by making contact with the governors of the states, but insisted that the candidates must meet our minimum requirements - upper second class degree or better in any field, to be considered. Many of these young people turned out to be BPE's best and brightest, and this goes to show that when merit trumps caprice in staff selection, the results can be phenomenal.

The consultants observed that our staff compensation levels were poor compared to the private sector. The BPE staff housing loans scheme and the institution's pension fund were both in financial deficit. Certain that by the time our staff get well-trained, many investment banking and consulting firms would lure them away, we submitted proposals to the privatisation council to raise the pay and allowances of BPE staff to levels near to those of financial institutions, and to acquire our own offices. The council approved our proposals. The compensation structure needed to be ratified by the National Salaries and Wages Commission to take effect, which was done. In 2000, we acquired the building that we named Hamza Zayyad House on Osun Crescent in Maitama District. Over time, we extended the building slightly, building a staff canteen and crèche, while the Muslim staff contributed and built a small mosque for the two afternoon prayers. I ate lunch regularly in the canteen thereby compelling the caterer to whom we outsourced it to maintain quality and good prices. Apart from providing the canteen building rent-free to the caterer, nothing else was subsidised. We also insisted that no senior staff would have exclusive toilets, thus ensuring that the environment was kept clean by outsourcing the function as well to a cleaning company. BPE operated like a private sector organisation but we still had a skills-gap problem.

In addition to all these, there were no operating manuals for transactions and no serious diagnostics on the enterprises scheduled for divestiture or restructuring. To make matters more complicated, the BPE had no funds available to do most of these important preparatory activities. It was at this point I began to approach donors for support.

USAID to the Rescue

Early in 2000, I called for a meeting with the Mission Director of USAID in Nigeria, Tom Hobgood, and asked to present the outlines of our federal privatisation programme. We met him in Lagos (for a few minutes because he had to leave for another meeting but handed us over to Mrs Ravi Aulakh, his number two) and our presentation and subsequent discussions led to a grant of US $10 million for BPE in support of the privatisation efforts of the government. The funds would be administered by a USAID-appointed consultant, IBTCI of Fairfax, Virginia. We proposed to hire some staff as 'consultants' and then IBTCI placed the advertisements, short-listed candidates, interviewed them and fixed their hourly rates of pay. We did not even know how much the consultants were paid! For me, as long as I could get Nigerians at home and in the diaspora to assist the implementation of the programme, I was interested in nothing more. That was how we began the two-track system of staffing the BPE - the regular, permanent and pensionable staff of BPE, and the 'core team' consultants whose pay was much higher but whose contract of employment was neither permanent not pensionable, and indeed could end whenever funds terminate! Some of the regular BPE staff like Roz Ben-Okagbue and Chinelo Anohu opted for this option and converted. It was under this programme that we hired many of our future bright lights, my assistants, Lai Yahaya, Aishetu Fatima Kolo, Dr. Abdu Mukhtar, and line staff like Hassan Musa Usman, Eyo Ekpo, Emeka Obi, Dr. Lanre Babalola and many others. By the time USAID funding was running out, DFID gave us a grant of ten million pounds so we were able to continue and also expand the scope of the programme. I am always disappointed when the whole 'core team' programme gets reduced to a dollar-salary story, conveniently forgetting its openness to all, and the urgent need for us to have qualified staff to deliver on our programme objectives and timelines.[30] Aishetu Kolo was particularly unfairly maligned and while I was in FCT, left Nigeria unhappy and despondent, to join the World Bank Young Professionals Programme. I was pleased when she returned to the country some years later to settle down to a career in the private sector.

However, the story of how the payment of allowances due to Dr. Abdu Mukhtar and Ms Aishetu Fatima Kolo became the subject of a Senate Committee investigation is best summarised by reading Appendix 3 which contains the last two pages of the entire file of six pages of what really transpired and what was truly paid. Years after, Jonathan's choristers falsely claimed I was paying a youth corper some N2 million per month as salary. I never bothered to respond as the person behind the false allegations, Senator Mamman Ali, had become governor and subsequently died of cancer, so was no longer in a position to defend himself. I have decided to simply reproduce extracts from the file on the matter for any interested reader to review and make up his or her mind.

The World Bank Steps In

The early successes of our programme attracted the attention of the World Bank country office then headed by Trevor Byer, a West Indian, who had some experience in power sector reforms. We met regularly and he raised the idea of a privatisation support credit just in case we get starved of funds by the legislature. I did not think it was possible bearing in mind the commitment of my bosses, both Obasanjo and Atiku, to the programme, but felt there was nothing wrong with taking an insurance policy, just in case. Am I glad we did? Discussions and approvals were sought and negotiations for the credit began in earnest, lasting about 18 months before the $110 million credit became effective. It was the shortest time a credit was ever made effective in Nigeria since it began relations with the Bank in the 1960s. The credit covered not just the BPE, but the Nigeria Communications Commission (NCC), and the Abuja and Lagos State Water Corporations. The BPE not only led and anchored the negotiations but met the credit-effectiveness conditions ahead of every other agency - a further confirmation of the competence and internal capacity of the BPE staff, for which I remain very proud.

With the credit in place, we could spend more on training and capacity building, hire advisers and consulting firms with expertise in sector reforms, pay for many more individual consultants and 'core team' members, and undertake more study tours. We still had our DFID grants available for first spending before drawing down on the credit - which attracted 0.5% interest, so it was almost nearly cost-free! And as correctly predicted by the World Bank, we began to face funding challenges from the legislature shortly after. Whenever we proposed an amount in the budget for privatisation transaction costs, the Ministry of Finance would either reduce or omit it entirely, and the legislature would either delete the reduced amount or just leave it at zero. Our representations to committees on privatisation as well as appropriations consistently came up with nothing. After two consecutive years of zero allocation for privatisation transactions costs, I was summoned by Hon. Nze Chidi Duru and his committee members to explain how we were able to finance such transactions! I explained that we had the World Bank credit to draw upon, whereupon I was asked to explain how we borrowed without the approval of the legislature. My one paragraph response was "Ask the Minister of Finance." After all, it was the Federal Government, through the Federal Ministry of Finance, and not the BPE that obtained the credit.

It was then I realised that the non-funding of the BPE transaction costs was deliberate, and unless we were willing to 'play ball' nothing was forthcoming either from the Finance Ministry or the National Assembly. The legislators in particular were quite clear that unless we were willing to provide pay-offs or appoint their friends as privatisation consultants or advisers, none of our budgets on transactions would be approved, and they never were. This was because our competitive, open and transparent selection process lent itself to no such prior 'arrangements'. The legislators also wanted various relations, cronies and friends hired, whether qualified or not, but our aptitude test and interview process reduced such opportunities to a minimum. The privatisation committee chairmen, Senator Haruna Zego Aziz and Hon. Nze Chidi Duru had a hard time reining in the anger and hostility of their members that were interested in both immediate cash and other non-cash benefits which were not forthcoming from BPE. Of course this created other future problems for me, being identified as a 'non-cooperating individual' by the political system, as we will see later.

We presented our 'no-win' situation to the Vice President and on the advice of the Attorney-General of the Federation who is a statutory member of the NCP, BPE was authorised to begin the practice of adding up all transaction costs associated with any sale, and deducting them in full before remitting the net amount of proceeds to the privatisation proceeds account at the Central Bank of Nigeria. The implementation of some of the smaller, less prominent but critical, transactions that could not be financed by the credit would have been impossible without this flexible and necessary interpretation of sections 9 and 19 of the Privatisation and Commercialisation Act.

Years later in October 2011, a Senate Committee investigating privatisation transactions ruled this legal opinion of the Attorney-General 'illegal' and the practice as unconstitutional, and recommended that I and other DGs 'be reprimanded' for the deductions of transaction costs. It was an absurd recommendation as one can only reprimand one's employee, which I and three of my successors were not any longer. My guess is that the committee was duty-bound to find something against El-Rufai, and that was all they could pin on me after examining my nearly four years at the helm in BPE.

An Encounter with Enron

One of my most memorable early experiences in BPE was a political baptism of fire - an encounter that put me smack in the middle of ethnicity, politics and policy conflicts, involving a company that became globally notorious for its internal misgovernance and deception - the Houston-based Enron Corporation. Electricity shortages have become a way of life in Nigeria, and Enron saw an opportunity to cash in on that misfortune. They did something similar in India in the 1990s and it went really wrong but they learnt some lessons and came to Nigeria with a more refined approach. What Enron proposed was to supply second-hand, barge-based generators (movable and easy to relocate in case of payment defaults) using diesel initially, to be supplied by Wale Tinubu's Ocean & Oil Ltd. (now Oando) until gas pipelines are extended from Egbin to the barges' location, to provide initially 90MW and expandable to 540MW of electricity exclusively for Lagos State.

The Lagos State governor, Bola Tinubu, his finance commissioner Wale Edun, budget commissioner Yemi Cardoso, Gbenga Oyebode of Aluko & Oyebode, Wale Tinubu and Tunde Folawiyo, all of them friends or acquaintances of mine, were involved in the transaction at various levels and capacities. There were only three hurdles that needed to be crossed. First was the legal reality of the time: that only federally-owned National Electricity Power Authority (NEPA) could buy, transmit and distribute power so the cooperation of the Federal Government (FGN) was needed. Second was that NEPA was notorious for not paying its bills (even to government-owned companies like the Nigerian Gas Company which supplies it with feedstock), so some payment security arrangements needed to be put in place in anticipation of NEPA's default, and finally Enron would require a sovereign guarantee in the event that NEPA fails to pay and the security arrangement fails to crystallise or is exhausted by multiple defaults. Enron and Bola Tinubu found a way by getting Chief Bola Ige, a fellow opposition AD party leader working in a PDP administration, to get Obasanjo to sign off on the transaction without any cabinet review or rigorous inter-agency discussions. Bola Ige also obtained the president's consent to sign a sovereign guarantee on behalf of the Federal Government of Nigeria - something only the Minister of Finance was legally authorised to do.

There were no loud protests from NEPA management who could foresee the dangers of potential corporate insolvency because they all believed resistance was fruitless since Minister Bola Ige had the ears of President Obasanjo. Everything was signed, sealed and delivered and we all read about it in the newspapers. I was concerned that this could negatively impact the future privatisation of NEPA and requested the VP to obtain copies of the agreements signed for our review. This was barely two weeks after I resumed, and then early in December 1999, we received the 'power purchase agreement' (PPA) of over 100 pages including annexes, annexures and other attachments. We could not make any sense out of it. We approached Norton Rose of the UK, and two local law firms, A B Mahmoud & Co. based in Kano and George Ikoli & Okagbue of Lagos to undertake a review of the power purchase agreement. Norton Rose needed several weeks, and instinctively I knew we had to figure this out before it got too late, and several weeks might be too late.

The local law firms submitted the outcome of their reviews within a short period, but what we got were not very helpful in isolating the potential impact of the PPA on our power sector reform programme. The agreement was highly technical with enough equations and integrals to scare all but the most mathematically proficient of lawyers. At this point, I approached the World Bank country office for assistance. Trevor Byer, the country director who fortuitously had been involved in power sector reforms elsewhere before his posting to Nigeria, was very helpful, proactive and immediately responsive. Within a couple of weeks, we received a summary of the agreement, its impact on privatisation, what the equations and annexes meant in terms of tariffs, security arrangements, dollar payments and contingent liabilities. I immediately briefed the Vice President who was alarmed at the findings, and he instructed me to draft a memo for onward transmission to President Obasanjo.

Within five weeks of taking over the headship of BPE, I drafted the first of many memos which would be forwarded to the President, drawing attention to surreptitious steps being taken by line ministries to frustrate sector reforms and privatisation. The Lagos State-Enron case was particularly dangerous as it would have bankrupted NEPA almost overnight! The president immediately put the transaction on hold and commended the vice president for briefing him on the implications of the deal. The VP set up a ministerial committee chaired by Minister of State Danjuma Goje, with BPE, the Federal Ministry of Finance, and Lagos State Government represented as members, to review the agreement. Enron immediately hired GoodWorks International, the global advisory firm co-founded by former US Ambassador to the UN, Andrew Young, to influence the outcome of the review, while Bola Ige and some sections of the South-West media got busy attacking me, the vice president and the BPE for 'depriving Lagos and Yoruba people of steady electricity'. We declined to respond, focusing on fixing what we saw as a potential stumbling block to reforming and privatising our electricity supply industry. I am glad we truncated the original deal, but even the better and revised arrangement which reduced tariffs from 8.5 cents per kilowatt-hour to just 1 cent a kilowatt-hour ended up placing huge financial burdens on NEPA years into the future – and the undertaking we extracted from Lagos State to share part of the burden was subsequently challenged in court, and remained in dispute until we left office.

My Enron experience was an education of sorts. I learnt many new lessons that dispelled my naivety. Well-informed and trusted friends put pressure on me to look the other way because they were advisers or consultants to Enron, or were potential beneficiaries in the transaction. My explanations and passionate representations that the transaction was inimical to national interest, negatively impacts the long-term viability of NEPA and threatened the reforms of the electricity industry were neither important nor relevant to their position. I saw starkly how government officials were willing to pervert the interest of the country to impress foreigners, or obtain preferences for those they thought were their kinsmen. It was an early sobering experience and an appreciation of the reigning dictum of every one for himself, and no one for the country.

The hypocrisy of multinational commercial interests that think 'contract sanctity' overrode Nigeria's laws, our national interest and the voidability of a contract based on a mistake also came to the fore. The even-handedness of the World Bank officials was commendable; for their efforts however, some of them were moved out of Nigeria, and some reportedly took early retirement due to pressure from the Executive Director representing the US on the board of the World Bank, as a result of complaints filed against them by Enron. It was gratifying (and I felt that it was divine judgment for the sleepless nights and media attacks we in the BPE were put through by their executives and Nigerian collaborators for no reason other than their narrow commercial interests!) that I had to witness the collapse of that evil corporation. I remember vividly I was in Houston, Texas when on December 2, 2001, Enron filed for bankruptcy protection.

The Swiss Tycoon and the Nicon-Noga-Hilton Hotel

Another early case which taught me a lot about the penchant of the Nigerian elite to subordinate public interest to their individual greed involved a businessman with a long history in Nigeria. Nessim Gaon began exporting groundnuts from Nigeria in the 1960s when the marketing boards were in charge, and quickly became a close friend and business associate of many northern leaders, including a prominent prince that became the Sultan of Sokoto in the 1980s, Alhaji Ibrahim Dasuki. Gaon, a Swiss-Jew, diversified into trading, construction and hotels development. He was awarded the $320 million contract to build the Nicon-Noga-Hilton Hotel in Abuja in the early eighties. This was to become what is now the Transcorp Hilton Hotel - Abuja's premier hotel destination. The Noga in the name is derived from Gaon's name, even though his company, Aprofim, and its sister, Afro-Continental Construction Ltd., did not invest a penny in cash in the hotel company's equity, and the hotel design, construction and furnishing ought not to have cost more than about $120 million then. In the estimation of a reputable quantity surveying firm, Gaon may have walked away with at least $100 million from the project after netting all expenses, kickbacks and other payments back in the mid-1980s. Yet, his company claimed to be a 25% shareholder in the hotel-ownership company, Nicon Hotels Ltd., under a very questionable management contract executed with the Nicon Insurance Corporation, which was never approved by the regulator – the National Office of Industrial Property, Iponri, which has now been renamed NOTAP.

By 2001, when preparing to privatise Nicon Insurance, and its associated companies including the hotel property itself, I was directed by Vice President Atiku Abubakar to meet with Gaon to resolve his alleged ownership claim, something which Nicon Insurance denied explicitly. Gaon's petition to Atiku Abubakar, cataloguing the injustice done him by Nicon Insurance were referred to me, and two of the VP's aides including his Special Assistant, Economic Matters and former secretary of PIMCO, Dr. Ajuji Ahmed, came to the meeting uninvited, on a 'watching brief' so to say. Within the BPE, our minds were open to logic and evidence of ownership. Even if Gaon owned 25%, we still had 75% to sell; as long as there were no provisions for pre-emptive rights exercisable by existing shareholders, we concluded that we could proceed. By the time we reviewed all the evidence and arguments, it was clear that Gaon had no legally-defensible ownership stake, was contestably allotted shares, never paid cash for them, but claimed to have provided some 'technical services' in lieu that were not lawfully registered, something Nicon Insurance's future management and board never accepted. After two meetings, I was advised by BPE's lawyers and advisers to rule that (1) in our opinion as BPE, Gaon had no claims we could sustain, (2) but if he disagreed, should feel free to pursue that in court. (3) However, we hinted that as attorneys for the government in respect of the shares, BPE intended to join as co-defendant in his suit and would counter-claim for the balance of the historic over-pricing of the hotel contract - about $200 million plus accrued interest from 1985. Gaon was incensed, mumbled his shock and surprise at the BPE having the temerity to treat him that way, and left. The VP's guys appeared disappointed, and by the time we made a formal report of our findings, Atiku accepted the findings and Gaon's suit in court was dismissed in the end, enabling the privatisation of the Hilton as a 100%-owned asset of the Federal Government to proceed. Many other incidents in BPE helped clarify my attitude to some of these, but more would come my way.

Success Factors in Public Service

As I settled down in BPE, I came to realise that success in public service differs from that of the private sector in many ways, but could even be more satisfying. Whereas a successful business person can be judged by the size of his organisation, its profitability, jobs created and shareholder wealth amongst others, the public sector success indicators are far less visible or measurable. That is why I think we have very bad public leaders getting away with crass incompetence, and sometimes even the destruction of the system they were meant to develop without many citizens quite realising the damage done!

Over the years, it has become clear to me that to succeed in public service, one must have acquired a certain level of anger with our failures as a society, and be willing to damn all consequences to change things for the better. To do so, the public leader must be competent and prepared academically, professionally, and experientially for this leadership role, that is, one must be a round peg in a round hole. Then the person needs staff, both the core around him and support staff that are smarter than him in many areas, younger and harder working possibly, older and more experienced in other areas, to handle the sub-tasks needed to succeed in the leadership assignment. A lot of luck comes into play here because in the public service one has limited room to choose every person one works with, except for a few personal staff and aides. The third is a support structure of peers. As a director-general, for instance, the cooperation of permanent secretaries eases dealings with ministries and ministers. As a cabinet minister, enjoying the trust and friendship of the finance minister and the head of the procurement office are helpful to one's success in getting funds released and implementing capital projects. Finally is the most obvious factor - the unflinching support of the boss, which in my case was the Vice President initially; and ultimately, the President. I was most fortunate to have all four factors working in my favour in my eight years or so in the two terms of the Obasanjo-Atiku administration. Anyone wishing to take the plunge into the public sector at senior levels from a nongovernmental background and experience needs to think through these 'success factors' carefully. Otherwise, the person would go in, and fail to achieve much, thereby damaging an otherwise stellar academic or private sector career!

The legal and institutional framework for running the privatisation programme took the President out of the decision-making loop, with the buck stopping on the desk of the Vice President and the National Council on Privatisation. Obasanjo was clearly unhappy with that arrangement and tried at least twice to have the law amended to take the powers away from Atiku and require more participation of his office. On our part in the BPE, we decided sometime in 2000, to prepare weekly briefs for the VP and President and persuaded Atiku to endorse the briefs to Obasanjo for 'comments and approvals' even though the law did not require such. We thought, wrongly it turned out, that bridging the information asymmetry about the programme between the two offices would smoothen the implementation path. I am sure the briefs helped somewhat, but impediments placed by ministers, sometimes with President Obasanjo's inadvertent support, continued to confront us. We soldiered on nevertheless.

The BPE was staffed by largely competent and professional people. My task was to deepen and broaden the skills base, and fill any identified gaps. I was lucky to have high-calibre colleagues, staff and assistants as confidants and co-travellers. Whether they were old TCPC/BPE hands or brought in to strengthen the team, they shone in their roles and were recognised accordingly. Others that failed to perform after successive warnings were sent out. It was an exciting period seeing otherwise shy young men and women gaining confidence and developing into real technocrats. We did what we thought were great and exciting things - building what was without any doubt the most efficient public service institution in Nigeria at the time. On the whole, it was a great period in my life, made so by lots of experiences – both good and bad.

Chapter Five

"You Will See the Meaning of Power"

"Corruption and hypocrisy ought not to be inevitable products of democracy, as they undoubtedly are today"
— Mahatma Gandhi, 1869-1948

There is an old joke, sometimes featuring Winston Churchill, in which a man approaches a woman at a cocktail party and asks her if she will sleep with him for one million pounds. "Perhaps," she replies coyly, adding something to the effect of, "but of course we would have to discuss the terms." The man then asks her if she will sleep with him for one pound, to which she replies, "Of course not! What sort of woman do you think I am?" The man's response: "We have already established what sort of woman you are. All we are doing now is negotiating the price."

Those who swear by the rule that everything has a price would have found much to contemplate during my early years in BPE. By that point, the public service had transformed dramatically for the worse. Back in Daudawa during my childhood, government was staffed with mostly honest people. Of course, we realised that most of the rich people around us either worked for the government or were contractors to the government and very early on I had an impression that public service was one route to being comfortable — even then there were rumours of some corruption in the public service, but generally, in the 1960s and 1970s, the civil service was perceived as clean. Indeed, civil service work was the honest pathway for belonging to the middle class. I am sure in Lagos there were people living comfortably who were not in the civil service, but in most of the north, other than the traditional commercial centres of Kano, Gombe, Gusau, Maiduguri, Jos and Funtua, this was mostly the case.

This began to change around the middle of the 1970s largely due to two forces. The first was the massive forced retirement of civil servants the Murtala-Obasanjo regime undertook in 1975. The road to hell is paved with good intentions. While a shake-up of the civil service might have been justified, the mass retirements had one devastating and long-lasting unintended consequence: from that moment on, the civil servants who remained got the unmistakable signal that their jobs were no longer secure. At that point, people realised that they had to feather their nests while they still could because they might be fired by the military governor or head of state at any time without recourse to due process, or recompense.

The second force was that public service pay did not keep pace with increases in inflation or the general cost of living, while economic activity in the private sector and its pay did. People were paid much higher in private sector jobs while public service pay stagnated. When Babangida came into office, and in the late 1980s devalued the nation's currency, the deplorable situation only worsened. The unsurprising result was that Nigeria's best and brightest no longer aspired to the prestige of a career in public service – indeed, there was no prestige anymore as far as they were concerned.

By 1999, what we had was an economic and political incentive structure that paid rents to an elite few in whose best interest it was to perpetuate the system's dysfunction. Anyone entering public leadership in Africa, particularly Nigeria, beginning from that period till today, really has two choices. The first is to join the dysfunctional and corrupt system, derive some illicit and substantial income from it, enjoy a comfortable standard of living, retire with some assets and cash tucked away, and hope to live happily ever after. The second choice is to want to change the system for the better in a way that benefits the many rather than the few elites but this choice has high probability of failure and earns for the 'deviant' aggravation, frustration and other retribution. Any success or failure in Nigeria in any aspect of governance derives precisely from people making any one of these two choices.

By the time I came to the BPE, my thoughts and life experience had already aligned in one particular direction, which can be summarised in four points. The first was that although Nigeria had a population then of some 120 million people (now more than 160 million), over 500 languages and more than 300 ethnic groups, I had come to the conclusion through my experiences up to that point that there are simply two kinds of people in Nigeria. There were good people and there were bad people, period! Each can be found speaking every language, in every religion, every ethnic group, every village, every town, and every city. In my private sector career, I had been helped more by people from the south of Nigeria despite the fact that they knew me as a 'northerner', and I had more often than not been let down by fellow 'northerners' perhaps because I grew up knowing more of them. I therefore do not perceive my country and its population through tribal or ethnic lenses.

Secondly, I believe that human beings are generally about the same, and to a large extent, strategic and rational in their thinking and conduct. Everyone pursues what he or she perceives to be in his or her best interest. An effective way I have found of relating to people is to consider what I would do if I were in their position pursuing my rational strategic interest. Any negotiation that bears that in mind will result in a deal being made. Our common humanity suggests that people of all religions, ethnic groups or races, are essentially all the same, which leads to my third point.

Thirdly, human beings respond to incentives and sanctions, and shape their conduct accordingly. People like to say Nigeria is a corrupt country, but I really do not believe there is such a thing as a corrupt country; it simply is a matter of incentives or absence of sanctions. I have seen many British, Italian and American citizens who have come to Nigeria and were they to be judged strictly on their corrupt tendencies and actions, one might easily then think they were born in Nigeria, which proves that environment trumps race or ethnicity anytime. They conduct themselves simply in response to the incentives they find, a person looking around the system and subconsciously asking, "What can I get away with?" The reason people are more honest in one society than another is because there is a very high chance of being caught and sanctioned somehow, for dishonesty. In Nigeria, the unfortunate verdict seems to be that if you are dishonest, not only is there very little chance of getting caught, there is a very high chance of being rewarded with senior appointive or elective positions in politics or public service, honoured with chieftaincy titles, and with the praise and respect of one's community. As a nation, we have become unquestioning of wealth, no matter how ill-gotten, and generally forgotten to name, shame and ostracise bad people, while failing to recognise and adore the good - those that sacrifice and resist all temptations in order to be decent and serve the nation honestly.

Finally, whatever worked in Nigeria and seemed to be improving every day was what was owned or managed or under the control of the private sector. Whatever did not work, or was barely working and mostly deteriorating over time, was owned or managed and controlled by the public sector. This became particularly pronounced as the quality of public servants deteriorated at the time the scope of state capitalism was deepening due to rapid build-up of oil revenues in the late seventies and eighties. Conversely, the quality and capacity of the Nigerian private sector improved during the period, further widening the comparative performance gap with the public service.

These four principles were wired into my brain well before I was appointed to head the BPE. They played guiding roles in defining our hiring practices, in the pursuit of restructuring the BPE, and in the design and aggressive implementation of the privatisation and commercialisation programme from 1999 to 2003. I do not think it is any coincidence that by the end of my nearly four years there, people across the political spectrum considered the Bureau of Public Enterprises to be one of the most respectable public institutions in the country, a big change from what it had become towards the end of 1999 after the departure of Zayyad - a dysfunctional and low-morale institution with more deputy directors than real staff.

There was, of course, a price to pay for this. Understanding someone else's best interests does not necessarily mean endorsing them. Within the public sector in Nigeria, a person is more trusted when it is known that the person will be a team player - take bribes, bend rules here and there - because then it means the person cannot expose anyone else doing anything wrong. When a person acquires a reputation for not taking bribes, as I did right from our construction industry consulting days, it arouses not only suspicion, but outright disbelief and anger.

"We are not Kaduna boys anymore"

One of the first such incidents to test 'my price' (if I had any) occurred just a few months into my BPE tenure. There was this guy I knew from Kaduna simply as Captain Abdul. He claimed to be an airline pilot. I do not know whether he ever qualified to be a pilot, but knew him as one of those who often hung around important people acting big and spending big, claiming to be 'businessmen' while doing no visibly productive work. One day, Abdul walked into my office and I thought he was one of my Kaduna friends and acquaintances who had come to congratulate me and wish me well in a new assignment. Instead, he sat down and after brief pleasantries said, "Well, I am one of Atiku's (the vice-president's) men."

"Good. What does that mean?"

"Well, I handle his businesses. I do stuff for him."

"Oh well, congratulations," I said. This is seriously how the Abduls of Nigeria speak and operate.

"Well, I am here because we hear that you want to buy a guest house for your council members."

"Yes, we have been thinking about it."

We had four privatisation council members (Akin Kekere-Ekun, Dr. Ejike Onyia, Alhaji Umaru Ndanusa and Comrade Adams Oshiomhole) who travelled from outside Abuja to attend our meetings, they would meet at least once monthly, and often more frequently when council committees met in between, which can be few times monthly. It was costing us a bundle because they usually stayed at the Hilton. So Ibrahim Njiddah, who as director of council affairs was in charge of managing the expenses of the members, suggested that perhaps if we bought a guest house, and placed it under private management with catering services, it would be easier and cheaper for us. I thought it worthy of some consideration and just mentioned it in passing at one of our BPE management committee meetings that we should consider buying a four bedroom house and keep these guys there, rather than paying these huge hotel bills. A sub-committee was tasked to study the idea and report back. Apparently, this went out of BPE's walls and this was the reason for Captain Abdul's visit. So I admitted to him that we were indeed considering it but had not yet come to any decision on the matter.

"Well the vice-president knows about it and I have a house that you should buy."

"Ok, we will look at that, but let us decide on it first," I said.

"No, you are not listening to me. I handle the VP's business, he has heard about your intentions to have a guest house. Write to him, he will approve it, and I have the house that you will buy."

"Fine. Leave, Abdul. I have got some work to do"

And he left. We had the sub-committee report back the desirability of a guest house and had further discussion in the management meeting. Though I had some reservations, we resolved to go ahead with the acquisition of the council guest house. I did not even remember the conversation with Abdul when we wrote to Atiku as chairman of the privatisation council about it, and the memo came back approved. As did Abdul.

"You've got your approval. I have the house."

"Four bedroom house?"

"Yes."

"See the director of council affairs, Ibrahim and he'll send our people to look at it and if it meets our requirements, then give us an offer."

"No, all this 'long grammar' is not necessary; this is the house you are going to buy."

By that point, I began to get really irritated, so I just put the whole thing on hold. A week or so later, Abdul came to my office and what he did was quite dramatic.

"Nasir, we are not Kaduna boys anymore," he said. "We are grown up now. I am telling you what I do for a living."

He dug into his pocket, brought out a diplomatic passport, put it on the table and said,

"This is a diplomatic passport. Take a look at it, it is my passport."

So I looked at it, and yes, it was a diplomatic passport with his picture and his name and personal information.

"Congratulations", I said. So what is your point?"

"How do you think someone you think is a loser like me can get a diplomatic passport? You think I am a loser, don't you?"

"Abdul, you are a loser, and always will be."

"I have a diplomatic passport and you do not because I act and make money for the vice-president, and I am telling you, the reason why he approved your proposal to buy a guest house is because you are buying this particular house that I will show you. I will tell you the price you will pay."

"Are you done? If so, then get out of my office or I will have you thrown out."

"You are talking to me like that?"

"Yes. Get out of here. Otherwise, I will have you bloody thrown out."

He left. I decided I was not going to move on the acquisition of the guest house, I just left it unattended. Abdul did not come back to me. After about a month, the staff working on identifying the choices of potential guest houses came back to me with a report of five houses that they had identified, and there was one in particular they said was the best due to its proximity –within walking distance actually from the BPE office. I circled it and suggested contacting the property owners so that they could give us an offer. The offer came in at 2.8 million US dollars, then equivalent to some 294 million naira.

"Are these detached houses that expensive?" I asked. I was incredulous, but referred it to the committee chaired by BPE's internal auditor, Edwin Azodo, to review and negotiate.

The committee then wrote to either the valuation units of the FCDA or the Federal Ministry of Works and Housing for advice, and we hired an estate surveyor and valuer to give us an opinion on the purchase value of the property. What came back was a valuation ranging down from ¦ 180 million as capital value, through ¦ 140 million as forced sales value to ¦ 80 million as replacement cost (excluding open market value of land). The committee recommended that we counter-offer the owners of this house at a price above replacement cost but less than the forced sales value - we agreed to make the firm offer of ¦ 109.5 million.

I do not know how it happened, whether the property was really the best or if it was rigged within the BPE system, but the house that was highly recommended by our staff committee was Abdul's house. The offer of ₦ 294 million came from him. He came back to see me.

"I do not want to see you, Abdul."

"Well, you are buying a house from me, you better see me. Look, my price is ₦ 294 million, and the valuation was ₦ 180 million, how can you offer me ₦ 109.5 million, what is wrong with you?"

"That is the maximum we can offer," I said.

"You are going to buy this house at my price. You will see the meaning of power." And with that, he stormed out of my office. I was incensed that Abdul would come to my office, talk to me in this way, while raising his voice. At this point, I called Dr. Usman Bugaje, my friend, who was Atiku's political adviser.

"You know, our people have a saying," I said to him in Hausa language, "Biri yana kama da mutum" literally translating into "the monkey sometimes resembles a human" or "if it looks like a duck, walks like a duck, then it must be a duck."

"What do you mean?"

"Well, this Abdul has been coming to my office, dropping words and issuing threats. I know him as a scammer from Kaduna, but I am beginning to take him and his statements seriously. I am compelled by how events are unfolding to believe some of his stories."

"Why?"

I explained to Dr. Bugaje everything that had happened, ending with the question. "Is Atiku involved in this? If he truly is, I am not going to be in this job for much longer. I am not going to work like this." Usman appealed that I should calm down, promising he would look into it and get back to me.

Bugaje spoke to Atiku, who then called me and said, "Nasir, about this guest house business – I know Abdul. I know him, he brought the house, he wanted it purchased, I heard you were looking for a guest house, and I said I would introduce him to you, but he said he knew you from Kaduna. I thought you were friends."

"I know him. That is all" I said.

"I have no hand in determining at what price the house should be bought and I did not encourage him to insult you in any way," said the Vice-President.

"Well, Mr Vice-President, this is what he said: he said you got him a diplomatic passport because he does many things for you, he said that I will buy the guest house at his price, he said he will show me power."

Atiku said Abdul was lying and he was sorry Abdul spoke to me that way; that he was going to cut Abdul off, and I should go and decide whatever I wanted to do about the purchase of the house.

"We will offer to buy the house, our staff like it, I have not seen the house, but we will buy it at our price - one that we can defend before anyone on behalf of the Privatisation Council."

"Whatever you decide is fine. I just want you to know that I am not involved in anything to do with the house or Abdul's conduct in this instance."

This was the first time Atiku or someone associated with him came close to suggesting that I become part of any impropriety but I am convinced he initially acquiesced to it. It is just that he saw it going out of control and did not know what kind of man I was. I think he remembered that at our very first meeting in April 1999, I had the temerity to argue with Obasanjo and he may have just decided to back off. I never saw Abdul again. Nobody on the VP's staff ever came to my office to boldly ask for anything inappropriate until I moved to the FCT. I think Atiku probably called Abdul and just said, "Keep off this guy. He is mad."

At this point, we decided to send a memo to the Vice-President to the effect that further to his approval to acquire a guest house, we had examined the housing market, and finally identified this guest house, the government valuers and our consultants have appraised it at between 80 and 180 million naira, so please kindly approve that we offer 109.5 million naira for the house. The memo went to the VP on June 28, 2000 and returned the next day, approved.

In a way, that early 'Abdul incident' enabled me to buy my peace. I think Atiku understood I was not going to do these dodgy things and I was going to face him with any such issue anyway. To this day, I still do not know what arrangement, if any, Atiku may have had with Abdul, but I was still willing to give him the benefit of the doubt and move on. It was not long before another incident presented itself that raised more questions than it answered.

The Cost of Doing Business

When it became clear that the state of our electricity was such that the resources of government alone would not be adequate to address the deficit and that without private sector investment, it would be impossible to solve our electricity problem, we decided to attempt deregulating electricity. We hired NERA of South Africa- a consulting firm, and worked with Anil Kapoor and Trevor Byer of the World Bank, as well as our BPE staff to draft the new Electric Power Policy that would be the basis for legal and regulatory reforms of the electricity supply industry. The BPE team, initially led by Abdulkareem Adesokan, made very important inputs leading to the final version which was approved by the Electric Power Sector Steering Committee (EPIC) and published in 2000. CMS Cameron McKenna of Washington DC led the consortium that was retained to draft the new Electric Power Sector Reform Bill in 2002. The bill sought to deregulate the electricity industry, establish an independent regulator for the sector and create a framework for privatising NEPA.

The next step was to begin discussions with the National Assembly committees on power and privatisation to get the draft law passed. The privatisation committees already knew us, but the electric power committees did not. We presented our plan first to the Senate Committee with the consultants present and they asked questions, because it was a very complicated and technical piece of legislation. After we finished, the committee asked everyone to leave because they wanted to meet with just me - the DG alone, 'in camera'.

'In camera', the senators led by the committee chair, Dr. Nnamdi Eriobuna and his colleague Jonathan Zwingina, reviewed our groundwork and observed that $100 million plus credit that we had from the World Bank to support privatisation and policy reforms was a positive development. Therefore, by the committee's reasoning, Senator Eriobuna suggested that the BPE finds a way to 'lobby' the committee members with a payment of $5 million if we wanted a speedy passage of the electricity bill. I was taken aback, but recovered quickly enough to explain that this was impossible for at least four reasons.

One, as a matter of personal principle, I explained, I do not do that kind of thing and the institution I head does not do that either. Two, this legislation was not some special interest pitch that would benefit some elite few; the legislation had universal beneficiaries – every Nigerian, including them, would benefit. Electricity is a problem for everyone in the country, and I did not think that there were any beneficiaries willing to pay that "lobbying cost". Third, even if we wanted or were willing to, we did not have this $100 million sitting in the BPE bank account from which we could just write a cheque. I explained that the World Bank kept the funds and would disburse accordingly to a beneficiary of a contract after compliance with established procurement and disbursement approval procedures. Finally, when all these obstacles are cleared, the vice-president, as my boss, would have to know about this $5 million payment, its purpose and would have to approve it. I thought that bringing the vice president into the picture would make them back off somewhat from this preposterous position.

The committee's chairman responded that on the first two, the BPE had to make a decision on whether or not it wanted this bill passed – as though I or the BPE were the special interest. On the third item, one of the senators' opinion was that because I knew the World Bank and its inner workings, we should be able to fashion a way to get them $5 million out of the kitty, somehow. On the final point, they agreed to meet with the vice-president and directly request him to approve their demand of a $5 million kickback. The vice-president, as always, appeared shocked when I briefed him on what the senators demanded, and he agreed that this was something he wanted to hear and see with his own ears and eyes.

We did convene the meeting and the vice-president refused to play ball. He said flat-out that no such transaction would take place. Instead, he suggested we took the committee members on a study tour abroad to appreciate the intricacies of power sector reforms. The chairmen and deputy chairs of the electric power committees in the Senate and the House of Representatives were therefore sponsored by the BPE on study tours to Chile and Canada to 'observe' the functioning of privatised electricity markets at a cost of about $76,000 in March 2002. While the House Committee chairman Abdullahi Idris Umar took the assignment seriously and did a lot to make the bill pass through the legislature, Senator Eriobuna was only interested in cashing in his flight ticket and pocketing the per diem! Tijjani Abdullahi suggested that we met with ABU alumnus and friend, Speaker Ghali Umar Na'Abba to solicit his cooperation in getting the EPSR Bill passed. We scheduled an appointment and he promised to support the bill in a meeting with many principal officers of the House in attendance. After the official meeting, Na'Abba asked to meet with me and Tijjani in private, during which he indicated interest in acquiring government stake in one or two oil services companies listed for privatisation. We informed him that we were working to resolve some outstanding legal issues surrounding the OSCs and would advertise them for sale as soon as practicable, advising him to express interest at that point.

I do not know if there were any other meetings between the vice president and the senators about this topic in my absence, but at a point, Atiku asked one of his political associates and Anambra State 'godfather' Emeka Offor to meet us for a briefing to 'assist in getting the EPSR bill passed'. The VP also suggested we deposit some funds on 30-day call in a bank in which Mr Offor had substantial interest. We complied as we saw no ethical violation since we placed un-remitted funds on call in various banks anyway. Mr Offor never got back to brief us, but when the bill was passed about 15 months later, months before I left the BPE, the president simply refused to sign it into law. After 30 days, the bill lapsed and did not become law at that point, but was re-presented in 2005 and subsequently passed into law, virtually unaltered from the 2003 version. The reason the president withheld his approval the first time was because the bill gave Atiku, as chairman of the National Council on Privatisation, 'too much power' in determining the course and pace of the reform of the electricity supply industry. It was Dr. Olu Agunloye, who was appointed Minister of Power shortly before the bill was passed, who created this myth in President Obasanjo's mind to protect his own power and interests which in the opinion of the BPE staff, served at least two purposes - (i) the ministry of power maintained control of the electricity industry and the benefits of the procurement contracts associated for at least another year or so, and (ii) the overall reform of the industry was delayed for at least two more years with grave consequences for the country - something which we are still experiencing and suffering from.

As for Senator Nnamdi Eriobuna who demanded the $5 million kickback, I was reliably informed that Atiku ensured that the PDP did not re-nominate him to contest that Senate seat and he has not been seen nor heard from since then in the political space.

A $20 Million Hole

The very first state-owned company we attempted to sell saw more shenanigans. African Petroleum was once upon a time known as BP Nigeria. President Obasanjo nationalised the company in 1978 as a retaliatory manoeuvre against Margaret Thatcher's British government for allegedly selling our oil to South Africa during the apartheid era and changed the name to African Petroleum (AP). For some 20-odd years the Nigerian government, through its national oil company, the Nigerian National Petroleum Corporation (NNPC), owned 100 per cent of the company, with a minority portion of it subsequently listed on the stock exchange. In 1999, the BPE plan was to sell 40 per cent of the company to an investing group that would also have management control.

We advertised the sale and received responses from a handful of companies interested in participating in the bidding process: BP South Africa, a company called Sadiq Petroleum, and a third company which then bowed out before we even got underway. Sadiq Petroleum was a Nigerian company owned by a man named Peter Okocha, a very close friend of Vice President, Atiku Abubakar. Both BP South Africa and Sadiq Petroleum passed our pre-qualification hurdles without any difficulty. However, just before we began the bidding process, the representative of BP South Africa whose task was to conduct the due diligence – a Nigerian – surprised all of us by submitting a curtly-worded letter withdrawing from the bidding process. In a meeting with me, he explained that they were going to write a more detailed letter explaining their withdrawal but there were at least two reasons that he could cite up front. The first reason was that the health, safety and environmental (HSE) standards of the company were so poor that if BP South Africa bought the company, upgrading the company to be aligned with BP's global environmental standards would cost so much money that the bid price they would have to submit to justify it would be so low that they were going to lose the bid anyway. This was the official reason the forthcoming letter would detail. The second reason, which would not be mentioned in the letter, or anywhere, really, outside of our private conversation, was quite disturbing:

"In addition to this reason that we intend to make official, off the record, since you have been so helpful to us, you need to know that African Petroleum has a huge financial hole in its accounts of more than $20 million. At least, some twenty million dollars have been systematically stolen from the company. We discovered this while conducting our due diligence. The money is reflected in the books as income but it does not exist anywhere in cash or assets, and was never ever there."

I took a moment to digest this. "Wow. Can you give me the financial due diligence report which reveals that?"

He promised to send it to me as a favour and 'unofficially'. Then he disappeared and the next time I saw him was about four years later at an oil and gas conference in London. He had moved to another major oil company, and explained that there was no way he could have shared the report with me then. Even though he failed to send me the report, I had the unconfirmed information in my consciousness. In the meantime, we ended up with a single bid from Sadiq Petroleum. Aware of this new information about AP's finances, and because it was our very first 'core investor' transaction, a single bidder situation would send the wrong signal, particularly if that single bid came from a friend of the vice president. We therefore decided to be cautious because if there is only one bid, there can only be one winner, which would defeat the entire purpose of competitive bidding at this early, critical stage of our programme. I consulted with the chairman of the privatisation council's technical committee, Mr Akin Kekere-Ekun, who agreed with me that we should abort the bid process, re-advertise the sale of the company and re-bid at a future date. Without informing any of the BPE staff or council members, I went with Akin to see the vice-president.

"Mr Vice-President, we have ended up with only one bid. Our recommendation would be to cancel the auction and advertise again at a future date."

"But why? You went through all the required steps," he asked.

"Yes," Akin said, "but you know; if we end up with only one

bid and the winner is your friend, it will look like it was all pre-arranged, so it is not in your interest as the chairman of the privatisation council for us to go ahead with this."

I joined Akin Kekere-Ekun in weighing in along similar lines, and Atiku agreed with both of us, that we should cancel and rebid in the near future. He suggested that we bring the matter to the privatisation council for discussion and ratification.

Quite honestly, to me, at the time (and indeed throughout most of my time in BPE), Atiku came across as a fairly objective person for accepting the recommendation. After the council approved the cancellation of the bid process, the vice-president made some comments before the council that struck me as quite strange but commendable for its openness.

"I am happy the council has approved the cancellation of this process and we particularly appreciate the efforts of the chairman of the technical committee and the director-general," – that was me – "for having the courage of conviction to bring this recommendation to the council." He continued, "Let me tell you a story. Just before this council meeting started, the president called me and said one of the members of this council, and he was not going to reveal who it was, went to him yesterday and said, 'Mr President, Sadiq is the same name in Arabic as Abubakar. So Sadiq Petroleum is owned by the vice-president, whose name happens to be Atiku Abubakar.' One of the members, one of the people sitting here, went to the president and said I owned this company. I hope that person will go back to the president and say that I presided over the cancellation of an open and fair process which this company would have undoubtedly won."

Everybody was silent. We started looking at people and began suspecting who may have said what. God forgive me, but I thought it was a certain cranky member of the council that I did not get along with. It was not until many years later, at some point that President Obasanjo and I were between quarrels that I learned who told him the story: it was not any member of the council – it was another senior government official familiar with Arabic names. Indeed, in the Islamic world, it is true that Abubakar and Sadiq are interchangeable names, but Abubakar was not Atiku's name but his father's.

Months later, we re-advertised African Petroleum for sale. We again received an expression of interest from Sadiq Petroleum, as well as from Consolidated Oil, which is owned by Mike Adenuga. We went through the pre-qualification process and Sadiq Petroleum submitted a much higher bid price than Consolidated Oil, so Sadiq ended up buying the 40% stake afterall.

But this time, with the fore-knowledge of suspicions about Sadiq's ownership, we decided to conduct more extensive investigations into the company to accompany the memo to the council. We found that Sadiq Petroleum was incorporated in late 1980s or thereabouts and that the original subscribers were Peter Okocha and his family members, including his son, Sadiq Okocha, among other names. BPE's lawyers obtained the original incorporation documents and looked at all the changes filed in directorships and ownership of the company's shares over the decade of the company's existence. Atiku Abubakar did not feature even once, at any time in the history of the company as a shareholder or director. In fact, we found out where the Sadiq name came from - the son of Peter Okocha. It may well be that the son was named in honour of Atiku's deceased father, a practice common in our culture between friends,[31] but found nothing more to establish a factual nexus between Atiku and the company.

Our memo to the council concluded accordingly and noted that the fact that the chairman or owner of the company happened to be a friend of the vice-president's should not disqualify him from bidding for privatisation assets. The guidelines for the privatisation had been published and did not exclude friends of council members from buying shares or privatisation assets. Under the rules and regulations (and our self-imposed ethics), only the vice-president, council members and BPE staff were disqualified from bidding on or buying any assets. Any other person, Nigerian or foreign, had a legal right to bid if technically qualified. In fact, technically, even the president could purchase any privatisation asset since he was not a member of the Privatisation Council or within the decision loop of the divestiture process. I made a very passionate case for approving the transaction and it was approved without much comment. After we approved the transaction and announced it, Obasanjo called and asked me to see him.

"I hear that you have given AP to Sadiq Petroleum. I got the papers," he said. "I have seen all your arguments, you've done a very good job, but you know, are you sure that there is nothing and no-one behind this company?"

"I can't be sure of anything that is behind the company, sir," I said. "I can only deal with facts, logic and what I can see. Only God knows everything. I can't know what is not documented; neither can we rely on beer-parlour rumours. Those that allege should come out and provide proof. Based on every document that we came across, what I presented was what we saw. I do not see how Peter Okocha would be so foresighted that he would incorporate a company in the 1980s for the sole purpose of waiting some 16 years later to buy a company when his friend would be vice-president. If he had that kind of foresight, then we really should concede and give the company to him in spite of our unproven suspicions."

Obasanjo seemed satisfied with this. "But you know what, Mr President?" I continued. "I have not mentioned this in the memorandum because I am yet to have the documentary evidence, and could not therefore put it on the record anywhere. But that company is suspected of having a $20 million hole. So if they bought it – the VP and this man – they might be in for a surprise. Only a person with deep pockets and commitment can clean up that company. It has some valuable assets that could be sold to cover the financial gap; it is an old company, the first company to sell gasoline in Nigeria. It is British Petroleum, remember, so they have assets, particularly real estate assets, all over the place, petrol stations, two lube blending plants, and so on. With good management and financial reengineering, they may be able to get out of it, but there is a big hole there."

"Really? How? What happened?"

I proceeded to relate to him the story the BP South Africa representative told me. Obasanjo looked visibly more relieved.

Prior to the second round of bid, I had quietly and privately counselled Peter Okocha that I have heard rumours of a financial hole. This information neither surprised nor alarmed him. He seemed to be vaguely aware of it, and was nevertheless determined to go ahead with the bid. As soon as Sadiq took control of AP, we hired an accounting firm to undertake a governance audit into the affairs of AP. The findings were sobering to say the least. It was found that the company's NNPC-appointed management had made unauthorised borrowings of 11.75 billion naira through the issuance of Commercial Papers and Bankers Acceptances and obtained other bank loans without following due process. It had also purchased and sold assets without providing adequate details of sale proceeds and the identity of the buyers. In addition, it not only failed to reconcile huge debts owed to NNPC (estimated at between four and ten billion naira) but was also alleged to have been involved in insider trading, diverting revenues from bunkering and marine activities, and other general abuses. Sadiq Petroleum, the core investors, claimed that not only were these issues not disclosed, they were actively concealed from them during their pre-sale due diligence on the company. In order to establish the legitimacy of these claims, BPE held meetings with the core investors, Mr Umar Abba Gana (the former Managing Director of AP), the issuing house which supervised the due diligence exercise and Ernst & Young, the statutory auditors of the company, to resolve the conflicting records. For months, none of the parties could agree on the money owed to NNPC, the banks and other creditors and this remained unresolved throughout my tenure.

Sadiq Petroleum was not an innocent victim in this whole imbroglio either. The company was found to have colluded with the issuing house (NAL Merchant Bank) and the registrars (IMB Securities Ltd.) to corner the 20 per cent shares sold to the public on the open market; withheld refunds to unsuccessful applicants and went as far as forging NIPOST despatch records to facilitate these dubious transactions. We reported the capital market operators to the Securities & Exchange Commission (SEC) and the Attorney-General for further action.

In the end, neither the management of Sadiq Petroleum nor the findings of the governance audit fully established the size of the accounting hole until a couple of years later, after I had moved on to administer Abuja. Of course, this discovery was compounded by other issues which led to Sadiq demanding an immediate refund from the government. They found the hole largely because the NNPC, a government-owned company, supplied products to African Petroleum on credit, had better records and insisted on full payment of all outstanding accounts. AP's successive managements simply sold the products on to dealers and distributors, but apparently failed to remit the proceeds into AP's accounts, but allegedly diverted the proceeds to various private pockets – those running African Petroleum since 1978 were all seconded NNPC staff. They simply collected products from their parent company on credit, sold, and did not pay NNPC back - and literally stealing the money, and many of them had retired and were living happily ever after, in affluence.

Sadiq first approached BPE for a refund of purchase price, but we referred Peter Okocha and his directors to the disclaimers in the contract that BPE sold the company "as is, where is" and my warnings to him about the existence of the accounting hole. Sadiq Petroleum even engaged political operator and PDP chieftain Abba Dabo as consultant to facilitate the cancellation of the sale but he too was rebuffed. In the end, a couple of years after I left BPE, the company was re-nationalised and the government directed the BPE to refund Sadiq Petroleum the original proceeds of the sale. AP was then re-privatised a few years after that, this time sold to Jimoh Ibrahim, someone alleged to be close to Obasanjo, and similar speculations began, except that this time, it was Obasanjo rather than Atiku that became the suspected 'owner'. It was all very amusing to me. Subsequently, AP was acquired without any involvement of the BPE by Femi Otedola, another close friend of successive presidents, who has renamed it Forte Oil.

The rumours of Atiku's interest in the AP deal continued to make the rounds until we left office In any event, Atiku was a sitting vice-president at the time, there was nothing anyone could do because he had constitutional immunity from prosecution even if pursued. At any rate, even if true, I am not sure any crime was committed. A breach of administrative rules and NCP's code of conduct, yes! Unethical behaviour, perhaps, but not a violation of any law that I know of since any public servant can be a shareholder in any business, but is prohibited from being a director while in office, except it is an agricultural enterprise. By the time Atiku left office, the whole thing became a moot point and Nuhu Ribadu, who would have had the courage to pursue the matter further, got kicked out of his job anyway.

Nobody was going to take on somebody like Atiku Abubakar except the US Senate,[32] which has now published a report showing that his wife, a US citizen, laundered some $40 million through her personal bank accounts in the United States, including a $2.8 million wire transfer acknowledged by Siemens AG of Germany. Atiku and his wife, Jennifer, left the US in good time before the FBI got to ask them some questions. He is back in political contention in Nigeria as a leading member of the ruling party and a presidential hopeful for 2015.

Mike Adenuga Sends Cash

Not all manoeuvres in BPE's universe were as covert as the vice-president's alleged stake in Sadiq Petroleum. When the time came to put National Oil (Nolchem) on the auction block, the attempted bid rigging and kickback schemes could not have been more open.

National Oil was the former Shell Nigeria downstream business in which the government had bought a majority stake though Shell remained technically a partner and shareholder. The first bidding round yielded no actionable prices from our perspective. We cancelled the auction, waited a few months and re-launched the bidding. I do not know what's so difficult to understand about the concept of an auction, but this time around we had a group of potential buyers who were under the impression that 'highest price wins' does not necessarily have to mean that the highest price actually wins.

Engen of South Africa, which was the former Mobil South Africa, pre-qualified, as had Mike Adenuga of Consolidated Oil and another friend of Atiku's, Chief Igweh, the owner of Bolingo Hotels in Abuja. Shell and a consortium led by Mr Kola Abiola also submitted bids. When we opened the bids and were writing the evaluation report, President Obasanjo sent for me. He asked what was going on with National Oil, because Shell's management had come to him complaining that they wanted to buy it back, but we had frustrated them. From Engen's corner, South African President Thabo Mbeki had also called President Obasanjo and said Engen's bid was being unfavourably considered.

"Mr President, Sir. Let me explain what is going on." I said. "This is what Shell wanted to buy the company for and we think it is worth more than that, it is even below our reserve price, which is why we cancelled the bid in the first place. I cannot recall the exact numbers but think Engen was bidding something like 28 naira per share, Bolingo was bidding 34 naira per share and Mike Adenuga was bidding something like 36 naira per share and that was the highest price. This is the deal we're being offered. We are recommending the highest price for acceptance because all the bidders have submitted sound business plans and so are technically qualified."

The president waited a moment to see if I had anything else to say, which I did not. "Ok," he said finally. "This is what is on the surface. Now tell me what is behind the scenes. Who is behind which company?"

Obasanjo always wanted to know what was happening behind the scenes – he never entirely believed what was on the table was all there was. I think this was when I had begun to know him a bit better and he also had begun to trust me a bit more. My sense was that he began to realise I was open with every piece of information I had. I did not hide anything because I did not care who won the bid, I just wanted to sell the companies I thought were draining the economy and move on.

"Well, the face behind this company is Bolingo, - Chief Igweh, Atiku's friend and PDP financier, ConPetro is Mike Adenuga's and this company is Engen South Africa."

"Has the vice-president spoken to you in favour of any particular company?"

"Yes, he did. He told me that both former President Ibrahim Babangida and Oba Sikiru Adetona, the Awujale of Ijebuland, had asked him to intervene in favour of Mike Adenuga, for Consolidated Oil/ConPetro. I had told the vice-president that no one could do anything to influence the outcome, so just to tell Adenuga to submit the highest price that he could pay. There was no other way to cut corners. ConPetro did submit the highest price and we therefore intend to recommend that the company be sold to him."

Obasanjo appeared satisfied with my explanations.

That is what happened. Everything was all properly done, bids were publicly opened, and the highest bid price won. We signed and sealed the agreement and payments were made. The six-month transitional period embedded in the share sale agreement during which sudden board and management changes needed prior BPE approval began. That should have been the end, right?

Wrong. Mike Adenuga had no intention of complying with the transitional provisions regarding board reconstitutions and job security during the period to enable a proper governance audit. He stormed the company's head office with a detachment of armed mobile policemen like a cowboy, and asked the managing director, Mr Ojo, to vacate office immediately and leave the building, and also demanded that respected former Head of State, General Yakubu Gowon, should step down as chairman of the board without the prior knowledge and approval of the NCP. I was away from Nigeria on assignment and was livid on being briefed of these violations of the sale agreement. I therefore directed that the share certificates conclusively evidencing the sale should not be handed over by the BPE to ConPetro, until the Director of Legal Services reviewed the agreement, recommended options for us and appropriate sanctions. That was when the games started!

First, Mike Adenuga sent one of his senior people with an envelope containing cash to Tijjani Abdullahi as his 'thank you' and demanded for the share certificates. Tijjani declined both the offer and the request. Then a couple of days before my return to Nigeria, the vice president called Tijjani, over-rode my directives, and instructed him to hand over the share certificates to Mike Adenuga without further delay. Thirdly, a day after I returned to the office, a BPE deputy director, Charles Osuji came to me to say he had a message from Mike Adenuga – a person I was quite upset with at that point. I was a little surprised because Charles was not working on the NOLCHEM transaction, but on the privatisation of Nigeria Airways. The message he carried was a Zenith Bank account statement with twenty five million naira, then the equivalent of about US$250,000 in an account in some name I did not know.

"What is this?" I asked.

"Well, Mike Adenuga gave this to me to give to you as a 'thank you gift' for selling the company to him, so I opened an account to receive the money." he said.

"I did not sell the company to him," I replied. "The federal government sold the company to him and everything was done properly until his violations of the share sale agreement. We all did our job, and that was nothing special. We do not need anything from him. We are reviewing the agreement to decide on the next steps." I looked at the bank statement. "Whose name is this?"

"Well I went and opened an account in this bank with a fictitious name. It is to show you that I will transfer the money anywhere you want."

"No, I do not want anything." I said. "Charles, you are a nice guy, a good staff, do not get involved in this kind of thing. I will consider this as a first serious infraction and not report to the council, so just go back to Mike, give him his money back, tell him I do not want it, I do not work like that. And advise him not to test our will by violating the share sale agreement again."

So Charles left. A few days later, he was back.

"Mike said in addition to the money in the account, he wants you to have an additional one hundred thousand dollars in cash. He thought the amount will now be adequate." Charles said.

Furthermore, Mike had apparently given him the $100,000 in cash, and it was sitting right outside in his car parked downstairs. I was supposed to go with him and collect it.

"Charles, you are not listening. Did not you understand what I said to you? Take back the money. If you do not take back the money, I will have to report this first to the privatisation council and you will be fired. You will lose your job, and possibly, be prosecuted as well."

"You can't do that to me, Sir. I am trying to help you. You have nothing. Since you came here, what have you got?"

I shook my head.

"I do not need anything. Did you think I came here because I needed something? I am here voluntarily to work, not to collect bribes. Who appointed you the custodian of my interests? Did I ask you to do this?"

"No, but it is my duty as your staff to look after your interests because you are being foolish."

I may be naive, but till today, I believe that Charles believed he was doing the right thing, and probably thought he meant well for me.

"Look, thank you very much, take back the $100,000 and give him back his 25 million naira and bring me zero balance in this account you have showed me so that I know he has got his money back."

"Ok sir, but Sir, you are making a mistake. Nigeria is not worth suffering for."

"Just do it and come back quickly."

The next day Charles came back.

"Mike said he will not take the money back and that I should tell you that the vice-president, Atiku Abubakar, was consulted before offering you this gift."

As chair of the privatisation council, the vice-president was my boss.

"Really?" I said.

"Yes."

"Tell him I still do not want his money. Bring me the zero balance tomorrow."

I then went to the vice-president's office and told him the story. At the end, I said,

"Now, I have just been told today – I was going to report this to you if he did not do what I said. I am keeping it under wraps because I think I can handle it. So I am giving him a chance to just get out of this and we will retain his services, which is why I have not yet reported it formally to you and the council. I have just been told that Mike Adenuga had your prior consent to offer this money. Is this what you are doing? Your administration is verbally fighting corruption and encouraging this kind of offers?"

The vice-president appeared shocked. "Nasir, he is lying. It is not true."

"Well, Mike sent Osuji to tell me that you knew about the cash offer."

So he picked up his land-line phone and said, "Get me Mike Adenuga." On getting a connection, he put Mike on speaker phone.

"Mike, how are you? Did we ever discuss Nasir El-Rufai with you?"

"Yes sir," said Adenuga through the speaker.

"And what did I tell you?" asked the vice-president.

"Sir, you told me he is a straightforward person and that I should not try to give him any money or try to thank him in any way."

"So why did you send him money even though I told you not to?"

"I am sorry sir. I just thought they did a good job and I ought to thank him as the leader of BPE. I am sorry sir."

The vice-president hung up the phone, turned to me and asked, "Now do you believe that I told him to do it?"

"Well sir, what do we do now?"

"Well, Charles must be fired immediately. You should bring a memo immediately to approve his disengagement."

Charles was a deputy director, so I could not fire him; I had to bring a request showing cause to the council to authorise his firing. The vice-president said, "Bring it, I will approve as chairman of the council and the council in full session will ratify it at the next plenary session. He has got to go, this conduct is not acceptable in a privatisation agency." As instructed, Mrs Modupe Abiodun-Wright took all the steps leading to drafting the memo for VP's approval and Osuji's appointment was terminated.

A few weeks later, I reported the matter to the council for ratification in full session. Some members of the council were very angry. The attorney general, Bola Ige, opined that both Charles and whoever offered the cash should be prosecuted. Furthermore, the VP and I were obliquely accused of being too lenient with Charles and the council accordingly decided that Charles' termination was to be converted to dismissal. Now, dismissal means he had lost everything – he receives no terminal benefits, he receives no retirement benefits, nothing. That was what finally happened. He lost everything. As for Adenuga, when I reported the matter to the council, I did not reveal his identity; I just stated the facts of the case. Once the attorney-general realised who was behind the scenes pulling the strings and sending the 'thank-you' cash, his resolve to prosecute considerably weakened, contrary to the desires of the council at large. The extent to which Adenuga's attempted payment served to not only thank me but to give a taste of what was to come from successful bids of his in future privatisation ventures I do not know, but at the BPE we became cautious with anything related to him from that point on. He did finally get a telecommunications license which was not issued by the BPE but another regulatory agency, with the help of the vice-president and concurrence of the president.

As for whether I ever gave receiving the money a second thought, I can say in no uncertain terms that I did not. This is where some people have a difficult time understanding me to the point of disbelief, but I am really very proud of my parentage, person and my family name and would hate a situation in which I would be caught red-handed doing something dishonest. I do not know how I would be able to live with myself. I was really more concerned with Charles' bad judgment and future consequences on his career than anything else. I was and am still convinced that he was misguided into believing there is anything like free cash. He therefore situated himself as the negotiator and conduit of the gratification, thought I deserved to have it, convinced delivering it would make him look more useful in my eyes, and saw nothing wrong morally with his actions. I was quite certain he was just a pawn and at the end of the day he would be the loser because anyone worth a billion dollars has the capacity to limit what damage can be done to him. Mike Adenuga was worth more than a billion dollars at the time and I therefore knew nothing adverse would happen to him in a country like ours, while Charles would ultimately be the fall guy, and that was exactly what happened in the end. I tried my best to avoid that outcome, but Charles just did not see it.

As soon as I left the BPE, Charles launched an effort to get back into the organisation using the usual route in Nigeria - petition to a parliamentary committee headed by someone from his ethnic group. That attempt at reinstatement failed in spite of the willingness of BPE's leadership at the time to accept him. He made another attempt during the Senate Ad-Hoc Committee hearings on privatisation from 1999 to 2011, which I understand was set up to 'nail El-Rufai' (again!). Charles Osuji appeared before the committee, and admitted under oath on national television - that he took monies from Adenuga to pass on to me, but never did. The committee chairman and members appeared shocked, one even called him a criminal - yet he walked out of the Committee Room a free man, suggesting that he was procured by my political adversaries to give that testimony in the hope that the pre-arranged newspaper headlines the following day would damage my reputation. The DG of BPE, Bola Onagoruwa, who was Assistant Director (Legal Matters) at the time of the incident, and therefore familiar with the case immediately discredited the testimony there and then, and testified that Charles lied under oath about the details of what happened.

Once the National Oil saga was over, there were not many more attempts to bribe me in that manner while I was at the BPE. Word about this got around and everybody got the message, not unlike my days in the private sector. The construction industry – and this seems to be the case in any country around the world, for some reason is widely acknowledged to engage in practices that were not always above board. At El-Rufai &Partners, we were constantly offered money in virtually every construction consulting job we had in the first five years of our practice. We always politely refused. Quantity surveyors keep the construction industry books, the financial accounts, so anyone wanting to do anything financially dishonest needs to have the quantity surveyor on his side. Eventually, word went around that these El-Rufai & Partners guys are crazy, they do not accept money, will not be compromised, and we began to get clients who heard that we could not be bribed. Anyone who took us on as consultants would be comfortable in knowing that we would not allow his or her money to go to waste, so we got a lot of work, particularly from private sector clients, because of that reputation. We also lost other opportunities particularly in the public sector for the same reason of "not playing ball". It is a double-edged sword, but we chose what makes us sleep well at night!

In government, I began learning that there were a couple of twists on this dynamic. Firstly, word got around much quicker – as I said, as soon as people heard, there were not many more overt attempts. Secondly, this did not mean there were not more attempts, period. The attempts to coerce and compromise an honest official would take on different forms, some of which I will discuss shortly. Thirdly, there is outright bribery which became rare, and then there are covert methods of gaming the system to one's advantage. Fourthly, there is the meta-statement of what this all means. Some of my friends in the West have asked me or suggested that perhaps what sets Nigeria, Africa, or the developing world apart is that so-called corruption has come to be viewed as a sort of 'tolerated ugliness', but I do not think this is really accurate. I just think it has gotten to a point, particularly in the last few years, that only the fool does not do it. Finally, quite apart from bribery, kickbacks or anything else that would fall under the very broad-stroke 'corruption' umbrella is the simple premise that certain people have a certain emotional investment in seeing certain projects done a certain way, or not done a certain way, as the case may be, and this can set the stage for a big conflict of interest. This last point can be particularly challenging when that conflict of interest is with the president of Nigeria.

Nigeria Airways or Two and a Half Planes

The two different arguments we had the very first time I met President Obasanjo was clearly some sort of foreshadowing of what our relationship was destined to become, for we had constant quarrels over all manner of things. Someone recently asked me if I could boil down my relationship with President Obasanjo into three simple words, and the closest I have come so far is to simply say, 'a roller coaster' or a 'love-hate relationship'.

One of our first big disagreements was over the proposed privatisation of Nigeria Airways. President Obasanjo clearly had an emotional attachment to the airline. When he was military head of state in the late 1970s, he expanded its fleet from a handful of planes to more than two dozen aircraft. He also expanded government contribution to GDP from 22 per cent to 44 per cent, so he was very interested in state-directed development then. He also purchased 16 huge merchant ships for Nigeria's national shipping line, established six automobile assembly plants, built 22 airports and a steel plant. He really believed that only government could be fair, only government could be just, so government should be big in business - and do everything.

Shortly after he assumed office as president in 1999, the joke among us at the BPE was that Nigeria Airways only had two and a half planes – 'two and a half' because two were flying and one was grounded as it was due for 'D check', which is what a plane goes through every five years after logging a certain number of flying hours. We did not have the money to pay for the D check though, so we had the plane, it was fine, it could fly, but no pilot could be willing to fly it without that inspection. So really we had two planes flying and neither one was flying any international routes. Nigeria Airways' total fleet had gone from nearly 30 in 1979 when Obasanjo left office the first time, to two and a half in 1999 when he returned to the presidency.

As a result, the president had great difficulty seeing this child that he had raised die, and was, therefore, very reluctant to see it privatised. His attitude was, "Look, why can't we get Boeing or Airbus to give us some planes and we pay them back over time?" How we would pay them when Nigeria Airways staff siphoned off the revenues into private pockets I suppose was an afterthought. Nigeria Airways managers were known for giving free tickets to friends and relations and nobody paid for excess baggage or any cargo on their flights. The only way out was to take the national carrier license, bilateral air services agreements and the two and a half planes as assets, get some private sector entrepreneurial spirit to acquire them so he could then use his balance sheet to borrow and buy more planes, and hopefully keep it as a going concern, and preserve some of the 2,000 jobs.

The IFC had been appointed as transaction advisers in the privatisation of Nigeria Airways. This sent a very positive signal to the rest of the world that Nigeria was serious about privatisation. As we all soon learned, President Obasanjo did that just for show, so that he would look good internationally, but had no intention of allowing the sale to happen quickly. Perhaps his plan to drag it out would have succeeded if not for the fact that some two weeks later, he appointed me as BPE's director general. When I came onto the scene, I honestly thought selling off a near-dead airline was a no-brainer!

Once I took over, we were going too fast by Obasanjo's mental timeline. There were a number of obstacles to privatising the airline. To begin with, it had a staff of 2,000, down from 6,000 at its peak, and two aircraft, making for an average of 1,000 employees per plane. Meanwhile, the international standard was 200 employees per plane. This meant that in the short term, something on the order of 1,500 people would have to be sacked, and their terminal benefits settled prior to privatisation.

Obstacle number two was the psychological process of coming to terms with a major asset sale like that - a privately-owned national carrier meant no free flights for ministers, officials and their relations. President Obasanjo had a minister of aviation who was very close to him, Dr. Olusegun Agagu. Agagu was not interested in hastening the privatisation of Nigeria Airways, despite the fact that it was an airline with two aircraft and no revenues, and the reason was very simple - money!. In the airline industry, each country signs bilateral air services agreements, commonly referred to as BASAs, with other countries. In a given country, any foreign airline that earns more than the host country airline pays a fraction of its excess revenues to the host country.

This quasi-socialist framework was set up to prevent bigger countries from taking advantage of smaller countries. In the case of developed country revenues flowing to underdeveloped countries, the purpose of these monies was intended to help develop infrastructure for the poorer countries' aviation industries. Nigeria Airways, in 1999, received about $35 million just on the basis of this agreement, paid in from Lufthansa, KLM, British Airways and others – essentially free cash for doing absolutely nothing. Contrary to the provisions of the Nigerian constitution, these funds do not go into the distributable pool of revenues or even the treasury of the Federal Government. Much like oil money, it just rolls in freely, but into an unaudited account under the control of the ministry of aviation.

As the money is off-budget (it does not go into the federal treasury to be accounted for and appropriated by the National Assembly), it could be spent pretty much entirely at the discretion of the recipient-agency. This was what the successive ministers of aviation were feasting on, and it was not a bad chunk of revenue for a person or two or even ten. So there was obvious resistance to the privatisation of Nigeria Airways in the Ministry of Aviation because of that annual $35 million income. Minister Agagu consistently made a case to keep the airline for sovereignty, pride, and 'national security' reasons – everything other than BASA account, and what not, and Obasanjo listened. Approvals needed to terminate excess staff, close high-cost centres, fund terminal benefits and so on returned with questions and further questions.

To say there were huge tensions would be an understatement. Soon enough, Obasanjo replaced Agagu with a woman and I was initially relieved because I knew I was being successfully obstructed on account of Agagu's closeness to Obasanjo. We later learnt that this woman was even closer to Obasanjo, with a longer history of family connections, which worsened the challenges of privatising the airline. The new minister, Dr Kema Chikwe, is the sister-in-law of Ajie Ukpabi Asika, the Administrator of the then East-Central

State during the civil war, and had been close family friends with Obasanjo from the 1960s. We therefore made little progress, and decided within the BPE, and in the interest of our institutional credibility, that we had to go public with the ministerial obstructions and our frustrations. The IFC was equally bewildered by the attitude of the Nigerian leadership and the conflicting signals about the political will to privatise moribund public enterprises.

At one point, one of Obasanjo's domestic aides came to me and said, "Look, just slow down on this Nigeria Airways thing, because you will never win with this lady. The president will never consent to any action that she is opposed to. It is not a question of whether you are right and have a better argument or not. You will simply never win." But I did not care, I believed I had a job to do, and it was not Obasanjo's but Nigeria's.

Our arguments over Nigeria Airways even made several headlines in Nigerian newspapers – that was how open the quarrel was. President Obasanjo was quoted as saying that if I ever insulted his minister again he was going to fire me, and I responded that I was going to privatise Nigeria Airways, no matter what. I asserted that I was sure in two years the airline would be dead unless it was placed in private hands. Many people thought I was crazy but the truth was at that point, I really did not care if he fired me. In the end, the airline was never privatised, the lady minister tried setting up another airline, Airwing, with the airline's assets and BASA, which we successfully foiled, and Nigeria Airways finally ceased operating in 2003, shortly after I left BPE, much as predicted. The chief of staff to the president reconciled Dr Chikwe and I in May 2003 and asked me to write her a letter of apology on 'the inappropriate use of language' since she was older than me, even though I felt she was wrong. I had no problems with that and wrote the letter, as life must go on and one must not hold grudges for too long, or be seen to be unforgiving.

Years later in 2006, Kema Chikwe confidently visited me to seek the support of our group – the economic team - in her bid to run for the governorship of Imo State. My friend and perceived nominee, Hakeem Belo-Osagie, had been appointed the chairman of the PDP gubernatorial screening committee for the South-East zone, and Kema needed my help to discredit and discountenance some petitions filed to disqualify her. I was gracious and mentioned the visit to Hakeem who went on to do a professional job of the screening exercise. The nature of political relationships is dynamic and susceptible to change sometimes overnight, and often unpredictably.

The ending to this story I did not fully know until I was in exile, when I met one of the air transport union leaders deployed by the aviation minister to resist the sale of Nigeria Airways. He was abroad for medical treatment. He complained that all his union members were then not only unemployed, but had not received their terminal benefits – even the negotiated fraction of what they were entitled to on paper. I was unsympathetic. I felt that it served them right, and told him so. He admitted that they erred, but was honestly persuaded by Kema Chikwe that the government would bail out the airline with the acquisition of new planes and fresh injection of funds with the BPE as the only stumbling block. The union leader admitted that the Ministry of Aviation financed the union's campaign against the privatisation of Nigeria Airways and their support of the 'turnaround' option. An example of such media campaigns was a paid advert on page 7 of the Daily Champion of 25th September 2002 titled – "Air Nigeria, El-Rufai, BPE and the Rest of Us: What Does El-Rufai Want?" He admitted that they felt swindled when Obasanjo approved the liquidation of the airline shortly after I left the BPE, a process that resulted in job losses and substantially discounted terminal benefits.

Nigeria Telecommunications Limited (Nitel)

One of the underlying reasons for my quarrels with President Obasanjo those first few years was his constant suspicion that the vice-president and I were up to no good in the privatisation implementation. I do not fully know where he got this idea but my sense is that it was a combination of the president's generally suspicious nature and the fact that unlike some other senior government officials, I never made a practice of paying him regular visits just to chat, or more correctly, gossip about others, despite his frequent invitations. This all changed – not our quarrelling, but his suspicion of me – as a result of our flagship privatisation transaction for 2001: Nigerian Telecommunications Limited, better known as Nitel.

Nitel was the telephone monopoly and the effort to privatise it was a huge challenge, because Nitel, like Nigeria Airways, was a big cash cow that had made a lot of politicians, generals, bureaucrats and business persons very rich. Those who were benefiting from the status quo therefore saw our effort to privatise it as a threat to their livelihood and rent-seeking. But because I came into my job in the BPE with a telecommunications background, I knew the industry well and what needed to be done. We rewrote the national telecommunications policy, and actively spearheaded the deregulation of the telecommunications industry[33] such that licenses would be issued to other operators to compete with Nitel because we did not want to just make it a private monopoly as other countries have done. Instead, we proposed to both deregulate the industry and privatise Nitel in parallel. We were fairly successful overall though the Nitel privatisation did not succeed as well as the deregulation path.

The moment we invoked the provisions of the privatisation act, all of Nitel's shares came under the finance minister's oversight, who in turn gave the power of attorney to the BPE since the intent was to auction off majority shares of the company. Because BPE effectively became the sole shareholder of Nitel, I joined the board of directors. Shortly thereafter, we dissolved the board (made up largely of politicians) and constituted our own technical board to steer the company more directly onto a path toward privatisation.

Of course, the main element of the privatisation process involved auctioning off 51 per cent of the company itself, plus management control. While this sale over the years has morphed into something that I do not think anyone could have foreseen, the very first bid attempt ended up actually quite indicative of the sort of dynamics to expect. A consortium known as Investors International London, Ltd. (IILL) bid $1.317 billion to acquire a 51 per cent stake in Nitel in 2001. The terms of the sale dictated that 10 per cent of the bid price be paid in immediately as a non-refundable deposit - $131.7 million – with the other 90 per cent due within 60 days. Failure to pay in the balance would result in the deposit being forfeited and the company being offered, hopefully to the second highest bidder - the reserve bidder - someone hopefully more solvent.

After paying in the nearly $132 million deposit, the consortium failed to comply with the 60 day deadline, even after being granted a 30-day extension, approved by the NCP. The consortium's leader, Chief Bode Akindele, then attempted to get the deposit refunded, despite the fact that everyone was warned well ahead of time what the rules were. I did not find out until later, but he apparently was offering $10 million in cash to anyone who could convince the BPE to change its mind. When this did not work, he appealed to First Bank Nigeria to discuss the matter with me since First Bank had made an unsecured loan to Akindele of about $92 million for part of the initial down payment.

Had the lender been a small bank, we might have debated the issue or reconsidered, and made a case to the Privatisation Council for reconsideration to avoid systemic risk. But First Bank had the balance sheet and financial strength to take the hit and should have known better, really. In short order, we paid the $132 million into the treasury, so the only way for anyone to get the money back would have been via an appropriation bill requiring National Assembly approval.

I do not know what it was about the rules we devised, but the procurement process for Nitel's GSM equipment suffered similar difficulties. We got a GSM license reserved for Nitel without auction and since by then it was competing with private companies, Nitel had to invest in and deploy its GSM network. The vice-president, as privatisation council chair, approved a bid process for the first phase of the procurement of GSM equipment. While we were pre-qualifying the companies interested in participating, he called me in an attempt to rig a system specifically designed to be open and transparent.

"I have been approached by the Ericsson people," Atiku began. "They are really interested in doing this Nitel job, and they have done more GSM equipment than anyone in the world."

He continued for a few moments with what was more or less a sales pitch for Ericsson, and ended with the question - "In what way can we assist them?"

"There is no way to assist them, other than just tell them to submit the lowest bid price for the equipment."

"DG, you never help, you only say 'submit the highest price' or 'submit the lowest price,'" he protested.

We laughed about it and I thought that would be the end of it. A few days later, his aide-de-camp, a police officer named Abdullahi Yari, came to me and said Ericsson had approached him to 'intervene' on their behalf.

"Yes, the vice-president had spoken to me about Ericsson, but these bids will be opened publicly, so just advise Ericsson to submit the lowest price that they can afford," I said. "The only way to win is to submit the lowest price because that is what we will recommend, consistent with the bid specifications."

On bids opening day, we conducted our usual procedure of publicly opening the final bids with the media in attendance. Motorola submitted the lowest bid for about $38 million. The next lowest bid was Ericsson for about $41 million. The others, including Siemens, were even more expensive. So we evaluated the bids and recommended Motorola be the supplier of the equipment for Nitel's GSM network. The final step was to convene a meeting with the president to approve a final decision a few days later.

"We are meeting here to take a decision on who will supply equipment for Nitel for first phase of their GSM network," President Obasanjo said. Without looking up from the memorandum placed before him, he added: "BPE director general, please present your findings and recommendations."

The BPE team leader for the Nitel transaction, Hassan Usman, led the presentation and detailed every step that had been taken leading up to the recommendation in favour of Motorola, because the company submitted the lowest bid price, had supplied equipment in countries all over the world, and was a pioneer in cell phone technology. He also listed the other bids and explained that all of these companies were equally qualified to do the job, so it was simply a matter of price.

The floor then opened for comments and the president looked at me and asked me if I specifically had any comments. I said not really, just that the team had done a good job, and that I was simply the messenger passing along their recommendations. The vice president looked grim but said nothing.

"Our decision is as follows," he said. "We approve the award of this contract to Ericsson Nigeria, but at Motorola's price."

He looked at me again and asked if I had any objections.

"Mr President we do not care who is the contractor as long as it is at the best price and the job gets done. It is just the price that matters, Nigeria should not lose money because any one of the pre-qualified bidders has the technical capacity and competence to do the job."

"Fine, then we are decided and the contract awarded."

The meeting closed and we left.

The immediate effect of this was a letter of protest from the American ambassador[34] to President Obasanjo, saying the government of Nigeria was discriminating against American companies: how could a US company, along with European companies, bid competitively, and despite submitting the lowest bid, the contract still went to a European company at the price the American company offered? What has the American company done wrong? If this is not discrimination then what is?

A few days later, a former US ambassador to the UN and an old friend of Obasanjo's, sent a team to Abuja. His firm had been hired by Motorola management out of Chicago, to be their consultant to figure out how and why they lost the bid in which they submitted the lowest price.[35] The leader of the American team came to meet me separately to understand what happened during the bidding stage. I explained that we did what we could as technocrats, but the award of the contract was a decision reserved for our political masters. He informed me that the US government would protest the decision, to which I wished him luck, but as far as BPE was concerned, this was the end of it. A week or so later, the gentleman returned to my office just before he left to report back to Motorola. What he told me about the high-level intrigues was quite revealing.

"We have seen Obasanjo and he said to us that the vice-president had come to him and told him three things," my American friend said. "The first was that you (that is my humble self) had been on Motorola's staff and therefore had rigged this bid so that Motorola would win. Two, Ericsson had offered some financial contribution to Atiku, (it later turned out to be $3 million) for the ruling party's war-chest for the 2003 elections while Motorola had been quiet on this matter. The vice president therefore suspected that Motorola planned to pay you that sum of money instead. Third, the vice-president was convinced that your older brother Bashir owned 10 per cent of the common stock of Motorola in the US, so it is in the best interest of your family for Motorola to win this contract. You were therefore conflicted but failed to excuse yourself from overseeing the bidding process."

I was incensed. Responding to him, I explained that I had worked for Motorola, which was of course true. My last job before I joined the government was as a business development manager for Africa for Motorola, but both the president and vice-president knew that when they appointed me to the position and directed me to oversee the bidding. Secondly, the bid could not have been more open – bids were received and opened with all the mass media represented. How could I have known in advance what price would be low enough for Motorola to win? Finally, Bashir did not own any Motorola stock as far as I knew, and even if he was able to buy a few shares on the New York Stock Exchange, I am certain only major US mutual and pension funds, and the Galvin family that founded the company owned more than 1% of the company – certainly no individual in the whole world owned 10 per cent of Motorola. Regardless, Motorola had annual sales well into the tens of billions of dollars, so I doubted if a measly $38 million contract would be so important to any Motorola shareholder. However, as I would come to learn later, these were the ways in which people like Atiku Abubakar seek to manufacture fiction, manoeuvre and manipulate situations to create false scandals in Nigeria. I was understandably enraged at this high-level accusation by the vice president which benefited them. I was determined not to let this go without a response.

"My short friend, I have a duty to train you"

In short, Atiku was spreading falsehoods about me for reasons I could only surmise, but it made me very angry. I decided not to go to Atiku but to Obasanjo, with my letter of resignation.

"On this Nitel contract, I have heard stories that the vice-president said about me," I said.

"I did not believe him," he replied.

"Oh but you did, Sir. You believed him. If you did not believe him, sir, why did you award the contract to Ericsson instead of Motorola? You believed him, Mr President."

"Yes, but I did that not because I believed him but because he is my vice-president. I cannot fight with him because of you. But I made sure it was at Motorola's price, so whatever financial arrangement he may have had with Ericsson, he will not be able to get it. The country does not lose anything. You said so yourself on that day."

"Well, anyway, the reason why I came here is to tell you that I have my resignation letter here. I can no longer work with Atiku Abubakar. If you want me in the government, get me another job," I said. "Or if you say I should hold the resignation while you redeploy me, I will wait, but I cannot work with this man. Anybody who would do what he did to me for no reason is simply mean-spirited and not someone I want to work with."

I also told him about the vice-president's request to help Ericsson win the bid and sending his aide-de-camp to me. The President then showed me a petition addressed to the Vice President and sent in by Ericsson, signed by one Kenneth Awara, alleging that I rigged the bid against his employer.

What happened next is what I consider the first really personal, candid conversation I had with President Obasanjo. He stood up. I was escorted to see him by my friend Steve Oronsaye, then the principal private secretary to the president. Obasanjo locked his office.

"Well, my short friend, I am not going to discuss any resignation and I am not going to redeploy you," he began. "You know why? Because I am the father of everyone here, and I have a duty to train you. I have a duty to make sure you learn to work with everyone, not just people you like. In public service, you meet people you do not like and you must learn to work with them. This is not your company, this is not your quantity surveying firm where you can choose who you work with, this is the government of Nigeria, and everyone - good, bad and ugly have equal right to be part of it. It is my duty to teach you to learn to work with people like Atiku."

"But Mr President, why learn to work with people I do not like?"

"Because you see, you are a good man, a clever man. One day, if you play your cards right, you will do even greater things in government than where you are today, so I have a duty to develop you, smoothen your rough edges and reduce the obstacles you will face in future public life."

Steve and I listened attentively. He continued,

"Listen, let me tell you – you know, you have three problems. Each one of them is enough of a problem by itself, but you have all three. Your first problem is that you are very clever. People generally do not like clever people. You are clever. That alone will attract you enemies."

"But you have a second problem – your second problem is that you look clever. One look at your face and a person knows that this one is very clever, and that is a bigger problem. Look at me. In my time, I was not as clever as you are. I have gone through your grades in school. You are very bright. You got A's in high school, A's in A levels, first class honours. I did not go to university but I took my high school graduation exams a year in advance and I also got A's so I was also clever in school. But I am lucky – God gave me a not-so-clever face. People think I am stupid. So you can't look at me and know what is going on in my brain. But in your own case, you do not have that luck. You know what I do? I behave like a bushman. See what that has done to me. I am here, far smarter people than me are out there. There is nothing you can do about your face, but you can reduce the enemies you have by avoiding the problem of being too clever."

"Your third problem – you speak clever, you act clever, you are impatient with people who are not as smart as you. You talk down to them. You do those things. So you have these three problems. That is why Atiku won't like you. You are smart; you look smart, talk and act smart. Many people will not like you. You must learn to look simple, to be patient with people who can't think as fast as you. You must learn to talk less and listen more and agree even more with not-so-clever people. Unless you do that, you will continue to have problems and it is my duty to protect you, and to develop you, because you are a good person. If I let you go, you will remain unchanged, learn nothing and suffer more for the rest of your life. So, go back to your job. Go and manage Atiku Abubakar. You do not like him? Learn to work with him, prove that you are learning something, and prove that you are a real man by working with him, in spite of your misgivings and the fact that he had been mean and unfair to you."

I was in absolute shock. I did not know what to say.

Finally, he said, "But have you noticed something? I kept

asking you if you had any objections to awarding the contract to Ericsson. Why did you not object?"

"Because I had no objections, I really did not care who won."

"Do you not see, for me; that showed you had no interest in the matter, that he was being unfair to you? But he is my VP. I will not fall out with him because of you. I will not give him any reason to think I will not do what he wanted. But I know what is going on. I want you to know that by coming here and speaking up about the matter, you have earned my respect and confidence."

In many ways, that conversation was not only the first deeply and candidly personal conversation I had with him, but it also made him begin to trust me just a little more, and appreciate that I was not in cahoots with Atiku to subvert the privatisation outcomes. Up until then, there were all these stories about the vice-president buying up companies and Obasanjo believing that somehow I was a part of it. He was constantly asking questions, checking up on things, and even though I was upfront with him, I could tell he still felt that there was something else going on. This was a ground-breaking moment in my relationship with Obasanjo because he knew from then that I was not Atiku's boy, and that Atiku was mean to me, but that I would henceforth be managing the relationship and be tolerating working with him. As a result, he gave me stronger political support in many other ways.[36]

Now the rest of the Nitel transaction became a much longer story that I must take up in a separate book on my BPE years, and which even as I write is still in process. The point here merely is that the Nitel transaction fundamentally changed my relationship with the president and the vice president. On a personal level, I decided firmly on resigning from service after a three to four month gap, to avoid any connection between this incident and my leaving. I therefore began to devolve more responsibilities to the directors of BPE, particularly Tijjani Abdullahi whom I considered the most capable and honest of my six direct reports. I had meetings with some of the trusted BPE directors, my inner circle of friends, the US Ambassador Howard Jeter, and UK DFID Director William Kingsmill, intimating them of my plans to leave the BPE after a while. All were unanimous that I reconsider and wait until the anger of that period subsided, which I did.

On further reflection, I also decided to defer resigning until I attended the Advanced Management Programme (AMP) at the Harvard Business School (HBS) in the early part of 2002 to prepare me better for a private sector life. One of the considerations that compelled me to defer resignation was the threat by the US Ambassador Jeter that if I resigned, the $10 million grant funding by the USAID to support the privatisation programme 'may be in jeopardy'. I had met with Ambassador Howard Jeter over lunch to review the GSM contract debacle involving Motorola, Ericsson and Atiku Abubakar. I thought it would negatively impact the BPE's operations and training programmes if that funding is lost on my account. Aspects of this conversation appeared in the Wikileaks release of classified US diplomatic cables in 2011! But things turned out quite differently as subsequent events would reveal.

Chapter Six

The Enemy of My Enemy is My Friend – Unless the Friend is El-Rufai

Luck is what happens when preparation meets opportunity.

– Seneca (Roman Philosopher, mid-1st century, AD)

My disagreements with the president did not end, but for the most part they were about process. We still broadly agreed on where we wanted to go, we just disagreed on how to get there and how fast, but I suspect he knew deep down that the way I went about things was without any personal interest, and generally for the better, even when it was inconvenient for him. He discouraged me from resigning in late 2001 after the dust-up over the NITEL GSM contract, and he seemed to have more confidence in me. Even so, I did not expect to be part of a second Obasanjo term. I had started packing my bags to leave the BPE as my tenure was due to end in November of 2003. This was why I went to Harvard Business School in April 2002 to undertake the Advanced Management Programme. I was happy to meet three other Nigerians in the programme – Ado Wanka, a friend and classmate from my 1984 MBA graduating class, Funke Osibodu, a woman banker of repute, and Akin Osuntoki, an executive of Vigeo. I had no intention of staying in BPE for a second term of office, and I was certain that Obasanjo would not re-appoint me even if I wanted.

Then one day, President Obasanjo called me up to see him in the residence.

"You know, you are a useless man, you are a bad man, you insult people, you have no respect for my ministers and I do not like you," he said. "But I am going to nominate you to be a minister."

"What?"

"I want to nominate you to be a minister."

"Why?"

"Well, ask me. I do not like you. You seem to have no respect for elders, you argue too much, you think you know everything, but there is a job I want done in my second term as president and I think you are the only one I know who can do it. I have struggled inside to find someone, but, much as I dislike you, I think you are the only one who can do it."

So I just laughed and said it was ok.

"You won't ask what the job is?"

"No, Mr. President, you will tell me when you are ready."

"Ok. Well, I just wanted you to know, I am nominating you to be a minister."

Of course, I did not believe him, but then things happened in quick succession. We faced an interview panel of Obasanjo, Atiku and party chairman Audu Ogbeh. A few weeks later, the names of his proposed cabinet were read on the floor of the senate, for the screening and the confirmation process to begin. As was the custom, we were invited for finger-printing and documentation and the rest of the standard procedures for engaging ministerial nominees. I went back to the president.

"Is this for real?"

"Yes."

"Ok, I can now ask you, what is the job?"

"I am sending you to FCT."

"Why? Because I am a quantity surveyor and the FCT is a huge construction site?"

"Well, that is part of it, but that is not the reason why. Let me explain. You see, Murtala and I thought of a new capital that became Abuja because we realised that the seat of government had to leave Lagos because Lagos was not working. Lagos would

T: Barewa College Table Tennis Team B: L-R(Standing): Lateef Ajibade, Hambali Faruk, Author, Yomi Awoniyi, Ayo Elelu, Nathan Chukwuocha. (Sitting): Yekini Olatunji, Abdullahi Ajisafe, Mr. Clement Dehinnugbo, Hassan Dikko, Nnamdi Nwuba.

Barewa Graduation Day: Receiving BOBA Academic Achievement trophy from Emir of Kano

Matriculation Day 1977 standing next to future wife Hadiza, with Alwan Hassan, Fatima Hassan and Hafsa Hashim.

With friend, classmate and future business partner Husaini Dikko at School of Basic Studies, Zaria

ABU Graduation Day 1980 with Barewa classmate, Abdulkarim Lawal Kaita

Abuja in the 1980s: Hilton Hotel under construction in the background. With Hadiza and friends

Days of Private Practice (Quantity Surveying Consulting) I

Days of Private Practice (Quantity Surveying Consulting) IIt

Yasmin.... a few hours old with her mum

With Saidu Abdu Jae in the days of when we lived on Rimi Drive, Kaduna

With Yasmin at Adesoye College Offa

T: Harvard OPM graduation. B: L-R: Professor Bruce R. Scott, Author of Capitalism and the Business Government and International Economy professor and his wife

L-R: With Sule Allahbamulafiya, Bashir El-Rufai, and Mallam Ibrahim Aliyu at the Motorola office, US

Receiving the OFR national honour for contributions to construction industry

Receiving honorary D.Sc from the University of Abuja. R: Sultan Maccido, Pro-Chancellor

With Carl Masters and Akin Kekere-Ekun, chairman Technical Committee of NCP

never work unless something miraculous happens. So we decided to build a new city, a new capital in the middle of nowhere that will be planned from day one and will not be disorganised, and will not be chaotic. This new capital is going in the direction of Lagos right now. I have appointed two ministers and instructed them to try to restore order in this city and none of them has done it. I think you can and I think you will. That is what I want you to do. I want you to clean up this city and make it work. Do not let it slide toward the direction of Lagos. Can you do that?"

"Of course I can. I am not sure I will succeed but I will certainly try."

"Good. Now, you know you will have to be cleared by the senate so try to speak to as many senators as possible so that they do not say you are arrogant, aloof and too proud to go and talk to them."

"Of course. Whom should I speak with, should I talk to my senator, Dr. Tafida?"

"No, go and see Senator Mantu."

Senator Ibrahim Mantu was the deputy Senate President and was very close to Obasanjo. I did not realise this suggestion would begin a very interesting relationship with the upper chamber of the National Assembly that remains till today.

Softening the Ground

Everyone knew Senator Mantu. He was a skilled political operator and bridge builder. I knew him from a distance and met him regularly at official events. He was always friendly and full of compliments. After listening to one of my presentations on privatisation, he walked up to me and said something to the effect that he thought I had the wisdom of Solomon without the age of Methuselah. I had his number, so I called him and requested to meet as suggested by Obasanjo. He was effusive in his congratulations and we agreed to meet at his house in Maitama District. When I arrived, Jonathan Zwingina was there. A one-time member of the Senate Committee on Power in my BPE days, Zwingina had by now been promoted to deputy Senate Majority Leader. Both men congratulated me for the nomination and said they heard I was going to head the Federal Capital Territory. I claimed ignorance because I did not want to admit to them just yet that the president already told me. I simply said I did not know where I was headed, only that I had been nominated to be a minister.

They continued by complimenting me on my work at the BPE, and we all went through the standard pleasantries and discussed how much we all were looking forward to working together. We concluded with Mantu saying he and Zwingina would do some 'ground work' and talk to me in a couple of days. Mantu then called me some days later to see him, but on arrival at his office, he kept me waiting for four hours without attending to me. Then he stopped taking my calls. I reported back to Obasanjo who just shrugged and said he had done his bit by nominating me. At this point, someone suggested that I meet Senator Mantu's influential and gentle wife, Zuwairatu, who quietly practises law in Abuja, but I refused. I was prepared to leave things as they were until a mutual friend came to the rescue. Senator Bala Adamu had served as chair of the Senate Services Committee between 1999 and 2003 and therefore knew both Mantu and Zwingina quite well. He called Mantu and arranged to see him with me. Mantu could not refuse his colleague wishing to visit his home. So we got there on a pleasant Abuja afternoon.

"Distinguished Senator, Mallam (referring to me) is my friend and he is a really good man," Bala told Mantu.

"I am sure he will make us proud as a group, community and as a country if he is given the opportunity to serve as minister."

He asked Mantu not only to facilitate my clearance but help guide me through the minefield of legislative intrigues, of which Mantu is known to be a master. Mantu nodded agreement, repeating his Methuselah line.

Zwingina then walked in and after exchanging pleasantries, the duo asked Bala to excuse us so that we could speak alone. Bala left me at the Mantu residence.

> "Well, we promised that we would do a lot of groundwork," Mantu began. "It seems that there is going to be a problem with your confirmation."
>
> "Why is that?" I asked.

"Well, in the BPE, you did not carry people in the Senate and House of Representatives along. You have insulted many legislators and made so many enemies. You were fighting everybody and selling companies in which our people were employed and our people were benefiting, so there will be some resistance from some of the senators," was the response. "We have spoken to many of the senators and they are not going to do this (confirmation) unless they see a change of heart or see you as a potentially changed person."

I thought I knew what was coming, but still asked. "And in what way am I going to be a changed person in their eyes?"

"You know, in your current job at the BPE you have been selfish, you sold all these companies to your friends, you took care of yourself, but you did not spread the goodies around. The feeling is that you made a lot of money as head of BPE but you did not share it. You and Atiku bought everything, cornered all the companies and you did not consider other interests in the legislature."

"Well, I think those who say that are wrong, because I have not made any money in BPE, and as far as I know, Atiku bought nothing from BPE." I said.

"In fact, to tell you the truth, my company (El-Rufai & Partners,) was paying me a regular supplemental to work in BPE. If anybody thinks I have made any money, please explain to them that they are wrong and – well where is the money? I have nothing, and there is nothing in BPE except long working hours and tons of reports."

"Well, even if what you say is the case, none of our colleagues will believe it so you will have to do something," said Zwingina.

> "You will have to raise some money and give it to us so that we can give it to the more recalcitrant senators to soften the ground."

That was the phrase – 'soften the ground.' Mantu was quiet all through, but now more helpful, he jumped in.

> "You know, there are 109 senators. If you give us 54 million naira, we will have 1 million naira for each of 54 senators. On the urging of the president and the vice president, both Zwingina and I will vote for you, so you do not have to give us anything. With 56 senators out of 109, you are through. So we do not need to take care of everybody. There are those who do not like you, but for those that are indifferent or like you a little bit, by the time we give them a million naira each you will be fine, you will be home and dry."

I thought Mantu truly just wanted to help me through an environment he believed I do not understand. Perhaps in his eyes, he was looking out for my best interest and no more, and complying with Obasanjo's request to tutor me through screening.

> "Well, I do not have 54 million naira, I will not find it and even if I had it, I would not give it to anyone to be a cabinet minister," I said. "For me, being minister is a great opportunity but a huge burden. I am the one sacrificing for my country. I did not ask Obasanjo to nominate me as minister; he did it because he said he wanted me to do a particular job."

> "Yes, you are being sent to FCT. You know, FCT is a big job, you can make this money on just (selling) one plot of land." Zwingina chimed in.

> "Well I am not going to FCT to do that kind of stuff. If I get posted to FCT, it will be to get serious work done, not selling land. So thank you very much, I appreciate your efforts, thank you for the feedback and the groundwork, but you know what – I am not doing this. But really, I appreciate your efforts."

And they were visibly shocked, that much I could see. "If there is nothing else, I would like to go." I added.
They resisted.

> "No, sit down, why are you being unreasonable? How can you say you can't find such a small amount, you have friends, you know people, one of your friends can pay this," one of them— I don't now remember who— remarked.

> "I know but do not care; it is not about the amount of money, but about the principle of it." I said. "I can ask a friend to pay, but I will not be able to live with myself. I just won't do it. I cannot do what you want. I am sorry."

Mantu and Zwingina looked at each other, and then asked, "Ok how much can you get?" They thought it was a negotiation! I was livid, but did all I could to remain calm.

> "Nothing! Not a penny. I won't do it."

They looked pensive. These were politicians, and to them everything was negotiable. They eventually relented and we shook hands and I left.

I immediately called President Obasanjo, explained that I had just seen Mantu and Zwingina and there was a problem that I wanted to come talk to him about.

> "No, I am not handling this senators' thing. I have done my part and nominated you. You should go

and tell the vice-president about whatever has transpired. He will handle it."

I had the distinct impression that he suspected what may have happened but did not want to be a part of it.

"I know Mantu, I know Zwingina," he added. "They are funny people, do not let them upset you, just go and tell the vice-president everything."

The next day I met with the vice-president and told him what had happened. "I am grateful to you and the president for considering me worthy of being in the federal cabinet but if this is what it takes to be confirmed, then I am out of this game, I cannot do it," I said.

"Do not worry," Atiku said. "Mantu is so greedy, he loves money so much that if you put 1,000 naira in the mouth of a lion, he will try to take it even though he knows that the lion will probably eat him up in the process. But do not worry, we know how to deal with these people, we will have our way and still not give them a penny."

That was that. I left and went back home. I consulted with Senator Amah Iwuagwu, spoke with a couple of other friends of mine who knew some senators, and they told me to leave it to them and not see anyone else. Not too long after that incident, the vice-president asked me and Senator Zwingina to come by his house. Atiku first went into a closed-door meeting with Zwingina for a few minutes and then emerged to tell me simply that Zwingina and Mantu would henceforth leave me alone. Nobody would ask me for any money, so I should go prepare for the nomination hearing because my name was not going to be withdrawn. That was the last I heard of it. On the 8th of July, 2003, Ngozi Okonjo-Iweala, Nenadi Usman and I went for the confirmation hearing. The senators asked me several questions and my screening process lasted for about 45 minutes. Senator Jibril Aminu asked the most insightful questions and was helpful and supportive in his comments. Most other nominees spent less than 10 minutes. At the end of it, I left the chambers and was confirmed, sworn in on the 16th of July, 2003 and reported for duty at the Ministry of FCT on 17th July 2003. I had handed over BPE's affairs to Tijjani Abdullahi since June 16, 2003 when the cabinet nomination became official.

One day, barely a fortnight after I assumed duty at the FCT, a friend of mine, a senior manager of a leading bank who had served in one of our many privatisation council committees, and was close to Atiku, came to visit and wish me well in my new assignment. In the course of conversation, he dropped a bomb:

"Did Atiku tell you what he did with Mantu and Zwingina?"

"On what account?" I asked.

"In connection with their request for money before you were cleared as minister."

"No, he just told me not to worry about it."

He laughed. "I think he paid them off."

He then went on to explain how Zwingina went to my friend's bank and collected 50 million naira from one of the accounts operated on behalf of the ruling party and controlled by the vice-president.

"Fifty or fifty-four?"

"Fifty."

This absolutely incensed me. They were paid! I thought to myself about what to do and decided I was going to expose it at the time of my choosing. I made up my mind to go public with the request made of me, and that I refused to pay it. Before I did, I ran the idea by Obasanjo.

"Mr. President, I am sorry to raise this again, but do you remember that meeting I had with Zwingina and Mantu and you told me to report it to the VP? I just found that he paid them."

He was surprised and asked how I knew. I related the story to him and he said, "Yes I see. Your source is well-known as a senior manager in Atiku's bank. So what are you going to do now?"

"If you permit, I will expose it. In my next media interview I will mention it and draw all of them out."

He was quiet for a moment and then agreed. I did not know it then, but by that point, Obasanjo and Atiku had had a falling out of sorts, so Obasanjo would encourage anything that would complicate Atiku's political life. As far as I was concerned, I had to make sure nobody thought I was part of the cash exchange. I was very angry because I felt if Atiku was going to do that, he should have told me and given me the choice of withdrawing, because that was what I offered to begin with. Like most practical politicians, Atiku would justify his actions on two grounds - my offer to withdraw is politically naive, and the bribery is just a price to pay to get a 'good man' into public office to do even greater good. Atiku would also calculate that N50 million is worth paying to have one of 'his boys' in the cabinet! Like Mantu and Charles Osuji, these 'practical' people believe they have the best of intentions, but it is this kind of conduct that has under-developed our nation and is now accelerating our descent into ruin.

A couple of weeks later, around the middle of August of 2003, I had been on the job for about a month or so when the Abuja Bureau Chief of *The Guardian* newspaper, Martins Oloja, came to interview me. Martins had shown uncommon commitment to the development of Abuja, first as editor of the defunct *Abuja Newsday*, before joining *The Guardian*, which was among the most credible newspapers in Nigeria at the time. I decided to blow the whistle through the paper. Oloja asked all sorts of questions, including about the unproved allegations that Sadiq Petroleum fronted for the Vice President in acquiring African Petroleum. I gave a lengthy explanation of the process that led to the emergence of Sadiq. I ended with the assertion that ..."We operate in a climate of suspicion; and no matter what you do people will always suspect (you of corruption)."

Now it was my turn to drop the bomb.

> "It was like when I was nominated for ministerial appointment. A couple of Senators called me and said I had made money as D-G of BPE and so to make sure I get cleared, I had to pay them N54 million. I was asked this question because people think if you are in (such) position, you make money.

> But what they do not know is that I actually came out of that job in debt. I still have debts but nobody believes that."[37]

Oloja was shocked. He asked if I really wanted this statement published, because the Senate would surely ask me to prove it.

> "Martins, nobody looks for witnesses when asking for a bribe," I told him. "I can't prove anything directly but I am prepared to do so circumstantially. It happened. I can tell my story, if people believe it, fine, if they do not, that is fine too."

He did not ask for the senators' names. I did not offer their names. I just told him to go ahead and publish it. He came back a week or so later to tell me that that portion of the interview had been removed before sending it to Lagos. I shrugged, knowing that I will have other opportunities to repeat the allegation. But the bribery demand story subsequently appeared in the *Sunday Guardian* a few days later, on August 31, 2003. All hell, needless to say, broke loose.

The senators at first attempted to sow confusion. Two newspapers, the *Punch* and *Guardian*, published stories based on a fictitious official statement purportedly issued by my chief press secretary, Kingsley Agha, denying the substance of the interview.[38] We later learnt that Mantu and Zwingina were behind the stories. So we immediately issued a certified statement of our own explaining that the other statement was false. I confirmed that I did give the interview and I was prepared to appear before the Senate and name names. All through September 2003, nothing captured the imagination of the media more than the "Senate Bribery Scandal." Other newspapers latched onto it. *ThisDay* newspaper published an editorial titled *"El-Rufai and His Bribery Allegation"*, while Eniola Bello, one of the nation's most respected columnists, weighed in, demanding: *"Will the Distinguished Senate Rise?"* It became clear that this matter would not go away as the senate leadership no doubt wished it would.

Of course, I started to receive threats, which I still on occasion do to this day. Obasanjo was enjoying all of this drama thoroughly. It was only then that I began to figure out what was going on between the president and his deputy. Obasanjo had kept a safe distance from it all, quietly and constantly assuring me of his support, which he publicly signalled by accompanying me to flag off the demolition exercise to clear illegal structures within days of the publication.

Soon after I gave the interview to *The Guardian*, I met Atiku and shared what I learnt from my banking sources and asked him why he paid off the two senators.

"I did not pay off any one."

"No, my friends at your bank confirmed that you paid 50 million naira to Zwingina around the time they made the demand of me."

"True, we paid him such an amount, but it was campaign debt," the vice president responded. "It has nothing to do with you or your confirmation. Zwingina was the coordinator of the Obasanjo-Atiku presidential campaign in the North-East zone including my state, Adamawa, and there were debts incurred for which we had not reimbursed him. The debt was 150 million, we still owe him another 100 million, that payment was part of a payment for that debt, go and check."

"And how exactly do I check?"

"Look, Nasir you better believe me, that is all there is to it. How much did they ask you for?"

"Fifty-four million."

"What we paid was 50 million. Why was it not 54?"

"I just figured you had negotiated it down."

"No, I do not even know anything about this; you're the one who told me about the demand made. I called them, met with Zwingina and told both of them off. I did not know the exact amount of money they asked you for."

"Ok, Your Excellency," I said. "But this thing is out in the public space. I will be invited to the senate to testify. I will be under oath, and if they ask me whether I know you have paid, I will say I do not know, but I have heard"

"They will not ask you that."

What happened subsequently is amply documented in newspapers, but it culminated in a Senate committee investigation into the matter. I appeared before the committee, swore on the Qu'ran, and read a prepared speech, in which I recounted what happened and named the senators who asked me for N54 million. I did not go beyond that – without any mention of what I had learned about Atiku paying them off because I had no direct evidence. I just narrated exactly what I witnessed.[40] Seated with me during the testimony were my lawyer and trusted friend, Asue Ighodalo, and colleagues in the economic team, Finance Minister Ngozi Okonjo-Iweala and "Madam Due Process", Mrs. Oby Ezekwesili.

Senators Mantu and Zwingina were then invited by the committee. Mantu is a Muslim as well, but he declined to swear on the Qur'an, which, to every Muslim meant that whatever he said was unlikely to be the truth. Any Muslim who wishes to speak the truth will take the Qur'an in his hands to affirm or swear by it. Zwingina also declined to touch the Bible but simply affirmed his intention to truthfulness. In the end, I learnt from another senator, that the senate went into what is called "executive session," in which the public gallery was cleared so that the senators could have a frank conversation. In that session, both the accused senators admitted to their colleagues that they had indeed demanded payments from me and other nominees, but then asked their colleagues to cover them because the reputation of the entire senate was on the line, and in any case, other senators have been as culpable at other times. The Senate therefore cleared them of the allegations, on the basis that I had no proof other than to say God was my witness.

I was neither surprised nor disappointed by the Senate's decision. For me personally, the most significant support at this time came not only from some of the friends already mentioned, but my immediate family that stood solidly by me throughout. Mallam Yahaya Hamza, the father-figure who brought me up and educated me, granted an interview to the *Punch*[39] after Mantu and Zwingina got their 'not guilty' verdict, stating,"I am ready to swear by the Holy Qu'ran that Nasir, my son, did not lie." He added: "...I can tell you that Nasir does not lie and so he cannot wake up to cook such a lie against the two senators without it being true." Other newspapers similarly ran editorials on the matter.

Such was the inauspicious beginning of my relationship with the Senate, which has remained so to this day. They had clearly felt affronted, but over time I became even more convinced that the behaviour of the legislature of the Fourth Republic is partly driven by some selfish elements united in one vast conspiracy to pillage the country. Many are complicit. The only time they break ranks is if one of them cheats the others, collecting money without spreading it around. That is treasonable felony in our National Assembly. Otherwise the mafia code of silence, *omerta*, is scrupulously observed.

Obasanjo won't complete his term; the Marabout said so

Why was Obasanjo indifferent to my leaking this senate bribery story to the press? Let's start at the beginning.

When Obasanjo began his first term, the unwritten compact he had with Vice-President Atiku Abubakar was that Obasanjo would be Nigeria's face to the outside world and spend most of his time repairing Nigeria's badly disfigured image, courting investors and getting us external debt relief. Atiku was essentially to run domestic policy. This meant tactically that Atiku would be the politician, the domestic policy guru, and dealmaker, and would take charge of building the network and accumulating the war chest both Obasanjo and Atiku would need for re-election in 2003. Obasanjo, international statesman, would go hang out with the likes of Tony Blair and Bill Clinton, focus on regional stability, national defence, foreign policy, the UN, fighting malaria, wrestling with the AIDS pandemic — that sort of thing. Obasanjo, a co-founder of Transparency International, would remain clean and above board, while Atiku, the former customs officer, would do the deals needed with the politicians, the legislature, and the contractors, oiling the political machine and preparing the ground necessary for re-election.

For a while, it worked. Atiku was very influential in the first Obasanjo term. Anyone who wanted any sort of contract with the federal government or some important board appointment had to go to Atiku. If Nigeria were France, Atiku would have essentially been the prime minister rather than a VP. Eventually, I think Atiku's circle got a bit carried away because they had all this influence, power and money at their disposal and they thought these were natural, and normal entitlements of the VP's office, and the financial, physical and political perks that came with it.

I recall that one day, after an especially vile quarrel I had with Obasanjo over the frustration of the privatisation of Nigeria Airways, I came to the point at which I had seriously considered resigning from the BPE. When I walked into Atiku's office, and while still standing up expressed my frustration and intentions, he motioned for me to sit down.

"Where are you going? You can't leave," he said. "We are about to have the whole thing."

I was taken aback as I was not sure what he meant.

"What do you mean, Sir?"

He then told me about a marabout in Cameroon who had been in touch with him since the very first time he contested for state governor in his home state of Gongola, now Adamawa and Taraba States. At the time, the marabout had told him not to waste his time because he was not going to win, and he lost. The second time he tried, the soothsayer supposedly told him he was going to lose, and lo and behold, he lost again. The third time he attempted to be governor, so the story goes, the marabout told him he was going to win the election, but he was not going to actually become the governor. And so it came to pass. Atiku won the election, but before he could take office, Obasanjo chose him to be his running mate. On the strength of this fable, Atiku appeared to have placed his faith in the predictions of this marabout.

"Nasir, this 'mallam' has been consistently right in his predictions."

"Wow, that is very interesting sir, but what does this have to do with my resignation?"

"Because the same mallam said that Obasanjo will not complete his first term."

"Really?"

"Yes. So why do you want to go? When I am president, we are going to take charge of this place and fix it and I will need you. You are one of my best people."

Personally, I do not believe in all this marabout stuff, though many people I know do. After Atiku shared this momentous prediction with me, what could I do? My hands were effectively tied from taking any immediate action. So I said, "Fine, Mr. Vice-President, I will hang in there." One must never under-estimate the influence of both Islamic and Christian spiritualists on African politicians. For instance at the height of the Obasanjo-Atiku feud between 2005 and 2006, Uba Sani, my friend and Special Assistant to Obasanjo on Public Communications, shared a one-page list of predictions by a mallam purportedly obtained from Atiku's camp, predicting that Obasanjo would die in March 2007, with Atiku being sworn in as president. With all this floating around, it was easy for the unwary to become intoxicated, and for vaulting ambition to prevail over common sense.

In August of 2002, Atiku called a meeting of what he called his three closest advisers: Dr. Usman Bugaje, who was his political adviser and a close friend, Nduka Obaigbena, the publisher of *ThisDay*, and I. We met in a guest house off Aso Drive, which some years later I would purchase as part of the federal government sale of houses programme. Atiku thought his residence may not be secure enough so he asked us to meet him at the guest house because he wanted to speak freely and very confidentially.

At the meeting he told us that he had been having meetings for the past several months with two groups of politicians. One group (called G4) consisted of President Ibrahim Babangida, and General Abdulsalami Abubakar, both of whom were former military heads of state, as well as General Aliyu Gusau, who has been National Security Adviser almost forever. The four of them had been meeting to review Obasanjo's performance and they had concluded that Obasanjo's first term up to that point had been a disaster, the National Assembly had twice tried to impeach him, and the four of them had just thought that Obasanjo should not have a second term. In their meetings, according to Atiku, they decided that since Atiku was the incumbent vice-president, he should have the first shot at the presidency.

Now, it was a well-known fact then that President Babangida harboured a similar ambition. Yet, Atiku believed that Babangida, who is also older, would step back for him to have the first shot. He did not see it as a trap. The moment he told us, it did not sound right. As I learned much later, this was Babangida's ploy to prove to Obasanjo that Atiku, given the slightest opportunity, would stab him in the back. When the four of them began meeting and discussing Nigeria's problems, Babangida allegedly called Obasanjo and informed him. Obasanjo had repeatedly told anyone who tried to question Atiku's fidelity to him that their partnership was a Catholic marriage, indissoluble, till death do them part. Babangida is reported to have said, "You see, we have started something. I will keep you briefed, but at the end of it, your VP will betray you."

Some years later, Obasanjo confirmed to me that Atiku had come when the meetings began and recommended that Obasanjo should reach out to the other three, because they did not seem pleased with him. Up to that point, either Atiku was faithful to his boss, or was simply taking out insurance by providing partial information. When they had the second meeting, he reportedly went back to Obasanjo and said, "I think this meeting is becoming regular and they have named the group G4. I do not know what the objectives are but I will keep you briefed." So up to that point, Obasanjo had full confidence in Atiku. But IBB allegedly kept calling Obasanjo, telling him that they would get to a point whereby Atiku would abandon him. This implied that G4 was nothing more than a manufactured illusion that the three others would support an Atiku take-over so that Babangida could get Atiku to bury himself without having to make any effort at it.

Meanwhile, Atiku had been meeting with a second group of politicians, 17 governors from the ruling People's Democratic Party, who all wanted him to be the next president, in return for assurances of a second term for themselves. These governors were very powerful because they controlled the selection of voting delegates to the party's national convention, which then determines the presidential nomination. So when he called Nduka, Usman and I together, he wanted our opinion on this because he knew that three of us were not only well informed but were likely to give frank advice. Usman Bugaje said, "Sir, I think you should go for it. I think Obasanjo is a disaster and you should just go for it, and with 17 governors on your side we would have a fighting chance."

Nduka Obaigbena was more careful. He felt that the support of the governors was vital but asked,

"Excellency, do you believe Babangida would not want to run for president and let you run first?"

"Well Babangida said he would not want to run against his boss and in any case since I am a sitting vice-president, they think it is only fair that I go for it now," replied Atiku.

Atiku asked me what I thought and I said,

"Quite honestly, this is not an area that I have a lot of competence in, but it does not sound right to me, just gut instinct."

We debated it at length and at the end, Nduka made a very brilliant suggestion.

"Look, we need to know if this is all for real," Nduka said. "So we should assume governors are on board. However, we should not listen to what Babangida says, but make him walk the talk."

'Walking the talk' meant the following: Nduka suggested that Atiku go back to the G4 and tell them that he had done some consultations within Nigeria and it was positive so far, but that he needed to now undertake international consultations. So Atiku should tell them that he was sending Nasir to the US, because of my contacts within the US government and in Washington – friends in the US Congress and the Clinton Administration, the World Bank and the IMF – and that Usman was being sent to the UK because Usman did part of his Ph.D research at the School of African and Oriental Studies and had some good contacts in the UK parliament, and a few people in the British media as well. Atiku should say that he did not have good contacts in Germany and France. Babangida had very good friends in Germany and France – he knew Presidents Mitterrand and Chirac, and former German Chancellor Helmut Kohl, as well as senior management from some of the major construction companies in those countries - Bilfinger & Berger (Julius Berger in Nigeria), Fougerolle and

Bouygues, in addition to rumoured connections with major financial institutions like BNP in France.

So Nduka essentially suggested that Atiku should pass the buck back to G4 and IBB. He should ask IBB to arrange for Atiku to visit President Chirac, former Chancellor Kohl and incumbent Gerhard Schroeder to discuss this planned challenge, to get their take on whether it made sense for Atiku to contest the presidency against Obasanjo while Nasir and Usman took care of the same issues at lower levels in the US and the UK respectively.

"If Babangida arranges the appointments for you, then you know it is serious, and he is not leading you on." said Nduka. "If he refuses to take your calls from that day on, then you know it was a set-up all along and you better just go to Obasanjo and explain everything."

It was very sound advice. We all agreed to move forward on this front. I was immediately instructed to purchase a ticket to go to Washington to start this consultative process and Usman was to go to London. We never got to the point of having those consultative meetings abroad because before they even took place, Babangida had already failed the Nduka test.

"What are you going to do now?" I asked Atiku.

"Well, from the very first time they invited me to these meetings, I told Obasanjo about it and asked him what he thought they wanted to discuss. Obasanjo had no idea but said, 'go and discuss with them and brief me after the meeting.'"

"And have you been briefing him fully?"

"Yes, but not including every little detail."

"I think you better go and come clean."

"No, I still think that he should go for it," interjected Usman Bugaje.

Dr. Usman Bugaje, Atiku's political adviser, was pushing for it because he truly believed that Nigerians at the time were fed up with Obasanjo. He worked with Atiku day to day, while Nduka and I only saw Atiku once in a while, so he had greater capacity to influence him. I think that Usman was probably right in the sense that Atiku could have pulled it off, as he had the bulk of the PDP governors. In the end, I learnt that Atiku had to reconsider because he could not get the broad support of the northern political elite. I was made to understand that Adamu Ciroma, Mallam Liman

Ciroma, Chief Sunday Awoniyi, Alhaji Isyaku Ibrahim and Etsu Nupe, Umaru Sanda Ndayako, on behalf of the various political tendencies in the North, signaled to Atiku that the North had largely agreed to support a southern president in 1998. Since he was not constitutionally barred from running again, unless Obasanjo decided not to run, they would not go back on their word and support any northerner. The reference to Obasanjo's position in 1999 that he would run for only one term 'to stabilise the country' was not helpful in convincing the northern political leaders.

The Only Currency in Politics

This essential argument was that a deal was made to zone the presidency to the South. In our country, geography is destiny. Zoning is a political philosophy that has saturated every sphere of our national life, and has become insidious and destructive. I personally think zoning as the overriding consideration in identifying leaders is nonsense, for reasons that I have stated publicly several times. While accepting that zoning as a policy of inclusion has contributed to stabilising our fragile nation, giving everyone a sense of belonging, it has on balance not served the nation well. It has been stretched to such unreasonable extents that qualifications, experience and merit have taken back seats. The perverse application of zoning and federal character principles has unleashed the exact opposite of the competitive forces that would throw up the best people to lead our nation. It has led to compromises that ensured the primacy of mediocrity, rewarding the worst prepared or the least threatening, and not the most competent, for leadership at all levels.

Despite my misgivings, however, an agreement is an agreement in politics and in life, and one should not be capricious about breaking it. If necessary, one should negotiate one's way out of it – but until then, a bargain is a bargain, to paraphrase the old TV drama, *Village Headmaster*. Many northern politicians understand that the currency of politics is keeping to verbal, even if legally unenforceable agreements, because politicians always sit and agree all kinds of deals and arrangements. A successful politician keeps his word, no matter how inconvenient. That is the only currency in politics – keeping one's word.

Though Atiku was a northerner and, at that point in 2002 could possibly have taken the nomination of the PDP, many of the political leaders in the north, the religious leaders, and traditional rulers, essentially said to him, "You can't do this." The message was, "We agreed in 1998 to cede power to the south. The constitution says Obasanjo can do two terms. Unless Obasanjo says he does not want a second term, you cannot challenge him. That would be dishonourable."

In any event, we told Atiku that it was best if he dropped the whole thing, go to Obasanjo, come clean about what had transpired and declare that everything was now back on track. He nodded, but subsequent steps he took indicated that he did not agree with that position. From that point on, we never talked about the issue, but relations with Obasanjo got worse when Atiku got several governors, led by Orji Uzor Kalu, Boni Haruna, Lucky Igbinedion, Joshua Dariye and James Ibori, to suggest to Obasanjo that he should not run for a second term, mere weeks to the PDP national convention. The political brinkmanship got so bad that Obasanjo had to visit Atiku's residence unannounced to plead for Atiku's support. Upon arriving at his deputy's residence, he reportedly knelt before Atiku and begged the vice president to remain onside, thus guaranteeing the support of the 17 PDP governors. In return, Obasanjo had to agree to retain Atiku as his running mate (he was rumoured at the time to be considering an alternative.) The stakes were high enough for Obasanjo to swallow his considerable pride and go to Atiku on bended knee..

Obasanjo had no problem going down on his knees to beg for what he thought was impossible to obtain any other way. As president, he would threaten to kneel before his subordinates if that was what it took to get them to do something they would otherwise be reluctant to do. At the back of his mind, Obasanjo was no doubt saying, thinking of Atiku, 'Okay, enjoy your temporary power. I am going to be president again in a few months and I am going to get you.' There is a Hausa saying "Durkusa ma wada ba gajiya wa ba ne" and a corresponding Yoruba maxim to this effect which says: k'á dòbálè fún arárá, kò'pé ká dìde k'amá tun ga ju lo. (Prostrating before a midget does not make us shorter than him when we rise up.)

And that was what happened. Obasanjo did whatever it took to get Atiku's support, until he secured the nomination, was declared winner of the 2003 presidential election, and set about politically decapitating Atiku day by day, shortly after their second term started. Compounding this tension was the fact that once their catholic marital vows were renewed, Obasanjo expected that the bulk of the money for the re-election campaign would come from Atiku and friends. Atiku basically gave him open palms and said, 'What money?' The money was gone – spent, according to Atiku, on oiling the political machine, keeping the party activities going, stopping the National Assembly from impeaching Obasanjo not once, but twice, and - this was not stated but alleged by the EFCC in 2006 - acquiring material assets to enhance Atiku's personal and political status. So when I, all of a sudden, and unknowingly had a way of making Atiku's life a bit more complicated by going public with the Senate bribery scandal, Obasanjo was more than happy to be more than a reluctant bystander. He relished every second of the embarrassing drama.

I think the missing money may have been the real tipping point. Even with Atiku's treachery, if he had provided the money supposedly raised for the elections, maybe they would have co-existed in relative peace from 2003 to 2007. But when Obasanjo concludes that you have cheated him out of even a penny, he never forgets, and tries to extract his pound of flesh. Unknown to us at the time, the stage was set for a divided presidency in the second term. With General T Y Danjuma unwilling to be the financial benefactor for the 2003 elections, Obasanjo had to resort to raising money from other sources and that was how Aliko Dangote came into prominence in the government. From 1999 to 2003, nobody had heard of Dangote having anything to do with the federal government in any significant way.

Indeed, when the BPE sold the federal government's equity stake in Benue Cement Company in 2000 and the transaction became mired in needless controversy, Obasanjo wanted it reversed, because at that point, Aliko was closer to Atiku Abubakar than to him. In the BPE, we refused to cancel the transaction because we were convinced that the objections raised by the Benue State government were political and driven by blatant ethnic bigotry. The Benue State government preferred a foreigner to a

Nigerian citizen because of his birthplace or religion. We therefore quietly paid the proceeds of sale to the treasury to make the sale reversal more difficult. About a year later, we sold Savannah Sugar to Aliko as well, much to Obasanjo's discomfort at the time.

In 2003 and thereafter, Aliko Dangote became increasingly prominent in governmental circles because, on the suggestion of the late Waziri Mohammed, Aliko allegedly financed Obasanjo's 2003 re-election, nearly single-handedly and without any strings attached. He did it because his friend Waziri said Obasanjo needed help and that was all it took.

So by the time we took office in July 2003 for the second term, Obasanjo took very clear, systematic steps to demystify Atiku and make him a totally irrelevant and disempowered vice-president. My encounter with the Senate over the bribery demand ahead of ministerial confirmation, amazingly and inadvertently, wound up playing a small part in this effort.

Chapter Seven

The Economic Team – Key Players

Here is to the crazy ones. The misfits. The rebels. The trouble-makers. The round pegs in the square holes. The ones who see things differently.

They're not fond of rules, and they have no respect for the status-quo. You can quote them, disagree with them, glorify, or vilify them. But the only thing you can't do is ignore them.

Because they change things. They push the human race forward. While some may see them as the crazy ones, we see genius.

Because the people who are crazy enough to think they can change the world, are the ones who do.

– Steve Jobs, Co-Founder of Apple Computer

A cornerstone of President Obasanjo's second term was creating an economic reform team that brought together a number of cabinet and sub-cabinet staff to debate and coordinate economic policy formulation and implementation. There were 12 economic team members but five stood out initially as the prominent figures: Ngozi Okonjo-Iweala, who was appointed finance minister and, later, foreign minister, following a stint as a vice-president and corporate secretary at the World Bank; Nuhu Ribadu, the executive chairman of the Economic and Financial Crimes Commission; Oby Ezekwesili, who worked with the economist Jeff Sachs at Harvard University before taking charge as presidential assistant on procurement reforms and later as minister of solid minerals and then minister of education; Charles Chukwuma Soludo, an economist who started out as a member of several privatisation council committees, then chief economic adviser to the president and, finally, Central Bank governor. As minister of the Federal Capital Territory, I also was part of this team; the government intended to use Abuja as the laboratory for testing and adjusting the nationwide economic reforms being proposed. Other key but lesser known members were Steve Oronsaye (then principal secretary to the President), Funsho Kupolokun, who ran the state energy company, the NNPC, Dr. Joe Nnanna of the Central Bank, as well as the heads of the Debt Management Office, my former agency, the BPE, the tax authority, and the budget office, led at the time by the accounting genius, Bode Agusto.

The questions we asked at the outset of economic reform design were essentially: "What is wrong with us as a country? Why do some countries do well, and others poorly? What 'good' policies, programmes and attitudes differentiate the performing countries from the non-performers? What bad policies, programmes and habits are prevalent in the poorly-performing economies? What can we do as a country to leapfrog to the ranks of middle-income nations within the shortest possible time?"

After a lot of research, debates and reflection, we came up with what we identified as six country conditions that successful developing nations had in common:

- Basic levels of political stability – a stable and legitimate government. This stability and legitimacy need not necessarily be achieved through democratic means.

- Very strong protection of rights across the board; whether they are property rights, human rights, contracts or any other.

- Consequences were predictable - there is 'rule of law' and a fair, affordable and predictable legal system.

- Investment in human infrastructure - in education, healthcare and near equal opportunities available to all citizens, including social safety nets.

- Investment in physical infrastructure - particularly electric power, communications and transport infrastructure like railways, roads, sea and airports and the like.

- Pragmatic reliance on markets allocating resources and pricing of goods and services in competitive sectors, as no sustainable development was found to exist under any conditions without economic freedom and political inclusion.

These six findings informed the design of our economic reform programme throughout Obasanjo's second term, which came to be known as the National Economic Empowerment and Development Strategy, or NEEDS. This period, 2003-2007, recorded the fastest rates of economic growth in Nigeria's history. And while we like to say that was the evidence of our hard work— which was no doubt the key factor— we also got very lucky that our hard work coincided with a period of galloping oil prices, which reached historical highs.[40]

The implementation of NEEDS further split out into the categories of economic stabilisation, public sector reform, governance/anti-corruption reform measures and then finally investments in physical and human infrastructure. As we attempted this, we were also trying to change the incentive structure of a society in which a privileged few sit around extracting rents by doing nothing, to a society where hard work, innovation and an orientation toward results become the norm. We knew that important people, particularly our parasitic political elites, would fight us, but we made the choice to engage the fight. Little did any of us know the lengths to which this fight would continue, but we were nevertheless determined to improve the state of Nigeria through sound reform policies.

During this period, Abuja could not have worked as decently as it is said to have without the critical support of the other economic reform team members. Each one contributed in his or her own way, and whether they realise it or not, it has occurred to me several times over the years that many people really do not know the full stories behind each of the team members, nor how they helped run key government departments and to a large extent, helped Obasanjo run the country.

Nuhu Ribadu, Chairman of the Economic and Financial Crimes Commission (EFCC)

Most people think that Nuhu and I have been friends from childhood, but as a matter of fact, I only met him in late 2002 or early 2003, years after I had started running the BPE. I had, however, heard of him in my university days. When I was pursuing my master's degree at Ahmadu Bello University, a story went around Kongo campus about an undergraduate law student having an encounter with armed robbers attempting to hijack his friend's car. The story was that Nuhu and his friend went out for a drive – Nuhu was driving, while his friend sat in the passenger seat – and soon enough found themselves held up by armed men who wanted to take the friend's car. The men made Nuhu stop the car pointed their guns at Nuhu and his friend and demanded they get out and hand over the keys. Nuhu and his friend dutifully did as told, but then one of the bandits slapped Nuhu in the face, just for added measure. So Nuhu slapped him right back. It seemed to be instinctive, but it was also perceived as courageous because someone holding you at gunpoint ought to be in the position of slapping you without expecting to be slapped in return.

The stunned gunman threatened to shoot Nuhu, whose response, according to this version of events, was not unreasonable, though perhaps foolhardy, in the circumstance:

"You are stupid. You wanted the keys, I gave you the keys. Why did you slap me?"

"I have a gun, I could kill you," replied the gunman.

"Go ahead and kill me then."

The leader of the gang then stepped in and told the gunman to back off.

Nuhu could have been shot dead that day and the world would never have known he ever existed. But he lived, and the rest is a pivotal part of our recent history.

This story of the confrontation spread rapidly around Kongo campus. Even though Nuhu and I are about the same age, we did not move in the same circles since he was an undergraduate when I was a graduate student, and so we never met. And now years later, when BPE director Ibrahim Shehu Njiddah asked me to meet his friend Nuhu Ribadu, I thought the name sounded vaguely familiar. Nuhu had just been appointed chairman of the Economic and Financial Crimes Commission, a brand new law enforcement agency that would lead a sustained and consequential war against money laundering and advanced fee fraud (419) scams.

On meeting Nuhu, he confirmed that he was the same Nuhu Ribadu who was an undergraduate student at Kongo Campus of ABU about 20 years earlier. After introductions and exchange of pleasantries, Nuhu went straight to the point.

> "I am a police officer and just been appointed to this position, but all I got is this letter," he said, showing me a basic form letter from the Secretary to the Government appointing him chairman of the EFCC, congratulating him and wishing him success.
>
> "I have no budget, I have no office, I have no personnel, nothing. But I have this important job to do," he said.
>
> "What is this job about anyway?" I asked.

Nuhu took little time to explain. "Well, Nigeria has been on the list of non-cooperating countries of the Financial Action Task Force (FATF), and for this reason, there are some international financial transactions that Nigerian banks cannot conclude and we have to get ourselves off that list," he explained. "One of the conditions is the enactment of the Money Laundering Act and the Economic and Financial Crimes Commission Act. The EFCC is supposed to be the law enforcement agency for the money laundering legislation. So I am supposed to fight the 419 scam letters, the resultant money laundering and all that. But I have nothing, I have been running up and down, I have met the secretary to the government, I have met the finance minister and they both say they can't help me, I am not in the budget for this fiscal year, 2003."

"But certainly there are contingency provisions or service-wide votes from which the authorities can get you some money?" I asked.

"Well they have not been able to. I do not have anything. I think that if I am able to do something that can show results, maybe I will have support, but as of right now, I have a commission on paper and nothing else. I have not even been able to see the president."

Nuhu was appointed to chair the EFCC without ever meeting Obasanjo, so he actually did not know the president at all at the time. Obasanjo made a lot of such key and high level appointments based on recommendations of others he trusted. In the case of Nuhu, the Attorney General, Kanu Agabi, was the chief advocate for his appointment, and Obasanjo nominated Nuhu for confirmation by the Senate based solely on trust in Kanu Agabi's judgment. Obasanjo was like that – if he trusted your judgment, he took major decisions and made appointments based on your recommendations without asking many questions. I got many people into government in that manner once he began trusting my judgment as well. Before the EFCC appointment, Nuhu was just a regular cop – an assistant commissioner, which is basically a middle management position in the Nigerian police.

Nuhu Ribadu was Kanu Agabi's gift to Nigeria. Agabi remains one of our country's leading lawyers and a man of principles, courage and unimpeachable integrity. He wrote the foreword to the White Paper published in 2009 by Robert Amsterdam[41] on my persecution by the Nigerian government. I am therefore always amused when Atiku Abubakar's supporters claimed he 'got Nuhu his job' and then 'Nuhu betrayed Atiku.' Both assertions are false. In the first place, Atiku did not even know when Nuhu got nominated and was cleared by the Senate. He admitted as much to me when I went to persuade him to approve for some BPE funds to be lent to EFCC for it's start-up. Furthermore, even if he got Nuhu this job, should Nuhu not investigate him if he gets involved in money laundering and other activities under the purview of the EFCC? The assumption that getting a person appointed to a government job means perpetual slavery to that person's interests and preferences is simply absurd!

After hearing all this briefing from Nuhu, I asked, "What do you want me to do?"

> "Well I need help in institutional design. I am convinced that you are running the best public service institution in Nigeria. Everyone talks about BPE, everyone knows about how it is transparent, and has efficient and highly motivated staff. I want to learn that from BPE and you. So I need you to help me design an appropriate structure for the EFCC, so that it can work like the BPE. That is one."

I liked what I was hearing from this man.

> "Secondly, I need an office. I do not know if you have any space here or in one of your satellite offices."

This was a reference to BPE's other office building that was purchased in 1995 or thereabouts, and which we were not using, a four bedroom house in Imani Estate, which we were in the process of converting to house one of our departments because we had grown too large for our premises on Osun Crescent in Maitama District.

> "I also need money. But I do not know what you can do to get me money because I do not have staff, I..." he went on cataloguing what assistance he would need from BPE.

Something about the way he spoke really hit me – there was a real passion, anger even, for wanting to do something, to prove that something could be done in our country's political space. For me, visible anger about our nation's state of affairs and the desire to change it are the most important qualities in a public servant. Nuhu captured my attention right away.

> "Yallabai," he said to me, using an honorific in his native Fulfulde, "look, if I just get a minimum level of support, in three weeks, I will shut down and arrest all the leaders of these scam letter operations, because I know them," he said. "The senior officers of the police force know who and where they are but they pay our bosses and have become untouchable but I know them, I know where they are, I will get them. I will shut them all down. These letters are giving the country a bad name. We have to do something, right away."

This was all it took – this one meeting to persuade me.

> "Nuhu, I am convinced. I believe that you will do what you said. We must support your new commission. I will give you two of my assistants to work with you to design an organisational structure. We will give you two rooms downstairs to use as your temporary office and our staff will work with you until you are fully set up. Let me think about how we can get you some money."

Nuhu was very grateful. I went to see the finance minister, who said the new budget had just been passed and it did not include the EFCC because the budgeting cycle is January to December and the budget is usually submitted in August or September the previous year. By that point, the EFCC Act had not been passed yet. Nobody even gave the EFCC a second thought. I met with the secretary to the government and suggested a search for funding under the contingency or service-wide votes or something, but the then minister of finance did not give us much room to pursue that further.

I then remembered a little-known clause in section nine of the Privatisation and Commercialisation Act that empowers the BPE and the National Council of Privatisation to do whatever was necessary to further the interests of privatisation. It is an omnibus clause in the legislation, which gives some flexibility. After clearing it with the BPE attorneys and obtaining an *en principe* consent of the vice president, I went back to Nuhu to find out how much he needed to take off.

"We have good news. I think we can get you some money, how much do you need?"

"Twenty million naira."

"Twenty million?"

"Yes."

"Are you sure?"

"Yeah, that is all I need."

"Ok, I think you are new in this business. Let us get you 100 million. If you do not need it, keep it in the bank and return it at the end of the fiscal year. But I do not think we can ask for this kind of money twice. I have asked, I have tested the waters, we are going to get it, let's ask for a lot. We will get you 100 million."

"No, it is too much, what am I going to do with that kind of money?"

"It is better to have money and not to need it than to need it and not have it. So let's get you 100 million." I smiled, surprised at Nuhu's modesty, and financial naivety.

We knew Atiku would not approve whatever amount we asked, but would cut it down to feel like the decision maker. So we sent a memo requesting 200 million and sure enough, 100 million was approved. We then issued a cheque to Nuhu and, in addition to the two office suites, assigned him a couple of BPE staff to assist him to get up and running. Nuhu's very first employee was Dr. Abdu Mukhtar, my special assistant, who continued to work for the FCT after I left office in 2007. The BPE staff (Mukhtar, a medical doctor and Harvard MBA, and Toyin Ibrahim, a youth corps member) worked with him to design EFCC's organisational structure, programmes and plans, salary, remuneration levels and the rest of the details that we had spent the past couple of years fine-tuning at the BPE. Two staff became three with the addition of Hadiza Dagabana Sani, a senior BPE lawyer, who I have come to value for her intelligence, dependability and work ethic. This started a tradition which yet survives, because many ex-BPE staff have remained in the employ of the EFCC, and other federal government institutions. Nuhu's first secretary, and Staff Number 4, was Rakiya, another BPE staff. These four were EFCC's pioneer staff, and helped lay the foundations for its future success.

Typically, in the Nigerian government, any new agency, on receiving its first budget allocation, is then faced with the challenge of showing the ministry of finance at year's end that all of the money was, in fact, necessary. If the agency cannot show that it needed that entire amount of money, it stands the risk of having its budget allocation cut in succeeding years. In the case of Nuhu, even the 100 million naira was too little for him. He needed more money before the year ran out. The miscalculation was nothing more than inexperience – he had not ever done anything like that before. When he worked in the police force, his salary came in, and I do not think he had an idea of the concept of running such an operation with budgets and stuff. This was the first time he was running such a potentially large organisation, but he learnt quickly.

Now, technically speaking, what we did – lending EFCC some money, was barely legal. We found a loophole and the doctrine of necessity to justify it, but our constitution makes it very clear that public funds could not be spent without appropriation by the legislature. What the BPE did, for which the Vice President is accountable as the approving authority, was to in effect take public funds (without appropriation), hand it to another agency (without virement), which then spent them without appropriation either. Legislation is normally required to approve these sorts of actions, but this provision in the Privatisation Act enabled us to collect monies and remit them only at the end of a transaction-closure period. Sometimes we would sit on these huge amounts of cash that had to be placed in banks to earn interest.

For instance, we would receive a down payment from a core investor, while the final payment would be due the following year. This meant we had to wait until the whole transaction sum was collected because the transaction could fail and we might have to make full or partial refund of the deposit. For these reasons, we often had huge amounts of money in partially remissible funds at the BPE, (which, according to our lawyers had not become "public funds" yet) and this was part of what we used to support EFCC and Nuhu. It was basically a short-term loan to the EFCC to reimburse the BPE in future, because we could not give them money outright, and I do not think the money ended up being paid back until 2006 or thereabouts.

The irony of the pre-eminent anti-corruption unit on the African continent receiving its take-off funding in this manner is not lost on me, but frankly, it was the only way I could think of to help it get going. If we had not supported Nuhu the way we did, the entire commission might have died before it even got started. When the FATF finally removed Nigeria from its blacklist, it was almost entirely due to the EFCC's efforts. The BPE gave him his first push, and three weeks later Nuhu had shut down all the leading foreign letter scam (419) operations in Nigeria. He conducted a coordinated arrest of about a dozen well-known leaders of these groups that basically had factories and home-offices churning out scam letters. All of a sudden, everybody knew the name Nuhu Ribadu. The EFCC was born.

Money was not the only obstacle Nuhu faced in getting started. Shortly after his appointment, the Inspector General of Police, Tafa Balogun, who was Nuhu's boss, complained to Obasanjo that Nuhu's appointment and rank were inappropriately matched because the EFCC Act made the Inspector General of Police (IGP) a member of the board of the EFCC, while Nuhu an officer junior to the IGP sat as chair. For the inspector general, that was a problem. His subordinate would sit in a Commission board meeting as chairman and, he, the inspector general, would have to seek Nuhu's permission before he could speak. Because of that complaint, the commission's inauguration by the president was postponed and the Inspector General began pushing for Nuhu's appointment to be reversed so that a more senior police officer, a former inspector general of police or someone who was retired from the police could be appointed the chairman.

Nuhu still did not know Obasanjo, but had enough appreciation of power to know that to do his job, he needed access to and the confidence of the president. He really needed to get close to Obasanjo. He came to me one day early on and told me his new job was already being threatened and he had nowhere to go.

At that point, the president and I were in the middle of some quarrel, so I could not help him out, but did the next best thing. I went to the chief of staff to find out what real threats Nuhu's appointment faced and explored what could be done.

"Well you know, we in the military and the police, we are very hierarchical," the chief of staff said. "We respect hierarchies and it is just not right for an assistant commissioner of police to sit as chair of a meeting while the IGP sits as a member."

"But that is nonsense," I said. "What if I or a classmate of Nuhu's from the military or the SSS was appointed the chairman of the EFCC. Would Tafa Balogun say he would not sit at the meeting?"

"No."

"So it is just in his imagination. Nuhu is not there as a policeman."

"What you are saying makes sense but you know what? No one has put it quite in this manner. I suggest that you write to the president on this subject. He respects your opinion."

The fact was the hierarchy issue was deeper – it was not just the inspector general, but also the Director General of the SSS and the heads of virtually all law enforcement agencies that would sit as members of the EFCC board with a person they see as junior as chair, which made it a major structural problem. Tafa Balogun was the first to make the pitch, but all the other members had the same concerns. The BPE then wrote an appeal to Obasanjo making the case for the EFCC board to be inaugurated forthwith as its activities would ease the attraction of investors for our privatisation programme. The letter also addressed the structural issues and made suggestions. The president got the Attorney-General to inaugurate the board right away, while addressing the structural issues by legislative amendments. We had surmounted the hurdle and Nuhu was grateful he could take off.

Ultimately the original EFCC Act 2002 was amended in 2004 to provide that 'a representative of' the inspector general of police and 'a representative of' the DG, SSS were to represent the agencies rather than the agency heads themselves. The opportunity of the amendment also enabled Nuhu to work quietly with Senator Lawal Shuaibu to substantially increase the breadth and scope of EFCC's powers to include anti-corruption and miscellaneous offences mandates, and confer the arrest powers contained in the Police Act on the EFCC, in addition to its original but narrow money laundering mandate.

> "Yallabai, thank you for all these efforts," he said to me when all the issues had been sorted out. "You have been very helpful to me. You know why the inspector general of police was against my appointment? Because he is corrupt. He is a very corrupt person and he is scared that if I am in this job, I may go after his corruption and money laundering activities. I was not planning to, but now I am going to go after him and I am going to put him in jail in the next two years."

Within two years, Tafa Balogun was out of his job and in prison, but this could not have happened without passing one more crucial hurdle: Nuhu had to get to know and secure the trust and confidence of the president. At that point in time, Obasanjo and I were embroiled in the Nigeria Airways saga and were hardly speaking, so I gave two suggestions to Nuhu. "First, do not tell Obasanjo that we share an office, or that you even know me; second, to get access to him, you have to meet Oby Ezekwesili first." He was thankful and requested an introduction to her. I went to Oby and asked her to take Nuhu to meet Obasanjo.

"I will not meet that man," she said. "This your Nuhu is Atiku's man. Atiku got him the job. Atiku is dodgy and generally promotes corrupt people in government."

Oby despised what she believed Atiku represented. She thought Atiku was a blemish on the administration, that he was this untiring customs officer who just collected kickbacks from everywhere and thus created a credibility problem for a government that claimed to be serious about tackling the menace of systemic corruption.

"Oby, Nuhu did not get his job via Atiku," I said.

"No, Atiku got him his job!"

"No, he did not and I should know. I went to Atiku to talk about Nuhu getting some money from the BPE and Atiku was oblivious to the fact that Nuhu was already in the EFCC. He only knew that Nuhu was from his state. But he did not even know about the EFCC so I had to brief him. If Atiku had gotten him the job, he would have at least known something about the institution and its head. Furthermore, Nuhu did not go to Atiku for the money, he came to me. If he was Atiku's boy, he would have just gone to him direct. Nuhu is a good guy - someone we should be working with, Oby."

After three such conversations, Oby listened to my appeal and finally said, "Ok I will see him, but my brother, it is just because of you."

Nuhu met with Oby and like with me, made his pitch to her, and Oby, like me, was convinced that the man was passionate, genuine, and meant well. That was the beginning of the friendship between Nuhu and Oby. She introduced him to Obasanjo and kept facilitating access until he developed his own direct relationship with the president. Of course, over time, I made up with Obasanjo so it became a team effort. These were the defining moments of our relationship that brought the three of us even closer.

It may come as a surprise to some, but the EFCC is actually the second anti-corruption institution the government established. The first was the ICPC, the Independent Corrupt Practices Commission, and frankly, it was generally seen as just a quiet, toothless bulldog. It had been in existence since 2000, but had made no major arrests, no prosecutions, nothing up to that point - lots of noise about investigations, but no real action. Nuhu came and almost overnight transformed the anti-corruption war and its landscape, and the EFCC became synonymous with the fight against corruption.

The moment he began taking action, he moved out of our offices and received money to buy an office building in order to set up his own office. He needed another office for the financial intelligence unit, so as FCT Minister some months later, we got him a building as well and assisted him to renovate and equip it. Within two years, Nuhu had a much bigger support base partly from the government in general due to the higher profile he had created for himself and the EFCC and partly from my suggestion to Ngozi that EFCC, rather than ICPC, be included in the membership of the president's economic reform team.

The idea of the economic team was to have the economic ministers and those running economically-related agencies involved in regular brainstorming, coordination and monitoring activities. In constituting the team and what agencies to be invited to the table, I argued for including the EFCC because everything we were planning to do would not really matter in the eyes of Nigerians and the rest of the world unless the public image of Nigeria as a corrupt nation was fixed, or at least be seen to be improving. So I introduced Nuhu to the rest of the team and the five of us became what Ngozi called the core of the economic team – Ngozi, Oby, Nuhu, Charles Soludo and me. She insisted that we meet regularly, support and have absolute trust in each other.

Ngozi Okonjo-Iweala, Minister of Finance

The first time I heard of Ngozi was in 1998 when I was advising the Abdulsalami transitional administration. I was in Washington DC, attending the World Bank annual meetings with my friend and PIMCO colleague, Amah Iwuagwu, when the name was first mentioned. Amah, who went into politics and got elected senator in 2003, knew Ngozi from years back when they were students in the Boston area at the same time. She was completing her Ph.D at MIT, while he was studying for his graduate degree at the Harvard Kennedy School. They got to know each other quite well. He mentioned this Nigerian lady who was a director in the World Bank named Ngozi, and he wanted us to meet, but we never got to meet her on that occasion.

I always remembered the name though, because I was impressed at the prospect of a Nigerian rising through the ranks to be a director at the World Bank. A year later, when I was running the BPE, I got a call from another ex-classmate and ABU alumnus, Dr. Mansur Muhtar,[42] informing me that Ngozi was coming to Nigeria to work with Obasanjo for six months. Mansur wanted me to help her settle down, and look out for her because she had never worked in Nigeria and never lived in Abuja. Before leaving Washington, she had asked Mansur which Nigerian government officials she should meet while in Abuja and he mentioned my name, explaining that I was the new head of the BPE.

When she arrived, she called me and I went to meet her at the Abuja Hilton. She had been granted a six-month leave of absence from the World Bank to work with President Obasanjo to do two things: draft an economic strategy paper for the new administration and set up a debt management office. Obasanjo was very concerned about our Paris Club debt burden and wanted it resolved, so one of the recommendations to him from the then president of the World Bank, James Wolfensohn, was to set up a debt management office. Obasanjo requested Wolfensohn to lend him someone who could help do this and Wolfensohn offered to send Ngozi free of charge, for up to six months.

Ngozi and I hit it off straightaway. Ngozi is charming, thoughtful and intelligent. She outlined what she came to do in Nigeria, and asked me to help link her up with other "reformers". In consultation with Finance Minister Adamu Ciroma, she set up a committee to draft the economic strategy paper and I, as the head of the BPE, was a member of the committee, along with Steve Oronsaye and Akin Arikawe - future members of our 2003 economic team. We worked on developing the economic strategy paper and collaborated on setting up the debt management office, including serving on the top management hiring committee. The first head of the debt management office we interviewed and recommended to Vice President Atiku Abubakar to appoint was Akin Arikawe. Similar to Nuhu at the inception of the EFCC, Akin had no clear budget and no organisational structure and asked the BPE to help him with the drafting of an enabling law, design of an organisational structure, and propose compensation levels – every agency wanted BPE to be the model to adopt. Since the ministry of finance already had a department managing our debt, they transferred the budget of that department to the debt management office, so he did not have to take money from the BPE. Dr. Mansur Muhtar was hired as one of the directors, effectively Akin's deputy, by our selection committee. Tony Phido, then of UBA Trustees, was also offered a directorship position but he declined. Anyway, that was how the Debt Management Office began.

During her six months in Abuja – this was during the 2000-2001 period – Ngozi and I became close friends and remained in touch when she went back to Washington. As head of BPE, I was officially tagged "Alternate Governor" of the World Bank/IMF group and therefore invited to the World Bank annual meetings, so we always had a chance to catch up. Whenever I was in Washington, I would go to her house, have dinner, spend time with her children and husband, and we became close family friends.

Just after the 2003 presidential elections, while the nation was still awaiting the results, and the president and I were at the height of one of our frequent disagreements about privatisation, Suraj Yakubu, another ABU alumnus and friend, who was then the CEO of the Nigerian Investment Promotion Commission (NIPC), called on behalf of the president to say that I, along with him (Suraj) and Oby Ezekwesili, were to meet with Baroness Lynda Chalker in her capacity as the chair of the Presidential International Advisory Council on Investment in London. The purpose was to discuss issues related to the reforms that would help attract private sector investments during the second Obasanjo term. Baroness Chalker,[43] a close friend of President Obasanjo, was the secretary for international development in Margaret Thatcher's government and has considerable international clout. Baroness Chalker had already started work in London with a team of consultants preparing an economic plan. The president wanted the three of us to join them to have a look at the plan and make it 'more grounded, real and Nigerian.' Suraj made it clear that this trip was to be secret – we were not even to tell our spouses about the purpose of the trip. Indeed, the NIPC covered our travel expenses to conceal the real purpose of the trip from our direct reports (Steve Oronsaye in the case of Oby, and VP Atiku Abubakar in mine.)

We spent two days in London reviewing and editing the plan that Baroness Chalker and her team had already prepared and on the third and final day it became clear that while we all liked the plan itself, we still had not come up with the appropriate structure and staff needed to implement it. One of the main objectives was to have Nigeria's $30 billion Paris Club debt written off inside of the ensuing four years. All of us agreed that the minister of finance, the economic adviser to the president and the governor of the central bank of Nigeria would be the three key appointments to ensure that the leadership remained focused on achieving the debt write-off. The governor of the central bank had a secure tenure that would not be up for renewal until 2005.

Baroness Chalker first mooted the idea of who she thought should be the finance minister and the economic adviser. She added that she had discussions with Obasanjo about me remaining at BPE and Obasanjo said he definitely would not have me in BPE during his second term. We found the suggestion of Obasanjo appointing the persons Baroness Chalker mentioned near impossibilities and told her so. The finance minister is the president's treasurer and bookkeeper, and therefore should be pretty close to the president. Given that Obasanjo did not particularly like the persons mentioned, we told the baroness that this was an unlikely outcome. In any case, we argued, the country needed a finance minister who had good relations with bilateral and multilateral financial institutions, and I suggested that Ngozi should be the natural choice. Until that moment, Lynda had never heard of Ngozi. Oby and I gave her a brief biographical profile which excited her beyond belief. Oby then hinted that there was already serious lobbying for the position of Minister of Finance and that to ensure we succeeded in having the President consider Ngozi for the position we needed to move quickly. Baroness Chalker then immediately placed a call to President Obasanjo who was spending time at his Ota farm. She went on to inform him that she had got him a finance minister. She was persuasive in establishing the link between the priority Obasanjo attached to the debt relief and the good relations Ngozi had with the creditors, by virtue of her position at the World Bank. Obasanjo bought into the idea immediately, telling the Baroness that Ngozi worked for him earlier in his first term.

We ended the meeting in the afternoon of April 23rd 2003, and I left for Washington for other meetings with the World Bank, and to put Ngozi on notice that a ministerial offer was likely to be made. Oby, whose focus was on the corruption in public contracts, immediately hinted that all she wanted to do was continue with the 'Due Process' reforms she had been working on. I was indifferent because I was advanced in my plans to leave the administration, complete my LL.B degree in London, and then go to the Harvard Kennedy School.

I arrived in Washington and took a cab straight to Ngozi's office. She had been promoted to the vice presidency of the World Bank, and had before then chaired an important committee on Low Income Countries under Stress (LICUS) whose report I was invited, along with other African reformers, to critique in Paris, months earlier. While waiting to see her, she was summoned by Wolfensohn to break the news about Obasanjo's request for her to be finance minister. She came back to her office, looking visibly shaken and confronted me with the information. I admitted to my role in the whole affair and appealed to her to accept the offer. I could see then that she was both excited but subdued and reluctant. Excited because it would be a great honour to serve one's nation in that capacity and many World Bank/IMF staff had done this, and went on to be prime ministers and presidents of their countries. Reluctant because with three children in university, or about to enrol, the cost of tuition, even with her neurosurgeon husband's substantial income, would prove burdensome if she accepted the ministerial offer and its low pay. She shared these and other concerns right away. One was the pay. The other was her limited knowledge of Nigerian politics and public service, and third was the need for a competent team, not just a one-person show taking place in the Finance Ministry.

Based on my experience at the BPE, I knew it was possible for her to get a decent salary in US dollars, funded largely by donor agencies, and I told her so. The two other issues we could resolve by working to get 'a few good men and women'[44]. Ngozi tasked me to work on them while she consulted her husband, children and parents. This aspect of the assignment was easy because as part of his rapprochement with Obasanjo, Atiku Abubakar informed Akin Kekere-Ekun and me that he had been asked to constitute an Economic Policy Coordination team that will improve collaboration among the various government departments that were concerned with the economy. The final team selected by Atiku to craft the economic strategy and design improved coordination mechanisms for the Obasanjo-Atiku second term was chaired by Professor Anya O. Anya, and included Fola Adeola, Asue Ighodalo, Akin Kekere-Ekun, Bode Agusto, Bashir Yusuf

Ibrahim and myself. We met regularly late into the nights working on the policy document which was handed over to Atiku just before the elections. Nothing more was ever heard of that plan. But from that interaction, I had a shortlist of a few 'good men and women' for discussion with Ngozi almost immediately.

A couple of weeks later, Ngozi flew into Abuja to discuss and conclude the issues related to the appointment with Obasanjo. After cutting through some administrative issues, Ngozi accepted the offer, and was set to take the job and Obasanjo now had the task of putting together an economic team. Ngozi convinced him first of the need for the team, and he agreed, asking her to come up with some names for him to consider.

> "For this to work, we need a team," she again emphasised to me when her position was all settled. "And I do not know many Nigerians so you have to identify the bulk of the people that we will bring in to constitute the team."
>
> "Ngozi, I will be happy to do a list of prospective team members for you, but mind you, I will not be in the next government, because of frequent disagreements with Obasanjo and I am all set to leave," I said. At this point, I believed the prospect of continuing to work for the president to be non-existent. "As soon as I finish my term at the BPE in November, I am moving on."

Ngozi would not have this. She went to Obasanjo and suggested that with my skills, experience and passion, I had to be part of the team. So Ngozi was one of those who made the first efforts to reconcile me with Obasanjo because Obasanjo said I was a stubborn and disagreeable person, and he wanted to have nothing to do with me, other than send me on intellectual errands to London, I guess! Ngozi told me of her efforts, and I told her that she should stop wasting her time and focus on moving things on without me. No one was indispensable, after all.

At this point, Oby Ezekwesili and her husband Chinedu[45] got involved in the same cause. They spoke to me on the need to accept to be in the administration if Obasanjo made the offer and suggested that we see Obasanjo together to discuss our seemingly irreconcilable differences. We then had what Oby calls till today a lengthy 'reconciliation discussion'- we had been estranged for a very long time - and that meeting lasted quite a while with lots of bantering before Chinedu then said, "Baba, we have brought your son back to you," and Obasanjo said, "Do not mind the stupid boy! He is just argumentative and self-opinionated." Oby and her husband then left the two of us to talk. We had our fill of trading issues as to who upset whom the most. I realised then that the man really liked me, had a soft spot for me even, because he thought I reminded him of a younger version of Obasanjo in one way - he saw a lot of his youthful stubbornness in me, and paradoxically that was the side of me he despised. In Obasanjo's eyes, I was an *enfant terrible*. But that meeting cleared the air and prepared the ground for Obasanjo to nominate me to the cabinet. A few weeks later, he informed me and Oby that he was sending me to go clean up the nation's capital.

So depending on who tells the story, both Ngozi and Oby can claim some credit for the reconciliation that led to my nomination. The chief of staff, General Abdullahi Mohammed, also counseled Obasanjo on my personal courage and effectiveness in getting difficult things done. Atiku Abubakar told many people that Obasanjo wanted a 'madman' to clean up the FCT and he suggested me, and so on and so forth. What I know for sure is that both Ngozi and Oby made a determined push to ensure that I remained in the administration.

Ngozi's initial preference was for me to be the Petroleum Minister so that together we would clean up the nation's finances. She even approached and convinced Atiku of this because he told me soon after quite authoritatively that he had agreed with Obasanjo that I was going to the Petroleum ministry, to which I had no response, as Obasanjo had already told me he was posting me to the FCT. Frankly, until Obasanjo told me of his intention to assign me to FCT, I thought I would end up being Ngozi's Minister of State. Shortly before we were sworn in, Obasanjo revealed to me and Ngozi the portfolio assignments and his decision to have Nenadi Usman in that position instead. Interestingly, a couple of days before we were sworn in, Obasanjo informed Ngozi of a change in portfolios. He was now assigning another woman minister as her Minister of State on Atiku Abubakar's insistence. Ngozi drafted me to persuade Atiku to drop the idea because she had got used to Nenadi by then and had taken a liking to her. Besides Nenadi was much younger, and appeared more humble and deferential. The other woman was a retired permanent secretary, older and more experienced than Ngozi. I went to Atiku and made a pitch and he changed his mind. Ngozi and Nenadi went on to work well together until the former was reassigned to the Foreign Affairs ministry.

Ngozi proposed that the economic team meet twice weekly - with the president early morning on Wednesdays before the plenary meeting of the Cabinet with other cabinet level 'members',[46] and in her office on the same day at 3pm. The inner core of five also met at least once a week, in her house, no matter how busy we were, to review everything going on in the nation's political economy. She also made us commit to a pact of sorts. We had to have absolute trust in one other. If anyone came to Ngozi and accused anyone of us of any wrongdoing, the default position should be not to believe it, and for her to defend the person under attack without reservations. The same applied to each one of the five of us and other members of the economic team. Ngozi's thinking, and I agreed fully with it, was that nobody outside our team should see any signs of rift among the five of us.

We also committed to the principle of all for one and one for all. For example, if circumstances required one of us to resign, then we would all resign collectively and leave the government. For us to resign collectively, we had to have a discussion. If anyone felt he or she needed to resign, we would discuss and agree that the situation justified that person resigning, in which case, all five of us would resign together. She felt that in an administration surrounded largely by corrupt, self-seeking politicians, we would not survive without one another. She opined that the reforms we planned to undertake would be very difficult, going against the tide, against entrenched interests and they would fight back. So we would have to face the situation with a united front.

Ngozi was visionary. Her intelligence, sound education and World Bank exposure made her appreciate ahead of many people the challenges that we would face and the price we would pay in undertaking reforms, particularly economic reforms. Ngozi also had a preference of negotiating and winning over adversaries rather than confronting and fighting them. Whereas Oby and I would prefer to confront, fight and defeat an adversary, Ngozi preferred to be nice, sidestep and move on anyway. Her approach was that often 100 percent victory is impossible or too costly, but if 60 percent victory can be achieved without too much blood on the floor, then we could compromise with the bad guys, and should still move on. As an illustration of this, Ngozi had a very good relationships with all manner of politicians, including the likes of the convicted felon and then governor James Ibori, and she indeed had excellent relationships with some of the 'corrupt' legislators and governors, many of whom the rest of us would not say hello to. She is a realistic student of power and wanted to be on the side of the powerful - the winning side, all the time. A few contradictions that irked us were persistent rumours that her brothers were doing deals in the ministry of finance and making money and she did not think it necessary to seriously investigate such allegations.

On the whole, she turned out to be a sensible strategist and a good leader and galvanizer of people to achieve set goals. She did not do much day-to-day work, personally, making her really more of a coordinator-in-chief rather than executor. But her strength I think derives from her exposure and experience in development matters, knowing in advance where the reform challenges are likely to be, and because she had access to the information and institutional memory of the World Bank and other multi-laterals, she came across as knowing quite a lot. Where she proved invaluable was in leveraging her personal contacts within the international financial institutions to get increased donor attention to Nigeria, and assistance to fund the economic reform programme. The concessions we got from the Paris Club were in large part because she knew how to get everyone in the Paris Club, all the G7 finance ministers, and Gordon Brown of the UK became a strong supporter and advocate, and remains a personal friend of her's.

Unfortunately, in the end, our relationship took a turn for the worse beginning from the fateful day Obasanjo moved her to the foreign affairs ministry. One morning, in May of 2006, shortly after the third term effort collapsed, Obasanjo called me aside after the economic management team meeting and said he was going to reshuffle the cabinet that day. The plan he had, he confided in me, was to move Ngozi to the ministry of foreign affairs to fix some persistent problems in our international relations, Oby to the ministry of education and Nenadi Usman, who was Ngozi's number two, to take over from Ngozi as full cabinet minister of finance. Obasanjo said he needed me to help manage the emotions and reactions of those affected. Taken together, these three were known as 'my sisters' in the cabinet. He also knew that Ngozi, Oby and I, were the three independent and 'uncontrollable' ministers in the cabinet. If he had reshuffled without warning us, we may well have responded by just saying, "Thanks Mr. President, we quit," and he did not want that embarrassment, so he needed to do this the way he did it - recruiting me as the interlocutor and persuader.

So about half an hour to the commencement of the cabinet meeting, I called Ngozi and Oby aside, outside the Council Chambers for a chat. I broke the news of the impending reshuffle to them. Oby who had just undergone stress sorting out the Solid Minerals ministry through an intense reform agenda, was both angry and sad that she was being thrown into another tough assignment. She was terribly unhappy, tearful and nearly broke down. "Why am I being thrown to another zoo again? Why is Baba doing this to me?" she said amidst tears. I counseled her about the importance of education to our nation's future and why she needed to be there to begin to get the place sorted out. She calmed down and subsequently with the intervention and support of her husband, quickly adjusted to her new assignment. Ngozi was shocked as well, but as a pragmatic student of power, recovered almost immediately and asked me who would then chair the economic team. I did not have an answer so I went back to Obasanjo to ask. He said that Nenadi as minister of finance must chair the economic team, unless she was unwilling to do so. I then went up to Nenadi who seemed to have a foreknowledge of the reshuffle and looked like she knew she was going to replace Ngozi, and talked to her. I confirmed to her that Obasanjo had just told me about it and we needed to meet to agree a few housekeeping issues. She followed me to the location outside the Council Chambers where Ngozi and Oby were tearfully talking in inaudible tones. We then had a four-person meeting where Nenadi agreed that Ngozi should not only continue to chair the economic team, but maintain the interface with international financial institutions until she felt ready to take that over. I reported our consultations and decision to a reluctant Obasanjo, who agreed to the arrangement but only as "an interim measure". This would be the beginning of our team tensions. This arose largely because unlike Oby and I, who clearly put our feelings on the table, subsequent events showed that both Ngozi and Nenadi were not entirely happy with the arrangement, but merely pretended to be. Ngozi never ceased to think of herself as finance minister to the exclusion of Nenadi, and Nenadi resented the suggestion that she could not chair the economic team. The seeds of failure were already sown.

Rearranging the power structure of any organisation is rarely smooth, and this was no exception. While the president's objectives may have been legitimate, they posed some issues for us as a team. This reshuffling opened the question of who was going to chair the economic team – this was where the power was, and Ngozi, as both the team's conceptual founder and minister of finance, was the official and unofficial chair. Furthermore, Ngozi, as a student and strategist of power, was not likely to give up this position easily. There was the additional question of whether or not Nenadi was ready to be both minister of finance and chair of the economic team, should Ngozi have no problem giving up the chairmanship and should Nenadi be comfortable taking on that role – neither of which held to be true. I was put in a very difficult position. To begin with, Nenadi Usman, the junior minister of finance, a younger politician from my home state, was receiving a promotion, so I was elated, and did not hide it, and therefore raised Ngozi's suspicion that I had taken sides. Nenadi also knew I was closer to Ngozi than she was to me, so did not entirely trust me either. This had fatal consequences for my attempted role as honest broker when the tensions over turf subsequently escalated.

Meanwhile, Ngozi soon became increasingly unhappy in foreign affairs. While she did a good job, it was clear that her heart was in the ministry of finance. She was essentially trying to run two ministries at once and as one might imagine, this was causing problems. When the IMF came for consultations, she got them to come to the foreign affairs ministry instead of finance.

"Listen," I said to her one day. "You are not the minister of finance, so when the World Bank and the IMF teams come, tell them to go see Nenadi. When they are done, whatever is outstanding – do it within the framework of the economic team. Do not ask delegations to the finance ministry to come to you in the ministry of foreign affairs. It will cause unnecessary problems."

When rumours started circulating in Lagos media circles that Ngozi was transferred out of the finance ministry so that Obasanjo would be free to do some dodgy financial deals in preparation for the 2007 elections, I got worried. I poked around and got reliable feedback that it was media people linked to one of her brothers and media aide Paul Nwabuikwu who were spreading these rumours. At an event in her honour in her hometown of Ogwashi-Ukwu, I berated her brothers Chichi and Chude for it, reminding them that there is nowhere in the world that being foreign minister of one's country becomes a situation for mourning or complaining. I counseled that unless these stories stop, they would ultimately get to Obasanjo, who was already upset with us in the aftermath of the collapse of his designs for a third term, and would direct his venom at Ngozi and the rest of the team. They denied all involvement but agreed with my assessment.

It appeared no one listened to my appeals because a similar allegation appeared in an article in *The Economist* shortly after. The final straw occurred when Ngozi was in London negotiating the write-off of our modest London Club debts. She made that trip unbeknownst to Nenadi. She just took the team she needed from the finance ministry, obtained Obasanjo's permission to travel as was usual, and went to London, in her capacity as chair of the economic team. Nenadi may have complained to Obasanjo about being kept in the dark. On the spot, Obasanjo decided to remove Ngozi as chair of the economic team – right away, without any discussion, consultation or notice, as Ngozi was in the middle of the crucial negotiations. All of the major newswires carried news of the firing of Ngozi from chairing the economic team and in the midst of meeting with her European counterparts; everyone was looking at their BlackBerries and asking her if she was still authorised to continue the negotiations. It was no doubt a totally humiliating moment for Ngozi. When I heard about this, I was distraught and went straight into the president's office.

> "Mr. President, what is going on with Ngozi and the economic team?"
>
> "Nasir, look, she can't do what she has been doing, acting as if there is no finance minister." he said. "We all agreed that chairing the economic team would be for a short period. What she has been doing is not fair to the finance minister. She should have handled this better. They worked together with her as minister of state, and that is why I thought it was a good idea to elevate Nenadi. Why can't they work out a way to work together? Why is Ngozi behaving as though she is the minister of both international finance and foreign affairs?"
>
> "I agree that Ngozi could have handled it better, but you could have allowed her to conclude the negotiations first, Mr. President, and then tell her to handle things differently in future. You should have given us the chance to work out the interface with Nenadi." I added.
>
> "No. She has been humiliating the finance minister. I had to deal with the situation."

Oby and I felt that Obasanjo handled it the wrong way. Oby was so angry with the president that she did not speak with him for days and constantly afterwards was somewhat withdrawn. I had to work with her husband, Chinedu, to bring her out of the anger that followed the catastrophic breakup of the economic team we had all so invested ourselves in building. In a way, Oby had always looked on Ngozi as the elder sister she never had, and really never fully recovered from the loss and anguish of that period. Many of us felt this also, though to a lesser degree.

To be fair to Obasanjo, Ngozi truly did not manage the transition well either, but she also did not think he managed it well, because there was no need to treat her the way it was done. It was clear that her situation was no longer tenable, and at the end of the day we lost her. She felt thoroughly humiliated in the international community that mattered to her, and understandably so.

She called Obasanjo from London and informed him of her decision to resign. He did nothing to dissuade her. She returned to Nigeria, submitted her resignation, packed her things, and just left, at first for Lagos, then went abroad. She was very angry at the president, at the situation, and at all of us. She expected all of us to also resign as part of our pact, but she forgot the part of the agreement that required us to consult, to talk, to discuss, and agree together. If Ngozi had talked to us, we probably would have resigned with her, because by then we were all weary, jaded and tired anyway. This was the end of 2006, the second Obasanjo term was almost over, and I honestly would have left and taken an early break. I am fairly certain Oby was jaded and unhappy, and would have left too. All Ngozi needed to do was to come back to Nigeria and say to us, "Well, because of what Obasanjo has done," – which we all would have agreed was humiliating – "I have to resign." We would have gone along with her.

I am not sure Nuhu would have resigned, because by then Nuhu, as a policeman, had become closer to Obasanjo in ways that the rest of us were not, but I know that Oby and I would have resigned. In any case, Nuhu's resignation would only require him to move from EFCC back to his career in the Police, which would not have been too difficult to do if he chose to. Unfortunately, Ngozi did not feel the need to consult us and, therefore, we did not feel the need to blindly follow her. This we suspect has remained a source of mild bitterness between Ngozi and the rest of us till today

Oby Ezekwesili, "Madam Due Process", Minister of Solid Minerals and Education

Oby was the first of the core team members that I met. Unlike Nuhu and Ngozi, who were both introduced to me by someone else, we met accidentally and she introduced herself directly to me. My lawyer and dear friend, Asue Ighodalo, had mentioned her as his sister and promised to link us up. He never got round to it. I had just been appointed to run the BPE and was making the rounds of national assembly committees to convince them on the need for privatisation of state-owned enterprises. I was at the House of Representatives' Committee on Privatisation to make a presentation on our programme, and Oby was in attendance as a guest. She had come to Nigeria on a project of assistance to President Obasanjo from the Harvard Centre for International Development, where she had been hired by Jeffrey Sachs directly after graduating from the Kennedy School in 2000. The Centre for International Development had put up some money for an economic reform assistance project in Nigeria and Oby was in Abuja directing that project. Oby was also personally close to Obasanjo as they were the founding directors of Transparency International back in the 1990s.

After I finished my presentation, she walked up to me and said, "I am Oby Ezekwesili," and presented me with her business card. It had her name and read Harvard Nigeria Project, Director.

> I looked at the card and said, "I am Nasir, and very pleased to meet you."
>
> "You are a very good man", she said. "Everything you said in the presentation makes sense. This is great, I did not know that there is someone like you in this administration. When can we meet and talk some more?" She would later tell me that on that day, she felt like she had found her long lost brother.

The next evening, we had dinner in her home, and I met her husband Chinedu - a pentecostal pastor, and her three wonderful boys.[47] We bonded instantly.

Oby got me involved in the "due process" work she was doing, which was basically trying to reform our broken public procurement system. In her opinion, the biggest problem in Nigeria is associated with lack of transparency in the government's procurement of goods and services – every year the government spent billions of dollars buying goods and services and there was no competitive bidding, no price intelligence, nothing. A kilometre of road costs half a million dollars to build in Ghana and more than two million dollars in Nigeria. Why should that happen?

That was the crux of her work. We began meeting regularly, comparing notes, and I appointed her to the BPE committees dealing with competition and regulatory reform, industry and manufacturing, and several of the other policy reform committees. When we began the reform of the electricity supply industry, I got Oby appointed to the board of directors of NEPA. She was brilliant, she had a lot of value to add, so I used her as a resource and we also became one family. Shortly after, Ngozi came for her six-month stint in Obasanjo's first term and then the three of us related and became like siblings.

Since Oby had been living and working mostly in Lagos, and I lived and worked mostly in Kaduna and Abuja, and because she made her name in civil society, while I had been focused mostly on the construction industry, I had never even heard of her before Asue mentioned her to me. I think her first degree was in business education. She was then employed and trained at Deloitte, and qualified to be a chartered accountant. She later studied international law and diplomacy at the University of Lagos. After she founded the Nigerian chapter of Transparency International, she was promptly hounded out of the country by the Abacha regime. While in exile, Oby gained admission into the Harvard Kennedy School Mason Fellows programme in 1999, the same programme I would enrol in nine years later.

Oby is one of the most honest people I know. When, as FCT minister, I encouraged her to apply for a plot of land, she did, in her own name. She did not use a pseudonym or the veil of a company like many others who equated that pretense with being clean. Oby does not play games, what you see is what you get. Oby is an amazingly talented woman. She is hard-working and focused on problem solving. She is one of those rare persons who combine skills in numeracy, literacy and oratory. She is also very forthright and courageous. Oby's only clear weakness is her inadequate 'people skills' - she can be impatient and brusque with people she considers of low standards, either ethically or professionally.

Oby is also one of those who could speak to Obasanjo in any manner she wanted, and Obasanjo was very tolerant of her. She says it like she sees it, is straight to the point, sharp, and gives it as much as she can take it, and she would give it to Obasanjo. Obasanjo was alleged to have told someone that in his cabinet, there were two people who, any time they raised their hands to speak in cabinet meetings, his heart would go into his mouth because he did not know what to expect: Oby and myself. I swear I am not one-quarter as bad in that respect as Oby. She really had no political guile at all. When it became clear that Obasanjo was plotting for a third term, she did not hesitate to go straight to the man himself.

"Why have you allowed the devil to take you over? This third term attempt will fail!"

That is the sort of person she was. Tony Anenih, who was the project manager of the third term campaign, had a TV commercial produced to promote the idea that a third term was good for Nigeria because some of Obasanjo's ministers had laid solid foundations which needed to be built upon. The very first advert featured Oby in a very positive light: Oby had done procurement reforms and saved Nigeria two and a half billion dollars in three years; she was a task master, a hard worker, a true patriot. Most people would be flattered, but not my sister! Oby called up the heads of both the AIT and the NTA and warned that their commercial was broadcast without her permission and that she was vehemently against third term. She further warned them that should they put her name or picture anywhere near any third term propaganda ever again, they could expect a very public lawsuit to be brought upon them. The television stations pulled the commercials and called Tony Anenih to explain. Chief Tony Anenih could not confront Oby directly so he called on Andy Uba, who allegedly controlled the purse strings for the campaign and was also from Oby's home state of Anambra.

"Did you call NTA and AIT to stop the advertisement of the party?"

"Yes. I did"

"You are a minister of this government," he continued.

"You are very silly to say that, Andy. Who told you that you could use my name to propagate your evil thinking without even so much as the respect of asking my permission?"

Oby dropped the phone but was not done. She went straight to Obasanjo and complained bitterly about the incident.

"Tell the third term people to never ever mention my name in any of their schemes..."

"Who? What did they do? – I did not know."

"You know! And you know that I am totally against what those vultures are doing with you in that stupid campaign."

None of us would go that far. We would dissent but there would be no such confrontation, but Oby did that. That was Oby. She in fact often acted like a moral conscience for President Obasanjo and was truly like a daughter to him. Her no-nonsense attitude earned her a lot of enemies within the administration, some of whom are as angry as, or even angrier, than my enemies. There are certainly worse flaws to have.

Oby, always took her obligations seriously. She completed her Kennedy School degree on a partial scholarship. She was already in exile when she applied and was admitted, but she was broke. At the end of the programme, when she went to work for Jeffrey Sachs, she owed about $40,000 to $50,000 in student loans. With her Harvard job, she began to pay off part of it, came back to Nigeria, and continued to pay the balance. She told Obasanjo, "Mr. President, when the project is over, I need to go back to the US to continue working for Jeffrey." By then, Jeffrey Sachs was planning on moving to Columbia and had offered her a job. Instead, as her project neared its end, Obasanjo offered her a job to be his special assistant on budget monitoring and price intelligence, to continue the due process work she had articulated. But Oby still owed about $40,000 in student loans. Obasanjo assured her not to worry about the debt, he would take care of it. He never did.

One day, I found Oby in her office crying. She told me about the student loan and Obasanjo's promise. If it was another person promised, Oby would have been at the forefront of asking Obasanjo to pay up, but she could not speak for herself. I went to the president and told him, "You have to pay this money – you promised."

"Well you know I do not have the money either."

Obasanjo was always claiming he had no money.

"No, you must do something Mr. President," I said.

Two days went by and Oby still had not heard anything about her loan problem. I went back to Obasanjo.

"You have to do this, sir," I said. "And I am not leaving until you give me $40,000 to pay into her account and liquidate this debt, because debt collectors are calling her, harassing her and distracting her from doing her job."

If I had it, I would have paid off the loan myself, but I did not have the money at the time. Obasanjo agreed and said he had some money. He gave me $10,000 and told me to give it to Oby.

"No, sir, please give it to her directly," I said.

Oby took the $10,000 and made a partial payment. Nothing else was heard of the balance up until we left office. The amount was not settled until Oby had secured a better-paying job as World Bank vice president.

Many people would say that only someone like Oby could be the final hurdle in approving billions of dollars in procurement in Nigeria for four years and then have difficulty paying off a loan of $30,000. Oby was simply incorruptible. She worked for six years in the government in positions that, if she wanted, she could have allowed herself to be tempted. But that was not Oby Ezekweisili.

Charles Chukwuma Soludo, President's Economic Adviser and then Central Bank Governor

Ngozi it was who first introduced me to Charles Soludo in 2000. He was something like a student or protégé of Ngozi's father while pursuing his Ph.D. in economics at the University of Nigeria, Nsukka. Ngozi's father then introduced Charles to her and over the years, Ngozi reportedly assisted him in securing some consulting assignments with the World Bank and other multilateral institutions. At the point she introduced us, he had done a stint lecturing at Swarthmore College, then an attachment with the Brookings Institution in Washington, and had subsequently returned to Nigeria with a vision to build a think tank similar to Brookings. He named it the African Institute for Applied Economics – the AIAE – and he wanted me on the board of directors. In addition to Ngozi and myself, he had invited Jan Piercy, the executive director representing the US in the World Bank, and a friend of the Clintons, as well as a few other people that I cannot fully recall now, as we had only one board meeting in Washington DC that I am aware of.

I protested that I was not an economist, but both Ngozi and Charles pointed out that I was in effect an applied economist, having served as privatisation czar. I also appointed Charles to a couple of BPE steering committees. There were other issues related to the privatisation programme that I involved him in, which kept bringing him regularly to Abuja. He impressed me as a very bright macro economist and strong speaker. Though he had earned this Ph.D at a very young age, and had this international pedigree, hardly anyone in Nigeria then knew who he was. There are many such intelligent, homegrown brains in Nigeria waiting to be discovered and given an opportunity. Charles got his through Ngozi's introductions.

A lot like Ngozi, Charles was also very clear-eyed when it came to power relationships. He started as economic adviser to the president and was initially a reluctant member of the Villa inner circle, but soon became one of the people closest to Obasanjo, possibly closer than many of us, because we did not take the time to ingratiate ourselves with Obasanjo as much as Soludo deliberately did. He joined Obasanjo's circle of regular Villa Chapel attendants, going every morning to pray with Obasanjo and discuss ideas with him. He figured out quickly that Obasanjo liked staff who praised him effusively and attributed every good idea and policy initiative directly to him. Always bubbling with ideas, Soludo would have them debated rigorously by the team and then present it first to Obasanjo. Once accepted, Charles would spin it in a way that it was Obasanjo's vision and ideas, and Obasanjo liked things like that – great ideas to be appropriated by him, or attributed to him. In short order, in no time at all, Soludo needed no further intermediaries to gain access to Obasanjo. By mid-2005, he was appointed governor of the Central Bank— without Ngozi or any economic team member being involved in the discussion.

His path to the Central Bank was not without its bumps though, and the first time his name was mentioned as a possible appointee to be economic adviser – during the meetings with Baroness Chalker – Obasanjo initially objected to him on the basis that he did not want his finance minister and economic adviser both being from the same ethnic group. We felt strongly that merit should override these considerations and Charles was the best macroeconomist we knew, and could vouch for. It was not that easy though. It took some convincing and in Ngozi's absence, it was Oby who repeatedly took Charles to Obasanjo and got her pastor husband involved in the mission of getting Charles appointed as economic adviser to the President.

For a while, this seemed to work out. Our economic strategy, NEEDS, the National Economic Empowerment and Development Strategy, was a great success due in large part to Charles' enthusiasm and hard work. We all contributed to the substance of the NEEDS document,[48] but he was the editor and task manager. His job was to bring coherence to the overall strategy. We received a grant from the Canadian International Development Agency, and engaged academics in developing the strategy; we invited former ministers of finance and former economic advisers, and debated the draft thoroughly. In the end it was a very widely consultative document, and one of the most widely debated economic reform documents in Nigeria's history. Everyone commended us for it.

When we presented its outline[49] to Tony Blair and Gordon Brown in Lancaster House, London in July 2003 and again in the autumn of the same year, Prime Minister Blair promised that if we faithfully implemented the economic programme we had outlined, the UK government would champion debt reduction for Nigeria. I think he said it because he was so sure we could not do it, but we knew we could because we thought through and designed the programme on our own, without any input from the IMF or the World Bank. When the Fund subsequently reviewed it, their staff said that it was more comprehensive than any IMF-designed economic reform programme. Two years into its implementation, we had achieved nearly 70 percent of the targets and Blair was compelled to lead the lobbying for our Paris Club debt relief. Because Britain was our largest single creditor, the rest of the Paris Club fell in line and it became a matter of how much of a discount we were going to get. We aimed for 80 percent, better than the typical terms for highly indebted poor countries and wound up with 60 percent of our debt written off.

Soon enough, however, fissures began to appear in our team. Both Charles and Ngozi were politically-savvy economists who equally craved the limelight when it came to how economic reforms and our team were portrayed. Oby did not care for the limelight and as FCT minister I was regularly in the news whether I liked it or not. But Charles very clearly wanted some attention as well and he came to see Ngozi as a person who was making the team work collectively while she got the sole credit. As economic adviser, he was the principal author of the NEEDS programme, but he was not content to just do this without a public acknowledgement that he was the team's principal economist. Thus began a period of constant friction. We met two or three times to try to sort it out, and both Oby and I took sides with Ngozi in the matter, as she was our team leader. We all agreed on these things in the beginning, but as Charles got more involved, gained more confidence and got closer to Obasanjo, I think he decided to develop his own public profile, somewhat like a musical group that splits because one of the members wants to develop a solo career. Ngozi obviously was not going to live with that.

The final time we tried to reconcile them was the most telling about what was going on in Charles' mind. Charles, Oby and I met in Ngozi's suite in the Bolingo Hotel.

> "Look, you are telling me to do all this work and just hand it over to Ngozi to summarise in four or five sound-bites and nobody knows all those that did the work," said Charles. "It is easy for you to support this, Nasir, you are minister of FCT, you are doing all these demolitions, and everyone knows you in Nigeria. Oby, it is easy for you, you are in charge of due process, no contract gets awarded unless you sign on it – you are Madam Due Process. Ngozi is the minister of finance. Does she have to be the sole public face of these economic reforms?"
>
> This assessment of our individual situations by Charles was in fact accurate and we had no response.

We sat there not quite sure what to say, but pretty much at our wit's end. Then he really put the nail in the coffin of our core team:

> "Why can't I also be acknowledged and publicly recognised? What does that take from Ngozi or any of you? Must there be only one voice for the team?"

At that point, it was clearly hopeless for him to work with us and what we were trying to achieve. Each played important parts: I focused on the FCT and the fact that Abuja was the laboratory for every reform we wanted to implement across the country; Oby spoke, not about economic reforms, but about the aspects of governance reforms that she was spearheading; Nuhu would speak about economic reform from the standpoint of anti-corruption and money-laundering law enforcement. We thought that Charles should be our spokesman on the macro economy. However it dawned on us that Charles wanted more and what he wanted was not unreasonable, but we were blinded by our loyalty to Ngozi to be flexible about it. As he himself said in not so many words, he wanted recognition and being the number two economic voice in the government - what he essentially was as de facto minister of the economy - was simply not visible enough.

One day, in December of 2003, after less than six months working together, Charles fell out of the core group:

> "I am done. I cannot do this. I have to chart my own course," he more or less said, and stopped attending the weekly economic team meetings in the minister's office and the core group meetings at her residence.

Five months later, he was appointed governor of the Central Bank of Nigeria.

Assessment of Charles' Falling Out

As time went on, it became clear why the conflict between Ngozi and Charles was bound to happen. Both of them are in many ways very similar, not only because they are both economists with good Ph.Ds, but they were ambitious, very concerned with public perception and far more politically-astute than Oby, Nuhu or I were. Once those two began to butt heads, the rest of us considered it our problem, but having tried everything to resolve it and failed, we eventually made peace with the fact that they could never fully reconcile. Ngozi was the one who made us work to bring him in, she sold him to us, so we pretty much took him at face value on her own recommendation.

Apart from the fact that we had all agreed on Ngozi being our team leader and spokesperson, another reason we sided with her throughout was that she had done so much for Charles – she more or less created whatever initial positive perceptions we had about him. Even his opportunities with the World Bank, which led to the fellowship at Brookings Institution, she was said to have played roles in making them happen. I think Ngozi was the one who got heartbroken about the falling out because at the end of it, it had to do with her judgment of character and she knew that. The rest of us were around the same age, but Ngozi was much older than all of us – was it really too much to defer to her for that period? Charles felt it was, and made his choices. We did not judge his choices, we simply disagreed with them at that point in time.

Quite plainly, the man had his long-term political agenda, unlike most of us, who were content to just get the job done. Charles was a politician at heart, and therefore loved to be vocal and visible, and his attire – even his style of dressing was designed to make political statements, all the time. As a central bank governor, who should traditionally, neither be seen nor heard too frequently and certainly not loudly, Charles would mostly wear expensive bespoke suits, complete with a bright red tie. I think this was his way of being very visible and having his image etched in the public eye for that ultimate future political contest.[50] Charles is brilliant and leaves no one in doubt about that, and I think nothing would have stopped him from shining anyway. Charles' very colourful tenure as the central banker, though initially acclaimed, eventually became tarnished. Unbeknownst to the wider public, Charles had effectively allowed the Central Bank to be 'captured' by the banks it was supposed to be regulating. Bank chiefs were acting like rock stars, and all restraint was tossed out of the window. Many large banks had become insolvent, but the public knew nothing until Soludo failed to secure a second term as governor and everything came crashing down. To bail out the banks and prevent a national economic meltdown would cost some N4 trillion.

Lessons Learned in Team-building

When I think of all the Nigerians who are extremely talented, want to improve the country and are dedicated to it, it is striking to me how short the list has been so far. The people I have described above were the ones I had a real pact with, like blood brothers and sisters, to serve together and constrain one another's behaviour. All that eventually fell apart, starting with Ngozi's departure. The cost has been steep, because unfortunately there's almost no one that I absolutely trust anymore. As time went on, we all discovered some truths about one another that led each of us to think of one another maybe not in terms of absolute trust, but relatively high levels of trust. I still trust these people more than any Nigerians, because quite honestly, by whatever standard, these are really decent people and true public servants. I trust Oby still, perhaps more than anyone. With Oby, nothing has changed because she has not changed significantly, only older and wiser.

I am not in touch with Ngozi as much as before because she left us a little embittered and was disappointed that we did not follow her out of the government, so some distance grew between us. Ngozi and Oby also had some needless tensions while working as colleagues in the World Bank, but I hope that their relationship has gotten better since both left the bank's employment.

We had differences with Nuhu on political issues in 2011. He moved from the position of embarking on a one-man crusade to make me the president of Nigeria at all costs to being bitter that I did not support his bid four years later. What led to the position I took to support General Muhammadu Buhari instead will be explained in detail in a later chapter. However, many have asked why Nuhu badly wanted me to be president in 2007. I would like to think that he appreciated all I did to support the EFCC's take-off and early success. Secondly, Nuhu had grown to be one of my closest friends and our families had become one, so indeed, it was better to have one's close friend as president than not. Finally, I believe Nuhu thought highly of my abilities and was initially starstruck at what we were able to make of our assignments in the BPE and the FCTA, and thought that could be applied at a higher level.

Nuhu is essentially a good man and by the standards of public service in Nigeria, he is still one of the best law enforcement officers I know, but I am convinced he has issues that need working on for him to succeed in public leadership at even higher levels. This is why I think, and I told him, that both of us needed healing, more experience, some exposure and a lot of internal reconciliation of the bitter experiences and betrayals we suffered before returning to public service, if at all.

For now he has gone his own way politically by first running for president without carrying us along and then joining the Jonathan administration in a role that may end up having an adverse effect on his public image. On reflection, these decisions are consistent with Nuhu's character though, that dining with the devil if necessary in this way is justifiable - to get power no matter the cost, and when one gets power, it could then be used to fix things right. In this regard, even Ngozi was at least initially on our side, despite the fact that she is a very realistic, open-eyed person about power. Even she thought on July 31st 2010[51] that while PDP was definitely not the political platform to move our nation forward, Nuhu was not taking the right path to joining the Action Congress as organised then, and in the way and manner he did - all alone. She opined that we stood for something in public service - integrity and performance. The opinion of our group was that whatever political platform we chose to join should be consistent with our public service record. We were all convinced that going to the AC as a lone wolf would hurt Nuhu in the long run. If we had all agreed to go into AC together as a group, there was a fighting chance that the party's orientation may be improved by the collective injection to make Nuhu's aspiration more plausible. Unfortunately, because of the way he handled his entry, without consulting us - much like Ngozi's unilateral resignation in 2006, we all chose not to go with him.

One thing the economic team could have done to avoid breaking up would have been for the key players to understand each other better. We did not. We knew each other barely, but trusted each other absolutely. We were too busy to understand the tell-tale signs of personal weakness and human failings that needed remedy rather than trust. It was both good and bad. If we knew that chairing the economic team was so important to Ngozi, maybe it could have been structured differently. When a team works closely enough to feel bonded together, in which everyone grows to respect and love one another the way we did, each member's flaws aren't always so noticeable. If they were noticeable, steps could have been taken to remedy them in good time. In our situation, I was in a position to go to Obasanjo before it went out of whack to suggest institutionalising the team and rearranging everything appropriately, but I did not get that it was that important to Ngozi with enough time on the clock. If I did, I am not sure if Ngozi's feeling of entitlement to be finance minister had any solution once Obasanjo decided, quite appropriately in my estimation, that her talents and contacts were better deployed to fixing our broken and dysfunctional foreign relations, once the Paris Club debt relief deal was done.

I also did not realise that Ngozi's understanding of our pact was that it did not apply to her. Obasanjo is capable of the same attitude – I am your leader so the rules apply to you, not to me and I saw this often. I do not know whether there is any remedy for it, really, because in teams these issues will come up in different ways but I thought that if we had stepped back and really understood the flaws in each of us – and I am sure that Ngozi, Nuhu and Oby could speak very well to my many flaws – maybe we could have worked harder at remedying the flaws and plugging in the gaps, but we did not. It took a lot of pain to fully realise how each person truly was - months and years after we left office.

The team's foundation is still there. Oby is very passionate about Nigeria. She was planning not to extend her term in at the World Bank in 2010 because she wanted to come back to Nigeria and I asked her, "To do what?" As long as there was nothing concrete to do, she may as well go ahead and get a couple of years' extension. Ngozi was always willing to come back to Nigeria if there is something significant to do, like being finance minister again and again, so, I think if we have another opportunity to regroup as we did in Pastor Bakare's residence in July 2010, to fight the bigger evils destroying our nation, it will bring us back together. Only Nuhu thought he could go it alone - he had not realised then that we needed each other, but I hope he has learnt some lessons after the political baptism of the 2011 presidential bid.

It is yet another illustration of one of the core lessons of my experience: to those aspiring to a career in public service, be ready for heartbreaks. If you understand those you work with and understand that they are human, they have weaknesses and you take pre-emptive steps to remedy those weaknesses or plug in the gaps, the heartbreaks can be minimised, but will never be completely eliminated.

This is life. Putting group interests above personal interests is the ultimate challenge. Nowhere was this more prominently on display than it was during Obasanjo's second term.

Chapter Eight

Abuja – The Economic Reform Laboratory

Wisdom, compassion, and courage are the three universally recognised moral qualities of men.

– *Confucius*

Faced with what is right, to leave it undone shows a lack of courage.

– *Confucius*

Getting appointed to high office in our country is often entirely based on caprice, as I have indicated earlier. In Obasanjo's second term however, an attempt was made to at least formalise the process. Each ministerial nominee, prior to Senate confirmation, first had to submit to a job interview with the president, the vice-president and the chairman of the ruling party.The first question they asked me was, "What is your favourite city in the world and why?" I said I had two favourite cities: Paris and Singapore. Paris, to me, is unparalleled for sheer beauty, and as a romantic getaway. Singapore addresses what I suspected the interviewing panel was really after: I like Singapore because it runs efficiently, is green and it appeals to my sense of order. I did not know then that Obasanjo considered Lee Kuan Yew to be one of his role models. Audu Ogbeh, the party chairman at the time, then asked me how much time I would need if asked to turn Abuja into Singapore, if appointed the Minister of FCT.

> "Well, Singapore took about 30 years to happen," I said. "But I think that if we have two years in Abuja, we can begin to show a difference."
>
> "Well, you know that for you to do that, you will have to demolish many buildings," Obasanjo interjected. "Would you be able to do that?"
>
> "Mr. President, that question is for you," I said. "Would you be able to do that?"
>
> "What do you mean?"
>
> "Most of the buildings were erected and are owned by retired generals and big men. They would run to you once the restoration starts. Would you be able to stand the pressure?"
>
> "What about customs officers and politicians?" Obasanjo asked.

Mind you, he was sitting next to Atiku, an ex-customs official, and Audu Ogbeh, the best-ever chairman of the PDP in my opinion, and a politician of some thirty years' standing.

> "Yes, there are a few of those too but most of the problems will come from your colleagues, the retired generals," I responded.

Obasanjo looked at Audu Ogbeh and said:

> "You see, I told you, he is mad. He has started abusing me already." He then turned back to me. "Well as long as you treat the retired generals as

you do the customs officers and the retired politicians, I will back you up."

That was the whole interview. At that point I knew for sure that I was going to be in charge of the FCT. A few days later, our names were read on the floor of the Senate by the Senate President Adolphus Wabara. We had already been quietly investigated by several security agencies and been given a clean bill of health. No medical examinations were required of ministerial nominees so we submitted to none. Of course I went through my backroom drama with Mantu and Zwingina, the attempted shakedown and the eventual poisoning of my relationship with the National Assembly.

The interview was only the first of a number of things that made minister-level public service different from anything I had done previously, and it began virtually the moment I was sworn in. As I came out of the Executive Council Chambers that evening on July 16, 2003, two men approached me. One was in a black suit and introduced himself as Widi Liman, my chief security officer. The other, in flowing *agbada,* said he was Sagir Hamidu and in charge of protocol. They showed me my convoy of four vehicles - my official car and Isa the driver, accompanied by a police outrider on a motorbike, plus two other vehicles, one with a flashing siren, and the other full of bodyguards. This caught me completely off guard. This was when I first decided something had to be written about this ministerial experience some day. I had met other former ministers who said they wished someone would have warned them about what to expect. Every new minister gets to meet three people within the first day of his appointment, his security officer from SSS, his police orderly and the protocol officer. The minister of FCT has the biggest contingent because of his special position as 'governor' of Abuja. I did not know any of that.

How I met the FCT

I made a point my very first day at the FCT to signal what sort of workplace I expected. I arrived at seven o'clock in the morning to a completely empty building. Everyone else arrived at around nine or so. Those first couple of weeks, and this is the case for any cabinet level minister, I spent most of the time just listening to various briefings from all the different departments – who spent how much money last year, what the problems were, how many staff each department had, these sorts of things. In between briefings, I was going on so-called 'familiarisation tours' to get a sense of the workplace and key projects.

The biggest lesson I took away from those first weeks was to read the briefing books - "Handing-Over Notes" in Nigerian public service parlance, before being briefed and have my questions ready when everybody else arrived. To those of you reading this expecting to serve as cabinet ministers, let me repeat that: READ THOROUGHLY, FIRST, and watch out mostly for what is omitted that ought to be there.

The second big lesson from that initiation period was to insist on physical evidence. For example, if I was being briefed on a road construction project on which I had questions, I would suspend the briefing for an hour so that I could go and see the project in the flesh. For the most part, the item in question was indeed what my staff claimed it was. But I can tell you that the moment I started doing that, word got out very quickly that I was not going to be the sort of minister who just sits in the office all day. Furthermore, I was fortunate that the FCT was a ministry whose geographical scope is limited to not more than three hours' drive to any location. The federal ministry of works, to take one example, has projects underway all over the country, so a similar insistence on physical evidence of every ongoing project is not always feasible.

Regardless of what lengths I went to set an immediate tone, however, certain games that civil servants played during those initial days, I am convinced, are just part of the fabric of the office. The very first thing they tried to scare me with was an apparently large looking number that represents the FCT ministry's 'liabilities'. All this is a sum of monies owed for projects over the entire lifetimes of each project. So for example, a 150 billion naira project that is meant to be paid in installments of 15 billion naira over each of 10 years is counted as "commitment" - the full, current liability of 150 billion naira - even though not everyone in the FCT will be on hand to see the project through to completion and even though our four-year administration would be only accountable for 50 billion naira out of it, if at all. The reason for presenting it this way is to scare the new minister into not looking at the details, and to conclude that it was hopeless to even try solving all these problems. The subliminal message - just take care of yourself with what is available and let life continue!

After listening to the initial briefings with my personal staff, I decided to visit former FCT ministers who I thought did well in office, mainly to ask what they wished they had done but could not, or what they would have done differently. In addition, I requested the president's permission to set up an honorary ministerial advisory committee. This committee met every two or three months to look at our policy directions, brainstorm new initiatives, and advise us accordingly. I did not attend their meetings but my chief of staff was the secretary and briefed me regularly. Periodic town hall meetings and frequent dinners with business leaders and FCT staff[52] from various sectors and departments respectively also helped inform our priorities and planning.

This is not to say that I did not already have some semblance of a plan before arriving at the FCT, quite the contrary. My point is simply that anyone expecting to step into a ministerial role should be prepared to be flexible, always question everything and make sure there are people in very close proximity who are not afraid to speak the truth to him. Anyone who steps into the role that truly does not care will find a system that will make it easy to perpetuate an environment of zero achievement. The system is designed to keep the minister desk-bound: there are more than 100 visitors and 200 phone calls a day, in addition to four to five daily meetings with various departments, summons to the presidential villa, seeing other ministers and what not. The whole week would be filled with routine activities with little time to think or plan and in any event one will be told that this should be what civil servants take care of. There are lots of memos for anything and everything, and unless one puts in the hours and figures out a management system, the likelihood of remaining desk-bound, achieving very little, approving travel and petty cash advances becomes very high. It is a completely debilitating structure and a minister can quite easily pass four years doing nothing more than going to banquets and dinners in the evenings and sitting all day for 7 days weekly, at a desk reading files, and approving a thousand requests for expenditures of N50,000. You would think you are busy working, but doing nothing really productive!

'Protocol issues' can also hamper one's effectiveness. One of my first decisions was to visit the Chief Judge of the FCT, Justice Lawal Hassan Gummi, also a Barewa old boy, to brief him and the FCT judiciary on our planned reforms. My goal was to ensure that the judiciary was fully on-board with our reform directions, guide us on the limits of our actions from time to time and hopefully minimise situations in which *ex parte* injunctions would be issued by FCT judges to slow down the needed restoration of the Abuja master plan. My staff agreed on the need for the briefing, but suggested that protocol demanded that the CJ and his team should be invited for the briefing. I considered the recommendation in my mind and decided to over-rule them on several grounds, but announced only one – the CJ was by far my Barewa senior, and our old boys' protocol trumped all others they may have in the FCT. So I visited Justice Gummi, met with his team of senior judges, laid out our reform programme and prayed for their support. The FCT judiciary supported us strongly throughout my tenure. We also decided to budget an annual grant to support our judiciary to procure court recording and automation equipment. We encouraged land disputants in FCT to utilise the Abuja alternative dispute resolution courthouse, the Multi-Door Court House, which was initiated by the CJ with the support of the Chief Justice of Nigeria, Mohammed Lawal Uwais.

To manage an inevitably heavy schedule, I asked my personal assistant, Peter Akagu-Jones, two special assistants Abdu Mukhtar and Aishetu Kolo, as well as my confidential secretary, Hadiza Cole, to file incoming memos into three different categories – routine, ambiguous but required reading, and serious. The routine items, things that simply required my signature, such as signing certificates of occupancy or minuting to another department head for advice or action - constituted about 60-70 percent of all the correspondence I received. I very quickly got into the habit of carrying with me everywhere I went the memos and documents dealing with such routine matters. As long as I could get those out quickly, I would have more time for the other more important issues. Once that system was in place, things went pretty much like clockwork. We had weekly Monday night meetings in my house with aides to go through a constantly evolving task list to keep all focused on what was really important.

Establishing the working environment of the FCT

Getting down to the nuts and bolts of FCT issues, a number of matters required attention as we got our administration up and going. Some of them were relatively quick fixes that were simply a matter of everyone rolling up their sleeves and getting to work. Others were deeper and more structural in nature, requiring significantly more groundwork to be done. I came into the job with some kind of unpredictable 'mad man' reputation, which gave me a rather large space within which to manoeuvre. Also in my favour was that I think everyone, including FCT staff, understood that I could get the president to support anything I wanted to do in the course of getting the job done.

The most immediate issue was that the FCT administration was overstaffed – about 26,000 employees – and most of the people were doing nothing. In fact, some staff had been employed for one or two years and did not even have a desk. For example, in an office for five staff, there would only be one table and one chair, so they would each come to work one day a week. I could have immediately disengaged some of the staff if I wanted to, but I did not. I took my time to work with them and only picked on a few bad eggs. When they were ultimately fired about a year later, the bulk of the staff understood that it was not a case of intimidation or victimisation. Among those remaining, many got promoted, went on career development programmes and they were also proud of what they were doing. More importantly none of my staff ever suffered for disagreeing with me or was punished for questioning me publicly or privately. I encouraged them to vigorously argue and disagree and give their own points of view. If their points of view were superior in logic, we accepted them and moved on. Whenever any of our staff over the course of doing their job got into trouble, I stood by them. Our staff knew that if they demolished the house of the ruling party chairman, nothing would happen to them because I would say I gave the order and would take full responsibility for what happened. I think that helped in getting staff committed to the same vision we had.

Equally as important was that we made a point to always provide the resources for a job we needed to get done. We would first make sure we were all clear on how much it costs, and since we knew there would inevitably be a bit of padding, we would try to reduce it as much as we could and then authorise that the money be made available. I was not the sort to strong-arm my friends, preferred contractors or subcontractors into any jobs – I never, throughout my years as Minister of Abuja, asked any of the heads of department to award a contract to any particular person or company because we were more interested in results, and definitely, we were not driven by patronage. It helped that I was not a politician as such. I did not have any constituency of followers that I had to appease. I just focused on getting the results. The staff seemed to like that because it left them free to do what they wanted as long as they delivered the results. In the process, someone may have been skimming a little bit of money, but we have no evidence of that, nor did we encourage it, and in any event that is something that can never be completely eliminated in any system. At the end of it, we got results.

In retrospect, there are people who seem to think I was some sort of magician, but I was far from it, and not alone. We had a good team, clever people and we encouraged them to express themselves, while holding them accountable for measurable outcomes. I was not personally interested in any contract or programmes, ensured resources were made available, and would take no excuses for failure. There were very few failures.

One protocol I did away with, and which took people in the FCT time to get used to, was the civil service tradition that demanded that the most senior person in a meeting always does the talking. The "desk officer" - usually an entry level officer, the one who does most of the writing and researching, was not allowed to talk but must write down comments and questions and pass them to the most senior officer. I broke that tradition the first time we convened a meeting because I wanted to hear from the person who had the closest look at the issue at hand. There was a junior level staffer sitting at the end of the table quietly, so I called on him.

"You – what is your name?"

"Ikechukwu, sir"

"What do you do in the department?"

"I am the desk officer sir."

"Give me your views."

He looked at the director. I said, "Do not look at him, I want your own views. Talk to me."

After I did that a few more times, even the departmental directors realised that when they came to meetings with those young officers, I wanted to listen to their views, because I knew they were the ones who wrote the memos. The directors just edit, initial or sign them, and pass them upwards. The result was that many of the young guys became much more confident, knew they had access to the minister and that helped raise morale all around. The directors were unhappy about it at the beginning, but they got used to it because they realised that I was not trying to undermine them, I just wanted to get every side of the story and I encouraged people to disagree with me. In the beginning, the very few who were bold enough to disagree with me thought they would be redeployed or not have a job the next day, because that was generally what tended to happen to people who openly disagreed with ministers. What those dissenters soon found was that I was bringing them closer. The more anyone reasonably disagreed with me, the more they spoke their minds objectively and intelligently, even if I disagreed, the closer I brought them and supported them. When someone is in a leadership position, the scarcest commodity available is hearing the truth, so when someone is bold or confident enough to speak the truth, that person is the one I treasured, and would engage and encourage. I consciously and deliberately did a lot of that. Most people, not just in the Nigerian civil service but in general, do not have the self-confidence to tolerate disagreement or dissent by subordinates. This is the price the leader pays in the constant search for the truth.

In taking charge of Abuja, our very first big move was to computerise the land registry. The land administration situation was really dire; we had no choice but to suspend any new land grants or transfers while we undertook electronic conversion. This meant nothing was going to happen on this front for about nine months, a measure that both the president and vice-president approved. I was still prepared to approve land grants for some commercial and public buildings because those must continue, but residential land, which constituted a majority of the land allocation, simply had to be reorganised, cleaned up and digitised. This was a major policy step that subsequently became a model for many states, and it bears spending a few moments exploring it.

The Price of Lawlessness

The restoration Obasanjo wanted me to focus on arose due to the physical distortions in Abuja – the violations of the city's master plan. Abuja's plan was prepared by International Planning Associates (IPA), a Virginia-based consortium of architects and planners. The central area of the city was designed by the prominent Japanese architect Kenzo Tange, a winner of the Pritzker Prize and one of the greatest architects of the 20th century.[53]

Everything was well thought out and properly designed. In the process of developing the city, however, the 'Nigerian factor', if you like, emerged, namely, that rules are made to be bent, or even oftener, broken.

Addressing these problems necessarily meant hurting people – removing illegally erected buildings that threatened public safety, firing people who should not have been employed to start with, though they had dependents and it was hardly their fault that they got jobs. Fixing these problems also meant coming up with cash to compensate people for mistakes made that in some cases were not their fault. For example, there were distortions of the master plan such that a residential building was put up in a location meant for an office building. It is not impossible to change the land use on the title, but what happens when a huge residential mansion is built by a very important man – Dr Amadu Ali, the chairman of the ruling party, in one case – but that building sat on a main water supply line. The risk of that building settling and blocking the water supply to the whole Asokoro District of the city was real. Is it really sensible to wait and take the one in twenty-five chance that a blockage of the water supply happens in the next 25 years, just because a very important man illegally built a house there?

Furthermore, what if that man did not really know he was building on a water line? What if he was properly allocated that land, by erring officials who should have known there was a pipeline underneath, and he innocently built his house? It means that the homeowner would need to be compensated with another plot of land and cash, if we, the FCT authorities, took his house down. All these costs added up and the money had to come from somewhere. The debate surrounding these issues and the implementation of the solutions of course caused a lot of pain and heated criticism. The biggest problems I had were not so much with ordinary people whose huts and houses we took down, but with important people who felt affronted that we had the audacity to do what we were doing. It did not matter that we were doing the right thing, nor did it matter to them that they could have been wrong. It was just disrespectful, an affront, for us to do what we did. But we had to do it. We did it, and in this regard, I have no regrets whatsoever.

Now here is an especially tricky one: what if the federal government itself is violating the master plan and building codes? Specifically, what if the Federal Ministry of Works has a building precisely on the spot where, according to the master plan, the right of way of an interchange is supposed to be? Of course, the ministry said it would not be possible to demolish their building and that we simply would have to reduce the curvature or direction of the interchange. The contractor handling the project, Julius Berger and the FCDA engineers had even designed a compromise that would reduce the curvature and avoid taking the building down. The problem was that the reduced curvature would make the interchange gradient a little bit steeper and more dangerous to negotiate when driving. This is likely to cause fatalities from accidents during the life of the interchange, but the officials cared less about that. It was my call as minister to approve the redesign as it would amount to an amendment of the master plan. Of course, I disagreed with their "solution" – and insisted that the federal building had to go. If I ordered the demolition of a building of a private individual because that individual had violated the law, how could the government or any of its departments walk away scot-free? I believe strongly that individual citizens have more rights than government departments. Predictably, that minister initially resisted, and some of the officials, including one close to me, even stopped talking to me for some time after we removed the building.

In the end, the minister, Adeseye Ogunlewe, saw the point and practically forced his officials to relocate in time for us to do what was needed. Taking down one of the buildings housing the Ministry of Works went a long way toward establishing our street credibility because it showed that the federal government was even willing to accept similar punishment meted out to citizens for any violations of the Abuja master plan. Obasanjo kept his promise – he gave me a lot of support to do the job. He wanted the job done; he knew it was difficult, he knew it was tough. All I extracted from him was that he backed me up 100 percent, and he did. In this respect, he never once let me down. Not once.

Over the course of four years, we took down more than 900 buildings, not the thousands that the Senate Committee hearings falsely alleged, most of them sitting on utility lines. Situations where the only offence was a simple land use violation, that is, a different type of building was built there than was meant to be built there, we just left alone but imposed land use violation charges, payable annually. Of utmost importance was removing buildings that posed a threat to public safety. If a building was on a water line, a sewer line or under high tension electrical lines, or on the right of way of the future Abuja rail line, we had to take it down, and most of those affected were really important people because it was mostly the political and economic elite that had houses in the centre of Abuja.

There were people who thought I was on a power trip of some sort, that I enjoyed what we had to do – in fact, quite the opposite. What ended up happening was that the poorest were the worst hit, and I cannot overstate the difficulty of knowing that what I was doing was the right thing to do while also knowing that those at the receiving end were suffering and would not understand. Furthermore, in a society where people are used to getting away with every violation of rules, the notion of someone coming along and saying, 'you were wrong, this is why I am doing this' was very alien.

By law, the only way we could provide compensation to anyone losing a building was if the person had a clear title to the land and government-approved building plans before the building started. Anyone who did not have these two items got zero. The result was that we paid billions of naira in compensation over four years because many of the buildings we took down belonged to people who had proper title and approval to build, so the error was on the part of the authorities at the time. As it happened, though, most of the buildings in the low income areas were just illegal structures that resulted from someone seeing a piece of space that nobody seemed to own and essentially squatting – and these people, regardless of income level, were not entitled to any compensation.

Unfortunately, while it is true that ignorance of the law is no defence, most of these people truly did not know they were in the wrong. In a culture of lawlessness, breaking the law had come to seem normal, even legal, making this part of the process particularly painful to execute. Many of the squatters came from rural communities where the notion of ownership of property via title is nonexistent – the village head just says this belongs to so-and-so now take it and build. When people like that see a piece of land in Abuja, they see nothing wrong in doing a deal with the local chief, particularly if nobody tells them not to. But Abuja is different. Every square millimetre of land in FCT is vested absolutely by the Constitution in the Federal Government to the exclusion of everyone else, so those land deals with local chiefs were all violations of the law and could not be upheld.

Another thing that made the demolitions painful was the knowledge that the home is invariably a family's biggest, and often the only, real asset, so approving the demolition of these buildings, illegal though they were, was a heavy burden for me. I have no regrets though. No society makes progress without rules, and if rules are violated, there ought to be consequences. Secondly, the fact that most of the buildings we took down in the centre of Abuja belonged to the affluent meant that I would have to face retribution sometime – I knew this. But my faith in God tells me that at the end of the day, God is my ultimate protector and I just did what was right. I knew for a fact that many influential people tried to put pressure on President Obasanjo to restrain or even fire me, claiming that I was causing him political problems, making him unpopular, but that did not work. Others claimed I was not for real, that I was simply punishing those that were not my friends or enemies of Obasanjo. President Obasanjo asked for the evidence and he quietly got the security and law enforcement agencies to investigate me. I was investigated at least five times on his instructions during my nearly four years as Minister of Abuja.

Needless to say, the reports he always got were that there was nothing personally-motivated, illegal or untoward on my behalf. He shared the findings with me only after the investigations.

Next on the hit list were 70 mosques and about 300 churches. Mind you, many of these were not real buildings as such, but situations in which a Muslim or Christian cleric saw a piece of land reserved for, say, a park. This person assumes the piece of land is available; they put up a tent and begin a church service or prayers there that before long become a daily event. After a while of not being bothered by anyone, they then begin laying bricks around it and if still nobody speaks to them, they then roof it and bingo, you have an illegal structure – but a very religious one. And because in Nigeria we are squeamish about religion, nobody touched illegal mosques or illegal churches until I came along and removed all of them.

On receipt of the list of the illegal religious buildings, I called a meeting with the religious leaders and shared the data with them. I informed them that, according to our records, there were many illegal mosques and churches in Abuja. The Muslims were represented at various times by either Justice Murtala Orire or Bashir Sambo on behalf of the Jama'atu Nasril Islam, while Bishop Ola Makinde of the Methodist Church and Reverend William Okoye led the team representing the Christian Association of Nigeria. In a meeting held on 19th November, 2003, we discussed the allocation of plots for religious institutions, recovery of plots that had been wrongly converted to other land uses, the demolition of illegal places of worship, the HIV/AIDS pandemic in FCT, and completion and rehabilitation of the national Cathedral and Mosque respectively. Another follow-up meeting took place on 9th December, 2003 on the same subjects. Not surprisingly, they did not think any church or mosque building should be designated as illegal. They asked us to explain what was meant by an 'illegal' mosque or church.

> "'Illegal' means no FCT agency gave the occupant the land, nobody granted approval to build. Either of those omissions makes the building illegal," I said.

> "But these are God's buildings"

"No, they are not. Anyone can make that claim on His behalf. God put me in charge here to make the city to work for everyone – that there should be rules and some orderliness. So please do not mention God as justification for violating the rules and regulations. The fact is this: in my religion (Islam) and in Christianity, we have all been enjoined to comply with rules and obey constituted authority. The FCT ministry which I head is the constituted authority around here. If you know anyone other than that, please tell me."

They agreed that FCDA represented the symbol of authority in the FCT administration, so I said, "Fine. Go and tell your members to remove those buildings within four weeks or we will remove them without further notice." We also agreed clear guidelines on allocation of plots for places of worship, the pre-screening of applications first by the religious bodies, and completion of the National Cathedral as well as the rehabilitation of the National Mosque. I briefed the president regularly on all the discussions and suggested next steps.[54]

We always had robust discussions in our meetings with religious leaders, quoting both the Quran and the Bible, and in the end the religious leaders agreed to support our reforms. They also agreed to preach and propagate in support of HIV/AIDS control programmes. The support and understanding of Bishop Peter Akinola of the Anglican Communion, Archbishop Onaiyekan of the Catholic Church, Bishop Ola Makinde of the Methodist Church, and Reverend William Okoye on the CAN side were invaluable at all times in these regards. On the Muslim side, Justice Bashir Sambo, Justice Murtala Orire, Sheikh Ahmed Lemu, Adamu Adamu, Sheikh Musa Mohammed, Akilu Idris, Alhaji Muhammad Mairami and Professor Ibrahim Mukoshy were extremely helpful in resolving many issues and supporting the FCT administration through difficult reform challenges. I will always be grateful to them all.

Most of these illegal churches were not put up by the orthodox denominations. We found that no Catholic, Anglican, Baptist or Methodist churches operated in this fashion, but rather it is this new generation of pentecostal churches that in the opinion of many

Nigerians are mostly 'faith scams,', basically business enterprises selling salvation on this earth without paying taxes, that were prevalent in perpetrating the illegalities. The illegal mosques were mostly attached to residences, offices and markets, put up without approved building plans. So we began removing them. Some mosques in particular consistently condemned me and prayed for my downfall. One or two declared me an apostate for daring to demolish a mosque, conveniently forgetting that Prophet Muhammad himself ordered the demolition of an illegal mosque in Madina Al-Munawwarah, some 1,400 years earlier.

Many of the affected 'churches' prayed that "by God's grace, El-Rufai will go down, El-Rufai will lose his job, El-Rufai will die in Jesus' name." I was there for nearly four years and we removed all of them. Some religious leaders rose to my defence even earlier than others. I was particularly touched when I learnt that one of Abuja's leading churches, Family Worship Centre, led by Pastor Sarah Omakwu, preached in defence of what we were doing in Abuja. Many of her parishioners affected by our demolitions left the church in protest and anger, but she remained resolute and persisted. I had not met her then, but subsequently visited her church to express gratitude for its support. I remain grateful to Pastor Sarah for her courage and early vote of confidence, and that coming from an influential leader of the Christian community was an important validation for our policies.

By the time I had spent two years in the FCT, I had become this mythical character who many people apparently believed had supernatural powers. How could all of these churches and mosques be praying for my downfall and nothing happens? Voodoo did not work on the man, praying against him did not seem to work either. All kinds of stories were going around that I had terminal cancer, and even AIDS – I remember one newspaper even published a cartoon of me, allegedly sponsored by the campaign organisation of one of Obasanjo's prospective successors to the presidency, depicting me as being very thin and dying of AIDS. The attacks never relented, and the anger never subsided.

The Tortoise in My Office

Without a doubt the funniest rumour that went around began when I came to my office one day and found something that looked like a small tortoise on my seat. This was supposed to be some voodoo curse meant to scare me. I do not know how it got there; I just removed it, settled down and started working on the files on the desk. The very next day, one Nigeria' newspaper, the *Daily Times*, had a story about how I came into my office, saw a tortoise, collapsed, and had been flown out abroad in a coma. The *Daily Times* has since gone out of print, but it was the oldest newspaper in Nigeria and this was its back page story.[55] I could not stop laughing.

When I arrived at the office the next morning, many people called inquiring about my condition. "You're supposed to be abroad!" they said. I assured them it is a complete lie. Just to keep things simple I did not even want to tell them that I saw the tortoise in my office. The curious thing is that the story was filed by the newspaper's FCT correspondent, so I invited him to drop by.

> "My friend, I am supposed to be on sick leave," I said.
>
> "I am sorry sir," he said.
>
> "Ok, but you filed the story. What was your source? Who commissioned you to write this fiction? Somebody that had something to do with this tortoise in the office thought that what would happen would be my going into a coma on seeing the tortoise. You wrote what you heard and sent it to Lagos, without cross-checking. Even when my media aides denied the story, you chose to ignore them."
>
> "Well sir, this was what I heard."
>
> "Heard from whom? Who told you?"

He would not talk. My CSO wanted him arrested and interrogated, but I did not see any sense in that. How can writing a false story amount to a crime? On what grounds would the reporter be detained without an offence disclosed? Instead, the Press Secretary, Kingsley Agha, wrote the *Daily Times* and asked that the reporter be withdrawn from covering the MFCT due to professional misconduct. He was redeployed elsewhere and the paper published a prominent retraction the next day. Access to my office was thereafter tightened by CSO Widi Liman, who thought that the secretary and cleaners must have had something to do with 'the security breach'. It was all amusing to me. I encouraged Widi to do his job, but made no personnel changes in the office. A friend then gave me a ceramic model of a tortoise which I kept on my desk throughout my time in FCT, as a reminder of the incident!

The rumours of ill-health, discovery of strange creatures in the office and attacks on the pages of newspapers did not affect our focus on the assignment to clean up the FCT. The removal of illegal structures of all kinds and descriptions was what dominated the media, but the challenges of dealing with the unintended consequences of these actions occupied our team throughout those early months. We had figured out how to handle the resettlement of the original inhabitants and other displaced residents of Abuja amidst scarcity of financial resources and time. This need to maintain momentum on all fronts remained paramount in my mind as we pursued the assignment with vigour.

Squatter Relocation as Safety Nets

Of course, I completely understood the anger of people on land-related issues. Aside from the 900-plus buildings we demolished, we probably took down twice as many shanty structures, which could not really be called buildings as some were nothing more than temporary accommodation on the outskirts of the city. Toward the end of my term, we modified the resettlement policy (applicable to the original inhabitants of Abuja) to include the "relocation" of squatters and other illegal occupants of land. This enabled displaced people to be entitled to alternative land within the FCT regardless of whether or not they had title.

The reason for this was largely because we realised there were so many people without title who had been made homeless, so we had to find a way to give them preferential allocation of alternative land, even though they were not entitled to it as a right. We even built low income housing in Pegi in Kuje Area Council, which we did not consider in the beginning because we initially viewed the squatters as strictly legal violations, rather than a social problem. To be honest, this was one of the few things I think we really could have done a better job on – starting the relocation and social housing programmes much earlier in our tenure.

Our initial focus on the mandate to clean up Abuja city, make it more orderly and pristine, led to an unintended consequence – we did not invest early enough in satellite towns. Abuja was designed to be an administrative centre, with low and middle income satellite towns around it. Not a lot of effort was put into developing the satellite towns at the beginning because a lot of the committed investment was concentrated in the city itself, which was mostly empty until about 1996. Even though we worked on the infrastructure for six satellite towns, I now realise we started too late and it was not enough. If we had made the satellite towns more affordable, serviced land there more available and connected them with affordable transportation infrastructure, the cost of living in Abuja would have dropped even more drastically than it did while I was running the FCT. If I had the chance to do this again, I would start investing in satellite town infrastructure and the build-out of a metro system from day one, rather than putting a lot of the resources toward trying to make the city centre and its network of roads and bridges to work better first. Alas, rarely are all facts known at the beginning of a project's undertaking.

Restoration of Wuse Market: 'It's Impossible, Hon. Minister'

If tearing down one of the buildings of the federal ministry of works was the beginning of earning street credibility with the people of the FCT, the turning point was undoubtedly the restoration of Wuse Market, the oldest market in Abuja. Wuse market was another of the early distortions of the Abuja master plan – its location was earmarked for a school, but a traditional market emerged instead. Wuse Market was originally designed to have some 1,800 shops, but over time, by continuous additions of illegal structures and shops, there were more than 13,000 shops. The car park had been converted to shops with the acquiescence of successive ministers and FCDA staff. All the walkways that were meant for people to enter and exit the shopping areas freely and securely had become shops. The situation had quite simply become as chaotic as might be expected of something that multiplies from nearly 1,800 to over 13,000.

When we first inspected Wuse Market and compared it to what was originally planned, our biggest concern, which became a nightmare, was that in the event of a fire, everything in the market would be destroyed. No fire vehicle could get in because there was no access. No one would be able to get out or take out anything and it would just be a major disaster. We discussed the options available with my staff and the line directors in the FCDA. What many of the directors advised was to leave things as they were, build more markets and de-congest the Wuse market gradually.

This was understandable since I was aware that some of them owned many of the illegal shops. In my view this was a "do-nothing" solution, and is a typical civil servants approach to any serious problem – protect their interest first. I had another "inner circle" session with some of my closest colleagues, including Idris Othman, Isa Shuaibu and Hadiza Abdullahi, and agreed an alternative course of action, to restore the market to its original design. To lay the basis for this, I convened a meeting with the market men and women and the shopkeepers' associations. I outlined the level of distortions, the dangers inherent, and concluded that something had to be done.

> "Ladies and Gentlemen, this situation in Wuse market cannot continue," I said.
>
> "Well what do we do then?"
>
> "We will relocate some of you," I said. "We will start work on building more markets so that some can move, but we have to restore Wuse Market back to what it was originally."
>
> "It is impossible to go back to that, honourable Minister."

'Impossible' – I learned to love hearing this word. I remembered what one Nobel Laureate said - "impossible only takes a little longer," and smiled at the shopkeepers because I knew we were going to do it anyway. Through an open bid process, we got four private companies to build four markets contracted on Build-Own-Operate-Transfer basis.[56] We did not pay them a penny; we just gave them the land and a 60-year lease with the understanding that on expiration, the land and buildings would revert to the FCTA. We also invested public funds to expand two more markets then under construction in Gudu and Garki II, making a total of six markets that will be able to absorb these 13,000 shops and more on completion. Once that process was under way, we began planning the clean-up of Wuse Market. The first market in Gudu was ready and we put up the shops for sale. The shopkeepers in Wuse were reluctant to move. "This is the market that our customers know," was the common refrain.

> "Have you heard of advertising?" I asked. "Just tell your customers that you are moving from point A to point B."
>
> "No, no, we are not moving from here."

Now, had I been asking a question, as in, 'will you please move from here?' saying 'no, no, we are not moving from here' would have been a perfectly legitimate response. Unfortunately for them, we had given them all the required notices under the law and we were not asking a question, but making a statement: "You have three weeks from today to move. By midnight, three weeks from today, we will start removing every illegal addition - whether shop and structure in Wuse Market and we will shut down the market for about three weeks."

They did not believe us. Until then, something like this – some official saying that a government department was going to do something difficult and then actually doing it when people were resisting, arguing, fighting or running to a general, a senator or president, or whatever – this was simply not done. Nevertheless, midnight arrived and we started. In the end, it took us five weeks but we cleaned up Wuse Market and got it back to what it was originally. Nobody in Abuja could believe it. The original shopkeepers became our biggest advocates because now they had proper shops, with no other businesses blocking them and an open customer thoroughfare.

Furthermore, the market became clean, organised and a pleasure to visit and shop at. That was when I first began to get any commendation from the people of Abuja. Before then, shopping in Wuse Market was hell on earth, because shoppers had to constantly squeeze between people just to pay for something and pickpockets ran rampant. Driving and parking became easier too – possible, actually. It was impossible before because of the sprawl of the shops, so parking took place a kilometre or so away.

The overwhelming response to the restoration of Wuse Market was positive. The demolition exercise, while more vital to the safety and functioning of the city, did not intuitively make sense to a lot of people and I recognised that. It took us another two years before we were able to restore some of the parks though. When we started recovering parks in Abuja, everybody said I was crazy, that Nigerians were too busy trying to earn a living to go to parks, or that Nigerians were too poor to care about going to parks or engage in any family relaxation in such parks. But we recovered the parks, planted grass, flowers and trees, and got wireless Internet hotspots[57] installed. And guess what happened?

Once the parks were commissioned, the citizens of Abuja trooped there in large numbers. The parks were full all the time. Many people could not believe it. Yet some people kept telling us then that Nigerians were too busy to go to parks! One of the parks, Millennium Park, the largest park in the city, gets so busy on Saturdays and Sundays that a traffic jam around it develops in the mornings and evenings as people arrive and leave.

With the demolitions, the restoration of Wuse Market and the parks behind us, cleaning the streets of unsafe motorcycle taxis - the ubiquitous *okada* was a piece of cake. This just had to be dealt with, because having motorcycle taxis carrying multiple passengers, unlicensed, unregulated, was just reckless and dangerous no matter which way you looked at it.[58] Furthermore, by the time I approved the proposal to ban them, they had become tools of bag snatchers and armed robbers. They were operating illegally anyway, in violation of the Road Traffic Act 1961, but had done so because nobody had been in charge of transportation regulation in Abuja. More disturbing were reports from the police and hospitals, indicating that a large proportion of fatal accidents were *okada*-related. I began consultations on how and when to ban them.

I distinctly remember the chairman of the ruling party in FCT telling me we could not ban them. Even my politically-savvy friend, Bashir Yusuf Ibrahim, thought that such a decision would not only fail but amounted to political suicide. When I asked the FCT PDP chieftain why not, his meek response was simply that the motorcycle taxi association – the okada association – was the most powerful political force in Abuja and we needed them for a variety of events around the city. In short, they had the capacity to make the city ungovernable. I retorted that there was no way anybody would make Abuja ungovernable under my watch. For me though, the overriding consideration was to reduce fatalities on our roads connected with the reckless behaviour of the okada riders.

Before we set the deadline for the okada ban, we put in place three bus concessions, concluded the deal to construct the Abuja Metro System and introduced the Abuja Green Cabs scheme. Then we announced three months in advance that on the first of October, 2006, we were giving the people of Abuja an independence anniversary present: there will be no more okada in the city of Abuja. From the day we made that announcement, huge trailers started moving motorcycles out of Abuja. In the final three days, it was a scramble, most okada left town.. Of course, we were ready, we had the police, the VIOs, Road Safety officers and traffic cops ready; we had everyone standing by on the first of October and in the first week we seized about 600 motorcycles that violated the ban. By the end of December 2006 we had seized 5,000 motorcycles. They never stopped trying, but the bulk of the okada riders, over 80 percent, left the city. The direct result of this was that fatal accidents associated with motorcycles decreased from the rate of 140 per month in September 2006 to just 14 in October 2006, – a 90 percent drop.

There is an old saying that imitation is the sincerest form of flattery. Well, since we left office, at least nine other states in Nigeria have copied what we did with the okada ban, with varying degrees of effectiveness. Even Lagos, ground zero for *okada* drivers, has announced that it is banning them from plying major roads.

Keeping the Capital Safe

Our aggressive first steps, as any mayor in the world would tell you, would have been impossible without the cooperation of the police. How does one get the Nigeria Police Force to cooperate in Abuja, and indeed anywhere else? Honestly, a lot of it comes back to certain core principles of leadership.

Specifically, I believe a large percentage of leadership effectiveness is signalling. When a leader is appointed or emerges atop any organisation – that organisation could be a club or a country – the leader's subordinates are looking to see what signals the leader sends that define the sort of person he or she is; the limits of the leader's will; and the leader's boundaries and power. Does the leader have the will to do what he or she promises to do? If the leader does something politically risky, will the political master or masters support his position or sacrifice the leader? Subordinates will be watching out for these things in the first few days or weeks or months on the job.

In our case, as I mentioned before, I came to the FCT with a lot of credit in the sense that I had already made a name in the BPE as a stubborn no-nonsense manager that is willing and able to take difficult decisions, and this is why Obasanjo sent me to the FCT. The FCT staff, whether good or bad, would start by looking closely and trying to figure out how much they could compromise me with some of the things I was not privy to while in the BPE.[59] It was a constant game of sending signals and receiving them. I also had the advantage of coming in with a reputation, for better or worse, of being a little crazy – I privatised government companies and fought openly with cabinet ministers, even though I was a level below a federal minister, and survived. Meanwhile, some of those ministers I fought with like Kema Chikwe and Ojo Maduekwe lost their jobs. When that scare factor precedes a leader's entry to a job, it tends to make people a bit apprehensive in facing him and come down a notch - then they watch how the leader takes the first steps. Coming back to the police, as any Nigerian knows instinctively, they are hardly a well-resourced and motivated force. The centrally controlled administrative structure, as opposed to its duties which are local, further complicates matters. The commissioner of police for the FCT (as with any state), was neither employed by nor subordinated to me but to the Inspector General. The police commissioner was expected to cooperate with me, but he's not directly accountable to me. He too - like others - will be searching, though, asking himself, 'Can this guy El-Rufai get the president to direct the inspector general to reassign me to a less important job? Can he influence my promotion? Can he provide resources that will enable me succeed?" If I could do any or all of these, then as far as the commissioner was concerned, I was indeed a surrogate for the president, deserving of cooperation.

Early in my ministerial tenure, a memo came to my desk requiring me to approve an eight million naira payment to the police. I asked what this was for and was told it was what the FCT ministry paid the police every month from our N600 million 'security vote' for the 2003 fiscal year. I asked to see the commissioner to ascertain why and what he needed the funds for. The commissioner came along with his deputy in charge of operations and a mutual friend of mine and Nuhu Ribadu's, Danjuma Ibrahim.

"What is this for?" I asked.

"Well you know, we moved a couple thousand mobile police officers before the 2003 elections to Abuja to enhance security and this is their relocation per diem."

"Well, send them back, elections are over. I am not approving the payment of this from next month," I said.

"Sir, I need these men to continue to maintain law and order in Abuja," he said.

I asked if he was sure the mobile police officers actually received the stipend. He said he was.

"If I call them, any of the policemen, will they confirm to me that they get the money?"

"Yes."

"Ok. What else do you need to support our work in Abuja? What are your problems and constraints?"

"I do not have vehicles."

"How many vehicles do you need?"

"Sixteen. I need sixteen cars, all our cars are old and breaking down, they are always in the garage."

So one of the first things we did was to approve his eight million naira, bought him 20 cars and many pick-ups. We also got my former employer, Motorola, to donate communications gear, and install some additional transmitters to improve police internal communications. On the police commissioner's suggestion, we commenced the design and roll-out of a phased closed circuit TV system that would cover the whole city footprint by 2010. All these were accomplished within 12 months of my reporting for duty in the FCT. As soon as these steps were concluded, we called him up for a security review meeting.

> "We have addressed all the logistics, communications and critical financial needs of the Police in FCT. Now, the Police have everything needed to ensure and enhance security in Abuja so you have to deliver without fail. Is there anything else you need?"

The response was negative, so I went on.

> "If you fail, I will go to the president and request that you be posted to another state. I hope we understand each other. Ok?"

Thus, began my relationship with the commissioner of police in Abuja. We gave him the support he needed and more, but demanded from him the results needed. We also increased the monthly allowances payable when requested, and extended the gesture to other law enforcement agencies like the SSS and even the EFCC. I chaired monthly security committee meetings to discuss routine security matters and be proactive on others. I received regular security briefings from the FCT Director of the SSS and read them carefully, noting and taking actions, and ensuring follow-up. One of the earliest incidents I recall was a security report of repeated theft of explosives from various construction company stores in FCT. This also coincided with a report from the FCT Immigration office of an observed influx of 'North African and Arab' nationals into Abuja a few months before the All-Africa

Games and the Commonwealth Heads of Government meetings within the last quarter of 2003. I convened an emergency security committee meeting to get to the bottom of it. This is an instance where "the security vote" is supposed to be used to facilitate the work of the SSS[60] agents, and also pay off the 'informants' - commercial sex workers, bartenders, hotel receptionists and the like.

Within two weeks, suspects were arrested. To our relief, we discovered these were mostly petty thieves selling explosives to other smaller construction companies and stone quarries. We approached security issues with single-minded focus because in my view, the first and most important duty of any leader is to make his community more secure.

Any time the security agencies had a problem, we took care of it because I realised that was the way the system worked. As a result, the police acted on any law enforcement request we made.

I had the misfortune of having to deal with three different commissioners of police for various reasons, and not necessarily because I wanted them moved, but because of one incident or the other or they had served out their tour of duty. In one particular case, there was a case of opposites when my friend, Danjuma Ibrahim, one of the senior policemen in te FCT, was allegedly involved in extrajudicial killings, so the commissioner of police and all the top echelon had to be removed by the inspector-general of police on the orders of the president and posted to other states. Danjuma and some of his subordinates are being prosecuted for the homicide as I write this. Apart from that, I tried my best to politically protect all the commissioners I worked with, and when one of them was going to be moved from Abuja by police headquarters, I went to the president and asked that he should not be moved. I was enjoying working with him and he was going to retire in less than a year, so why post him out and dislocate his family? Why not let him stay out his time in Abuja till he retires? The president overruled the inspector general of police and the officer remained and became one of the best commissioners of police FCT ever had.

Proud Moments

Of all the things we did during my tenure at the FCT, the four things we did that I am without a doubt proudest of came about halfway through the term. One was giving up – or as the chief of staff to the President put it at the time - 'donating' - the Dornier 228 aircraft of the Ministry of the FCT to the presidential air fleet, thereby saving at least N150 million per annum in overhead cost.

Another was the street naming and house numbering system that we implemented, enabling easier identification and location of residences and facilities and delivery of mail and goods. Abuja is till today the only city in Nigeria with such clear addressing system. The third was a freak incident. And the fourth had to do with addressing the water supply challenges in Abuja.

The 'Orphanage'

A friend of Jimi Lawal's, Ms. Sonia Chikelu, who lives in London came home to Abuja in December of 2004 for the Christmas holidays to give presents out at orphanages listed on her local church's registry, as she had done every year. As she approached one of the orphanages, she saw right in the window a child that really looked on the verge of death. The owner-manager of the orphanage was nowhere to be found and the staff on hand was not at all helpful. When she went back the next day, not only did she see more of the children, several of whom looked really on their last breaths, but when the orphanage's owner-manager finally came around, she was not at all open to receiving Christmas gifts – quite the opposite of what one might expect from someone in such a position. What we eventually discovered was that this was a private orphanage run by a woman who was in the business of collecting abandoned children and pregnant young girls who did not want their pregnancies to be made public. She would pay these young mothers, take their babies and starve the infants sufficiently so that she could use photos and videos of them in donor campaigns to get western organisations[61] and countries to give her 'aid' - free money for the running of the orphanage. She was actually making a lot of money doing this, but for her to make the case that she needed the money, she decided she had to starve the children. The more malnourished they looked, the more pity and guilt the foreigners felt, and the more money she received. She was the 'Reverend' Frances Charity Ibe.

On learning of the condition of the children, I sought permission to leave a cabinet meeting early and drove to the orphanage accompanied by a distraught Sonia Chikelu and a very angry Jimi Lawal. We immediately took three of the most malnourished children from the orphanage straight to a private hospital because FCT doctors were on strike at the time. We then ordered the Social Development secretariat to undertake a detailed investigation into the matter. We discovered that apart from the fact that this 'orphanage' was not licensed, the building was an illegal structure that had no title and no building plan approval.

Unfortunately, there was no legal framework enabling me as minister of FCT to take compulsory possession of the children for their safety. The only lawful option available was to remove the building housing the orphanage, being an illegal structure, but this may put the children under greater risk. We had to be creative - finding a legal way to protect the children, within the provisions of the Child Rights Act.

Enabling the evacuation of the children required me as Minister of FCT to acquire the powers of the Minister of Women Affairs in the FCT. Since the president was empowered to assign responsibilities to ministers at will (See section 315(2) of the Constitution and section 2(1) of the Minister's Statutory Powers and Duties (Miscellaneous Provisions) Act), I approached him with a detailed brief on the orphanage situation and proposed a solution. He took immediate action in support of the proposal of our legal department, approving subsidiary legislation[62] giving me such emergency powers within 48 hours. We, therefore, legally took control of the children and their welfare under the Child Rights Act, 2003.

Bola Onagoruwa[63] as Secretary for Social Development took charge of the situation. As a mother, she approached the situation with uncommon passion and focus. She proceeded to draft subsidiary legislation and guidelines on the establishment and management of orphanages, crèches and other childcare facilities which we enacted and published in the Federal Government Gazette. We then established a government orphanage, which the remaining 42 children were quickly moved into. We had to rent a building, fit it out and furnish it in less than two weeks. We also got a trained child psychologist to manage the orphanage and proceeded to remove the illegal orphanage from the face of the earth by its demolition. We then instructed the FCT legal department to begin immediate criminal proceedings against the Mrs. Ibe for offences under the Child Rights Act.

Clearly, if we had not come across that information and done what we did, some of those children would have died and the rest substantially damaged. Now they are all in school, thanks to Sonia's concern, Jimi's anger and Bola Onagoruwa's vigilance. We set up a system to take care of their education until they get to college, if they are able. In the Jabi Orphanage, they lived as comfortably as any middle class family with a safe place to sleep, a playground and the rest of the basics necessary for as normal a childhood as is possible.

This was not about building infrastructure or anything like that, but it deals with the vulnerable orphans and homeless children. It is for this reason that I am most proud of it. The fact that these helpless children were being exploited and we did something about it is one of the few memories I have that counterbalances all of the dark days of exile and Yar'Adua's smear campaign. When I think about those children, and that maybe one of those children might be the president of our country one day, and knowing that they would not have had that chance had we not taken the actions we did, it makes all the heartache and sleepless nights of the past 10 years worthwhile.

Water Supply

One other decision I am proud of involved finally contracting the expansion of Abuja's water treatment capacity. Abuja's population had grown so fast that we had water shortages because treatment capacity was not expanding as fast as the population was. Thus one of my most important responsibilities was to increase the potable water supply. Contracts had been awarded to pipe the water 75 kilometres from Gurara River in Kaduna State to Abuja since Abuja has no natural water source. Construction of the dam and the pipe work were nearing completion, but we had not expanded the treatment facility to deliver the water to residents. We, therefore, launched a procurement process to build a treatment facility to increase potable water delivery capacity from that of a population of 600,000 to about 2 million. While going through the tender process, a friend - Kashim Ibrahim Imam - approached me lobbying for an Israeli company called SCC to handle the water treatment contract. SCC has been in Nigeria for a while and had constructed the pipeline from Gurara to Lower Usuma Dam, among other projects.

It was both normal for the company to be interested in building the water treatment plant and not unusual in Nigeria to ask a friend to speak to another on their behalf. Furthermore, the FCDA had commissioned separately in 2002, an Israeli engineering consultant - Tahal Consultants - to undertake the engineering design of the water treatment plant and associated facilities. I told Kashim the same thing I tell everyone since my BPE years: there is very little I can do, it will be a competitive process, bid your best price, in this case the lowest possible, as we will select the lowest price bid consistent with technical compliance. As the tender process got underway, Atiku phoned me. This was early in 2005 and our relationship then was not close, but I kept a civil interaction with him in deference to his position as the vice president of the country.

"Nasir, a friend of mine needs your help."

"What can I do, sir?"

"It is about the bid for your water treatment plant project. You know Levi has been my neighbour in Lagos while I was still in the customs, we lived in the same block of flats."

"Who is Levi?"

"Oh, he is the managing director and owner of SCC."

"Oh, ok, yes, they are indeed bidding for our water treatment plant."

"Yes, that is what I wanted to talk to you about. I would really appreciate that you do whatever you can to ensure his company gets the contract because we are very good friends and during the Abacha period, our difficult times, he really was very helpful to me."

> "Ok sir, but you know this will be a competitive bid process and we have a shortlist of six or seven companies that have been pre-qualified and any one of the companies can do the job. So it just really boils down to a mix of price and completion period. You know me, sir. Please just tell them to give the

best possible price. That is the only way I can be of help."

By then, the competitive bidding and evaluation system I had designed for the FCT Administration was pretty much tamper-proof. Shortly after, Levi, the SCC CEO, came to see me at Atiku's urging. I gave him the same advice I give everyone. They were doing other work for us anyway, and they had already proven themselves as competent engineering contractors, so there was no issue about their qualification. I told him to just put out the best price they could. He thanked me for meeting him and said he would do his best. But my concerns were raised when I escorted him out of my residence to his car. He whispered that they would pay me 5% of whatever they bid. I advised him to discount his bid by the same percentage and he drove off, looking a bit perplexed.

Our initial specification was to build a 10,000 cubic metre per hour treatment plant that could be expanded to 20,000 in the near future. We received a bid from a British company called Biwater for about 8 billion naira. The Atiku-friendly company, SCC, bid about 12 billion for the same plant. A German company, Julius Berger, bid 18 billion, and other bidders' prices came in between. We opened the bids publicly, announced the prices, and referred the bid documents to the consulting engineers and an FCT review committee for evaluation. That was when the games really started.

The first thing the consulting engineers did was to disqualify the lowest bid as too low to be realistically achievable. The consultants were supposed to give the engineers' estimate which would be the basis for evaluating the bids and they came up with 14 billion as the estimate for the 10,000 cubic metres per hour plant. I suspect the two Israeli companies - SCC and Tahal –probably agreed beforehand what the consultant estimate would be so that SCC could come in just under it. I got the preliminary report disqualifying Biwater and I immediately wrote back. As a one-time consulting quantity surveyor, I knew how to do this bid evaluation stuff, and I directed that since all the bidders had been pre-qualified for technical competence, no bid could be disqualified or precluded from detailed evaluation. I instructed that the consulting engineer should just evaluate the submitted bids for technical compliance and bring them to the FCT Management

Committee. I requested to meet with the consulting engineer to justify his estimate of 14 billion naira by providing a breakdown backed by submitting fully-priced bills of quantities.

The consultant was clearly colluding with SCC and was feeding them information. When I responded to the attempted disqualification, the consultant must have informed SCC about the step I had taken and encouraged SCC to write a petition to the president that I was interfering with the 'technical evaluation process'. SCC alleged that I did not want the technical people to do their jobs and I had a pecuniary interest in the bid outcome. It did not occur to them that a bidder should not have such information. This petition they filed through Atiku to bring to President Obasanjo, which he did. Obasanjo, of course, called me.

"Minister, do you have a water project in your budget this year?"

"Yes sir."

"So, has it been awarded?"

"No, it is still being evaluated by the consulting engineers. I have not received the appraisal report yet."

Obasanjo was a little surprised.

"So you do not know how the evaluation is going?"

"I do not have anything conclusive yet."

"Ok then, take this petition." He gave me the petition. "Take it and study it, and do nothing for now. Just for information" So I took it and I glanced through and said:

"Mr. President, you know, we have a low bid of about seven to eight billion naira by a reputable company and we have a high bid of 18 billion naira. This is the range of bids we have. We have our consultant's estimate coming in between and I just want to consider everything. I do not want to declare any price as unfit. I want to consider everything."

After all, FCT was footing the bill.

"Seven billion and eighteen?" asked the president.

"Well that is the range. I just do not want the engineers disqualifying anyone and pushing the price up. I just said I wanted every bid evaluated."

"Oh – and that is why they are petitioning against you?"

"Yes sir."

"Why would they do that?"

"Mr. President, let's wait for the evaluation to be completed and I will brief you in full."

Obasanjo did not tell me who brought the petition to him, but I already knew the moment I saw it that it would be either Kashim Imam or Atiku Abubakar, as both had access to him.

> "Let us not comment until we receive the report, Mr. President. I would like to respond to this but I can't because the process is not yet done. When it is done, I will give you a comprehensive response and a background briefing because I have a feeling I know where this is coming from."

Obasanjo agreed. Shortly after, I received the bids evaluation report, which suggested that since the engineers' estimate was ₦ 14 billion and Biwater was bidding at about half that amount, the engineer did not believe Biwater could do it so cheaply, even using an alternative treatment technology, and should therefore be disqualified. The report recommended SCC for the award of the contract. I reviewed the report, looked at the detailed pricing structure and technologies offered and decided to modify the entire procurement outcome. I instructed FCDA to request the consulting engineer to direct all the bidders to submit an alternative offer for a 20,000 cubic metre per hour plant. Since we had budgeted ₦ 12 billion, and we had a bid for 10,000 at seven to eight billion naira, I thought maybe we could get 20,000m^3 per hour at or near 12 billion naira. We also requested that the bidders should include proposals for contractor financing of a portion of the project cost, just in case oil prices suddenly dropped and our short-term liquidity dried up.

A week later, the bids came back and Biwater bid to double the capacity at about 11 billion naira, with some omissions and detailed design services totalling another three billion naira. SCC had moved to something like 18 billion naira. At these price ranges, the consulting engineer could not disqualify any bids, but still submitted a report, supported by the FCDA in-house evaluation team, that SCC should be awarded the contract at a price about four billion naira higher than Biwater! For the first time since 1998, I was challenged to be a quantity surveyor all over. I personally took the bid documents and evaluation reports and wrote line by line queries, accompanied by hard, detailed questions. By the time the queries list got to the evaluation team, they realised that this minister knew the game. The final report came back recommending Biwater at the lowest bid, 14.3 billion naira, for a water treatment plant with a capacity of 20,000 cubic metres per hour that would adequately supply two million inhabitants of FCT with potable water. We got twice the capacity at a little above our initial budget with an offer of financing if we met certain conditions.

The moment I sent back my queries of the internal evaluation report, a second petition went to the president, this time, accusing me of changing the specifications, shifting the goalposts, being unprofessional, unfair and unrealistic and, most critically, that this sort of plant and the treatment technology proposed by Biwater has never been built anywhere in the world.

Obasanjo sent it to me with a cover letter this time requesting for an explanation, in writing. As it turned out, about a year earlier I had visited Malaysia and went to Kuala Lumpur for a totally different reason - to visit their Abuja-like capital under construction - Putrajaya and their technology park, Cyberjaya - but part of that trip involved inspecting the largest water treatment plant in the world at the time, more than 30 kilometres from the city, on the recommendations of our High Commission there. It was built by Biwater Malaysia, using that very same filtration technology that would be proposed for Abuja. So when Obasanjo received my response and invited me for a final, face-to-face briefing – Obasanjo studied civil engineering by the way, so he knew the technical issues pretty well – I started from the beginning, told him about Kashim and Atiku and the tendering process, all the issues and I explained all the technical issues and he understood clearly.

> "But we now have this," I said. "We can get twice the capacity we planned for the same amount we would have paid SCC, and just a little over our initial budget, Mr. President. These SCC guys just wanted to rip us off. So subject to your approval, I intend to fire the Israeli consultants because they were clearly

not working for us, they were working for SCC. I propose to appoint the French engineering consultant supervising the construction of the Gurara dam to supervise the water treatment contract."

Obasanjo understood and agreed to all of it, approving my recommendations a week later which were then subsequently ratified by the Federal Executive Council. We announced the award of the contract to Biwater on 14th July, 2005 and works started on 5th of August, 2005. The contract was due for completion by August 2007. It was at that point that Obasanjo said, "Do you know who was bringing me those petitions?"
"Either Kashim Imam or VP, sir."
"Yes, it was Atiku."

I was incensed. On my way home that night, I kept thinking and wondering why Atiku did these nasty things to me. Right from my days in the BPE, he had actively undermined me and accused me of inappropriate behaviour simply to get contracts for his friends – Ericsson in BPE and now SCC in the FCTA. What I was angry about was the ease with which he fabricated fiction and falsehood against me once I refuse to violate procurement rules and regulations. What wrong had I done him?
It was at this point that I decided that I have had enough of Atiku's games at my expense, starting from the NITEL GSM tender while I was in BPE. I vowed that, henceforth, I would fight his smear attempts aggressively. But I did not need to, as it turned out. Atiku's comeuppance hardly needed my involvement.

Obasanjo, Atiku and the PTDF saga

Perhaps the falling out between Obasanjo and Atiku became public knowledge in September 2006 when what came to be known as the Petroleum Technology Development Fund (PTDF) saga dominated media headlines. The whole affair started innocuously when the FBI raided the home of US Congressman William Jefferson, in May 2006, and found $100,000 cash stashed in a freezer, plus certain documents pointing to some business deals in Nigeria.

Under the terms of a mutual legal assistance treaty subsisting between the governments of the USA and Nigeria, the US Department of Justice requested the EFCC to assist the US Attorney's Office and the FBI's on-going bribery investigation of the Congressman.

The FBI specifically requested the EFCC to locate and provide documents and information on some government officials and institutions, private companies and individuals in relation to the activities of the congressman in promoting US business ventures in Nigeria. The joint ventures between some Nigerian and US companies were specifically mentioned in the request: I-Gate/NDTV and I-Gate/Rosecom technology ventures in Nigeria, among others. The request for information revolved around 31 individuals and companies, including, most prominently, Vice President Atiku Abubakar and Obasanjo-Atiku confidante, Otunba Oyewole Fashawe.

In compliance with the request, the EFCC undertook the investigation and interviewed as many of the named persons and companies as possible. In the course of its assignment, the EFCC then stumbled upon likely violations of Nigerian laws relating particularly to alleged conspiracy, fraudulent conversion of funds, corrupt practices and money laundering by some Nigerian public officers and other persons. The relevant information was provided to the US authorities and a comprehensive report submitted to President Obasanjo.

The EFCC report, dated 24th August 2006, identified several persons who may have violated various laws. Obasanjo therefore decided to establish an Administrative Panel of Inquiry to review the EFCC report and make recommendations for the Federal Executive Council to decide on next steps. The panel was chaired by the Attorney-General of the Federation and Minister of Justice, Chief Bayo Ojo, with me, Otunba Bamidele Dada, Minister of State – Agriculture, Major-General Abdullahi Sarki Mukhtar (Rtd) – National Security Adviser, and Oby Ezekwesili, Minister of Education as members. The panel's secretariat and meeting venues were the NSA's secure offices and facilities.

We were empowered to interview anyone concerned if necessary and request for more information from any quarter to enable the discharge of the administrative nature of its mandate. In this regard, Obasanjo voluntarily provided hitherto classified copies of correspondence exchanged between himself and Congressman William Jefferson to assist the panel. The panel was given one week to submit its report, but this was extended to allow time to undertake a thorough review of the Report and other supporting documents as well as meet with key individuals. We re-invited several of the people mentioned in the EFCC report and visited Atiku in his office to ask questions that may exonerate him and others associated with him, of the indictments in the EFCC report which have been extensively documented in the ensuing media war between Obasanjo and Atiku, culminating in public hearings by an Ad-Hoc Senate Committee and litigation up to the Supreme Court of Nigeria. I will focus on what we essentially found in the course of our panel's assignment.

The PTDF was established in 1973, for the sole objective of building capacity in the petroleum industry through manpower training in engineering, geology, science and management. Atiku Abubakar supervised the activities of the PTDF and inaugurated its Interim Management Committee in September 2000, and gave approvals for the management and expenditure of its funds, and must therefore take primary responsibility for whatever may have gone awry.

Of the $125 million approved for the PTDF in 2003, Atiku instructed the fund to deposit $10 million into Trans International Bank. The balance of $115 million, he instructed, should be placed in Mike Adenuga's Equatorial Trust Bank Ltd. The vice president was unusually detailed in his involvement, instructing further that out of the deposit in Adenuga's bank, $100 million should be converted to Naira at ¦ 128 to $1 (but not sold through the Central Bank) and the proceeds invested under Term Deposit at 14% interest per annum. In October 2003, Atiku instructed the Accountant-General of the Federation to release another $20 million to the PTDF, without the consent of the president or the approval of the FEC. These decisions became intertwined with the joint ventures between NDTV and I-Gate, and linked to the Jefferson investigation for various offences in the USA.

Congressman Jefferson promoted I-Gate in Nigeria which sought to do business with two companies – NDTV, promoted essentially by Otunba Fashawe, and Rosehill owned by Sulayman Yahaya. What EFCC concluded from its investigation was that funds meant for training manpower for the petroleum industry, provided to PTDF by the Federal Government, were not being used for that purpose. Instead, some of the monies were deposited in favoured banks that were not AAA-rated, at lower-than-market rates of interest, while the banks granted unsecured loans to NDTV, Otunba Fashawe and other companies under his control. The EFCC also attempted to establish business links between Otunba Fashawe, Atiku and Mike Adenuga's Globacom, which our panel thought needed further clarification and confirmation. We submitted our report to Obasanjo which essentially held Atiku responsible for unauthorised accretions to the Fund, mismanagement of monies since the deposit in TIB was lost, while monetary losses were incurred through agreeing to lower-than-market interest rates and exchange rate conversions for the balance of the funds.

Atiku fought back the Nigerian way, which essentially is not to deny having done something wrong but claim 'selective targeting' – "I am not the only one doing it, Obasanjo was involved too" was his message in the local media. Atiku even hired an expensive international media team from the US— Frank Mankiewicz, Ed Weidenfeld, Craig Smith and Paul Clark— to schedule interviews with leading international news-magazines to spin his message with the objective of emerging from it as the democrat, anti-Third Term champion and Obasanjo's victim. The highly politicised and divisive public hearings that followed in the Senate ended up damaging both Atiku and Obasanjo, and widening the gulf between them. An initiative of Bashir Yusuf Ibrahim, Dr. Usman Bugaje, Nuhu Ribadu, Frank Nweke and I to work out a truce and reconcile the two leaders around October 2006 fell through after a second meeting in my official residence with former minister and Atiku loyalist, Yomi Edu leading their team. Atiku ended up decamping from the PDP to the Action Congress and running for president on its platform in 2007. Less than three years after these blow-outs, Atiku went to Abeokuta to reconcile with Obasanjo and returned to the ruling PDP!

Winding down

The sensational stories that receive the most publicity are rarely the stuff that effective public service is made of; indeed, if public service is practised correctly, it should rarely even make the news. More important than specific acts that I take pride in, though, is the feedback that I get from the public. Even today, people in Abuja recognise me and remember the things we did as an administration and they come up and thank me, which really means a lot. There was a clear sign of someone in charge, and we took care of business, we managed the city – it worked. There was order, orderliness and rule compliance, generally, in every sphere. We did that by being resolute and taking some painful decisions and treating everyone equally. We did not care who you were, if you violated any regulation or broke the law, we sanctioned you. Nobody could accuse us of anything else.

Minimising discretion and focusing on outcomes and results rather than processes and procedures – this was the guiding philosophy in everything we did, from selling Federal Government houses to reforming the public service to computerising the land registry to introducing e-government in FCT, particularly in making land available to every Nigerian that qualified and applied. When I first came to the FCT, a plot of land in Abuja city centre typically sold for between 30 and 50 million naira (at the time between $300,000 and $500,000). By the time I left office in 2007, the same piece of land sold for less than ten million naira (about $100,000) because we made land more easily available to more people. We nearly eliminated land speculators and middle-men! As minister, I was solely in control of land in FCT and I could allocate it more or less on a discretionary basis. We allocated a lot of land to the largest number of applicants in FCT's history. The 11 ministers before me allocated less than 19,000 plots of land, in about 25 years. In my four years as minister, I approved the allocation of more than 27,000 plots of land, much more than the 11 preceding ministers put together. We saw the solution to high land prices as a supply issue, so we just increased the supply, and it worked!

It was not until about 2006 that people began to see the effects of some of the difficult and often painful policy decisions we took. As the city improved, FCT staff became more proud and noticeably began walking around with more of a bounce and swagger. I would like to think that everybody got credit all around, if the comments from outsiders were anything to go by. I know for a fact that one of the questions even current FCT employees ask is, 'why is Abuja not running like before?' It is nearly all the same staff there as when we were in charge. So what is the problem? I have a sense that one problem is that the staff no longer feel protected as they did when we were in charge. They now feel that if they did their job and it affected a "big man" or they made a genuine mistake, they would be immediately sacrificed – quite different from our management style. We made a point to never sacrifice my staff, even when someone did something wrong. I always believed it was better to protect the staff from the outsider and then discipline the staff internally than to let go any of my staff or sacrifice them or publicly blame them.

Nowhere is this aspect more vital than in preparing to leave office. Because of the way we worked, we knew that once I was out and my successor came in, staff who loyally obeyed my directives would surely face retribution. So as I was winding down my term, I had a number of things to see to, as I believe that the signals one sends upon exit are just as important as the signals sent upon entry. Apart from ticking off items from my to-do list, I also tried to get all my aides jobs in the private sector or other parts of the public sector, because I knew that if they stayed on, their continued survival would be subject to political forces beyond their control and mine.

Most importantly, I also had to keep an eye on the books and make sure that money did not disappear because the last days of an administration are when the crazy spending proposals start rolling in. From January to February, we started slowing down the spending and I wound up leaving behind over N50 billion in the bank accounts controlled by the FCT –a huge amount of money – for my successor. I also ordered audits of FCDA, Sales of Houses and all other accounts so that internal control infractions are identified to guide our successors. Had I done it any other way, I would have been accused of other crimes in addition to the false and fictitious ones that were subsequently manufactured against me.

Also important, I had to keep accurate and useful handing over notes, which are basically the outgoing minister's briefing to the incoming minister. My handover notes ended up filling 54 bound volumes and to this day I am not convinced that any of my successors read beyond page one. I do know that part of the reason the various Senate hearings targeting me had trouble finding anything to pin on me was because I could refer to my detailed handing over notes - and they were too lazy to read them and could therefore nor contradict them.

Finally, as far as the discussion of Abuja as a laboratory for economic reform goes, I would cap this off with what many consider a heretical statement but I say it with confidence because I ran a city: rural development is an oxymoron because ultimately everyone in the world will live in cities. In my view, the phrase, 'rural development' was crafted to ensure that Africa remained underdeveloped. We should all work to develop our human settlements into cities and try to get everyone to move to cities except those who choose to remain in the countryside, or those like farmers whose livelihood is off the land and the forests.

As of 2005, more than half of the world's population lived in cities. This is because cities are centres of economic opportunities, so it stands to reason that most people will naturally gravitate toward cities. We therefore must find a way to manage cities better. As someone who has run a city, I would like to think that ultimately all the cities in Nigeria will be like Abuja, or better. We used Abuja as the laboratory of our economic reforms, so whether it was public service reform or fighting corruption, or land reforms, we applied all those in Abuja first. We tried to have a city, the only city in Nigeria that works. We attacked the culture of impunity of our elites. We decided to restore the master plan of Abuja to the extent we reasonably could, which necessitated taking down buildings. We carefully selected our first targets – a minister who had violated the rules, a senator, a retired general and inspector general of police, and we took down their houses, which sent a message that we were either crazy or for real. Either way, it did not make a difference, the signalling ensured that we had a city that worked before our four years ran out. This is an accomplishment even our enemies cannot take away from us.

Chapter Nine

Land Reforms

"In Haiti, untitled rural and urban real estate holdings are together worth some $5.2 billion. To put that sum in context, it is four times the total of all the assets of all the legally operating companies in Haiti, nine times the value of all assets owned by the government, and 158 times the value of all foreign direct investment in Haiti's recorded history to 1995."

– Hernando de Soto, 'The Mystery of Capital'

The responsibility for administering the FCT was, for me personally, an intensely satisfying experience. Running a territory gives one the opportunity to change it not only physically through investments in infrastructure, but also through effecting social improvements in the attitudes of people, security, rule-compliance and human capital formation. Some of these we achieved by studying problems and attacking the fundamentals - the roots of the problem, the cause of the disease rather than symptoms. So for instance, instead of 'fighting corruption' in the FCT land administration, we chose to lay foundations to make it more difficult for corruption to happen or thrive. This we did by cleaning up and computerising land administration, increasing the supply of land and making an example of those employees most notorious for the abuses in land administration.

Background to Land Reforms

Within six weeks of taking over the administration of FCT in September 2003, I briefed the cabinet on the discovery of widespread forgery of land records, fraud in allocation of land and collection of land-related revenues. The cabinet observed the need for drastic reforms of the land administration system in the FCT. Indeed, during the session, the president suggested that we consider the cancellation of all certificates of occupancy issued in the history of the FCT, with a view to issuing new and more secure documents as evidence of title to land. The political and economic elite, along with the bureaucrats, had distorted the land management system so badly, and then taken advantage of the confusion - anonymity of applicants, using powers of attorney to enable effective transfer of land titles, and many other legal shenanigans to acquire huge tracts of land for themselves.

We were mindful of the fact that the fundamental problem of the land management system in the FCT is the reliance on 'paper-based' records that were susceptible to manipulation and forgery. We therefore sought the president's approval to accelerate the engagement of Julius Berger as lead consultant for the computerisation of the cadastral and land information system of Phase 1 of the Federal Capital City (FCC). Incidentally, the president had directed that this be done since 2001, at the cost of about N265 million, but the ministry chose to set up committees to study the issue instead, and retained two consultants for the purpose. We decided to take decisive action. We first inaugurated a committee to review previous studies, reports and everything on the subject and recommend how to computerise and restructure our land title and related documents. The committee was headed by Usman Sabo Ago, a one-time director of planning and survey for the federal capital. My friend and top Lagos lawyer, Asue Ighodalo, and a US-based urban planner, Dr. Ismail Iro, were members, along with a few others. We terminated the endless studies and ended the contracts with the consultants. The committee undertook a detailed study, and submitted its excellent final report in April 2004.

We then proceeded to engage Julius Berger to undertake the turnkey computerisation assignment whose scope covered Phase I of the FCC. This included the Central Area, Garki 1, II, Wuse I, II, Maitama, and Asokoro Districts. The project entailed the acquisition of relevant data, satellite pictures and aerial photographs, the supply of required computer software and other hardware, and staff training. The project required the turnkey delivery of a state-of-the-art land information system, geographic information system, and integrated land maps with comprehensive data on land title holders in digital form and hard copies.

We constituted a 16-person counterpart team comprising staff of the land-related departments of the MFCT to work with the consultants. We selected each member of the task force based on technical competence, integrity and record of previous limited involvement in land racketeering in the FCT. As the implementation of the project went under way, it became clear that much more was achievable with the hardware and software already supplied and the resources available if additional data capture activities were tagged onto the main project. For instance, we realised that unless plots in Phase II of the FCC (Mabushi, Utako, Gudu, Katampe, Jabi, Gwarimpa I, II, Karmo, Wuye, Kukwaba and Durumi) and other new contiguous districts like Katampe Extension, Guzape, Mpape and Asokoro Extension were covered, the problem of double allocation of the same plot of land and similar fraud could not be fully addressed.

Therefore, I persuaded President Obasanjo of the need for the 'add-on projects', which we funded partly from the contingencies in the contract and our 2004 statutory budget. These entailed the mass data entry of all land records in Phases I and II of the FCC; the field verification of status of all plots in Phase I and parts of Phases II and III of the FCC; the digital photographs of all buildings on all plots in Phases I and II; and the procurement of satellite imagery for Phases II, III and IV of the FCC. Other major settlements outside the city like Zuba, Lugbe, Kubwa, Karu, Nyanya, Gwagwalada, Kuje and Karshi were also to be similarly covered. The assignments were completed without any cost over-runs. In the process, our 16 staff were fully trained and certified to expert level in GIS and LIS. By July 2004, we were able to submit a comprehensive memorandum to the Cabinet containing the following findings:

As at April 2004, the FCT had over 105,000 applications for land, for which only 21,470 had been granted rights of occupancy. We had over 85,000 applications un-attended, some filed since 1980 – an 80% failure rate.

The manual record-keeping system and resultant corruption had led to multiple allocations of the same plot of land to more than one applicant. Over 866 cases of multiple allocation involving individuals, companies, embassies and even Federal Government were documented by the task team. There were 2,149 cases of multiple plot numbering and 119 cases of multiple file numbering.

There were rampant cases of forgeries of land records, theft of files and smuggling in of forged files into the Land Registry. The FCT branch of the EFCC under Assistant Commissioner of Police Amodu had to shut down a printing press in Kaduna, and began prosecuting some members of the syndicate.

There were several other unauthorised bodies within the FCT involved in the allocation of land contrary to the provisions of the Constitution, the Land Use Act and the Federal Capital Territory Act, which stipulated that only the Minister of FCT and no other person or authority could approve the allocation of land in the territory.

Vital facilities provided for in the master plan for respective districts and neighbourhoods had been converted to other uses, mostly residential – seriously distorting the Abuja master plan and putting pressure on designed facilities.

Encroachments and violations were found wherein buildings were erected on water and sewer lines, road reservations and under high-tension electric lines. We uncovered the more disturbing, wholesale of conversion of flood plains, railways and transit way reservations by untitled squatters into buildings of sorts. About 200 buildings had to be demolished in the city to remove these encroachments.

Land-related revenue generation had been poor due to breakdown of record keeping, which provided ample room for non-payment of charges due, fraud and diversion of revenues. We found also that more than 70% of land title-holders were in arrears of payments of ground rents and other land charges, without any reminders, consequences or sanctions.

We were conscious of the fact that some of the 85,000 reportedly pending applications for land included those filed by staff of MFCT land administration department, sometimes using passport photos obtained from FCT Pilgrims' Board using all manner of fictitious names. Furthermore, due to the age of some of the applications, we recognised that even some of the genuine applicants might have passed away, changed addresses and other contact details. We therefore needed to take steps to correct some of these anomalies as part of any clean-up process.

We drew the attention of the cabinet to the existence of nearly a dozen different agencies, departments and authorities allocating land within the FCT. These existed and operated while the relevant professionals in the land administration department were helpless, leading to the distortion of the Abuja Master Plan, multiple land use violations and threats to public safety, health and order. These unauthorised 'land allocation organisations' included the following:

- the Federal Housing Authority (FHA) that alienated land within residential estates allocated to it;
- Abuja Environmental Protection Board that 'allocated' parks and gardens for irregular use;
- Development Control Department of FCDA which 'allocated' corner shops and open spaces;
- Federal Ministry of Housing and Urban Development, which alienated land within residential estates allocated to it;

- Department of Engineering of FCDA , which controlled and temporarily 'allocated' 'life camps' to construction companies, electric sub-station plots, transit ways, and roads rights of way;

- the six Area Councils had until 2001 control of land outside the city footprint, previously allocated what was called "Rural Land" in FCT;

- Department of Economic Development which 'allocated' Agricultural Land, and alienated plots within any FCT Market;

- Department of Public Buildings of FCDA which sometimes alienated land within various FCDA residential estates;

- the various task forces on resettlement extensively allocated land illegally in Dei-Dei, Zuba and Kubwa),

- Department of Maintenance, FCDA also engaged in land alloaction within some FCDA residential estates; and

- The Chiefs, Village heads and other traditional rulers in FCT granting what they called "customary title" to various illegal squatters and occupants of land.

The Cabinet accordingly approved that the next stage of the computerisation of the cadastral and land information system should proceed, such that the rest of the FCC and the FCT would be digitally mapped and formal title, called Certificates of Occupancy, issued to all those who qualified.[64] On completion, we established the Abuja Geographic Information System (AGIS) in the Minister's office, to be the sole custodian of all geo-spatial data in the FCT.

Taking advantage of the existence of multiple land allocation points and the confusion arising from it were several land syndicates operating with impunity in the FCT. Two such syndicates stood out - Engineer Amuchie Success, who operated in Asokoro, Wuse II, and Maitama, while Alhaji Muhammadu Kamba, who specialised in Wuse I, Garki 1 and Kubwa plots. These syndicates operated with the assistance and connivance of staff of the MFCT cartographic unit and FCDA planning and survey department. Indeed, the syndicates even printed their C of Os, which were identical to the genuine MFCT certificate, and were alleged to have the capability to forge the signature of virtually any Minister or official of the FCT, past and present. With the assistance of the Economic and Financial Crimes Commission, we put these syndicates under pressure and on the run, and Engineer Success was arrested and was being prosecuted by the EFCC as at when we left office. In the course of investigations, the EFCC found that several tracts of land within Asokoro, Maitama and Wuse II District of the FCC had been fraudulently 'allocated' by these syndicates to several high-ranking Nigerians.

Some of the victims of Amuchie Success, according to an EFCC report dated November 30, 2003 and addressed to President Obasanjo, were Senators Anyim Pius Anyim, Jonathan Zwingina, Evans Enwerem, Maina Ma'aji Lawan, and Abubakar Mahdi. Others included my predecessor-in-office, Mohammed Abba Gana, former governors Chukwuemeka Ezeife and Lucky Igbinedion of Anambra and Edo States respectively, the late Stephen Shekari, then Kaduna State Deputy Governor, as well as other prominent individuals. The syndicate leaders targeted senators, governors and important people that had the connections and capacity to 'launder' their allocations by getting properly regularised titles issued to them *after* they had completed their buildings with forged offer letters, titles, and building plan approvals. An instance was the case of Senator Jonathan Zwingina. Mrs. Altine Jibrin, then Assistant Director and Deeds Registrar, resisted all pressures including ministerial directives to register (and therefore launder) Senator Zwingina's fake title in respect of land reserved for a park on which he had built his mansion. The other alleged land racketeer, Muhammadu Kamba, mysteriously disappeared, and was rumoured to have fled from Abuja in fear of the EFCC. On receipt of the EFCC's report, Obasanjo directed the MFCT to recover all illegally acquired plots and keep him informed.

Following the finalisation of the computerisation of cadastral and land information system of Phases I and II of the Federal Capital City, and the establishment of the AGIS, we redesigned the form and substance of the FCT title document – the Certificate of Occupancy (C of O), - and withdrew all evidence of land titles, while preserving the titles themselves. We invited every title-holder to submit documents for re-certification. To give legal effect to this decision, we gazetted FCT Land Use Regulations 2004, pursuant to the Land Use Act, and embarked on a nine-month programme of title re-certification, which started on July 5, 2004.

Many initially questioned the legality of our re-certification exercise, but none succeeded when they challenged it in court. In fact, before arriving at this drastic but necessary decision, we ensured full legal review and compliance. I was merely exercising the powers of the minister of FCT which the president statutorily delegated to me under section 18 of the Federal Capital Territory Act and sections 9(1), (2) and 46(2)(d) of the Land Use Act, not only to grant Right of Occupancy (R of O) and C of O, but to make regulations with regards to, among others, the forms to be used for any documentation.

Land Allocation Criteria

We also looked at land allocation criteria and proposed steps to reduce the level of discretion vested in the FCT minister in granting titles to land. In the Federal Capital Territory, the basic principles guiding allocation of land were originally designed to ensure the achievement of the following objectives:

- Provision of adequate infrastructure, services and facilities;
- Development of a functional, beautiful city at all times, and viable satellite towns around the city;
- Promotion of national integration in residence and business ventures;
- Integration of the original inhabitants into the mainstream of economic and social life of the Territory; and
- Observance of relevant provisions of the Land Use Act, and full compliance with those of the Federal Capital Territory Act.

These principles enjoyed different interpretations in the previous 28 years by successive administrations of the FCT. In the Second Republic, the Shagari administration's two ministers that first began the allocation of land in the FCT adopted the following criteria:-

- Date of Application (i.e. first come, first allocated),
- Ability and capacity to develop within 2 years of allocation,
- State quota with 40% of allocation based on population.
- Equality of states to ensure national unity, with 50% of available plots for allocation.
- Minister's Discretion: 10% of plots available for allocation at the minister's discretion to take care of presidential priorities and other political considerations other than (I) – (iv) above.

Even though the criteria were fair and equitable, empirical evidence indicated that political considerations trumped the stated criteria. The criteria also failed to classify for instance, what identity to assign to firms and companies in which the state of origin of the owners and registered office of the business may be different. Other applicants like embassies, international organisations and foreign persons like the United Nations became similarly difficult to classify.

Indeed, in the previous 20 years until I took charge of the FCT Administration, ministerial miscretion was virtually 100%, instead of the 10% in the approved guidelines, with the result that speculators, rather than capable developers, got land allocations within the FCT. Evidence available of registrations of power of attorney and deeds of assignment indicates that nearly 40% of all land allocated in the FCT in the previous two decades had changed hands at least once before development.

After a careful review of the 28 years of experience and considering the backlog of 85,000 unattended applications, we proposed the criteria for the fair, just and equitable allocation of land within the Federal Capital Territory - assuming that infrastructure provision for a particular district was financed with public funds - which were approved by the Federal Executive Council:

- Equality of states – 60% of plots
- Population of states - 10% of plots
- Public Servants resident in Abuja – 10% of plots and
- Ministerial Discretion – 20% of plots

I have gone into some detail in explaining the logic behind our land reforms for two reasons. First, many states have attempted to implement what we did, with limited success as far as I know, and I hope that this will help point them in the right direction. In addition, the attempt by the Yar'Adua administration not only to reverse what we did, but to imply that we were driven by anything other than the best interest of Abuja and Nigeria, needs to be debunked. I had cause to write President Umaru Yar'Adua on November 30, 2007 on these and other matters, long before the Sodangi Senate Committee was procured to go on the revenge mission called 'investigative public hearings'. I will refer to parts of that letter because its contents would complement the story of the land reforms.

I had assumed that President Yar'Adua meant well but was simply being misled, and with all sense of responsibility, I wanted to prevent the creation of more serious problems for his administration in attempts to demonise, smear and discredit a single individual - that is me. I love Abuja and gave nearly four years of my life to its restoration, orderliness and development.

Land Administration in 2003

When President Obasanjo appointed me as FCT minister he gave me the mandate to clean up amongst other things, the FCT land administration system which he adjudged to be a major source of corruption and rent-seeking within the Federal Government. In the FCT, we found that the President Obasanjo's judgment was largely correct. For instance, we discovered that:

> Many Nigerians, particularly the political and military elite had been allocated plots of land, which had remained undeveloped for years. These plots of land were in every way developable and the title-holders were persons of financial capacity evidenced by their generally expensive life styles!
>
> Notwithstanding the terms of grant requiring development within two years (unless there are practical physical or technical hindrances), these "big men and women" held on to Abuja plots that

they were selling for tens and even hundreds of millions of Naira.[65]

While these persons held on to these undeveloped plots, over 85,000 applicants for land (some as far back as 1980), remained in MFCT without any allocation. Indeed, we found that even staff of FCT had no plots of land allocated to them even though some have been in Abuja from its inception.

The endemic corruption and the largescale distortion of the Abuja masterplan meant that our capital's physical development suffered, rents were wildly inflated beyond the levels seen even in Lagos and Port Harcourt. A few connected speculators got rich. The fat cats did not even care to pay requisite ground rents to the FCT. The scam was well entrenched.

In addition to the Land Administration and Resettlement Department, every department in the FCT system from Engineering to Development Control, and agencies like AEPB and Water Board were all engaged in the 'allocation', sub-leasing or otherwise alienating land with the attendant confusion, record-keeping nightmares and total disregard of the provisions of the Constitution, the Federal Capital Territory Act and the Land Use Act which vested the president's delegated power by statute only in the Minister of the FCT and no other person or authority.

Staff of the defunct Ministry of the Federal Capital Territory (MFCT), the FCDA and other FCT agencies all joined in the land speculation swindles. Multiple applications for land by staff in various names with passport photos obtained from States' Pilgrims Boards were common. An example was when the EFCC discovered in the house search of a middle level staff of the MFCT, - Musa Audu - 132 land allocations in various names!

> Diversion of people's allocations by MFCT staff, hiding of files to facilitate allocations of the same plot of land to more than one person (double allocation), and even the allocation of government-designated plots to individuals and companies were the order of the day. Federal civil servants lobbied and bribed to be posted to MFCT, and those posted returned the favour by facilitating allocations to those that posted them, and the cycle continued.
>
> Such allocations were then laundered via a "stock market" within FCDA premises – which by the way also provided trading floors for MFCT/FCDA contracts and employment letters, amongst others. The use of powers of attorney and deeds of assignment to launder and transfer these fraudulent allocations were the order of the day.

The revelation of the extent of abuses in Kubwa land allocations by Musa Audu mentioned above shocked all of us in the MFCT. In a letter, reference CB: 3940/EFCC/FCT/ABJ/Vol.1/25, dated March 24, 2005, titled "Progress Report on Investigation Activities relating to Land Fraud involving Engr. Success O. Amuchie and 5 Others," the EFCC named Musa A. Audu, the planning officer in charge of the Kubwa Resettlement project, as being in possession of 132 allocation papers in various names. Audu, Success and some MFCT staff involved were charged to Federal High Court by the EFCC in 2005. The prosecution had not been concluded by the time we left office.

Nevertheless, we moved quickly to take immediate corrective measures with President Obasanjo's strong support at all times, while seeking sustainable, longer-term solutions. Amongst other steps:

> We set up several committees consisting of outside and internal staff experts to study the problems observed above and make recommendations.
>
> We sought the assistance of the Police, ICPC and EFCC in the investigation of all valid cases of

corruption in land matters. The FCT is one of the first 'states' to have a resident EFCC branch to handle such matters.

We abolished all disparate departmental discretions in land matters and centralised all land allocation under the Minister's Office supported by all the relevant technical departments.

We established a Task Force to computerise the land register and all land-related records, and while the project was on for about 10 months; suspended new land grants, except the most critical commercial or public building needs.

We ordered a review of development control regulations which had remained unchanged since the early 1990s. Consequently, in April 2007, the revised FCT Development Control Regulations 2007 were debated and approved by the FCT Executive Committee, and published pursuant to the FCT Act and Nigerian Urban Planning and Development Act.

We gazetted two FCT Land Use Regulations pursuant to the Land Use Act, revising the ground rents, compensation rates and other land-related charges to encourage physical development in the territory. For instance, we lowered ground rents and development charges on industrial, recreational and agricultural land to encourage agriculture and other job-creating activities.

These efforts led to far-reaching land reforms – at the time, arguably the most advanced in Nigeria – the fulcrum of which was the computerisation of the Land Information System (LIS - the paper file records) and this was supplemented by satellite-supported Geographical Information System (GIS), the recertification exercise to sanitise the records, the updating of all pending land applications and the enactment of the legal framework to guide its design and implementation.

Legal Basis for Land Reforms

On 30th June 2004, almost a year after I assumed office, I sought President Obasanjo's approval to recertify all titles to land in the FCT and related matters. These and other subsequent reforms in land administration and management led to the creation of the Abuja Geographic Information System and the gazetting of the *FCT Land Use Regulations 2004* in the Federal Government *Official Gazette No. 15, Vol. 94.*

Everything we did that was described as "inconsistent" by the Yar'Adua administration was based on well considered recommendations of senior FCT staff. Some went out of their way to mislead our successors-in-office. Furthermore, each decision and action we took was guided by these laws, land use regulations, and development control guidelines. Throughout our tenure, I never operated outside these guidelines, nor did I ever go beyond the scope of my authority whether it had to do with allocation, revocation or re-allocation of any land.

The legal grounds for revocation of title to land are listed in the Certificate of Occupancy. Any of the contraventions listed below could lead to the exercise of discretion by the Minister to revoke the title:

- non-payment of annual ground rent or such other revised rent

- non-payment of penal rents imposed by the Minister

- non-payment of rates (including utilities) etc.

- non-development within two years of grant

No title was revoked during my tenure without being found in contravention of one or more of these conditions.[66] Moreover, these rules were applied blindly, without looking at the personality involved. Indeed, when I directed that all plots in Asokoro Extension that had infrastructure that were undeveloped should have their titles revoked, the plot allocated to me in 1998 by the Mamman Kontagora administration was included and revoked accordingly. I never ever received the revocation letter because the FCT staff thought it was a mistake! It was not. I knew the particular plot allocated to me would be affected but still approved the revocation. It was reallocated to an applicant I do not know, and has since been developed by the new owners. President Obasanjo often told the story of how a plot of land belonging to him was similarly revoked, using the same neutral criteria. That was how we operated, applying rules to everyone, ourselves included, without favour or discrimination.

Districts without 'infrastructure'

The existence or lack of 'infrastructure' does not affect in any way the ministerial discretion to revoke. This is because – (i) infrastructure is not mentioned as a condition precedent for development in the C of O, or in the regulations as fettering the minister's discretionary power, and (ii) existence of infrastructure while an important input in the decision to revoke or not, is a matter of fact, not desk-based speculation of general application. As an example, the Central Area, Gwarimpa and Mabushi Districts have no comprehensive engineering infrastructure so no undeveloped plots allocated there may be revoked. However, the reality is that parts of these districts, depending on location, had adequate infrastructure and if an allottee has a plot in those areas, there was no general excuse not to develop.

Clear examples of these are the FCT minister's official residence in Gwarimpa-2 district. The Mabushi Ministerial Quarters and Federal Ministry of Works were located in Mabushi District and several buildings like the National Mosque, Federal Mortgage Bank and even the Federal Secretariats had been built in the Central Area – all districts 'without infrastructure'. It makes no sense to argue that if a person has a plot in these districts, but near these facilities, and fails to develop, he could hold on to the title forever. With respect, this position is wrong in law and in fact. We were careful in revoking titles to land taking into consideration the surrounding facts, but fully applying the law. Though the regulations do not require this, we only revoked plots in districts without infrastructure when ground rents of years have remained unpaid and the special cases of *"un-issued R of Os"* below.

Un-issued Letters of Offer (R of O)

In the course of the recertification exercise, my attention was drawn to about 2,500 cases of missing files and un-issued letters of offer (or R of O in FCT parlance) – AGIS recommended that the cases and allocations be reviewed, temporary files created or existing files vetted and cleared, or otherwise cancelled based on available information. We took the decision to cancel some of them because many had no subsisting applications for title in FCT, several were suspicious allocations, and the beneficiaries had no valid addresses. Most of these plots under the "un-issued R of O" cases fell within the districts without infrastructure. There was really no way many of the allocations could stand scrutiny post-recertification and updating of all application records for land in FCT. The revoked plots were subsequently allocated to applicants with valid and subsisting applications. It was absurd for our successors to reinstate titles that were void in the first place – to persons that either never applied for land, or never bothered to update their applications when notified to do so!

Failure to Re-certify Titles

By the time we left office, we had revoked 5,604 plot allocations due to the failure of allottees to come forward for identification and recertify titles. The logic behind recertification is similar to a nation changing the design, name or colour of its currency, but not the face value. In my lifetime, Nigeria has gone through this more than once. It is necessarily a *time-bound* exercise designed to expose, for instance, staff of MFCT that acquired plots in fictitious names, senior public servants with land ownership not declared in their asset declaration forms, 'big men' - money launderers and those hiding the proceeds of corruption, and so on. Our conclusion at the end of the exercise was that most of those who failed to come forward had something to hide and largely fell amongst one of the suspicious classes mentioned above. There were genuine cases like lost certificates, deaths of title-holders and estate issues, delayed registration of assignments and powers of attorney that were considered on a case-by-case basis after the expiration of the deadlines, and only on the recommendations of AGIS.

It was, therefore, tragic that the Yar'Adua administration decided to reopen recertification and made it 'a continuous exercise' - not only an absurdity, but a violation of gazetted regulations and accordingly, unlawful. The decision suited the corrupt and fraudulent title-holders amongst FCT staff and other elite just fine as they had a fresh opportunity to launder their fraudulent titles. It also created a fresh onslaught of litigation between the FCT and new allottees since many of the 5,604 revoked plots had been allocated to new allottees that then held valid and subsisting titles over them. Surely, anyone could see that this was a self-serving decision that only legitimised years of land racketeering in the FCT for the benefit of a few, but it was done by our successors-in-office.

One of the land issues we had to deal with concerned the category of plots known as ONEX site yards. ONEX refers to the Outer Northern Expressway – the main road from Suleja-Kubwa coming into Abuja up to Maitama District. The plots adjoining this road were provided to contractors doing work in Abuja as *'temporary site yards, renewable every five years'* – they were not meant to be permanent titles. No city worth its salt grants plots of land along the principal access to construction companies with their heavy equipment, and increased risks of accidents and attendant pollution. The Department of Urban and Regional Planning drew my attention to this and recommended the withdrawal of all offending titles and the re-planning of the whole corridor.

While the plots were to serve as temporary site yards, many of the allottees built without development permits and in contravention of the terms of their grant – with the result that the area was littered with mixed-use developments, factories, etc. contrary to the "site yard" land use authorised by the FCT. The temporary allottees, mostly FCDA contractors, were assisted by staff of the Engineering Department to get away with this illegality. We, therefore, took the decision to revoke the titles and relocate those in gross contravention, while upholding those that were compliant with the land use for the corridor. We granted some of the construction companies alternative plots in Idu Industrial District and directed them to relocate. What remained uncompleted was the relocation of those who violated the Master Plan, that is those assisted by FCDA Engineering Department to convert the temporary allocations to 99 year leaseholds, which ought to be reversed. Any re-consideration would be a disservice to the efforts to preserve the serenity of the main highway of entrance into our nation's capital. Sadly, our successors again reversed all these decisions, for which the city will pay a heavy price in the future.

Accelerated Development Programme (ADP)

The ADP was one of the initiatives approved by President Obasanjo to enable commercial developers of land have easier and cheaper access to land for development in Abuja. The programme sought to ensure that land was allocated directly to the developer [eliminating the middle-man syndrome] and the development is required to be conducted within a specified timeline. The terms and conditions for the grant were the result of consultations and focus group sessions internally and with outside investors. The conditions attached vis-à-vis the equivalent open market value of the plots on offer clearly confirms the programme's attractiveness.

The conditions, though strange to those used to discretionary allocation of commercial plots in Abuja, were, therefore, not stringent by any reasonable commercial standard. The programme was initially marred by the misconduct of some of the officers charged with collating applications for the PPP Technical Committee to make recommendations for my approval. We undertook investigations and dismissed the erring employees. A revalidation exercise was subsequently conducted to ensure the validity of the title-holders and ascertain any contravention of the terms of offer. By the time we left office, many of the plots – nearly half were at advanced stages of being developed, and some had even completed the buildings which the programme targeted for development.

We also moved against government agencies that were illegally converting land to unintended uses. We revoked titles to residential plots allocated to government agencies for residential purposes that no longer needed them, subdivided and allocated them to various applicants for land.

Many rushed to subdivide and share out the plots to their senior officers, while others sought to transfer the vacant, undeveloped plots to their pension funds. The more criminally minded agencies joined the land speculation business by attempting to go into 'joint ventures' with private organisations to develop the land, often outside their core mandates and enabling statutes. We took the decision to reject all these attempts and comply with the letter and spirit of monetisation – that no government agencies should directly or by proxy develop land other than what they needed for their administration, which will be funded via appropriation acts and no other way.

'Functus Officio,' – the Great Land Grab

It is now history that these detailed explanations submitted to President Yar'Adua neither made any difference nor stopped him and my dear friend and successor as FCT minister, Dr. Aliyu Modibbo, from initiating, guiding and motivating the Sodangi Senate Committee to probe my tenure under the pretext that they were responding to petitions received on the administration of the FCT from 1999 to 2007. Even a fool knew I was the target of the investigation, and the proceedings clearly demonstrated it. For instance, when my predecessor, Abba Gana, was asked by a senator whether he had approved the allocation of any plots of land to his family members, he answered in the affirmative, and added that "charity begins at home!" The senators laughed and let the moment pass. At the end of their proceedings, however, the one 'scandal' contrived against me was the fact that I had approved the allocation of a plot of land for my wife. This same action admitted to being taken by FCT minister Abba Gana elicited a totally different reaction for the obvious reasons that I was a target and he was not.

Some of the members of the Senate Committee, like the chairman, Sodangi, Smart Adeyemi and Ikechukwu Obiora, came into the assignment with conflict of interest and some personal grudges against me and decisions of FCTA during my tenure, and contrary to the Standing Rules of the Senate, neither declared the conflict nor disqualified themselves from participating in the proceedings. These are matters still before the courts, but I will provide documents here[67] that I hope would speak to the various instances of misconduct of selected senators, without being '*sub-judice*'.

Part of what we inherited in the FCT was a huge backlog of applications for land, which had not received allocations. I was determined not only to clear the backlog but also to reduce the waiting time for allocation of land to between three and six months from the date of filing a complete application and payment of fees. We therefore not only got all the nearly 85,000 un-attended applications updated, but inaugurated a task force on October 30 2006, headed by Baba Kura Umar, then an assistant director at AGIS, to recommend the allocation of plots in the FCC and satellite towns to all the qualified applicants. Of the backlog, we concluded that about 22,000 of such applicants qualified for land allocation, and we were determined to try to clear the backlog by the end of my tenure, on May 29, 2007. Until the inauguration of the task force, only about 8,000 plots had been allocated in my entire time as minister. The task force worked round the clock putting up recommendations for my approval up until the eve of our departure from office. While trying hard to clear the historical backlog, we did not realise we were setting up ourselves for misrepresentation by the professional mischief-makers who succeeded us in office. As an example, I was accused by my successor of allocating over 3,000 plots in the month of May 2007. He conveniently forgot that, since the task force began submitting recommendations to me in November 2006, I was approving a similar number every single month to May 2007.

The goal of my successor and the Senate Committee was to find a way to invalidate these allocations so that they could re-allocate to the senators, new FCTA leadership, chosen friends, family and companies that they owned or controlled. Since the mere accusation of last minute allocations was not enough to render the exercise of ministerial responsibility illegal, FCT minister Modibbo and Senator Sodangi had to create a huge lie – that the Federal Executive Council of which my successor and I were members till the 29th of May 2007 had been dissolved on the 15th of May 2007. This was both an outright and disingenuous lie and a perjury to boot, for several reasons. First, such a significant event happening would certainly have been reported in the media on the 16th of May 2007. No newspaper or web-based medium reported such. Secondly, the Cabinet met on 23rd May 2007 with my successor, Dr. Aliyu Modibbo, then minister of commerce and industry, in attendance. Finally, Cabinet meetings are a matter of public record and only morally-flexible people would lie so blatantly and attempt to wish away such records.

All these did not stop my successor and Sodangi misleading the Senate Committee, the Senate as a body and the whole country by declaring that: (1) The FEC was dissolved on May 15th 2007. (2) Nasir El-Rufai became *"functus officio"*[68] and therefore ceased to be Minister of FCT on 15th May 2007. (3) All the allocations made during the period were therefore void. The shameless contradiction in all these claims was that other actions that I took during the same period, including signing letters of offer for sale of houses to a couple of ministers and other officials in the Yar'Adua administration were, conveniently, not deemed invalidated.

In Appendix 6 of this book, I have provided the attendance list for the cabinet meeting of Wednesday, 23rd May 2007. The cabinet met again on Monday, May 28th 2007 with no agenda other than to adopt the conclusions of this meeting. We then had a valedictory photograph and video session widely reported in the print and electronic media. My successor, Dr. Aliyu Modibbo, was at that meeting as well. In addition, Yayale Ahmed, Major-General Abdullahi Sarki Mukhtar, General Abdullahi Mohammed, Dr. Sayyadi Abba Ruma, Alhaji Ikra Aliyu Bilbis, and Dr. Hassan Mohammed Lawal, all part of the Yar'Adua cabinet, were also in attendance, but miraculously and conveniently forgot this post-May 15th meeting ever taking place, while the falsehood of *"functus officio"* was being bandied around as gospel truth.

This contrived lie was however convenient because it enabled the FCT ministers that succeeded me to unlawfully "revoke" over 3,000 plots already allocated to qualified Nigerians and 're-allocate' them to Sodangi and others[69] based on the falsely procured Senate Resolution. Under the leadership of Adamu Aliero, officials of the FCT administration quietly drew attention to the minutes of the last meeting of the FCT Executive Committee dated May 22nd 2007 to debunk Modibbo-Sodangi's fictitious *"functus officio"*. Aliero wanted to allocate some of the plots too in like manner and was therefore reluctant to accept the truth.[70] He chose to write the Cabinet Secretariat in the office of the SGF asking for clarification on the purported dissolution of the Cabinet on the 15th of May 2007. The response from the SGF's office was unequivocal – the Cabinet met on Wednesday May 23rd in its final plenary session, was never dissolved at any time, and met for the last time on Monday, May 28th 2007.

This was not the reply any of my successors-in-office wanted, so they ignored it and proceeded with the unlawful revocation and re-allocation of the plots of thousands of innocent citizens, while giving the impression that the allocations were 'hurriedly made' to my fronts, friends and family members. Many cases are in the courts challenging (and successfully reversing) these unlawful actions. What continued to baffle me when these lies about 'cabinet dissolution' were being propagated was not the shamelessness of those that seek to benefit from them, but the silence of some other Obasanjo ministers that were re-appointed to the cabinet by Yar'Adua, and even Obasanjo as well about a clear and simple issue. A one-line statement from him that he never dissolved the cabinet in his second term would have ended the falsehood and the injustice to thousands of land allottees that depended on it. However, it was clear though at that point in time, it was everyone for himself and no one for truth or country. What is sad about this is that those that fabricated these lies to acquire undeserved ability to tamper with the property rights of others, or kept silent while falsehood was allowed to prevail over truth somehow believe they were "smarter" than the rest of us, and that societies ran that way can make progress. They are surprised that life quite does not work that way.

Correlation between Policies and Outcomes

Our principal goal as FCT Administration was to accelerate the orderly development of Abuja by eliminating land racketeering, reducing rent-seeking and land speculation, and giving genuine developers easier access to land. This we did by ensuring that over 27,000 out of 30,000 verified and valid applicants were allocated land during our tenure. We revoked the titles of persons who considered themselves sacred cows. We did not care about how they felt because the public interest of Abuja and the country overrode that of a few greedy and self-serving individuals.

We know that they will neither forgive us nor forget until they extracted their pound of flesh. We have no defense against their wealth, power and capacity for mischief except the truth. We are ready to face them any time with facts, figures and documents. We have nothing to hide and no one to fear. As human beings, we must have made mistakes. However, to suggest that anything we did was driven by any motive other than public interest is patent injustice to us. I insist always that those that attribute any such motives to us should do so with facts, figures and documents not innuendo, rumour and repeated character assassination.

The correlation between our policies and development outcomes are clear. I invite the reader to review the table below to see the relative efficacy of our decisions and actions. Between 1980 and 2005, nearly 19,000 plots were allocated to private individuals and organisations in FCT. Slightly over 11,000 were developed by 2005 - an average of less than 500 plots developed per annum. In comparison, during the second half of my tenure, when our land reforms began to take full effect, over 2,000 plots were developed within less than 2 years. This created a construction boom in Abuja with jobs and economic opportunities for many more than the few greedy land speculators of the past. This is how we measured the efficacy of our policies, decisions and actions.

TABLE 1: PLOTS DEVELOPMENT IN FCT

S/no	District	Plot	Built 1980-2005	2005 - 2007 Completed	Under Construction	Fence Work Only
1	CBD	720	192	29	86	15
2	GARKI	1328	1240	30	21	9
3	WUSE	2671	2660	15	6	3
4	GARKI II	940	735	81	51	6
5	ASOKORO	2769	1900	192	88	25
6	MAITAMA	2260	1998	113	107	15
7	WUSE II	1598	1460	65	44	11
8	GUDU	750	450	39	23	15
9	DURUMI	850	10	37	32	6
10	WUYE	866	185	15	14	4
11	JABI	620	185	116	145	50
12	UTAKO	750	210	86	113	30
13	MABUSHI	850	28	16	35	13
14	KATAMPE	1100	10	10	6	11
15	SECTOR CENTRE C	70	Nil	2	3	2
16	SECTOR CENTRE B	77	7	2	4	4
17	SECTOR CENTRE A	140	Nil	Nil	2	8
18	SECTOR CENTRE D	158	5	6	15	20
19	IDU - INDUSTRIAL	440	33	5	35	10
20	NEIGHBOURHOOD CENTRES	21	corner-shops	2	6	1
	TOTAL	18,978	11,308	1059	1036	558

We institutionalised AGIS as the sole custodian of geo-spatial data in the FCT, and erected the AGIS headquarters building at the southern tip of the Cultural Zone – near the FCDA offices to house the operations of the organisation. We submitted legislation to the National Assembly to convert AGIS from an administrative entity in the minister's office into an independent statutory agency, but the legislation was never passed until we left office. Related legislation like the Abuja Property Tax Bill, Abuja Board of Internal Revenue Bill, and another to create the FCT Public Service Commission were similarly and sadly ignored by the legislature. I hope those that care about Abuja's sustainable governance would dust some of these and move on with getting them enacted.

One other development that saddens me is that all the reforms we carefully thought through and implemented in land administration have unravelled under the repeated assault of our successors-in-office. Incompetent cronies were appointed to replace competent, well-trained AGIS management, former staff that were laid off for involvement in land racketeering were reinstated, and all manner of well-connected people were imported to enjoy the newly created gravy train in AGIS. The careful and limited access to land data we had put in place was liberalised in 2008. The audit trail capabilities built into the system that enabled tracking of those that altered land records have been removed. The results are disastrous. Today, double allocation has returned even more easily because it is simpler to alter digital records without trace than create fake paper files. Moreover, those that took these destructive decisions thought they were simply undoing our legacy, hoping that they will unearth some smoking gun of corruption in land allocation - but found there was nothing. It is only the FCT and its residents that may have been the worse for it, not El-Rufai and his team.

Chapter Ten

Sale of Government Houses in Abuja

The acquisition of a home is usually the single largest investment made by most people in their lifetime and home ownership is what catapults people to middle class status. Owning a home also presents an opportunity to alienate it and raise money for investment in other real and financial assets, thereby leveraging societal resources and encouraging entrepreneurship.

– Housing for All? – El-Rufai on Friday, ThisDay, September 30, 2011

One of the cornerstones of the economic reform programme of the Obasanjo administration in 2003 was the restructuring, reorganisation and reorientation of the Federal Public Service from a bloated, expensive and inefficient bureaucracy (67% of the federal budget was spent on recurrent expenditure) to a leaner, more professional, and efficient service delivery organism. A key component of these reforms was the restructuring and monetisation of public sector personnel benefits and entitlements to eliminate waste and the opportunities for abuse.

Accordingly, two of the largest items identified for elimination were the direct provision of individual transportation and housing, particularly as these had proven to be the most wasteful, inefficient and uneven benefits in the public servant's pay package. Consequently, over the period between 2004 to 2006, virtually all 'official' government cars (with the exception of pool cars and a few sensitive, utility or essential vehicles) were withdrawn from individual officers and sold by public auction, with the previous assignees being granted a right of first refusal in most cases. The second, larger and more important, item was that of housing in the form of numerous residential properties, scattered across the country that had over the years been built or purchased by various federal agencies for the use of their staff or as investment items.

The replacement of the government's flawed, inefficient and woefully inadequate staff housing policy, which accommodated less than 10 per cent of its staff, with the policy of the monetisation of housing benefits, left the Federal Government with a considerable pool of residential properties. These vary in form and quality (from marble and stone stand-alone mansions to plywood barrack-style single rooms), but which now had to be properly disposed of. Disposing of them necessarily requires putting in place a mortgage system to enable the purchasers to finance the acquisitions in what would turn out to be the largest single transfer of wealth from the government to its citizens on the African continent.

These residential facilities constituted a major government investment and were a significant drain on scarce resources. Furthermore, they had proven grossly inadequate for the purpose of providing fair and affordable housing to the Federal Government's 600,000 civilian public servants, as there were only about 40,000 government-owned houses across the country, with an estimated 32,000 of these located in Abuja.

We set about disposing of this stock of houses in a manner designed to balance the need to recoup some of the government's investments with the desire to provide affordable permanent housing to as many public servants as possible in an even, fair and efficient way. The programme aimed to cause minimum dislocation and inconvenience to existing residents and beneficiaries of the old system. In addition to reducing waste and empowering public servants, additional benefits expected to emanate from the sale exercise included the creation of a viable mortgage system in the country that had hitherto been non-existent. For the FCTA, the sale would also assist in restoring the Abuja Master Plan, as over the years many houses in residential areas had been converted to offices by MDAs. By retrieving and selling these offices as houses, the land use would therefore be partially restored.

At the end of 2003, the latest addition to the government's housing stock in Abuja was the Games Village, built to accommodate African athletes for the All-Africa Games we hosted in October 2003. Early in 2004, President Obasanjo approved a memo we wrote to dispose of Games Village facilities as a dry run for the sale of all the government houses in Abuja. The MFCT then mandated Abuja Investment & Property Development Company Ltd., to handle the sale. With Tijjani Abdullahi as CEO and his competence in privatisation, we all thought it would be a piece of cake. We were wrong.

As soon as the sale guidelines and conditions were advertised, several ministers, senators and politicians made representations to Obasanjo to take the responsibility away from AIPDC and transfer it to a more flexible body. Obasanjo had either forgotten his approval for MFCT to handle the sale or did not link AIPDC to my ministry and promptly queried the steps taken. I was incensed, and responded in writing attaching his earlier approval. In the end, he decided that I should hand over the sale of Games Village to the Minister of Housing, Mrs Mobolaji Osomo. This decision made no sense at all since it was MFCT that had the details of the land, design and construction of the Village, and would issue survey plans and title deeds to any purchaser. We let it go, knowing that Osomo would have to approach us for title documents and other geospatial data.

In July 2004, the President directed me to proceed with the sale of all Federal Government residential facilities in Abuja. He also instructed that I should be the vice chair of the committee to sell all other residential buildings outside Abuja with the Minister of Housing as chair. I reminded him of the Games Village debacle, and obtained his assurance that on this occasion, he would not reverse his decision. By then the Games Village sale had floundered and become mired in controversy.

We immediately assembled a team chaired by Jimi Lawal to develop a strategy and framework for the sale, followed by detailed guidelines, which I sent to the President as a memo on 17th January

2005. After waiting more than a month without receiving a response, I sent a reminder dated 21st February, 2005 which returned approved vide a State House letter dated February 22, 2005. A cabinet memorandum was then presented to ratify the president's anticipatory approval, which substantially modified the earlier approved guidelines, in March 2005.

Implementation Framework - the Ad-Hoc Committee

By this decision, the Federal Executive Council mandated the FCTA to oversee the disposal of all the 32,000 non-essential federal government-owned residential houses in Abuja, and an Implementation Committee to that effect was set up. The President-in-Council (FEC) constituted the highest authority with regard to the sale exercise and all major policy decisions had to be sanctioned by him and the FEC as circumstances dictated. The FCTA executes its mandate to conduct the sale exercise through the Ad-hoc Committee on the Sale of FGN Houses in Abuja, made up of representatives of the FCTA, Presidency and mortgage institutions. In November 2005, the first person running the sale secretariat, Jimi Lawal, left the country, and the operations and leadership of the Ad-hoc Committee were reorganised. This led to the introduction of a special Auction Monitoring Group to oversee the public auction and bid opening exercises in order to improve its integrity and transparency. The sale exercises were handled by a team of consultants based in my office under the supervision of one of my special assistants, Dr. Abdu Mukhtar.

I have gone to some length to outline the approval process from the president and the cabinet, the elaborate steps we took to make the sale as neutral and transparent as possible. The guidelines were published in the *Official Gazette, Vol. 92, No. 82 of 15th August 2005*.[70] In December 2006, the Cabinet expanded the mandate of the FCTA to include the disposal of a balance of 49 houses in the Abuja Games Village remaining from the earlier sale exercise carried out by the then Federal Ministry of Housing and Urban Development. However, only 37 of these houses were eventually handed over to the FCTA for disposal.

Database for the Sale Implementation

Prior to the commencement of the sale exercise, the Secretary to the Government of the Federation had commissioned a group of private real estate firms as consultants to carry out an extensive audit of all the FGN houses in Abuja. The firms were to create a database of all the information, including a census of the buildings, tenants, specifications and status of the individual houses, property values, maintenance and repair requirements and the like. The original idea involved the subsequent provision of organised facility management services to these properties by professional facility management firms. However, these steps were overtaken by the introduction of the monetisation programme. Therefore, the incomplete initial results of the consultants' work on the database were transferred to the FCT Administration together with the burden of settling the consultants' claims as earlier negotiated with the SGF. The information acquired by the SGF's office together with the existing data with the FCDA and the allocation records from the Office of the Head of Civil Service of the Federation was to form the bedrock of the sale exercise, as they provided the principal database on which the entire exercise was based.

In addition, the FCTA and the Implementation Committee variously wrote and invited all government agencies to submit detailed information on all the houses they may have bought, built, been assigned to or occupied by their staff, in Abuja over the years. Not all of them responded. During the course of the sale exercise, the Abuja Geographic Information Systems (AGIS) came in handy in compiling additional information on FGN houses in the FCT that had not already been captured in the committee's database. In a number of cases FGN houses were discovered (including whole estates) only when the occupants expressed interest in buying them. Furthermore, the FCT Committee on Street Naming and House Numbering also discovered several undisclosed FGN houses that were then added to the database.

Valuation of the Properties for Sale

As explained above, the Secretary to the Government of the Federation had originally commissioned a group of 26 private real estate/facility management firms as valuation consultants to conduct an extensive audit of the FGN houses in Abuja. The 26 Firms eventually submitted their valuation reports to the Implementation Committee after the mandate for the sale was granted to the FCTA. In addition, copies of the valuation reports were later passed to the Federal Mortgage Bank of Nigeria (FMBN) for assessment, towards floating a Federal Government bond to ease the provision of loan and mortgage facilities for the public servants.

In all, 32,581 housing units were identified and valued based on the list of houses disclosed by Federal Government MDAs. This figure included houses not disclosed to the Valuation Consultants by some MDAs but were captured via information from AGIS reconnaissance and other independent FCT sources. It is pertinent to note that the houses valued also included 515 houses occupied by public servants in areas outside the FCT such as New Karu and Mararaba in Nassarawa State and Suleja in Niger State. These were handed over to the Federal Ministry of Housing and Urban Development to take further necessary action.

In line with the guidelines for the sale of houses, two methods of valuation were employed for each individual property using the Current Replacement Cost method, and then Open Market Value approach. The Current Replacement Cost (CRC) valuation or the Quantity Surveying approach ascertained the estimated cost of replacing, or rebuilding the entire property again at the prevailing cost of labour and construction materials. This method excluded the cost or value of the land and the differential effects of location on value, and therefore usually produces a lower price than market value, for the building in question. However, in some of the Satellite Town locations the reverse may be the case as replacement cost may be higher than market price of property in the particular location. This valuation formed the offer price granted to career public servants (CPS) on 'first right of refusal'. The open market value (OMV) or the Estate Surveyor's approach is an estimation of the current market price for the property given the prevailing demand, level of supporting infrastructure, location and therefore cost or value of land. This valuation constituted the reserve price, or baseline price, for offers granted to political office holders, POHs on 'right to match' and public bid participants in the Auction/Bid Rounds. The OMV was generally higher than the replacement cost of a house as it took local conditions, locational advantages, market demand levels and other factors into consideration. However, in rural locations such as the distant satellite towns where land values were lower and demand very weak, the OMV could and does fall considerably below the replacement cost of the property. A total of 980 houses were also captured as "Essential Housing Units" and excluded from the sale exercise as required by the approved guidelines.

The Sale Process of Government Houses in Abuja - Guidelines and Categorisation

The approved guidelines classified the beneficiaries of the sale exercise into three broad categories: Career Public Servants (CPS) that were eligible for a grant of offer based on the 'first right of refusal'; Political Office Holders (POH) that were eligible for a grant of offer based on the 'right to match' a winning bid; and Public Bidders (PB) that were eligible for a grant of offer on the basis of a 'winning bid' in a simple public auction/sale.

The sale exercise commenced in April 2005 with the processing of CPS expressions of interest and a total of 20,661 offer letters were issued to qualifying CPS. Out of this, 1,944 CPS had made full and final payment, about 17,000 had made payments of a minimum of 10% or more, and 1,361 were unable to make any payments by 20th October 2006 and consequently those offers were forfeited and withdrawn. A total of N37.6 billion had been realised from payments by CPS. The second phase of the exercise, which was the Public Auction/Bids, commenced in September 2005 and the last round was held in December 2006. A total of seven General Public Auctions/Bids and one Special Auction/Bid were held, with 4,175 offers being granted to winning bidders who had made payments of about N10 billion by April 2007. Also dependent on the outcome of the public auctions were the offers to POH, whose houses had to be advertised prior to consideration for an offer. 722 offers were granted to POHs, but only 567 had completed payment for their houses by the time we left office.

Gross Revenues from Sale of Houses as at May 2007

In all, about 27,000 CPS, POH and other Nigerians acquired houses under the programme. About N68 billion had been realised from the sale exercise by March 2007, and N25.5 billion had been remitted to the Federal Government under the terms of the exercise, while some N30 billion in mortgage facilities originated by different banks were still domiciled with the banks pending their repurchase by the FMBN.

As part of government's efforts to facilitate the acquisition of the FGN houses by a large number of public servants, the Federal Government, through the FCTA, Ministry of Finance, CBN, SEC and FMBN initiated a mortgage bond that would enable prospective buyers access the mortgage market to finance the purchase of their houses at reasonable (single-digit) interest rates. This bond was successfully issued on the 21st May 2007 with UBA Global Markets as the lead initiator.

Pilot Mortgage System

At the beginning of the sale exercise, the administration expressed the desire and commitment to providing the funds required by buyers to pay for the houses on sale through the provision of affordable mortgage facilities via a bond to be floated by the Federal Mortgage Bank of Nigeria (FMBN), initially proposed to be about N100 billion. The combined sale and mortgage support strategy was designed to encourage home ownership through mortgage finance in order to rebuild and stabilise the middle class in the FCT and Nigeria, particularly in the face of the dismal home ownership rate of less than 5% and housing deficit of 16 million units in the country.

Under the financing structure, the FMBN issued a N100 billion bond, fully guaranteed by the Federal Government, which was then underwritten by banks and other financial institutions. These financial intermediaries were expected to purchase the bond. At the retail end, mortgage originators were to first create the mortgages with their own funds under the FMBN's uniform underwriting standards, while FMBN will subsequently purchase such mortgages from them using the proceeds of the bond issue, thus providing the liquidity for the creation of further mortgages.

Where an underwriter/investor decided to originate mortgages, the FMBN will accord priority to acquiring and refinancing its qualifying mortgages up to the amount of the bond underwritten by such an institution. The flotation of the proposed bond also sought to expand on the overall economic reform agenda to drive innovation in, and increase the depth and breadth of financial intermediation. It was our expectation that beyond the bond flotation, which would have the acquirers of the FGN houses as ultimate beneficiaries, many more Nigerians would become home-owners through a robust mortgage finance system that evolved from the Abuja pilot and experience. Unfortunately, the bond flotation was unduly delayed because the Central Bank of Nigeria refused to provide the forbearances required by the banks to subscribe massively in purchasing the bond. Therefore, we had no time to expand its application to other jurisdictions outside the FCT.

After we left office, my expectation that Tanimu Yakubu, then FMBN CEO who became Yar'Adua's Economic Adviser, would push the process to completion and mainstreaming to cover the rest of the country, did not materialise. So in spite of our best efforts, Nigeria is yet to put in place a national mortgage system, and we are all the worse for it.

Challenges Faced and Some Lessons Learnt

The sale exercise had not been without its fair share of problems. Indeed, a project as extensive, complex and sensitive as this was bound to be problematic, and the FCTA and the Sale Implementation Secretariat expended great energy to resolving as many of the issues as possible in the most efficient, transparent and equitable manner possible. Some of the most significant problems included: the reliance on a flawed and incomplete database of houses in the FCT primarily compiled by valuation consultants engaged by the SGF and complemented by the efforts of FCTA agencies and agents; the low level of understanding of the guidelines displayed by career public servants, political office holders and members of the general public, as well as, the managements of the various MDAs; delays in the issue of the FMBN bond; pressures from different quarters to modify or manipulate the guidelines; and the general indiscipline and corruption displayed by some participants in the exercise.

On the eve of the transition to the Yar'Adua administration in 2007, the Sale Secretariat had successfully transferred legal title in the form of Certificates of Occupancy to 1,500 individuals, while a further 11,000 were at various levels of processing for C-of-O, having completed payments on their houses. At the time we handed over, I never anticipated that this exercise would become the source of the biggest smear on my name and reputation to date - the allegation that "N32 billion was unaccounted for" under my watch.

The mercenaries in the Senate Committee, FCTA and the Yar'Adua administration were careful not to accuse anyone of embezzling the money since they knew they were lying, and all the funds were intact, but, by appropriate "purchase" of newspaper headlines - suggested that I stole the money. I sued both the National Assembly and the Federal Government when their Finance Minister discovered N46 billion in 15 bank accounts that my successor-in-office had hidden to prove the disappearance of the funds. By then, I had in my possession the joint audit report of the Sale of Houses programme prepared by Akintola Williams Deloitte & Touche and Aminu Ibrahim & Co., dated July 2007, confirming that not a penny was missing.[71] The matter is still being argued before the Federal High Court, with all government agencies doing all they can to delay its closure.

The Justice Bashir Sambo Saga

Perhaps the most publicised controversy arising from the sale of houses programme was the ejection of Justice Bashir Sambo, in August 2006, from his official residence located at 1, Aso Drive, Maitama District. At the time the carefully choreographed media war led by the *Daily Trust* newspaper was going on, I chose to maintain silence, and just directed the secretariat to take out full-page adverts explaining what it had done and why. I thought that was the end of it. Sadly, less than a year later, Justice Sambo, who was chairman of the Code of Conduct Tribunal, died on 29th April 2007 in a Cairo Hospital. He was 76 years old and had been ill for some time. For that reason, I decided never to join issues with those who thought that the ejection of the deceased jurist was inappropriate and went as far as suggesting that it caused his 'premature' death. I remained silent because the man could no longer defend himself if I chose to speak out. I will not go into the detailed history of the interactions and interlocking relationships between our families or the record of our previous interactions in the FCT in his role as head of Jama'atu Nasril Islam in Abuja and the Abuja National Mosque Management Board. These are matters of public record in FCT Administration's file, with living witnesses and the institutional memory of the public service.

I will simply tell my side of the story on the sale of the house in question, subsequent cancellation, and the actions that followed naturally with reference only to letters written by Justice Bashir Sambo himself and other officials in the government. These exchanges of correspondence culminated in my directives to the Sales Secretariat on 7th July 2006 to eject him immediately from the house in question because he had by then, become an illegal occupant.

Justice Bashir Sambo was appointed chairman of the Code of Conduct Tribunal (CCT) in May 1996 by General Sani Abacha, after a long career in education in the old North Central State and Sharia Courts of Appeal in Kaduna and the FCT. He was appointed for a second and final five-year term by President Obasanjo. His term was deemed to have ended in April 2006 or thereabouts. The CCT is one of the federal executive bodies created by the Constitution to put on trial any political office holder who abuses his office, including those, like the president, the vice president, the governors and their deputies, that have immunity while in office. Its decisions are subject to appeal, making it the equivalent of a High Court. What is unusual about the CCT is that even though it operates as a court and imposes sanctions including asset seizures and disqualification from holding public office, it is part of the Presidency and not the Judiciary.

The approved guidelines exempted from sale all houses occupied by judges of superior courts of record - the Federal High Court, High Court of the FCT, Court of Appeal and Supreme Court. The guidelines were not specific on CCT, National Industrial Court, Sharia Court of Appeal and Customary Court of Appeal of the FCT. However, since all these but the former were under the Judiciary, we had no difficulty exempting all their houses from sale. The CCT, being under the executive branch was treated like other parastatals, and the chairman and justices treated as political office holders with rights to match open bids for the houses they occupied.

The CCT houses were, therefore, advertised in national newspapers on 2nd September 2005. They were put on open bid and thereafter, through an offer letter dated October 5, 2005, Sambo along with one other justice were given up until 19th October to exercise their right to match the bid price by making a downpayment of 10 percent. In the case of Justice Bashir Sambo, this amounted to 6,525,200 naira. That was when he took steps to lose the opportunity he had to purchase the house he was occupying. The first wrong step taken by the CCT was to write to FCT complaining that the chairman and members of CCT were "....*not political office holders but judicial officers....*" and demanded similar treatment. When we did not respond, the CCT reported the matter to President Obasanjo who referred it to us on October 24, 2005 with a benign comment[72] and no directives. In the circumstance, Justice Bashir Sambo collected his offer letter, and made the first payment on 22nd November 2005, about a month later than he should.[73] It was nonetheless accepted.

The issue, I suppose for Justice Bashir Sambo, was simple. His neighbours on Aso Drive who were career public servants were paying a little above N20 million for the same house he was being asked to pay N65 million, and he wanted the same "preferential" treatment. He first visited me to make the argument that he was a civil servant when the houses were advertised for public bidding in the media. When I reminded him that the retirement age for civil servants is 60 and he was well over 70 years old and that his appointment, promotion and discipline were not within the purview of the Federal Civil Service Commission, he left disappointed and visibly upset. At that point, the CCT came up with the new argument of their chairman and judges being "judicial officers" and expecting that would earn them the same treatment as "career public servants."

Before making the second payment on 19th December 2005, Justice Sambo had sent a petition to the president making the case that CCT members were "judicial officers" whose houses ought not to have been put on bid, and should be sold on Current Replacement Cost basis not Open Market Value. The President referred his petition to me for comment, and sought the legal opinion of the Attorney-General of the Federation, Chief Bayo Ojo. Obasanjo also sought the views of the Chief Justice, Justice

Mohammed Lawal Uwais, on the status of CCT. Based on the verbal opinions and views he obtained, the SGF conveyed the decision of federal government to Justice Sambo, to withdraw the offer made to the CCT judges in a letter, reference 597001/T.9/215, dated 3rd April 2006, and copied me. I was accordingly directed by Obasanjo to withdraw the offer letter and refund any monies paid by the chairman and members of the Code of Conduct Tribunal.

Justice Sambo promptly responded to the SGF in a letter dated 4th April 2005, then claiming that (1) CCT members were not judicial officers (2) he had a subsisting contract with government which must be respected, as soon as he paid the balance of 80% of the sales price. We wrote on 11th April 2006, withdrawing the offer and suggesting that another house could be purchased by Sambo. In effect, by trying to get the house at a cheaper rate, Sambo managed to lose the opportunity to buy the house! Justice Sambo then wrote an interesting letter to me, dated 18th April, 2006, accusing me of treating government property as my personal property, rejecting the withdrawal letter sent to him by the Sales Secretariat, restating that he was NOT a judicial officer, and ending with a statement which would have invalidated the sale even if there were no other breaches or grounds: *"As a matter of fact I have already sold the house in order to get the money to pay the remaining 80% as others have done."* Justice Sambo then surreptitiously submitted a certified cheque constituting the final payment of N52,201,600 on 25th April 2006 to the Ad-Hoc Committee to strengthen his mythical contractual claim. I suppose he thought that the payment would enable him have documents to tender in court in a future litigation. By then Sambo had retired from public service and 90 days after retirement, he became an illegal occupant - a trespasser in occupation of government property and liable to ejection without notice.

Observing Sambo's persistence and capacity for intrigue, I advised Obasanjo to obtain the legal basis for the decisions in writing and for the Cabinet to formally consider and decide on the status of CCT vis-a-vis the sale of houses programme. He agreed and requested written briefs from both the AGF and CJN on the matter. Meanwhile, the two payments collected from Justice Bashir Sambo were refunded on 16th May 2006 and collected by his assistant, Yahaya Abba. The Committee never banked the third certified cheque for N52, 201, 600 dated 25th April, so no refund was necessary and it was simply returned to Yahaya Abba who duly signed for it on the same date.

The Attorney General's legal opinion was conveyed to the SGF in a letter referenced HAGF/SGF/2006/Vol. 1, dated 16th June 2006. The legal opinion and the CJN's views were deliberated upon by the Cabinet and a formal decision taken to add CCT's houses to the list of exempted "essential houses." Meanwhile, Justice Constance Momoh had been appointed the new chair of CCT, and she was incurring huge hotel bills which were unjustifiable. Having refunded the monies collected in full to Justice Sambo, and having retired from service in May 2006, he was considered a trespasser from July 2006 and ejected from the residence after several notices to vacate. Justice Sambo claimed in the media that he had filed a suit against the FCT, but if he did, we were never served any processes. I was certainly never personally served as required by the FCT civil procedure rules. In the end, I think, I decided to leave the judgment of what transpired between Justice Sambo and I to the Almighty God, knowing that He Knows everything that may be hidden in the hearts of men. I merely invite readers to peruse all the documents in Appendix 10, and let Sambo's letters and the opinions of other officials involved in the matter speak for themselves. I had never commented on this matter before, and will say no more because as lawyers would say – *"res ipsa loquitor"*

Chapter Eleven

Restoring the Abuja Master Plan

Courage is not the absence of fear, but rather the judgement that something else is more important than fear.

– Ambrose Redmoon

It is the action, not the fruit of the action, that is important. You have to do the right thing. It may not be in your power, may not be in your time, that there will be any fruit. But that does not mean you stop doing the right thing. You may never know what results come from your action. But if you do nothing, there will be no result.

– Mahatma Mohandas Gandhi

President Obasanjo's passion for Abuja and his concern that it was becoming another Lagos was certainly one of the reasons behind my appointment to administer the Federal Capital Territory. At the peak of the 'silence is the best answer to a fool'[74] controversy, I had cause to ask him why he cared so much about Abuja and why he was willing to apologise to the Senate to ensure I remained on the job. He told me a compelling story starting with his tenure as Federal Commissioner (now Minister) of Works under Gowon.

The government witnessed the demographic explosion of Lagos after the civil war, the impact of the oil boom from 1973, and the need for the construction of Eko Bridge in Lagos. He spoke of Eko Bridge being Julius Berger's first major civil engineering project in Nigeria and the beginning of a long friendship with the then JBN project engineer Hans Whitman that has remained.

Abuja and Obasanjo - A Touching Story

Obasanjo described the challenges he faced in making Lagos liveable with massive infrastructure investments eagerly supported by the Head of State, General Yakubu Gowon. However, it was a losing battle, as Lagos grew faster than the rate of infrastructure build-out necessary to make it work. Obasanjo had proposed to Gowon a system of ring roads around Lagos, a railway (metro) system, and ferries to take advantage of its Lagoon and waterways, but the cost was horrendous. That was when the thought of moving the capital out of Lagos to a brand new location as a solution, began to form in his mind and Gowon's. Less than a year later, Obasanjo became one third of the Murtala-Obasanjo-Danjuma troika that succeeded General Yakubu Gowon in a bloodless coup on 29th July 1975.

As Chief of Staff, Supreme Headquarters, Obasanjo was not only the equivalent of the vice-president of Nigeria, but in charge of supervising the governors who administered the twelve states of the federation, which later rose to 19 states. Obasanjo therefore initiated the debate on the need to relocate the federal capital from Lagos, and the triumvirate accepted the idea. From that point on, in what would appear to be a politically astute decision, Obasanjo took the lead in selecting the members of the panel to study the matter and make recommendations to the government. Obasanjo ensured that all but two of the members were from southern Nigeria, but knew each would be objective in assessing the continuous suitability of Lagos as federal and state capital, as well as administrative and commercial centre of Nigeria. Only two persons from the North – Justice Owen Feibai based in Jos, and Muhammad Musa Isma[75] from Kano, were members of the Justice Akinola Aguda Panel. The other members were Dr. Tai Solarin,

Col. Monsignor Pedro Martins, Dr. Ajato Gandonu, and Professor O. K. Ogan. The acceptance of the Justice Akinola Aguda Panel Report led to the promulgation of the Federal Capital Territory Decree No. 6 in 1976 that created the Federal Capital Development Authority, charged with the responsibility of planning, developing and maintaining Abuja as Nigeria's new capital.

The Pioneers of Abuja

Nine days after signing the decree creating the Federal Capital Territory into law, General Murtala Mohammed was assassinated in an abortive coup and Obasanjo became Head of State, but his interest in the Abuja Project did not wane. He appointed Mobolaji Ajose-Adeogun as Minister of Special Duties in the office of the Head of State to be in charge of the new Federal Capital Territory project. For day-to-day supervision and control of the project, Chief of Army Staff, Lt-Gen. T Y Danjuma, was assigned the responsibility of midwifing Abuja to a successful birth. Under T Y Danjuma's watch, the key decisions taken included the appointment of consultants for the preparation of the Abuja Master Plan, the ecological surveys, demographic audits and river blindness eradication schemes. The resettlement of original inhabitants and the policy modifications all had the thoughtful, decisive and balanced imprints of T Y Danjuma, a public leader highly respected in our nation.

Obasanjo, therefore, considered Abuja almost like his own child. He had appointed two ministers – an architect and civil engineer in succession, between 1999 and 2003 to restore Abuja back on its originally planned path and roadmap of order and orderliness, but nothing much happened under their watch. Obasanjo was somehow confident that I could take on the assignment. That was the reason he selected me – a person that he ended up supporting like his own son - for the FCT assignment, and he added, that up to that point in time, I had not disappointed him.

As earlier mentioned, the planning and development of Abuja were guided by the Master Plan that was prepared by International Planning Associates, an American firm. The Master Plan was to enable the emergence of a new City that would function better than Lagos. Though Abuja was conceived as a *"Garden City"*, it was also meant to be a functional and efficient one in terms of movement of people and vehicles within its boundaries. Obasanjo's anger was that the vision of Abuja's founding fathers was being lost due to the distortion of the Abuja Master Plan over the years. This was essentially the situation until July 2003 when our administration assumed office.

Challenges Abuja Faced in 2003

At inception, the challenges before us were rooted in every facet of the development of the FCT - as referred to severally in this book, not just in Abuja City itself but the surrounding 'Satellite Towns'. As the territory's population had far exceeded the planned capacity of available infrastructure and other facilities, the city had become filthy and unruly, surrounded by unplanned squatter settlements, with over-stretched infrastructure. While the planned population of the city by the end of Phase 4 was projected at three million inhabitants, we were informed in our ministerial briefings that the territory contained over six million people, with only parts of Phases 1 and 2 completed in mid-2003.

There were many other infrastructural and social challenges. For instance, there was congestion in FCT schools; some had 120 students in classrooms designed for 30. The FCT had 14 hospitals with about five under construction, at various stages of completion. The roads were congested. The water supply plan envisaged the building of ten storage tanks around the city as well as the orderly expansion of the water treatment capacity, which by 2003 could only serve 650,000 people.

Many buildings, structures and shanties in the city were built on water pipelines, sewer trunk lines, under high-tension electric lines and on green areas. Violations of land use regulations were rampant, with plots designated for schools or religious institutions developed as residential or commercial facilities and so on. Most of these were overlooked in the past due to the immense cost of removal and the compensation payable by the government as many of the structures had approved Building Plans and Certificates of Occupancy.

The restoration of the Abuja master plan meant demolishing some of these buildings, recovering parks and green areas, clearing squatter settlements and expanding infrastructure and social services to meet the needs of the rapidly expanding population of Abuja and its environs. I will describe briefly how we planned and executed this controversial programme, which, as Machiavelli rightly observed of citizens' resistance to beneficial change, only attracted due recognition and accolades years after we left office.

Preliminary Review and Early Signals

The two volume handing-over notes I received from the then Abuja Permanent Secretary, Dr. Babangida Aliyu,[76] had little to say about illegal structures and other master plan violations. I realised that unless I asked questions and dug deeper, no one was willing to talk about these thorny issues. Consequently, on the 5th of August 2003, I asked Mallam Sani Kalgo, the Director of Land Administration & Resettlement, to brief me on an international conference he had co-hosted on behalf of the MFCT on the review of the Abuja Master Plan in 2001. After the briefing, during which Mr Kalgo handed me a copy of the publication of the conference proceedings, I directed the permanent secretary to furnish me with the several studies and reports related to the design, implementation and distortions of the Abuja Master Plan. By the time my aides and I reviewed, digested and summarised these reports, we realised that non-compliance with the Master Plan was inhibiting Abuja's potential to provide basic services to residents. The city's green corridor had been abused, for instance, by locating army barracks in areas for a national monument and landscaping for tourism and the addition of unplanned districts like Guzape, Kpaduma and Kurunduma. Obstruction of flood plains by buildings would lead to major flooding in areas like Kubwa. The misappropriation of green areas and construction of corner shops had deprived Abuja of proper parks and shopping malls respectively. The squatter communities that have emerged to overwhelm the satellite towns of the FCT have become unsanitary urban sprawls that must be removed and relocated sooner or later. Garki Village, a slum within the Federal Capital City, had become unmanageable, reminding everyone of Obalende near South-West Ikoyi, Lagos. All these issues needed to be addressed in addition to the expected attention and interest in the demolition of some visible buildings.

The good news was the realisation that all the information needed to begin the restoration programme had always been available in the ministry. A meeting with the Director of Development Control, Olu Ogunmola, produced a list of over 300 illegal structures already identified for revocation of title, notification and immediate removal. He was eager to start, but I decided otherwise. First, I briefed President Obasanjo and Vice President Atiku Abubakar of what we had found, and what the next steps were going to be. I then obtained the consent of the president to begin the restoration exercise on 30th August 2003, with the removal of some buildings on a trunk sewer line along Accra Street. We picked this location for its double demonstration effect – the street smelt from the odour of raw sewage, so there was little dispute of the impact of the distortions, and the recovered area was to be converted into a park for the enjoyment of the neighbourhood. I requested President Obasanjo's presence to bless the kick-off of the restoration. He confirmed immediately, cancelling a planned weekend in Ota to be there.[77] We then approved the removal of buildings and fencing put up by some high profile Nigerians[78] to send the signal that no one was above the law in FCT.

Task Force on Master Plan Enforcement

With our signalling phase over, we ordered a suspension of the exercise for a week. Then we constituted a task force to oversee and execute the programme to ensure that from then on, every case went through rigorous inter-departmental review and recommendation before I approved removal. This 'task force' approach also served another purpose common in public service – sharing of blame and responsibility for what we knew would be an unpopular, controversial course of action. All the key MFCT directors were members of the Task Force,[79] and we gave them the mandate to co-opt any officer needed to execute the assignment. The task force met initially weekly, which became daily when I gave the deadline of December 31, 2003 for the completion of all restoration operations within the Federal Capital City. The Task Force sent me weekly reports and daily memoranda to approve the removal of structures that violated the development control regulations. We could not remove every building that violated the master plan as they were many and would have been too heavy a burden on our resources. We therefore had to prioritise and decide which buildings constituted the most serious threats to the inhabitants of Abuja – these were those sitting on sewer lines, water trunk lines, under high tension electricity lines and transportation (road, transit way, flood plains, etc.) reservations. Some parks and green areas were recovered, but many were lost permanently because of the quantum of compensation that would have been payable if we chose to revert strictly and completely to the original Master Plan.

The Results of Enforcement Efforts

In the end, we removed some 945 buildings within the Federal Capital City, about 300 in Kubwa and about 12,000 shanty structures and buildings in some of the squatter settlements in Idu-Karmo, parts of Jiwa, Gwarimpa, Jabi and Anguwan Mada. In addition, about 11,000 illegal structures and containers were removed to restore Wuse Market to its original design. Additional new shops were also built in the market. We relocated 30,215 traders occupying the site of the Abuja Central Shopping Mall in Central Area to Dei-Dei, thus clearing the fire-prone Bakassi Market.

We recovered 33 green areas, developed and commissioned twelve recreational parks all over the City and the satellite towns. We developed an irrigated tree nursery with over 30 indigenous varieties of plants at Wuse II, the first of its kind in Nigeria. We procured, propagated and nurtured to maturity about one million seedlings to trees that were planted in the city. When the parks became very popular, we introduced park rules and regulations alongside a policy document that guided the development and management of parks in the FCT. We had great ambitions for Jabi Lake, but sadly, we were unable to get both banks of the lake developed with the recreational and tourist facilities we had dreamt of.[80]

We cleared all illegal buildings on transit ways,[81] removed three wrongly located petroleum stations[82] that compounded the traffic congestion at AYA junction, and built an overhead bridge and roundabout to ease traffic in the area. We recovered and secured the Gudu and Gwarimpa cemeteries, and clearly demarcated them between Christian, Muslim and Unclaimed corpses with Abuja Environmental Protection Board in charge of their management and maintenance. We re-introduced the regime of house-to-house sanitary inspection in the City and outskirts, inspecting some 68,856 houses at the end of 2006, initiating prosecutions and issuing abatement orders for violations to 23,749 households.

As part of our efforts to restore orderliness to the City, we implemented a street naming and house numbering scheme for Phases 1 and 2 of the Federal Capital City. Many people are unaware that Abuja has a naming system for districts, expressways, streets within districts and so on. All districts derived their names from the original Gbagyi settlements nearest to, or within the districts like Maitama, Wuse and Garki. Expressways and parkways in the FCT were named only after former presidents and vice presidents respectively like Murtala Mohammed (ONEX) and Nnamdi Azikiwe Expressway (Ring Road 1). Arterial and collector roads honoured some of our founding fathers and foremost nationalists. Each district had a street naming scheme. For instance, street names in Maitama originate from natural features – rivers, lakes, mountains and the like.[83] Garki's are named after local government headquarters in Nigeria, and Wuse streets recognised African cities and so on. I will now take a few cases of the master plan enforcement that became controversial to throw some light on what really happened and why.

Corner Shops and Neighbourhood Centres

In the context of the Abuja Master Plan, the neighbourhood centres were the lowest point in the hierarchy of community facilities and services within the territory. Each neighbourhood centre was to contain at least a primary/nursery school, police station, post office, clinics and grocery shops. When the government could not immediately construct the neighbourhood centres as planned, the Gado Nasko administration sub-divided the neighbourhood centre plots into smaller plots – for 'corner shops', and issued five-year licenses to develop these small shops as stop-gap measures. The intention was to remove these as soon as conditions permitted for properly-designed shopping malls to replace them. The plan, according to former minister Gado Nasko[84] was to withdraw the licenses on expiration of the initial period to give way to the development of truly modern neighbourhood centres.

Instead, corner shops assumed a life of their own and became permanent features of the FCC, going beyond occupying neighbourhood centre plots to include the wrongful conversion of parks, green areas, flood plains and transit way reservations. The list of corner shop allottees read like "who is who" of Nigeria, and blighted the landscape. An interdepartmental committee on Corner Shops and Neighbourhood Centres[85] was therefore formed to study the whole issue and make recommendations. They reviewed and inventoried all corner shop allocations by AEPB, Development Control and all MFCT Departments, submitting a report in August 2004. On 13th August 2004, we published a six months' notice in national newspapers revoking and withdrawing all development permits for corner shops and open spaces in the FCT.[86] As our plans to remove the corner shops progressed, I received a report from the State Director of the SSS dated 17th May, 2005 titled – 'Imminent threat to law and order by Amalgamated Neighbourhood and Corner Shop Owners Association in the FCT'. The association, led by one Kola Martins, had met and issued a press statement urging us to reconsider the decision to remove the corner shops. On June 2nd 2005, we invited all corner shop owners and tenants to a meeting and agreed on strategies for the redevelopment of the neighbourhood centres. We restated that there would be no going back on the decision to remove the corner shops. We persuaded those that attended that we intended to give them the first opportunity to redevelop the locations of their business, and not take the land back for our friends and cronies, as they had alleged.

The resolutions from the meeting were widely published in several newspapers.[87] We maintained a standing committee to continue engagement with the corner shop owners and tenants throughout the removal and redevelopment period. We then removed more than 1,215 such shops, and encouraged the licensees and occupants of the corner shops to form incorporated associations to redevelop the plots into shopping malls that they could own jointly or as tenants-in-common, in accordance with guidelines issued by the FCT Administration.

Abuja Investment Company prepared Prototype Preliminary Designs for the Neighbourhood Centres to guide the associations and reduce the time taken for developing design briefs and schematic designs. The terms of conditional grant required the associations to move to site and begin development within six months of offer. Thereafter, they were to proceed diligently with the works to the satisfaction of the Department of Development Control. At the time, plots similar in size and location to those of these centres were being alienated for at least N100 million each in the open market. We were interested in serious developers and took a decision to grant these titles in three steps. Upon a payment of N1 million, a license to develop would be issued to qualified developers. As soon as they begin work on site within six months of initial offer, a firm letter of offer (called R of O in FCT parlance) would be issued when buildings reach a certain level. A firm title in the form of a Certificate of Occupancy with a 99-year tenor is then issued upon achieving more substantial completion.

In general, we found that the physical progress on site of the various associations at the dates of withdrawal (more than 12 months after initial offer) fell below expectations. We therefore withdrew the 'licenses to develop' for violating the terms of offer and invited other reputable business organisations to take over under conditions that were even more stringent. Virtually all the reputable developers had already achieved substantial progress by the time we left office.

How did these companies achieve greater progress under more stringent conditions than the Neighbourhood Centre Associations? For us in the FCT Administration at the time, the lesson we learnt was that getting many people to collaborate and cooperate to execute such construction projects just did not work. Instead, it appeared better to allocate land to individuals and organisations and hold them accountable for better results.

Kuruduma/Kpaduma/Apo Tafyi Layouts

These layouts were created out of the green buffer zone around the FCC by my predecessors and the Abuja Municipal Area Council (AMAC). AMAC did so in violation of the Court of Appeal's decision in *Ona v.* Atenda, which declared illegal any land allocation in FCT by anyone other than the Minister. We found that it was mostly favoured staff of the FCTA, well-connected persons in the Villa, and in the National Assembly that were the principal beneficiaries of that illegality and abuse of the green buffer zone around the city of Abuja. Throughout my tenure as minister, I withheld assent to assign, mortgage or sell any of the plots in these layouts, filed them for study when submitted for re-certification and requested AMAC to hand over details of their 'allocations' for a holistic decision. Our plan was to take inventory of all the allocations and provide alternatives on the completion of the regularisation of area council land 'titles'. The allottees of these illegal allocations were not notified of any revocation so could not be offered alternative plots because we had not sorted out all the issues by the time we left office.

Illegal Land Conversions in Kubwa

Kubwa was originally a new town to resettle original inhabitants of Maitama and Wuse villages when city infrastructure construction in the districts began. The resettled citizens were usually provided with facilities like houses, schools, markets, social and medical facilities, along with tracts of farmland so their agrarian lifestyles were not unduly disrupted. However, the decision to accelerate the movement of federal ministries to Abuja converted Kubwa into a de facto satellite town, and most of the original inhabitants sold their homes at premiums and relocated to other parts of the FCT, thus compounding the overall resettlement challenges.

We found that illegal land conversions were therefore taking place, not only within the FCC, but in the satellite and resettlement towns. In Kubwa, nearly 100 hectares of erstwhile agricultural land statutorily allocated to Fresh Fruits Ltd - a company owned by former minister of FCT, Air Vice Marshall Hamza Abdullahi,[88] had been wrongly converted into residential land. The farm was re-designed, laid out and 'allocated' to gullible citizens with the active connivance of past and current staff of the MFCT and FCDA. Over 60 hectares of this land had been occupied by illegal developers with hundreds of buildings. The situation needed to be acted upon, resulting in the extensive demolition operations in Kubwa.

We began by setting up a task team to ascertain the extent of encroachment and illegal conversions in Kubwa, and received a progress report in March 2004. The team identified 24 people, many of whom were MFCT/FCDA staff, that were engaged in various land-related malpractices in the old resettlement town. The report established that more than 200 houses were built in parts of land set aside for agricultural purposes for three organisations, including the International Institute for Tropical Agriculture (IITA). The team recommended that the minister of FCT accepted the reality of the rapid and unexpected growth of Kubwa from a small resettlement town into an urbanised satellite town. The committee also recommended that the farmlands be redesigned as residential areas, the grants revoked, and the allottees relocated to Kuje, Kwali or other agricultural parts of the FCT. The report suggested that Kubwa should then be completely re-planned into the proper satellite town it had organically evolved into.

We accepted the recommendations, but agreed to limit the land holdings for large residential estates (then renamed Mass Housing) to a maximum of 50 Hectares and directed that new, modified but residential titles be issued to Fresh Fruits, General Gado Nasko and IITA. We then inventoried the illegal buildings already constructed, pegged boundaries and informed the Kubwa Residents Association (KUREWA) that no more buildings should be erected in the area.

President Obasanjo wanted all the illegal residential buildings demolished and land reverted to the MFCT. We argued in the FEC that this would amount to waste of resources, as those allocated the land had to develop it into residences after excavating the foundations anyway. We made the case that we should live with the infractions but make the law-breakers pay as if they were acquiring the buildings afresh from the government. This was derived from the legal maxim of *"lex situs"*, that is 'whoever owns the land (the government) owns whatever is built on it by any other person (the illegal developers)'. We saved thousands of citizens from being traumatised and the FCTA made hundreds of millions of naira in revenues from persuading the cabinet to take this pragmatic decision. We got approval of the cabinet to issue titles to all the pegged, illegal buildings upon payment of the current replacement costs of the buildings plus normal land charges. We got our staff and outside team of valuers to value each property, and issued offer letters.

Unfortunately, members of KUREWA began building fresh settlements, enlarging the encroachments, sometimes during the night to avoid detection. We had to put a decisive stop to this. Therefore, we deployed bulldozers to Kubwa and took down the illegal additions. We also used the opportunity to begin the clearance of other illegal structures in Kubwa, causing uproar in the House of Representatives.[89] This was understandable, because we later found that many influential members of the House had several such illegal properties there. This pattern of clothing private, self-interest as public concern has sadly become a repeated pattern of conduct of politicians in general, including those in the national assembly.

Early Vindication by Unexpected Flooding in Kubwa

Our incessant enlightenment campaigns on the dangers of violations of the Abuja Master Plan got a boost from a most innocuous occurrence – an unexpected flooding that caused massive loss of property in Kubwa, about a year after the House of Representatives had condemned our corrective actions in the town. On 7th August 2006, a section of Kubwa town woke up that Monday morning submerged by water due to heavy overnight rains and flash floods from the surrounding hills. Happily, no lives were lost but properties were destroyed, routine activities disrupted and productive time lost in the process. The worst hit areas were those along the banks of Usuma River and its tributaries, which traversed Kubwa Town.

The FCT administration intervened in the rescue operations and the temporary resettlement of those affected. We then proceeded to remove structures that appeared to obstruct the free flow of the river, while carrying out a study to address medium term needs for the prevention of future occurrences. About three weeks later on 22nd August 2006, I received a comprehensive report prepared by the quietly efficient, intelligent and competent Deputy Director of Development Control, Yahaya Yusuf[90] with analysis of the situation, recommendations and schedule of remedial actions. Mr Yusuf recommended the complete removal of 159 buildings, partial removal of 35, shifting of 23 fence lines, and the relocation of four non-residential land uses. Outlined was a four-week programme of removal and clearing of rubble that would then be followed by planting and landscaping of river banks and proposed recreational grounds, and construction of walkways along the river and its tributaries by the Bwari Area Council. I approved all the recommendations on 6th September, and this time around, no one in Kubwa or the national assembly raised any objections. God in His Mercy had come to the aid of the righteous FCT administration by showing what happens when rules, regulations and issues of orderliness are taken for granted.

Public Toilets

Early in my tours of the FCT, I noticed a young man urinating on the side of the road.[91] I made a mental note to ask whether the Abuja Master Plan made no provisions for public toilets in our weekly management committee meetings. The discussion confirmed that indeed, public toilets had been provided for in the plan, but like everything else, had been distorted, converted to other land uses or not built at all. This led to the establishment of a committee to ramp up the provision of public toilets in the Federal Capital City on 3rd May, 2004, under the chairmanship of Mrs Maimuna Ajanah, the Director of Municipal Affairs and Environment of MFCT.[92] The committee submitted its report in June 2004.

The report indicated that nine public toilet facilities were first constructed by the FCDA between 1996 and 1997, and allocated to private operators and managers upon payment of N12,000 per annum. The public toilets had been converted into shops, business centres and laundromats. The allocations were accordingly revoked, and quit notices served on the violators. The committee observed that there were only 13 such facilities in the entire city and these were grossly inadequate for a daytime population of nearly two million. The report made far reaching recommendations for the MFCT and the private sector to construct several public toilets in locations all over the city with easy connections to sewer lines. In parks, bus stops and recreational areas without access to sewer lines, the committee recommended the deployment of prefabricated 'waterless' toilets. The FCT management committee approved all the recommendations and these were faithfully implemented, with little or no demolition.

Chief Igweh Comes Calling

One of the earliest challenges we faced in restoring the Abuja Master Plan was a confrontation with a leading politician and businessman now deceased, Chief J. U Igweh, the owner of the

Bolingo Hotel in Abuja. Chief Igweh was a very close business and political associate of Vice President Atiku Abubakar, a leading member of the PDP and reputedly one of the party's original godfathers in the southeast. His case was typical of many influential Nigerians who wanted things done their way without regard to the rules. In my BPE days, he had bid to acquire controlling interest in Unipetrol, but lost to Ocean & Oil (now Oando). To be fair to him, he did not blame me entirely, as he felt Atiku ought to have given me orders to simply sell the company to him. In spite of this, I think our earlier unprofitable interaction may have coloured his attitude to our efforts to sort out the issues relating to violation of the land uses around Bolingo Hotel. I will now explain this in some detail.

In November 1990, Bolingo Hotels and Towers were allocated Plot No. 597 of approximately 1.2 hectares within the Central Area, AO District, for the development of a hotel building. Four years later, in 1994, after the commencement of the development of the hotel, the company applied for and obtained approval for the adjoining Plot 598 of approximately 6,400 square metres as an extension of its premises [Plot 597]. Plot 598 was designated in the Abuja Master Plan as a Central Area Night School, so the city lost the benefit of having such a school. This allocation brought the area of the land allocated to the hotel company to 1.8 hectares. In November 1995, barely one year after the first extension was granted, another request followed. This time the company sought for extension into Plots 599, 600 and 601. In the Master Plan, Plot 599 was reserved for green park and Plot 600 for a church, and infact had already been allocated to ECWA Church. Plot 601 was reserved for the transit railway park. Plots 599 (green area) and 600 (ECWA Church), with total size of about 1.3 hectares were revoked and reallocated to Bolingo Hotels, while Plot 601 was not for obvious reasons. With the new addition, the total size of land granted in favour of the hotel increased to 3.1 hectares. By these allocations, the ministry changed three prescribed land uses of the Master Plan in favour of Bolingo Hotels, namely: Educational, Green Park [also reserved as corridors for underground utilities] and Religious Institution [already allotted to the ECWA Church]. In terms of size, the allotted land area increased nearly three times over the original allocation. It should also be noted that Bolingo

Hotels insisted on separate certificates of occupancy for the extensions granted [that is Plots 599 and 600] instead of a mere adjustment to the TDP for the first grant [that is Plots 597 and 598] to incorporate the new extensions, as is customary in FCT land administration.

In spite of the concessions made by the ministry, another letter in 2000 from Bolingo Hotels and Towers sought for further extension into Plots 601 [this was the transit way park plot that was earlier refused] and 602 reserved as rail terminus. It was obvious that the request was against basic urban planning principles and could only be granted in further gross violation of the Abuja Master Plan. The application was, therefore, not granted and this was duly communicated to Bolingo Hotels. In early 2003, just before my predecessor left office, Bolingo Hotels re-applied for the allocation of Plots 601 and 602 that had earlier been refused in the public interest. Unfortunately, the staff of the Surveying Division of MFCT misunderstood the Minister's written directive to 'process' Bolingo's new application as an 'approval for allocation' and proceeded to prepare a title deed plan (TDP) and issued a bill for the Certificate of Occupancy in respect of Plots 601 and 602 without any formal approval and letter of allocation. It is important to note, however, that without finally obtaining the required ministerial approval, the purported 'processing' of Plots 601 and 602 TDP in favour of Bolingo Hotels was of no effect, as the mere possession of the TDP could not have passed title of the plots to Bolingo Hotels.

That was the situation I inherited in July 2003 when Chief Igweh paid me a courtesy call and complained that corrupt officials of the MFCT were delaying the issuance of his certificate of occupancy, thus delaying his expansion programme for the hotel. I think his expectation was that I would instruct the expeditious issuance of a C of O, which would have remedied the fatal omissions in the 'allocation' process. Luckily, I did not. I promised to look into the matter and requested for a full briefing by all the land-related departments. What I found – the almost insatiable land grab and flagrant violations of development control regulations both amazed and intrigued me.

Bolingo Hotels and Towers obtained the building plan approval for the development of a hotel on Plot 598 in 1996. Bolingo had since then had a series of confrontations with, including physical assault on, staff of the Development Control Department due to various development control contraventions. Some of the contraventions included:

- Development without setting-out approval. The application for setting-out approval for the development of Plot 598 could not be granted due to inappropriate access to the plot. Temporary access was taken by Bolingo Hotels through Plot 596, which belonged to an adjoining allottee. Despite the ministry's disapproval, Bolingo Hotels proceeded with the development. Bolingo Hotels even went further to obtain an injunction from the Abuja High Court restraining the lawful allottee of Plot 596 from denying Bolingo Hotel trespassory access through his plot.
- Erection of Fence without due approval. In September 2003, Bolingo Hotels built, without planning approval, a fence and other structures on Plot 599 reserved as corridors for utilities. The Development Control Department reacted by demolishing these structures.
- The development of Plots 599 and 600 without planning approval. Several contravention cotices were served on Bolingo Hotels with regard to the development of Plots 599 and 600, done without proper title or the approval of the Department of Development Control. As usual, most of the notices were ignored by Bolingo Hotels. Only a big man in Nigeria, with wealth and political connections, could behave with such impunity.

However, there were more complaints from other departments of FCDA about Bolingo and Chief Igweh.

The Bolingo Hotels building was set-out and built on natural ground level, which is inconsistent with engineering regulations. The access to the hotel was from Road AR-14 [which was yet to be constructed then] where the road finish level would be about eight metres above the natural ground level on which the hotel was set-out. This was the ground for Development Control's refusal of approval for the setting-out, but Bolingo Hotels ignored the department and proceeded to develop. The problem was that when

Road AR-14 would eventually be constructed, the hotel would then be at least eight metres below the road level and susceptible to flooding, plunging vehicles downwards into the hotel in the event of accidents and other risks.

Bolingo Hotel's management refused to acknowledge these problems, which would be germane to the safety of its customers and the viability of the hotel itself in the long run! Another engineering problem created was the attempted extension of Bolingo Hotels and Towers to Plot 599, a green park reserved as corridors for utilities within the Central Area of the City. Bolingo was duly informed of the danger posed by such development to the overall functioning of the city, but the FCDA was ignored. Bolingo's argument that this problem had been solved by the provision of a culvert running through the plot was not acceptable because utility lines would require periodic maintenance and it is vital that the FCDA has a free access to them for its men, plant and machinery. This was not the case because the lines would be enclosed within Bolingo's premises. In addition to housing the utilities, the plot is a green park and should be so maintained.

On my instructions, we wrote Bolingo inviting their team for a meeting. During the long and stormy session in which a visibly affronted Chief Igweh shouted and insulted me and our staff more than twice, we maintained our calm and communicated the decisions we had taken with regards to the land allocation, land use and development control violations as they affected the hotel. Chief Igweh stormed out of the meeting and petitioned President Obasanjo and Vice President Atiku Abubakar, claiming that I was engaged in violation of his rights to the land already allocated to him, victimisation and discouraging investment in Abuja and Nigeria. My seven-page response, dated 11th October 2004 and addressed to Obasanjo, was accompanied by engineering drawings, survey maps and previous correspondence, explaining everything, and the actions we took. President Obasanjo once again upheld our decision and actions.

The Ministry acted immediately after the meeting, revoking the rights and interests of Bolingo Hotels over Plot 599 designated as green park/corridors for utilities and Plot 600 designated as a church, both plots measuring 1.2 hectares. We also withdrew Bolingo's purported rights and interests over Plots 601 and 602, designated as transit railway park and public park/rail terminus respectively, measuring 8,733.51 square metres. Plot 597, measuring 1.2 hectares, and Plot 598, measuring 6,400 square metres, were to be retained by Bolingo Hotels. These two plots are fully developed and accommodate the main building of the hotel. Though Plot 598 constituted a distortion of the Master Plan, having regard to the consequence of revoking it, which would require demolishing a part of the main building of the hotel and payment of compensation, it was reluctantly conceded to Bolingo Hotels.

Contrary to the widely-reported claims of Bolingo Hotels of the value of assets affected by the revocation [which Bolingo put at N6.6billion], the affected structures, comprising the boiler room, generator house, fencing, and the like were valued by the Ministry in the sum of about N103.4 million. This amount was to be paid as compensation to Bolingo Hotels had we established that the affected structures were built on titled land and approved (before construction) by the Development Control Department as required by law. When we found otherwise, Bolingo Hotels was in the end not entitled to any compensation. Chief Igweh died, almost two years after we took these decisions, in an air crash. In the FCT, we all prayed that his soul and that of other passengers rest in peace, and I visited the family to convey our condolences.

The Rules Apply – Even to the PDP Chairman

Amadu Ali, Barewa old boy, medical doctor, Nigerian army colonel, and pioneer director of the National Youth Service Corps (NYSC) in the Gowon administration, minister of education in the Murtala-Obasanjo regime, senator in the Second Republic, and senior special assistant to President Obasanjo, became the chairman of the ruling party, the PDP, in 2005. Due to our common membership of the Barewa Old Boys' Association, I looked up to him as an elder brother, and we got on well, even though I preferred his predecessor, Audu Ogbeh, who remains the only truly reformist chairman the PDP has ever had. Our excellent interpersonal relations were to sour in the course of the restoration programme because one of his houses in Asokoro District was built on a trunk water line, and had to be removed. Like every Nigerian "big man," particularly the ultimate Abuja big-shot, the chairman of the ruling party, that action was a slap in the face that he neither forgave nor forgot.

Senator Amadu A. Ali was granted right of occupancy over Plot 1613 in Asokoro District in 1994. He proceeded to erect two residential buildings on the plot in accordance with the terms of grant and approved building plans. Later, it was discovered that one of the buildings sat squarely on the main water trunk line supplying the Asokoro District. We therefore issued the required notices, valued the violating structure for compensation and thereafter removed the building. It was an unprecedented action that Obasanjo used to good effect to prove that the reforms of the federal government were blind, not selective, and spared no one, including the chairman of the ruling party. For me, it was another show of political will and support by Obasanjo for the master plan restoration programme. As I say to anyone who cares to ask why I decided to leave the PDP in 2010, it was because the party had evolved within four years into a totally different party, more toxic, self-centred and controlled by a tiny clique of morally-flexible people. Is it possible in the PDP of 2010, I always ask, for any minister of FCT to take down a building owned by the chairman of the ruling party? "No way!"– virtually everyone would respond. However, we did that, and life continued like nothing had happened, as it should. Rules should apply to everyone without fear or favour.

Diplomatic Pressure – the French Embassy/School Plot

Another restoration decision that became a subject of controversy was the revocation of the title of the Embassy of the Republic of France to a piece of land in Maitama District that the embassy had earmarked for the ambassador's residence. The decision to revoke the title was misunderstood at the Ministry of Foreign Affairs, and an angry Obasanjo summoned me to a meeting to explain. Jacques Chirac was a close friend of Obasanjo's and it looked like I had ruffled not only diplomatic relations with France, but the warm friendship between the two statesmen!

The Embassy of France, like other foreign missions, was granted two plots of land nearly gratis in the FCC, to build their Chancery in the Diplomatic Zone of the Central Area District, and for the construction of the ambassador's residence in either Maitama or Katampe Extension. The French Embassy's residential allocation was granted in December 1993 - Plot 929 in Maitama measuring 4,829 square metres, a sizable plot. A year earlier, in November 1992, the embassy was granted Plots 376 and 377 in Central Area District, measuring 1.49 hectares, to build its Chancery. The embassy was granted another plot elsewhere for a French School as well. For some reason, the embassy wanted a much bigger plot for the Ambassador's Residence, which the MFCT could not provide, so they acquired one in the open market, Plot 122 of 1.88 hectares, earmarked for a primary school in Maitama A6, along Mississippi Street, allocated to Professor Albert Ozigi. Professor Ozigi was a prominent educationist and a Barewa old boy. He had acquired the plot in 1990 to develop a primary school. He sold it to the French Embassy on 30th December 1993. The Embassy intended to build its Ambassador's Residence and Chancery on this plot, but had not done so until we revoked the title on 8th November 2005.

The French ambassador, Mr Dominique Raux-Cassin, wrote me on 9th December 2005, appealing for reinstatement of the title, restating the resolve of the French authorities to build the chancery and ambassador's residence in that location reserved in the Master Plan for a primary school. In what smelled like diplomatic blackmail, the Ambassador reminded me that Obasanjo had escorted French President Chirac to the location to perform the foundation laying ceremony in July 1999. In the New Year, we met with the ambassador and his team and gave them the option of building a French Primary School on the plot, reminding them that they already had separate allocations for chancery and residence. The ambassador was unwilling to take our offer. We, therefore, reconfirmed the revocation, which led to the summons by Obasanjo. By the time we put all our explanations forward with documentation not controverted by the French Embassy, Obasanjo upheld our decision and subsequently sought the understanding of the French authorities that the FCT Administration was trying to sanitise our capital city the way their forebears had made Paris so beautiful. That was the end of the matter.

Nonetheless, I was certain that unless we got that school built on that plot, the French Embassy would probably appeal to a future president or minister of FCT to get the revoked plot back. It was middle of 2006, and we had no budget for the year to build such a school. I, therefore, put out a search to find a developer ready to build a school IMMEDIATELY on the plot. The only condition I insisted must be met was that the person would provide designs, construction documents and a signed contract before I approved the grant of conditional title, and full title when the project achieved 50% completion.

We got lucky. Lucky Omolewa, a wealthy defence contractor, was looking for land to build a top-class basic education school, and was therefore ready to meet our conditions. We granted the title and today, I am proud to see the school in operation – Centagon School – any time I drive to Chopsticks, one of my favourite restaurants in Abuja, or to visit any of my friends in that neighbourhood. The circumstances surrounding the revocation and reallocation of the plot sparked rumours that Lucky was merely a front for me. Indeed, a couple of people have approached me to help gain admission for their children into 'El-Rufai's school.' Some are embarrassed when I tell them that I had never met the owner of the school until I retuned from exile in 2010. Sometimes I wish all the buildings in Abuja and other businesses in Nigeria whose ownership were at one time or another credited to me truly belonged to me. I would be Nigeria's wealthiest man, and would need not struggle every autumn to pay the school fees of my children and myriad others that I sponsor. But *c'est la vie*.

We Did What We Had To Do

People often observe, in some cases correctly, that many of our decisions and restoration efforts have been reversed or allowed to flounder by my successors. The corollary to that is whether our effort was worth the pain and suffering— whether acquiring all the enemies that we inevitably did was all for nought. I do not agree. Firstly, I do not think that for anyone in a leadership role, there is any alternative to doing what is right, for its own sake. Secondly, it is posterity in this life, and Almighty God in the next, that will ultimately judge our decisions and actions, not those timorous souls too quick to render opinions based on the short term. Thirdly, there is an important message for the discerning arising from the corrective actions we took. It would teach a lesson that although a 'big man' may presume to have clout to violate the regulations today, but sooner or later, the law would catch up with him, and often at greater cost. Finally for me, restoring order in the chaos that we found many aspects of living in Abuja at the time, was simply consistent with my personal philosophy of life, a preference for rules and orderliness–a burden that I needed to discharge personally so I could sleep well at night. It was without question worth giving four years of my life to pursuing. Therefore, I have no regrets for attempting to do what we did. We did what we believed to be right at the time we did it.

Chapter Twelve

A Large Construction Site

> *The city is a fact in nature, like a cave, a run of mackerel or an ant-heap. But it is also a conscious work of art, and it holds within its communal framework many simpler and more personal forms of art. Mind takes form in the city; and in turn, urban forms condition mind.*
>
> – Lewis Mumford (American Writer, 1895-1990)

My professional background, as a chartered quantity surveyor and construction project manager, proved invaluable in the administration of Abuja, particularly in addressing Abuja's infrastructure development needs. The Federal Capital Territory was without doubt the single largest construction site in Nigeria, if not in Africa. Indeed, successive ministers of FCT have focused more on infrastructure development of the Federal Capital City than anything else. In spite of this, the influx of people into FCT had accelerated since 1999, outstripping the FCDA's capacity to provide not only physical infrastructure, but also other social and human services in acceptable quantity and quality.

A focus on city infrastructure build-out often led to inadequate attention to the development needs of the satellite towns. In spite of this, many city districts with plots allocated had incomplete infrastructure, thereby driving up the cost of serviced land, rental levels and real estate values to unsustainable levels. Moreover, the existing infrastructure, mostly built in the 1980s and 1990s, was falling apart because of neglect. Apart from roads, no other component of the city transportation master plan, including bus ways, transit ways and light rail system, had been designed, let alone built. Every aspect of social, economic and physical infrastructure – hospitals, schools, markets, roads, water and water management— were in short supply and under increasing pressure. It was clear that addressing infrastructure deficits would be a principal challenge in administering Abuja.

A week after I took control of Abuja, on 24th July 2003, it was the turn of the Executive Secretary of the FCDA, Charles Dorgu[93] and his team of planners, engineers and surveyors, to brief me on their core function of planning, development and maintenance of the infrastructure and facilities of the FCT. They first presented me a huge "welcome card," then got down to business. The briefing focused on FCDA's problems and then proposed a schedule of visits to all their major projects. Like every agency of the MFCT, the FCDA complained of inadequate funding, excessive debts of nearly N50 billion, and unresolved resettlement issues that had further hindered the execution of some of their infrastructure projects. We visited all of FCDA's projects a couple of weeks later, between the 21st and 28th of August, 2003. I studied the briefs and took copious notes, asked questions and began to form plans in my mind how each of the projects could be managed better, challenges addressed, and the bottlenecks cleared.

Firstly, I decided that we would not embark on any new projects unless we completed some of the existing ones. This decision became necessary due to the scarcity of funds – the FCT was entirely dependent on the Federal Government for its financing needs.[94] We attempted changing that by clawing back the personal income tax of private and public sector employees resident in the FCT[95], introducing property taxes in the City, and exploring other sources of revenue, in addition to improved collection of land fees and rents. Secondly, I needed detailed briefing on the thorny subject of resettlement of the original inhabitants of the FCT. It was not only an issue of fairness to the indigenous people, but the lingering problem hampered the orderly development of the City.

Resettlement of Original Inhabitants

The briefing revealed that at the inception of Abuja, the entire territory was a sparsely populated area of less than one hundred thousand people - one of the reasons for its choice as our future capital. The territory's Master Plan assumed that all the original inhabitants within the nearly 8,000 square kilometres of the FCT would be relocated to neighbouring states. Professors Akin Mabogunje and S. I. Abumere of the University of Ibadan were engaged to undertake demographic and ecological surveys to ascertain the exact number of people to be resettled outside the territory, and determine appropriate compensation. However, this policy of total evacuation was shelved, largely because the estimated N300 million compensation was deemed unaffordable. General T Y Danjuma, then in overall charge of the new capital project, recommended that only original inhabitants living within the city footprint – the 250 square kilometres containing phases one to four of the Federal Capital City- would be resettled in the future, when required by infrastructure development.

Original inhabitants living outside the city might choose to remain but would have no indigeneship rights because every citizen of Nigeria living in the FCT shall enjoy the equal residency status. Consequently, those entitled to resettlement under the revised policy fell into two categories: those who had opted to be moved out of the FCT and had received compensation between 1976 and 1978, and those who remained but would be resettled within the Federal Capital Territory (FCT), outside the Federal Capital City (FCC), whenever their places of abode were affected by city development projects. We tasked a committee[96] to look at all the locations where infrastructure projects have been delayed by resettlement issues, and recommend immediate remedial actions. The committee was also required to revise and update resettlement and compensation fees that had been unaffected by inflation since 1979. The committee submitted its report in April 2004, once community leaders were finally persuaded to sign on to it. Implementing the recommendations was not without difficulties. Due to incessant obstructions created by two recalcitrant local chiefs— the District Head of Galadimawa and Sapeyi of Garki— I took the unprecedented decision to invoke the powers I had under the act guiding the appointment of local chiefs and deposed them both, in

December 2005. The Sapeyi was exiled to Abaji for a period. We reversed the decision in 2007, after repeated representations by other traditional rulers and assurances of good behaviour on the Sapeyi's part. Infrastructure development projects in the FCT proceeded unhindered as soon as we took the deposition decision.

Satellite Towns Development

A major recommendation in the FCT Regional Development Plan Report was the establishment of satellite towns to serve as "growth poles." The Abuja Master Plan had envisaged that the informal sector would, by the year 2000, make up 43% of the total labour force in the City proper. It was, therefore, envisaged that the City's support population would have to be accommodated in specially designated Satellite Towns of about 100,000 – 150,000 population each. In order to reduce the pressure on the city and ensure compliance with the Master Plan and the Regional Development Plan, the creation of new Satellite Towns and upgrading of existing ones had become imperative by July 2003. Some of these Satellite Towns could serve as resettlement centres for the indigenous population to be relocated from areas covered by the FCC Master Plan.

We sought Obasanjo's approval (and budgetary support) to establish new Satellite Towns, in Kuje, Gwagwalada and other areas. We also sought approval to upgrade some existing settlements to Satellite Towns, considering such factors as proximity to existing infrastructure, such as transportation.

The Satellite Towns Development Agency received unprecedented support and attention from President Obasanjo and I, and had an exemplary team headed by Buhari Dikko, who was one of FCDA's pioneer civil engineers. Ongoing road improvement projects were concluded.

We also made progress in infrastructure development within the City and rest of the territory. We were especially determined to improve the environment, completing sewage treatment plants, landfills, and water treatment plants, in addition to clearing the landscape of thousands of broken-down vehicles and other eyesores.

We improved and expanded public buildings and facilities as well. Notable examples include new administrative wings for the National Assembly, additions to the Federal Secretariat complex, and commenced work on the showcase Millennium Tower.

As was typical, many of these projects faced headwinds from entrenched interests. A case in point was the permanent building of the FCT Administration, which was planned for a plot in the Central Area that was illegally occupied by Bulet Construction Company. After we ejected Bulet, the company obtained a court order followed by a judgment that found a way to justify the continued illegal occupation, even in the absence of any title to the land. Bulet, a company owned by Ismaila Isa Funtua, a politician, businessman and friend of the powerful, had been given a licence to occupy the plot as a temporary site office for the construction of the neighbouring federal secretariat building. But the license had long expired. Funtua had approached me in my first month as minister, complaining that the permanent secretary, Dr. Babangida Aliyu, had refused to "regularise" the allocation of the plot to him. But I established, upon investigation, that the plot was in fact earmarked for the FCT building in the Abuja Master Plan. What was more, no private organisation could be allocated a plot in the Ministries Zone. Though I patiently explained this to Funtua, the logic of the Master Plan meant nothing to him as the ultimate Nigerian big man. One of our judges, in his infinite wisdom, has allowed him to so far have his way, and the FCT Administration building remains unbuilt.

Abuja Technology Village

The Abuja Technology Village, or ATV, was a Federal Government-promoted project. The FCT was mandated to anchor it in order for it to achieve speedy implementation. The project was aimed at establishing Nigeria as the technology hub for Africa, and was billed as a free trade zone. The vision of the ATV was to establish a platform for creating a sustainable knowledge economy.

We commissioned Aim Consultants in 2005 to prepare the master plan and urban design of the village, as Nigeria's first technology park, our future Silicon Valley. An excited President Obasanjo named it Abuja Technology Village. We awarded the infrastructure development contract for the construction of the ATV to Gilmor Nigeria Ltd., and persuaded the Nelson Mandela Institute to locate the first campus of the African University of Science and Technology within the village.

All the major global technology companies with presence in Nigeria, such as HP, Cisco Systems, IBM, Microsoft and Oracle, committed to locating their operations in the ATV, while Nigerian companies like Zinox Systems and SocketWorks confirmed their interest to do the same. The ATV project was still ongoing, had acquired "Free Zone" status and attracted massive private sector interest by the time we left office. We explored the promotion of a 600MW independent power plant for Abuja to ensure stable power supply to the ATV and accommodate the typically voracious appetite of tech firms for power. A state-owned Chinese engineering company, CGC, expressed willingness to finance, design and construct a gas pipeline from Ajaokuta to Abuja, to supply the power plant. We began discussions with three companies to go into joint venture with Abuja Investment Company Ltd., to implement these projects, but did not conclude the arrangements by the time we left office. Luckily, after we left office, Yar'Adua's economic adviser Tanimu Yakubu, focused his interest and high-level attention on the ATV, ensuring it was not left to wither on the vine, like many of our other initiatives. The ATV may well be a reality sometime soon, under the able leadership of my former special assistant, Hauwa Yabani.[97]

The technology village currently hosts the African University of Science and Techonology, an initiative of African diaspora academics under the aegis of the Nelson Mandela Institute. Taking a cue from MIT as well as the Indian Institute of Technology, their vision is to establish four campuses of excellence for the AUST to train high quality engineers, scientists and humanities professionals. The initiative enjoyed the early support of the World Bank, African Development Bank, the UK government, and the European Union. Dr. Frannie Leautier, then Director of the World Bank Institute who now runs the Africa Capacity Development Foundation out of Harare, was the lead promoter of the project. She coordinated bilateral and multilateral efforts to realise the project. Abuja competed with Tanzania to host the first campus and won, by offering serviced land along the Airport Road, twice the size offered by the Tanzanian government.

However, the promised support from the bilateral and multilateral sources was late in materialising, so the FCT Administration and agencies of the Federal Government bore most of the set-up costs of the university. In 2005, the FCTA spent over N100 million for offices, furniture and equipment, vehicles, staff salaries and consulting fees for the planning and design of the university. Another N200 million was expended by the FCTA in 2006 for staff salaries, various consultancy fees for environmental impact, topographical survey, hydrological studies, architectural designs, land clearance and fencing, and the meetings and conferences of the African diaspora professors that came to Abuja for the project's ground breaking ceremony in December 2006. FCTA also signed an infrastructure construction contract with Gilmor Nigeria Ltd., for the ATV, which included the AUST. We relocated the Chinese construction giant, CCECC, from the proposed AUST site, but persuaded the company to leave behind their buildings for the immediate take-off of the university.

The FCTA, therefore, provided virtually all the initial setup funding. The government-funded Petroleum Technology Development Fund, or PTDF, then headed by Adamu Maina Waziri, granted $25 million to build the Gulf of Guinea Institute (G2i) within the AUST campus. The institute is to serve as a continental centre of excellence in petroleum engineering and related technologies. The first set of masters degree students of the AUST, drawn from several African countries, enrolled in September 2008. The university has proudly graduated at least three sets of masters' degree holders from several African countries by 2011.

The Abuja Transportation Plan

Similarly determined efforts went into tackling transportation challenges. We reviewed and updated the Abuja Transportation Plan to include new settlements like Nyanya and Karu whose unexpected growth and rapid urbanisation were not envisaged by the Master Plan. This led to the creation of a bus system comprising three integrated lines and concessions - National Unity Line (Green) FCT's Abuja Mass Transit Company (Red) and Sonic Global Company[98] (Yellow) - to connect parts of the city, satellite towns and major population centres within and outside the FCT. We granted the companies land for their maintenance and parking terminals, obtained import duty, VAT and tax waivers from the Federal Ministry of Finance for them, encouraged banks doing business with FCTA to finance the acquisition of their fleet. Our plan was for the bus operators to continuously expand their fleets so as to reduce bus-waiting time to not more than 5 minutes anywhere in Abuja by December 2009. The once ubiquitous 'El-Rufai' Cabs - a territory-wide taxi system using the London Taxis and Dark Green Peugeot 307 as the two acceptable prototypes also came out of this effort. The goal was to get all the rickety second hand taxis off Abuja's streets, inculcating the habit of hire purchase and deferred payment acquisition, making regular payments and encouraging entrepreneurship. This we achieved by securing import duty, VAT and tax waivers for Peugeot Automobile Nigeria, Kaduna, thereby enabling the Abuja Leasing Company Ltd (a public-private partnership with a handful of commercial banks) to lease the cars to owner-drivers upon the payment of three hundred thousand naira – about the price of a second-hand vehicle. We also brought in safety training and street location experts from London Taxis to train the first batch of drivers in safety, security, locating street names and numbers, and customer service, at our own cost and only those who were fluent in English, and had passed the final test were allowed to acquire or drive the cabs.

Finally, we also embarked on the establishment of a light rail network, which groundbreaking was presided over by President Obasanjo in the waning days of his administration, in May 2007. When operational, the Abuja Metro system was to be powered initially by diesel, convertible later to electricity, with the capacity to transport about 20,000 passengers per hour at very affordable prices. Had the project been allowed to proceed, it would have been completed before December 2010, and Abuja would have joined over 100 cities with metro systems including London (which commissioned its Underground in 1863) and Cairo in Africa (that commissioned its own system in 1987). Regrettably, the project later fell victim to a particularly destructive Nigerian disease, the *successor abandonment syndrome*, as a result of which the light rail network project remains "ongoing".

Human Capital Development

The Education Secretariat was established in June 2004 as one of the mandate secretariats in line with FCT's administrative reform programmes. This was informed by education being an instrument of economic, scientific, technological, social and political empowerment for the individual and the society at large. We wanted to ensure the provision of qualitative, accessible and affordable education to the entire inhabitants of the FCT at primary, post-primary and tertiary levels.

The FCT education secretariat achieved a lot under its two secretaries between 2004 and 2007. We increased budgetary provision for education from 5% of FCTA's total budget in 2003 to about 20% by 2007; a total of 250 new classrooms were constructed between 2004 and 2005, with hundreds more under construction by 2007; 987 sets of classroom furniture were provided for 237 primary schools in all the FCT area councils; and 145 classrooms were constructed in 75 primary schools in the FCT area councils

We also rehabilitated 462 classrooms in 75 primary schools and introduced a school shuttle bus system to convey uniformed students to and from schools; not only to provide succour to those who could not afford the high transport fare, but to also check cases of truancy and lateness on excuses of transportation difficulties. We acquired buses for senior secondary schools in the FCT to ease the transportation difficulties of staff and students who needed buses for academic and recreational activities such as excursions, inter school academic and sporting competitions and for emergencies.

We equipped schools with computers to promote information and communication technology (ICT) and expose students to modern trends in teaching and learning in order to stimulate their urge to engage in research. This was actualised through collaboration with Intel Corporation, World Computer Exchange Programme and Professor Nicholas Negroponte of MIT, and sponsorships from MTN, Zenith Bank and the Education Tax Fund.

We improved the quality and quantity of teaching staff throughout the FCT by recruiting 700 qualified UBE teachers and 590 teachers in key subject areas in the senior secondary schools. An additional 1,200 teachers were contributed by the Federal Ministry of Education through its Federal Teachers' Scheme as we sought to reduce the student-teacher ratio to a reasonable level. In terms of welfare, teachers enjoyed a 25% increase in pay compared to 15% for other public servants in the FCT engaged in non-teaching activities and an award system for students and school teachers was instituted in the 2006-2007 academic year with the star prize of a brand new car for the winner. This was an effort to encourage students to strive for good results. Teachers, principals and staff of the education secretariat were also recognised for exceptional performance. We also trained teachers on modern teaching methods, principals and vice principals on management principles and non-teaching support staff on relevant ancillary competencies.

Finally, we had an education sector plan (ESP) prepared in collaboration with the World Bank and the United Kingdom's Department for International Development (DFID). The ESP was addressing the gaps in the FCT education sector and budgeting for a 10-year development plan. The Education Management Information System (EMIS) was designed and installed to address the problems of incorrect data, which had contributed in the past to faulty decision making. The purpose of the EMIS was to collate all education data into a single unified integrated information system. We also upgraded the financial accounting systems in all FCT public schools. This project was aimed at improving the financial accountability and transparency in the management of school funds.

With respect to the health care component of human capital development, the Health and Human Services Secretariat, which succeeded the MFCT Health Department in 2004, with the responsibility for overseeing the health sector of the FCT in all respects, granted operational and administrative autonomy to the FCT general hospitals. This enabled patients to get more than 90% of their drug requirements in the hospitals and incidences of 'out of stock' medication were significantly reduced. The secretariat's intensive inspectorate and monitoring functions aided the closure of over 30 fake and unregistered pharmaceutical premises. Several unlicensed patent medicine stores were also shut down. Hospital manpower planning was considerably improved, enabling all the hospitals in the FCT to run 24 hour services with all the shifts covered.

We were conscious of the need for trained personnel for the sector. We trained 150 health workers, 25 each from the six area councils, 189 doctors and 669 nurses/midwives in various healthcare disciplines in 2006 alone. The Disease Control Division trained over 600 general health workers on the prevention of malaria, tuberculosis (TB), leprosy, HIV/AIDS, guinea-worm infection and schistosomiasis. This helped to improve early disease detection, treatment and treatment outcomes in the FCT We also set up a Public Health Department, which carried out all planned immunisation activities through the administration of oral polio, and Hepatitis B vaccines to children under the age of five. Over one million children were immunised in the four year period.

With the revamp of the FCT Action Committee on AIDS (FACA) and donor support, we established primary health centres in the FCT area councils and voluntary counselling and testing (VCT) centres in secondary health facilities to provide free counselling and testing services to pregnant women and free infant formula for babies with HIV-positive mothers. We provided free screening procedures, re-confirmation of HIV status, free immune boosters, food supplements, workshops on positive living, micro-credit and grants, free food items and referrals for prompt attention. I became personally involved in interactions with people living with HIV/AIDS, attending their network meetings and hosting them to dinners in the minister's residence a few times. This served to reduce the levels of stigmatisation of the disease in the FCT.

We made progress in stimulating a vast job-creation engine focused on enabling the private sector. Among the key drivers of our activities in this regard were the revamped Abuja Investment Company, as well as the Abuja Enterprise Agency. We invested heavily also in agriculture and social services for vulnerable groups, and paid particular attention to quality of life issues.

A Better Life for All

The purpose of government and public leadership, after all, is the constant pursuit of a better life for all citizens, to be an enabler, not an obstacle, and to ensure security, fairness and justice, and social harmony. These were our guiding principles, pursued rather singlemindedly, and often requiring the ruffling of many feathers and the stepping on many toes, big and small. Our commitment to rapidly accelerating infrastructure investments in Abuja was to remove one of the biggest bottlenecks to Nigeria's progress. We ramped up investments in education and healthcare because an educated population is a society's most important resource. This may sound like a cliche but it is no less true for that. We believed that the private sector should lead in economic activities and job creation. We therefore took steps to make life easier for businesses through tax breaks, import duty waivers, cheaper access to land and more responsive municipal services. We acted not for personal benefit, or to create any special advantage for our friends or unfairness for our foes. We believed that a measure of idealism was necessary for public progress.

We restructured the FCT administration into a slim, efficient and effective bureaucracy that treated citizens as customers. It comprised four organisations: the FCT Administration itself undertakes policy, residual administrative and final decision-making functions; the FCDA plans, designs and builds city and territory-wide infrastructure and facilities; the Satellite Towns Development Agency (STDA)[99] delivers on infrastructure outside the City boundaries while the Abuja Metropolitan Management Agency (AMMA)[100] maintains infrastructure within the city and territory and provides essential municipal services like water, garbage collection and recreational facilities. We tried to be public servants and did not behave like lords of the manor. We engaged extensively with the FCT's citizens through telephone helplines, radio and TV call-in programmes, and quarterly town hall meetings. I tried to lead by example. I never used sirens or motorcycle outriders. I obeyed traffic lights as I expected of ordinary citizens, and discouraged having an army of public servants in centipede-like convoys of vehicles accompany me everywhere, settling typically for only one additional car carrying security personnel. We did not, as is routine throughout our political establishment, spend the FCT's security funds for the benefit of anyone of us in the leadership. We did not allocate plots of land to ghost companies for our benefit, or used fictitious names or companies to allocate same to our friends or family.

We instituted a fair system of rewards for good conduct, and imposed sanctions – including firing and prosecution - for unethical and criminal behaviour. We applied the rules evenly and neutrally, without fear or favour, and without regard to social status. We got rid of staff with clear cases of incompetence, corruption or abuse of office, even when they happened to be our friends or relations.[101] These principles form the basis of how we believe any organisation, city, territory and country should be run. We preached it. We lived it. And our record bears witness to it. The rest we leave to Almighty God, who is final Judge of all humanity.

Chapter Thirteen

Reforming the Public Service

The trade of governing has always been monopolised by the most ignorant and the most rascally individuals of mankind.

– Thomas Paine

The Civil Service are the Opposition in residence.

– Anthony Jay

The reform of the public sector was one of the key components of our economic reform programme – the National Economic Empowerment and Development Strategy (NEEDS). With my background and experience in privatisation and parastatals' reform in the BPE, the Economic Team assigned this sub-task to me, and I drafted the sections related to privatisation, commercialisation and public service reform in the NEEDS document. When it came to implementation, we debated and agreed that instead of attempting a blanket reform of the public service all at once, we would conduct a pilot with a few government departments, learn from them, and then do a phased rollout to the rest of the service. Naturally, with the structural and service delivery challenges we faced in the MFCT, we offered to be the guinea pig. This led to the adoption of Abuja as the laboratory for trying out the reform components within NEEDS, before mainstreaming into the rest of the Federal Government.

First, we had to answer a few questions in designing a public service reform programme from scratch. Sequencing was a key issue. Do we start with the smaller but more resistant civil service or reform both the civil service and parastatals concurrently? What about the scope and priorities of the reform programme? How do we select which departments for the pilot? Should we be concerned with quality of public servants (qualifications and training-focus) or their quantity (right-sizing focus)? Finally, how do we ensure institutional sustainability by both injecting new blood into the service, and then creating reform champions to continue when we leave? Unfortunately, for us, we found no successful models of public service reforms that were easily applicable to our situation. We found that a country either has a great public service from day one like Singapore's, and then works to preserve it, or a good one like New Zealand's and then reform to improve it, or nothing. Once your public service becomes dysfunctional, it is very hard, like humpty-dumpty, to put it back together again, and that was precisely the situation with Nigeria. We realised that we were in a grand mess, but must do 'something' even if there was no record of accomplishment anywhere in the world of a successful turnaround of a broken public service. It was my duty to take charge of trying that 'something'.

Since 1999, President Obasanjo had intended to reform the public service. In fact, he initially had a minister for the civil service (Bello Kirfi, *Wazirin Bauchi*) but nothing appeared to have come out of it. In 2001, a human resource audit of the federal civil service at the behest of the IMF revealed that about 20 per cent of the nominal roll consisted of "ghost workers". Nothing was done about the audit, and like most things related to the civil service, these and similar abuses continued quietly growing unabated.

In 2003, Obasanjo tasked Yayale Ahmed,[102] the crafty head of the civil service of the federation, with the job of reforming the service, with a huge budget to support it. Yayale ensured the monies were expended travelling all over the world – visiting Malaysia, Singapore, Australia and New Zealand, among other nations, to learn "international best practices," sent beautiful 'progress reports' to Obasanjo, but implemented zero reforms at home. In fact, the situation continued to worsen, with reported corruption in postings done by the head of the civil service and even malpractices in promotion examinations undertaken by the Federal Civil Service Commission.[103]

Public Service in Context

It is a truism that no nation develops beyond the capacity of its public service, and there is still today, broad consensus amongst Nigerians that our public service is broken and dysfunctional. The quality of public servants and the services they provide to our nation are both below expectations. From the glorious days at independence when the best and brightest graduates competed to join the administrative service up until 1970s, our public service is more recently perceived as the employer of the dull, the lazy and the venal. In 2003, we were well aware of this need to retrieve our old public service that was effective, well paid and largely meritocratic, attracting bright people, imbibed with a spirit of promoting public good.

We began by looking back in time to see where we went wrong. The Nigerian civil service evolved from the colonial service with its historical British roots of an independent, non-political, and merit-based administrative machinery for governing the country. Each region then had its civil service in addition to the federal service. We asked some fundamental questions. What is the public service, anyway? How did our public service evolve from inception at independence to excellence and now to its current abysmal state of ineffectiveness? How can the public service be reformed, re-skilled and right-sized to provide the basic social services that will earn the public trust?

The Public Service - An Overview

The public service consists of the civil service - career staff whose appointment, promotion and discipline are under the exclusive control of the Federal Civil Service Commission (FCSC)- the national assembly service, the judiciary, public officers in the military, police and paramilitary services, employees of parastatals, educational and health institutions. By September 2005, when I became the chair of the Public Service Reform Team (PSRT), the number of federal public servants was slightly above one million. The estimated number working for the 36 states and the FCT was another 2 million. Adjusting for the increasing numbers of aides of the president, ministers, governors and legislators numbering anything between a low of 10,000 and a possible three hundred thousand, it was not unreasonable to put the total number of those working directly for governments then at about three million. Therefore, while our national population has increased by about 160% between 1960 and 1999, the size of our public service increased by 350% in the same period.

Crafting solutions to the problems of the public service required careful thought, thorough collection and analysis of data, and political will. The initial diagnoses and findings were sobering, to say the least. The civil service was rapidly aging, mostly untrained and largely under-educated. Their average age then was 42 years, and over 60% were over 40 years. Less than 12% of the public servants held university degrees or equivalent. Over 70% of the service was of the junior grade levels 01-06, of sub-clerical and equivalent skills. About 20% of the public service employees were 'ghost workers' - non-existent people on the payroll whose emoluments were stolen by staff of personnel and accounts departments. In the FCT, as will be detailed below, out of an initial headcount of 26,000, we found 3,000 ghost workers in the first round of audit. By the time we introduced biometric ID and centralised, computerised payroll, we found an additional 2,500 who failed to show up for documentation.

While the public service pay was low relative to the cost of living, the overall burden of its payroll as a percentage of the budget was huge. We found that in most states other than Lagos, Kano, Kaduna and Rivers States, an average of 50% of the annual budget went towards the payment of salaries and allowances to about 1% of their population. Employees of parastatals, including educational and health institutions, consumed nearly half of the money spent on staff compensation. The military, police, and other paramilitary groups consumed more than a third, while the core civil service took the rest.

The team which I chaired faced the daunting prospects of reforming a federal public service whose central management organs - the civil service commission and the office of the head of the civil service, had become corrupt, inept and ineffective. We learnt that appointments, promotions, postings and discipline were bought and sold by civil servants almost the same way shares are traded on the stock market.

Surprisingly, and with some relief, we did not see these levels of malfunction in the armed services. The human resource management systems of the Army, Navy and the Air Force were better and, to some extent, even the police and other paramilitary services were in much better shape than their civilian counterparts. However, first, I had to deal with the problems of reforming the largest and most unwieldy ministry in the federal public service - the Ministry of the FCT and its affiliated public service. The MFCT had been selected by the economic team to apply the template for reforming the public service. The success of the experiment led to the decision by the president in September 2005 to ask me to take overall charge of the public sector reforms.

Guinea Pig: The Ministry of the FCT

The MFCT was an ideal pilot for public service reforms for several reasons. First, it was an administrative basket case, giving rich opportunities for learning. The MFCT with its estimated 26,000 staff was also the largest single ministry of the Federal Government. Its single location in Abuja made it an attractive pilot. The MFCT also operated as a hybrid— functioning in many cases like a state and, in others, like a typical federal bureaucracy. This made it a plausible provider of lessons relevant for the 36 states. Our hope was that if we succeeded in making Abuja run better and look better, the regular gubernatorial and other visitors would seek to replicate such gains in their states. Finally, the leadership of the MFCT - that is our own team - had shown enough reformist antecedents for the Economic Team to have confidence that we would champion the change process.

The state of service delivery in the FCT was poor. Essential services like education, healthcare, environmental quality and security were not adequately provided by the MFCT. For me, it was qualitative indices like whether our grasses and hedges were of the same height on both sides of the road and whether the shortest cul-de-sac in Garki 1 was always clean and garbage collected daily that indicated that the administration was working. It was quantitative indices like how long it took to replace a broken street-light, the time patients spent in our hospitals before seeing a physician, and the number of students that made five credits in WASC and NECO examinations that would measure our administrative effectiveness. Did our staff regard the residents of the FCT as "customers" that they should be responsive to politely, and not with the arrogant indifference seen in most government departments? Were we thinking through policies to address observed problems, and seeing through implementation? These and similar considerations guided our thought processes throughout.

We, therefore, designed our FCT public service reform programme around six activities, with some pursued as "quick wins" to send the right signals, and others medium and longer-term in orientation. The activities were: planning, budget and procurement reforms; structural reorganisation of MFCT and agencies; modernisation of internal administrative processes, waste reduction and e-government solutions; performance measurement, monitoring and evaluation; privatisation of services and promoting public private partnerships wherever possible, and pension reforms, training and re-professionalisation strategies. The goals of all these were to improve service delivery and make the FCT run as a model city and territory in Nigeria.

Quick Wins ahead of Painful Reforms

We recognised that the reform programme will not have credibility until visible and sustained improvements in service delivery and the "look and feel' of the city are demonstrated within the shortest possible timeframe. We therefore focused our first six to nine months on six groups of decisions and actions to send the message that there were new people in town, and they care about delivering results quickly.

Beggars had become a huge nuisance in Abuja and even though the AEPB Act 1996 made begging and street hawking criminal offences in the territory, they had continued unabated and become an industry of sorts. At traffic lights and junctions, beggars and newspaper vendors struggled for space to attract the attention of motorists. We studied several reports of previous 'beggar deportations' and rehabilitation. We then made public our intentions,[104] and then designed a destitution management programme with three components - rehabilitation, empowerment and enforcement. We gave all the beggars the opportunity to attend the vocational training school in Bwari free of charge, with free feeding and lodging for the duration of the training, and paid them a monthly stipend. On completion of training in various trades, the FCTA gave the graduates tools and equipment, and some seed capital to start their small businesses. The programme trained hundreds this way. Those that rejected our offer were arrested and fined until they stopped showing up to beg. The others were repatriated to their states of choice if neither option was acceptable to them. Those affected by leprosy had a special settlement built for them at Yangoji in Kwali Area Council, complete with school, clinic[105] and other essential facilities. Within nine months, there were no beggars on Abuja streets.

The quick greening of the city to take advantage of the rainy season was another quick win. We invited construction companies that were beneficiaries of FCT's procurement contracts and other corporate organisations, and requested them to help with city greening and in developing our parks and recreational facilities as part of their corporate social responsibility. We made it clear that this was all we required from them - no kickbacks, no free tickets to Europe and so on. Many enthusiastically accepted and we developed and put into use sixteen neighbourhood, district and city parks within the first nine months. Some of the recovered areas were also restored as parks. Among those was Accra Street, where Obasanjo flagged off the widely-publicised demolition exercise on 30th August 2003,[106] and which became Ukpabi Asika Memorial Park. We intensified efforts to make Abuja cleaner and greener.[107] We launched a programme to plant one million trees in Abuja within four years, and published a tender to privatise garbage collections. We also invited tenders for the private maintenance of our streetlights to improve response time in changing expired lamps and so on. We completed all these processes within the first nine months as we were undertaking internal structural and administrative changes within the Ministry of FCT and its agencies.

We also paid off a large number of contractors and suppliers who were owed relatively small sums of money by the MFCT, as part of our "quick wins" programme. On assumption of office, I was briefed into believing that the MFCT had total liabilities in excess of N150 billion. On digging further and requesting for an aging analysis of the debts, I found that a substantial percentage of the debts were small-contractor claims of less than N10 million for work done or goods supplied. These contractors happened to constitute most of the under-capitalised, briefcase carrying, overnight contractors that take up a lot of executive time bearing notes from ministers, senators and governors, requesting payments for what had been due. I thought it made sense to just clear the backlog and get everyone to focus on bigger challenges. We, therefore, set up a committee on outstanding liabilities headed by Mr Sylva Ameh, Director Finance & Accounts, which submitted a report in October 2003. We tasked another committee headed by Yusuf Tsaiyabu, Head of Internal Audit, with making the payments, but there was one hurdle - there was no money voted for that purpose in the 2003 budget that I inherited.[120] We reviewed the spending priorities, cut down on purchases of tea and coffee, domestic and international travel, and so on. We then approached the national assembly to approve the virement - transfer of funds from one budget head to another. We effected payments in two batches in the total sum of N1.8 billion, in addition to some N700 million in normal liability payments by 31st December 2003, and succeeded in getting hundreds of companies off our backs.

I have gone into these details to demonstrate the link between sequencing the implementation of public service reforms, the organisational context and the outcomes. Pursuing public service reform as a standalone activity without visible improvements in other areas will be interpreted as simply laying off large numbers of people, and no more.

With regard to the core reforms in the MFCT, we first reviewed the nominal roll from the HR departments and compared them with the payroll of the Finance & Accounts Department. We ordered that a pay parade be undertaken for the months of August to October 2003 requiring every employee to collect his pay in person with staff ID card and letter of first employment. This was then followed by cheque-only payments to designated bank accounts, and then biometrics - about 3,000 staff failed to show up. We saved about N756 million in 2004 from these steps taken in 2003. For instance, the ministry's nominal roll showed 13,855 staff, but only 11,722 cheques were cashed.[108] Other parastatals and agencies accounted for the balance. By the time we concluded the restructuring and reforms within the FCT Administration, our nominal and pay rolls were capped at about 18,000 employees. We then undertook detailed process reviews, looking at our budget and spending priorities, and reversed the structure in favour of capital spending.[109]

The Ministry of the FCT was then dissolved by Executive Order and about 1,500 staff of the Federal Civil Service were given the option to convert to the FCT Public Service or return to the office of the Head of Civil Service for posting. Most of them chose to leave the FCT Administration. We then restructured the entire FCT Administration and right-sized the workforce, disengaging redundant staff and those engaged in corruption, land racketeering and declining performance.

Intensive training and pay reform followed, enabling our teachers to be better paid than any in the Federal Government. We collaborated with computer vendors to introduce government-assisted purchase of computers and motorcycles for FCT staff, with flexible payment terms. On the whole, our pilot was deemed successful and similar templates were followed by the other pilot MDAs - the State House, the Federal Ministries of Finance and Information, National Planning Commission and the Federal Inland Revenue Service.

Creating the Public Service Reform Team

In the course of implementation of reforms in the pilot MDAs, we learnt a few lessons. Obvious ones included the resistance to change and issues of trust in the reformers. The public servants considered us hostile outsiders intent on messing up their lives, work and careers. Only continuous interactions and evidence of good faith can change that perception. The rigid civil service rules and systems did not help matters, and we realised the need to rewrite and update the rules for the twenty-first century. Issues of federal character, regional and religious balance in staff disposition constrained decision-making sometimes, amidst shortage of skills and inadequate resources within the public service. These all needed to be taken into account when mainstreaming the reform processes to cover the entire public service.

On 8th August 2005, I submitted a fourteen-page memorandum[110] to the President reporting the status of the reforms in the FCT and other pilot MDAs, and recommending changes in the implementation arrangements for the public service reforms. The proposal to change the reporting relationship such that the Bureau of Public Service Reform reported to the Economic Team through me was approved. Thereafter, the head of the civil service, in a September 27, 2005 letter to the president, reluctantly gave his status report. This was transmitted to me and the Secretary to the Government a week later. By then I had already taken charge of supervising the Bureau of Public Service Reform, and instituted the reform team.

Like most citizens, I considered myself a victim of the corruption and inefficiency of the public service. I, therefore, approached the PSRT assignment with single-minded focus to effect reforms in the service. In this role, I received the support and assistance of many wonderful and capable people. Segun Peters of the World Bank combined passion for Nigeria, uncommon dedication and intellect that enabled him break down complicated policies into measurable, implementable strategies. Dr. Goke Adegoroye,[111] an academic scientist turned civil servant, brought commitment, integrity and competence, in addition to emotional intelligence, in navigating the minefields and traps of the civil service establishment, represented by Yayale Ahmed, the intuitively obstructive head of the civil service. It is my humble opinion that the imperative to reform the public service for effectiveness is still very much on the table. I will therefore go into some details about what we did, lessons learnt, and what is left to be done.

In a State of Denial

One major problem with public service reform is the belief held by most public servants that they are not to blame for the sorry state of affairs. The bulk of the public servants continue to be in denial and have refused to take responsibility for their ineffectiveness, blaming their political masters for the dysfunction in the public service. They blame the collapse of merit and excellence in the public service on the Murtala-Obasanjo retirements "with immediate effect" that occurred in the mid-1970s. Others attribute the current situation to the Civil Service Reform Decree No. 43 of 1988 of the Babangida administration. The deterioration of pay and fringe benefits relative to the cost of living as a result of the Structural Adjustment Programme in the late 1980s has also been identified as contributory to the de-motivation, deskilling and dispiriting of the public service.

The truth may be a combination of all three and more, compounded by the inability of the public service to update its methods, skills and technology. The public service has been short-term in its vision, self-centred in policy formulation and corrupt in programme implementation. Instead, its leadership (the permanent secretaries and successive heads of civil service) have consistently focused on taking care of themselves and their narrow interests to the detriment of the nation, the public service and the governance system which sustains it.

The public service failed to reform itself between 2001 and 2005 when two successive heads of the civil service were tasked to do so by President Obasanjo. It was therefore inevitable that driving the public service reforms of 2005-2007 had to be transferred to the economic team, with President Obasanjo leading the charge himself. I, as an 'outsider,' was needed to administer the required medicine. But even that needed the cooperation of the patient, which was not forthcoming.

Public Service Reforms in Summary

It was incontestable that the public service became dysfunctional following years of neglect and failure to reform. The public service was both large and unwieldy, accountability was weak and professional standards low. The federal bureaucracy had also sprawled, with considerable overlap of functions between agencies, and between tiers and arms of government. There was an urgent need for both civil service and parastatals reforms, and in spite of all efforts, little progress was made in that regard.

The need to improve the overall efficiency and effectiveness of the public service had been recognised from pre-independence days, and over time there were several attempts at reform. The first of these was the Tudor Davis Commission of 1945-46. The

Morgan Commission of 1963 not only revised salaries and wages of junior staff of the federal government, but introduced for the first time a minimum wage for each region of the country. The more recent ones include the commissions headed by Simeon Adebo (1971), Jerome Udoji (1972), Dotun Philips (1986) and the Allison Ayida Panel (1995). The Dotun Philips reforms properly and correctly aligned the civil service structure with the constitution and presidential system of government, designating permanent secretaries as directors-general and deputy ministers. Unfortunately, the reforms devolved human resource functions with respect to employment, promotion and discipline of the junior cadres to ministries with disastrous consequences which needed dealing with by 2005.

The Bureau of Public Service Reforms (BPSR) was established in September 2003 as an independent agency in the Presidency to ensure the reform of all ministries, departments and agencies (MDAs) of all arms and branches of the federal government, and submitted quarterly reports to the President. The Public Service Reform Team (PSRT) had the BPSR as its secretariat and met weekly every Tuesday to deliver on its mandate. Some of the achievements of that round of reforms include:

Restructuring of Pilot Ministries, Departments and Agencies (MDAs): The PSRT produced two generic guidelines approved by cabinet in March 2006 for the reform and restructuring of MDAs and parastatals. Initially five pilot MDAs volunteered for restructuring and this was expanded to 14. This entailed cleaning up the staff headcount and payroll, and redesigning the MDA structure to have between four and eight departments and two to four divisions per department. These were approved by the cabinet on May 16th, 2007 and became applicable to all government departments immediately.

Cleaning up of Civil Service and Parastatals Nominal Rolls: A committee of the reform team, headed by Steve Oronsaye,[112] developed eight criteria for the retirement of public servants to enable the clean-up of the headcount and reducing the negative impact of the devolution of human resource management functions to MDAs in 1988, and the failures of the FCSC and OHCSF to

With late Senator Amah Iwuagwu and Asue Ighodalo

Senate Bribery Hearings: Senator Ibrahim Mantu taking the oath without touching the Quran

Senate Bribery Hearings: Senator Jonathan Zwingina taking the oath without holding the Bible

Senate Bribery Hearings: Author with Peter Akagu-Jones, Asue and Timi Austen-Peters

With CJN Uwais, VP Atiku Abubakar and Senator Ibrahim Mantu at the Eid praying ground, Abuja

Obasanjo launches the demolition exercise at Accra Street, Wuse Zone 5

With Obasanjo commissioning Abuja Mass Transit System

With Obasanjo and Tijjani Abdullahi commissioning Abuja Mass Transitt

Mass Transit: the Green and Red Buses (later added the Yellow Buses)

Performing Hajj with Idris Othman, Bolaji Anibilowo (RIP), and Yusuf Ahmed

Welcoming Queen Elizabeth II to Commonwealth Heads of Government Meeting (CHOGM), Abuja December 2003

In a handshake with UK Deputy Prime Minister John Prescott

Presenting Iranian President H Khatami with the Key to City of Abuja

Welcoming Brazilian President Lula to Abuja

With Bono, Gordon Brown and Ngozi at a DFID-aided village in the FCT

Wesley Snipes visiting Abuja in 2005

discharge their central management functions. An appeals process was put in place to minimise victimisation and errors. For the civil service, about 45,000 names were prepared by MDAs and forwarded to BPSR for consideration and approval by PSRT, and then forwarded to the FCSC for removal from the service. An initial batch of 36,843 officers were put through pre-retirement training, disengaged and paid about N24 billion as their severance entitlements. Unfortunately, about 20,000 of these severed civil servants have found their ways back into the civil service, thereby defeating the clean-up exercise and wasting the monies spent. These 'staff' now draw both pensions and current pay explaining partly why the federal payroll has ballooned from ¦ 600 billion in 2007 to N1,600 billion in 2012, nearly three times the size in five years. For the 400 or so parastatals and paramilitary services, the estimated number of staff to be severed was 75,575 at a cost of about N57 billion. Parastatals reform and right-sizing was to be undertaken jointly by BPSR and the Bureau of Public Enterprises (BPE). Sadly, this was never fully realised.

Monetisation of Fringe Benefits: All benefits-in-kind like free housing, furnishing, car and driver for various cadres of public servants and political office holders were abolished for ministers, permanent secretaries and equivalent cadres and below. All government-owned houses except thirteen classes of official residences were sold to occupants or via public bids. All official vehicles were discounted by 50% and sold to officials. Other pool and utility vehicles were auctioned in public bids. Personal drivers, cooks and cleaners were laid off and made personal staff of the affected officials.

Pay Reform and Medium-Term Pay Policy: The Ernest Shonekan Pay Review Report was referred to PSRT for consideration and implementation. Shonekan found that public service pay was on average 25% of private sector pay for the same or similar jobs. A pay increase of 15% went into effect in January 2007, with a plan to increase pay by 10% per annum but linked to productivity such that in five years, near pay parity with the private sector would be achieved.

Integrated Payroll and Personnel Information System: This is a computerised, biometric platform intended to provide a reliable and comprehensive database of employees in the public service to facilitate manpower planning, and eliminate headcount and payroll fraud. The electronic platform was approved by cabinet in February 2006 and implemented in phases. The first phase covering six agencies and the central management organisations of the public service went live in April 2007, saving N416 million from the payroll of the 12 agencies in its first month. Sadly, the vested interests[113] in the public service have since frustrated its mainstreaming to cover all government departments and other public service organisations.

Review and Update of Public Service Rules and Financial Regulations: The BPSR undertook a holistic review of the Public Service Rules and Financial Regulations and produced a White Paper which was amended and approved by the cabinet on 9th May 2007.

Next Steps in Reforming the Public Service

The next steps are clear. Learn from the recent past, build on foundations laid by PSRT and correct any errors we may have made. The quality of the public service must be improved by attracting the best and brightest from our educational institutions and the private sector. This requires reducing the current pay disparity between the public and private sectors of the economy. To rejuvenate the service, new blood must be injected at all levels from the academia, private sector and the Nigerian diaspora, based on merit. This will be impossible unless the aging and un-trainable public servants take early retirement.

Who can perform in today's work environment without the knowledge of IT, and the ability to use search engines like Google, social media platforms like Facebook and Twitter, and messaging tools via BlackBerry? Any public servant who can't use the computer — and there are entire legions of them— ought to give way to our army of unemployed young people who can. The number of government agencies duplicating functions, and their staffing levels, must be reviewed downwards to enable our nation afford the higher pay that our public servants deserve. We cannot maintain the same numbers and pay them any higher.

After we left office, another civil service review committee appointed by the Yar'Adua administration and chaired by Mallam Adamu Fika lamented the low morale and widespread malaise in the service and observed that the integrity deficits in the Federal Civil Service Commission and the Office of the Head of Civil Service of the Federation were responsible for inefficiencies and corruption that have become pervasive in the service. The Yar'Adua-Jonathan administration lost a unique opportunity to correct some of these gaps. Sadly, the multiple appointments of heads of civil service (about five heads in about five years) made continuity of reforms impossible since 2007.

Chapter Fourteen

Covert Battles

> *"The wish to acquire more is admittedly a very natural and common thing; and when men succeed in this they are always praised rather than condemned. But when they lack the ability to do so and yet want to acquire more at all costs, they deserve condemnation for their mistakes."*
>
> *– Niccolo Machiavelli*

The only way a constitutional amendment allowing a third presidential term would ever be plausible, from the standpoint of what is politically palatable to Nigerian voters, is if the president pushing for it does not benefit from it. The only way for this to happen is if the amendment takes effect only upon the incumbent's exit from office. This is assuming a critical mass of people actually wants any president – regardless of political party – to have the option to run for a third term, with all that such an amendment would imply. From a legislative standpoint, in order to pass any constitutional amendment, it must gain support from two-thirds of the Senate, two-thirds of the House of Representatives and two-thirds of the nation's state assemblies voting in favour of it. The bottom line here is that anyone trying to game the constitutional system in pursuit of tenure elongation faces very long odds.

My vested interest in this was precisely that any perceived weakening of Obasanjo's political stature that derived from anything, whether it was a grab for a third term, a huge corruption scandal, a key legislative defeat or any number of other obstacles a Nigerian president faces, was going to inhibit me from continuing to do my job effectively. Therefore, it was in my best interest to, after abiding by my oath of office to the constitution, see to it that Obasanjo conducted the affairs of the country in accordance with the best democratic practices. I also believed that Nuhu, Ngozi and Oby felt the same way.

There were three possible decision paths Obasanjo could have taken with regard to his tenure. The first and obvious path was to simply do nothing and play by the rules, serve out his second term, hand over power to the next democratically elected president, and resume basking in the international acclaim he enjoyed when he voluntarily stepped down from power in 1979. This was the easiest and most predictable route for him to take and, frankly, the smartest, and I do not need to lean on hindsight to make that assessment – indeed, I was saying the same thing while it was all happening. Who the best person for him to hand power to and which part of the country that person should be from was an entirely different matter, which I will take up shortly. For the moment, I am concerned solely with the structural options that were at hand.

The second route he could have taken was to make a case for a constitutional amendment allowing a third presidential term for future presidents to come – and not for his benefit. Since Obasanjo is a 'southerner', this action would have required significant support from the political leadership of the south in exchange for very clear and unmistakable reassurances that he was not pulling the wool over their eyes for the north's benefit. This action was not theoretically out of the question, in my opinion. He could have made a plausible case that after spending as much time as he had as president of Nigeria, he had concluded that eight years were not long enough to take Nigeria where it needed to go and he did not want to see future leaders of our nation similarly constrained. He could have made this case and it may make sense to many if it did not appear self-serving. Whether the north and south would have bought it, I do not know, but on its face, it was a plausible stance.

The third route he could have taken was to push for a constitutional amendment allowing a third term, applicable to his own tenure. For the reasons stated above, the chance of this path succeeding was not impossible, but highly improbable, to say nothing of the potential damage it could do to our institutions. This necessarily meant that any reasonable person directly affected by the outcome of this action must assume and prepare for failure. This is precisely what we on the economic team decided to do. Indeed, by August 2005 there were really no loud denials that the Third Term Project was in full bloom. Though we still had no confirmation, we had access to a document prepared by the Africa Department (Equatorial) of the UK Foreign and Commonwealth Office, dated 22nd June 2005, which suggested that Obasanjo "might just be pressed into (amending the Constitution) late in 2006" as the lesser evil of handing over either to "Atiku, his deeply corrupt Vice President or Babangida, former military dictator." The FCO added that "we judge this unlikely, though possible."

As I narrated in the prologue, we decided that we were going to be outwardly neutral towards "the Third Term project" yet work behind the scenes to help unravel it in a way that would enable the president to save as much face as possible. Specifically, we wanted him to be able to still have enough influence with the ruling party and the populace to have some limited say in who would succeed him. We believed that once it became clear to him that he was not going to get a third term, he would select someone who could build upon the foundations we had laid during his tenure in office.

In order for this to take place, the third term initiative had to end as quickly and painlessly as possible. The more protracted the effort was, the more damaging it would be to Obasanjo and our administration. Furthermore, we had to be concerned whether a quick end would not leave the president and his project managers enough time to formulate a clear strategy to punish the country for not giving them a third term. So the timing issue was two-fold: keep Obasanjo's dignity and political capital as preserved as possible, yet also ambush any plans for causing further political problems in the country going forward. The more time the president and his managers had to engineer after the effort's failure, the more time there would be to think about other problems in Nigeria that might be used as an excuse to declare a state of emergency and remain in office.

Once we agreed on that position, we then had to set about our strategy for achieving this objective, and we immediately knew that the cooperation of the National Assembly would be instrumental in ending the initiative. We immediately began a dialogue with Dr. Usman Bugaje of the House of Representatives, who was the main champion of the group in the House opposed to a third term; we also approached Ken Nnamani, the Senate president, and Aminu Masari, the speaker of the House, to ascertain what their sentiments were on the 'third term' amendment question. Their attitude was that they were elected by the parliament to lead the body and they were simply the first among equals – neither claimed to have a voice except in the respect that they represented the wishes of the majority of the legislature. Both of them believed the National Assembly was dead against extending Obasanjo's tenure and, therefore, it was doomed to fail. We made it clear to them that we were likewise against the idea, but that we did not want the president to emerge so weakened and disgraced that he would have no influence on the direction of his succession. We insisted that the opposition effort be executed in such a way that the dignity of his office would be preserved, though we knew he would not be able to get away from this completely unscathed.

Every few days, Nuhu and I would go around meeting with various parties we knew to be involved in the project, both in support and against it. Everybody in the pro-Third Term camp spoke freely with us as they assumed that we were close enough to Obasanjo, and were therefore trusted members of the team. Obasanjo himself never said much to us about it, but those involved in the project on his behalf would tell us openly what was planned and how they were going to address various issues and challenges. Almost every night between two and three in the morning, after everyone had gone to sleep, we would drive to Senator Nnamani's house and the three of us would update one another on what we had all learned that day. Senator Nnamani would update us on what was discussed in the legislature and we would inform him of the latest manoeuvrings in the executive branch. We would also visit Speaker Masari's guest house on a similar mission.

Engaging the Ex-Presidents

From my end, I wanted to get Obasanjo to at least confirm to me that there was such a project as the 'Third Term', but he would not until much later. In an effort to get some kind of conversation or admission, I asked him at one point what sort of contact he had with any former presidents, and in particular regarding 'the proposed constitutional amendments.' At the time, there were many provisions to the constitutional amendments on the table, so I just threw the generic term out there to see how he would respond, if at all. He was silent, so I felt encouraged to probe further.

> "If you want to amend the constitution to what appears to be to the detriment of the northern politicians, you must secure the support of at least seven northern states' legislatures to enact it. You are not talking to the political leaders and the impression being created is that this whole thing is just to get you a third term; and no more," I said. "The whole thing will be dead on arrival in states' legislatures unless you obtain their prior buy-in. You can neither get anything through by force or by deception. It can only be through discussions and negotiations"

> "Well, I am in touch with Babangida, but all the other former presidents I am not in touch with," Obasanjo finally responded.

> "The most important person you need to talk to is General Buhari and followed by perhaps President Shehu Shagari. If you are thinking of something as significant as this - our very first amendment to the constitution, nothing would be more compelling than the advocacy of people who have been presidents before you," I told him. "If with respect to something as contentious as term limits, one or two of them would say something like, 'I wish I had stayed longer' or something like that, it will help the legislatures in moving the amendments forward."

> "Well, Buhari does not talk to me."
>
> "Why not?"
>
> "I do not know, but he won't even take my phone calls."

Most of the country's political leaders particularly from the north were so angry with Obasanjo, first for ignoring them after many of them did everything to get him elected, and then with the third term grab they just switched off from him. Certainly, for a few of them, it was like taking dinner off their table, while for many others it was just a principled response to what they considered Obasanjo's disappointing performance in office. At this point, Obasanjo suggested that I would serve as emissary to the ex-presidents and selected northern leaders to re-open that channel of direct communication - particularly with Buhari and Shagari.

I went first to meet President Shehu Shagari and His Eminence Muhammadu Maccido, the Sultan of Sokoto, the leading Muslim traditional ruler in the north. We were on familiar enough terms that arranging the meeting was no problem, but of course, the moment they see a government minister approaching them, they would assume he was coming to them to convince them to support an Obasanjo third term. Knowing this, I began by telling them that the president had sent me to meet with them.

> "Why is he sending you, why can't he talk to us directly?" one of them asked.
>
> "I do not know, but let me tell you what he would prefer I talk to you about and then let me tell you what I want you to talk to him about."

I explained to them my position. To Obasanjo, I was being sent to sensitise the leaders on his behalf on constitutional amendments to. In my mind, my duty required a different mission, to try to advance the national interest as I saw it. I noticed that these leaders did not realise the danger we were in as a nation, that there was a chance, albeit very small, that Obasanjo could succeed in getting his 'third term' because many legislators were unprincipled, and politicians were easily swayed by money. This was why the president's third term team spent a lot of time raising huge amounts of money – more than $300 million by Nuhu Ribadu's informed estimate. I thought the nation's political leaders needed to think through a response to each of the two possible outcomes. Shagari and the Sultan of course said yes, they saw the point of engaging with Obasanjo but reaffirmed they would not be part of anything that enabled him to get a third term.

> "Of course not," I said. "In fact, you can make it very clear that you do not support it. Just be talking to him. When this third term effort dies, you can then be in a position to prevent him from doing damage to the whole system. My sense is that when it fails, he would be very upset and would identify objects of revenge. Only people of your standing can mitigate what damage he can do."

The Sultan promised to engage Obasanjo directly. President Shagari encouraged me to visit and brief Dr. Umaru Dikko, and maintain all future contacts with him on the subject.

I enquired about General Buhari, and learnt that Buhari had not spoken to Obasanjo since 2003. No one seemed to know why, all I learnt was that they were not talking. Buhari was a different kettle of fish. I did not know him well then. I had never had any meeting with him, no interaction with him at all prior to this turn of events. I did know that the man still commanded national respect and near reverence in the north – he is probably the only politician who could announce that he wanted one million people to come out in the streets for some event the next day and two million would show up - without being paid to do so. I had to go through Dr. Mahmud Tukur, who remains one of my intellectual guides and is very close to General Buhari, to arrange a meeting. I went with the same message, but could tell from the very beginning that dealing with him was going to be very different.

> "I am here because I had a conversation with President Obasanjo and he said you have not been talking," I said.

> "Minister, if you are here to talk to me into supporting Obasanjo's third term ambition, you are wasting your time," said General Buhari.
>
> "No I am not here to talk about third term, sir." And he relaxed.
>
> "Ok, but he sent you to me?"
>
> "Yes. He said you two have not spoken for two to three years."
>
> "When his wife died, I sent him my condolences."
>
> "Yes but you have not spoken with him."
>
> "Well what does he want to talk about?"
>
> "I do not know, but you two should be talking. You are a former president, he is the current president. You were his petroleum minister. You were very close, and enjoyed mutual respect. You should be talking."
>
> "Ok, true. One day I will talk to him."
>
> "No, you should talk to him now."
>
> "Well, let me think about it."

That was the first time I ever met General Buhari and that was about all we discussed. I had to visit him three or four times in Kaduna before I could convince him and it was the same core message that was communicated to Shagari and the Sultan.[114]

> "Excellencies, you are national leaders, but in addition you are also seen as our community leaders by ordinary northerners," I said. "And we have a situation here. Obasanjo wants to get a third term. He might get it. He might not. Whatever the outcome, as northern community leaders, you should be interested in engaging with him. As national leaders, you have a duty to manage the success or failure of this attempted power grab."

"He will not get a third term," Buhari said.

"I believe you. But what if he gets it?"

"No, he can't get it."

"I am sorry General, your job as a leader is to open your mind to the possibility, no matter how remote, that he could get it. After all, he has the resources of the state, corruptible people in the political space, and control of coercive instruments of power to force his way. What if he gets it? What will be your reaction? What will be the response of northern community leaders? What will be your response as a national leader?"

Buhari was silent. He had no immediate response.

I continued, "General Sir, this is my point. As community leaders, you need to be thinking of a strategy, a response, just in case he gets it. As national leaders you have a duty also to engage with him, and be talking to him, so that in case he does not get it, you would prevent him from becoming a bull in the china shop of the Nigerian state. He could destroy everything. He could endanger our democracy, he could make wrong choices or unleash vengeful policies that will negatively affect the people of Nigeria as his revenge on them for openly opposing his third term bid. You are our leaders, you should be thinking about this, considering options and scenarios, Sir, not sitting back and saying, 'he won't get it.' This third term attempt is very real, Sir."

I believed this pitch got him thinking.

After nearly three years of the silent treatment, this conversation may have convinced General Buhari to engage with President Obasanjo. He knew his former boss well. He was careful.

First, a delegation representing General Buhari consisting of Dr. Mahmud Tukur, Adamu Fika, *Wazirin Fika,* and Dr. Suleiman Kumo had an initial meeting with Obasanjo at the Banquet Hall, near the State House. It was after that exploratory meeting that Buhari finally took a call from Obasanjo and I stepped completely out of the picture. I learnt from Obasanjo that the trio led by *Wazirin Fika* reportedly told him off, informed him that he had derailed, and assured him that his Third Term project would be defeated. At this point I was not looking like a successful emissary in Obasanjo's eyes, but my job was done. Merely by reaching out, we succeeded in recruiting Buhari[115] to spearhead the guerilla warfare that helped end "the Constitutional Amendment" debates in the National Assembly.

Buhari remained available to engage with Obasanjo while making repeated trips to Abuja to visit legislators in their houses, or call them, making a pitch for them not to support the third term attempt. His first basic argument was that the American Constitution, which was what we modeled our constitution on, started without a term limit provision, but over time the Americans realised these term limits were necessary and this was why it is in our constitution and we should not change it. Secondly, if we amend the constitution to allow a third term, what stops Obasanjo from trying to get a fourth term, or a fifth or a sixth? Where will it end? When does the work of government end? When does the work of a leader stop? At some point, one must draw a line and hand over to a successor. Buhari had considerable moral authority and was completely disinterested in the outcome of the third term debate, so having him available and physically in Abuja to oppose it helped a lot in defeating Obasanjo, Tony Anenih, Amadu Ali, Ojo Maduekwe, Senators Ibrahim Mantu, Dalhatu Sarki Tafida and other third term protagonists. What was impressive about Buhari was that he did this all very quietly and effectively without the desire to claim any credit. In the House of Representatives, the most vocal and articulate opponents of Third Term who rallied around Dr. Usman Bugaje (PDP) included Farouk Adamu Aliyu and Bala Ibn Na'Allah of the ANPP, and Femi Gbajabiamila of AD. They all did a great job, were courageous and took great risks to openly oppose the third term project, while others like Atiku claimed victory.

How the Third Term Project was initiated

With this new communication channel I was shepherding, Obasanjo now had to let me in a bit more on some of the things they were doing. A public communications management group was formed and I was included as a member. Circulated at one of the meetings was a public relations budget for media spending to the tune of 1.2 billion naira that was drawn up in support of the third term. I was amazed and wondered how it would be funded. The response was that NNPC and the FCT Administration were expected to provide the funds and I was given a copy of the budget. I had no intention of using FCT's security budget for such an endeavour. I was, therefore, relieved when *Leadership*, one of the newspapers in vehement opposition to the third term project, obtained the budget and it was front page news a few days later. The chief of staff to the president summoned me and suggested that the president had been informed that I was the source of the leak.[116] I did not bother to deny anything as I had got used to being credited for any leaks that emanated from *ThisDay* and *Leadership* newspapers.

At another point, I asked Tony Anenih, who was the minister of works during the first Obasanjo term and one of the project managers for the third term effort, how things were progressing. He produced a list of all the National Assembly legislators with crosses and ticks to denote which ones were supporting the effort and which were against it. He suggested that I sway some of the legislators against the effort by offering them plots of land in Abuja in my capacity as FCT minister. I took the list, but did no such thing. I did, however, share this list with other interested parties.

Meanwhile, we generally knew Obasanjo's people would pay lots of money to the National Assembly members to try getting the two-thirds majority they needed, but beyond that we did not know how they would do it and we did not even know who was going to be paying out the money. Nuhu directed the financial intelligence unit of the EFCC to track cash movements, mostly from the states to Abuja, which accounts most of the money ended up in, and so forth. Most of the money was allegedly going to companies and bank accounts controlled by Andy Uba, who was the president's special assistant on domestic matters that handled those things for him.

All of these actions and efforts were being undertaken without any of us really having a full picture of just how, legislatively speaking, the third term amendment was going to be packaged. Obasanjo's managers finally made their first move on this front. They dusted off a very old report commissioned in 1999, 'to look at the 1999 Constitution and suggest various amendments'. The idea was to hide the term limits provisions by mixing them up with other more desirable constitutional amendments.

For instance, at that time there was a lot of discontent about how governors were using their constitutional immunity to engage in grand corruption. Many state governors were involved in money laundering and diversion of public funds, and our Constitution gives them immunity from prosecution while in office. The Supreme Court of Nigeria had ruled that they could be investigated and the findings, no matter how dire, could be published, but they cannot be charged in court until they leave office. There were huge levels of anger throughout the country about that.[117]

As a result, there was a provision in the amendments to remove the immunity of sitting governors, along with a few aspects of our Constitution that most people agreed needed changing. Buried with these was the provision to remove term limits or to allow up to three terms of office, which was what Obasanjo wanted. The president's legal team even came to my office one day to discuss questions relating to Abuja since, from a constitutional standpoint, Abuja does not have quite the same powers or rights as states, but rather is an entity unto itself as the Federal Capital Territory. In the end, a bill[118] containing several amendments went before the National Assembly with hundreds of millions of dollars raised to procure its passage. Most of the money came from governors friendly to Obasanjo, but some also came from Lagos-based businessmen. The idea was to use this money for not only bribing legislators, but also for public relations, such as the production of jingles and movies depicting Obasanjo as moving the country in the right direction – mentions of debt relief, his role in ending the civil war – without explicitly stating that he just wanted to stay longer.

Some National Assembly members were reportedly recruited and paid large amounts of money to spearhead the effort, so as to make it look as if the idea came from the National Assembly rather than from the administration. Deputy Senate President Ibrahim Mantu, (of "54 million naira" fame), took the lead in the Senate, Bako Sarai from Kano in the House of Representatives, while Tony Anenih, as the chairman of the PDP board of trustees, reached out to the electronic media, the state governors and other political heavyweights. Obasanjo did not directly meet with anyone until very late in the game.

As the debate progressed into the month of April 2006[119] and voting day to refer the bill to committee for second reading approached, the struggle to ensure passage became so desperate at one point that Aminu Masari, the House speaker, was invited to a meeting with the PDP national chairman, Dr. Amadu Ali, and Tony Anenih and other PDP apparatchiks. In the meeting Ali and Anenih pressed Speaker Masari to just call for a voice vote on the term limits clause and then declare it passed regardless – no show of hands, no electronic vote tally. Masari was very direct.

> "I can't do that – there is an electronic counter," Masari said.
>
> "We'll disable it the day before the debate," Amadu Ali said.

But Masari, to his credit, would not budge.

> "Whenever there is such doubt or confusion or an important matter like that, or any provision in a controversial bill of this nature," he explained to them, "we do a division – we do not do voice votes or even do a show of hands. We say those for, stand to the left, those against, stand to the right."
>
> "Do not do that, just do a voice vote," said Amadu Ali

We heard the details of this incident directly from other persons who attended the crucial meeting, as by then, both Masari and Nnamani were reluctant to confide in many of their colleagues because they were no longer sure which ones would go back and tell the Obasanjo crew. So we took this information to Dr. Usman Bugaje to share with the House opposition and craft a response in case any of the two presiding officers buckles to pressure. Two days later, Bugaje came back to us.

> "I have 152 members of the House that have signed a pledge to write individual letters stating that they would be withdrawing participation in the business of the House, until this provision on tenure elongation has failed," he declared. "Then they will resume attending the House and join the rest of the sessions. They are prepared to debate the other amendments. But as soon as debate on term limits begins, 152 members will withdraw from the House."

Since the House had 360 members, if at least 121 members withdraw, less than two-thirds of the chamber remains in session, disabling any constitutional amendment from passing. The Bugaje group's plan was that 152 members would not even be in attendance – they would each write letters officially to the speaker stating that for the period in which this particular issue was being debated, they would be withdrawing from participation in the proceedings. In this scenario, the speaker would take a count and declare that attendance was less than two-thirds full and therefore a vote can either not be taken, or taken and not passed. It makes it easier on the speaker because it removed any burden of responsibility from his discretion. In short, nearly half of the House of Representatives were willing to protest this – and they were not just from the north, but from all over the country, both Christian and Muslim. When Dr. Bugaje furnished the list of 152 members, we agreed that it would be prudent to bring the list to Obasanjo's attention so as to give the president the opportunity to tactically withdraw and just end the 'third term' madness.

> "Mr. President, this thing is going nowhere. These 152 members are not going to support this no matter what," I said, showing him the list. A vote still had not been called yet – that stage was yet to come.

"They plan on withdrawing from the chamber so that the term limits provision will be impossible to pass under any presiding officer. So why not just end this?"

"No, your information is wrong," he said, shaking his head. "Go and see Tony Anenih. He will give you a different picture – your information is wrong."

"No sir, these guys are our friends. They have told us that this is what they plan to do."

"No. They cannot do it. Your friends are misleading you."

I went to see Tony Anenih and he brought out his own list of people that committed to vote in favour of third term: 85 senators and about 260 members of the House of Representatives.

"I do not know where you got your information but I have 152 members here that have signed statements to the effect that they intend to withdraw from the proceedings."

"No, your information is wrong," he said.

"No, it is not wrong."

"Look, minister. By the time we give them money, all of them, they will change," he replied. "Maybe your information is right, right now, because we have not distributed the money yet." said Anenih.

He believed so much in the power of money to modify the principles and actions of political actors. He did not realise that the situation at hand went beyond money politics.

There would be no penalty for the 152 members signing a pledge not to participate and then changing their minds to the affirmative at the last minute. This was Tony Anenih's point – they still had not received any money. I left and went back to Obasanjo and relayed to him my conversation with Tony Anenih, but gave him my own views.

"I do not believe him, Mr. President. Even when he gives these guys money, they are unlikely to change their position. I am convinced that the situation in the House of Representatives is settled firmly against the amendments. I think his assessment of the support in the Senate is too optimistic as well. Who is your most reliable person in the Senate? I want to assess the situation in the Senate."

We were more familiar and much closer to the state of play in the Senate. Senator Saidu Dansadau led the opposition in the Senate, accompanied by the late Senator Sule Yari Gandi and Senator Lawali Shuaibu,[120] but they were from the opposition party, the ANPP. From the PDP, we had Senator Uche Chukwumerije, and the Senate presiding officer, Ken Nnamani was also firmly with us. Senator Nnamani was against the third term, but as the presiding officer he had to appear neutral, yet unwilling to do anything unethical for or against the constitutional amendments.

Obasanjo suggested I meet with Senators David Mark and Tunde Ogbeha and even personally set up a meeting for me with them. I met them in Senator Tunde Ogbeha's residence, in Apo Legislative Quarters, along with Nuhu Ribadu. We briefed them about the visit to Tony Anenih and Obasanjo's reliance on that source of information.

> "Tony Anenih showed me this list of legislators who will supposedly vote for third term," I said. "I told him we had been provided a different picture with 152 members of the House of Representatives not interested in supporting the amendments and they plan to withdraw from the chambers the moment the debate on term limits begins. Tony Anenih assured me that in the Senate, he has 85 senators who will vote in support. So I have here the entire list of all 109 senators and I'd like to go through with you which ones these 85 senators are."

David Mark was quite blunt, as usual.

> "Minister, I have told President Obasanjo the truth, but he has decided not to believe me," Senator Mark said.[121] "There are not more than 37 senators who would vote for this third term thing. That means 72

senators are against it. We barely have one third of the senate and we need two thirds. I am in the Senate and have told him but he does not believe me, he believes Tony Anenih who is not in the Senate, and has never been in any legislature. I know my colleagues. I know each of these guys; I can walk up to them and ask what their position is. But Tony Anenih, who is not a senator, tells him that there are 85 senators."

I asked him to go through the list and tell me which ones he knows, for sure, would support the removal of term limits. We came up with I think 35 or 37 names.

"Why are we wasting our time?" I asked. "Why can't you tell him that this is a futile effort?" Nuhu interjected.

Tunde Ogbeha responded, "because he does not want to believe us. Obasanjo and Tony Anenih are convinced that if they give legislators money, it will change their position. Maybe it will sway one or two, maybe even a few more. But to move from 37 to 73 or 74 is very hard. We can't double the numbers of those in support no matter how much money is given to the senators. There are some challenges that money just cannot overcome."

I went back to the president and said to him,

> "Mr. President, I do not know what people are telling you, you have told me twice to see Senator David Mark. David Mark, you said is your most reliable man in the Senate."

> "Yes."

> "He has just told me that between 35 and 37 senators would support what you want. Senator Tunde Ogbeha agreed with him."

"That was what David Mark said?"
"Yes! Just call him and talk to him!"

From that point on Obasanjo stopped talking to me about the constitutional amendment project. I think he concluded that either I was simply a naïve bearer of bad news or a closet saboteur of the Third Term project. A week or so later, we – Ngozi, Oby, Nuhu, Aliyu Modibbo and I – went to the chief of staff, General Abdullahi Mohammed, with the following set of facts: We had spoken to Senator David Mark, Tony Anenih and Dr. Usman Bugaje; we had the list of senators David Mark was convinced would support President Obasanjo's third term and it struggles to reach one-third of the Senate, to say nothing of two-thirds; we have the list of House members that are definitely going to walk out once debate on term limits starts; in short, this thing is going nowhere.

"Please, please, please let us go to the president and convince him to stop this."

"Well, Obasanjo has never admitted to me that there was a third term project," he said.

I told the chief of staff that Obasanjo had admitted it to me and Nuhu confirmed that he had had a similar conversation in which the president even used the words, "No third term, no Nigeria." Since the two of us could confirm that Obasanjo had told each of us separately, there was no need to beat around the bush and we could face him. But the chief of staff had been in the military with Obasanjo and had known the man for 40 years. "Ok look," he replied, "I do not think we should all go and see Obasanjo with this. You guys leave me with these pieces of information and I will talk to him. If it becomes necessary, then we can all go and see him together."

I do not know what the chief of staff actually said to Obasanjo and till today never asked, but the following morning, when Oby and Ngozi went to the chapel in the State House to pray with Obasanjo as they were accustomed to doing almost daily, Obasanjo called them aside, berated them for being weak-hearted and not being loyal. He told them that 'the constitutional amendments will pass' and they should not be thinking of failure. He then called me up and denounced me as the 'head of the coup plotters.'

"You have to solve this"

The legislative agenda consisted of starting the debates in the Senate and then, contingent upon early passage in the Senate, moving on to conclusion in the House. While this was happening, President Obasanjo was scheduled to be travelling on state business to South Korea and France. Days before he left on his trip, the first of two meetings convened between the party hierarchy, the leadership of the legislature and the president. At issue was the fact that the debate in the Senate was going to be televised, a decision obviously made without the input of the executive branch. The clear implication was that some of the senators secretly agreed to vote in support of the term limits amendment, but as soon as it was known that all of this was to be shown on national television, that support went out of the window. Nobody wanted to be seen voting for this "third term" project. The house had not passed a resolution to televise their debates.

"Why are we televising this debate?" the president demanded.

"Well, this is the first time we are amending our Constitution and we think it is of general public interest and everyone should know about it," said Senator Nnamani. "So it was proposed to the Senate and the Senate approved it as a motion."

"Well, as presiding officer, can't you go and stop it?" said Obasanjo.

"I can't stop it, sir. It has to be tabled as a motion to the Senate – a proposal to end the debates and even that in itself will be debated and voted for and against, live on national television."

"No, you must just stop it!" Amadu Ali insisted.

"I can't, sir. It was the Senate that decided, I am just the first among equals, I can't decide. Some senator has to go back to our colleagues and say something like 'this thing is heating up the political temperature of the country, do we really want to televise this?' And then we'll take a vote." Nnamani continued, "We therefore need somebody to table a motion that says that televising the debate is good, or not good, and that will start a debate about the merits of televising the debate. You can then get those in support to push for a vote to end the live coverage. I hope you have the numbers to pass a motion against the live transmission of the debate. The first step is to get a senator to table the motion as soon as possible."

Tony Anenih then stepped in. "No problem, I will ask Professor Osunbor to table the motion."

Professor Oserhiemen Osunbor was a senator from Tony Anenih's home state of Edo. He had ambitions to be next governor of the state, and Anenih is the political godfather of Edo PDP. It was therefore expected that Senator Osunbor would do anything Anenih asked him to do in the Senate.

"Fine," said Nnamani. "Once Senator Osunbor gets it onto the order paper, it will be my duty to present it. Then we will debate it, we'll see. But you know this is the most popular reality programme awaited on Nigerian TV. I do not think a motion to stop the telecast will pass, but you know, if Osunbor will table the motion, I will put it up for debate."

The following day, we learnt that Professor Osunbor went to the clerk of the Senate and asked that a motion be raised of urgent national importance, with no topic. This is allowed – any senator can move to table a motion of 'urgent national importance' with no further detail. The clerk put the motion in the order paper to be raised onthe floor the day after. On the appointed day, Professor Osunbor fell miraculously ill and had to be admitted to hospital, so there was nobody to raise the motion. The televised transmission of the debates continued.

The second meeting convened before Obasanjo's trip clearly indicated that the president was then coming to his senses. At this point, a day or two after we went to the chief of staff with evidence that a third term amendment was a futile effort, we were declared enemies in Obasanjo's mind. The president and his team wanted to discuss tactical options since at this point, they had distributed the money. Each House member we learnt was to receive 50 million naira, and each senator 75 million naira. It was from Andy Uba's house that the payments[122] emanated. Many of the senators declined the money, saying that they did not want it because they were not going to support the agenda anyway. Some decided to take the money and still vote against it, because there is no legal recourse – this was bribe money, after all, and no one will ever admit it was paid or get sued for it in the event of non-performance! Of course, some took the money and in return were prepared to vote in support of it. Even with the distribution of the money, the amendment's success was not looking as certain as it should have, and so a final meeting convened. One thing even his enemies will admit about Obasanjo – the man is not stupid. He may have preferred to hear what he wanted to hear, but every so often he stops the show, reflects honestly and asks for a straight assessment.

> "All the information I am getting is that this thing is not going the right way," said President Obasanjo in his opening remarks. He even shared the information that we had passed to him via the chief of staff.
>
> "I do not like the way this thing is going, so what can we do to salvage the situation?"

Listening uncomfortably were party chairman, Amadu Ali, Tony Anenih, Ojo Maduekwe, Senator Ken Nnamani, Speaker Aminu Masari and Obasanjo.

Amadu Ali, the chairman of the ruling party, turned to Senator Nnamani and asked,

> "How do you intend to call for the votes?"

> "We'll either do electronic voting, because each senator has a button that he can press green for yes,

red for no," said Senator Nnamani, "or we call for a division. If it is too controversial and people do not trust even the electronic vote, we call for a division."

"Do not worry about the electronic voting, we will disable it. We will get it disabled," said Ali. "So do not worry about that. Is there not anything you can do to just rule that it has passed?"

"No sir, I can't do it. Because if they say no, and I say they said yes, I will not get out of the place as Senate President, maybe not even alive. It is a very combustible issue. I can't do it."

They looked at the Speaker Masari.

"Excellencies, I cannot do it as well," said Masari. "We can't do any of these things that you are asking us to do. We are not like the presidency where the president is number one and everyone else is below him. We are in parliament, we are there as presiding officers because we are elected by them. It does not work the way you operate in the executive arm."

President Obasanjo then turned to the Speaker Masari.

"Tell me the truth. Forget about all these people and what they are saying," he said. "Tell me the truth – do we have enough people supporting this amendment in the House of Representatives?"

"Mr. President, this is the first time you have asked for the truth. So I will tell you – you do not even have one-third. They are my colleagues, they confide in me. Surely, not all of them have spoken to me on the issue, but my reading is that you do not even have one-third. That is the truth."

Obasanjo then turned to Senator Nnamani.

"Mr. Senate President, what about the Senate?"

"Mr. President, it is about the same in the Senate. We do not have enough votes supporting this to obtain a two-thirds majority."

"Ok what can we do about it? I am going on my trip. Party chairman, chairman of the board of trustees – you go and figure out what needs to be done about it. When I come back, I need to see a plan on how to solve this. You have to solve this."

Judgment Day

We had wanted this to end as soon as possible, preferably before the bill went to the legislature. On this front, we failed. When it got to the legislature, General Buhari and other antagonists of the third term project tried to block it from ever being debated, and failed. Bills have to go through three readings: there is the first reading, a vote is then taken before agreeing to send it on for a second reading in committee, then come the public hearings, followed by a third reading, and then it is voted upon. We wanted it to end with the first reading. The longer the process took, the more damaging it would be to Obasanjo and the administration. We had greater certainty about the bill dying in the House of Representatives and as such were preparing for it to die there by having the 152 members walk up to the Speaker the moment debate on the third term clause began, present letters, each of which would state that they would be withdrawing attendance until the debate on that section and the vote on it was taken, and then walk out. This was the only way to guarantee that it would not be passed – the opposition in the House, led by Dr. Usman Bugaje, did not even want to chance a voice vote. They had 152 members, which was what Dr. Bugaje had recorded, and we had their names and phone numbers and they had all written their letters and were waiting to just walk up to the Speaker and hand over the letters of withdrawal. They would then address the media and explain why they were withdrawing and making it publicly known that the term limits clause could not and would never pass in the House of

Representatives, since more than one-third of the members had withdrawn from the debate. That was the plan.

In the Senate the debate was progressing remarkably well and the whole bill was considered and all Senators that wished to comment made their contributions. It was then the time to take a vote on whether to proceed further or not. The morning of the vote arrived, and the first reading of the bill was completed. At its conclusion, Senator Nnamani said, "We have finished reading the bill, we have done the first reading. Now I want to put the question. Do we refer it to committee for second reading? Those that are for this, say aye, those that are against it, say nay."

There were no ayes. Everyone kept quiet.

"No ayes?" he said. "What about the nays?"

From the depths of the Senate chambers came a resounding "NO!"

He repeated the question.

"Distinguished senators, I am putting the question, those who want this bill to go to second reading should say 'aye'. Those that are against it should say 'no.'"

There was no question: the no's had it. Live on national television.

Once it was clear that the bill had failed in one house of the national assembly, there was no point continuing the debate in the other house since both houses would have to pass it with two-thirds majority for it to move on to the state assemblies. We had no idea it was going to end that dramatically and so easily, but for us, that was about as graceful as it could ever get.

Obasanjo returns to face the music – With a Speech

That is, until the infamous speech. Obasanjo came back from his travels a couple of days later and everyone – the Tony Anenihs, the Amadu Alis, Ojo Maduekwes, and Andy Ubas – went into hiding. On our part, we all just kept away from Obasanjo because we did not know what he would do next. What he did was he wrote a speech - no speechwriters, no drafts. He authored it himself and then delivered it on national television. He congratulated the National Assembly for doing a commendable job of deliberating over the constitutional amendments, how some of the amendments were desirable, but they have not been passed and we have to accept the will of the people; he also mentioned how people had been accusing him of wanting a third term, but that in fact he never wanted it. It was all very strange, but the strangest bit he saved for the end: whatever he wanted, he would ask God for it and God would give it to him. Therefore, went the implication, he clearly had never wanted a third term. That speech, I must reiterate, I know he wrote all by himself. We were nothing less than completely shocked.

As a result of presenting that speech,[123] Obasanjo had to pretend nothing happened. The next day we all saw him and some ministers commended him for the speech: "Mr. President that was a very good speech."

"Yes, imagine," he exclaimed, "They said I wanted a third term!"

We just smiled. What was there really to say? What would we do when someone accused us of being coup plotters a few days earlier, because we had suggested that the third term amendment was going to collapse, and then some days later looked at one of us and said, "Ha! People said I wanted a third term!" – Really, what more was there to say?

His chief of staff called me that next day.

"Nasir, you see what happened with this? God works in mysterious ways."

"Yes, He does."

"Let me give you a piece of advice as someone who knows Obasanjo very well: he thinks you are behind that group that came to my house. Be careful. Be very careful from now on, please."

I thanked him and promised to heed his counsel.

I was not the leader of the economic team – Ngozi was the leader. We all went together, indeed she did most of the talking and I gave out the information to back our position.

"You and Ngozi, you are in trouble. He will exact his revenge. So just be careful."

The chief of staff never really liked Ngozi – I do not think he gave her this warning.

"I know him, I have known him for 40 years plus, he's going to try to get you, so just keep your head down, do your work, get out of his way," he said. "He never lets anything like this go without retribution."

Of course, less than a year later, Ngozi was more or less forced out of her job. I stayed. Even as we speak today, there remains the grudge. I think after the whole initiative collapsed, Obasanjo figured out that Nuhu Ribadu and I played some role in its demise, in addition to the 'coup plotting' discussions with the chief of staff, which he considered unforgivable enough, anyway.

I said this at the beginning and I will keep saying it: I am indebted to President Obasanjo for all of the things he did for me, for giving me the opportunity to achieve national prominence, for standing by me and providing the support to do my jobs effectively and serve Nigeria well. However, I took an oath of office which required my loyalty to the federal republic of Nigeria and the rule of law and the constitution. I was loyal to President Obasanjo throughout our tenure and will always respect him, but that loyalty is not without its limits. Specifically, that loyalty ends where the national interest and preserving our constitution and our laws begin. I cannot, out of loyalty to a friend or to a mentor, break the law or violate the constitution or do something that in my assessment could be wrong and against Nigeria's interest.

President Obasanjo and I have never addressed this issue head on since leaving office, so if he reads these words, I hope that he will finally understand my position on this matter. As for the retribution that the chief of staff warned me about – well, I will never know for sure whether the president ever sought retribution against me.[124] What I do know, though, is that the two years immediately following our exit from government were the most difficult two years of my life. Many people close to Umaru Yar'Adua[125] have suggested that Obasanjo might have had something to do with what Nuhu Ribadu and I went through. That may be true, but I do not hold Obasanjo or any other person (other than Yar'Adua) responsible for what happened. After all Yar'Adua was the president and must be held responsible for everything, good or bad that happens under his watch to any citizen. In any case, he did not do everything Obasanjo expected him to do. My belief is that he must have pursued us politically because he wanted to, even if someone else had planted the seeds.

Chapter Fifteen

From Bad to Worse

"When you're going through hell – keep going."
– Winston Churchill

With the third term distraction out of the way, attention could only then turn to who would succeed Obasanjo. There are those who say Obasanjo's revenge for his third term defeat was intentionally picking two incompetent people to be president and vice-president, but I do not fully agree with that. I think Obasanjo picked them for a different reason: he thought they were weak people he could control and through whom he could continue to exercise power. I think that he thought Yar'Adua would be an acceptable president, but would be weak and subservient to him in many policy areas and would be consulting him regularly so that Obasanjo might be a Lee Kuan Yew sort of figure, exercising power from behind the scenes. I do know that Obasanjo and Lee Kuan Yew are friends and he admires Lee Kuan Yew – whenever he spoke about a great, visionary leader, it was always Lee whose name he brought up.

If I am just naive and the ticket that ended up succeeding Obasanjo was meant to be a third term revenge, it did not exactly work out. Yar'Adua revolted against him, reversed virtually everything he did and even began investigating him.[126] Obasanjo recently admitted to another close friend of ours that throughout the years Yar'Adua was in power, he was constantly in fear of being arrested because it was clear to him that at some point, Yar'Adua was after him.

While Goodluck Jonathan has so far behaved a little differently, he has also not exactly been subservient to Obasanjo either. It certainly has not quite worked out the way I think Obasanjo envisaged it, but many people think he chose them in particular for those more sinister reasons. Personally at the end of the third term adventure, I was more worried about other things: Would Obasanjo create some chaos that would enable him to invoke the state of emergency provisions in our Constitution to stay on? I had all sorts of nightmare scenarios running through my head. What will he do next? - was a nagging thought in the early post-third term days.

In any event, Obasanjo chose Yar'Adua for reasons that to this day nobody can be sure of. One of the times I visited his Abeokuta home with my friend, Ulysses, in October 2010, he asked him why he chose Yar'Adua. Obasanjo said that Yar'Adua was the candidate who was a) northern, b) not Atiku and c) in the best position to keep Nigeria unified. Take that for what you will – I did not really buy it. What I can say is that after the third term project collapsed how the aftermath unfolded only served to heighten the already existing tensions within the administration. The first step involved a group of about a dozen people,[127] businessmen and senior government officials, including our economic team, who decided to meet to discuss the way forward. I do not remember why, but Obasanjo was not directly privy to the meeting, though Andy Uba was invited to participate in our first meeting. The meeting was scheduled to take place side by side with the meeting of the Honourary Presidential Advisory Council on Investments (HPACI), hosted by Baroness Chalker in London. We met and brainstormed ideas for how to approach the succession strategy and agreed to follow up with a second meeting in Abuja at Ngozi's house.

That second meeting never happened. Obasanjo found out presumably from Andy Uba about the substance of the first meeting, was incensed that anyone would convene such a gathering without his authorisation and told everyone – except me – that he did not need anyone's advice on succession and therefore this second meeting was unnecessary. It was Nuhu's idea to begin this discussion group, but I am fairly certain that Obasanjo must have heard that I was involved and immediately concluded that I must be leading the proceedings.

All that Obasanjo said regarding succession was that he would fast and pray for 30 days for God to guide him on his choice. One day, in November of 2006, Tanimu Yakubu, who eventually became Yar'Adua's economic adviser, came to my office and said that Yar'Adua would be coming to see me, which from a traditional as well as protocol standpoint, was unusual – it was usually I who paid visits to him, whenever he came to Abuja. On pressing Tanimu further, I understood why this apparent reversal of protocol and tradition became necessary on that day. What made this time different was that he was coming to ask for my support of his candidacy to be president of Nigeria. Obasanjo had made his decision.

Umaru came over to my house that evening looking like a man who had just had the weight of the world thrust upon him. He told me that Obasanjo had called and asked him to submit a nomination form to run for president and that he really was not expecting this and felt totally unprepared, but that if he was to go ahead with this, he would need me by his side, along with the economic team. I congratulated Umaru and assured him that support from the economic team should not be a problem. I honestly did not think it would be any problem. In spite of my misgivings about his personal shortcomings, I did not think he would make a bad president.

He was a bit hung up on the fact that no one else who had officially declared candidacy was, as he put it, 'impressive,' and wanted to know why I was not in the race.

"Well, I have never thought about this and I am not really into competitive politics."

"At least if two of us are in the race, one of us will get it," he said.

"No, I am really not into this game, Mallam."

"Ok. Well listen, I am going to Katsina tomorrow and will be passing through Kano to inform certain others about this. From your end, whom do you think I should talk with before I leave Abuja?"

"Please see Nuhu Ribadu, definitely. Also, see Tony Anenih and tell him."

"Do you think he (Anenih) does not know?"

"The president has not told any one of us and we are probably the closest people to him in the government. If he has not told us, I would like to assume that he has not told anyone else. So I think it would be good to go and see these two people. When you return to Abuja, it would be nice to see Nenadi Usman who as Finance Minister is the head of the economic team. But that is mere formality."

Umaru Asks Nuhu for Support: the Beginning of Our Problems

Now, I do not know what happened between Umaru and Tony Anenih, but I can say that what happened then between Umaru and Nuhu was probably when the seeds of our future problems with Umaru were planted. When Yar'Adua broke the news, Nuhu's response could hardly have been any less gracious:

"Well, Obasanjo has not told me, and as far as the presidency is concerned, I have my candidate for president, and that is Nasir El-Rufai. I am going to have to speak to Obasanjo about this."

When Yar'Adua left Nuhu's office, Nuhu immediately called Obasanjo to see if he was available to talk. Obasanjo invited him over, but by the time Nuhu got to the Villa, Nuhu was not allowed past the gate. For two days, Nuhu tried to see Obasanjo and Obasanjo avoided seeing him. When they finally saw each other, Nuhu demanded to know how and why he would make such a choice. Nuhu's logic was that if we had performed creditably at the federal level, Obasanjo should pick the successor from amongst officials at the federal level, not anoint someone from amongst those he considered to be poorly-performing state governors. Obasanjo initially denied that he invited Yar'Adua to run. He said Yar'Adua came to him like everyone else and said he wanted to run, but Obasanjo did not invite Yar'Adua to run. Nuhu was relieved and left Obasanjo in peace. He then called me up directly after.

"Umaru was lying! Obasanjo did not ask him to run for president!"

"Nuhu, I have known Umaru since 1972. He would not come to my house and lie about something like that."

"So are you saying Obasanjo is lying to me?"

"Yes, Obasanjo is lying to you. I am sure of it."

It took sometime before Nuhu figured out Obasanjo's games and what was really happening. Nuhu's instinctive reaction was that of a typical policeman - dust off EFCC files and comb for petitions against Umaru. Nuhu did not realise it at the time, but he was the one in trouble, not Obasanjo or Umaru. He dusted off all his files and found petitions against the Katsina state governor and launched investigations. He even arrested some local government chairmen from Katsina as part of his investigation of diversion of local government funds by the state governor. He was clearly trying to take Yar'Adua out of the race and narrow all options to zero except for El-Rufai. This was all a one man show on the part of Nuhu – he never told me, he never confided in anyone until it was too late to counsel him otherwise. As soon as I heard that the chairman of Mashi Local Government, a young man that my sister living in Mashi town knew very well, had been arrested, I figured out what my friend was up to.

"Nuhu, what the hell are you doing?"

I asked him, wanting to know why the chairman of Mashi Local Government and a family friend had been arrested and detained in Abuja.

"Yallabai, we can still take charge of this. No, we can't allow Obasanjo to do this," he said.

Nuhu was still delusional about what he could do to override a strong-willed president.

> "Look, we had a problem. Obasanjo wanted 'not to leave'. Now he has got someone he is comfortable with to run for president, which means he has accepted that he would leave. We all wanted Obasanjo to leave, and with this development, there is a chance he would leave."

"Asking for anything more than this – it is just being selfish. You want me to be president because I am your friend, not because you think I am quite different or better than Yar'Adua. Leave this thing alone. Whatever your plans are, whatever your plans were, they have not worked partly because you have not made it open and inclusive - for everyone to know what you were thinking, planning, and doing. You were doing this alone. It is now over. So drop it. Anything you do henceforth will only just confirm what people say about you – that you target people that threaten certain interests. If you had been investigating Yar'Adua for a year beforehand, that would be different, but you were not. It is too late to start now. Please stop it."

I was not the only one – Oby and several others urged him to stop, and he eventually did. If Nuhu had trusted anyone with whatever his vision was and we had jointly come up with a plan for me or indeed anyone we settled on to run for president, perhaps we would have developed an overall strategy that might have worked. However, Nuhu never trusts anyone with his plans. He preferred to plan and act alone if he could – this is simply how he is. By the time we realised what was going on and Nuhu had even recruited a couple of my wealthy friends to support and agree to bankroll his "last man standing" strategy, things had gone really bad, for me and all of us.

Breakfast with Obasanjo: the 'transition' period

A few days after Nuhu's showdown with Obasanjo, the president invited me over for breakfast. Typically, people come by the residence early for morning prayers and stay around for breakfast, but that morning, he made a point to clear everyone out, leaving just the two of us in the main dining room of the residence. Obasanjo was generally a simple eater at breakfast time, some boiled yams and fried eggs. That day, I remember I just had a healthy bowl of Quaker Oats.

"You know, your brother came here, he was very angry about my choice of Umaru Yar'Adua," he began, referring to Nuhu. "He accused me of all sorts of things, he was angry that I did not pick you to be the presidential aspirant that I was backing."

"I was not an aspirant and never in contention, Mr. President."

"I know. You have never spoken to me or hinted at anything like that. But Nuhu somehow felt that you should have been the one."

"That is his opinion that I do not share, sir. But it does not matter. It is fine."

"Well, let me tell you something. I thought about you but I decided that this is not the time. The next four years – 2007 to 2011 – is just a transition period. The nation and our politics are not ready for someone like you. I feel you still have a few more things to experience, to learn."

"Transition period?"

"Yes."

"I do not understand. Please explain, Mr. President."

"Well, nothing will change, you know? I will be in Ota but we will be running things. Everything will remain the same, you know, you will remain in the government, the economic team will remain. Nothing will change. Only I will move to Ota and Yar'Adua will be here but we will be running things."

"I see. Well you know Mr. President, I will not be part of this transition."

"What do you mean?"

"Well I have my plans. I have personal things to do and frankly I think I have given enough of my life to this government business, I need a break."

"No, no, all of you will be here. You need to be here."

"No, Mr. President. I will not be here. I am taking a break - at least two years."

"Ok, well I just thought I should call you and explain to you that the next four years is just a transition period. The real change in government will happen in 2011. Not now."

"Ok. I do not understand what you are saying, but if you say so, it is ok."

What is amazing about this conversation is that Obasanjo had similar ones with at least two others – Nuhu Ribadu and Osita Chidoka. By sharing that view with Osita, who is one of his trusted co-conspirators, he was not just telling me and Nuhu that line to calm us down; I think he truly believed it - that "we" (that is, Obasanjo and his boys) would be in charge, while Yar'Adua remained a figurehead! Not knowing Umaru Yar'Adua as I did, I thought Obasanjo had gotten that wrong, smiled all the way back to my house, and accelerated my plans to get out of Nigeria as soon as the handing-over process was completed.

Obasanjo's final night in power

Of course, what he was saying was that he did not plan on leaving the scene entirely. On Obasanjo's final night, the 28th of May, we had gone to the guest house where Yar'Adua was staying to put finishing touches to the inaugural speech. Up to that point, Yar'Adua was consulting me virtually every day, on things in general and also on his inaugural speech. I had asked a friend of ours, Dele Olojede, who later became the publisher of Next newspapers, to help draft the speech, and we were going over it, debating the level of detail we wanted it to cover. For instance, there was a debate as to whether 54 percent of Nigerians lived above the poverty line, or if it was a higher number, and whether it was appropriate to even mention what percentage, or simply stating the need to eradicate poverty would be enough. Those were the sorts of debates – little issues here and there. We debated the words to use to admit that the elections that brought Yar'Adua into power were not exactly picture perfect. Some of us were of the opinion that we should not even admit that the elections were flawed. At the end, we settled on the use of the word, "flawed", rather than to say that the elections were outrightly terrible.

To Yar'Adua's credit, he delivered a speech that called the very elections that brought him to power, 'flawed.' We finally convinced him to accept this, then follow it up with a pledge to set up a high powered commission so that we learnt from the mistakes. We adjourned at around two in the morning and while I was driving home, Nuhu called me to ask me to join him and Obasanjo at the State House. When I arrived there, I could hear them shouting at each other the moment I got out of my car.

"You are wrong! We will recover them!" Nuhu said. He was banging the table.

I entered the room and all of a sudden they both went silent.

"What are you guys arguing about?"

They brushed it off for the time being and quickly moved the conversation to other matters. This was just hours until power was handed over, so we discussed the few years we had been working together, focused mostly on the good things we did, and a bit of logistics for the next day. After about an hour, Nuhu and I left and that was when Nuhu alluded to the essence of the conversation they were having before I intruded.

Many of us felt that Obasanjo made four huge mistakes in his presidency. The first was that Obasanjo had borrowed money to purchase shares in Transcorp, a company known to have plans to acquire certain government assets. The shares were offered to many government officials. Atiku Abubakar was offered, Ngozi was offered. I dissuaded both of them from taking up the offer because they were chair and vice-chair of the Privatisation Council respectively. Ngozi actually considered borrowing money to buy the shares until I dissuaded her. I felt strongly that as government officials, we were sitting on councils, committees or in the cabinet that would approve some of these transactions. In my opinion, even if there was nothing wrong legally with it, there were ethical issues. Part of this came from my experience at the BPE, where we had a self-imposed rule that neither BPE staff nor privatisation council members could buy shares of government companies being privatised. This was one of the first rules that we tightened upon entering the BPE, so I personally persuaded both Atiku Abubakar and Ngozi to reject the Transcorp share offer as well. We also told the president that we disagreed with his intention to purchase shares in Transcorp.

What was even more troubling about the Transcorp deal was that the shares were offered to selected officials and "promoters" at one naira per share. We all had inside information that in a few months, these same shares were going to be listed on the stock exchange at six naira, so that would be 500 percent capital gain practically overnight for doing nothing. I just thought it was immoral. Oby, Nuhu and I were never offered since the promoters knew our position on the share offer. Most economic team members declined to buy the shares and we told Obasanjo that much. Yet, he went ahead, using corporate entities and borrowed from banks and bought some seven hundred million shares. Assuming he sold not long after the company was listed on the stock exchange, he would have made billions of naira in profit. As I write this in early 2012, Transcorp shares trade for less than one naira each, which meant all those who bought early and did not sell immediately got burned.

This Transcorp share acquisition made Nuhu very angry and this was what he was arguing about with Obasanjo when I arrived that night, as well as the other three mistakes of Obasanjo's presidency: the third term effort which we all thought was a blemish for us as an administration, the fundraising for the Obasanjo Presidential Library while he was still in office, and the mistake of handing power to persons who had no idea or any experience in the running of the federal government. Nuhu and I parted ways for what remained of the rest of the night to catch a few hours of sleep before meeting for our final breakfast at the presidential villa.

The fundraising for the Obasanjo Library was one issue on which Oby, Nuhu and I made separate and joint representations to Obasanjo not to proceed with. We felt that it was inappropriate and unethical for a sitting president to raise funds for something of which he would be a direct beneficiary. I was strongly of the view that Obasanjo should have arranged with his successor (Yar'Adua) to organise that in his honour after leaving office. Obasanjo did not even think twice, as he told me that no one would donate to the project once he was out of office. For me that admission confirmed the inappropriateness of the fundraising. Nuhu tried, appealed and even threatened Obasanjo to get him to cancel the planned event. In the end, Obasanjo, with the encouragement of Carl Masters of GoodWorks International, went ahead and raised billions of naira, at least on paper, for the construction of the library, hotel and residential facilities in Abeokuta. Nuhu attended, watching as each state government (excluding the FCT) donated ten million naira each, Nigeria's richest men - Aliko Dangote and Mike Adenuga donated huge amounts, along with the NNPC, and the international oil companies. The Nigerian Ports Authority and other government institutions lined up to give away public funds as gifts to a sitting president. It was disgusting. Nuhu was incensed, but at that point, we all just wanted Obasanjo to hand over and leave. That last night we were together in the Villa, Nuhu raised this as one of Obasanjo's errors as president. I agreed with him.

As I said, at the time, though I had my reservations derived from his past and personality, I did not think Yar'Adua was a bad choice at all, particularly after he was willing to admit that the 2007 elections were flawed. I was legitimately optimistic he was going to build on the foundations we had laid as a government from the same party, and correct any of our mistakes, but keep moving in the same broad direction. Surely, I thought, what we did was largely positive, and in the best interest of the majority of our citizens. Personally, I was also looking forward to taking a break from the hectic life of the previous years. Even though the third term effort was successfully defeated for the time being, we still had the sense that Obasanjo had not really given up and as such were all sitting at the edge of our seats expecting him to pull out something at the last minute. So we made a habit of meeting with him every day – it was like a game of chess in many ways, in which we had to be watching and checkmating him at every point every single day because we were not sure what he was up to, or what he would do next.

So by the time we went to the presidential villa for breakfast, there was a giant sense of relief. I also realised how exhausted I was. While the work was challenging, exhilarating and inspiring in many ways, working for the president of Nigeria necessarily forces one to lose some freedom and control over one's life. By then, Obasanjo and his vice-president had become estranged, and the vice-president had moved to another party and was contesting for the presidency, leaving no effective vice-president in our final year. I was doing more or less whatever the president usually assigned the vice-president to oversee, like serving as a liaison with the electoral commission, monitoring preparations for the population census, and at various points running the ministries of interior, commerce and industries and several other assignments – Obasanjo was throwing everything at me and it was really stressful and I had never felt more overstretched in my whole life. The prospect of a break from this was very appealing, to pursue what I love doing – studying, travelling, and enjoying music, movies and the theatre, in the company of my lovely wives and wonderful children.

Though I do not regret it, the way my role evolved was not something I had ever aspired to or sought out. Mine was a perpetually growing role because Obasanjo saw me as a person who got things done. Whenever he had a problem, whether it was the census being delayed or the preparations for the elections not being up to speed or electricity production going down by 50 percent at the end of 2006, he just assigned me to resolve it. I did – each and every issue somehow got resolved to Obasanjo's satisfaction.

Indeed, in the final year of Obasanjo's presidency, I was not just running the FCT but involved in an array of activities - I was required to handle the portfolios of the minister of commerce and industry (twice), minister of interior, chair of national or cabinet committees on electric power supply improvement, sale of federal government houses in Abuja, national ID Card, development of a national mortgage system, public service reforms, review of salaries and emoluments in the public service (including the military and the police), destruction of contraband, and was at various points the oversight and liaison with chairmen of the Independent National Electoral Commission and the National Population Commission. In the eyes of many, including some of my cabinet colleagues, I had by default become a de facto vice-president. The more I sorted out these issues, the more Obasanjo threw others at me, and it just became too much. I was always tired, sleep-deprived and exhausted.

While I was being overworked, some of my other colleagues were becoming restless that I was getting all the attention of the president and perceived public recognition. Being the final year of his presidency, people did not have to make too big of a leap to conclude that Obasanjo was preparing me for anointment to succeed him. Obasanjo even sent me to the Niger Delta to work with James Ibori to find a way to create jobs in Warri. He established a presidential commission on job creation in Warri and made me chair of it, so I ended up having to make three or four trips to Delta state just to meet with the state government and youth organisations to try replicating the job-creation and entrepreneurship programmes we introduced in Abuja that spawned many new small businesses and thousands of construction-related jobs. The flaw in this presidential initiative was that Abuja was a growing city under construction, enjoying inward migration of skilled people, and lots of construction workers who had come in looking for work.

Warri is a much older city, then conflict-ridden without any one in charge, and the youths had a sense of entitlement due to oil exploration and production taking place next door to their homes. Obasanjo's stance on it was simply, 'I want to solve it,' so we had to go and conduct interviews, engage in consultations and studies, and submit a report on how to create jobs when the real problem was an overall governance and accountability deficit. Nevertheless, Ibori welcomed the commission and was very nice to me. I later learnt that he usually gave cash to visitors like me, but since he knew I would not take that, he gave me a beautiful bronze statuette as a gift instead. I never had any relationship or disagreements with him and at that point his issues with the EFCC had not yet emerged – he was still good friends with Nuhu. His problems started after leaving office, when he lost the immunity from prosecution he enjoyed as governor.

While people thought Obasanjo was preparing me for something, the truth really was that no anointment was being contemplated. I knew that I was simply an overworked machine and nothing more, because I know my boss very well. The truth also really was that Obasanjo would never even in his wildest dreams think of supporting me to be president, largely because he knows that he would not be able to control me in that or indeed in any position. If, as president, I were to find that he did something seriously wrong, he knows as well as I do that I would not overlook it simply on the basis that he used to be my boss. This professional independence and loyalty to principle, I believe, made Obasanjo very uncomfortable with me and people like me. My boss is uncomfortable with anyone he is not absolutely certain he could control. Unlike others who led him on to believe he could control them, I am incapable of pretending to be servile to get ahead. Only focus on work and the results constitute my testimonial in any situation, and thus the explanation for the roller coaster relationship I had with Obasanjo. He loved the fact that I got difficult jobs done but hated my independence of thought and fidelity to principles higher than blind loyalty to him.

The record of extra-ministerial assignments listed above and the history of my apparent closeness to the president neither endeared me to Atiku Abubakar, who was estranged from Obasanjo at the time, nor some of my ambitious cabinet colleagues. In the future, the same reasons made it more difficult for an insecure Umaru Yar'Adua as president to feel comfortable with me visibly walking around in Abuja, and hence the need to cut me to size.

The final breakfast
The sentiment of the final breakfast was for the most part upbeat, though it struck me that Obasanjo that morning looked like he

had grown several years older. He looked as if he was about to face death – his skin was sallow and it was very clear that this was difficult for him, like someone in the final hours before heading to the electric chair. He did not eat any breakfast, he just had some tea. I never thought of losing power as being that painful, but he was visibly pained. He delivered a nice speech about how the administration's success was due to the efforts of some of us, that people abused him and said Obasanjo had achieved nothing, yet in the same breath they say Dora Akunyili, El-Rufai, Ngozi, Nuhu and Oby had really turned things around in their various areas; he gave a nod to Femi Fani-Kayode, the minister of aviation, for ending the series of plane crashes that had afflicted the country's aviation sector; and he said to us that he expected us to remain in the government. Oby had left for the World Bank by then, so she was not at that breakfast, and of course Ngozi had already been long gone, thanks to the London fiasco. Obasanjo gave the clear impression that he had spoken with Umaru Yar'Adua and everyone who wanted to stay in government employment would stay.

Toward the end of the breakfast, as we were preparing to go home and ready ourselves for the inauguration, Obasanjo called Femi Fani-Kayode to stay on for a few minutes after everyone left.

When Femi joined us at the inauguration, I could see he was upset about something, but he would not tell me about the incident until some weeks later. The long and short of this brief meeting was that Femi had had an unpleasant encounter with Obasanjo after we left for allegedly refusing to do something that Iyabo Obasanjo requested of him as aviation minister..

That final morning, those two faces of Obasanjo – one in which he was sitting with us, praising everyone and being gracious and the other, exacting retribution from one of his cabinet ministers even as he was leaving office – was not the first time that I learnt of Obasanjo as being capable of such quick changes in demeanour. For a while, I simply thought of this as an isolated incident, but I eventually learned that it was more than just an individual thing. It was actually a recurring characteristic of such leaders throughout history. However, there were still some other things that had to happen before I would understand that. Perhaps, these are some of the lessons and experiences Obasanjo thought I needed to understand.

My Relationship with Yar'adua Pre-Nomination

Leading up to Umaru's elevation to the presidency, I would not say we were very close, but we were very cordial to each other. Any time he came to Abuja, which was not often - he would send his aide for me and I would go visit him at the governor's guest house, we would have dinner and catch up on things. I never went to Katsina just to visit him. In fact, he hosted me only once while he was governor.[128] Nevertheless, we always had a decent, professional relationship, sort of a brotherly relationship.

This brotherly relationship went back many years, to when we first met in late 1972. I had just been admitted to Barewa College in January of that year and he had just graduated from Barewa a month earlier. Even though he had already graduated, since he was the immediate past house captain in my hostel – Mallam Smith House - he was liked by everyone, I heard a lot about him. His nickname was "Bad Man" – he drank all the time, smoked a lot, was not a strict disciplinarian at all and that was why all the students loved him. He was quite bright though, and despite reportedly sleeping away his two years of A-Levels and mostly missing classes, he still made good enough grades to be admitted into university at a time when most people failed all four A-level papers. During his time in secondary school at Keffi and later at Barewa College, he got involved in student politics and eventually ended up as president of the Katsina students' union.[129]

The reason I got to meet him was because his cousin, Sani Maikudi, a mentor, who later became a partner in our consulting firm, became my senior guardian in school. While we were at Barewa, Bad Man had enrolled at Ahmadu Bello University to study chemistry-education, so Sani used to take me along to go visit him during the next two years that Sani was in Barewa. Bad Man was always a quiet type of guy, measured with his words and would not really say much unless he was with people he knew for a long time. What struck me when we first met was his austere, untidy appearance and the debilitating skin disease – some kind of eczema that gave him a blotched, discoloured aspect. I got to know him, I concluded that he was very untidy, dirty even, rarely bathing and never caring to ever dress neatly.

It was precisely those characteristics that many of us admired about him because in our minds that sort of comportment connoted someone who was down to earth and humble. His father was a first republic minister and his brother ended up being the number two man in the Obasanjo military government. He came from an important and well known family, but refused to let it get in the way of how he wanted to be seen. Because brothers of military governors and heads of state and generals in those days drove fancy cars in universities and wore expensive designer clothes, we interpreted Umaru's austere bearing as modesty and humility and it was quite endearing. Those of us from more modest backgrounds were always put off by rich boys showing off their family's money. To meet someone who could have done that but chose not to amounted to a breath of fresh air. As a result, I always saw him as a much revered older brother and related to him as such. I respected him as much as I respected Bashir El-Rufai and Sani Maikudi. All of them were more than brothers to me – they were mentors that I never saw as competitors at all.

Years later, Bashir drew my attention to the relationship between Umaru's father and our father. Apparently, they not only worked in the same ministry but had a student-teacher relationship. The letter evidencing this, written by Musa Yar'Adua in 1953 to our father to sympathise with him over the loss of some of his cattle, is in Appendix 13.

Umaru was also very shy, particularly with girls, but when he and Turai married, I recall being invited to attend the wedding because of my closeness to Sani Maikudi. I did not know this until much later in 2007, but at some point around 1997, he and Sani had a bad falling out. Neither Sani nor Umaru mentioned the estrangement to me at any time and I maintained my relationship of respect and affection for both.

Knowing Umaru better over time and longer than most people that worked with him as president, I was convinced that working with him would damage our cordial relationship. One of Umaru's basic problems was that he was insecure and could therefore be irrational about many things. Part of the reason I think he failed as a president was that this deep insecurity prevented him from surrounding himself with enough numbers of competent, independently-minded people who could disagree with him. This is because good people often have strong opinions and necessarily disagree with others, including their leaders. They are naturally confident, outspoken and will not always agree with the leader's views and will say so. Umaru had no tolerance at all for people who argued or disagreed with him. Once a person disagreed with Umaru once or twice, that person would never have access to him ever again, he just blocked him out. These deep insecurities led to all kinds of things and I think maybe Sani took many things for granted that may have led to the falling out.

Thinking back and recalling that evening in 2006 when Umaru came to my house asking for help – this was not a political thing, but just a show of support that he was requesting, which, all things considered given our past together, was a totally reasonable thing to do. I even managed to get Nuhu to come around and support Umaru's candidacy in the end, though I do not think Umaru ever really forgave Nuhu for that first reaction – first impressions, after all, last forever. In the end, virtually each one of us supported Umaru's candidacy and Obasanjo then established a presidential campaign council and then proceeded to appoint all but one of the members of the council. As Obasanjo was the one who picked these people, Umaru did not feel it was his campaign council and therefore needed a smaller team of his own to be thinking about the campaign. This led to my second meeting with Umaru after a dinner in my residence with Tanimu Yakubu in tow. Umaru then asked Bukola Saraki, Aliko Dangote, Andy Uba and James Ibori to invite me and Nuhu Ribadu to another "inner circle formation" meeting in Andy Uba's house a couple of weeks later.

It became clear, at these meetings, that Umaru did not have access to the campaign funds Obasanjo was raising purportedly on his behalf. He was finding that he had to hire aircraft to take him to various places and he could not pay. He called me and mentioned this, then sent Tanimu to ask for financial contribution. We ended up raising N50 million (then about half a million dollars) twice, and both times got the money handed over to Tanimu Yakubu in cash.

There also came a point at which Umaru confided in me that he was not happy with the communications strategy that his campaign was implementing and asked for help. I suggested that the Yar'Adua team hire a team comprising a British campaign strategist, Nigerian communications consultants and an American pollster to review and revamp the Yar'Adua campaign plan. The campaign spent some two million pounds sterling to do extensive polling nationally, undertake focus group sessions that led to the production of multi-lingual radio jingles, videos and a comprehensive campaign strategy for candidate Yar'Adua, all paid for by a friend of mine who still prefers anonymity. Apart from the instances when Umaru requested me personally to assist, I did not have any hand in the campaign's strategy, which was neither here nor there as far as I was concerned. My role in his presidential campaign, to the extent that I had any, was coming up with the ideas, contacts and resources and handing them over to his team, and on one occasion campaigning with him and Obasanjo when the campaign team spent the day in Abuja. Given the many other things I had on my plate at the time, I was perfectly fine with this level of contribution.

President-Elect Yar'Adua

Immediately upon announcing Umaru's election victory, I congratulated him and informed him of my medium-term plans, mainly because I did not want him to offer me a job that I would have to say no to. I explained to him that I had a law degree to finish in London followed by attending a graduate programme at the John F. Kennedy School of Government.

"But I am going to need you here," he said.

"Well, I will be available by phone or email any time you need me but I need to do this," I told him. "This is my life that I have put on hold for nine years."

"Mallam Nasir, you know I can't do this job alone, I need experienced people around me and I was relying on you to be there."

"Sir, you know I will always be there, just a phone call away. I am available to research and write a paper on any problem. Just anything you want as long as I do not have to take a full time job."

He indicated that he did not like this answer, but we agreed to discuss it again when things became more settled.

Two days later, he called with a request to initiate a transition committee to begin planning how he would take over and he wanted me to co-chair it along with one other person. He gave me the names of those he wanted to be on the committee and we started meeting up. After two or three meetings, I noticed that

Tanimu Yakubu, who was one of the closest people to Yar'Adua, and Aliyu Modibbo, who was supposed to be my co-chair,[130] stopped attending the meetings. Clearly, I concluded, Yar'Adua was no longer interested in this transition committee.

When a new president is elected, many people come to him seeking influence, seeking relevance, and expecting a job in the administration. There may have been some people convincing him to set up another transition committee without some of us as members. I did not think much of it at the time as I had enough other work to do and if Umaru was not interested in what we were doing, we might as well get on with our lives. Our committee stopped meeting and eventually I went to see him to discuss the matter.

"Mr. President-elect, it does not seem to me this transition committee is working because your guys have been too busy to attend and we cannot do it well without the input of people from your side," I said. "So we will just tidy up whatever we have done and I will hand it over to you and you can continue from there."

His response was brief and telling – he basically just said that sounded fine and thanks, which confirmed to me that this was what he wanted. There was no explanation. We assembled all the reports and sent them to him and that was it. This was the first sign that something was amiss.

Nevertheless, Yar'Adua continued to consult me on other matters including some key appointments. When he was appointing his secretary to the government, he called me to ask for names – explaining first that he was looking for a career public servant with experience in politics to be his secretary to the government. He also called looking for a meeting with the UNDP and the country director for the World Bank because he wanted to begin exploring what the World Bank could assist him with when he took over. The World Bank country director had become a good friend of mine, an Egyptian named Hafez Ghanem, so I brought him to see Yar'Adua. He basically called when he wanted something that was relevant to my network, expertise or connections and that was pretty much it.

During Yar'Adua's first few weeks in office, I went ahead with the plans I outlined to him. I first traveled to Saudi Arabia to perform the Umrah, followed by a two-week programme at

Harvard Kennedy School, and then with Hadiza, went on a North Atlantic jazz cruise courtesy of Hakeem Belo-Osagie. I was doing what I had wanted to do for years, but could not. Yar'Adua and I remained in touch and every time I saw him that summer, it seemed to be the same story with him: he perpetually needed to see me, to request for help, but then when we would finally sit down again, it was as though the previous conversation had never happened and we would start all over. "I need you around here," he uttered this phrase to me more than thrice that summer and then periods of radio silence followed, despite the intermittent requests for some involvement. What was happening behind the scenes, and I say this only after hearing it from multiple sources who were on the inside, was that after those first 100 days or so, Yar'Adua had given up on being able to run the federal government. His first week, the amount of paperwork that came to his desk was so overwhelming. He could not believe that the president was required to read all those memos and approve or comment on each one.

Obasanjo, the taskmaster, did, indeed, do all of that. Obasanjo was a very hands-on president who wanted to know everything. Anything that ought to concern the president, Obasanjo wanted to be briefed on, and he worked 20 hours a day to make sure he did not miss anything. Umar was certainly intelligent but had limited capacity to work long hours. In Katsina, such an approach was not going to be problematic because it was an easy, laid-back state, everyone spoke the same language, virtually everyone was Muslim, and everyone was related somehow –akin to one large extended family. Running the nation at large was a little bit more complicated, and it did not matter how well one delegated as president of Nigeria, one must work sixteen hours minimum, every day, Sundays included.

As one of the people I know who had been on the inside in the early Yar'Adua days put it to me, "By the end of the first month, we were panting. It is as if we were involved in a long sprint. By the second month, we were shaking our heads with disbelief. We could not believe how difficult things were that needed doing. By the third month, we had pretty much given up and decided that we would go after three or four things that were important to us and focus on them: petroleum, agriculture, various Chinese deals and electric power, because there were lots of contracts there and presumably some money to be made by the inner circle." That was it. The rest of government basically got ignored so that Yar'Adua could focus on these four areas that his inner circle felt they could make money from, would enable them to show some results, and sleep the rest of the time.

Two other signs that something went wrong, though I still had yet to piece it all together, were revealed very soon after we left office. The first was about a week after I turned in my diplomatic passport. The ministry of foreign affairs wrote to the president to say that many former ministers had not turned over their diplomatic passports and some of them could constitute security risks to the new administration. This was before Yar'Adua's ministers were even appointed. The foreign ministry approved the cancellation of all the diplomatic passports and recommended that such should be impounded upon presentation to Nigerian immigration. My name was apparently number one on the list of former ministers in question, even though I had already turned in the passport in question. When Umaru sent his chief of staff instructions to recover the diplomatic passports, the chief of staff complied, but informed him that I had already turned mine in. As at then, most of my colleagues still had their diplomatic passports.

The second indication that something was amiss came that summer. One day, a detachment of police officers from the presidential villa came and surrounded the house I had just purchased in the federal government house sales programme. The policemen declared that no one was to enter or exit the house, because it was the vice-president's guest house and my occupation of it was illegal. The house was formerly allocated to the vice-president's office, but all such guest houses were approved for sale, and had been sold. I bought it at a price approved by the cabinet and on terms identical to the terms offered other political office holders and at more than twice the price paid by career public servants. My family was at home at the time and ended up being detained for some four hours. My wife tried calling me but could not reach me as I was out of town, so she called Nuhu. He came to the house and called the president's chief of staff, who called the head of the State House police and ordered them to withdraw.

What prompted all these, allegedly, were people from Atiku's camp starting a media campaign, raising questions about the house, which caused then-vice-president Goodluck Jonathan to enquire as to why he did not have guest houses. He was not the one who gave the orders to the police, though. To this day, it is unclear who gave the orders.

One day in September, Tanimu Yakubu called me to say Umaru wished to appoint me to the membership of the National Energy Council. Obasanjo had recommended to him that I should be so appointed, because of the results achieved when I chaired the cabinet committee on power supply improvement. It was a part-time obligation, which perfectly fit my plans. What I later learned was that there were a number of other dynamics happening, even with something as seemingly innocuous as this. The council consisted of the chairman, which would be Yar'Adua, the vice-chairman, who was the vice-president, several ministers and four outsiders. I was one of the four outsiders.

The original intention here was that Yar'Adua wanted to make me 'alternate chairman' and then basically just hand over day-to-day running of the council's operations to me. Mind you, I had no idea about this at the time, as it was nothing close to what I had personally negotiated. Only through conversations after the fact with two people close to Yar'Adua did I learn of this. Apparently, everyone that Yar'Adua had spoken to told him that I could help him resolve the electricity problem and other power issues, so he wanted to inaugurate the council, then step back and allow me to run it as alternate chairman, and then probably take all the credit afterwards. This would have approximated to being a full-time assignment, something I was unwilling to accept at the time. Frankly, I had no opportunity to decide on the matter as no one bothered to inform me of the plan.

Where it all fell apart was, according to a minister close to the situation, when Yar'Adua told Obasanjo what his plan was on the matter. Obasanjo counselled against this – he had recommended that I should be on the council, but not as alternate chair because according to the source, that would make me 'too powerful' and would turn out to be a problem for Yar'Adua. As a regular member of the council, I was quite able to contribute technically to the work of the council, but in a position of leadership, Yar'Adua would have problems with me, in Obasanjo's opinion, according to the former minister. So within hours, Yar'Adua's stance on my role in the council had changed, and by the time the council convened its first meeting, I had no idea of what had been happening behind the scenes. In any event, I ended up attending only one meeting of the council - the inaugural meeting in September 2007. That was the last time Yar'Adua and I saw each other. I subsequently learnt of all the intrigue after my return to Nigeria, exactly four days before Yar'Adua's death.

The Smear Campaign Begins

From that point, I honestly do not know for sure what went wrong. I have thought about this over and over and I have no concrete answers. What I have are anecdotes about events that happened, some observations, some deductions and a certainty that my life from then on was never the same.

The hint that I had a potential problem on my hands was when my successor in the FCT, who had been a friend of mine for over 27 years, Aliyu Modibbo, started suggesting that some decisions of mine on land matters while I was in charge of the FCT were inappropriate. The moment I saw that I called a meeting with my close friends and I warned them, "Yar'Adua has decided to 'get' me. We should organise right away to confront him."

Everybody in the group said I was jumping the gun, that I had no basis to draw these conclusions, and that this was just Modibbo's adventurism, and there was nothing to worry about. But I knew Yar'Adua very well, I knew his style. The moment it started, while I did not yet have a full view of everything that was likely to happen, I knew that Yar'Adua did not like open, public fights. He's a surreptitious fighter, one who gets up to attack you while you are not looking, and then steps back before you turn to identify him. I said to them we should make this an open fight, otherwise it would get worse. But all my friends insisted I was wrong and that I was overreacting.

The next red flag was the public hearings in the first half of 2008, which Aliyu Modibbo initiated at what we suspected and later confirmed were Yar'Adua's behest. At that point, it was very clear to me what was happening, I just did not understand why. I later understood that Yar'Adua wanted some independent basis to persecute and if possible, prosecute me. He did not want to be the one to point the finger at me, rather, his style was to find someone else's accusation to latch onto. So in this particular case he personally commissioned the National Assembly to do his bidding and then took the report and said he was only doing what the legislature insisted he should do. Had I met with him that first day, he would have denied any involvement and strictly leaned on the National Assembly's findings as being something he was obligated to act upon as a constitutional duty.

Nuhu was still in the EFCC then and had become somewhat chummy with Umaru. So he thought then that the situation could be managed. Personally, I knew it was going all the way wrong and that there was no point in attending the public hearings because whether I attended and answered questions or not, knowing both Umaru and Aliyu Modibbo, the report had already been written. I was convinced that it was a kangaroo hearing that would do Umaru's bidding - "get Nasir at all costs." Nuhu disagreed with me and persuaded my inner circle that more or less forced me to agree to attend the hearings. My initial position was to go to court and challenge everything about the legality of the investigation. The group decision was that since we had nothing to hide, and we had all our facts, I should appear before the Senate Committee and defend our tenure. They did not realise that my earlier history with the Senate ensured that I would never ever have a fair hearing. I think now my group of friends knows better. I have been a victim of my belief in the wisdom of crowds and group decision making but have no regrets. I have learnt to live with it.

In any event, the administration clearly decided that the easiest way to destroy me was to go after precisely what I had going for me and cared most about, which was my personal integrity and record of performance. Once they started the public hearings, hysteria of course took over and nobody realised that the reason the FCT was then functioning properly was because the remnants of the orderly, auto-pilot system we had put in place there still worked. The city was running and people thought someone was running it, but no one was running anything. It was the system we put in place which the new gang was unable to destroy overnight. So the differences in performance were not apparent at that point in time. Secondly, if they could smear, without any proof or evidence, that was fine – that was why they investigated me – the gang was not in pursuit of truth, but the achievement of false and sensational headlines.

They investigated me for financial corruption, for missing monies and tried to find people who had bribed me while in office. They called all the major contractors in FCT and asked them how it all went down, and nobody could say anything because nobody had ever been involved in that sort of thing with me. They called the banks, because the bank managers all were supposed to pay brokerage, commissions and kickbacks to ministers for deposits in their banks and none of them could point to any sort of such relationship with me. I never met any bank manager before starting any banking relationship with the FCTA. These functions were delegated to my special assistant on economic matters and the FCT director of treasury, who remained silent, like true civil servants, when I was falsely accused by the new boss. Aliyu Modibbo, a friend of many years, led the charge not only to 'put Nasir's arrogant ass in the right place,' as he told a mutual friend, but to please his employer, Umaru Yar'Adua.

The administration's presecution battalion, led by Dr. Aliyu Modibbo, Senator Abubakar Danso Sodangi, Attorney-General Michael Aondoakaa, and EFCC chair Farida Waziri (who took charge after Nuhu had been forced out) were quite frustrated because they could not find anything unlawful with which to tar and feather me. Umaru thought that I was either very clever or extremely lucky, and he kept asking everyone, "How can anyone run Abuja for four years and leave no trace of any money missing?" Even the attorney general said he was unable to find anything to prosecute from all the investigations by the EFCC and the police. Umaru's reply to the attorney general was that nobody could be that honest or that careful, and they must keep digging.

As an example of how desperate the administration was for any sort of dirt on me, they concocted a story hinting that I had misappropriated funds from the sale of federal government houses in Abuja. We sold houses on behalf of the federal government for 96 billion naira, and yet only 64 billion naira was in the bank, so in their eyes, 32 billion naira was still 'unaccounted for.' What they conveniently left out of this snappy little accusation was that house sales of 96 billion naira did not necessarily lead to 96 billion naira in cash, as some mortgages had not been fully funded. However, it was a good headline, which they paid some newspapers a great deal to put on the front page. Their argument when audits and bank accounts revealed where all the funds were was that they did not actually say I stole anything, they had simply alleged that it was "unaccounted for."

We know this is unnecessary innuendo that is only perpetuated by people trying to distract attention from some inconvenient truth. When this accusation failed and Yar'Adua's hit men still had not found anyone who could testify to bribing me, they then went through the entire database of plots of land I allocated while I was at FCT – this is over 27,000 plots of land – and they picked out 19 beneficiaries named Rufai or El-Rufai, assumed that they were all my relations and ignored the fact that half of them received land before I was even running the FCT, and my family never had the monopoly of the name "Rufai". The numbers of plots I purportedly allocated to my family members kept changing due to protests by, for instance, Senator Rufai Sani Hanga from Kano State, who was listed as my brother, and a Sharia Court judge named Ali Rufai who was certainly not my brother with the same name, who had retired from the Nigerian Air Force as an air vice marshall. In the latest EFCC smear story, the number of plots allocated to my extended family members had come down to less than eight out of more than 27,000 plot allocations I approved during my tenure.

In short, nobody could find anything substantive that spoke to any wrongdoing of mine. This was why when I went back to Nigeria and was approached to get the government then under the acting presidency of Goodluck Jonathan to drop the charges against me, I refused. "I do not want the government to drop the charges against me," I said. "The charge against me is that I have committed an offence by approving the allocation of a plot of land to my wife. That is the kernel of the charge against me. I want a judge to rule that it is an offence to do so. Every Nigerian is entitled to a plot of land in Abuja if he is above the age of 18. If my wife applied in 2001, and I got to the FCT in 2003, and she finally got a piece of land in 2006, I do not see how that can be an offence. It is not like I got there and on my first day I said to people, bring my wife's papers to approve an allocation for her." I still stand by this position.

I never had a chance to confront Umaru directly about this so, as I said, the most I can do is make some observations and draw certain conclusions from what I have learnt from those close to him. The first thing I would say is that Umaru and I had a historical problem in that from day one, he considered me a competitor. I still do not think he ever forgot or forgave Nuhu's initial reaction to his presidential candidacy, and then to top it off, he was misled into thinking that Obasanjo's short list of successors consisted of two people: him and me. Yar'Adua, with his deep feelings of insecurity, came into the job feeling that I was a potential problem – I was not only a past competitor, but could be a future competitor. Yet he kept trying to bring me in close, and when I told him I was not interested in working for him, I think that persuaded him that I was up to no good, I was retreating to re-arm. Even when I thought it was better to leave town, that did not work either, because he thought I was going abroad to get this big arsenal of American, British and other 'imperialist' friends that I am supposed to have. Quite honestly, I really did not care and I never had, about this sort of thing.

Secondly, there was the Obasanjo factor. I had no doubt in my mind, and I had a variety of indications of this, that Obasanjo told Yar'Adua the truth - I was difficult to control. I also think that when I outlined my plans to be studying abroad for at least the first two years of his tenure, he felt snubbed and it would be typical of Yar'Adua to take my retreat additionally as a sign that I had no regard for him. Putting all these things together with Nuhu's attitude and investigations, he likely considered us two dangerous northerners that he could not trust and who needed to be taken care of. It was a simple matter of making sure he covered all his angles. Southerners would be waiting until 2015 regardless, so there was no need to worry about any of them. Northerners posing a potential threat had to be eliminated.

I know that he had plans to at least do his two terms, but I do not think he factored in his health. Had he known he was going to die before his first term was over, I do not think he would have bothered with it all, but this is all just supposition. I am now quite certain that he knew he was not going to do much work, so he would have plenty of time to devote to knocking out everyone else. I had the reputation of getting things done, his doing nothing evoked memories of our accomplishments, particularly in Abuja. Everyone in Nigeria was concerned about electricity and everyone, even my own enemies, was writing opinions suggesting that I was one of the few that had proven capability to fix it. That kind of thing would certainly worry a president who had given up on delivering.

More than just an inconvenience

There is, of course, a difference between suspecting a smear campaign is being waged against you and knowing that you are in danger. While I was studying to complete my LL.B. in London in May 2008, I was also arranging to return to Nigeria in June to retrieve my student visa so that I could go to Harvard that summer to begin a master's degree programme. Nuhu had asked me not to come back to Nigeria in June 2008 out of concern because of certain things he was noticing already underway. He was not in the EFCC and thought that if I came back to Nigeria I would be in some danger. Jendayi Frazer, who at the time was the US Assistant Secretary of State for African affairs, was aware of the danger of going home and told me I could collect my visa from the American embassy in London if I wanted, but I insisted on going back. Once I was there, the EFCC came to my house to ask me questions about particular land allocations, which I had already answered during the public hearings, so I gave them a pre-written 118-page explanatory document and we all left it at that. When I went to the airport to return to London for my LL.B. exams, something was definitely not right. I had checked in, my baggage was already on the plane and when I handed over my passport for my exit stamp, internal security informed me that they had been told not to allow me to fly out that day.

"Ok. Am I under arrest?"

"No."

"Well I have to travel. I have the right to travel. If you are not arresting me for an offence, then I have a right to travel." The SSS does not have the power of arrest.

"Well I am sorry sir, I am following orders."

I called my lawyer, Abdul-Hakeem Mustapha, and informed him that I was being illegally detained at the airport and was going to miss my flight, so he should get ready to sue the federal government for violating my civil rights. I then called the head of the internal security service in Nigeria - the Director General of the SSS, Gadzama, who was my senior at Barewa College.

"I have been detained by your people, what is going on?"

He knew nothing. Five minutes later I still had not heard from him, so I called the chief of staff to the president, who was the chief of staff when we were in government. I told him what was happening and he became very upset. He too knew nothing but promised to check on it and get back to me. After about 15 minutes, I was permitted to board and was still able to catch my flight. I did not know when I would come back to Nigeria again, but I knew this incident at the airport was not a mistake.

As the plane took off from Nnamdi Azikiwe International Airport that morning and turned northwards, I knew I would not be able to return to Nigeria for quite a while. It turned out to be 23 months of exile.

Chapter Sixteen

Exile

"To me, there is something very powerful about being totally alone and far from home. It gives you a perspective about life you could never have any other way. It is a rush, partly because you have no identity or connections to where you are. You could be anyone, anything. You could be nothing."

– *Owen P. Grover*

When I left the country, thoughts of exile or asylum did not cross my mind as I was embarking on a 12- month course of study. Exile is what happens when circumstances have forced you to keep away from your country, but on a temporary basis. Asylum, on the other hand, is permanent, but like exile, also involuntary. You accept that your life, limb or property is in danger in your country and you are driven to live in another country so you request for political asylum and intend to never return unless circumstances change. Being a refugee I think is voluntary, either as a political imperative or because economic circumstances force you to leave your country willingly and move to another. So exile and asylum are involuntary, while being a refugee is to some extent voluntary, broadly speaking.

This is why I considered myself an exile. I was now an exile, but would not seek asylum. The Yar'Adua government, of course, wanted me to apply for asylum, and the attorney general even alluded to the fact that I was attacking Yar'Adua because I wanted to justify my application for political asylum in another country.[131] I did not hesitate to respond that I would never seek asylum, I would come back, because I would not live permanently anywhere else.

I do not know why, but when Nigerians leave Nigeria for more than a few days, we really begin to miss our country. This I noticed my first time in England as a married man, in 1985. Nigerians I knew abroad or at home, were and still are fond of complaining all the time about our country, and yet we miss it. A friend of mine recently told me a story that I thought captured this quite well. She used to work for me in the BPE and has dual Nigerian-British citizenship. She had her first daughter when she was in her early twenties, the daughter was born and raised in the UK, and grew to be 28 or 29 without ever having visited Nigeria as an adult. A couple of years ago, the daughter visited Nigeria for the first time since she was a young child. When the daughter came back to the UK, she packed her bags, sold her house and moved to Nigeria.

> "That is very strange," I told my friend. "I would like to ask your daughter why she made such a drastic decision."
>
> My friend said, "Well I asked her the same question and she said it was very simple – she just loved the lack of order. She loved the anarchy, the fact that you do not have to pay your bills, the fact that if you drive too fast or beat a traffic light, you can negotiate it. She said in England, if you beat a traffic light, you are sure to get a ticket or you pay a fine at the end of the month, and if you do not pay that fine, you will get dragged to court and could go to jail. But in Nigeria, everything is negotiable. She loves that about the country."

I am a law and order type of person, so I do not think I can say that I miss the same chaos about Nigeria. But I did miss home terribly— the networks of friends and family, the food, especially my favourite jollof rice, the climate, the sight and sound and smell, the contentious jostle, the hustle and flow, the sense that you belonged to your own corner of earth.

Prior to my exile, the longest I had ever been away from Nigeria at a stretch was about three months, so the idea of exile of indefinite duration I found really tough to handle. I had great difficulty accepting that anyone could say that my country was not mine to live in – it was an affront to my sense of citizenship. The thought that President Umaru Yar'Adua would attempt to deprive me of my citizenship and residency rights enraged me. I had to face him and we had to sort it out one way or the other, even if it meant one of us dying, more likely me.[132] If I was not at Harvard attending the Mason Fellows Programme, and was instead just living idly in the US, I would have returned immediately to Nigeria the moment the persecution started. But I was certain that if I had returned to Nigeria, I would not be allowed to go back to the US to complete my degree programme and I was determined to do that because I had been waiting ten years to do so. So I thought, first things first, I will first complete my academic programme, not be distracted, and put it behind me - then face Yar'Adua full time and end it - one way or the other.

A Lonely Year on the Charles River

Among the things that made my exile easier was that first, one of my sons, Mohammed Bello, was studying for his undergraduate degree in the Boston area and my wife Hadiza, eventually joined me. I had an austere two-bedroom apartment in Peabody Terrace, one of Harvard's many graduate apartment blocks in Cambridge, but my wife did not like Boston very much, so she would frequently visit Washington where her sister lives, as well as family friends like Dr. Angela Onwuanibe, Stella Ojukwu, Oby, Ngozi and many acquaintances working at the embassy and at the World Bank. In the end, she moved to live in Bowie, Maryland as she increasingly found DC to be more liveable. She at least had family and a community of friends there. From my end, I really spent most of the time reading. My graduate programme required the reading of some 300 pages of course material every day, which gave the sense that Harvard really overworked its students to make them feel like they had come to the greatest school in the world. I do not think they believed that everyone would read it all, but I did end up reading almost all of it, which left me little time for anything else, Yar'Adua and his goons included. I was and remain very grateful to God and Harvard for the lonely experience of exile, as painful as it was, because the programme kept me very busy and left no room for me to be unhappy about what was going on in Nigeria. My summer programme of seminars went quickly and the master's programme required me to take eight classes, which equated to eight credits over twelve months, two semesters. The school recommended very strongly that each student takes three or four classes per semester. I decided to take five credits in the Fall Semester which included the winter and my logic was simple: I hate winter, I hate the cold, and I knew that I was going to be unhappy and be mostly in my room, so I thought I would take five classes and just stay focused on the readings. I figured that if I passed the five classes, I could then take three classes in the spring when the weather would be much better, and I would be able to go out and enjoy it and go to Washington for the weekends.

In addition to taking five classes, I was also a teaching assistant, which effectively meant taking six classes. I had to attend the sixth class, prepare for it and also set aside what was called in Kennedy School lingo, 'office hours'. This meant I sat with my classmates on Sunday and assisted them with their homework because the assignments were due on Mondays, and the professor knew from experience that most people waited until Sundays to do homework. This meant I could not go to Washington for weekends in my first semester. When spring came, instead of taking three classes, the minimum I needed, I ended up taking four and did not enjoy the weather as much as I had thought.

The Politics and Ethics of Statecraft

It was only as a result of this intense studying, coupled with my physical withdrawal from the street-level manoeuvrings in Nigeria, that I was able to learn many lessons and come to certain conclusions about the past number of years. One of the most revealing came in the form of a class entitled, 'The Politics and Ethics of Statecraft.' The course was taught by a Catholic priest named Brian Hehir. I became curious about it during the 'shopping' period, in which all professors spend a week teaching a sample class for 45 minutes so students could get some feel for each professor's style. Since I had never in my life actually studied politics or political science in a classroom, I thought I should take a class on politics – after all, this was the Kennedy School of Government. Joe Nye had a politics class but it was Americo-centric, the whole soft power thing. I had read enough about the US and I needed something more, something different in political science. On a lark, I attended Professor Hehir's class during the shopping period and he totally swept me off my feet.

The syllabus focused on the characteristics of a handful of great leaders in history: Otto von Bismarck, Charles De Gaulle, Henry Kissinger, JFK, Woodrow Wilson, Tony Blair and Jimmy Carter amongst others. What was most compelling about this class is that it helped me understand that leaders in general possessed huge components of both good and evil in their character and leadership styles. Of that group, there was no one leader that did not have a significant blemish. Some had a little bit more evil than others – Bismarck was amazing, and De Gaulle was a huge egomaniac. That was when I began to understand Obasanjo a little more. I always had difficulty understanding how Obasanjo could sit with us and preach about sacrifice and transparency one moment and then the next, sit with Gaius Obaseki, the GMD of NNPC, about how to get some payments to the PDP from some oil or LNG deals. I never understood how a person could do this and sleep well. How can one have Obasanjo's complex personality and sleep well at night? Studying Bismarck, De Gaulle and the rest helped me make sense of this duality in leaders.

The class also had one advantage: no end –of-term written examinations. Instead, each of us was required to write a final essay about a leader, dead or alive, that we had studied on our own. I wrote on Obasanjo and I received an A, one of only two in the class. I was also the only student who had actually worked for the leader he or she wrote about and since it was first-hand, I had an added advantage.

The bottom line was my realisation that anyone who achieved that sort of leadership level tended to have certain character traits, indeed, to even arrive there required a certain moral flexibility. In discussing this with an American friend of mine not too long ago, he pointed out to me that when Bill Clinton came into office, the word, one of the many, that entered the American political lexicon in the 1990s was 'compartmentalisation'. Clinton was a famously adept practitioner of this craft. The general concept of this is apparently the ability to mentally isolate certain ideas and behaviours in certain compartments and not have the terms of engagement that govern one compartment spill over into another compartment where they may not be necessary, relevant or convenient. It appears that this is a skill that must be possessed to be able to ascend to a certain leadership level. I am hoping that this is a skill that can be acquired, as I would very much like to master it someday.

The Theory of Second Comings

Another major revelation, which came partly out of this class, but also just from having some more distance, both mental and physical, from Abuja, was what I have come to call the theory of second comings.

The Obasanjo I met in early 1999 and worked with from end of 1999 until the middle of 2005 or thereabouts was a totally different person from what emerged after that. The presidency and the circumstances changed him. Now, it is easy to fall back on the usual tropes about power, corruption, egotism and the like, but as befitting my activities during my years in exile, I came to take a more academic approach to this. Many people I have studied with or worked with in public service, who left with a decent record of integrity or achievement the first time around, often came to grief when they returned to public service a second time. Obasanjo, who ascended to the presidency the first time because his predecessor was assassinated, did a decent job for the most part. He kept to the democratic transition programme they agreed upon; he presided over a government that was overall decent. He organised acceptable elections, handed over power and then retired to his farm while enjoying international acclaim for being the first African military head of state to voluntarily hand over power.

Obasanjo became one of the most revered persons in Africa – Mandela was still in prison then. He also went broke in the intervening years. Why did all this happen? As military president, he reportedly did a few things to prepare for life after retirement –

buying shares during the indigenisation programme, some real estate investments and such rainy day activities – to prepare for the future, but in the broad scheme of things, he did not engage in nearly as much corruption as he was accused of in Fela Kuti's songs. Perhaps he had every opportunity as a military dictator to do so. As a basic example, as petroleum minister for the 14 month period between August 1978 and October 1979,[133] he could have set himself up very nicely. During his first outing, Obasanjo and his troika colleagues did not do things like that. They were angels when compared to today's gang.

After handing over, Obasanjo retreated to his Ota farm and got involved in all sorts of leadership foundations, international NGOs like Ford Foundation, Transparency International, and the like. Twenty years later, once he came back as an elected president, one could safely speculate that the thought may have crossed his mind that he did not adequately take care of himself the first time around. It would surely have occurred to him that he borrowed from banks to set up his farm and nearly went personally bankrupt. He would almost certainly have entertained the thought that Nigerians did not much care that he had served them honestly and well. He was accused of corruption anyway. Everyone danced to Fela's *Zombie*, *International Thief Thief* and *Coffin For Head of State*, and his defenders were few. It would not have been entirely shocking if he had allowed himself to entertain the thought that, this time, it would be different. I see this pattern in many people—career civil servants, cabinet ministers, presidents, and governors, very decent by Nigerian standards the first time out, but who, if they get a second chance, decide to take the fullest advantage, and then we see abusive acquisition on a large scale. This is the essence of my theory of second comings.

Why? How does one come to this point? How can anybody, who has a demonstrably clean record, purposely tarnish it? It is a phenomenon that I began to observe while practicing as a quantity surveyor and it continued to intrigue me while in government. I spent nearly two years in exile thinking about this issue. What I have concluded is that it is a combination of a few things that I only ever could have understood by leaving government and having some distance from Abuja. The first is that being in government is deceptive, financially and materially. There are so many things that come to public servants for free, one does not have to be corrupt and accept bribes to have them. Put simply, there are waves of gifts that come on one's birthday, on Christmas, Eid el-Fitr, Eid el-Kabir, during other religious festivals, weddings and wedding anniversaries, and children's graduations; and the culture and the ethics in government service allow one to accept a pen, a simple watch, and things of that nature on these sorts of occasions. Nobody has a problem with this. What everyone frowns upon is when a person collects a box full of cash. When a person is offered a watch as a birthday present and rejects it, this will be a big issue – what is wrong with this man? How can he reject the gift of a simple watch on his 40th birthday?[134]

One example from my own experience: because of the public way I fought senators who asked me for N54 million, I was not offered bribes as people were scared of giving me such 'gifts'. During the Muslim festival of Eid el-Kabir, everyone who can afford it is expected to slaughter a ram. When I was head of the BPE, I used to receive many rams every year. Everyone knew I could afford a ram or two, so I really did not need people to give me any. However, companies, banks, and everyone we did business with or wanted to do business with would send me two rams each, as it was one of the few opportunities they had to give me a 'token gift' that I could not decline, without appearing needlessly disagreeable.

What I did was I kept all the rams within the BPE premises. Two days before the festival, we would distribute them to the staff, starting with the lowliest and working our way up. All of the junior staff got a ram and it went up the hierarchy from there until the collection was all exhausted. During the eight years I was in government, I never had to buy a ram because I always got between fifty and a hundred every year, and even after giving away a lot to my staff, I still had some left over after the festivals. A minister would typically receive dozens of diaries and calendars each year, and deliveries of truckloads of rice and beans, so would not even need to buy much food. Even if one constantly gives them away, one would still have bags of rice in the store that would remain from the Christmas gifts of the previous year. During my public service years, my wives had instructions on how to handle these and usually gave them to our employees, the domestic staff and our relations immediately, but they kept coming in as long as I was in public office, often without my knowledge.

'Why Is My Phone Not Ringing?'

Once a government official leaves public service, however, this generosity vanishes overnight. The guy who sent a Merry Christmas card last year will not send another card now that the government official is out. In any given year in office, one might receive some 1,000 cards; the next year out of office, perhaps only ten. That rough ratio applies to all gifts, from rams to cash (for those who took bribes.) It is not difficult to understand why people feel deeply deprived after they leave government. Any friends a person thinks he or she made while in high positions of power in government are nothing more than a deception. After receiving a couple of hundred phone calls a day and scores of visitors to one's house when in office, these phone calls and house visits drop to near zero the morning it is all over. The only friends are the ones who were there before that person even contemplated being in these positions. There is such a massive change in the attitude of people that it hurts. Unless one is properly grounded, there can be a huge emotional letdown.

There can also be a lot of financial turmoil for anyone who becomes dependent on those gifts. It is not uncommon for many high officials, the relatively clean ones, to go completely broke within a few years of vacating their posts. You get accustomed to the high life, the adoring crowds of hangers on, the official cars and police escorts, the constant refrain of "Honorable" This and "Honorable" That, the rams and the Christmas cards and the supplicants waiting on you constantly in the outer office or your living room, and when the music stops, the silence can be deafening. Many will be depressed and many will be both broke and depressed, spending money they do not have to keep up appearances of their former high life.

I have a friend who was a principal officer in the National Assembly. As such, he was entitled to a convoy of policemen and aides to go with him wherever he went. He lost his position in the next election cycle, but he felt compelled to still maintain his convoy of cars, policemen and aides so that he did not look depreciated. When he was a principal officer, those cars were bought and maintained, and the aides were paid by the National Assembly. The moment he insisted he wanted to maintain them and he was not entitled to the police escorts, he had to pay them out of his own pocket. Within two years, he became broke and had to start selling off assets to maintain the standard of living to which he was accustomed. This happens to lots of former high officials.

Personally, even before I became minister, I had a fixed list of people I would give gifts to during the Muslim festivals: my mother, my stepmother, Yahaya Hamza's family, my six sisters, a handful of other relations, and that is all. Those are the ones I felt were my direct responsibility, no one else, and I have never expanded the list in 22 years. Even when I was minister, I kept to that list, and I did not, on account of being minister, give any of them two rams instead of the one I was used to and could afford on a sustainable basis. I obviously had the additional rams to give while in office, but I knew that one day I was going to leave that office, and I would have to try harder to maintain this if I started giving them two rams instead of one, so I never started that habit. Many people make the mistake of starting what they cannot feasibly sustain without the freebies of public office.

The next element of second comings is that when one leaves public office, one's universe of people all of a sudden shrinks to something equal to or less than what it was prior to entering public office, which for most people, is not very large. As minister one would receive between 200 to 300 phone calls a day. The day after one became an ordinary citizen, one would receive maybe a dozen. One would even think the phone system was down – 'Why is my phone not ringing?' Even people to whom one has been especially helpful and supportive, and in some cases trusted, would not so much as call to say hello. In my case, some of them actually became part of the smear campaign against me, and actively fabricated stories to make me look bad in order for them to get favours from the new government in power. They knew that they were lying, but they did not care because I was no longer in a position to be either threatening or useful to them.

When all these dynamics converge, most people out of public office easily become embittered. If they get the second chance, many of them think to themselves, 'This time, I will not repeat my earlier mistake.' The thing is, it was not a mistake – the ethical way one behaved in public office that first time was the right way to do it and there should be nothing to be regretful about. It is simply the nature of human beings. It should not be an excuse for anyone to move from one extreme of doing things right to the other extreme of doing things the wrong way.

I'll be the first to admit that there are some things I miss about high office. One was the influence I had to get things done for the benefit of others. For instance, when someone needed a job and would send me a CV, I could make one or two calls and the person would have a job the next week or month. I missed that once in a while, because there are many people who need such help – we have a broken system where merit does not get you what you deserve, and being qualified alone is not enough to get you past the door. So everyone needs help getting simple things done - like being interviewed for a job. The rest, the material and financial freebies, I did not benefit much from and have lived without. My experiences during the six months' break after serving in General Abdulsalami Abubakar's government and the five years since the end of the Obasanjo administration have given me a lot more food for thought about second comings and the risks attached to them. Whether this theory is generally applicable is still open to question, but I am personally acutely aware of it all the time.

"You are an inappropriate person to be in our programme"

This theory of the tragedy of second comings I only fully understood when I left office and went to study at Harvard. Of course, not all of my time at Harvard was spent studying and theorising; I still had the matter of my reputation and name to look after. I kept getting stopped from entering or exiting many countries, particularly the UK. Three or four times, I landed in the UK and the immigration officer would take my passport, disappear for 10 or 20 minutes, re-emerge, and stamp my passport for entry. I did not know why until much later, when another friend in the know informed me: I had been red-flagged by Interpol, on the request of Yar'Adua's government. I suppose when immigration authorities check an Interpol flag and see the flag is for a politically-related 'offence' – as opposed to being a drug dealer or a terrorist – they just conclude that this is a political thing and let it go. Regardless, going through the process everytime just made me angrier and angrier at the Yar'Adua regime. Just as I had predicted, there were a lot of continuous, slow-burning tactics Yar'Adua and his administration deployed to keep the campaign on, even though I was out of the country and not even in the public eye. One of them never even made the news, but it was an inconvenience all the same.

A year earlier, during the summer of 2007, I had escorted my son, Mohammed Bello, to the US to begin his undergraduate studies in Norton, in the Boston area. I went to the Bank of America branch at Harvard Square and opened an account for him and for myself. Since senior government officials are legally barred from operating bank accounts outside Nigeria – it is prohibited by our constitution – when I was appointed to the BPE, I had to close all my foreign bank accounts. The only one that survived was in the UK, a joint account with my wife, opened in 1985, from which I withdrew my signature and my wife became sole signatory, since she was not a public officer. All other accounts I closed as legally and ethically required. So in 2007, once I left office, I opened a new bank account in Cambridge and put a couple of thousand dollars into it, and then opened another for my son. When I came back to Harvard a year later for my master's programme, I had wired about $85,000 of the $145,000 my company gave me to cover tuition and living expenses at the Kennedy School, only to learn that I did not have to pay the entire fees immediately, so I had over $50,000 balance in my account.

One day during the fall of 2008, I received a letter from Bank of America informing me that they had decided to close my account. I showed this letter to my local branch manager who was shocked because the letter came from Bank of America's corporate headquarters. The branch did not even know about it. The manager logged on to the system and confirmed the order to close my account, with no reason to be given to me. My contract with the bank stated that the bank could close the account any time, so I had three weeks after which the bank would freeze the account and issue a banker's check for the balance in my favour. I did not understand what was going on but I walked across the street to another bank and the Harvard University credit union and opened two accounts on the same day, depositing a bit of cash in each. I did not think much of it then because as a Nigerian I was used to being treated that way – you never know what some Nigerian somewhere in the world has done in some bank to cause it to put a red flag on all Nigerians, so I let it go.

A couple of months later, I received a phone call from an unfamiliar number in Nigeria. It was a lady who worked in the office of the secretary to the government of the federation. She introduced herself, told me that we had never met, but she lived in Abuja, thought I did a wonderful job as minister and that during my tenure she was able to buy her own house, so she thought the world of me because this changed her life. I thanked her and explained that I was just doing my job. She said she worked in the registry of the office of the secretary to government of the federation and she came across a letter written by the secretary to the government of the federation to two banks in America. She thought that the letter was most unfair and that was why she decided to call me. She then read the contents of the letter to me.

The letter was addressed to the presidents of Bank of America and Citibank. The title of the letter was something to the effect of, 'Nasir Ahmad El-Rufai, Nigerian fugitive.' I do not remember the exact wording of the letter and I am still trying to obtain a copy of it – she promised to keep it for me – but it explained that I was a cabinet minister in the previous administration that had become a fugitive from justice and was known to be living in the United States, spending hundreds of millions of dollars that the Nigerian Senate had investigated and found I had embezzled. The letter then went on to state that the Nigerian government had information that I may be operating bank accounts in that bank and to be advised that any monies in such bank accounts may be the proceeds of crime that the federal government of Nigeria had a claim or an interest in.

Now, I did not operate any bank account with Citibank. I think they just took a shot. But I presume that when Bank of America received that letter and then saw me in their system as a student with $52,000, this probably gave them pause. Frankly, if I were in their shoes and did not know better, I probably would have done the same. The lady asked if I had a fax so that she could send me the letter, but I did not. I offered to have someone pick up the letter from her on my behalf, but she refused. "I will not give it to anyone. I do not trust anyone with this, I could lose my job," she said. "But I will keep it for you anytime you are coming to Nigeria, or if I am going abroad, I will carry it along with me." I still have not had a chance to retrieve the letter as I lost contact with her when my phone was stolen in Boston some months later.

Around that time, my statistics professor at Harvard, a famous Mathematics professor and author, Deborah Hughes Hallett, had asked me to be her course assistant since I was one of the top students in the quantitative methods class during the summer programme. One of the officers of my mid-career Masters' programme eagerly approved and remarked how pleased she was with how much value I was adding to the programme. I responded that I was just glad to be there and in the course of that conversation, the official revealed something that up to that point I did not know about.

> "You know, shortly after we admitted you, we got a letter from your government saying you were an inappropriate person to be in our programme," he said. "We looked at your references and concluded that they had far more credibility than the Nigerian government, so we just ignored it."

My recommendations were written by Oby, who was then vice-president at the World Bank, Rosa Whitaker, who was assistant US Trade Representative under Clinton and Bush and a good friend, and the third one from Hakeem Belo-Osagie. Both Oby and Keem were successful Harvard alumni, which counted for a lot in the eyes of the Kennedy School. I had obtained a written reference from General Abdullahi Mohammed, the chief of staff to the president of Nigeria. Instinctively, I declined sending it to Harvard, and returned it to him unopened after being admitted to the Mason Fellows programme. Hearing this comment, I am glad I trusted my instincts and did not use that 'government' recommendation.

I was shocked. "Really?"
"Yes, it is true."
"May I have a copy of this letter?"
"Not on your life."

This response was to be expected I suppose – Harvard is always wary of being involved in needless controversy or the prospect of being sued. But anyway, these smaller things I found to be far more irritating than the bigger things. The bigger things, the public things, are easier to handle because they were out and I could respond, but this sneaky underhanded stuff was typical of Umaru Yar'Adua and his cowardly gang. The more I saw that, the more I was convinced that even though he denied any involvement, Umaru had to be behind this. My friends in Nigeria still recommended I restrained myself, but my anger kept rising. This was beyond smearing my reputation; it was taking deliberate steps to reduce my ability to live, even though I posed no threat, immediate or distant, to the Yar'Adua Administration and Umaru's craving for absolute power.

Then in October my lawyer forwarded to me a letter[135] from the EFCC requesting me to return again to answer some questions on some unspecified land matter beyond what I had made a written submission on. Since I knew this would be the end of my programme if I went back to Nigeria, there was no way I was going to physically go back until I finished school. My lawyer wrote the EFCC to inform them that I was busy in a graduate degree programme, but would be happy to answer any questions they wished to submit through my lawyer. The EFCC's response advanced the request a step: I had to come back physically or else the EFCC would declare me wanted, which they eventually did at the end of 2008. The EFCC's Director of Operations, Tunde Ogunsakin, and Farida Waziri's spokesman, Femi Babafemi, gleefully announced that I was a 'wanted man' and they would not take any questions from the media about it, save to claim that I had 'N32 billion unaccounted for.' I knew they wanted to grab headlines, but I really did not think that Yar'Adua would want to make this a protracted fight because he was really not the type to engage in open confrontations. At heart, he knew he had skeletons, his wife and daughters had even more and he had no stomach for open fights which could reveal more of these.

Of course, the fight did become protracted, which was against the wishes of both Umaru and I. One of the reasons for this was that my political friends in Nigeria did not agree until much later on - around April 2009 - that it was Yar'Adua that was behind everything. Had I started open attacks against Yar'Adua immediately, maybe it would have ended faster because he would not have stood for too much of that. Everyone around me except one or two of my closest friends, were against my attacking the president for a variety of sensible as well as undisclosed reasons. Some were simply scared of the prospect of confronting a sitting president, and the powers he had to deal with an ordinary citizen. Some had commercial interests – existing or prospective – that they thought would be jeopardized if I started attacking the president and they were well known as my friends. Yet others truly believed that the president was not a bad guy and that I should give him a chance – he had just appointed me to the national energy council, so where was I getting the idea that he was the one behind all of this? I knew, having been in government, that no minister or government official would take on a high profile ex-public officer like me without at least testing the waters with his boss that it was ok. So even if Yar'Adua was not the initiator, he had to have supported it covertly or overtly.

To me, the best way to solve the problem of this nature was to attack someone higher up in the hierarchy such that even if I lost, I stood a chance with an attack where he is most vulnerable. When an ordinary citizen fights a government, even if that citizen 'loses', the public at large will allow for the fact that the citizen tried to stand up to an entire government – the public loves a good David and Goliath dustup. No average person will sympathise with Goliath.

From my standpoint, attacking an EFCC chairman or a cabinet minister would not suffice. It would be beneath me to attack a sub-cabinet official like Farida Waziri. A cabinet minister was like my equal, four years late and I have always preferred to fight someone bigger than me so that even if he beats me up, everyone else will look at my opponent – much like they did when I fought Sunday the bully as a child – and say, 'This is not fair – it is a bully beating up a small kid.' But despite my natural instinct to attack Yar'Adua, I deferred to the wishes of my friends as I did not want to jeopardise whatever they had at stake, whether personal, relational or commercial, because it would not have been fair for them to be punished for a fight that was never theirs to begin with.

For the time being, I had to be patient and take a lot of hits from Yar'Adua while I waited for each of my friends to catch up to my view and realise I was right all along. That finally happened around April of 2009, when one of my friends' contacts in the EFCC confirmed that Yar'Adua had personally directed Farida Waziri to charge me for any criminal offence – even if it was a traffic offence – because he no longer cared about my innocence. He made it clear, and his Attorney General Michael Aondoakaa confirmed it to me in September 2010, that he did not care if there was a good case against me or not, and whether the government would succeed in securing a conviction. He just ordered that I must be charged for any offence to facilitate my extradition so the EFCC staff went scurrying around to frame one. At that point, we all agreed that Yar'Adua was behind this, so I went for him with all I had – which was a lot.

The counterattack begins

I was engaging in a battle against a government, so I at least needed to enhance my communicative abilities to be equal to that of a government. This necessarily meant equipping me with people who were familiar with how to wage this counter-campaign at an international level. I hired people outside Nigeria who were instrumental in rolling out this element of the strategy, which had both offensive and defensive components.

At the beginning of 2008, through my Washington DC advisor, Riva Levinson, I met a lawyer named Robert Amsterdam, who specialised in international criminal cases that had a political element. At the time, one of his higher profile cases was representing the Russian energy magnate Mikhail Khodorkovsky, the former owner and CEO of Yukos, who has been in jail in Russia for more than five years. But at the time, what Bob was interested in was some oil deal in Nigeria. Nigeria then had approached the Russians to do some oil and gas deals and Bob knew the Russians well. His take was that the Russians were just going to sign a deal but will never actually get out any oil or gas because they had a lock-hold on Europe in terms of gas particularly, but also some oil. What they had been doing all over the world was going to countries that could be competitors to Russia as far as oil and gas supplies were concerned, and just locking the supply – pre-emptive strikes, so to speak. I arranged for him to meet with Tanimu Yakubu, the economic adviser to President Yar'Adua in London, so they could work out what they could do together.

Bob had been a regular visitor to Nigeria since the mid-1970s, so he understood what kind of environment it was and could do something about it. When my own problems with the Yar'Adua government started, retaining him was a no-brainer. I knew that when I told him that if I returned to Nigeria at the time, I would be detained and injected with a culture of hepatitis and HIV, he would not think I was crazy, because he knew that this kind of thing could happen where we came from. In the beginning, my idea was that Bob was retained to defend both Nuhu and I, because Nuhu's problems had also begun at that point and he had also escaped from Nigeria at the beginning of 2009.

Nuhu initially consented and even attended a meeting in London with Bob's team and me. Then he changed his mind and ended up going a different route. I knew that we both needed someone like Bob, a political lawyer with a track record of defending dissidents around the world, to do this for us. His role was to be a convenient and articulate speaker on my behalf in the international court of public opinion. He also assisted with some legal research surrounding our lawsuit against the government when the EFCC put out the story of 'the unaccounted for 32 billion naira', a case still underway that I may also pursue outside Nigeria.

Former Attorney General Mike Aondoakaa later admitted that they expended considerable resources to object to and slow down the lawsuit by signalling officials and agencies joined as respondents because it was clear that the government was unlikely to win. We had four or five of these sorts of cases – any time the government went public with an allegation, we got our lawyers to sit down, reframe the allegation into the falsehood that it was, and go to court to obtain a declaratory judgment disproving it. Unfortunately, the cases were dragging at slow speed through the system and the government may have been covertly interfering with the pace at which the cases were being heard, but Bob achieved what he was hired to do, which was: raise the cost of persecuting me - internationally.

Till death do us part

While Bob was busy doing what he did best, I turned to what I did best – inviting bullies bigger than me to take a swing at me in front of an audience. I knew I would go back to Nigeria as soon as my programme at Harvard was over. I also knew that when I got back, bad things were going to happen to me – I was likely to be arrested and detained at the minimum, of this I was certain. I also knew that if I was going down, I was not going down alone or without a fight. So I had to think of what I could do to make it emotionally painful for the other side and how to escalate the reputational cost to Yar'Adua for making my life difficult or putting me in danger. I knew he would do it, but I wanted it to cost him a whole lot. I wanted to ensure that if anything bad happened to me, Yar'Adua would become an international pariah and the Nigerian government would pay a heavy price internationally and domestically. I did not have control of any coercive power and I could not inflict pain on them as they would on me. The only thing I could do was to destroy Yar'Adua's reputation and that of his government. I, therefore, became the proverbial patriot who loved his country but hated his government.

In the end, that was what I did. All of my efforts, all of my essays at Harvard, the American radio talk shows I spoke in, all of the speeches I made at think tanks like the Centre for Strategic and International Studies, my op-eds in Foreign Policy and FT blogs, the several workshops I participated in, were all geared toward giving Umaru sleepless nights. One of the papers I wrote at Harvard about Yar'Adua is now part of every foreign intelligence agency's file on him. It was an essay in April of 2009 entitled, 'Umaru Yar'Adua: Great Expectation, Disappointing Outcome'[136] exposing Yar'Adua for what I believe he was, - a pretentious, marabout-dependent, incompetent man- and posted it in four parts on my personal Facebook page. I took my time and waited a week for everyone to read the first part and people immediately started calling me up commending me: 'This is great! When are you posting the second part?' I later learnt that it was eventually serialised in full in two national newspapers, *Leadership* and *Punch*, both of which enjoyed high circulations across Nigeria, at the papers' expense. Then I was later informed that someone who read the essay and liked it had paid half a million naira per page to publish it as an eight-page advertisement in a third newspaper, just so that more Nigerians could read it.

I knew Yar'Adua hated that essay (and its author) because it hit him where I knew mattered most to him: Umaru liked to be seen as the good guy, the nice guy, the kind, humble, gracious guy. He did not want anyone to know he used to drink a lot of beer, gin and whisky; he did not want people to know he smoked marijuana; he did not want anyone to know he was too shy to talk to girls; he did not want anyone to know he had a failed second marriage, that he had never worked a day in his life, that he had lived off and been kept by his brother Shehu, that he was a free thinker for a period, and believed more in marabouts than his professed Islamic religion. He had conned the whole of Nigeria into thinking he was this nice guy who was just really an innocent person while people around him would do all kinds of things and he was too sickly and weak to stop them. However, I knew that he was behind a lot of evil in the country at the time, and I could tell his story from childhood to sketch a character portrait that showed him for what he truly was. That was what I did and he was deeply hurt. He was also totally helpless since I was physically out of his reach. He was the all-powerful president of Nigeria, yet he could not touch me.

During his three years as president, Yar'Adua only gave two media interviews: one to the Financial Times of London in May 2008, to explain that he was still "planning" a year after taking office, and the other to the Guardian of Lagos in April 2009. The latter was in response to my essay published widely in the Nigerian media about him. That was the beginning of his unravelling.

Upon my eventual return to Nigeria, I confirmed from my media sources that Segun Adeniyi, who was Yar'Adua's special adviser on media and communications, would not comment on the essay. I learnt that when the essay was published, Yar'Adua called him and the minister of information, Dora Akunyili, and said, "Look, Nasir has published something about me. No one of you should respond, no one should comment. What's going on between me and Nasir is a quarrel between two brothers and we will sort it out. It is not your problem, it is my problem." No one in the government was allowed to say anything about this, not even to deny or confirm anything I had written. When one of the newspapers called and asked Adeniyi what President Yar'Adua's response was to this essay, he told the reporter, "I have been asked not to comment. You should not even publish 'no comment' from me."

After I completed my programme at Harvard, the situation at home was still not quite right for me to return, so I obtained a resident permit to live in Dubai and moved there in July 2009. Since four of my children were then studying in the UK, I shuttled between the UAE and UK a lot to see them, and by August, all the pages in my first passport had been fully stamped with visas and entry/exit notations. This posed a problem when some friends of mine in Austria invited me to visit them because I was going to need more space for a new Schengen visa.

Tampering with my citizenship

In August of 2009, my battle with the Yar'Adua Administration was in full force: before I left the US, I had spoken at the Centre for Strategic and International Studies,[137] and written op-eds in Foreign Policy.[138] I was speaking from Dubai on various network radio programmes in the US[139] about what was happening in Nigeria and Yar'Adua was becoming increasingly agitated because all of a sudden everyone knew about him and the not-so-nice things his administration was up to in Nigeria. When I went online to apply for my passport renewal, a thought occurred to me for a moment: Could these guys refuse to renew this passport? It was just a fleeting thought – if they were to do that, they would be playing right into my hands, but I never thought they would be so dumb as to try that. I went ahead and applied anyway, paid all the fees online, printed out the receipts and went to the Nigerian High Commission in London like every Nigerian would.

In doing this, I overlooked the assigned appointment date generated by the software, but because the high commissioner was someone I knew very well, I thought I should just visit the high commission and check whether I could have an appointment date or possibly renew the passport immediately. I did not realise the appointment date the system generated for me was there on the printed forms and very little flexibility was possible. I went to the high commission, and although the high commissioner was not in the office, I met with the head of chancery, a former classmate and friend, Ahmed Umar, who referred me to the head of the passport section, also another ABU alumnus and the head of the National Intelligence Agency (NIA) desk in London. He looked at my papers and circled the date I was supposed to appear for the renewal, still a few days away. I apologised for overlooking that. He offered to check the system to see if the details were there anyway so that processing could begin, but I told him not to worry, I could come back on the assigned date – I was in no hurry to leave London and did not want any preferential treatment. So I left.

The morning I was to return to the embassy, Ahmed Umar called me very early in the morning. After the exchange of pleasantries, Ahmed asked:

"Nasir you are scheduled to come to the high commission today to renew your passport, right?"

"Yes, I thought I could come around 10 or 11 o'clock. I hope that will be ok."

"Yes, this is why I am calling. The high commissioner got a call from Abuja this morning instructing that your passport is not to be renewed."

"Really?"

"Yes."

"Oh, that is great!"

"No, you did not get what I just said. Your passport is not to be renewed."

"No, I heard you right."

"So do not bother coming."

"No, I will come. You guys will have to deny me the renewal of my passport officially. I have an appointment, I will come for my scheduled appointment."

"Wow. Ok."

I went to the high commission and Ahmed started on about how he did not understand what was going on, that a passport is a right and consular services were rights that every Nigerian citizen was entitled to and how could they do this?

"Ahmed, do not worry about it. I was hoping they would do that."

"You were?"

"Yes."

"Why?"

"This now gives me an opportunity to make Yar'Adua look really bad."

"How?"

"Do not worry about it. Let me go see the high commissioner."

The high commissioner, Dr. Dalhatu Sarki Tafida, appeared very upset. He had received a call that morning from Imoehe, the director-general of the National Intelligence Agency, to the effect that the presidency had ordered that my passport was not to be renewed. He asked on what basis they were ordering this. After all, I am a Nigerian citizen and the high commissioner's job is to renew passports and offer similar consular services to Nigerian citizens. He asked if the president was depriving me of my citizenship. The response was simply that this was the decision of 'the presidency.'

"Well, what do you mean by 'the presidency'?" he asked them.

The 'presidency' is a huge place. That omnibus term could mean anything from the SGF, the sports commission, the NSA or the Chief of Staff.

"Who in the presidency gave the order?"

The answer was that the instructions came from the national security adviser, Major-General Abdullahi Sarki Mukhtar.[140] The high commissioner then called the general, who confirmed that my passport was not to be renewed because I was going around the world insulting the president and thereby making our country look bad. This, according to Mukhtar, was their God-given opportunity to ground me in one place.

The stupidity of this reasoning by Sarki Mukhtar was astonishing. The fact that my passport was full did not mean I could not go anywhere, but this was how they saw it – as my friend and former cabinet colleague Oby Ezekwesili observed at the time, the IQ of the Yar'Adua Administration was about 30. The administration also clearly did not realise that with the Internet, podcasts, videophones and satellite TV, I could be located anywhere and continue to effectively attack them. From the high commissioner's end, he explained to them that he did not take instructions from the NIA, that he represented the president of Nigeria. So the general told him to call the president directly and hear it from the ultimate source. This I learnt was exactly what he did. Yar'Adua's response was short and sharp: my passport was not to be renewed under any circumstance. Umaru added that I should go to Obama or Gordon Brown and ask them for a passport since that was where my loyalties lay rather than Nigeria. Yar'Adua was clearly under the illusion that he was Nigeria, and attacking him amounted to a declaration of war on the country.

The high commissioner explained all this to me and apologised, but made it clear that his hands were tied. He could not go against the direct instructions of Mr. President. He sought my understanding of his situation. I understood perfectly, but I had rights to enforce.

"That is fine. But you know I am going to fight this."

"No, why do you like fighting? Just leave it."

"No, I am going to fight it."

"Ok, but please do not reveal any of these conversations I have had with the national security adviser and the president because I am telling you all these in the strictest confidence. Otherwise I will lose my job."

"I promise not to share this with anyone unless you also get involved further in persecuting me," I responded.

"Of course not, Nasir. We are brothers."[141]

We are brothers – got that?

I called one of my friends, Sam Nda Isaiah, who publishes the national newspaper *Leadership*. Incidentally, he happened to be in London, so we met up for lunch. He immediately saw the newsworthiness of this passport renewal story. The court ruling on the Olisa Agbakoba case, in which Agbakoba, who was then president of the Civil Liberties Organisation, had his passport seized by the state security service, was still fresh in public memory. The Supreme Court had descended on the SSS, declaring that the ownership of a Nigerian passport was a right guaranteed under the Constitution because it comes with the rights of citizenship and freedom of movement, therefore the government cannot under any circumstances or pretext withdraw a person's passport. Was the Yar'Adua Administration really this dumb? Yes.

Of course the media picked this up. *Leadership* broke the story and then one or two other newspapers picked it up. The Nigerian government in Abuja stayed quiet hoping that it would somehow go away but it did not. Their only response was to put pressure on

High Commissioner Tafida – 'my brother' – to publicly say I was not denied the renewal of any passport. What did he do? He granted an interview to *Daily Trust*, a paper then widely known for despising me, claiming I came to the embassy and wanted my passport renewed on that day, and that they told me there was a one week waiting period but I refused because I wanted to be treated preferentially. In short, El-Rufai was just too big to wait his turn like every Nigerian; he wanted to jump the queue. I called Tafida immediately.

"Mr. High Commissioner, I just read your interview in the *Daily Trust*."

"Yes, I was forced to say that because you have been trying to make the president and government look bad on this passport matter."

"I did not try to make the government look bad, I tried to make the government look like what it truly is – a bad government. It denied me my right as a Nigerian to renew my passport and I made it public. If you guys were not proud of your decision, why did you take it?"

"But you know, you should not do that, Nasir. You are fighting the government."

"So you lied. You went to a newspaper and lied. You knew the truth, more than anyone. You spoke with Yar'Adua, you spoke with Sarki Mukhtar and you know that you were ordered not to renew my passport, yet you lacked the conscience to tell the truth! You lacked the courage to even keep quiet! You went on the record and lied against me!"

"Well I have to do my job. The job of an ambassador is to lie on behalf of his government," Tafida added in self-justification.[142]

"Thank you very much. So you now know that our deal about not revealing what you discussed with Sarki Mukhtar and Yar'Adua is off."

"No, no, you can't do that."

"I am going to do it. You know what? I will not say anything which you can deny. I am going to get firm evidence to nail you guys. You will be sorry you lied against me." With that, I ended the call, both upset and disappointed with the high commissioner.

The only question I had to answer then was how do I expose them 'magisterially'? Was this decision taken all orally or is there some written record? Generally, when a competent government wants to do some dodgy stuff like denying someone his or her basic rights, it will not keep a written record of it. Given the utter brainlessness that the Yar'Adua government had demonstrated up to that point though, I knew I had a fighting chance of finding written proof somewhere. So I activated all my contacts in Nigeria and asked them to keep an eye out for anything officially written on this matter.

For two weeks, I got nothing. Then, pay dirt.

Yet another former classmate of mine in one of the Nigerian embassies called me with what turned out to be a major breakthrough.

"Nasir, I just read a very disturbing cable from the ministry of foreign affairs. It was sent to every Nigerian embassy and diplomatic mission and instructed us to deny you and Nuhu Ribadu consular services."

"Wow, it has expanded."

"What do you mean?"

"Well I went to renew my passport three weeks ago and was denied. But I did not know that the scope of persecution has expanded beyond not renewing my passport to include all consular services," I said. "This means that if I get arrested, or into any situation, no embassy of Nigeria is supposed to come to my aid. Effectively I have been declared no longer a citizen of Nigeria by President Yar'Adua."

"You know, I thought it was very strange. In my two decades in the diplomatic service, I have never seen anything like this. I thought I should inform you and ask you to be careful."

"Can you get me this cable?"

"I have just come across it, I did not think of taking a copy, but I will try to retrieve it from the department I minuted it to and get you a copy."

"No, do not, because it will raise eyebrows and you are my classmate, and it is easy to suspect you as the source, so just leave this as it is, I will get it, somewhere, somehow. Thanks."

Since it had been sent to 120 Nigerian diplomatic missions, and at least three of my friends or classmates and a similar number who were ministerial colleagues were ambassadors, I figured I would be able to get it from at least one of them. I began to call all our diplomatic missions where friends, classmates and acquaintances served. I asked them all the same question: "Guys, there is a cable out there declaring that I am to be denied my consular rights. Can I have a copy?" The most courageous of them obtained the cable, got his son to copy it out in long hand and sent the transcript to me. All the others were too scared to send me a copy while a few even stopped taking my calls. I, therefore, started focusing on Nigeria and working my contacts within the federal government. Within a week, I got a batch of correspondence, scanned and sent to me as a pdf file, containing everything ever written and commented on the subject. The cable was only the latest product of the decision-making chain. Before the cable was sent to every mission, the director general of the NIA had written to the ministry of foreign affairs, conveying the directives of the president that consular services should be denied to Nasir El-Rufai and Nuhu Ribadu. Nuhu had not gone to renew his passport but he was included anyway. In addition to that memo and the cable, I also obtained the response of the permanent secretary of the ministry of foreign affairs back to the NIA saying this directive was wrong: 'You have instructed us to do it, we have done it, we have sent the cable, but it is wrong to deny a Nigerian consular services.' The diplomats did what they were told, but they put their objections in writing, and covered their backs.

Next, I released the first two documents – the cable and the NIA memo. Of course, Yar'Adua denied knowing anything and immediately got the head of the NIA, Ambassador Imoehe, fired. I knew Imoehe from his days in the Nigerian embassy in Washington. He also appeared like a nice guy, servile perhaps and lacking in self-worth, but not a vicious kind of guy. I have not seen him since I returned to Nigeria. He was the sacrificial lamb and all the blame was put on him and the ministry of foreign affairs, with Yar'Adua denying any personal knowledge, as was his practice. I then released the second letter containing the diplomatic corps' joint objection. It was addressed to the NIA and copied to the office of the president, so Yar'Adua could no longer credibly make any claim of deniability. I also added in subsequent media interviews that Yar'Adua had given the order himself to the High Commissioner.

"If he says he did not know this, he is lying." I said. "And he gave the instruction directly to the high commissioner in the UK.

The high commissioner said this to me himself."

The administration then issued a statement apologising and saying I should feel free to renew my passport anywhere in the world as all embassy and consular services were restored, and this is all a big misunderstanding due to some over-zealous official just going overboard – pure hogwash. It was the president all along who went overboard.

I called back 'my brother', High Commissioner Tafida.

"Well we can renew your passport now, when can you come?" he said.

"I will come. I am going to Dubai and when I come back I will come and renew it."

"But you said you do not have a passport."

"I did not tell you I did not have a passport, I only said my passport was full. I have alternatives."

"So why did you do all this?"

It could have ended there, and if the administration had any sort of sense, they would have let it drop there. But they did not. They set up an investigation committee to find out how the media got the documents. The newspapers told them how: "El-Rufai gave them to us." I told them all to feel free to tell anyone who asked that I gave them the documents because I wanted anyone interested to ask me how I got them. When I went back to Nigeria, one of the questions the EFCC asked me was, "So how did you get those documents on the passport situation?"

I just laughed and told them I had some of the many 'investigation reports' the EFCC had written about me and asked, "How did I get those reports?" They appeared to be shocked. Virtually, everything the EFCC had written about me, and the identity of those doing it, I was receiving regularly, so I knew everything going on. I guess many Nigerians were angry with the persecution that was going on and thought it was just unfair, so I got all these documents from people I did not even know – like that lady who called me about the letter to the US banks when I was at Harvard. This is one of the reasons why even when I get angry with the Nigerian authorities, I cannot afford to be angry with the ordinary Nigerian. Many people in the government took great risks to send me all those documents. I had many if not all of them. I will forever remain in the debt of these rare but courageous people who stood for truth and justice amidst great risk to their persons and careers.

When this was all over, I had a couple of other items to see to. One was to have one of my attorneys in the US draft a petition to the African Union and ECOWAS Secretariats reporting the Yar'Adua government for abuse of my human rights and then also file a petition with the United Nations to the same effect, which is still under consideration. Within domestic courts in Nigeria, I got my lawyer here to sue the minister of the interior and the comptroller general of immigration for denying the renewal of my passport and grounding me in one location for a few days, and asked for $150,000 in damages.[143] Nearly three years later, after overcoming several preliminary objections and several other delay tactics by the Federal Government and its agencies, we got judgment against the authorities. The ruling further limited the legality of the government's ability to tamper with the rights of the citizens – something that is very dear to me.

Ultimately, I always knew I could win this fight. I was confident I could win because I believed I was right and they were wrong and I knew I would suffer some inconveniences but in the end it would all work out. This passport saga particularly was a milestone in the sense that it brought out in very clear terms that the Yar'Adua government was persecuting me. I think that denial of a right as petty as a passport confirmed that other bigger violations must be in the works and any Nigerian could relate to that and could see it was unfair. I do not think anybody believed Yar'Adua when he said he did not know. Even if he did not know when it was done, when I shouted and complained and it was reported in the media, he could have fixed it if he did not give the order in the first place, or if he cared to discharge his oath of office.

Nevertheless, the only reason I was able to return to Nigeria when I did and remained alive and safe was because Yar'Adua was effectively gone. Had I gone back while he still was in charge and in control of the coercive instruments of state power, I would have been arrested, detained and I would not have got out any time soon. I do not think he would have had me killed[144] because by then, he had been weakened and I think everyone around him could see that it was a matter of time before his presidency ended prematurely, so nobody wanted the responsibility of my murder.

Yet, I was sure that the Sarki Mukhtars of this world would have had no problem detaining me, throwing away the key and torturing me while in detention.

I think, I hope, one of the positive results to come out of my fight with Yar'Adua is that I have bought for me some degree of permanent peace in Nigerian politics, much in the same way I did with Sunday the bully as a schoolchild. The difference with Yar'Adua is that there was no intervening authority, no equivalent to the school headmaster to step in and say, 'Ok, that is enough. This fighting must stop.' Such was the nature of standing up against the president of a nation, and since the president himself was the highest authority, there was really no other option but to keep the fight on until one side dropped. Well, I think we can now say that God's verdict came on 5th May, 2010. Contrary to what I know many people think, I really did not enjoy doing it. I will fight again for my citizenship rights if faced with no other choice and, well, I believe every citizen must be willing to fight these battles. It is not about me, but about others that might have been similarly treated in the future if I had not resisted the oppression of the Yar'Adua regime and its overzealous goons. In this particular case, the results speak for themselves and justify the struggle and pains of the experience.

Chapter Seventeen

Five Years of Invaluable Experience

> *"The best years of your life are the ones in which you decide your own problems are your own. You do not blame them on your mother, the ecology or the president. You realise that you control your own destiny"*
>
> *– Albert Ellis*

In my approximately ten years in public service, I certainly have a few regrets. What I regret the most was not any decision or action taken but the time spent working to the overall detriment of my family life and personal development. In retrospect, perhaps I should have devoted much more time to my family. This regretful feeling became particularly manifest when my loving, brilliant and near-perfect daughter, Yasmin El-Rufai, died suddenly in London in November 2011, a day before I was to visit her.

The first two years following my exit from government were a mixed bag – the stimulating intellectual experiences of completing my LL.B degree in London, and of the Harvard Kennedy School, the carefully contrived scandals of the Senate hearings on my administration of the FCT, the painful smear campaign by Yar'Adua and his surrogates, the emergence of loyal friends and betrayal by others, and the constant struggle to remain focused in the midst of several conflicting emotions and let-downs by family members and once-reliable allies.

The next three years, from 2009 to 2012, were periods of intense thinking, planning and haphazard activities in the political realm whose final outcome remains uncertain as I write this. What is clear to me though, is that the fresh knowledge, new contacts, mostly painful and turbulent experiences and the lessons of these last five years have changed my life in fundamental ways. So what happened? What have I learnt in my 50s that I did not know or experience in the first half century of my life? I would say that I learned a lot more in a few years than most of the preceding years combined. I will attempt to relate these events in chronological order, and leave the reader to draw conclusions.

The First Near-Fatal Error: Ignoring Politics

Halfway into my Mason Fellowship at the Kennedy School, I concluded that one of the biggest mistakes that 'technocrats' like me and Oby made while in government was not getting actively involved in party politics. Though as ministers, we were given overnight party membership cards, some of us abhorred politics because we did not want it to affect our performance or reduce the focus on our respective assignments. In that regard, Ngozi and Nuhu were the slightly smarter exceptions. Unknown to Oby and I, Ngozi regularly visited Wadata House, the headquarters of the ruling party. Nuhu was very much engaged in political conspiracies and late-night intrigues with Obasanjo, cultivating the friendships of unlikely allies like Andy Uba, James Ibori and Bukola Saraki in the process. Ngozi engaged the various state governors actively and maintained such contact even after she left the Cabinet in 2006. Oby and I like to joke in retrospect how naïve we were. We were '*mumus*'[145] who just never got it.

As minister of FCT, I had the unique opportunity to be engaged actively in partisan politics. My position earned me membership of the PDP National Caucus, the leadership of the party in the FCT and membership of its state Executive Committee. I pointedly requested Obasanjo to exempt me from all these partisan engagements and he kindly consented. So I never attended any one of these partisan political meetings. Perhaps, if I had not declined these opportunities, I would have learnt much earlier that politics, in the end, trumps everything – economics and friendships inclusive.

Though early in my ministerial term, I attended a few meetings of political office-holders from the North-West and sat with the governors and ministers of that zone, and of the North-Central Zone (in which the FCT is geographically located) to negotiate chairmanship of federal boards and parastatals, I consciously avoided any direct interactions with partisan politics and politicians. I never got involved in direct party activities until early 2006 just before the collapse of the Third Term project, when Obasanjo appointed me to several study groups and committees on succession, future political direction, reforms within the PDP and the like. One such was a group chaired by Senator Liyel Imoke, then minister of power, along with me, Femi Fani Kayode, Nuhu Ribadu, Bayo Ojo, and Ojo Maduekwe to think through a succession strategy for Obasanjo. We met in Liyel's guest house in Wuse 2. The group (T6) submitted a final report in August 2006.

Another was what Obasanjo and Amadu Ali called the "PDP brain trust" consisting of me, Oby, Femi Fani-Kayode and Osita Chidoka, under the chairmanship of Babagana Kingibe, who had just returned home from Darfur. This group was to focus on the reform of the PDP and the design of a political transition strategy. The committee met mostly in my official residence at the Life Camp but never submitted any report. I think it collapsed by November 2006 when Obasanjo asked Umaru Yar'Adua to run for president.

Obasanjo then formed another committee with me, PDP chairman Amadu Ali, Keem Belo-Osagie, Osita Chidoka and Ojo Maduekwe to review the branding and publicity strategy for the PDP and the Yar'Adua Campaign. This committee met several times in my Life Camp residence with the marketing consultant, Rosabel Advertising, with Umaru Yar'Adua personally attending a couple of the meetings. Obasanjo also appointed me to the PDP Reconciliation Committee for the North Central Zone in 2006. With a Second Republic minister, Professor Emmanuel Osammor, as chair, we toured Benue, Kogi, Plateau, Niger, Kwara and Nasarawa States attempting to reconcile feuding party members and leaders, and mostly failed.

Whether these last minute involvements in the workings of the ruling party and Abuja politics were helpful to me, or inadvertently served to make me appear threatening to others, is now open to speculation. The stories of what happened in those various committees, and what Obasanjo did or did not do will require another book that would chronicle the widespread political intrigue, the raising and dashing of hopes for real change, and the missed opportunities at critical junctures for our nation to be put on the path of sustainable progress.

The first lesson that I learnt the hard way had been written by philosophers and political economists for centuries – every citizen ignores politics at his or her peril. Indeed, thousands of years ago, Plato already concluded that when good people shun politics and governance, they will suffer under the rule of worse people. Edmund Burke reiterated this point centuries later in a different way, when he asserted that the only thing needed for evil to prevail is for good people to do nothing.

It was during my years of exile and after that I became convinced to get more involved than I had ever wished in partisan politics. It was perhaps this realisation too that persuaded Nuhu to decide to run for the highest political office as a reaction to our collective victimisation, persecution and exile by political operatives. Ultimately, as we became more involved in partisan politics, Nuhu and I ended up in different camps. This occurred as a result of differing personality traits and how we interpreted our public service experiences and their aftermath in completely different ways. How this political separation happened is a matter that I have reflected upon in the last couple of years and learnt some very important lessons from. In spite of this temporary political disagreement, we remain close family friends, and inseparable brothers.

January 2009: The Earliest Conversations about Nuhu running for President

I left Nigeria in June 2008 to pursue a masters' degree at Harvard, and had been declared wanted by the Yar'Adua administration before the end of that year. Nuhu had been forced out of the EFCC, first to study at the Nigerian Institute of Policy and Strategic Studies, in Kuru, Jos, and then unceremoniously replaced by his former police special fraud unit boss, Mrs. Farida Waziri in May 2008. By December of the same year, Nuhu informed me of two attempts on his life, the first being on the highway from Jos to Abuja, and that the bullet-proof car I left behind for his use practically saved his life! I counselled that he should leave the country before the bad guys got lucky just once. He finally slipped out of Nigeria and arrived in London in January 2009. After concluding some formalities on being admitted as an associate of St. Anthony's College, Oxford University, Nuhu met me in Washington, DC.

That was the first time Nuhu suggested that one of us should challenge Umaru Yar'Adua for the presidency in 2011. My response was immediate, simple, short and sharp – I was not interested. If he was interested, he should start working on it, I suggested. We met again with our group of friends in London in early April 2009 at the Marriott Park Lane, where we decided it was time for me to begin an all-out street fight with Umaru Yar'Adua. My Abuja friends had proposed that I declare an intention to run for president as part of the offensive strategy. Their reasoning was that it would then politicise any action taken against me when I returned to Nigeria. This we hoped would be soon after my graduation from Harvard in June 2009. Nuhu appeared alarmed at this suggestion in light of our conversation that January in Washington, DC, but he made no contribution. I persuaded the Abuja group that we should not make empty declarations that we did not mean to see through just to score some political points. I insisted that it would be inconsistent with my character to say I would do something and not do it, and since there was no such aspiration, we should not be flippant about it. In the end, they saw my point and agreed, to the relief of both Nuhu and I, as the Abuja group members were not privy to our Washington discussion. On the sidelines of the meeting with the Abuja group, I asked Nuhu whether he had thought more seriously about running for president. He answered in the affirmative. I told him there and then that he should not under-estimate the gravity of such a decision and the seriousness of the endeavour. I opined that a serious presidential run required a huge amount of intellectual, experiential and emotional preparation, not to mention huge sums of money, and a massive national network of political elite and grassroots operatives. In my view, the first part requires a lot of personal preparation and self-discipline.

One must realistically deepen and broaden one's knowledge of the core components of governance – applied economics, politics, philosophy and law – and then add public service experience, general management skills and thinking through how to engage with, and unleash the capacities of the private sector.[146] Emotionally, I counseled Nuhu to fight and exorcise the demons of anger, disappointment and betrayal that afflicted both of us during that period. I added that it was on account of what I consider to be challenges in these areas that I felt ill-prepared to run for any elective office at the time he contemplated his run. I did not see any point running for office or being in government just to make a point, or worse still, if there is a chance however slight, that one would use the powers of public office to settle personal scores or pursue one's past or current enemies! I was not sure that the pain we both experienced at that point in time foreclosed such possibilities, and frankly would not test my resolve not to fall victim to a primordial, but completely human tendency, to avenge a perceived wrong!

On the intellectual and experiential preparations front though, I thought Nuhu was particularly lucky to be safely abroad, located at Oxford near Professor Paul Collier, and soon to join Nancy Birdsall at the Centre for Global Development as a Visiting Fellow. I suggested that he took advantage of the time out to learn, reflect deeply about our time in public service, and then consume the vast intellectual resources in Oxford and CGD as much as possible. He nodded in agreement, but responded that if an Umaru Yar'Adua can be president, he just did not see what I was worried about. In response, I ruefully reminded him that Umaru was not turning out to be a decent president and we must expect Nuhu as president to be very different, and much better. He appeared to have agreed with the observation and suggestions. I went back to Harvard for my final two months, and shortly after that published the Yar'Adua essay referred to earlier.

June 2009: Another Harvard Graduation[147]

In June 2009, Nuhu came to Harvard from Washington, DC for my graduation. We used the opportunity to hold a meeting with a Nigerian Diaspora organisation called 'Change Nigeria Project' (CNP), chaired by Dr. Isa Odidi. After the meeting, I asked Nuhu about his presidential aspirations and what contacts he was making in Abuja in pursuit thereof. He admitted being in touch with his old friends Femi Falana, Kayode Komolafe and Babafemi Ojudu. I suggested that we needed to team up with mainstream politicians in addition to activists and leaders in civil society and the media. Since I had just completed a degree at the Kennedy School of Government, I offered to prepare a political strategic plan starting with a concept paper for discussions within our group. We still had not shared our 'Washington Consensus' on Nuhu's presidential run with any of our friends and group up to that point. The first person that I shared Nuhu's presidential aspiration with was *NEXT* newspaper publisher, Dele Olojede when we met at Aspen, Colorado, on 12th June 2009.[148]

Dele had just got his newspaper in print, initially on Sundays, and then daily, but was despondent about the deterioration of governance under Yar'Adua. He thought there was too much 'static' around me, counseled that I should not remain outside Nigeria for too long, and not be bothered by the efforts made by the regime in Nigeria to attack my reputation. He was confident that nobody bought it and such attacks would fail in the end. He then suggested that we come together and support Ngozi for the presidency in 2011, with me as her running mate. I, was, therefore compelled not only to divulge the discussions I have had with Nuhu but enlighten him on the difficulties that Ngozi's candidature would have to overcome I was still working on the concept paper and promised to share it when completed. Dele was excited about this development, and promised to add whatever value he could.

I worked a bit more on the outline for this book in Aspen, and then returned to Washington DC to prepare for my relocation to Dubai. I met with my lobbyist Riva Levinson and discussed my plans and next steps in details with her. We agreed that during the next few months of the open fight I intended to have with Yar'Adua, I needed to retain her firm, KRL International, to sustain my messaging to the relevant people in the Obama administration. We discussed and agreed both the defensive and offensive strategies to confront the Yar'Adua administration, as well as approaches to accelerate the completion of the book I had decided to write. I then left for Dubai, hoping that I would complete writing the book in months and then head back to Nigeria for the final showdown with Yar'Adua and his gang.

July 2009: Formation of the Good Governance Group (3G)

By the middle of July 2009, I had not only finalised the concept paper but had personally recruited Senator Ken Nnamani, former Speaker Aminu Masari and former Yar'Adua minister Adamu Maina Waziri to lead a new political association that we named Good Governance Group (3G) in Nigeria. On my side, I convinced Tijjani Abdullahi and Balarabe Abbas Lawal to lead the start-up team. Nuhu brought in his nominees - Mrs. Najaatu Mohammed, Kalli Alghazali and Shehu Iya Abubakar to join the team. I then persuaded a civil society activist and trade unionist friend, Salihu Lukman, to be the organising secretary. We scheduled an initial set-up meeting in Dubai. Ken Nnamani was elected chair of the Steering Committee and, along with the start-up team, returned to establish 3G and its branches in Nigeria. Nuhu and I organised funding the start-up through our few close friends and well-wishers at home and abroad.

We met regularly in Dubai to fine-tune our plans and before the end of the year had expanded the leadership of 3G to include Babafemi Ojudu, Yinka Odumakin and Jimi Agbaje, representing the Afenifere Renewal Group (ARG) – an organisation that was introduced to us by Nuhu. In Nigeria, 3G captured the imagination of a depressed political environment and attracted many genuine as well as opportunistic politicians as members. What we conceived to be a platform for Nuhu's aspiration was acquiring traction. I was pleased with the progress recorded within just three months of starting 3G.

September 2009: Umaru considers a succession move

Once the 3G political network began to form and grow, we became even better informed about what was going on in the Yar'Adua government. We had inside tracks into the Villa, the legislature, the SGF's office, the petroleum ministry, the various oil and infrastructure deals with GE and the Chinese government, and even intra-family wrangling in the households of the president and vice president. We learnt about Umaru's dire medical condition, the various suspicions about his multiple ailments and the increasing frequency of his loss of focus and consciousness. However, the most interesting story, which on return to Nigeria I reconfirmed as truth, was the report of a meeting between Umaru Yar'Adua and a leading northern traditional ruler in September 2009. The first class Emir, who had unsuccessfully sought audience with Umaru for months, suddenly received a call summoning him to the Villa to meet the president. He came to Abuja immediately and met Umaru the same evening.

After exchanging pleasantries, Umaru first heard out the traditional ruler's reason for wanting to see him and responded positively to the request made. He then informed the traditional ruler that he was convinced that his deteriorating health would disqualify him from running for a second term in 2011. He, therefore, needed to carefully identify the person that he would support for the next contest in less than two years. The assistance of the traditional ruler, whose domain is nationally respected for the quality and quantity of its marabouts, spiritualists and mystics, was required to guide Umaru arrange his succession. He appealed to the traditional ruler to mobilise these human forces in prayers for him to be guided in making the right choice of a successor.

The traditional ruler has been through this quite a few times in his reign, which has spanned several years and through more than half a dozen presidents. The traditional ruler thought "Why can't these presidents allow the Will of Allah as expressed freely by the electorate to decide who leads? Why do we have to go through this over and over?" But his royal training from childhood has conditioned him not to raise such questions or reveal any such emotions, and his face remained expressionless. He expressed sympathy over Umaru's condition and prayed for his recovery. He pledged to instruct all the Islamic scholars in his domain to pray for the president's improved health, and to guide him in choosing a worthy successor, should that ever become necessary. Umaru was pleased.

Just before he took his leave, the traditional ruler requested Umaru to give him the names of anyone he had considered as successor, so that the mystics could pray appropriately and ascertain whether that person "can successfully wear the crown of leadership." Umaru thought carefully about this, got a piece of paper and wrote four names and handed them over to the Emir without another word. The Emir looked at the list expressing no emotion, pocketed the single page and took his leave. The names on the list were Umaru's wife, Turai, his sons-in-law Governors Saidu Dakingari of Kebbi State and Isa Yuguda of Bauchi, and Bukola Saraki, then governor of Kwara State.

On his way out, the emir was ambushed by Turai who wanted to know if Yar'Adua had included her on the list of potential successors. The emir was a little shocked, but went on to confirm that. Turai thanked him and suggested that she was the only person that could be trusted with Umaru's legacy, as the mother of his children. The emir returned to his hotel and left Abuja back to his domain the next morning. For us, the political significance of this story was that Yar'Adua had given up, thus improving the likelihood of leadership change. For others, it confirmed the suspicions of many that the contrived marriages of Yar'Adua's daughters to one governor after another were part of a grand dynastic agenda. Even the emir, a product of a dynastic oligarchy, was shocked at Umaru's choices. Less than two months after this incident, on 23rd November 2009, Umaru had a massive stroke, was flown out to Saudi Arabia in a coma, never uttered a word or recognised a soul until he died on 5th May 2010 – exactly four days after I returned from exile.

Honestly, Nuhu and I were not surprised that Yar'Adua collapsed when he did. We did not buy the tales about pericarditis because we were better informed than most about his health and medical condition. Our friends with access to sources in Saudi and American intelligence had predicted that Yar'Adua's medical condition was so dire that he was unlikely to live beyond October 2009. He outlived every medical prediction of his demise by nearly seven months!

October 2009: 3G out in the media and Todd Moss calls me

Early in September 2009, Obasanjo sent a message that he would be visiting New York for a Clinton Foundation event later in the month and would like us to meet in London on his way back. I flew to London from Dubai to see him. We updated one another on developments in Nigeria, and Obasanjo admitted that things were not going in the direction he thought he had carefully charted. He said he did not realise that Yar'Adua was 'duplicitous'. He warned me not to return home any time soon, until he thought it was safe, and advised me accordingly. He promised to link 3G up with some seven state governors that he said were still solidly in his camp. We had a late lunch of sumptuous Nigerian cuisine, and I left him at the Heathrow Hilton for his night flight that evening of 2nd October, 2009.

Meanwhile, as more and more people joined 3G from across Nigeria, we began opening up zonal and state branches, which naturally attracted the attention of the authorities, political mercenaries and the ruling party. Soon, we became news on the front pages of *The Nation*, a growing national daily allegedly owned and controlled by Bola Tinubu.[149] On the day the story broke, I posted it as my status on Facebook, and got several exciting responses. Later in the day I got a call from an old friend, Todd Moss, who had worked under Jendayi Frazier at the African Affairs division of the State Department. At the time we interacted very closely on many bilateral issues and mutually liked and respected one another. He had since the exit of the Bush administration moved to the Centre for Global Development. We had been out of touch for more than two years when I got a call from him to complain that my Facebook status seemed to confirm *The Nation* story that Nuhu and I were involved in some political association called 3G. He thought that such confirmation could jeopardize Nuhu's continuing work with CGD. I replied that what I posted was correct, and Nuhu did not inform anyone of us that his fellowship at CGD precluded his freedom to associate with any political movement. In any case, I added, if that was the issue, I would remove the status and wished him, Nuhu and CGD well. I was taken aback that Nuhu would not speak to me directly about something like this, but filed this for a future conversation. I archived the Facebook status and forgot all about the incident. Nuhu never raised it when we met, and as good Fulani men, we both let things be.

Visit to the Mayor of Dakar, Khalifa Sall

After a sweeping election victory in the 2009 municipal elections in Senegal, Khalifa Sall, who contested against the incumbent President Abdoulaye Wade's son, planned to bring about meaningful and long desired change to Dakar that will benefit the entire populace. The change, he anticipated, would bring a new face, new phase and new life to the people of Dakar, and eventually inspire other African cities and nations to emulate it. To this end, he put together a team of 'pro-bono' professional advisers and technical experts with similar passion to see to the fulfilment of this dream. I was invited by Mayor Sall to offer suggestions based on my previous experience as minister in charge of Abuja, the Federal Capital Territory of Nigeria.

Based on initial briefing by my classmate at Harvard, Naye Bathily, I began considering areas that may be helpful to consider during the visit. On arrival into Dakar on 26th of October, as we drove through the city, I jotted a checklist of preliminary thoughts and observations to guide the interaction with the staff of the mayor's office. These included garbage management and street cleaning, city greening and creation of recreational parks, street naming, house numbering and addressing system, siting of public toilets and enabling environment for employment generation. Thoughts of a coherent communications strategy, selection of projects and prioritisation and financing of such projects and programmes, also crossed my mind as we drove from the airport to my hotel.

I invited my former secretaries of Education and Health at the FCT, Dr. Auwalu Anwar and Mrs Amina Bala Zakari to join me in Dakar to interact with the mayor and his team. Amina made it to Dakar, my administrative assistant Peter Akagu Jones flew in from Canada, and we spent the next few days meeting with the mayor's staff and touring parts of Dakar. We then had sessions with the mayor, his deputy and staff on their key challenges and gave them our initial thoughts. We promised to submit a report containing our policy suggestions and recommendations for action within a fortnight.

The night before our departure after spending a week or so in Senegal, we were hosted to a dinner in the residence of Naye's father, a leading opposition politician, Abdoulaye Bathily, with Mayor Khalifa Sall, and other key political figures in Senegal attending. The week before I arrived in Senegal, the president Abdoulaye Wade had given a briefcase containing two hundred thousand euros to the outgoing head of the IMF as a parting "African traditional gift." The hapless IMF chief was uncertain what to do but handed over the briefcase on arrival in Europe to his superiors. Wade did not deny the gift, but justified it as a Senegalese tradition. The media were awash with the stories of the scandal and the opposition took advantage of Wade's deteriorating moral and political standing well before the next presidential elections scheduled for 2012. We had vigorous discussions about the future of Senegalese politics, the elections and the prospects of a united opposition against Wade's increasingly corrupt and incompetent government. We left Dakar for our separate destinations, and some weeks later turned in our report to the mayor. It was a most enlightening learning experience in urban management and opposition politics.

November 2009: Yar'Adua Collapses and is Flown to Saudi Arabia

Yar'Adua's manifest infirmity changed everything about our well-structured political plans and timelines. Activating several of our contacts in Saudi Arabia, we got influx of information about his condition, until it became a trickle with the tightening of security around Yar'Adua from December 2009. We shared the information with our 3G leaders in Nigeria and some of our media contacts. Yar'Adua left the country suddenly without transmitting the letter required under the constitution for the Vice President to take over as acting President. This created a constitutional lacuna that was effectively used by the Yar'Adua loyalists – Turai Yar'Adua, his CSO Yusuf Tilde, ADC Colonel Mustapha Onoyiveta, Economic Adviser Tanimu Yakubu, the NSA Major-General Abdullahi Sarki Mukhtar, the Abuja Minister Adamu Mohammed Aliero, the Principal Secretary David Ediebvie, Attorney-General Mike Aondaokaa, Umaru's childhood friend, business partner and member of House of Representatives Shehu Inuwa Imam, protocol officer Inuwa Baba, Agriculture minister Sayyadi Abba Ruma, Governors' Forum chairman Bukola Saraki and former governor James Ibori, supported by Dr. Bello Haliru Mohammed, the National Vice Chairman, North-West of the PDP - to hijack presidential power and refuse its timely and orderly transfer to then VP Goodluck Jonathan.

Meanwhile, Bukola Saraki was in touch with the US Embassy, feeding them what was clearly incorrect information about

Yar'Adua's health. He had informed Ambassador Robin Sanders on 30th November that Yar'Adua was no longer in the intensive care unit. He was then in coma.[150] Yar'Adua had been to Saudi Arabia thrice within five months, yet his inner circle remained in denial about his terminal medical condition. From our contacts working in the hospital in Jeddah, we gathered that Yar'Adua was incapacitated and had been in coma for weeks since arrival in Saudi Arabia, yet some newspapers were awash with stories quoting the Nigerian ambassador in Saudi Arabia Garba Aminchi[151] that Umaru had recovered and was eating *tuwo da miyan kuka*, a traditional northern dish that was rumoured to be the president's favourite. It was all false. Nuhu and I, therefore, concluded that these people would stop at nothing to sustain the deception about Yar'Adua's medical condition to hold onto power even if a national constitutional crisis resulted. We were concerned about avoiding any such occurrence that might derail our democratic continuity, and decided that we must do something as a people, as a group, and as concerned Nigerians.

December 2009: G53, G57 and Save Nigeria Group Emerge

That was when we began to network with other individuals and groups to form G53 which then became G57 that subsequently metamorphosed into the Save Nigeria Group (SNG) under the leadership of Pastor Tunde Bakare. The brain behind the formation of G53 was Yinka Odumakin, who was the publicity secretary of ARG, and a member of the 3G steering committee. I did not meet Yinka in person until February 2010, but had maintained regular contact with him by email and telephone from the moment we were introduced in September 2009. Yinka felt strongly that based on all we knew about Yar'Adua's incapacitation, we should issue a press statement calling on him to resign or require the national assembly to remove him from office forthwith for various constitutional violations.

I agreed, and we both began calling up people that would consent to add their names and backing to such a statement. Yinka did the first draft which I sent to a couple of people in Nigeria and the USA to comment on, expand and improve. The final statement was issued on 2nd December and made front page headlines in virtually all newspapers in Nigeria. Prominent among the signatories were the 3G leadership – Senator Ken Nnamani, former speaker Aminu Masari, former minister Adamu Maina Waziri and myself. Political and civil society heavyweights like Lt. Gen. Alani Akinrinade, Admiral Ndubuisi Kanu, Abdulkadir Balarabe Musa, Pastor Tunde Bakare, Femi Falana, Colonel Abubakar Dangiwa Umar, Festus Okoye, Uba Sani and Joe Okei-Odumakin, Yinka's understated but strong-willed spouse and leader of the Campaign for Democracy (CD), joined her husband and many other patriots to put their names on the statement. We experienced an initial setback within 48 hours, when, under pressure from the NSA Abdullahi Sarki Mukhtar, some of the people dissociated themselves from the statement, claiming that "they did not sign" any statement. In fact no one signed anything, it was all circulated via email and had the knowledge of all the people named. Festus Okoye, Col. Dangiwa Umar, Shehu Sani and Senator Ken Nnamani fell into this class for a variety of personal reasons.

We were not deterred by the setback and within barely another fortnight, we had recruited others to join the list including Femi Fani-Kayode and social media activist Roz Ben Okagbue. Nuhu Ribadu requested exclusion from the list because he was still in litigation with the Police Service Commission over his dismissal at the time, and made the argument that including his name might be prejudicial to the case in court. On 20th of December 2009, we issued another statement this time signed by Buba Galadima, Yinka Odumakin and Osita Okechukwu, on behalf of the expanded group – called G57 - restating our call for the immediate and orderly transition of power to then Vice President Jonathan.

At the 3G end, we convened another steering committee meeting in Dubai for the 3rd of December 2009 where we considered what our next steps would be bearing in mind the developments in Nigeria. We evaluated the options of operating within an existing major party, merging with other groups towards forming a new party, establishing our stand-alone party that will then seek to merge with other parties, or taking over and restructuring an existing party. At the time, there were several political movements like the NDM process, Bola Tinubu's CODER, the Mega-Party group and so on. CPC had not been registered then. We agreed to initiate discussions with Action Congress (AC) and Labour Party (LP). We also agreed at that meeting to reach out to personalities like Donald Duke, Olusegun Mimiko, Prof. Jerry Gana, Brig-Gen. John Shagaya and Professor Wole Soyinka, among others, with a view to forming a broad-based political platform.

There were discussions too about my plan to return home on 26th December 2009. The group members were unanimous that as an opposition linchpin at the time, the decision to return to Nigeria was not personally mine, and insisted that I called off my plans to go home. Nuhu was absent at this meeting, but I could see that he had worked on some members of the group to convince me not to return home then. The next day, the Sultan of Sokoto called and instructed me, as a Barewa senior,[152] not to consider coming home immediately. His reasons were simple and straightforward. No one was in charge in Nigeria at that point in time, so should anything untoward happen to me, it would be difficult placing responsibility on any person or authority. I had been successfully ambushed by the combined effort of Nuhu, my friends in Nigeria and some of my close family members. Rejecting their collective, near unanimous counsel would be simply unreasonable and insensitive. I was compelled to postpone my scheduled return in December 2009 to a future date.

January 2010: Save Nigeria Group Marches for Nigeria's Democracy

Yinka Odumakin called me again in the New Year. Yar'Adua had not returned. The 'Yar'Adua Cabal' kept planting mythical stories about his remarkable improvement and imminent return to Nigeria, but we knew better. Yinka suggested that G-57 organise a public protest in Lagos to push the cabinet to declare Yar'Adua incapacitated or the national assembly to impeach him. I concurred with the idea though I confessed to him that neither of the two paths would be taken by the two constitutional bodies anytime soon. Nevertheless, I had a personal challenge. Tucked away safely in Dubai, I felt unable to ask any person to protest on the streets and risk being assaulted, tear-gassed or shot at by the police or the army. I suggested that Yinka finds someone willing to lead the movement and protests, both materially and spiritually. He then asked me what I thought of Pastor Tunde Bakare leading the effort. I had heard of the name, read some statements credited to him, and remembered clearly that Obasanjo did not quite like him for reasons that I never explored while in government. I opined that Pastor Bakare is well known for his views about the state of the nation and I believed he had the courage to lead the G-57 effort onto the streets.

Immediately the first G-53 statement was issued, I was approached by a Nigerian in the diaspora – Dr. Baba Adam – who wanted me to contact him by telephone for 'an urgent message'. He turned out to be an emissary of the First Lady, Turai Yar'Adua. I ignored him until Turai directly emailed me a number in Nigeria to contact so we could speak. I did not call the number. She then concluded that the only way we could communicate was by email, and an exchange of messages (and signals) ensued between 15th December, 2009 and 17th January, 2010. Turai was aggressively engaged in an effort to disarm me and rally support for her incapacitated husband. She probably suspected that I was playing a substantial role in the organised opposition that G-53 became, or was perhaps just reaching out and offering carrots to those previously declared as Umaru's enemies.

For me, Turai's strange attempt to reach out confirmed that Umaru's condition must be so bad that she felt the need to make up with people she knew he had been unfair to.[153]

Then on Christmas Day, a young Nigerian, a secondary school friend of one of my sons, Umar Farouk Mutallab, attempted a suicide bombing of an American airliner headed for Detroit. It was the first time a Nigerian was involved either in suicide bombing or international terrorism. Nigeria had no president to speak or engage with an angry US government. When Nigeria was placed on the US terror watch list as a knee-jerk reaction to the Mutallab incident, I wrote a widely publicised letter on 8th January 2010[154] to President Obama, appealing for it to be reconsidered. I was also compelled by the circumstances of the time to follow up with a piece in Foreign Policy titled "Time for a New Nigerian President"[155] to articulate the dilemma of our country. Our nation was facing an unprecedented leadership crisis and it looked like primordial sentiments had taken over the minds and bodies of our political and economic elite. Sitting in Dubai, I kept reaching out to our friends, associates and 3G compatriots in search of answers.

It was in the midst of these efforts of organising the protests in Nigeria to promote constitutionalism and orderly succession that I became further blessed with the friendship and brotherhood of a truly remarkable and gifted man – Pastor Tunde Bakare. We first spoke on the phone and worked together over the next days and weeks coordinating street protests in Lagos, New York, London and Abuja. Pastor Bakare demonstrated the altruistic and impeccable leadership that made the various marches successful.[156] Those January protests along, with a mind-blowing piece of investigative journalism by *Next on Sunday*[157] about Yar'Adua's brain-damaged condition in Saudi Arabia, constituted tipping points that changed the entire mood of the country, leading to the intervention of former heads of state and chief justices that persuaded the national assembly to invoke some 'doctrine of necessity' that finally catapulted VP Jonathan to the acting presidency in February 2010. In between these, we closely monitored Yar'Adua's condition in Saudi Arabia and shared the information with our contacts in Nigeria.

February 2010: Jonathan is Acting President, Yar'Adua Returns

In February, my daughter Yasmin, Jimi Lawal and Chinelo Anohu worked together to organise a party to mark my 50th birthday. My mother, Bashir, sisters and children that could take time off school all made it to Jumeirah Beach Hotel in Dubai for the dinner. It was a night of reconnecting with friends, family and political associates. Dr. Aloy Chife flew in from New York; Roz Ben Okagbue flew in from London.Yinka Odumakin, Babafemi Ojudu, and Dr. Tunji Olowolafe surprised me by flying all the way from Nigeria, with fraternal greetings from Governor Raji Fashola. Pastor Bakare was unable to make it, but sent his best wishes. The organisers invited all my known close friends, former staff and associates. It was well attended and I was quite touched. Yasmin was in school so she called in from London, and wished me the best birthday on behalf of her siblings with a short speech broadcast on an amplified cellphone speaker. Mohammed Bello flew in from Massachusetts and was equally outstanding. The famous Nigerian comedian, Ali Baba, made us laugh all night, thanks to former BPE staff, Chinelo Anohu who flew him from Nigeria.

It was also on that day I had an email interview with Matthew Tostevin of Reuters in which I expressed my views about zoning and my personal attitude towards Goodluck Jonathan running for president. This is why I am amused when some of Jonathan's sympathisers who hailed my position as 'patriotic and nationalist' in February 2010, turned round a year later to call me a 'northern sectionalist' when I was unable to support the dual disappointment of an unreformed PDP and what turned out to be Jonathan's incompetence and incapacity to provide decent, inclusive leadership. I said then about leadership choices, and I meant every word, that:

> Yar'Adua is from the North but did nothing for the region, just like many before him. If Goodluck shows real leadership over the next few months, many of us will campaign for him to be our president. I think Nigeria and the West African sub-region will be the better for it[158]

In the same interview, I made it clear that I intended returning home soon, but not to contest for any office, be in any government or be Jonathan's running mate as Reuters claimed was the speculation all over Abuja at the time. I started active preparations to return home and over the next month quietly went round to my bank in the UAE and donated a power of attorney over all my accounts. I did this so that just in case I returned home and I was unable to travel or be otherwise incapacitated, Yasmin could operate my bank accounts in Nigeria and abroad and keep our family going without any legal hindrance.

About a week after the interview was published, Umaru Yar'Adua and his entourage had to depart hurriedly from Saudi Arabia. He had spent three months in hospital without any sign or hope of improvement. Indeed, his continued presence in the Kingdom without being accessible to multiple delegations sent by the Nigerian government was developing into a potential diplomatic disaster for the Saudis. In January and February alone, high-powered delegations from the ruling party, the House of Representatives, the governor's forum and the abinet were in Saudi Arabia and were denied access to Yar'Adua by his strong-willed wife, Turai.

The story of Yar'Adua's sudden return, sneaking into Abuja like a thief in the night is the stuff of a thriller movie. The only role I will admit to playing in the saga was confirming that the presidential jet had indeed left Jeddah, tracking its flight through Sudanese and Chadian air space, and along with Yinka Odumakin, Sam Nda Isaiah and Simon Kolawole, ensuring that the local and international media, with their cameras, were at the presidential wing of the airport to give Umaru a grand reception and welcome. In the end, the airport was thrown into complete darkness as soon as the plane completed taxiing, and a hapless and helpless Umaru was lifted like an infant out of the presidential jet into the brand new 'intensive care-equipped ambulance' that had just been acquired for him, and driven into Aso Villa, never to be seen in public until his corpse was buried in Katsina on 6th May, 2010. Whatever he may have done to me and others, I prayed for Allah to forgive his errors and rest his soul in peace. In the end, we are all mortals – something easily forgotten by many around Umaru, once they got drunk with the elixir of unexpected political and economic power.

March 2010: Meetings with Pastor Bakare, SNG and AC

Pastor Tunde Bakare and I finally met face-to-face at the end of March 2010 in Dubai. We bonded almost instantaneously. I found in Tunde Bakare a forthright and intelligent man, a gifted speaker, passionate patriot and one of the most honest men I know. He is straight and courageous in thought, speech and action. I knew I had found another elder brother to add to the blessings of Bashir, Ali and Sani Maikudi. He flew to Dubai along with Yinka Odumakin, Uche Onyeagocha, Wale Oshun, Jimi Agbaje, Dipo Famakinwa and Yinka Quadri, his assistant. On the 3G side, we had Dr. Isa Odidi who flew in from Canada, Jimi Lawal, Kalli Alghazali, Akin Osuntokun, Naja'atu Mohammed, Balarabe Abbas Lawal, Tijjani Abdullahi, Idris Othman and Salihu Lukman.

We spent two days debriefing each other and then thinking through options for active engagement with the political process.

At the end of the meetings, we decided to open discussions with AC and Labour Party (LP). The CPC had just been registered, and we agreed to keep it in view after concluding with the former parties or otherwise. We recognised even then, that it would take the merger of all the parties, or at least an electoral alliance, to successfully confront the ruling party. We also agreed to push forward and conclude the registration of a political party for which 3G had already filed an application with INEC.[159]

After the second day of meetings, I went to see Pastor Bakare in his hotel room. He had just ordered dinner when I arrived and had Jimi Agbaje keeping him company. I thanked him for coming to Dubai to meet with me and our group. I apologised that Nuhu was unable to make it because his family was spending the Easter holidays with him in Washington, DC. On completing his dinner, Pastor Bakare asked me a straight question. "Who are we doing all this political organisation-building for? Who is the candidate we have in view for President?" he asked. I replied that I expected whoever we will support to emerge from some democratic process within the party we finally join, but added that my preferred candidate was Nuhu Ribadu. Pastor was equally quick and sharp. "Nuhu will not be an acceptable candidate. He is seen as Obasanjo's attack dog and has made too many enemies of Lagos business elite." I disagreed and insisted that the perception was wrong. I asked Pastor Bakare how well he knew Nuhu and if he had ever met him and he answered in the negative. I, therefore, appealed to him to reserve his judgment until he met Nuhu and got to know him better.

He accepted that proposal and we said our farewells as they left for Lagos the following morning. One of the decisions we took was for 3G to meet as soon as possible with the leadership of AC and LP and report back. Akin Osuntokun was tasked with arranging the LP meeting while Wale Oshun, Babafemi Ojudu and Uche Onyeagocha would be the links to AC. We never heard from Akin Osuntokun but within a week, a meeting with AC's leadership was fixed for 25th April in Accra, Ghana.

April 2010: Meeting with AC in Accra, Ghana

Nuhu again could not make it to Accra even though the date was fixed with AC subject to his convenience and physical availability.

I, therefore, led the 3G team to Accra, while National Publicity Secretary Lai Mohammed led a smaller delegation[160] representing AC. We met for hours, debriefing one another on the situation in Nigeria and agreeing to explore a merger between AC and 3G. A joint committee of three persons on both sides was constituted to continue meeting in Nigeria to negotiate the terms of the merger. But from the very first meeting with Oshun, Ojudu and Onyeagocha in Dubai, it was clear that AC wanted 3G to present a candidate for president while they would provide a running mate. We on the other hand, perhaps naively so, preferred to collectively review the Party's primaries system to allow greater, more open competition – something AC seemed strangely and surprisingly uncomfortable with. Nevertheless, the two delegations then left for Nigeria while Jimi and I went back to Dubai after spending a few days with our host Aloy Chife, his lovely wife, Gesare and their son, simply known as Papa.

I had already decided that I would return to Nigeria by the end of that month of April 2010. I had, therefore, booked a one-way flight to London en route Abuja on British Airways. Apart from informing my daughter Yasmin, and a couple of others, I shared my travel plans with no one until I got to London and was a couple of days away from arriving in Abuja. Many of my close friends, Nuhu included, were incensed at my 'sudden decision', but it was neither sudden nor impulsive. I had simply learnt lessons from the last ambush led by Nuhu to frustrate my planned return to Nigeria. I was determined, at the risk of being accused by my friends of not trusting them, not to provide another opportunity this second time.

One of those I shared my plans with was Dele Olojede of *Next* newspaper because of his constant, unbending and committed support during the most difficult period of my life. *Next* and other newspapers[161] broke the story of my planned arrival. At Heathrow Airport on 30th April 2010, the night of my departure, I called General Aliyu Mohammed Gusau,[162] then Jonathan's national security adviser, to confirm that I was on the BA flight to Abuja. He was pleased that I was coming home and said I was being expected. He requested that I should visit him to catch up as soon as I settled down in Abuja.

May 2010: On May Day, I Returned to Face Umaru Yar'Adua, but......

Jimi Lawal and I arrived in Abuja the morning of May Day, the first of May 2010. I was cleared through immigration without any incident, pulled my trolley bag and stepped out to the warm embrace of a crowd of family, friends and political associates.[163] The person responsible for my 23 months of exile, Umaru Yar'Adua, had returned in the darkness of the night of 23rd February, but no one had seen him – not even acting President Jonathan. He was holed up in the Villa, with Turai organising visits of Muslim and Christian clerics to give the never-ending impression that he was going to be miraculously fine the next morning and would appear in his office to chase Jonathan away. Since we were still better informed than most about Umaru's pathetic, medical condition, we did not believe any of the fabrications emanating from some of the clerics. Meanwhile, I was alive, at home, healthy and receiving an endless stream of visitors – friends, family and even curious well-wishers. I remain grateful to God for His mercies.

On Tuesday, 4th May 2010, I drove to the EFCC office in Wuse to meet with my traducers at about 10 in the morning. Our session was uneventful as they had exhausted their investigation and in frustration found nothing to nail me. By one o'clock in the afternoon, we were done, but they made a show of detaining me till evening so the newspapers would report that I was grilled for nine hours. The questions they asked me were comical, some even ridiculous. I was amazed at the extent to which supposedly serious organisations relied on unfounded rumours as basis of law enforcement work! I was asked if I owned the *NEXT* newspaper which had been at the forefront of exposing the corruption within the EFCC since Nuhu was forced out of the institution for Farida Waziri to take over. They also thought that since I played a central role in nurturing the UAE-Nigeria relations that led to the grant of a telecommunications license to Mubadala,[164] I must be the real owner of Etisalat, or at the very least, a major shareholder in the company. It appeared that as far as the EFCC was concerned, that was how senior officials were expected to conduct government business – an incredulous assumption!

Now, even a brainless person knows that Etisalat is a state-owned telecom company based in Dubai, with operations in a dozen countries, and how I could suddenly own it in Nigeria only reminded me of Atiku's tale to Obasanjo that my brother owned ten percent of Motorola, Inc.! In any case, since I had filed suits against the EFCC and the federal government challenging some of these wild and defamatory accusations, it was sub-judice to ask any questions on those but they tried. I reminded them that they could not ask any such questions, but go to court and tell the judge what they knew. The leader of the team, Abdulkadir Jimoh, was gracious, even apologetic, implying that he did not believe in all the persecution but was "merely doing his job." I was released on 'administrative bail' in the evening. The criminal charges filed against Altine Jibrin, Dr. Ismail Iro and I were to be heard on 6th May anyway, so we were all to meet in court in a couple of days.

The next day, the 5th of May, I went to another court, this time the Code of Conduct Tribunal, to witness proceedings in the case filed by the Yar'Adua administration against Nuhu for allegedly not declaring his assets, a case that was withdrawn by the Jonathan government and was accordingly dismissed that day. I then joined Pastor Tunde Bakare at the launch of Save Nigeria Group's "Contract with Nigerians" at the Abuja Hilton Hotel. We spent the rest of the afternoon meeting with other civil society leaders like Solomon Asemota, SAN, and later in the evening with Pastor Bakare, preparing for a planned meeting between SNG and the then acting President Jonathan that day.

It was while in the midst of this that a call came through from the National Security Adviser, General Aliyu Gusau, to inform us that Yar'Adua had died a couple of hours earlier. He further informed us that he was on his way to pick Jonathan so they could pay a condolence visit to Turai Yar'Adua. He promised to keep us updated on developments. After absorbing this unsurprising yet unexpected piece of news, I quickly placed calls to three of my friends in the media – Ben Bruce of Silverbird Television, Sam Nda Isaiah of *Leadership*, and Nduka Obaigbena of *ThisDay* to break the news to them. Silverbird TV was the first to break the news, ahead of even the government-owned Nigeria Television Authority. We were all pensive for the next hour or so, and we knew that the planned meeting with Jonathan was not happening anytime soon.

In the end, Pastor Bakare and the SNG leadership met a few more times with Jonathan until 28th November 2010 when he sent Niger Delta minister Godsday Orubebe and Tony Uranta to give them an envelope that was found to contain $50,000 as 'transport money' back to Lagos. That ended any further interactions with Jonathan and any hope that he would be anything other than the usual transactional Nigerian leader! Perhaps, one day someday, Bakare will tell his story of the various meetings SNG had with Jonathan until they gave up on the man.[165]

Jonathan was sworn in as president on the 6th of May, 2010. A couple of days later, I met with him in the ADC's lodge in the Villa, with my old friend and his principal secretary, Hassan Tukur. It was a brief meeting. He looked tired and sleep-deprived. He welcomed me back home and promised that all the Yar'Adua persecution would be terminated since he had now fully taken over. He promised to make more time over the weekend so we could talk about pressing national issues. I thanked him for making time to see me, but suggested that he should not interfere with any investigations or prosecutions as I preferred to prove my innocence in court, rather than to appear 'guilty as sin, but saved by his friend'. I told him I looked forward to a longer meeting but added that I had no intention of returning to full-time public service any time soon. The next day, my state governor, former colleague and acquaintance from our ABU days, Namadi Sambo, invited me to accompany him, the Emir of Zazzau and others on a condolence visit by the people of Kaduna State to President Jonathan. I did and met Jonathan again briefly where he reiterated that he would set aside a weekend for our promised meeting. At the close of the visit, I was asked questions by State House press corps on many issues and once again my views about zoning.

My responses were widely reported, with Jonathan's sympathizers interpreting the views to be in support of Jonathan personally rather than any leadership selection principle, while the self-appointed defenders of 'northern interest' attacked me for being bought by southerners. One of my historically-consistent critics, Mohammed Haruna, wrote a very angry syndicated column[166] attacking me and chastising Sambo and Jonathan for inviting me to the Villa. As far as he was concerned, I was a fugitive from justice until recently and since in his peculiar type of jurisprudence, I must be presumed guilty unless I proved my innocence, the State House should be off-limits to me, and Jonathan and Sambo must keep a safe distance from felons like me! Jonathan clearly took the warning seriously and we never met again until October 2010, when he was looking to recruit me to support his presidential aspiration – something that I was unwilling and unable to do by then as I will explain shortly.

The PDP Reform Forum and Aftermath

Just before I returned to Nigeria, two of my 3G compatriots had formed the PDP Reform Forum, an association of ruling party members that were unhappy with the stranglehold of the state governors on the party. A new president, not particularly well-regarded by the PDP state governors, presented a window of opportunity for driving through internal reforms of the party. They invited my friend and former chief of staff, Balarabe Abbas Lawal, to join the steering committee, chaired by Senator Ken Nnamani. Former speaker Aminu Masari was the vice chairman. The governors-controlled National Working Committee of the PDP was sufficiently rattled by the emergence of the forum, such that the leaders and 'suspected financiers' were suspended from the party. Nnamani and Masari, both members of PDP's National Executive Committee, had promptly challenged the decision in court.[167] I was invited to join the forum's steering committee the moment I returned to Nigeria. I attended my first meeting on 12th May, 2010, and thereafter every week until August when the forum went voluntarily into abeyance.

Over the next few weeks, we worked hard at designing internal democratic processes that will remove control of the PDP from the godfathers, the governors and unelected apparatchiks and restore it back to the ordinary membership. The foundation of such a system is a clean, fraud-resistant biometric membership register of all party members nationwide. We approached several technology companies to propose solutions that would enable this and publicised our proposals in the print media. The forum leadership, consisting of Senator Nnamani, Speaker Masari and Dr. Raymond Dokpesi, kept briefing Jonathan on the direction of the reforms, persuading him that it was through implementation of these ideas that he would successfully wrest control of the party from the governors' forum which had been pro-Yar'Adua all through till the very end, and vest it in the membership. Our proposals were easily accepted by the PDP National Caucus and recommended to the Board of Trustees for consideration.

I was mandated to meet with BOT chairman Olusegun Obasanjo to brief him on the forum's activities and the proposals for his support, advocacy in the board and approval. He was enthusiastic, while regretting that Senator Ken Nnamani and Speaker Masari, his two third-term nemeses, were leading the group. Our proposals were approved by the BOT, but thrown out by the PDP NEC on 18th June 2010. The story of how Jonathan double crossed the Reform Forum following a deal he struck with twelve of the governors in South Africa while attending the opening ceremonies of the FIFA World Cup, would be better told by Nnamani and Masari who personally experienced it at the PDP NEC meeting.[168]

Suffice it to say, this became a behavioral pattern of Jonathan's that would become even clearer over the coming months and years -never expect Jonathan to keep a promise, never expect him to reciprocate a kind gesture.

What I have consistently counselled those that did not know Jonathan as well as a few of us was this - "Do what you believe to be right whether Jonathan happens to benefit or not, and do not expecting any political pay-offs if he did. Taking risks on his behalf would always lead to zero recognition, so it is best to do so out of some bigger conviction"! I am not suggesting here that Jonathan behaves this way out of any patriotism or fidelity to principles – he is just a person who quickly forgets a favour but remembers every little slight. In this regard, Jonathan and Yar'Adua shared more than a few things in common.

Some leaders of the forum left the PDP for the AC (Dr. Abiye Sekibo) and the CPC (Aminu Masari). Others remained in the PDP to pursue their disparate political aspirations. I was uninterested in either contesting for any office or seeking a political appointment, so I did neither. I devoted more time to civil society activities via SNG, got more interested in 3G's negotiation meetings with AC, and resuscitated my earlier plan to establish a policy think tank in Abuja. I was assured by the 3G team – Salihu Lukman, Dr. Sam Amadi, Kalli Alghazali, Tijjani Abdullahi and Balarabe Abbas

Lawal that discussions with the AC remained on course but were unduly delayed by the travel schedules of some of the members of the joint committee we set up after the Ghana meeting in April. This was before we learnt of some developments in Dubai of all places, involving AC and Nuhu.

June 2010: Nuhu Returns, and the Political Games Begin

On the 4th of June, Nuhu arrived back in Nigeria. He felt safe enough to return since Umaru had died about a month earlier and he had been cleared of all charges by the Jonathan administration. We joined him a few days later, 7th June, at Babcock University where he was conferred with an honorary doctorate degree. We returned to Abuja and had an emergency meeting of the 3G leadership in Senator Ken Nnamani's house with Nuhu, Adamu Maina Waziri, then Jonathan's minister of police affairs,[169] former speaker Aminu Masari, Balarabe Abbas Lawal and myself, amongst others. We reviewed the political situation including the status of the 3G-AC discussions and the progress made with the PDP Reform Forum at the time.

However, one of the decisions we took, which Nuhu did not object to, was to put on hold or at best slow down discussions with AC until we established that reforming PDP was a hopeless proposition. Nuhu left a couple of days later to return to Washington, DC. His plan was to tidy up the visiting fellowship with the Centre for Global Development and return for active, partisan politics. It was from that location that Nuhu went off on his own, literally abandoning the group we had formed, and the platform we had carefully designed and built – and collectively agreed was for his political benefit.

My friend Hakeem Belo-Osagie, who loved watching football and remains a passionate Manchester United supporter, had earlier in the year invited me and two of my children – Yasmin and Bello – to join his family in South Africa for the FIFA World Cup. Just as I was preparing to leave Abuja, I got a phone call from a mutual friend in Dubai that Nuhu left that day for Washington after a day's meeting with an AC team led by Senator Bola Tinubu. I took in the information, and awaited Nuhu's briefing as I was certain there was some explanation for it, if at all true. A few days after I heard this without any subsequent confirmation or otherwise from

Nuhu, I went to Lagos to catch the South African Airways flight to Johannesburg for my vacation, bonding with two of my lovely children, and cheering Ghana to win the World Cup! In Lagos, I saw Pastor Bakare to update him on our political discussions with AC, at which point, he, along with Yinka Odumakin, not only confirmed Nuhu's meeting with the AC leadership in Dubai, but the two agreements reached – that Nuhu will be handed the AC presidential ticket while AC chooses his running mate, and the need to keep this quiet until the seven or eight AC leaders went back to Nigeria, and briefed their other leaders like Tom Ikimi who were not privy to the deal. Nuhu had committed to AC that he would bring the whole 3G team on board to support the ticket, and needed the 'under-wraps' time to brief us as well.

As far as Pastor Bakare was concerned, he had established that Nuhu went to Dubai behind my back and the other 3G leaders', which to him constituted the ultimate betrayal. The fact that even after doing that, Nuhu failed to explain his visit and bring me up to date said everything about his character. Pastor Bakare never had a positive view of Nuhu in the first place, and with this incident, became even more convinced of Nuhu's unworthiness for serious leadership roles. I admitted to Pastor Bakare that I was surprised and disappointed but was confident that there would be an explanation at some point, sometime soon. I appealed to Pastor Bakare again to suspend judgment until he got to meet and know Nuhu a little better and more closely. Though by then I was compelled by the reality of the last few months to expect miracles, I told Pastor Bakare and Yinka Odumakin that I was sure Nuhu would have a perfect explanation for the whole Dubai episode. I departed for South Africa.

July 2010: Politically, Nuhu Goes His Own Way, Alone

We had a great time in South Africa and in retrospect, the quality of time spent with Yasmin in those weeks in Johannesburg and Cape Town, made coming to terms with her death less than 18 months later, just slightly easier. It was a great vacation on the whole, spent watching football, dining and debating with Jimi Lawal and his daughters, Keem and his family, Dele Olojede, his intelligent and charming wife Amma Ogan and their two daughters. We were in the month of July 2010. It had been two weeks since Nuhu went to Dubai, and I had not heard from him. Then Dele Olojede called me with exciting news.

His newspaper had just gotten an exclusive – AC had decided to give Nuhu Ribadu the party's presidential ticket. The scoop would be the paper's lead story the next day. I confirmed to him that I had heard about it too, and gave him additional details of the Dubai meeting that his paper did not have. Dele was upset. How could I forget to mention this important political development to him in the last week or so that I had been in South Africa? I explained that Nuhu was yet to inform me of the decision. At that point Dele's phone went dead, and within 15 minutes he arrived at the rented apartment we were using in Sandton. On hearing the entire story pieced together from Pastor Bakare and my friend's earlier call from Dubai, Dele felt disappointed too, but appealed to me to forget about the omission and move on with supporting Nuhu as a credible candidate for the next elections. After all, he added, this was what I tried to sell to him in Aspen a year earlier. I nodded, and just said "we will see how things pan out from now on. It would really depend on how Nuhu conducts himself from now on."

On the 9th of July, the day both *Punch* and *Next* broke the story of Nuhu's deal with AC, I got a call from him. He was in Washington and wanted to know how it felt to be watching the World Cup live and in colour. We chatted for some minutes and rang off. He did not raise the subject of his trip to Dubai or the story in the newspapers in Nigeria.[170] I did not ask him. I think Nuhu knew that I must have heard the news of the deal and therefore expected me to raise the subject. But by then, I had learnt that patience is the most important habit of the trainee politician, which I was. Nuhu called back the next day. I had a bad cold then and we talked about the flu, weather and vuvuzelas. He exchanged pleasantries with my daughter and son, and asked me to buy him a vuvuzela. He said he would be on his way to Nigeria shortly, and would pick it up when we meet. Once again, I thought Nuhu expected me to enquire about his adoption by AC as presidential candidate but I said nothing.

While in South Africa, Dele invited me and a few other Nigerians that were around for the World Cup to a dinner in his Johannesburg home. In addition to the company of Dele and his wife Amma, we had a pleasant evening of good food and reflection about the state of our nation. Amma acted as facilitator of the discussions with probing questions and prodding follow-ups. Keem Belo-Osagie and his wife Myma, Fola Adeola, Dr. Yele Aluko, Asue Ighodalo, Ahmed Dasuki and I participated. Udoma Udo Udoma could not arrive at Johannesburg until the day after, and Atedo Peterside and his wife Dundun arrived after we had nearly wrapped up. We agreed to do a follow-up meeting in Nigeria and continue exploring how good people could come together under a single political platform to rescue the country from the gang that was running and ruining the nation. Within days, the World Cup was over and we flew back to Nigeria. My two children went back to their respective schools.

Pastor Bakare Convenes 'the Arrowheads' Meeting

On arriving in Lagos, Pastor Bakare informed me and Jimi Lawal that he had thought of a need to bring together a few good men and women to brainstorm on our nation's governance predicament, look at some options and perhaps chart a way out of the situation. By then Bakare and the SNG leadership had practically given up hope that Jonathan and his PDP co-travellers would provide the minimum level of good governance that Nigeria so badly needed. Bakare proposed to convene a meeting of between ten or twelve people he thought could be "the arrowheads" of political change in Nigeria. He came up with about half a dozen names and we suggested a few more names. Pastor Bakare then sent text message invitations to Danjuma Goje, Dr. Pat Utomi, Dr. Ngozi Okonjo-Iweala, Oby Ezekwesili, Fola Adeola, Donald Duke, Nuhu Ribadu, Dr. Usman Bugaje, Raji Fashola and my humble self, to meet on 15th July, 2010. All ten confirmed attendance a few days later.

In the end six of us attended the meeting in Pastor's residence.[171]

In attendance at the meeting were other politicians apart from the "arrowheads" - Jimi Agbaje, Yinka Odumakin, Jimi Lawal and Olawale Oshun. We first had dinner, followed by hours of discussions which stretched till three in the morning. It was an evening of passionate discussions, debate and disagreements. All of us agreed on the strength in numbers and teamwork, and to explore as a united group the possibility of joining a political party other than the PDP. Nuhu made a case for the group to join AC. A couple of us were sympathetic to Labour Party, while Fola Adeola made a pitch in favour of a brand new platform – either join his Kowa Party or register a party afresh.

Nuhu informed us that within the next two weeks, the AC, DPP, parts of ANPP and APGA were merging or going into alliance to adopt one presidential candidate – and with the information already in the public domain, we thought that would have to be Nuhu. We could not agree on which one party to adopt, and were hoping that the other absentees would contribute to the decision. We agreed to meet again on 31st July at the same venue, hopefully with more of the arrowheads attending, to discuss further and finalise the way forward politically.

August 2010: The Arrowheads Agree to Disagree

We met again on 31st July. Oby and Ngozi called in from Jamaica. Fola who suggested the date and time of the meeting arrived from Abeokuta after we adjourned. Donald and Nuhu simply forgot about the meeting. By then, we had made progress in our discussions with Kowa Party and Labour Party. By mid-August when we were scheduled to meet in group plenary to decide on a common political platform, most of us had gone our separate ways, politically. With my encouragement, Oby extended her employment contract with the World Bank by another year; Nuhu was going round the country, visiting traditional rulers and political leaders to sell his arrangement with AC; Danjuma Goje, Fola, and Ngozi no longer returned our calls; Pat Utomi unilaterally announced his own presidential candidacy on the platform of Olu Falae's Social Democratic Mega Party (SDMP); and Donald, Jimi Lawal and I were left alone discussing with both Kowa and Labour Party.

Other persons in attendance at our first meeting had also moved. Jimi Agbaje was rumoured to be considering accepting a position in the Jonathan administration while Wale Oshun and Nuhu became more involved in the AC presidential contest. The 3G-AC discussions had ended when news of Nuhu's acceptance to be the party's flag bearer got confirmed. Our other 3G leaders had moved as well – Salihu Lukman to AC to contest a senatorial seat, Aminu Masari to Buhari's CPC, while Ken Nnamani and

Adamu Waziri chose to remain in the PDP and hope for the best. Pastor Bakare, Yinka Odumakin, Jimi Lawal and the rest of our 3G and SNG leadership were left standing alone. We threw in the towel not long after, terminating all discussions with Kowa and Labour Party. AC had merged with DPP to become ACN, and then approached 3G to continue our 'discussions'. Our response was simple – thanks, but no. Pastor Bakare, Yinka, Jimi and I conferred with Oby and accepted the reality that once again, the personal ambition made it impossible to unite against a common enemy – bad governance. We agreed to let things go and plan better next time.

September 2010: Buhari Courts Bakare and SNG

For the third time within three months, General Muhammadu Buhari met with Pastor Tunde Bakare, this time in Lagos. We met in the pastor's Ikeja residence on 23rdSeptember, with Sule Y. Hamma, Aminu Masari, Hadi Sirika, Joy Nunieh-Okunnu and Farouk Adamu Aliyu representing the CPC, while Yinka Odumakin, Jimi Lawal, and my humble self along with Bakare, represented the SNG. Pastor Bakare spoke passionately, as always, about Nigeria's unity and potential. He suggested that the way forward was for the CPC to work with other parties to confront the evil of the PDP. He briefed Buhari and his team about our efforts as SNG/3G to bring Kowa and Labour Party together. Buhari lamented the state of the nation and the self-centred and short-sighted attitude of our elites. He gave reasons why he left the ANPP and why CPC was registered: to ensure social justice for all Nigerians through good governance.

While lamenting the disappointing roles of the police, INEC and the judiciary in legitimising electoral fraud in the past, he expressed hope that with past examples of Bauchi and Kano States, a citizenry united with the local elite to demand change could result in fairer electoral outcomes. Sule Hamma added that SNG and CPC were ideological soul mates and should work together to deliver better governance for our country. He added that ACN-CPC talks were to continue, with electoral alliance and merger as imminent possibilities. We basically discussed possibilities of working together in support of Buhari's third presidential bid, and agreed it was worth exploring. On the SNG side, we agreed to present the proposal to our leadership and revert back as early as possible.

In the end, we decided that SNG should be preserved as a non-partisan civil society organisation, while 3G would be the political interface on behalf of our group. Further discussions and cooperation with CPC and other political parties would henceforth be with 3G, on behalf of the group. We therefore continued our discussions with both Kowa Party and Labour Party, on behalf of SNG, and hoped that we would bring both parties into an electoral partnership of some sort with the CPC. We also hoped that CPC and ACN would work something out so we can all be together again with Nuhu against the common enemy – the unreformed, governors-controlled, anti-people and undemocratic PDP.

October 2010: An attempt at humour generates unexpected furore

One of the earliest signs of the misplaced spending priorities and profligacy that would define the Jonathan administration appeared when it budgeted some N50 billion to celebrate our fiftieth independence anniversary. In the course of several days of celebrations, *Leadership* newspaper had an event of lectures at the Abuja Sheraton to which I was invited by the publisher, Sam Nda Isaiah. Among those invited to deliver keynotes and speeches were former presidents Muhammadu Buhari, Ibrahim Babangida and Abdulsalami Abubakar. Jonathan's NSA General Aliyu Gusau, who had then quit the job to contest the presidency, was also invited. Buhari was absent, but the others along with many political leaders including Governors Ikedi Ohakim and Babangida Aliyu filled the Ladi Kwali Hall. I declined the invitation to join them or sit in the front row because I planned to leave before the completion of the programme.

Imo State governor Ikedi Ohakim gave a long, boring and unapologetic speech in defense of his decision a week earlier, to lock out of the Concorde Hotel, Owerri, personalities like former Vice President Ekwueme and prevent them from holding a meeting that would have resulted in a statement inimical to Jonathan's emerging presidential aspirations. This gross violation of the rights of these south-east political leaders to associate and express themselves was further repeated when security men and the police prevented them from meeting in another privately-owned hotel in Owerri! Ohakim's conduct was not only culturally disrespectful, democratically intolerant but outrightly illegal and unconstitutional. He stood there justifying his act of impunity citing 'security considerations' as if the ever-peaceful and professional Ekwueme would be associated with anything violent, a threat to security or against the public interest! I was seething, and waiting for an opportunity to tear apart his nonsense. More speeches followed, and then it was the turn of former president Babangida (IBB), then, a PDP presidential aspirant, to speak.

The Babangida I knew was very intelligent, smart on his feet and an articulate speaker, an orator even. Whether in his smart military uniform in Dodan Barracks or some years later in traditional *'baban riga'* in his Minna living room, he captivated his audience with his charm, words and gestures. Though he thought of me and Nuhu as two sides of a bad penny, I have great respect for his intellect, self-confidence and great charm. I have always liked IBB the person, even though I thought in the end he had let himself and many of his admirers down, as president.[172] On that day, the speaker was not the IBB I thought I knew and had come to admire. His speech was nothing near what he dished out as president. It was then it hit me – what remained in my mind was the IBB of the 1990s and here we are 20 years later and I am assuming it has to be the same person, shining intellect, articulation and delivery! It became clear to me that he was simply past his prime. I became downcast and simply walked out of the hall to go home.

I was ambushed on my way out of the Sheraton Hotel by AIT and the *Sun* newspaper. They asked me questions about our independence anniversary celebrations and the aspiration of IBB to Nigeria's presidency. I expressed the view that Nigeria had something to celebrate even though we could have done much better. On IBB's presidential aspiration, I observed that both IBB and GMB were presidents some 25 years ago, when I had just started a family. Now with my grown children and with me having attained the age of 50, they still wished to lead the country again. I suggested that both should retire and support other candidates. I observed that more than 60% of Nigeria's population was below the age of 40, with a new generation of young people connected via new communication and social media tools. I concluded with an attempt at humour that many people of their age thought BlackBerry is a fruit! Those that saw the interview clip on AIT mostly had a laugh about it, but the *Sun's* headline the next day was provocative, insulting even – "El-Rufai to IBB, Buhari – You Are Expired!" or something to that effect.[173] The IBB media team just chose to ignore the headline, knowing the sensational orientation of the tabloid, and released a statement that I served an older man, Obasanjo, as president. The Buhari media team was angry and launched a vicious attack, not on my views – they were largely factual – but on my person and reputation. Daniel Aghanya, the protem National Publicity Secretary of the CPC, issued a statement insulting me, accusing me of non-performance when administering the FCT, with corruption and abuse of office as my trademarks. My political group and media people were incensed. We met to decide on a response and though I thought we should just ignore the attack and let it ride, my group overruled me on two grounds. Buhari had earlier granted an interview to *TheNews* magazine while Nuhu and I were on exile, containing statements that were unkind and uncomplimentary, and perhaps even accusatory on our persons.

Some members of my group had even then suggested taking legal action, but on consulting Dr. Mahmud Tukur and Abba Kyari – both people I respect and who remain very close to both Buhari, I quashed the idea as misguided. With this fresh assault, the group felt that our media team must respond, because GMB's media people seemed to relish destroying the reputation of others without regard to facts or the truth. Muyiwa Adekeye was accordingly tasked to issue a similar response which was widely published in the media.[174] This statement has been quoted by the Jonathan team repeatedly to establish my position about Buhari as if I could not change my views based on new facts, information or emerging circumstances. When circumstances led to Buhari and I having to work together, we discussed these instances of misunderstanding, appreciated that what we had in common was bigger than these incidents, and moved on in the interest of our country and have never looked back. Our team members had to come to terms with the decision of the principals – Buhari and my humble self – as if the incidents never happened.

My statement and the sensational slant given to it by the *Sun* newspaper led to the suspension of negotiations between CPC and 3G, on behalf of SNG. The visibly angry CPC team, which was ironically led by one-time 3G leader Aminu Masari, decided that my personal views, however sensationalised and 3G's must be one and the same, and discontinued further contact. Pastor Bakare saved the situation by suggesting that CPC and another development NGO he was part of – the International Centre for Reconstruction and Development (ICRD) – replaced 3G and the discussions continued.

The next few weeks were periods of intense political activities with lots of back and forth between the CPC, ACN, Labour Party and Kowa Party, to agree on some form of electoral cooperation. In the end, a cocktail of unhealthy personal ambitions, unrealistic optimism and misplaced confidence in the biometric voters' register to deliver credible elections, made it impossible to forge a common front against the PDP. By the end of October 2010, I was convinced that there was no hope of defeating the ruling party, but I was personally unwilling to continue to be even remotely associated with it. As a courtesy, I informed Obasanjo, my state governor Patrick Yakowa and my friends that I was done forever with the PDP, and did not care if the party ended up winning the next elections. I did not intend to be part of PDP's evil even if that seemed to be winning for the time being. Except for the one required for my ministerial screening documents, I had never really held a party membership card or been a registered member of any ward branch of the PDP, so there was nothing else to do other than walk away.

A few days after I had taken this decision, an old friend from our ABU days and a PDP chieftain, Ibrahim Sidi Bamalli, called and asked for a meeting with me, my chief of staff and political counsellor Balarabe Abbas Lawal. We agreed, and he came to my house with Niger Delta minister Godsday Orubebe, whose mission was to persuade me to publicly support Jonathan's presidential aspiration and join his campaign organisation. He thought it was necessary for 'credible northerners' that were agnostic towards zoning as matters of principle to support his boss, in light of the increasingly effective voice of the Northern Political Leaders' Forum led by Mallam Adamu Ciroma. I responded that even though I had voiced my opposition to zoning as a parameter in leadership selection, I also believed that merit must then supplant it. I was clear in my view that Jonathan had not shown enough leadership in political and economic matters to earn any public support. I gave Orubebe the history of my friendship with Jonathan to make the point that no one needed to be an intermediary between us. If Jonathan wanted to talk to me, he knew how to reach me through our mutual friend Hassan Tukur. As for joining the Jonathan campaign organisation, I explained that I had left the PDP and will never ever have anything to do with the party. Orubebe asked me what can be done about the Federal Government's charges in court against me, and I told him to leave it to the Federal High Court to decide, and added that I would not accept any withdrawal of charges. He concluded by saying he would not give up trying to woo me 'back to the fold' and asked that we meet again.

Subsequently, we met twice more and then had an audience with Jonathan on the same subjects. My position never changed, but as a friend, Jonathan asked for my honest views out of the quagmire he created by denying the existence of the zoning provisions that were clearly entrenched in section 7(1)(c) of the constitution of the PDP. I promised to write up my honest views and suggestions as to how he can begin to repair the damage he had wrought on the party and the sensibilities of many Nigerians. On 8th December 2010, I sent him a three page note which began with this introductory paragraph which addressed head-on, the observed parochial mindset of Jonathan and his inner circle :

> President Goodluck Jonathan's aspiration to be re-elected is in danger. Indeed, his chances of winning the nomination of his party, the PDP are low and at risk. And this has nothing to do with other Nigerians being unwilling to accept his candidacy. It also has little or nothing to do with 'Northerners' opposing his aspiration because he is from the 'South'. Indeed, Jonathan came into office enjoying overwhelming sympathy and goodwill of Nigerians, from every part of the country. Furthermore, it was 'Northern' leaders like Generals Abdulsalami Abubakar, Buhari and Yakubu Gowon that played leading initiative roles in defeating the so-called "northern" Yar'Adua

cabal earlier in the year to enable him move into real leadership. This current sorry state of affairs has more to do with political mismanagement and incompetent response to unfolding events.

I was then very blunt in pointing out where Jonathan and his team destroyed the goodwill they enjoyed in February 2010, and made suggestions that he took tough decisions and specific actions, with some deep thought and humility to unite his party and Nigerians behind any presidential aspiration rather than his preferred partners – the state governors, Obasanjo and other PDP godfathers. I knew that the memo will end further communication with me, and trigger subsequent harassment by Jonathan and his guys, since they were not used to being addressed in the very clear and frank manner that I did – and I knew it will come across as 'arrogant and disrespectful'. I did not see or hear from either Jonathan or Orubebe until November 2011 when I lost my daughter.

Yar'Adua administration's politically-motivated charges against me quashed

Meanwhile on October 20th, Justice Adamu Bello of the Federal High Court sitting in Abuja, quashed the politically-motivated charges that the Yar'Adua administration had filed against me in 2009. The kernel of the charges was that I approved the allocation of a plot of land in Abuja to each of my two wives – and that exercise of ministerial power or discretion amounted to abuse of office because I had "conferred corrupt benefit" on my spouses. The fact that every Nigerian adult is entitled under the laws, rules and regulations to an Abuja plot was immaterial to Yar'Adua, Aondoakaa and Farida Waziri. It was simply a "gotcha" charge to nail me, and was filed under a law that the government's prosecution lawyer admitted in writing as having been repealed. Even if the law remained valid, the charges were filed in the wrong court – the Federal High Court instead of the High Court of the FCT. The judge had no choice but to quash the charges and discharge me and my two co-accused persons.[175]

Some days later, on 29th October to be precise, I was invited along to another electoral alliance conference at the Abuja Sheraton, with heavyweights like Chief Lateef Jakande, former Governor Bukar Abba Ibrahim, Dr. Pat Utomi, Shitta-Bey, and several others at the high table. There were lots of speeches and expressions of commitment to unite against the ruling party, but, like other efforts, translating that into concrete actions and a unified political platform became a mirage. I left the conference to attend a pre-scheduled event, but the media reports wrongly claimed I walked out in anger.

November-December 2010: Alliance Discussions Intensified, then Collapsed

While these were ongoing, discussions with CPC, Labour and Kowa Party continued to unify them around a common platform. CPC and ACN were in discussions as well and it looked like a Buhari-Tinubu ticket, or Raji Fashola or Niyi Adebayo as possible running mates to Buhari. All kinds of political manoeuvrings were in the air in Lagos, Kaduna, Abuja and Minna. Rumours of all kind were in the air, and the Northern Political Leaders Forum had decided on its 'Northern Consensus' aspirant – former Vice President Atiku Abubakar. There were rumours that Atiku's huge financial war chest, legendary political network and deep roots in the PDP would enable him to defeat Jonathan and his godfathers – Obasanjo and the twenty eight PDP state governors. The Electoral Act[176]

had specified that presidential primaries would take place in respective states, and this would have ensured Jonathan's defeat. In a first show of impunity that would characterise Jonathan's utter disregard for extant laws and rules, the law was amended virtually overnight to have the primaries in Abuja.[192] And that amendment, coupled with alteration of names of delegates and alleged cash payments of seven thousand dollars to each delegate against Atiku's three thousand, and intimidation by state governors combined to give Jonathan a landslide victory over Atiku in the PDP primaries.

Former President Obasanjo came to Abuja and sent for me. He took me into his bedroom in the presidential suite of the Hilton Hotel for what he said were very important discussions. He appealed to me to support Jonathan for president. I responded that since I had left the PDP, the value of my support was zero. When Obasanjo insisted on what he called non-partisan expression of public support, I explained giving reasons why I could not support Jonathan even if I had been in the PDP then. Obasanjo did not disagree with me that Jonathan was personally ill-prepared and incapable of shouldering the burdens of the presidency and taking Nigeria as his constituency rather than his very narrow Ijaw mindset. I did not agree with Obasanjo that 'good people' around Jonathan could help him address those fundamental and personal inadequacies. I added that the last six to eight months have shown Jonathan only knew how to squander our national savings and borrow more to spend for zero results. I then made it clear that he would be on his own in this 'Jonathan for president' matter.

By mid-November, I was convinced that the opposition parties would never unite against the common threat to Nigeria's democracy and development – what I called in Jos the governors' dictatorship party – the PDP. I decided to terminate further active involvement in politics and focus on my personal, professional and family life. I revived work on setting up the policy think tank I have always wished to pursue. I persuaded Dr. Omano Edigheji, who ran the ANC think tank in South Africa, to help out in the set up and establishment of the global knowledge network to make the think tank successful.

On a personal level, I decided to marry a lovely woman I had been dating from my days in exile – Aisha Garba Haliru. I met her while still in the cabinet, but did not maintain any further contact. Ummi, as she is better known, had been in contact with me while I was going through my Mason fellowship at Harvard. She was sympathetic to my travails and called regularly to counsel and did everything to uplift my spirits. I was convinced that the care and concern she showed for me would add value to my family life. Some of my family, friends and children were unhappy with what appeared to be a sudden decision, but it was not that sudden. I had thought it through over a three year period before deciding. I therefore craved for the understanding and support of my family and friends, and we tied the knot in November 2011 in a very quiet ceremony in Abuja.

With these decisions taken and implemented, I refocused efforts at doing some writing and travelling to African countries where I have some contacts to explore business opportunities. In short, I began pursuing a new roadmap in which politics was a side show, an incidental activity, and not something that would take a lot of my time. I would never have guessed at the time how the next twelve months were going to be, but all my assumptions went out of the window on Remembrance Day - January 15th, 2011.

January 2011: ACN confirmed Nuhu, Bakare became Buhari's Running Mate

In January we all witnessed the conclusion of the primaries of the political parties, and I was under increasing pressure from our SNG colleagues to contest the presidency under the platform of the Labour Party (with or without Kowa Party). My 3G colleagues and the Abuja group agreed with me that the civil society leadership of SNG were getting it completely wrong. Civil society activists go into politics to make a statement. Politicians contest elections to win, acquire political power and use it for good (or sometimes for bad). I intended to be more of a politician and less of an activist. The reasoning, which my 3G colleagues concurred with, was simple and based on answers to basic questions. Why should anyone jump into a race that one had not really thought about? Should one contest an election knowing that one would lose just to make a point? Was it sensible to contest just because there was a free presidential ticket on the table, without the intellectual, emotional and resource preparation? Is there anything like a free ticket to contest a presidential election in Nigeria? And with my friend Nuhu in the race, what value could we add that could not be achieved by changing our minds, and joining and strengthening his campaign? The answers to all the questions were 'NO'. In the end, I wriggled out of the situation without upsetting the SNG leadership by giving them 'conditions precedent' that I knew they could not meet – related to mobilisation and fundraising, and then only if Nuhu was unable to secure the ACN ticket – a near impossibility in my assessment! By mid-January, I had reverted to my October -end condition and become a free Nasir. My inner circle of political collaborators - Pastor Tunde Bakare, Jimi Lawal, Balarabe Abbas Lawal, Husaini Dikko, Idris Othman and Tijjani

Abdullahi, were either depressed or relieved. Depressed because it seemed that the main opposition parties (ACN, CPC, ANPP and Labour) coming together to confront the PDP had become an impossibility, but relieved because we all knew we had tried our best to form a unified, patriotic platform and failed not due to selfishness or lack of effort. I recalled that Pastor and Jimi said we could now move on with our lives, and I responded that we should wait for the next 24 hours before concluding that it was over. My instincts were that something would happen that may yet change our political and personal situation.

On 15th January, Pastor Bakare received a surprising and unexpected call from Buhari asking him to be his running mate. Pastor rejected the offer right away, whereupon Buhari asked him to think about it and then call him later in the day. At that point I later learnt that Bakare called me, Jimi Lawal, Oby Ezekwesili, Ngozi Okonjo-Iweala, and Asiwaju Bola Tinubu among others, to inform us all of the offer and requested for our views and counsel. I told Pastor right away that he had no choice but to accept the challenge. I reminded him that it would be hypocritical of him to decline the offer when a few weeks earlier he was advising me and others to contest, or suggesting that Buhari should pick Ngozi or Oby as his running mate. In the end, we went to my house in Kaduna late in January 2011, prayed for God's guidance and thereafter a pensive Pastor Bakare met with Buhari and accepted the offer, on condition that Jimi and I would be on his side throughout the process. I reminded Pastor Bakare that Buhari and I still had some unresolved issues, but undertook to support Pastor Bakare and the ticket the best way I could.

The next few days and weeks were busy as we took over the debate and re-drafting of the CPC manifesto, campaign planning and fundraising because Buhari took the unusual decision of appointing Bakare to be the chairman of the Presidential Campaign Council. Bakare's selection as running mate and, by implication, the invitation of our group to the CPC met the stiff resistance of Buhari's inner circle, who felt both slighted and affronted that he picked Bakare over and above their preferred candidates and was vesting so much responsibility in the Bakare group.[177]

We soldiered on nevertheless and were active in the campaign nationwide. I joined the campaign train from Lagos on 15th of

March, 2011 and visited most of the south-west states with Pastor Bakare, reached out to financial donors, and delivered whatever we could muster to the party. We reached out to old friends and compatriots all over the country to support the Buhari-Bakare ticket as the best opportunity to change the nation's governance trajectory. In between these efforts though, many other interesting things occurred. The rest of the story of how a small group within the CPC leadership took capricious decisions that cost the party dearly in Kano, Katsina, Bauchi, Niger, Kaduna, Kebbi, Gombe and Taraba States is best told by the those more closely involved in the party and the campaign, some day. We supported Pastor Bakare to do the best we could as late-arrivals to the organisation and its structures and processes.

Obasanjo Makes an Interesting Move

The period between 15th January and the deadline for submission of nominations by political parties to INEC had its own version of intrigues. Pastor Bakare had not immediately accepted the offer to be running mate, but the media was awash with speculations that Buhari had chosen him. On 25th January, I was summoned by former President Obasanjo to his hotel room at the Hilton for reasons he said were both urgent and important. On arrival, I exchanged pleasantries with Steven Oronsaye and Akin Osuntokun in the living room and we went straight into his bedroom.

After greetings, Obasanjo asked if I was still in touch with Buhari. I replied that I was not directly but could reach him anytime I wished. He then asked that I resumed my role of emissary between the two of them and wished to know quickly if I could reach Buhari with a message. I responded that I could do so pretty quickly. Obasanjo then said that he concurred with my earlier belief that Jonathan would not make a competent president and that the best presidential candidate of the whole lot was Buhari. He expressed willingness to support Buhari and go public with it if CPC and Buhari are willing to consider his suggestions and implement them. Obasanjo suggested that I should convince Buhari to pick Ngozi as his running mate, enter immediately into an alliance with the ACN and ANPP, and then offer the Senate President's position to the South-West to secure Tinubu's support.

If Buhari agreed to these proposals, Obasanjo undertook to get three or four unnamed wealthy people to help with funding the CPC campaign, and Obasanjo would try bringing Labour Party to endorse the Buhari-Ngozi ticket. Obasanjo promised to resign from the chairmanship of the Board of Trustees of the PDP and announce his support for the ticket if it would be helpful. I took notes on the hotel notepaper and left, promising to report back the next day.

It was fortuitous that both Buhari and Pastor Bakare were in Abuja, so along with Pastor Bakare we met Buhari and delivered Obasanjo's message. Bakare, who until then was a reluctant running mate, saw the Obasanjo offer as good for CPC and Buhari, and hoped it would free him from the burden that Buhari had imposed on him. He added that since Buhari had not yet officially announced his name as running mate, he would be happy to step aside for Ngozi. I was simply an emissary so I was silent, hoping that Buhari would accept so I would be free of my commitment to be at Bakare's side! Buhari smiled and asked for my opinion as someone that knew Obasanjo pretty well. I told both of them that I thought Obasanjo was being honest in his recommendations as I would urge Buhari to take similar steps of merger with other parties and so on. I doubted if Obasanjo would deliver on the monies promised and the resignation from the PDP Board of Trustees, and did not even think the latter would help the CPC and GMB in anyway. I also added that Obasanjo's faction of the Ogun PDP had just lost all their tickets to contest the next elections and should this situation change, Obasanjo would renege on everything he had committed to. Obasanjo may also be making another strategic move of removing Bakare's name from the ticket, in addition to responding to Jonathan's failure to ensure that his faction got the ticket by hook or crook – something Jonathan simply refused to do, preferring to support the state governor, Gbenga Daniel and his faction.

Buhari restated that he thought long and hard before deciding on Bakare and would not change his mind. However, we all agreed to continue to engage Obasanjo and encourage contacts with Ngozi, while pushing to see real movement towards the financial and other political commitments made. The same evening I returned to Obasanjo to brief him. He was excited and promised to contact Ngozi,[178]

Labour Party, the ANPP leadership and a few wealthy benefactors.

February 2011: Obasanjo's Wild Goose Chase Ends in Abeokuta

Some days later, on 1st February, I got a call from Professor Julius Ihonvbere requesting a meeting to follow up on my discussions with Obasanjo on Buhari. We met in the 3G offices on 2nd February with Julius and Festus Odimegwu on the same subject. We exchanged information and updates on the political situation and ended with the question posed by Obasanjo to me, and then to Julius and Festus – "How do we stop Jonathan from getting elected, and thereby saving the country from state failure?" We discussed various steps, but unanimously recognised that Obasanjo would abandon the plan as soon as his temporary disagreement with the Jonathan administration was resolved. Since we believed in what we were doing, we agreed to soldier on under whatever scenario.

On 7th February, we all travelled to Abeokuta to meet with Obasanjo. Odimegwu and Julius had developed a clear roadmap about remedying the weaknesses in Buhari's organisation and campaign for Obasanjo to play his lead role in the anti-Jonathan effort. By then, a weird Federal High Court ruling had restored the tickets of Iyabo Obasanjo and other members of their faction in Ogun State. So true to form, Obasanjo simply back-tracked, rejected the roadmap he had asked us to prepare, and said we should now explore ways of "remedying Jonathan's weaknesses" and supporting his candidature. His commitments to Buhari vanished that day, just as we all predicted on 25th January. It was a very depressing drive late at night to Lagos for the five of us – Professor Julius Ihonvbere, Festus Odimegwu, and Professor George Obiozor with Otunba Akingboye driving. We lamented Obasanjo's consistency in putting his personal interest before that of the nation and agreed that never again will he get another opportunity to waste our time the way he just did.

We spent most of February 2011 getting the manifesto of the CPC drafted, debated and approved. Jimi Lawal did most of the initial drafting with the input of Suleiman Adamu, Professor Olivet Jagusah, Professor Okunnu, Lanre Tejuosho and Dr. Anthony Kila.

Nuhu had sent me his draft manifesto for comments as an email attachment. I printed it and sent it back with handwritten comments. Jonathan and the PDP neither prepared nor published a manifesto. Only the CPC had a proper manifesto[179] with clear policies, programmes and timelines for implementation. Unfortunately, the elections were not decided on that basis.

March 2011: Meeting Ibori in Dubai Jail and Speech at Chatham House

Early in March, I went to Dubai for a short break, and to write a bit. Former Delta State governor James Ibori had been in the custody of the Dubai Police since the 12th of May 2010 and I had quietly made a mental note to locate and visit him sometime. As I had planned to be in Dubai for about ten days, I decided this was sufficient time to try seeing James. This happened twice, on the 7th and 14th of March. We chatted about the past and the present, and how and why his circumstances changed overnight in Nigeria. James also threw some light on why Umaru Yar'Adua and his group went after me, confirming much of what Mike Aondoakaa shared with me in August 2010.

The Royal Institute of International Affairs, the world famous think tank better known as Chatham House, invited me to speak on Nigeria's democracy and prospects of the 2011 elections.[180] The presentation focused on the risks and opportunities the country faced at the time, but I made the flawed assumption that a biometric and accurate voters' register existed and that Jega and his staff in INEC were truly committed to conducting decent elections. I was confident then that it was unlikely for Jonathan to win the presidential election in the first ballot; that electoral fraudsters will be exposed in the tribunals using the biometric register and ballots as foundational evidence; and violence was likely to result if the elections ended up being manipulated or rigged as we witnessed in many states in 2007! I was wrong on the first two, but was sadly vindicated on the third when at least twelve states recorded outbreaks of avoidable violence – wanton killings, widespread arson and targeted attacks on political leaders, traditional rulers and marabouts suspected of being sympathetic to the PDP.

I returned from Chatham House to join the campaign actively starting with Lagos, and then moving through virtually all the states of the south-west. We travelled to Jos with Pastor Bakare to reach out to voters in that state after Buhari's successful campaign visit. Pastor and Jimi held meetings with electoral aspirants from Katsina and Kano to try resolving the crisis that arose from inconclusive or multiple primaries in these states. Bauchi was another state where the confusion over who was the legitimate candidate of the party for the governorship election was being addressed all through March. In the end, these acts of omission or commission led to the confusion that may have contributed to the CPC's loss of the governorships of Katsina, Kano, Bauchi, Kebbi, Kaduna, Taraba and Niger States to the PDP.

April 2011: Elections and Post-Election Violence

We went into the general election with the optimism that it would be much freer and fairer than past elections due to the confidence we all had in Professor Attahiru Jega and his team of INEC national commissioners. In the event of fraudulent elections, we relied on the availability of thumb-printed ballot papers for digital matching to the biometric register of voters to expose any corruption of the election process. When the first round of elections for legislative offices started on 2nd April, CPC virtually led in all constituencies in the north. It was going to be a landslide sweep amounting to near-control of most of the seats in the two houses of the national assembly. If that election had been concluded, CPC and ACN would have taken more than two-thirds of the House and Senate. The election was aborted and the partial results, made available by INEC to Jonathan and the PDP to the exclusion of other parties, sent shockwaves to those in power. Jega's decision to reschedule the elections gave the PDP adequate warning and time to re-arm and implement a desperate election rigging strategy. The first step was to militarise most of the states where CPC was likely to win landslide victories. The second was to send huge sums of money – three billion naira election 'gift' to each state governor in Nigeria of whatever party - to ensure that all agents of the state were adequately paid to look the other way. Third was to restrict general movement the night before elections and on the day of the election so that government agents and the security agencies could move around freely while everyone was grounded, and rig the elections without any challenges by the ordinary citizens – and all of these restrictions have no basis in any law and clearly violated the constitutional right of movement, association and assembly. The rest is now history that is better told by others.

The last-ditch efforts by the CPC and ACN to negotiate an electoral alliance also failed, thus giving the PDP free reign to rig the elections not only in parts of the north (to get Jonathan 25% of the total votes cast all costs), but even in the more difficult south-west where the ACN virtually abandoned its candidate, Nuhu Ribadu, in favor of allowing the PDP to win![181] Once again, the story of the failed attempt at an alliance is better told by those more closely involved in the negotiations. I just got to know about it only in the last two days of the process when Pastor Bakare came to my house around 11pm to let me know that he had just left Buhari and they have agreed that if we won the election, Pastor would resign as VP within three months to give way for an ACN nominee for the position, as the party's sacrifice to enable the ACN/CPC alliance come into effect. Pastor Bakare who had always been a reluctant running mate, had no issues with that, and we agreed to meet early in the morning to draft a carefully worded letter that would be acceptable to both the CPC and ACN. The letter was to be ready for a meeting fixed for 10 am the next day.

The wordings of the letter needed careful drafting because if Bakare signed the letter as Vice President (before being elected) it would constitute some legal violation and so on. By 8am, we had a suitable draft ready and GMB came to Pastor's hotel room in person about 9 am, collected three signed copies and handed Pastor ACN's draft alliance agreement and their preferred wordings of the "resignation" letter. The two drafts were referred to ACN and CPC's lawyers and negotiators to discuss and agree. The chairman of the ACN, national leader Asiwaju Bola Tinubu, governors Fashola, Aregbesola, Oshiomhole and Fayemi, among others, were in Abuja to conclude the alliance. CPC's team consisted of Sule Y. Hamma, Chairman Tony Momoh, Engineer Ife Oyedele and CPC national secretary Buba Galadima. Behind the scenes were General Ibrahim Babangida, Atiku Abubakar and Aliyu Mohammed Gusau, acting as interlocutors and honest brokers to nudge both sides to a deal. GMB took a back seat, and Pastor Bakare was not at the negotiating table. None of us was involved until the talks had broken down – largely on the exact wordings of the "resignation" letter, the leakage of the details to several newspapers by PDP agents in both the ACN and CPC that wanted the prospective deal scuttled, and late delivery of Bakare's letter to the ACN. Buhari and Bakare were both incensed by the leakage, and it raised GMB's suspicions about the intentions of both the ACN and the team of interlocutors. It never occurred to any of us that our guys may have been the source of the leak as well.

It was about 3pm in the afternoon of that fateful Wednesday that Sarki Abba, Buhari's loyal, trusted and reliable personal assistant came to Pastor Bakare's hotel room and asked to see me alone. He told me that the alliance being negotiated was about to collapse and GMB had become quite upset by the turn of events and no longer cared if it did. He implored me to see him right away and intervene to bring things back on track. I drove straight to the house in Asokoro that was rented for Buhari and sought to speak to him. We spoke for about an hour after which he was convinced that the alliance talks must be concluded at whatever cost, called up Sule Hamma who was leader of the delegation and instructed him accordingly. I left and immediately called the Oba of Lagos, Rilwan Akiolu, requesting his intervention to get Tinubu and his team back on the negotiating table. He directed me to see Tinubu and talk to him in Abuja, while promising to call Asiwaju and put him on notice. I placed similar calls to my father and one of the most respected traditional rulers in Nigeria, the Awujale of Ijebuland, and sought his assistance as well. I called two other friends with links to Tinubu and the ACN leadership and got their tacit support to bring pressure to bear on Tinubu and the leadership to do a deal. I guaranteed all these people that Buhari has assured me that he wanted the deal and will honour every commitment, written or unwritten, that would arise from the deal. I further assured everyone that as one of the closest people to Bakare, I guaranteed that he was willing to do whatever was needed as long as he is not required to break the law or his professional calling as an evangelical pastor. I then went to Lagos House in Asokoro to meet with ACN leader, Asiwaju Bola Tinubu. We talked for two hours and he briefed me on the circumstances that compelled him to seek for an alliance in the first place after several failed efforts to merge with the CPC earlier in the year. He dispelled the stories going round about his vice-presidential aspiration as the deal-breaker in the negotiations. He agreed that the alliance was necessary to save Nigeria from imminent collapse in the hands of Jonathan and the PDP, but regretted that the ACN team had already left for Lagos, feeling angry and slighted that once again, Buhari and CPC had failed to fulfill their promise to table an acceptable resignation letter by 2pm that day. He informed me that ACN had already addressed the media, informing supporters that the talks had failed. He asked why Buhari refused to lead the negotiations, or have me included in the team. He thought that if we were there and proffered the reasons I passionately made before him, the alliance may have been consummated.

I appealed to him to get the ACN leadership to reconsider the position taken, but he felt it was too late. With only two days to the presidential elections, he thought the voters would be further confused by any last-minute alliance announcement. I did not buy that, but seeing that his mind and that of the ACN was made up, I left depressed about the outcome of the elections and what it could mean for Nigeria's future. The Asiwaju left one opening though – he felt that based on the election results it would appear that there would be a run-off since he felt it was unlikely for Jonathan to win the plurality of votes on the first ballot. He therefore suggested that we resume our conversation immediately after the first round of the presidential elections. There was nothing to report to Buhari and Bakare that evening. I just went home, stayed in and tried to have an early night. It was one of the worst days of my life in recent times. The rest of course is history. My hope is that those more deeply involved in the failed negotiations will document the experience and throw more light on what went wrong so that we can all be better informed, and learn for the future.

Just before the elections, I had been invited by the Atlantic Council, a Washington DC think tank, to speak on the outcome of the elections. The event was organised on the mistaken belief of the Americans that Goodluck Jonathan was going to win the election fair and square and the seminar was expected to be merely celebratory, congratulating Nigeria and INEC for conducting clean elections. I did not know if there was any agenda and did not care, as we agreed, Buhari, Bakare and my humble self, that I should attend. I accepted to speak but informed the person through whom I was invited me, former US Ambassador Robin Sanders that I did not have a valid US visa. She intervened to have one issued.

I left the morning after we had all cast our votes in the presidential elections and the results were being released. It was the early morning BA flight from Abuja and I found myself seated next to a leading PDP apparatchik from my home state of Kaduna. After we exchanged pleasantries, he informed me of riots in Kaduna, with homes of PDP leaders and the palace of the Emir of Zazzau in Zaria, surrounded by angry youths. I had no clue at all that by then, these riots had broken out in several states. He admitted to me that they expected something like this happening in Kaduna, and the VP Namadi Sambo and many of his inner circle had left the city after voting, with their prized possessions – family members, the SUVs and other valuables. I was dumbfounded and asked him why. He confessed that they had added about 800,000 votes to Jonathan's real votes so that he could get at least 25% of the total votes cast. According to him, they did this because VP Namadi Sambo was determined not to be disgraced in his home state. Later, I found this pattern all through the northern states and this misconduct became the remote cause of youth anger and this was expressed through the spontaneous riots in at least twelve states. At the time, I did not realise how bad and widespread it was. My prediction at Chatham House in March 2011 had eerily come to pass in a way that no one realised. I had written then that:

> "If the 2011 elections turn out to be as flawed as those of 2003 or 2007, I do not think the opposition candidates have sufficient confidence in the Judiciary to take their complaints to the Courts. In fact one of them has publicly declared that he would not. In that case, the discontent will spread to the streets of the major urban centres. I predict massive protests in various parts of the country, as we have witnessed recently in Cote D'Ivoire and some countries in North Africa and the Middle East, until those that steal the elections vacate office."[182]

I slept on the flight and arrived at Heathrow with only one hour to make my connection to Washington. As soon as I switched on my phones, my Etisalat Dubai phone was ringing incessantly, while on the Heathrow transit train. It showed a blocked number so I thought I did not need to pick the call. After seven call attempts, I reluctantly answered to hear a clearly agitated Obasanjo on the line. "Where are you?" he asked in his standard line from my ministerial days. I said London. He then requested me to contact Buhari right away and tell him to come on national TV and radio to appeal to his supporters to stop rioting. Obasanjo told me that twelve states were on fire, and the north was in turmoil. All the governors had gone into hiding, many of the traditional rulers were holed up in their surrounded palaces, and President Jonathan and his security agencies were taken aback by the spontaneous response to the announcement that afternoon of Jonathan as the winner of the election. I told Obasanjo that I was en route Washington, had one hour to catch my connection but would try to reach Buhari. I told Obasanjo that I did not think it was Buhari's supporters doing the damage but a sense of general outrage at the blatant faking of results that occurred during the elections.

I called Buhari and passed on Obasanjo's message. He expressed sadness at what was going on, and agreed with the need for it to stop. But he prophetically warned that if he came out to appeal to the rioters, and the rioting somehow stopped, he or the CPC would be blamed for the whole unfortunate event. I noted his concern, but asked him to consider doing so along with other national leaders, just to save innocent lives and property. I called back Obasanjo and relayed Buhari's concern and told him that he would reflect and decide what to do. Obasanjo insisted that I should not get on the flight unless Buhari spoke, but I told him that I would not miss my connection for that reason. I felt I had done all I could. I switched off my phones, got on my flight and was incommunicado for the next eight hours. In the end, Generals Gowon and T Y Danjuma joined in appealing to Buhari to speak, which he did. Unfortunately, as he predicted, Jonathan and the media he had under his wings sought to blame everything on Buhari and the CPC, completely ignoring the blatant malpractices[183] that led to the violence in the first place. Jonathan even set up a commission of inquiry and tried to influence the outcome in that predetermined direction but failed. This kind of conduct was to emerge as a behavioural pattern of the Jonathan administration: create an avoidable crisis, run for cover while the crisis festers, beg others to help the administration out, avoid any responsibility, use money, religious or regional sentiments to procure the media to suppress the truth of what went on and then blame anyone naïve enough to help the administration out as 'the real cause' of, or the 'faceless' person(s) behind the crisis. From the post-election violence, to fuel subsidy removal protests, and the intensified Boko Haram insurgency, Jonathan and his team have continued to behave in accordance with this oft-repeated and worn-out script! It is no wonder no one - except the gullible or those greedy for governmental hand-outs or attention - offers ever to help Jonathan and his crisis-prone administration! Those who offer do so at their peril!

My speech at the Atlantic Council was an anti-climax for the Jonathan celebrants that assembled on that day to endorse the cleanliness of the elections.[184] Jonathan's aide Oronto Douglas, in a somewhat misplaced triumphalism, asserted that they had succeeded in redrawing the map of Nigeria, with a new northern boundary that included only the "Muslim" states. My speech questioned the credibility of the election, and assured the audience that the tribunal process would prove the massive rigging in many states. I thought the rigged election was a lost opportunity for Nigeria and meant every word. I cautioned against unnecessary triumphalism as that will further erode the social cohesion needed to govern decently and in peace. The Nigerian ambassador, Oronto Douglas, Reno Omokri and some of their American believers, merely suggested that we (the CPC, the north) were simply sore losers!

I returned to Nigeria immediately to review all that occurred - the elections, the violence that followed, and the contrived and sponsored script playing out in the media to place the blame on GMB and the CPC. I joined Yinka Odumakin, who was Buhari's spokesman during the campaign, and Rotimi Fashakin, the CPC's national publicity secretary, to oppose the carefully designed onslaught against our party and its leadership. I appeared on several radio programmes – both local FM stations and international – BBC Hausa Service, the VOA, Deutsche Welle and Radio France International – explaining how the elections were rigged, why there was spontaneous violence in the north and why Jonathan and PDP should be held responsible rather than the CPC and Buhari. I spoke to several newspapers, notably *ThisDay*, the *Sun*, *Vanguard*, *Leadership* and *The Nation* along the same lines. Many others spoke out, but my voice, as a former member of the PDP and minister for Abuja, stood out slightly more than the message others and I were articulating.

May 2011: Jonathan sworn in and I wrote an FT Op-Ed

In no time, I began to be referred to variously as a CPC chieftain, opposition leader and so on. Frankly, I was just angry at how everything went, and how those whose actions and inaction led to the deaths of many Nigerians, the maiming of others and destruction of property, were using the media to narrow the whole tragedy to the deaths of youth corpers in one state, Bauchi, and ignoring acts of violence and murder elsewhere whose victims didn"t exactly fit the preferred script. Yet, some gullible citizens, blinded by tribe or faith, were accepting it hook, line and sinker, without regard to any facts or logic. I felt that our common humanity required that we acknowledge and reflect upon every tragedy, and all victims.

On 29th May, Jonathan was sworn in as President. The CPC refused to congratulate him or accept the legitimacy of his election. We also declined to participate in his cake-sharing 'government of national unity', along with the ACN. We also primed our members in the legislature to collaborate closely with the ACN members to provide a bulwark against the dictatorship of the PDP. This was to prove decisive in defeating the PDP's plan to impose a south-west member as the Speaker of the House. We worked with independent-minded PDP members, the ACN and some ANPP members to support the emergence of Aminu Tambuwal as the Speaker later in June. On my part, on the 5th of May, I drafted a discussion memo to GMB and Pastor Bakare on the way forward for our party. The memo and many others were carefully studied by GMB as he thought about the next steps for the party. He had undertaken not to challenge the results of the election if he lost, but the party's NEC overrode him and decided to challenge the results. As party leaders, we insisted on this to prove the depth and breadth of the malpractices that took place. At the time, we did not know how far Jonathan and the PDP were willing to compromise the electoral and judicial institutions to preserve and protect their stolen mandate. Neither did we expect that men of integrity within those institutions would succumb so easily to be willing tools of conferring legitimacy on fraud! But that was what happened in the months to come.

I was also contacted by William Wallis, the Africa editor of the *Financial Times*, to write a short op-ed on Nigeria to be published as part of the paper's coverage of the swearing-in of Goodluck Jonathan. William, an old friend from the late 1990s wanted three points of view on Jonathan to be published – a midway view which he thought would be provided by Bismarck Rewane, a chorister's highly optimistic view provided by Atedo Peterside, and an opposite, pessimistic view of the Jonathan administration which he knew I held.

The article, which was heavily edited by the *FT*[185] to remove the political aspects I covered, was nevertheless well received. I then decided to publish the complete (and expanded) version in *ThisDay* when Atedo Peterside got his views published on that paper's back page. My piece titled "Jonathan's Tough Choices" was both so popular and outrageous at the same time that a couple of weeks later, the publisher, Nduka Obaigbena, requested that I make it a weekly column. He suggested the simple byline of *El-Rufai on Friday*[186] and I have been writing it regularly since then.

June 2011: 'El-Rufai on Friday' Debuts, GMB speaks at Chatham House

One of the pieces I wrote for "El-Rufai on Friday" was titled *"What Nigerians Pay the Federal Government."*[187] It was a cheeky title for what was a summarised analysis of the federal budget for 2011. It was an outrageous and incompetent budget by every measure and therefore an opposition party's delight. It not only showed the levels of waste in spending, but also the misplaced priorities and corruption. It related that mismanagement to the life of the average Nigerian in the most pedestrian way – that each Nigerian was paying for all that waste and corruption. Many Nigerians related to that immediately. The authorities were incensed by *"Jonathan's Tough Choices"*[188] and the subsequent one on the budget, and felt the need to deal with me. Ita Ekpenyong, the head of the SSS, made the case that El-Rufai had to be dealt with before things got out hand. But I did not know all this at the end of June when we left Nigeria to go to London with GMB and Pastor Bakare. A couple of months later, I would publish another critical piece that for the first time, opened up the federal security budget for Nigerians to see what our government was wasting in the name of security expenditure against the insecurity outcomes we had in another piece – *"Sleeping with both eyes open."*[189]

But before leaving for the UK, I was invited by Uba Sani to meet with Nuhu Ribadu and an inner circle of our friends in his house. The purpose of the meeting was to discuss all that happened between us starting from our exile years to the present, establish what went wrong and steps we both needed to take to avoid these recurring in the future. It was a soul-searching meeting during which we both learnt a lot about each other. Nuhu was bitter at my refusal to support his presidential aspiration, preferring Buhari instead, and so openly and publicly. I explained that the way and manner Nuhu pursued his ambition exhibited lack of trust in me and concern for my support. In the end, we understood each other and resolved to move forward as the friends and brothers that we have always been. I then left for the UK to meet up with Buhari and Bakare.

Our collective concern over the mischievous and flawed image of the CPC and GMB in the media persuaded us to accept another Chatham House invitation to GMB to speak at the think tank. He was initially reluctant, but agreed providing Pastor Bakare and I went to London with him and I agreed to join him to present the case of the CPC. We did, and Buhari gave a stellar performance during the question and answer session. He was as articulate as he was passionate about the country's problems and why he wept at his final campaign outing in Abuja. He made a case, both historical and factual, for the need for social justice in our country. We were all proud of him. It was the honest and patriotic Buhari we knew that came out that day in London – one that the Nigerian media had misrepresented so successfully. Many in the audience, including Jonathan's sympathizers, were blown away by his passion, patriotism and concern for the voiceless and vulnerable. Those planted to ask questions got appropriate responses from both Buhari and Bakare. I summarised the voting statistics from the "clean" April elections and showed the clear turn-out fraud and rigging particularly in the South-East and South-South states in very clear and incontrovertible ways. Our British and Nigerian audience was stunned and left the event better informed about the 'Deceitful Elections' of April 2011!

We also used the opportunity to meet with some British members of the House of Commons and the Lords. We hosted a dinner for the Nigerian Diaspora in the UK to interact with GMB at the Pearl Liang Chinese Restaurant in Paddington. Pastor Bakare and Buhari made some welcome remarks. My daughter Yasmin (now deceased) joined us and met Buhari for the first and what would turn out to be the last time. Kayode Ogundamisi and Dr. Garba Sani made passionate speeches about Nigeria's future, and Buhari's role in shaping it. Pastor Bakare made an eloquent speech that was cautiously optimistic about the country's future despite everything. We then spent a few more days after the Chatham House event to debate and discuss the future of our party and country.

We all believed that Jonathan's tenure would be a disaster, but hoped that on the whole it was going to be slow-paced, dull but largely peaceful – even with the expected massive looting and corruption. So long as Nigerians are left alone by the government to pursue their legitimate livelihoods, we could focus on rebuilding our party and hope democracy and the nation survive till the next election. But the outcome of the economic research for my weekly columns had convinced me that serious dangers lay ahead. The socio-economic data pointed to far too much poverty, inequality and waste of resources for the political and economic structure to be sustained without a change in direction. I felt that something would have to give, one way or another, though I was not sure what and when. What I did not expect was to be arrested at the Abuja Airport on my arrival from the UK!

July 2011: Arrested on arrival at Abuja, and saved by Twitter

I arrived at the Nnamdi Azikiwe International Airport, Abuja, around 5am on Saturday, 2nd July to be detained by officers of the State Security Service. I was taken to the headquarters subliminally called Yellow House, after being detained for nearly two hours at the airport. While waiting, I said my Fajr prayers, and got my BlackBerry charged. Once the ever-reliable Etisalat Dubai service came on, I tweeted that I had been detained and was being taken to the SSS HQ. I posted the same on my Facebook page and broadcast it to all my contacts via BlackBerry Messenger. The arrest and detention message went viral on all the social media platforms. Almost exactly seventeen hours later, the Nigerian authorities had to release me. My tweets immediately trended like crazy. Reuters, Associated Press, AFP, CNN, BBC World and Al-Jazeera all broke the news from the tweets, and the authorities began to receive frantic calls from within and outside Nigeria. The SSS had to issue an absurd statement saying I was arrested for writing something that was false and 'inciting' and later leaked to some selected newspapers that I would be charged for sedition. Subsequently I learnt that the Director General of the SSS, Ita Ekpenyong, got me arrested on the orders of the National Security Adviser, Andrew Owoye Azazi[190] who had cleared it with Jonathan in advance of my arrival.[191]

I later came to learn that Jonathan, Ekpenyong and Azazi had a nasty Saturday. As soon as the story of my arrest was broken by the global news outlets, they received incessant calls reminding them that they were not a military regime that could detain citizens at will; that arresting me for exercising the freedom of speech and expression protected by the Constitution was unlawful; and that the colonial era crime of 'sedition'- which the SSS was forced to admit via a statement issued that Saturday as the basis of my arrest and which they intended to charge me with- was no longer an offence in our laws as it violated the right to free speech entrenched in our Constitution. My party leader Buhari issued a very strongly-worded statement asking for my immediate release. Obasanjo was incensed. He called Azazi and Ekpenyong and told them that they had messed up big-time. He said that they just acquired an unnecessary and relentless adversary, and advised that I should be released and approached to mend fences. My friend and lawyer, Asue Ighodalo, reached Nduka Obaigbena to get to Abuja right away and get me out of detention. My friends Idris Othman, Tijjani Abdullahi and Balarabe Abbas Lawal, cut their weekends and kept vigil at the SSS headquarters until I was released. Dele Olojede called Azazi and Ita Ekpenyong to find out what was going on. Bashir Yusuf Ibrahim began reaching out to our friends and associates to organise a group response. Some other close family members and prominent friends of mine were surprisingly silent as if saying – "serves him right for daring to stand up to a sitting government." I got home around 10pm that Saturday with my lawyer, A U Mustapha, and my wife Asia, with *ThisDay* colleagues Nduka Obaigbena and Segun Adeniyi in tow.[192]

That was not the plan of Jonathan, Ekpenyong and Azazi. The SSS intended to arrest me quietly over the weekend, detain and torture me psychologically if not physically till Monday without anyone knowing about it or me having any access to lawyers, and then charge me for any trivial offence before a sufficiently-intimidated magistrate who would then remand me in prison custody with stringent bail conditions that would not be met for just a few more days. This is the *modus operandi* of the Nigeria Police and SSS which was perfected from the days of military dictatorship. That period of double incarceration then affords the authorities the time to smear the detainee some more, while he or she reflects on whether fighting on the side of the opposition was worth it. This plan was defeated - taken off the table by the availability of smartphone versions of Facebook, BlackBerry Messenger and Twitter!

Within the seventeen hours of my detention, my Twitter following increased rapidly - from about three thousand to over seven thousand, and since then has increased by at least one hundred followers every day. The SSS and Twitter made an overnight social media celebrity of El-Rufai with no effort on my part. The narrative of my time with the SSS has been widely reported by the Nigerian media and is available for anyone interested, but a few things became clear from the experience. First the Nigerian security agencies mistakenly equate national security with the protection of the narrow and personal interests of anyone in power. They have no understanding of overriding public interest or loyalty to the state. They thought and believed that Jonathan is the State, and an article insulting to him constituted an offence! Second, the senior officers I interacted with were driven more by primordial and ethnic sentiments than competence and overall national interest. One of those that interviewed me, a woman 'director' suggested that instead of writing pieces criticising the president, I should talk to "your people, Boko Haram, to stop all these killings." I simply asked, 'Are they not also your people?' and thereafter ignored similar remarks.

A few days later when I met the DG, SSS who once worked for me as state director of security at the FCT, the same sentiment surfaced, because as his justification for the arrest and illegal detention of a citizen, he asked me pointedly how I "would feel if a northerner was president and he was being attacked by south-south people"! Again, I was shocked that a national security chief, who had worked with me and ought to know that I have never in my life operated on the basis of such nonsensical sentiments, would now think, talk and act this way because he is DG, SSS under Jonathan! I knew then that the country was in greater trouble than I had estimated. I became more convinced than ever that the mindset and narrow worldviews of the key people in the Jonathan administration would manifest in deepening the divisions in the country and destroy all that some of us hold sacred. I was determined never to have anything to do with this brand of pathetic pretenders ever and further committed myself and all I have to holding them accountable for every decision and action till their last day in office, or until they change their attitude for the better and see Nigeria through more open, fair, just and inclusive eyes.

Thirdly, the Nigerian security agencies are neither updated in their knowledge of constitutional rights nor are they willing to obey the constitution and the law. The SSS has no powers of arrest. They need to obtain a warrant from a judge after showing justifiable cause to be able to arrest any citizen. So my arrest and detention were patently illegal. They also seized and kept my passport for three days in violation of the law, the Constitution and the Court of Appeal decision in the case of *Agbakoba v. The State*, which substance was upheld by the Supreme Court in *The Director of State Security v. Agbakoba*.[193] When I was informed at about 2pm that day that I was then formally under arrest, I asked to see the warrant and the lawyer quoted some secret Statutory Instrument signed by Obasanjo in 1999 granting the SSS powers of arrest as in the Police Act. I responded that no such delegated legislation could override the Constitution and I refused to say anything until I met with my lawyer. They were taken aback and shocked. Clearly they were not used to being so challenged and insisted that my "interrogation" must go on without consulting a lawyer. When I kept quiet and ignored all their questions, they succumbed and I met with my lawyer-wife Asia and A. U. Mustapha. I had intended to sue the federal government seeking a declaratory judgment for all these violations but was persuaded by my friends to drop it. We had too many cases against the government already. I let it go but there is no statute of limitation against constitutional violations, so I may pursue it someday. The thinking and practices of our officials must comply with the constitution and our laws, and this can only be achieved through serial litigation against oppressive behaviour and any kind of unconstitutional conduct.

The Last Few Months.....

Even with the financial support of El-Rufai & Partners and a few of my better-off friends, I found my liquidity in dire straits by the middle of 2011. I had to find means of supporting my immediate family, the think tank I wanted to establish and the many political activities I was engaged in. The breakdown of governance meant that from time to time, demands by relations and even complete strangers for financial assistance towards the payment of school fees, hospital charges and even purchase of grains and groceries have become common, daily personal challenges. Some years back, these kinds of demands were few and far between, but these days, the floodgates are impossible to bear conveniently. Since we are in opposition, federal (and even state) government officials are reluctant to or scared of having any business dealings with our firm, El-Rufai & Partners. The fact that levels of corruption have risen significantly since we left office, compounded by our reputation not to be part of any corruption-tainted business arrangements, has affected our corporate and personal liquidity. We were therefore forced to explore business opportunities in neighbouring African countries where my friends and I have contacts within the governments and with leaders in the business community. We also looked at consulting opportunities in East, Central and Southern Africa, using our offices in Dubai as springboard.

In November, the chairman of our party, Prince Tony Momoh, invited me to chair what came to be known as the CPC Renewal

Committee. The task given to us was to rebuild and strengthen the party's organisation, operations and processes at all levels, while preparing for upcoming governorship elections in Kogi, Adamawa, Sokoto and Cross Rivers states. I thought carefully about the assignment and accepted the challenge without any pre-conditions. The bulk of the membership was nominated by the national executive committee of the party, we added a few names of dedicated members that I know and got GMB's blessings to proceed. The assignment is ongoing as I write this, but it is clear that we would face serious internal and external challenges. Internally, self-acclaimed owners of the Buhari brand would think we intend to hijack the party and their product and would certainly attempt all kinds of political mischief and shenanigans. Externally, the ruling party would do everything to derail our efforts to rebuild and rebrand the party, including planting agents in our midst and deploying political mercenaries to distract us. I am determined that we remain focused until we deliver on our mandate sometime before the end of 2012 or in early 2013, by the grace of God.

....and Yasmin's Death.....

On 25th November, I traveled to Lagos to attend two events with my wife Aisha, Jimi, and his bride, Somi Obozuwa. Earlier in October, we had gone to Benin to begin the traditional rites for Jimi's marriage to Somi. The wedding fatiha took place in Ijebu-Ode some days after. Pastor Tunde Bakare decided to host Jimi and Somi to a wedding dinner at one of our favorite Chinese restaurants in Ikeja. We went to Lagos to attend that and participate at an annual youth event organised by Toyosi Akerele of Rise, a well-regarded young people's organisation. Pastor Bakare was a keynote speaker, and I was expected to make a few remarks as well. We attended the two events without any hitches.

The next day, 26th November, I was booked to take the British Airways flight from Lagos to London to visit my daughter, Yasmin, and her friend, Member Feese,[194] then in hospital. What I did not know until days later was that she had a massive seizure while getting dressed, slumped and died instantly in the bathroom of her apartment in Lisson Grove, London. As a child, Yasmin had been diagnosed with a mild neurological condition which unfortunately got more serious as she got older. She had been on prescription drugs to control the resultant seizures for years, and was doing quite well. Her sudden death was a great shock to all of us – particularly her mother Hadiza and I. I therefore canceled the trip to London, and went back to Abuja to receive the influx of people expected in our home on condolence visits.

For me and Hadiza, Yasmin was not just our first biological child, but was the centre, unifier and bridge builder of all the branches of our extended family. Everyone loved her – for she was kind, charming and intelligent. She was a humble child who never let the fact that her father was a visible public figure ever got to her head. I still remember the first question she asked me when I informed the children that I had been offered a public service job and wished to accept. Pointedly she asked – "Baba, does that mean my friends in school would say my father has become a thief?" Yasmin was very close to me, and everyone knew that I loved her more than my own life. She was fair to her siblings, and took the responsibility of looking after everyone else, - siblings, cousins, nephews and nieces with energy and commitment - sometimes even to her detriment. I still recall with great pride that Yasmin chose to study law after her masters' degree in political economy with the intention of pursuing a career in public service in Nigeria. She declined to consider opportunities in international development recommended by her two favourite aunties, Ngozi and Oby, because she felt Nigeria needed her skills first and much more. Yasmin is our daughter in every respect – she was completely detribalised and saw every human being as an individual worthy of respect and understanding. We were not surprised that the very first tribute published in her honour was by written Dipo Salimonu,[195] a Nigerian journalist living in London. The second was penned by Bashir Bala, then a young cadet at the Royal Military Academy, Sandhurst, who knew her and looked up to her as an elder sister.[196]

Yasmin's death brought all our old friends, ex-classmates and relations together in mourning. Dr. Angela Onwuanibe came all the way from Maryland, USA, concerned about my mental well-being and that of Hadiza and our children. Even friendships that went awry with people like my successor in FCT, Dr. Aliyu Modibbo, were repaired during the period of mourning. Pastor Chinedu Ezekwesili, Nuhu Ribadu, Femi Fani-Kayode, Shehu

Gabam and Kabir Shuaibu were by our side each and every day, from morning till night, praying and supporting us through that period of unimaginable grief. I was particularly touched by the show of affection and concern expressed by many, but particularly moved by General Buhari's attendance of prayers at the National Mosque and Yasmin's funeral at the Gwarimpa cemetery. Atiku Abubakar visited us to express his sympathies. President Jonathan called to condole, and followed up with a formal letter. VP Namadi Sambo visited in person. Several state governors, senators, representatives, ministers and prominent businessmen and women came in person in sympathy. Even one-time adversaries like Mrs. Turai Yar'Adua and Farida Waziri phoned to express their sympathies.

What can I say or write to prepare anyone for the loss of a truly loved one? One has to experience it to know the feeling. There is nothing or no one I held dear like Yasmin, and yet she is gone. What or who can hurt me anymore? What can I ever love and lose as I did with my baby – Yasmin? Till today, whenever I remember Yasmin – what she was, what she would have been – I break down emotionally and tear up. But as a Muslim brought up to submit wholly to the will of Almighty God, we are still learning to live without her, while waiting for our time to join her. I pray every day for Yasmin, and some days I wake up in the morning with thoughts of her as if she passed away the night before. In some way, Yasmin's death was both the end of a phase of my life and the beginning of another. My attitude to life, loved ones and relationships changed. Henceforth, it is hard for me to care too much about the worldly and the temporary struggles of this life. Yasmin's death had increased my faith and devotion to my religion of Islam. The rest of 2011 just moved on to end uneventfully. I remained in mourning, mostly keeping the company of my spouses and children as we came to terms with our irreplaceable loss. May Yasmin's gentle soul rest in perfect peace, Amen.

Epilogue

Paradoxes are nothing but trouble. They violate the most elementary principle of logic: Something cannot be two different things at once. Two contradictory interpretations cannot both be true. A paradox is just such an impossible situation, and political life is full of them."

– Deborah Stone in "Policy Paradox" – The Art of Political Decision making

What next? What is Nigeria's future? How do we make things right? I could offer the usual platitudes about the need to restore order, reduce insecurity, create jobs and make our economy more productive, but the fact is that that sort of discourse can be applied just about anywhere. In any case, I have written extensively about all these policy issues using various platforms on traditional and new media which require no repetition in this book. Instead, I would suggest we simply think about what Nigeria's strengths are, what make us unique to the rest of the world. As an old saying goes, 'When life gives you lemons – make lemonade.' So, what are our lemons?

Our Assets: Nigeria and Nigerians

Someone recently asked me how one could recognise a Nigerian in a crowd of Africans. My immediate response was, look for the most confident, loudest, boisterous person there, who is walking around as if he owns the place and generally behaving as if he was doing you a favour being in your country. That is the Nigerian. It is almost as if we were never colonised. In most other African countries, even today, there is a large, thriving and very visible community of Lebanese, Indians, French, and so on. In Nigeria, this is not the case – the foreigners are here, but they are not visible and cannot afford to be. They are making a lot of money, but they have to maintain a low profile. There are, quite simply, certain things about the Nigerian that makes him unwilling to take any nonsense from anyone, which makes me wonder why we are so patient with some of the corrupt and incompetent leaders we have had.

Now, why is this so? We are not rich, we are badly governed, we have failed to lead Africa – we are not the giant of Africa, but rather have turned out so far, to be the disappointment of Africa. What trumps this I think is that we are naturally a very competitive people, and this is something that is bred into us. Never mind the fact of our 160 million people or our 527 different languages negotiating constantly and daily for a piece of the pie. Before we even come to that, our culture of large families necessitates every child adapting to a Darwinian reality virtually the moment we leave the womb. Culturally, and even on a tribal basis, there has always been a lot of competition, negotiation and honing of survival techniques, even to survive within the family. This even applies to our Diaspora. We have a lot of countrymen abroad, and this is not a function of education, but of a resilience that drives people to go where the best opportunity is and make it happen. This was the case long before oil featured in an outsized way for us.

Another characteristic of the Nigerian that goes hand in hand with the competitiveness: entrepreneurship. We are natural entrepreneurs who unfortunately sometimes are led astray and if we do not acknowledge and embrace these positive traits, they can very quickly turn negative. I believe this is why one of the things that made Nigerians famous is the scam letters. People see the scam letters as some weird thing. I disagree – it is an avenue to discharge Nigerian entrepreneurship at its worst. We have young, clever people, college graduates without opportunities in their country. They have no money to go abroad. Those that could leave have left. Those that cannot – what can they do? They can't get a job; they can't compete for procurement contracts because the playing field is not level unless you know the president, a general or a minister. If lots of clever Nigerians have no opportunity, what can be done? They have to survive. When some clever Nigerian's neighbour just bought a new car from the proceeds of a fake letter sent to a gullible foreigner, it is not difficult to understand how such a shameful and dishonest activity can proliferate in no time: because it works, and there are no societal sanctions for the misconduct!

The knee-jerk reaction of the authorities at the beginning, in the mid-1980s, was to not take this seriously, but to merely view it as payback against white people for stealing from us in the past. They did not see it as something that could have a seriously negative impact on our country's image and so had no incentive to put a stop to it – after all, what's the problem with taking money from greedy foreigners who are just trying to do the same to us? The problem is that our continued failure to rally Nigerians around a unified leadership and a common vision has led to this fragmentation in which everyone is for himself, no one for the country, and the government is for no one. This is also what has led to the Area Boy phenomenon in the south-west, militancy in the Niger Delta, the misguided religious anarchism of "Boko Haram" in the north, endless cycles of violence in Jos and Kaduna, and a kidnapping problem throughout the south-east.

Perverse Incentives and their Consequences

This unfortunate misguided outgrowth of our natural entrepreneurialism is compounded by poor institutional structure, poor infrastructure and poor rule of law whereby a vicious downward cycle is created from which it is becoming more and more difficult to extricate ourselves. As a result, our country is being robbed of its potential in a significant way. Suppose we were to take a ready-made country in North America or Western Europe, where infrastructure and institutions were already up and running, we removed the locals and inserted Nigerians. What would happen? I honestly think Nigerians would not only maintain the country's stability but even improve it in dramatic ways. The successes of the Nigerian Diaspora clearly show that.

Part of the problem is that when people start from the scratch and have to act collectively, the incentives guiding them in the wrong direction can be so overwhelming that they become very difficult to overcome, and if the past number of years is anything to go by, we have not avoided them. Were we more patriotic as a people, we might have avoided them, but we are not really patriotic compared to citizens of many other nations and I think the reason for this is that we do not have any real sense of nationhood. Nigerians are very proudly Nigerian when they are outside Nigeria, and they defend Nigeria. But in general, we do not feel Nigeria as a nation has done something significant for us.

Take as an example the United States. If an American citizen is kidnapped in a foreign country, the American president will talk about it quite publicly and will promise to send the Marines, someone will call the American ambassador in that country, CNN will televise it around the clock, and the American government will do something – we have seen this happen. Now, imagine that I go to the US and get kidnapped. Do I need to finish this thought? The Nigerian embassy will just assume I was at the wrong place at the wrong time and, well, good riddance. For those who demand we change this attitude overnight, I would simply respond: like it or not, patriotism, like loyalty, is a two-way street. A country cares about its citizens and its citizens care about their country in return. The way for citizens to care is to be patriotic. If the leadership of a country does not care about its citizens, why should citizens care about the country? They cannot. We have not had many leaders who have persuaded Nigerians that the leadership and the country truly care about them.

The thing is Nigerians can also be a very discerning, observant and obedient people. When we see a person we perceive to be a true leader, an honest leader, we actually obey him, we support him and we may even be patriotic. We have had a few leaders, like General Murtala Muhammad between 1975 and 1976 and General Mohammad Buhari between 1983 and 1985, who had huge followings because they were perceived to be honest, straightforward, nationally minded people that applied rules to the big man and the small man evenly and did not care about status, religion or ethnicity. Part of the reason General Buhari is still popular with many Nigerians and part of the reason he could contest the presidency and can win is because as a military head of state, he was perceived to be tough on corruption, and tough on the big men. Every Nigerian knows what the problems are in Nigeria, and it is the big men and women who believe that rules should apply to everyone except them. The ordinary Nigerian – the common man and woman struggling to survive illiteracy, poverty and disease will line up and do the right thing under good leadership.

The Test of Leadership

This is all quite easy to talk about. But as is true of any great challenge, describing it is the easy part; actually doing it is where the real test begins. I am sure both my friends and my enemies would agree that many of the things I accomplished so far as a public servant were due to very unpopular decisions I took that caused some short-term pain for more than a few people. My friends might say it was bravery that drove me to do these things; my enemies might say it was egotism. I say it was neither – it was mostly driven by outrage and anger that my country seems not to work in spite of our many endowments, and the fact that I am not a typical politician. Among the many implications of that truth, the one I would like to focus on is that one cannot blame people for disliking a person who causes pain, and it is very difficult for a politician to not want to be liked. Maybe because I looked at my time at the BPE and FCT not as a politician, but as a short-term public servant who knew from the beginning that he would come in for a period and then get out. This is how I perceived the world and doing the right thing was far more important for me than being liked.

I know this strikes some people as arrogance, but I am really not sensitive to people not liking me. None of the hard decisions I took while in public service were done without a lot of thought, debate and widespread consultations. I met with my staff, we discussed and extensively debated all issues – nothing was off the table. Everyone was free to say anything, and part of the discussion would obviously include a consideration of who would benefit and who would lose or be hurt. It is impossible to have a situation in which nobody comes out losing something – that is the reality of public policy, that there will be a cost and a benefit and at the cost end will be people losing something or suffering some inconvenience. The key is to generally minimise those who bear some cost and maximise those who benefit. Once I aggregated all the views, I would decide which way to go, or we would vote on which way to go and then not look back. I have confidence in, and I'm a strong believer in, the wisdom of crowds. If there were ten of us in the room and nine of us agreed on a point of view, I got on with implementing the majority decision and did so with a very clear conscience.

There will always be detractors and sometimes they twist the truth into a version that suits their purposes. I ignore most of them. A few bad ones or those that have consistently defamed me, I sued, particularly when I was in government. But now, I take a dim view of them and mostly ignore them. These people cannot define me. There are newspapers that will never say anything positive about me in Nigeria, no matter what I do – the *Daily Trust* and its sister publications constitute such examples. At the other end, there are other newspapers, such as *Leadership*, which will generally depict me positively. In between these extremes, anything is possible.

I think people are discerning enough to understand this, particularly since I returned from exile. My sense, and I may be wrong, is that Nigeria is sliding toward a crossroads in which it will be more important to get things done, however painful, than to be liked. Despite the fact that I supposedly inflicted pain on people, the reality is that people still approach me and wonder why I am not running for public office – senate, governorship, even the presidency! How does this logic figure? 'El-Rufai demolished my house, I thought then that he was a wicked man, but now I know better, we need people like that to get things done without fear or favour.' – is that the thinking?

In environments like North America or Europe, where institutions are strong and things basically work, a politician must be liked to be elected. In Nigeria it seems that we are getting to a point where things are so bad that people really look around and just want someone who they know can solve their problems. Buhari's political appeal is largely for this reason.[197] In the last four or five years, my name has been mentioned several times amongst the persons that can fix our electricity problem, for example. It comes up so many times, it makes me laugh sometimes. I can only deduce that it is because my record in public service shows that I have shown the capacity to take very hard and unpopular decisions in the short term that may appear undesirable at the outset but wind up benefitting the majority of citizens over the long term, and some people have noticed.

Only time will tell whether people have drawn the same conclusion from this that I have, which is that we have a leadership problem in our country. Our positive traits, taken together with honest and transparent leadership, can be leveraged. We were very unpopular in Abuja for the first months of Obasanjo's second term, but toward the end, people began to appreciate what we were doing. Since returning to Nigeria from exile, it has become even deeper – when I walk around on the streets of Abuja, people come up to me and want to shake my hand and tell me how I have done a good job. All the positives are there, but if these positives are not properly channeled, they quickly become negatives. Nigeria has enormous potential that can be leveraged to make it a really great country, but we have not been lucky with the leadership to bring all this energy together and channel it in a positive way.

Our Bane: Too Many Critics, Too Few Doers

I came upon these words attributed to Theodore Roosevelt, the 26th US president, and they struck powerfully at how I have always seen myself. I have collected many scars during my decade in public service and its aftermath, in addition to many triumphs that I feel certain would have made proud that old man in Daudawa village, my dad, whose deathbed admonition to his little boy those many years ago have remained with me.

I see myself as a doer, even if an imperfect one – not a fence sitter, and I feel that in private and public sector careers President Roosevelt was speaking to me when he said:

> "It is not the critic who counts; not the man who points out how the strong man stumbles, or where the doer of deeds could have done them better. The credit belongs to the man who is actually in the arena, whose face is marred by dust and sweat and

blood, who strives valiantly; who errs and comes short again and again; because there is no effort without error and shortcomings; but who does actually strive to do the deed; who knows the great enthusiasm, the great devotion, who spends himself in a worthy cause, who at the best knows in the end the triumph of high achievement and who at the worst, if he fails, at least he fails while daring greatly. So that his place shall never be with those cold and timid souls who know neither victory nor defeat."

Our challenges are many, but our opportunities outstrip them. We will however have no chance of overcoming these obstacles without commitment and sacrifice from a critical mass of our people. Our country has amazing potential, and to watch these opportunities squandered each passing day I consider to be nothing less than tragic. We all know that when given the chance to help ourselves, Nigerians do it and do so enthusiastically. Perhaps we have been jaded into expecting nothing from our governments because we have had such bad governments. However, this view is necessarily a two-way street: as one friend of mine is fond of saying, 'a true democracy deserves whatever leadership it gets,' and I believe this to be the case with Nigeria. The more we choose not to care, the more we choose to opt out of politics, stay on the sidelines, or move abroad, the more we choose to resign ourselves to cynicism, the more our resignation becomes a self-fulfilling prophecy and our daily reality. The more we fail our children and their children. The more we decree a life of suffering and limitation for each child that wakes up in this land.

I hope this book has accomplished what I set out to do, which is make the case that public service should be something every serious Nigerian should consider if we are truly determined to put our country on the right track. All my working life, in both public service and the private sector, I have never sat on the fence with regard to any significant issue that affects my person, my neighbourhood, community, and my country. I have been consistent in expressing my views boldly and clearly based on the best information at my disposal at any point in time - no matter what discomforts some may have about such views, and at whatever costs they might impose on me. When superior information or better arguments convince me to change my position, I do so without hesitation, egotism or false pride. I never hang on to the illusion of yesterday's views and opinions when new information or circumstances prove them defective or outrightly wrong. I have never sought personal advantage at the expense of another person. I have never gone to bed with a grudge, because I express myself clearly and usually immediately. I wake up the next morning renewed, having forgiven the offender, and ready to start afresh again.

I have experienced the slings and arrows that come with life in the public glare, the victories and defeats that Roosevelt so eloquently described. I chose to never sit on the fence, but feel most alive when I feel the sweat on my face mix with the dust of battle, the battle for the public good. I have chosen, consciously and deliberately, to be amongst the troops who fight the battles to right public wrongs. I am fully prepared to lose some of them, but to push on and never surrender. I pray constantly for Allah to forgive my errors and strengthen my resolve to do right to everyone, including those that have hurt or offended me and those I love. The struggle to preserve a flicker of hope in every heart, and to ensure a better life for every citizen, requires many hands pushing forward together. I hope someday, and soon, some of you will join us.

Afterword

In 1978, Deng Ziaoping pronounced to a shell-shocked and demoralised China: "It doesn't matter if a cat is black or white, as long as it catches mice." With that, he unleashed the long repressed energy and single-mindedness of the Chinese people, so that in the three decades since, China has risen from abject poverty and social disarray to become arguably the second most powerful nation on earth, and still rising fast. Until the diminutive Deng and the Chinese Communist Party let their people go, China was in about as bad a place as nearly any country, having gone through more than a century of foreign domination, imperial dissolution, civil war, famine, repression, and general chaos. During Mao's famine-inducing Great Leap Forward, upwards of 45 million Chinese starved to death, and many were reduced to a desperate cannibalism. That was followed by another decade of social convulsion, the so-called Cultural Revolution from 1966 that ended only with Mao's death, in 1976. That chaotic decade saw the virtual destruction of the Chinese intelligentsia, and the final sundering of all measure of trust required to glue a functioning society.

So what has that got to do with Nasir El-Rufai?

This account of his near-decade in the inner sanctums of Nigeria's government, and the following five years in which he was pursued across the globe by his political enemies, can often make for depressing reading. This memoir has all the elements of a great Oyo tragedy: a talented but deeply flawed king blinded by hubris; his ambitious and politically adroit deputy who always carried about him a whiff of scandal; a powerful but politically naive band of reformist technocrats, determined to rebuild their country but riven by internal rivalries and the sin of unrestrained ego; a vast cast of unselfconsciously depraved courtiers and high officials with large snouts planted firmly in the imperial trough; a passive and ignorant subject people willing to put up with virtually anything— busy as they are with hanging on to the remnants of blighted lives.

For this reason, and though the narrative is also full of passages of great comedic power, as well as the inspirational accounts of almost superhuman effort in the service of the good, the inescapable sense the reader gets is of a country hurtling, eyes wide shut, towards utter failure.

It all should be rather depressing, but it thankfully isn't, for a couple of reasons.

One is that, just 30 years ago, China was in worse shape than Nigeria is today. It was far poorer, more dysfunctional, and arguably far more demoralised than anything our country is currently experiencing. And, left as we are to the tender mercies of our current political overlords, that is saying something. If the Chinese can rise from the ashes of a self-immolated country, so can we.

Which leads to the second point: The Accidental Public Servant makes clear to us that we have more than enough people who are committed, selfless and capable to lead our country to a better place. You'll find some of them in this book, women and men, high and low, who carved out areas of light in our overwhelming political darkness. Many of them are unsung, but their collective efforts gave us, from 2003 to 2006, a period of sustained and sometimes inspired government. Many of them carried within them the spark of the divine, and they showed that it is possible for us, current evidence notwithstanding, to build a country worthy of our children.

Nasir El-Rufai is to a degree chastened by his experience, but one gets the sense that this is a leader willing to bleed for the good society we all seek.

I will hazard a guess that, before too long, he will be back in the fray.

Dele Olojede
Johannesburg
Nov. 28, 2012

Endnotes

1. Chief of Staff's memo to Yar'Adua on withdrawing security guards and the explanatory memos can be found in Appendix 1 of this book.
2. This was reported inter alia by the Punch see: http://www.punchontheweb.com/Article-print2.aspx?theartic=Art20... See also Next, December 08, 2009 reported by Nicholas Ibekwe: "Police issue warrant for Ribadu, El-Rufai's arrest" - http://234next.com/csp/cms/sites/Next/Home/5493178-146/story.csp - Accessed on 11th November 2011.
3. Senate Committee hearings on the FCT (2008); the House Privatisation Committee planned hearings in 2009, but the chairman Hon. Yaro Gella fell ill and died shortly after the announcement; and the Senate Committee hearings on privatisation between 1999-2011 which took place in August 2011.
4. Examples are the Police, SSS and EFCC. The police report on NIPOST land re-allocation remains an anomaly wherein the Police was unlawfully procured to investigate a civil matter already before a court. The police report accused me of criminal breach of trust and requested the Attorney-General to prosecute. Even Aondoakaa knew that this would amount to malicious prosecution and abuse of judicial process and declined to do so. The EFCC investigated me twice under Ribadu's leadership and seven times under Farida Waziri's leadership. Some of these 'reports' are on this book's website. I was also investigated by the SSS (twice between 2003 and 2007), and the Code of Conduct Bureau once to check if I honestly declared my assets in 2008, upon leaving office in 2007!

5. Former Attorney-General Michael Aondoakaa admitted to me on November 7th, 2011, on a flight from Abuja to Addis Ababa, that the government sent a request to Interpol to list me as a "wanted criminal" on President Yar'Adua's insistence in 2009, along with the Senate Committee Report. The Interpol replied that the accusations were politically-motivated and declined to get involved in what is a "purely domestic political matter". Aondoakaa indicated that he was under the constant threat of being sacked unless he continued to mention Interpol and extradition in his public statements about me in spite of the Interpol rejection of the request of the Yar'Adua administration.

6. Aondoakaa's interviews in several newspapers, widely reported on 16th April, 2009. See for instance: http://www.ngrguardiannews.com/news/article01//indexn 2_html?pdate=160409&ptitle= Govt%20to%20 raise %20 panel %20over%20Halliburton%20scam - Accessed 16th February 2010. See also Tell Magazine No. 40, October 5, 2009 - "Nigeria - The Making of a Failed State", pp. 20-22 which stated - "El-Rufai's offence is that he was likely to be a presidential candidate in 2007 because he was close to Obasanjo." www.tellng.com

7. I have four pending lawsuits against the Federal Government or its agencies, the Senate, FCTA and the Attorney General of the Federation.

8. I have also filed a libel lawsuit against Suleiman Yahya and Rosehill, and at least two newspapers in High Court of the FCT. The suits are ongoing. I won a libel case against the Independent newspaper allegedly owned by James Ibori while still on exile in the FCT High Court. Damages of N6 million were awarded in my favour.

9. The case was thrown by the Federal High Court on October 20, 2010. The summary of the Ruling states inter alia: "The above quotation sums it all, that the charges brought against the Accused persons were without any foundation in law as the law under which the charges were brought ceased to exist since the 8th of May 2003. So the Accused persons could not have committed offences between the 13th day of December,

2003 and 14th of December 2007 under Sections 19 and 26 (1) © of the Corrupt Practices and Other Related Offences Act, 2000, that law having ceased to exist on 8th day of May, 2003. The 8 counts charge is therefore without any legal fulcrum. *Ex Nihilo Nihil fit* – from nothing, nothing comes. I hold that the charges are fundamentally defective. They were dead on arrival. No life can be breathed into them from the air of the repealed law under which they were anchored. I agree entirely with the submissions of the Learned Senior Counsel for the Accused persons that there is nothing to transfer to the appropriate Court in this case, the High Court of the Federal Capital Territory, Abuja. ...

... Consequently in view of all the facts adumbrated above, the 8 counts charge brought against the Accused persons be and is hereby quashed for lack of jurisdiction on the authority of Ikomi vs State (1986) 3 NWLR Pt (28) 340 at 342 ratio 9. The Accused persons are discharged accordingly."

The case was re-filed at the FCT High Court and it is ongoing.

10. This was early in the New Year after the holidays, sometime towards the end of January 2005.

11. In September 2004, a petition t against me was addressed to Obasanjo. It contained a plethora of allegations of wrong-doing in land administration, financial recklessness and administrative failings. My inner circle was convinced that it was the career public servants in the FCT that put together the petition. Our Villa sources informed us that the petition may have been handed over to Yayale Ahmed by Deji Omotade, my permanent secretary, who in turn hand-delivered it to Obasanjo. I never bothered to check the source and routing, and frankly did not care. The president forwarded it to me for comments and I sent a comprehensive response backed with documents to each of the allegations, many of which were simply false, and the rest the articulated mischief of civil servants. Obasanjo accepted my explanations and cleared me of all the allegations. Deji Omotade had to place stories in newspapers denying any involvement in the enterprise. See ThisDay, Sunday 17th October 2004, page 4 – "Perm Sec Denies Writing Petition Against El-Rufai", and the Tribune, Saturday 16th October 2004, p. 30 – "I Did not Plot

Against You", MFCT Perm Sec Tells El-Rufai. Both stories were based on the contents of a letter, reference MFCT/PS/2004/1041/116, dated 12th October 2004 addressed to me by Mr. Omotade. Six months later, the MFCT was dissolved by Executive Order and he was sent back to the Head of Civil Service for redeployment.

12. Sometime after this conversation, Obasanjo reconsidered this and thought of sending me on errands to the Sultan of Sokoto, President Shagari and General Muhammadu Buhari to brief them on the "state of the nation".

13. Fortuitously, the Financial Times of London had published a strongly worded editorial that morning asking Obasanjo to go, and appealing to world leaders that are his friends to encourage him to set a good example and leave. Seehttp://www.ft.com/cms/s/0/cc13086c-e477-11da-8ced-0000779e2340.html#axzz1wSfIutmA, accessed on 31st March 2012. Obasanjo had travelled, I think, to France or South Korea at the time the debate on the Third Term clause was going on in the Senate. The House of Representatives had not gone beyond preliminary consideration of the Bill at that point.

14. There is some uncertainty about my actual birth date. The date of 16th February, 1960 came from my deceased uncle, Alhaji Hamza Gidado, when registering me as a transfer student at LEA Primary School, Kawo. He swore a statutory declaration of age to that effect, and it has been part of my biographical records. Sometime in 2009, my brother, Bashir El-Rufai, found a piece of paper in our deceased father's books suggesting that I may have been born sometime in the middle of June 1959. I have maintained the "official" birth-date until further validation to justify amending all my personal biographical records.

15. The second copy of the handwritten letter of application using the Hausa traditional pen made from corn stalk, dated 1st November 1928, was found in our father's papers by Bashir El-Rufai and is reproduced in Appendix 2 (Translation included).

16. Indeed Arewa Hotels became the largest hotel management chain in Nigeria up until the 1990s.

17. Bank of the North is part of what is now known as Unity Bank PLC

18. Dr. Ahmed Gumi was my classmate in the School of Basic Studies, the pre-degree programme of Ahmadu Bello University, who joined the Army while in still medical school. He later resigned his commission and went to Saudi Arabia to study Islamic Theology. He is now a leading Islamic cleric, following his illustrious father's footsteps. Abdulkadir Gumi was a couple of years my junior in Barewa, and is now a general in the Nigerian Army and head of its legal services department.

19. The governor of Zamfara State between 1999 and 2007, Ahmad Sani, *Yeriman Bakura*, was the initiator of the Sharia movement in Nigeria, largely as a counter-force against PDP big-wigs from his state, like General Aliyu Gusau.. Amidst the poverty and income inequality raging in the North at the time, the movement became popular with the "talakawa", and within a year, 12 northern states had adopted Sharia into their criminal law. Sharia has always been part of our judicial system, but until then was only applicable to personal matters like marriage, inheritance and the like. Within two years, two women had been convicted for adultery in Zamfara and Katsina States, and sentenced to death by stoning. Both convictions were quashed on appeal largely because the evidentiary burden of proving adultery under Islamic law are nearly impossible to discharge - four independent witnesses must testify to seeing the adulterous couple in action, and no one would call another! Short of a voluntary confession, no one can be convicted of adultery under strict Islamic law. But the convictions made national and international headlines, and many lawyers made careers out of them! Within another two years, by 2004, the political sharia had lost steam. It is no longer an issue in Nigerian political and religious discourse.

20. The educational system then was 7-5-2-3, i.e. primary (7 years), secondary, up to WASC "O" Level (5 years), Higher School Certificate HSC/ "A" Level (2 years) and university

(3 years). Most people fail the HSC, and spend an extra year doing "prelim" in the university before proceeding with the degree proper. The HSC was abolished in the North and Schools of Basic and Advanced Studies were established for one or two year programmes, leading to the IJMB exams for entrance to ABU and Bayero University College, Kano. JAMB was introduced nationally in 1978 to replace the North's IJMB. The entire system was then changed to the American-style 6-3-3-4, thus abolishing 'A' levels in the late 1980s.

21. North-Central State became Kaduna State in 1975, and was split into Kaduna and Katsina States in 1987.

22. After a distinguished civil service career in education, spanning North-Central, Kaduna and Katsina States, Mallam Bello Kofar Bai retired and was appointed the chairman of the Federal Character Commission and served at the same time I was minister of the Federal Capital Territory. He died in January 2007. May his gentle soul rest in perfect peace. Amen.

23. NNDC is the New Nigeria Development Company Ltd., a development finance institution set up by the old Northern Region in the 1950s to fill the entrepreneurial and capital vacuum existing then. Under Hamza Zayyad, NNDC grew to be one of Nigeria's top conglomerates with investments in virtually every sector of the economy. It is jointly owned by the 19 northern states. I served as Joint-Secretary of two committees set up in the 1990s to restructure and revamp its operations under the chairmanship of one of its more successful CEOs, Mallam Musa Bello, OFR, a Harvard AMP alumnus, who retired as permanent secretary, Federal Ministry of Finance in 1979.

24. I left the cabinet on May 29, 2007 but was appointed to the super-ministerial National Energy Council by President Umaru Yar'Adua in September 2007. The National Energy Council was intended to be the coordinating body for energy policy and strategy, including electricity, oil, gas and renewables. Sadly, the council met only once as relations between Yar'Adua and some of us deteriorated. I resigned in

June 2008 as part of my preparations to attend the Harvard Kennedy School of Government.

25. Chief Bola Ige, then a leading opposition figure called the five parties 'the five fingers of a leprous hand.' Abacha clamped him into detention, along with my friend, Dr Usman Bugaje whose piece 'When Silence Is No Longer Golden,' is one of the best written opposition tracts of the time.

26. O. Obasanjo and A. Mabogunje (1992) – Elements of Democracy, p.133

27. According to Obasanjo, the group included Yaya Abubakar, Dr. Patrick Dele Cole, Dr. Tunji Olagunju and others I cannot now recall. This was his informal think-tank when he was Head of State between 1976 and 1979 in Lagos.

28. I suspect it was Steve Oronsaye who kept reminding him of the need to bring me into the administration. Steve and I have been close friends and he was returning a favour. Amah Iwuagwu and I intervened with Ismaila Usman to keep him in his position in the Finance Ministry after Abacha died. The civil servants resented Steve's position of influence under Abacha's finance minister, Anthony Ani, and they had served him a "quit notice" since he was not considered a "proper civil servant". Following representations by Amah and my humble self, Ismaila Usman reversed the decision and kept Steve on his team. Ironically, Steve went on to be the Principal Secretary to Obasanjo, Permanent Secretary in the Ministry of Finance and later the Head of Civil Service of the Federation under the Yar'Adua administration!

29. See Nigeria - Debt, Development and Democracy, FT Conference, May 4-5, 1999. The FT of May 6 mentioned my presentation on the proposed Nigerian privatisation programme - the first time my name appeared newsworthy in any newspaper was in a British newspaper! Antony Goldman wrote the story and it was the beginning of a long and enduring friendship.

30. A sample extract of the Weekly Briefs can be seen in Appendix 4 of this book.

31. It is normal in northern Nigerian culture to name our children after parents, grandparents, siblings and trusted friends. Many of my children were named in honour of parents, in-laws, uncles and aunts. Tijjani Abdullahi and Nuhu Ribadu named one of their sons Nasir as a tribute to our brotherhood and friendship. Peter Okocha is from Delta State but speaks fluent Hausa, Igbo and Yoruba. His three sons have Arabic (Hausa-Fulani), Yoruba and Igbo names - a mark of a true Nigerian.

32. See for instance this summary. Many Nigerian bloggers and newspapers have cited the full report. http://hsgac.senate.gov/public/index.cfm?FuseAction=Press.MajorityNews&ContentRecord_id=9a9a2e09-5056-8059-76f6-1b9eb33b29b2 accessed on March 29, 2012.

33. We drafted and published a new National Telecommunications Policy (2000) under the auspices of Communications Sector Reform Steering Committee, and hired a consortium led by Clifford Chance to draft a new Communications Bill (2001) which was presented to the National Assembly. This laid the foundations for the strengthening of the NCC to issue GSM licenses and the full deregulation of the telecommunications sector.

34. Ambassador Howard Jeter wrote a letter dated December 2, 2002 to Obasanjo, appealing he "ensures that irregularities in the early stages of the process do not unfairly prejudice (Motorola's) bid."

35. Motorola submitted a petition to President Obasanjo on the bid process dated October 17, 2002, hand-delivered by its consultant. Obasanjo directed the Minister of Communications, Dr. Bello Halliru Mohammed to ..."...look into this clinically and ensure no deviation and no corruption" on October 21, 2002. As the Siemens indictment later revealed, Obasanjo was unlikely to get any truthful responses to this directive!

36. Shortly after this incident, the BPE and the Minister of Transport, Ojo Maduekwe, had a head-on confrontation over the privatisation of Nigerdock. Like most ministers, Ojo was opposed to the divestiture and even published a disclaimer in the papers questioning BPE's authority to privatise. Both

Atiku and Obasanjo rebuked Ojo and supported BPE's decision to sell the enterprise. Ojo relied on Obasanjo's support to over-rule Atiku and the BPE, but unknown to him, by then Obasanjo was fully on our side. I was so confident of Obasanjo's support that I told the Punch – "Only Obasanjo can halt Nigerdock's privatisation" and it was reported on pages 1 and 2 of the newspaper on 24th October, 2002.

37. See the full interview titled "My mission is to build a clean, sane capital city - El-Rufai" by Martins Oloja in the Guardian of Sunday, September 7, 2003.

38. See The Guardian story of 9th September, 2003 filed by Alifa Daniel - "El-Rufai denies accusing senators of bribery" and the Punch story of same date filed by Sam Akpe - N54m bribery scandal: Senate to summon El-Rufai"

39. *The Punch*, October 13, 2003: "El-Rufai's family upholds bribery allegation".

40. The Yar'Adua-Jonathan administrations were luckier, enjoying even higher oil prices and increased levels of oil production but ended up earning and blowing over $200 billion in four years with little or nothing to show for it.

41. The White Paper titled "Reform vs. Status Quo – The Campaign against Nasir El-Rufai and the Degenreation of Progress in Nigeria" by Amsterdam and Peroff (December 2009).

42. Dr. Mansur went on to be the director general of the Debt Management Office in our time, and later minister of finance under Yar'Adua. He now represents Nigeria on the board of the World Bank as executive director.

43. Baroness Chalker remains a friend of Nigeria and Nigerian presidents. She continues to serve as chair of the Honorary Presidential Advisory Council on Investments, and is a director of Unilever among other involvements. Her consulting firm, Africa Matters, advises corporations and governments on investments in Africa.

44. The 11-slide presentation titled "Reengineering the Federal Government, 2003" undertook a situation review of 1999-2003, summarised the challenges for 2003 and beyond, listed

reengineering objectives, identified six priority actions, analysed key MDAs and reform sequencing, with a list 26 'good' men and women for consideration. Fifteen of the people ended up in the government. Two of them got elected governors, and another is now a catholic bishop!

45. Chinedu Ezekwesili was also some kind of honorary deputy chaplain of the Presidential Villa, ministering on Wednesdays, so he had a dual relationship with Obasanjo - as Oby's husband and as once-a-week pastor to Obasanjo.

46. We had Economic Management Team (EMT) meetings at 8.30am every Wednesday. The President chaired and the SGF took minutes. In addition to the 'real economic team', the ministers of Agriculture, Education, Health, Commerce and Industry, Culture & Tourism, Science and Technology and other ministers attended as needed, plus the Head of Civil Service of the Federation and some selected presidential aides. This meeting took broad policy decisions.

47. Oby's children - Chinwuba and Chinenmelum are twins and are recent graduates of two US universities. Chidera is about to enrol into his undergraduate programme in the US as well.

48. Charles's area was the macro-economy. Oby wrote the parts on governance, transparency and anti-corruption, including procurement reforms. I contributed the sections on privatisation, public enterprise reform and civil service reforms. Akin Arikawe and Mansur Mukhtar wrote the debt management sections. Bode Agusto and Steve Oronsaye covered public financial management and budget reforms. Ifueko Omoigui wrote on tax reforms. Ngozi coordinated the work and got us a mass of information from multilateral sources. Charles ended up being Mr. NEEDS!

49. Ironically, Obasanjo did not want me to be a member of the economic team. He thought that I had too much to do in FCT to have time for anything else. Indeed, the second time we were to meet with the British government in London, he recalled me to Nigeria when he learnt I was in London. At that second plenary at the Paddington Hilton Hotel in London, we considered the second draft of the Poverty Reduction Strategy Paper (PSRP) for Nigeria, and decided

we will give it our own name. Charles called it National Economic Development Strategy (NEDS). I suggested the addition of "Empowerment" so we ended up with the acronym NEEDS. It stuck! The irony of this is that both the strategy document and its name were largely conceived, written and developed in a London hotel!

50. Charles ran for governor of Anambra State on the PDP ticket and was almost certainly rigged out – a sad thing indeed, because I believe he would have governed the state much better than the person that ended up being declared the winner of the election.

51. At a meeting in July 2010 at Pastor Tunde Bakare's Ikeja residence, we debated these issues and five of us - Ngozi, Oby, Fola Adeola, Donald Duke and I thought AC was not the best platform as an alternative to PDP. Nuhu disagreed and assured us that four other opposition parties - factions of ANPP, DPP, Labour Party, APGA and AC were in discussions to adopt him as the alliance candidate and that was the way to go against the PDP. Subsequent events indicated that Nuhu was unduly optimistic about this 'alliance'. Indeed, we later gathered that no such discussions between the parties or with him were going on except with DPP.

52. These enabled me to meet with the entire top echelon – Assistant Directors and above – of the FCT over a twelve-month period. For instance, on 30th June 2004, I had an interactive dinner with Mrs. Helen Oloja, then Deputy Director – Legal, Francis Okuchukwu (Maintenance), Dr. A. M. Ahmed (Health), E. E. Volka (Finance), Umar Lawal (Admin), Francis Chogudo (Primary Education Board), J.O Fatigun (AEPB), Asma'u Usman (Education) and Engr. Obi Oduche (Engineering). I learnt a lot from them, and about them. Asma'u and Helen got promoted to full director positions before I left the FCT.

53. Kenzo Tange died in March 2005 as we were planning to celebrate 30 years of the creation of Abuja as our nation's capital. The urban design of the central area district of Abuja is listed as one of his principal design legacies. See http://en.wikipedia.org/wiki/Kenzo_Tange accessed December 30, 2011.

54. Based on the representations on the non-completion of the National Cathedral and the dilapidation of the National Mosque, President Obasanjo launched two separate fund-raising efforts for the two national monuments. The sum of N1.6 billion was raised for the National Mosque and I chaired the Technical Committee for the rehabilitation and submitted a comprehensive report in October 2004. Justice Bashir Sambo sued the government for excluding him from the committee, praying the court to compel the FGN to hand over the monies raised to Jama'atu Nasril Islam or the National Mosque Management Board. The suit was going through the courts by the time we left office.

55. See the back page of the Daily Times of Tuesday, 30th March 2004 – "Live tortoise found on el-Rufai's seat" reported by Simon Timothy.

56. The markets in Garki and Mabushi had been completed and nearing completion respectively. The other two markets had achieved remarkable progress by the time we left office. Access roads, water and sewage infrastructure were provided to their locations on a priority basis.

57. Abuja became the first African city to have citywide Wi-Fi hotspots. In return for access to tower sites allocated to Abuja Investment Compnay as the FCT's contribution to the CTAccess joint-venture, we persuaded the service-provider Suburban Telecommunications to give the service free to the people for six months, and then start charging about $1 per day for the Wifi service. It was still being built-out when we left office.

58. One of my friends from our Kaduna days, Dan Kunle, wrote me a congratulatory letter upon assumption of duties in the FCT, suggesting that the motorcycle taxis had become a problem crying for solution. I replied him promising to look into the situation. That was how the debate leading to the "okada" ban began.

59. One of the first officials to try was the Director of Development Control, Ogunmola, who within days of my resumption as minister approached me with a layout of corner shops carved out of a green area, with a list of some 'dignitaries' including

the wife of the VP. His assumption was that since I am supposed to be Atiku's boy, I would jump at approving the layout for immediate allocation. I took the layout from him to study. The next day, Atiku's wife called me to ask for a few corner shops for her cronies! I realised that the whole thing was well-coordinated and meant to test my stated resolve to 'clean up Abuja and restore the master plan.' That was the day I decided that Ogunmola would be one of the first to be disengaged from the services of the FCT administration once we settled down. Months later he was fired. He challenged the firing in a lawsuit and lost two years later.

60. The FCT Director of SSS then was Mr. Ita Ekpenyong who proposed that we advanced a modest amount of cash to investigate the incidents. I approved it without hesitation. Ekpenyong is now the DG of the SSS. On July 2nd 2011, he ordered his operatives to arrest me on arrival at the Abuja airport for writing articles critical of the Jonathan administration. According to him, my articles were aimed at inciting people against the government, and I did so simply because Jonathan was a 'southern president'! I marvelled at his transformation, and reminded him that inciting words do not constitute a crime under Nigerian law and that the Constitution protected the right to free speech, however inciting!

61. Investigations by FCT's Social Development Secretariat revealed that the orphanage received financial support from British Airways-UNICEF Change for Good programme.

62. This was gazetted as Statutory Instrument No. 15 of 2005 and titled - Child Rights (Transfer of Certain Statutory Functions) Order signed on 7th September, 2005. (See Appendix 9). It is still in FCT's statute books, and effective from 13th September, 2005

63. Bola Onagoruwa, an experienced lawyer and administrative workhorse, as at the time of writing this is the Director-General of the Bureau of Public Enterprises.

64. Under previous administrations, the Area Council chairmen were allowed to allocate 'rural land', i.e. outside the FCC,

but the landmark case of *Ona v. Atenda (Court of Appeal)* held that the whole of the FCT is federal land and an urban area, so local governments in the FCT had no jurisdiction to allocate any land, and in any case, the Minister of FCT who exercised "delegated powers" of the President in governing the FCT cannot delegate these powers to any other person or authority. All Area Council allocations were accordingly invalidated in 2002. Any such subsisting 'allocations' needed to be regularised by the FCT Minister to be valid. Sadly, this process was not completed within my tenure and the situation still remains the same.

65. In fact, I subsequently discovered that through various fictitious names and hastily-incorporated companies, successive political leaders from all over Nigeria owned a disproportionate amount of land in Abuja. It is not a violation of any rule, and officially not a problem if the plots were being developed, creating jobs and providing facilities for our citizens, but most are not. I threatened many with revocation and got some of them developed, but did not fully succeed in revoking or getting all of them developed.

66. And each case, no matter how controversial it may appear to be, based on one side of the story (including the revocation of the plots of former governor Ahmed Makarfi, the late Abubakar Rimi and others, which my successor in office mentioned in media interviews), was handled based on documented contraventions, and not on the settling of any perceived personal scores. I have never used my public position to pursue a person I am aggrieved with. I am no coward. In the unlikely event that I feel the need to settle any personal grievance, I would prefer to confront the person and settle the issue without the advantage of public office.

67. Appendix 5 contains correspondence between Senator Sodangi and the FCT administration, details of plots allocated (and revoked) with respect to some of the senators that are members of the committee, and the offers of plots and houses allocated by my successor to not only the committee but also the Senate leadership & bureaucracy to influence the outcome of the 'investigative public hearing'. As lawyers say – *'res ipsa loquitor'* – the documents speak for themselves!

68. *Functus officio*, Latin for "having performed his office," is a legal term used to describe a public official, court, governing body, statute, or other legal instrument that retains no legal authority because his or its duties and functions have been completed. The term is most commonly used by a higher court as a justification for vacating or overruling all or part of a lower court's opinion.

69. Appendix 7 contains the list of beneficiaries of the false "functus officio" plot re-allocations including Senate President David Mark, members of Senate Committee on FCT and Housing, several ministers and other officials. This went ahead despite a letter from the Secretary to the Government of the Federation debunking the lies!

70. Appendix 8 presents the attendance and the last two pages of the Conclusion of FCT EC (07) 18th meeting of the FCT Executive Committee of Tuesday 22nd May 2007 – clear evidence that I was the Minister of FCT after May 15th 2007!

71. See for instance: The Guardian of 24th November, 2008 - "Govt Recovers N46b from sale of FCT Houses" by Mathias Okwe, on www.ngrguardiannews.com/news/article03//indexn2_html?p - accessed on October 12, 2009. This was also reported by several national newspapers on the same date - including Thisday, The Punch, Leadership and Vanguard. See The Daily Independent - http://www.globe-expert.eu/quixplorer/filestorage/Interfocus/0-Societe/03-Territoires/030-Urbanisation/030-SRCNL-AllAfrica_ News_ Urban_ Issues_ and_Habitation/200811/Nigeria_ FG_Recovers_ N46b_From_Banks.html accessed on 19th March 2012

72. The correspondence between CCT, Justice Sambo and the FCT/Federal Government of Nigeria are appended, in chronological order for review by the reader. Please refer to Appendix 10 and make up your mind.

73. If we had any ulterior motives to avoid selling the house to Justice Sambo as he alleged, this simple breach of payment terms was enough to withdraw the offer and request the highest bidder to pay up and take possession. All these occurrences were lost in the cacophony of false accusations created by Justice Sambo and his sympathizers.

74. I made the statement in response to a question about the Senate Public Accounts Committee investigating the payment of accrued allowances of my two special assistants – Dr. Abdu Mukhtar and Ms Aishetu Fatima Kolo. The 'fool' referred to was the chairman, Senator Mamman Ali, who had visited my office a couple of weeks earlier to request for favours that I could not grant and had promised retribution. The Senate took the reference to one fool to mean 109 fools, and went on strike for two days, insisting that Obasanjo should fire me. He did not, instead he wrote an unprecedented apology to the Senate for whatever offence they took from my "inappropriate language'. Appendix 11 reproduces the Obasanjo 'letter of apology'. I later learnt that Obasanjo thought that I might quit if the pressure became too much. I did not intend to resign, as that would mean buckling to political blackmail and intimidation. I did not call ALL senators fools. At least two of them were former Vice Chancellors of Ahmadu Bello University, but the politics of mischief prevailed over common sense. I decided firmly that I would not submit to any sanction for what I had not said or done - their poor understanding of clichés in the English language is their problem, was my attitude. I was invited to the Senate in full session and I read a speech ending with I am sorry if you misconstrued what I said. Senator Mamman Ali went on to become the governor of Yobe State in 2007, but died of leukaemia in a Miami, Florida hospital in January 2009. I pray that his soul finds peace, Amen.

75. Alhaji Muhammad Musa Isma is the deceased father of my wife, Hadiza El-Rufai that I never got to meet. He died in an automobile accident in 1976, a few months after completion of the assignment as member of the Akinola Aguda Panel. Our family continues to pray for the repose of his gentle soul. Amen.

76. Dr. Babangida Aliyu has been the governor of neighbouring Niger State since May 29, 2007, and chairman of the Northern Governors' Forum – the regional club of governors of the nineteen northern states.

77. This show of political will by Obasanjo, and his unqualified support for the enforcement of development control

regulations in Abuja, sent a very clear message and was widely reported in the media. See *"FCT: Obasanjo Leads Demolition of Houses"* in *ThisDay*, 31st August, 2003 and *"El-Rufai Goes to War"* – Godwin Agboroko, *ThisDay*, 2nd September, 2003.

78. Those affected, whose houses were mistakenly built on trunk water lines, were former Inspector-General of Police Musliu Smith and former Chief of Defence Staff, Admiral Ibrahim Ogohi. Minister of Defence Rabiu Kwankwaso and Senator Daisy Danjuma had the fencing built on these lines removed. The proposed removals were leaked by our staff, and wrongly reported (See ThisDay, 1st September, 2003 – *"Demolition: FG Targets Retired Generals' Houses"* - ostensibly to cause problems, but everything went smoothly. All these allottees had proper titles and building plan approvals and had to be paid huge sums by way of compensation and replacement plots. Sadly, for some inexplicable reasons, the compensation payment took more than two years to settle.

79. The task force was chaired by Mr. O. S. Ogunmola, the Director of Development Control. The members were Dr. L. I. Ofoegbu (Education), Dr. M. O. Ayo (Health), Mrs. Maimuna Ajanah (Municipal Affairs), Mr. Nosa Ukponmwan (Water Board), Mr. Emmanuel Ovbiebo (Sewage), Mr. Emmanuel Chukwuocha (AEPB), Dr. Abdu Mukhtar (Special Assistant to Minister), Mr. Danjuma Ibrahim (FCT Police Command) and other staff of the Legal, Quantity Surveying and Survey & Mapping departments. The Task Force was inaugurated on 16th September, 2003.

80. The two companies we granted the right to develop the two shores of Jabi Lake into recreational and tourism facilities – Suburban Ltd and Duval Properties Ltd eventually failed to develop the facilities within the timeline we envisaged. One of our successors in office attempted to revoke the title to the land; and the matter has been in court since 2009, delaying the development even further.

81. Sadly, the transit ways are now being allocated to senior government officials to "build temporary structures", with the Nigerian hope of these then becoming permanent, and the risk that Abuja Rail system may never ever get built.

82. Two of the gas stations were in fact owned by a former minister of FCT, and were seized by the Federal Government in an asset recovery deal to avoid prosecution in 2001. This reduced our compensation payments substantially.

83. The only exception that was allowed was the naming of the Pope John Paul II Street and Close in Maitama A5 to commemorate the Pope's visit to Nigeria during the tenure of Lt.-Gen. J.T. Useni as Minister of FCT.

84. As part of my familiarisation meetings with selected former ministers of Abuja, I had a two-hour meeting with Major-General Muhammadu Gado Nasko on 24th February, 2004. He explained the rationale behind the decision to relocate the Presidential Complex from the Three-Arms Zone to a corner of Asokoro District near the National Arboretum. He also explained the basis of his ill-fated 'integration' of Garki Village, and introduction of corner shops in the Federal Capital City. He then mentioned for my intervention issues related to two farmlands in Kubwa, allocated to his company and Fresh Fruits Limited, owned by his predecessor in office, AVM Hamza Abdullahi, which had been illegally converted by MFCT/FCDA staff for residential purposes.

85. Ms Jummai Kwanashie, then Director of Development Control, chaired the committee. Other members were Kabir Maina, Jimmy Cheto, A. C. Ike, Isah Shuaibu, Hadiza Abdullahi and Tijjani Abdullahi. Messrs. A. I. Achu, B. E. Oteri and J. Agbonhense were the secretaries.

86. See page 61, ThisDay of 13th August, 2004 for Public Notice signed by Akumazi Martins, my special assistant on technical matters, effective 10th August, 2004.

87. See Page 49 of ThisDay newspaper of June 17, 2005 – 'Public Notice: Resolutions from the meeting of the Minister of FCT with Owners of Corner Shops in Abuja' – for example.

88. In my opinion, AVM Hamza Abdullahi was probably the best minister of Abuja. I therefore requested to meet with him immediately after we took office. We met at the guesthouse of a construction company on 9th September 2003. He not only gave me some of the soundest pieces of advice on administering Abuja, but a 25-page position paper titled –

"Abuja – The Way Forward" which I cherish until today. I will forever remain indebted to AVM Abdullahi for his counsel always. He did not once raise the issue of the illegal conversion of his farmland until I mentioned that I knew about it and would find a way to resolve the issues based on the realities of the time.

89. In fact, the House suspended sitting at the urging of Honourable Datti Baba Ahmed to visit Kubwa, led by no less a person than the Right Honourable Speaker of the House, Mr. Aminu Bello Masari. A motion condemning our action was passed without requesting us to brief the House on the reasons therefore, but with Obasanjo's tacit approval, we did not slow us down on our restoration of Kubwa.

90. Mr. Yahaya Yusuf, a low-key and effective manager, is currently the Director of Development Control, succeeding Mr. Isa Shuaibu that I had rapidly promoted and appointed to the position in 2005, after Mrs. Jummai Kwanashie had been made the CEO of the newly-created Abuja Metropolitan Management Agency.

91. This is a little-known criminal offence – a violation of the provisions of the Abuja Environmental Protection Board Act of 1996. Another even lesser known (and unenforced) crime is hanging clothes on balconies in Abuja!

92. Other members included my special assistant, Ms Aishetu Fatima Kolo, Mr. Bashir Haiba, Mrs O. A. Adebayo, Mr. Rabiu Usman and Ibrahim Bala. The secretaries were Salisu M. Dahiru and B. S. Ahere.

93. Charles Dorgu is an engineer by training and politician by vocation. He was appointed ES of FCDA via his political connections as one of the leaders of the PDP in Bayelsa State, and enjoyed the strong support of Obasanjo's powerful national security adviser, Lt-Gen. Aliyu Mohammed Gusau.

94. The FCT receives 1% of the Federation Account which, along with value-added tax and excess crude account, yielded about N14 billion in 2003. This constitutes the FCT's Statutory Budget. FCT's internally generated revenue was projected to be a mere N1.2 billion. In addition, like every state of the

federation, the FG budgets for projects located in the FCT, but these are payable by the Finance Ministry. In 2003, about N19 billion was budgeted for Abuja projects in the federal budget. This is referred to as the FCT's National Budget.

95. The Federal Inland Revenue Service (FIRS) collects all personal income taxes in the FCT which are then remitted to the Federation Account. We had several meetings to claw that back but were unsuccessful up to the time I left office.

96. The Committee was chaired by M. Sani Kalgo, the Director of Land Administration and Resettlement. Other members representing MFCT were Professor S. I. Abumere (Consultant), Jimmy Cheto (Engineering), Emeka Elobi (Planning & Survey), Mohammed Soso, Ben Ukpong, Abubakar Suleiman, O. Solomon, Lawan Ahmed, and U. D. Okafor as Secretary. Princess Esther Audu, J. S. Kaura, Micha Jiba and L. Z. Gaza represented the Abuja Municipal Area Council while Sapeyi of Garki, Usman Nga Kupi, Musa Barde (Galadimawa), Jacob Garki (Garki), Lazarus Nyaholo, John B. Bawa and Ishaku T. Yamawu represented the Original Inhabitant communities subject to resettlement.

97. I met Hauwa Yabani when she emailed a request to BPE for information on privatisation while researching her M.Sc thesis at the University of Warwick. She graduated and served out her NYSC year at the BPE in my office. When I moved on to the MFCT, I offered her a job as Technical Assistant, and later as Special Assistant. She is intelligent, conscientious and calm at all times. She is now General Manager of the ATV.

98. Years after I left the FCT, in early 2012, I met the owner of Sonic Global at Dubai Airport. I do not recall ever meeting him before he won the bid to be a concessionaire. He introduced himself and then told me how he was invited by the EFCC, threatened with detention unless he confessed that I was the owner of, or a shareholder in, his company. He refused and was released when Farida Waziri and her team failed in their intimidation. This seemed to be a recurring pattern of that persecution period because Charles Okah had a similar experience with the SSS in October 2010 (See

Appendix 14).

99. Mr. Buhari Dikko, one of the pioneer directors of the FCDA, was appointed to be the first Director of the STDA. A perfect gentleman, an experienced and competent engineer, he did a wonderful job, assisted by my senior professional colleague and Barewa Old Boy, Abba Dutsinma Abdullahi. Sadly, the enabling law to institutionalise STDA and AMMA were both ignored by the National Assembly.

100. Ms. Jummai Kwanashie, a hardworking and competent town planner that I had tested with previous tough assignments first as Director of AEPB and then Development Control, was appointed the pioneer Director-General of AMMA. She did not disappoint me, and laid a solid foundation for the take-off of the organisation.

101. An example is the retirement of my nephew, Lawal Zubairu Ahmed from the services of the FCDA. Lawal was one of the Zonal Land Officers, and his name was submitted along with others for retirement on the grounds that their activities messed up the land register. I was not expected to approve it. I did. Another example was approving the revocation of my Asokoro plot allocation when it remained undeveloped eight years after allocation.

102. One of the first persons I approached for help the moment I was confirmed by the Senate as minister was Yayale Ahmed, who had been a classmate and friend of my elder brother and mentor, Bashir El-Rufai. I therefore considered Yayale Ahmed a respected elder brother. I met him along with my assistant, Ms. Aishetu Kolo, on 10th July 2003 in his office for a long discussion. He was very helpful and frank in his assessment of the challenges I would face working with the civil service. He offered to help me in my future interactions with the Federal Civil Service. For instance, he gave me advice on restructuring the MFCT/FCDA, and promised to post out of the MFCT any person with whom I was uncomfortable. He suggested that I should ask the president to exempt me from protocol and politically-related duties incidental to the FCT minister's functions. I had already agreed with President Obasanjo on that exemption and on placing a distance from

partisan political engagements. In the end, Yayale did not fulfill any of his promises. In fact, at every stage of the implementation of the reforms of the FCT, he attempted to undermine and sabotage our efforts, with a smile and further broken promises - all the time.

103. Indeed, President Obasanjo wrote a letter, reference PRES/36-1, dated June 30, 2005 with the title: Stemming Malpractice in Civil Service Promotion Examinations, requiring the FCSC to investigate allegations of the exam malpractices. The letter was copied to me and the Head of Civil Service of the Federation.

104. See for instance *"FCT to prosecute beggars, hawkers - Minister"* in *Nigerian Tribune*, September 5, 2003.

105. The clinic building was a personal donation by Mahey R. Rashid, then Deputy Governor of the Central Bank of Nigeria. Alhaji Rabiu Karami Rabiu also donated a bus for the use of the Bwari Vocational Centre and the programme. I am grateful to them for their compassion and personal interest in our success in the FCT.

106. See for example The Guardian, 31st August 2003, pp. 10-11 - "Why We Are Demolishing in Abuja, by El-Rufai" and Vanguard of 1st September, 2003 - "El-Rufai unfolds plan to restore Abuja master plan"

107. We enlisted the support and participation of First Lady, Mrs. Stella Obasanjo, in launching the Keep Abuja Clean and Green programme. She was enthusiastic and mobilised the various women organisations and NGOs she related with to advocate for the programme. Obasanjo was also pleased that we kept his wife busy, productively.

108. See the *Report of the FCT Salary Verification Exercise, Ministry of Federal Capital Territory - 15th December 2003* and *"Responses to Salient Issues: MFCT Salary Verification Report dated May 2004, prepared by the Department of Finance & Accounts, MFCT* (just being wound up then!)

109. In 2003, the budget we inherited had only 25.13% earmarked for capital projects, and the balance for recurrent expenditure. In 2004, our very first budget, we had 67% for capital projects

and only 33% for recurrent expenditure, even though payroll went up by N1bn, and new provisions for school feeding and pensions amounting to N750 million were made. Japheth Omojuwa wrote a satirical piece on this feat titled: *"Nasir El-Rufai - His Past Finally Exposed!"* http://omojuwa.com/2012/nasir-el-rufai-his-past-finally-exposed/ *accessed February 2, 2012*

110. Moving the Public Service Reforms Forward - August 2005, was jointly authored by me and Mr. Segun Peters of the World Bank, with the assistance of Dr. Goke Adegoroye, Director-General of the Bureau of Public Service Reforms, after extensive debate and analysis of what was wrong with the implementation of that component of NEEDS. Every aspect had made substantial progress, and we had even secured the write-off of our Paris Club debts, but PSR lagged behind. We agreed something had to be done, and that meant taking control of PSR from the Head of Civil Service.

111. Anyone interested in more details of Public Service Reforms design, implementation and pitfalls should read Goke's highly informative book and a compendium of sorts about the Public Service Reform programme – *Beyond Yours Faithfully* publicly presented on his retirement in August 2010.

112. Steve Oronsaye was Permanent Secretary (State House) and was a member of the Economic Team. He went on to be the Head of Civil Service of the Federation between 2009 and 2011.

113. An anti-corruption team from the World Bank, led by Michael Stefanovic, visited me in 2009 in Dubai to ask questions about suspected corruption in the IPPIS procurement. They were investigating the conduct of one of the former deputy directors of BPSR, Mr. Tunji Olaopa, whose records showed had been to South Africa twice to meet with one of the prospective software vendors and was accommodated by the vendor. He tried to influence the bid in the company's favour but was unsuccessful. His dodgy conduct led to the decision to redeploy him to the OHCSF. I never got to read the investigation report but learnt from top-level World Bank sources that he was found ethically wanting. Unfortunately,

Tunji was protected by Yayale Ahmed's system and has been rapidly promoted and is now a federal permanent secretary!

114. Interestingly, after a couple of visits to Buhari, Obasanjo showed me a 'security report' sent to him by the DG of the SSS reporting me for meeting 'secretly' with Buhari to "protect Northern interests". The SSS neither knew that I was Obasanjo's emissary nor what I was discussing with Buhari. I was keeping Obasanjo apprised of the difficulties I was experiencing so he shared that one report with me.

115. From that day onwards I became the emissary between the two old soldiers. Whenever Obasanjo or Buhari had messages, I was called to deliver the message and the response. I have shed a little more light on this in the Epilogue.

116. It was well known that two newspaper publishers at the time were my close friends - *ThisDay's* Nduka Obaigbena and *Leadership's* Sam Nda Isaiah, so every leak in these two papers was blamed on me. I did not care and always told the President and his aides as much. I never deny my friends to avoid accusations like this.

117. On 13th September 2006, Nuhu Ribadu addressed the Senate on corruption in Nigeria and revealed that 31 out of the 36 state governors were being investigated for money laundering, corruption and other economic crimes. This was widely reported in the newspapers. See for example "The Ribadu Report" in *ThisDay* of 5th October, 2006

118. On 21st April 2006, the National Assembly Journal No. 9, Vol. 3 published the Constitution of the Federal Republic of Nigeria 1999 (Amendment) Bill, 2006 jointly sponsored by Senator Ibrahim Mantu and Hon. Austin Opara. The Bill was 33 pages long and contained about 100 amendments to the Constitution.

119. Other groups outside Abuja opposed to the Third Term project that we were in contact with included Dr. Mahmoud Tukur's PAL Group and the Arewa Consultative Forum which set up a liaison team with prominent political leaders from each of the 19 northern states led by General I B M Haruna, Senator J K N Waku and Dr. Umaru Dikko, coordinating the outreach to national assembly members.

One-time political rivals within the North and across the nation united for once to fight the Third Term project to a standstill. It was impressive.

120. Senator Lawali Shuaibu was the chairman of the Senate committee on economic and financial crimes and enjoyed very close personal relations with Nuhu Ribadu. I knew Senator Saidu Dansadau from the early 1990s in Kaduna, and he remains one of the most outstanding senators that emerged in this Republic.

121. Obasanjo relied on multiple, often conflicting, sources of information and then using the law of averages to aggregate and derive the truth. For instance, he encouraged the formation of a group of five of us to advise him on 'northern thinking' on the Third Term under the chairmanship of Lawal Batagarawa, with Adamu Maina Waziri, Mustapha Bello, Aliyu Modibbo and I. We met weekly at Lawal's house at Mabushi Ministers' Quarters. Another 'national group' of ten persons also met every Wednesday in the Villa with him to discuss "ongoing political reform" issues. Obasanjo enjoyed running these conspiracy cells from which he knew what everyone was doing and everyone else knew only a part of the whole story. He had similar cells headed by Tony Anenih, Senator Mantu, Governors Segun Agagu and Abdullahi Adamu, and many other party apparatchiks and federal government officials.

122. Andy Uba asked me to send an aide to collect a message from the President for FCT's legislators. My security details went to Andy's house along Ibrahim Taiwo Road to collect two aluminum brief cases containing N50 million each for delivery to the two members of the House of Representatives representing the FCT - Hon. Philip Aduda and Sidi Ali. Senator Isa Maina representing the FCT was one of the few well-known Third Term supporters and reportedly collected his own 'message' directly. I later gathered that the 'messages' were sent through me to "test my loyalty". I advised my security details to directly contact the two representatives and deliver the messages. Subsequently, none of the persons involved ever raised the subject or discussed the matter with me.

123. Obasanjo summoned a meeting of the national executive committee of the PDP and delivered a three-page address as 'the Leader' of the Party on 18th May 2006. He said among other surprising things -"Throughout the period (of the Third Term debate), I resisted the invitation to be drawn on either side and I maintained studied silence. I was maligned, insulted and wrongly accused but I remained where I am and what I am and I remained focused." Chairman Amadu Ali's speech was titled – "Time to move on," was along the same lines of total denial. Four days later, party Secretary Ojo Maduekwe addressed another press conference, and delivered an eight-page speech titled "That we may consolidate our democracy" that was more honest. He said among other things – "However, while we respect the decision of the National Assembly (on term limits), we as a party deeply regret the loss of a big and historic opportunity to restructure the foundations of our federation in order to build a virile and more united polity.

124. Our multiple sources in the Yar'Adua camp clearly informed us that early in the life of the administration, Obasanjo warned Yar'Adua to be careful and cautious in relating with Nuhu Ribadu and Nasir El-Rufai. As an army general and strong president, he allegedly told Umaru, he had great difficulty managing us. He added that we were strong-willed and stubborn - loose cannons if you like. Perhaps that was his idea of extracting revenge. I never asked Obasanjo about this and did not care. This is because I am quite clear in my mind that Yar'Adua selectively did what he wished, not everything Obasanjo desired!

125. My various conversations with many in the Yar'Adua inner circle, including Mike Aondoakaa and James Ibori, alluded to this. At the point in time I heard these, none of them was on good terms with Obasanjo and their views may have been coloured by that.

126. Indeed, many members of the Yar'Adua inner circle hold the view that Nuhu Ribadu's travails escalated when the EFCC submitted a report giving Obasanjo a clean bill of health of allegations of corruption after investigating a petition against

him by a civil society organisation. The petition was reportedly handed to Nuhu by Yar'Adua personally in late 2007 or early 2008.

127. The persons at the meeting were Ngozi, Oby, Nuhu, Jim Ovia, Tony Elumelu, Andy Uba, Tanimu Yakubu, Aliko Dangote, Nasir El-Rufai and Hakeem Belo-Osagie.

128. I went to Katsina for the wedding of the daughters of Alhaji Dahiru Mangal, along with Dr. Aliyu Modibbo and Inuwa Baba. Umaru offered the governor's guest house and we had lunch after the wedding fatiha.

129. It was in this role that Umaru caught the eye and affections of his future wife, Turai, then attending teachers' college. She was strong-willed and focused on her goals - to marry him - and she chased the shy Umaru to submission and they got married in 1976.

130. Yar'Adua had asked me and Dr. Aliyu Modibbo to co-chair a transition strategy team for him with Tanimu Yakubu, Bode Agusto, Femi Fani-Kayode, Dele Olojede, Dr. Isabella Okagbue, Senator Udoma Udo Udoma, Hakeem Belo-Osagie, Ifueko Omoigui and Lt.-Gen. Salihu Ibrahim. We held our first meeting on 6th May 2007, but discontinued within two weeks, when Tanimu and Dr. Modibbo stopped attending.

131. My reaction to Attorney-General Mike Aondoakaa's suggestion (see The Guardian, 16th April 2009 http://www.ngrguardiannews.com/news/article01//indexn2_html?pdate=160409&ptitle=Govt%20to%20raise%20panel%20over%20Halliburton%20scam) that my essay on Yar'Adua - Great Expectations, Disappointing Outcomes - was aimed at getting asylum was publicised widely in the media. See for instance - "El-Rufai: I am Not Seeking Asylum", ThisDay 17th April 2009, pp. 1 and 6.

132. Eventually the reverse happened, as Umaru died less than a week after my return to Nigeria. I landed in Abuja on 1st May 2010. Umaru died the evening of 5th May 2010. Many people do not even remember that I returned while he was still alive. Some think that Jonathan facilitated my return or I got back home at his invitation or returned only after Yar'Adua died - not one of these is true.

133. Obasanjo as military head of state oversaw the Petroleum Ministry as minister for this period when Colonel Muhammadu Buhari (as he then was) left office in July 1978 to attend the US War College. Obasanjo did not appoint a successor to Buhari and ran the NNPC directly. He repeated the same between 1999 and 2006 as an elected president.

134. Certainly if the watch is a diamond-crusted Rolex from a construction company or bank doing business, or expecting to bid for, business in one's ministry or agency, then that is prohibited by the Code of Conduct in the Constitution!

135. The letter, referenced CR: 3000/EFCC/ABJ/BF.2/VOL.33/189 and dated 18th October, 2008, requested me to report to Steven Otitoju, Deputy Director of Operations on Friday, 28th November 2008. The letter was addressed and delivered to my home in Abuja.

136. This widely circulated paper is available on http://el-rufai.org/2009/05/the-yaradua-paper/ and on the websites of several Nigerian newspapers and blogging platforms. It is an edited version of a term paper for the Leadership and Governance in Africa class taught by Professor Robert Rotberg of the Harvard Kennedy School. Professor Rotberg gave me an A for the effort.

137. My speech presented on 10th June 2009 was titled Nigerian Political Dynamics and Prospects for Reform. Both audio and PDF versions of the presentation are available on http://csis.org/event/nigeria-political-dynamics-and-prospects-reform

138. See "Time for a new Nigerian President" published in the web version of Foreign Policy on 1st April, 2010. http://www.foreignpolicy.com/articles/2010/04/01/time_for_a_new_nigerian_president

139. For example Jeff Santos interviewed me on WWZN Revolution Boston, with the audio downloadable from: http://revolutionboston.com/podcast_archive/2010/01/20100105/20100105_2.mp3on 5th January, 2010. I spoke several times on the nationally-syndicated Bev Smith Show between July 2009 and March 2010 as well.

140. After the collapse of the Third Term project, Nuhu Ribadu persuaded Obasanjo to appoint Sarki Mukhtar as the NSA once General Aliyu Gusau left in May 2006. We had met Sarki Mukhtar at the Aspen NLI Fellowship seminar in January of that year, where he impressed both of us with his unusual candour about the mistakes and missed opportunities of prolonged military rule in Nigeria. Two years later, in what amounted to a reversal of fortunes and an interesting turn of events, Sarki was the person that was tasked with the job of eliminating both Nuhu and me, physically if necessary, to ensure national security – a task he pursued with relish and single-minded dedication! He was fired by Jonathan in March 2010, and replaced by General Aliyu Mohammed Gusau!

141. Dr. Dalhatu Sarki Tafida, another Barewa Old Boy, former commissioner of health in my home state of Kaduna, was Majority Leader in the Senate when we were in the Cabinet. We had a decent relationship and I did my best to respond to his multiple requests for favours while I was in office. That is why he would call me his brother. It had nothing to do with being from Zaria, Kaduna or Barewa College! That is the language of Nigerian prebendalist politicians!

142. This is a common refrain in Nigeria. "I am just doing my job." Even if doing the act in question violates laws, rules, regulations and morality, the Nigerian thinks it is justified. Keeping one's public service job appears in the minds of many to be more important than doing what is right, lawful and moral. Why then do we wonder that our public service sucks and our nation is becoming increasingly dysfunctional?

143. The Federal High Court held that the Federal Government acted unconstitutionally and awarded me N1 million damages against each of the four agencies that we sued jointly. This was widely reported in the media. http://www.vanguardngr.com/2011/11/court-orders-fg-to-pay-el-rufai-n1m-for-passport-seizure/ and in Peoples' Daily, See: http://www.peoplesdaily-online.com/news/national-news/24220-el-rufai-gets-n1m-damages-against-fg- both dated 15th November, 2011. Nearly six months after the judgment, which was never appealed, none of the

government agencies has paid the damages! For me, the legal and moral victory exceeded the paltry amount.

144. What I learnt while in exile and this was subsequently confirmed from sources within the Yar'Adua inner circle was that had I returned in October 2008 when EFCC declared me wanted, there was a plan hatched in the NSA's office to inject me with cultures of HIV and Hepatitis viruses while in detention. That would accelerate and ensure my death through natural causes well before the elections of 2011, which Yar'Adua's marabouts had assured him I was going to contest against him.

145. 'Mumu' is a Pidgin English term popular throughout Nigeria for a naïve person – one that can be deceived or fooled easily and repeatedly.

146. My old friend from our Kaduna days, and experienced political operative, Bashir Yusuf Ibrahim, added knowledge of history to this initial list of necessary prerequisites for public leadership that I outlined to Nuhu. Bashir was secretary of the Northern Political Leaders' Forum that championed the observance of the zoning provisions entrenched in the PDP constitution.

147. The Harvard Alumni Association records list me as a 1996 graduate - when I completed the Owner/President Management programme – my first programme at Harvard. Since then my student ID has carried the same number through the AMP in 2002 and MPA Mid-Career/Mason Fellows Programme between 2008 and 2009. The June 2009 graduation was my third Harvard graduation.

148. Incidentally, it was also in Aspen, Colorado while attending the ACT II gathering of Aspen Institute Global Leadership Fellows on the 15th June 2009 that the first outline of this book was written.

149. *The Nation* newspaper of 5th October 2009 reported that Nuhu and I had formed a political group, with the backing of Lt. Gen T Y Danjuma, and Senator Ken Nnamani. I learnt later that the report caused some ripples in the State House. See for instance http://www.thenigerianvoice.com/nvnews / 1259/1/danjuma-el-rufai-ribadu-strange-bed-fellows-new-

po.html and the story reproduced in full on my website – http://el-rufai.org/new-governance-for-nigeria/

150. See for instance classified cables recently released by wikileaks.com – SUBJECT: PRESIDENT YAR'ADUA FLIES YET AGAIN TO SAUDI ARABIA FOR MEDICAL TREATMENT REF: A. ABUJA 1475 (NOTAL), ¶B. ABUJA 1760 (NOTAL), ¶C. ABUJA 1945 (NOTAL) ¶D. ABUJA 1962 (NOTAL), ¶E. USUN NEW YORK 1035 (NOTAL) - Classified By: Political Counselor James P. McAnulty for reasons in Sections 1.4 (B) and (D)

151. Garba Aminchi was the deputy governor to Umaru Yar'Adua in his time in Katsina.

152. Sultan Saad Abubakar III is the spiritual leader of Nigeria's Muslims and a descendant of Shehu Usman Danfodio. His father was the cousin of Sir Ahmadu Bello, the Sardauna of Sokoto. Sultan Saad was two years my senior at Barewa College, and is a retired general of the Nigerian Army. We maintained contact and good relations throughout my public service years.

153. The last time I met face-to-face with Turai was in February 2008 when Nuhu's problems with Umaru had begun with his forced movement to NIPSS, Kuru. At Nuhu's urging, I flew from Dubai to London to meet with her at Grosvenor House with the assistance of her aide and a mutual friend, Toyin Fagbayi. I appealed to Turai to advise her husband to focus and complete the NIPP projects Obasanjo started to improve electric power supply in the country. I explained to her that suspending the implementation of NIPP on any pretext was not in the overall interest of the country and Umaru's legacy. When I sought her intervention to repair Umaru's relationship with Nuhu, she attempted to end the meeting abruptly. I insisted that I was not done, and assured her that as a police officer and public servant, Nuhu would work well with Umaru. However, I could see that their mind had been made up on the subject. I called Nuhu and updated him, but noted the need for him to be very careful in his handling of the relationship with his new boss, President Umaru Yar'Adua.

154. See "Nasir El-Rufai writes Obama" http://www.nairaland.com/378773/nasir-el-rufai-writes-obama-u.s, accessed on 15th March 2012.

155. See Endnote 138 above.

156. Beginning in January 2010, the Save Nigeria Group (SNG) organised Nigerians protesting Yar'Adua's disappearance in Australia (12th January), London, UK and Lagos, Nigeria (15th January), New York, US (22nd January), and Abuja (10th March). Pastor Bakare personally led the protests, with his wife and children in tow in both Lagos and Abuja. Some of the videos are available on YouTube. For instance, see the following clips http://www.youtube.com/watch?v=Ovvq82hPUvQ and after Jonathan became acting president in February 2010, see http://www.youtube.com/watch?NR=1&feature=endscreen&v=DBTH2tv9OvQaccessed 31st March 2012.

157. See *"Yar'Adua is brain-damaged" in Next on Sunday, January 10 2010. The full story is available online at* http://www.jaguda.com/2010/01/10/yar-adua-brain-damaged-according-to-234next-com/ *accessed 18th March 2012*

158. *See Interview – "Nigeria's Jonathan could win backing as candidate" By: Matthew Tostevin, Wednesday, February 17, 2010. See* http://www.nigeriavillagesquare.com/forum/archive/index.php/t-48544.html *accessed 31st March, 2012*

159. The Good Governance Group had filed an application to register the Patriotic Peoples' Congress (PPC) as our left of centre political party, with Nuhu's friend and nominee Kalli Algahzali as Protem Chairman. The application was not pursued to conclusion once the group took other decisions on our political direction.

160. Accra was chosen as the location for our meeting rather than Dubai because, according to AC, their chairman, Bisi Akande, found the seven hour flight in Bola Tinubu's private jet too long. Asiwaju Bola Tinubu and AC National Secretary, Dr. Usman Bugaje, were expected to attend. None of the three party big-wigs came for various reasons. We took everything in absolute good faith.

Endnotes 525

161. See for instance Vanguard newspaper of 29th April, 2010 – 'El-Rufai Returns' http://www.vanguardngr.com/2010/04/el-rufai-returns/

162. General Aliyu Mohammed Gusau was very gracious and supportive of me personally during my difficult years. He called anytime he was abroad just to say hello, and encouraged me to 'hang in there'. When he was unable to reach me, he made a habit of leaving goodwill messages with my friend, Jimi Lawal. I will forever appreciate his open expression of concern towards my person and family always.

163. My return was widely reported in the media. See for instance The Nation, which we considered the EFCC's unofficial mouthpiece: Seehttp://thenationonlineng.net/web2/articles/45054/1/-el-Rufai-returns-dares-EFCC/Page1.html and The Sunday Tribune of 2nd May, 2010 http://www.tribune.com.ng/sun/index.php/front-page-articles/892-el-rufai-returns-visits-efcc-tuesday

164. Mubadala Development Company is one of the sovereign wealth funds of the Abu Dhabi government. Its board is chaired by Sheikh Muhammad bin Zayed Al-Nahyan, the Crown Prince of Abu Dhabi. We developed an excellent working relationship with the Crown Prince. We found him to be a thoughtful and decisive leader. Mubadala was granted the license upon payment of $400 million to the NCC. Mubadala then engaged Etisalat as operator of the license, and divested 40% of the operating company to Etisalat and 30% for Nigerians.

165. This was widely reported on several blogging sites like Sahara Reporters. Pastor Bakare's narration of what happened is on YouTube. See http://www.youtube.com/watch?v=5HvfOo1P-nQ, accessed on March 31, 2012.

166. "El-Rufai's Arrogance" was syndicated and published by The Nation and Daily Trust of Wednesday 19th May, 2010. It was also published by many online bloggers like http://newsdiaryonline.com/haruna_rufai.htm accessed on 30th March, 2012.

167. Other regular attendees at the steering committee meetings, which always took place in the conference room of Chief Dr.

Raymond Dokpesi's AIT, included Dr. Abiye Precious Sekibo, Prof. A B C Nwosu, Dr. Nora Obaji, Musa Elayo, Femi Fani-Kayode, Balarabe Abbas Lawal, Chris Ekpenyong and Nenadi Esther Usman. They were all threatened with suspension from the PDP at some point.

168. See for instance a newspaper report of the PDP NEC's communique in the Nigeria Tribune – 'PDP Dissolves Nnamani, Masari's Forum', on Saturday 19th June, 2010. See http://www.tribune.com.ng/sat/index.php/front-page-articles/1355-pdp-dissolves-nnamani-masaris-forum.html accessed on 30th March 2012.

169. Adamu Waziri as police affairs minister then initiated steps with the full support and approval of President Jonathan to reverse Nuhu's dismissal from the Police by the Police Service Commission, and the prior demotion, and to restore his AIG rank. Within weeks, Nuhu had been reinstated into the Force and restored to his rank of Assistant Inspector General of Police, then retired from the Police Force with full benefits.

170. This was the front page headlines on the Punch newspaper of Friday, 9th July 2010 – see *"2011: AC, others shortlist Ribadu, el-Rufai as candidates"* – By: Niyi Odebode. The Next newspaper story was more emphatic on Nuhu's candidature on its cover story of the same date.

171. Donald Duke, Ngozi Okonjo-Iweala, Oby Ezekwesili, Fola Adeola, Nuhu Ribadu and Nasir El-Rufai

172. And I had told former president Babangida so in 2001, when I visited him at Minna. We had concluded a BPE management retreat and I passed through Minna with one of my staff who knew him well to visit him. It was at that occasion that he intimated me of his plans to contest for the presidency if and when Obasanjo completed his term(s) of office.

173. The headline appeared in *The Sun* during the month of October 2010, but I could not retrieve it online.

174. See "Buhari should stick to the facts" – By: Muyiwa Adekeye on *Sahara Reporters* http://saharareporters.com/article/el-rufai-buhari-should-stick-facts *dated 4th October, 2010.*

175. See Endnote 9 above for the summary of the well-considered ruling delivered by Justice Adamu Bello of the Federal High Court, Abuja on October 20th, 2010.

176. Section 87(4) of the Electoral Act 2010 provided that: "A political party that adopts the system of indirect primaries for the choice of its candidate shall adopt the procedure outlined below:

   (a) In the case of nominations to the position of Presidential candidate, a political party shall,

   (i) hold special conventions in each of the 36 States of the Federation and FCT, where delegates shall vote for each of the aspirants at designated centres in each State Capital on specified dates.

   (ii) a National Convention shall be held for the ratification of the candidate with the highest number of votes.

   (iii) the aspirant with the highest number of votes at the end of voting in the 36 States of the Federation and FCT, shall be declared the winner of the Presidential primaries of the political party and the aspirants name shall be forwarded to the Independent National Electoral Commission as the candidate of the party after ratification by the national convention.

177. One of the self-acclaimed Buhari "brand owners" even said to the face of one of us that we "chopped" under Obasanjo and PDP, and are now rushing to "double-dip" just when they were about to reap the benefits of their years of investment in building the Buhari brand. We took many of these insults and similar snide remarks stoically throughout the campaign. The Buhari inner circle were certain that the election was a walk over and they would win, so did not want anyone they considered 'latter-day opportunists' near the General. This mentality frustrated many efforts to broaden the platform and enter into alliances with other parties, groups and individuals, partly contributing to some of the electoral challenges the party experienced in April 2011.

178. Obasanjo contacted Ngozi and she expressed interest in being the running mate, subject to consulting her husband and parents. A few days later, she flew to Nigeria to meet the first condition of being a candidate in an election – register to vote. By then, Pastor Bakare had been announced as running mate, so she left without meeting Buhari, but I gathered had a conversation with Obasanjo.

179. See the manifesto on the campaign website: http://buhari4change.com/wp-content/uploads/2011/02/CPC-OurCommitmentToNigeria.pdf accessed on 15th March 2011.

180. The full text of the speech titled *'Nigerian Democracy and Prospects for the 2011 Elections'* is available on http://www.chathamhouse.org/publications/papers/view/109637 accessed 12th March 2012.

181. With the exception of Osun State, the PDP surprisingly won in all the south-west states, and even Edo State, where Nuhu's good friend (and mine) Adams Oshiomhole was the sitting governor. The most positive interpretation of many observers was either that Asiwaju Tinubu negotiated a deal with Jonathan and the PDP, or sent clear messages to ACN supporters to vote any way they wished. Either way, regionalism and religion trumped competence and common sense!

182. Extracts from "Nigerian Democracy and Prospects for the 2011 Elections" by Nasir El-Rufai, and available on www.chathamhouse.org

183. These malpractices were widespread and even more apparent in the South-East and South-South regions of the country. In Rivers State, the governor, Rotimi Amaechi, complained of low voter turnout, yet the final results showed 76% turnout, out of which 99% voted for Jonathan and the ruling party PDP!

184. The paper I presented is available on Sahara Reporters website - http://saharareporters.com/article/nigerian-2011-elections-opportunity-lost-nasir-ahmad-el-rufai accessed on 30th November 2011. The audio record of the entire two hours of the proceedings is available for download on the Atlantic Council website - see http://www.acus.org/files/Africa/

041911_ACUS_NigeriaElection.mp3 accessed on 31st July 2011.

185. William Wallis introduced the three points of view; see http://blogs.ft.com/beyond-brics/2011/06/01/post-election-nigeria-whats-next/#axzz1wk41UhSz and my own abridged views titled "Nigeria – Muddling through or economic disaster?" - http://blogs.ft.com/beyond-brics/2011/06/01/post-election-nigeria-muddling-through-or-economic-disaster/#axzz1wk41UhSz accessed on 15th January, 2012.

186. *El-Rufai on Friday also appears on* my website, *the back page of 'Peoples Daily', Sahara Reporters, NigeriaIntel.com, Nigeria Village Square, Gamji.com* and *Huhuonline*. It also features on Newsdiaryonline.com, Facebook and Twitter. Several other bloggers like *omojuwa.com, Elombah.com* and *African Herald Express* regularly feature the articles. The series of articles aim to undertake factual analysis of key policy areas and are unique in their assemblage of history, fact-based arguments, data and prescriptions for better governance.

187. See "What Nigerians Pay the Federal Government" on the Back page of Thisday, 1st July 2011. It is also available online on my website: www.el-Rufai.org or http://www.thisdaylive.com/articles/what-nigerians-pay-fg/94277/ accessed on 16th August 2011.

188. *"Jonathan's Tough Choices"* attempted to sketch the challenges the new administration would face, and nearly a year later as I write this, my prediction of nightmare has become Nigeria's reality. See Back page of *ThisDay*, 10th June 2011 and available on my website and http://www.thisdaylive.com/articles/jonathan-s-tough-choices/92977/ accessed on August 17th, 2011.

189. See "Sleeping with both eyes open" on the Back page of Thisday of 2nd September 2011. It is also available on my website or http://www.thisdaylive.com/articles/sleeping-with-both-eyes-open-/97589/ accessed 17th September, 2011

190. Azazi was appointed the chief of army staff by Obasanjo in 2006. He was promoted to Chief of Defence Staff in 2007 and quietly retired by President Umaru Yar'Adua in 2008 due to his alleged involvement in the sale of guns and ammunition

to Niger Delta militants in November 2007. See *"Secret Army Report Implicates NSA Azazi, Ibori, Alamieyeseigha, Henry And Sunny Okah In Sale Of Military Weapons To Niger Delta Militants"* available for download on Sahara Reporters http://saharareporters.com/report/secret-army-report-implicates-nsa-azazi-ibori-alamieyeseigha-henry-and-sunny-okah-sale-milita accessed on 30th October, 2010.

191. I later learnt from officials of the administration that the real reason was our outing at Chatham House, and how we succeeded in changing the narrative about the "free and fair elections" of April 2011. The SSS was more interested in seizing my laptop and travel bag to search for 'subversive materials' than anything. Sadly, they were unable to lay their hands on either!

192. Some days later, on the 6th of July to be precise, we had a group meeting to undertake an after-action review of what happened. I was taken aback at how angry some of my friends and family members were at my writing for ThisDay, agreeing to be a member of its editorial board and being a weekly 'government critic'. I listened carefully, explained to everyone what I thought I was doing and we agreed to move on nevertheless in the same direction. I rejected any suggestions to soften my hardline opposition posture. Some of my friends did not realise how well I knew Jonathan and how certain I was about what his administration would turn out to be. Within months, vindication had bubbled to the surface and we are now all on the same page on most of these issues.

193. Those interested in a legal analysis of this path-breaking case, the different paths taken by the Court of Appeal and the Supreme Court to reach the same outcomes, please read *THE SUPREME COURT: WHITHER THE PRINCIPLES: A REVIEW OF DIRECTOR OF S.S.S V. AGBAKOBA"* – *TAYO OYETIBO, SAN* available online at tayooyetibolaw.com/admin/doc/1325672154.docx accessed 25th March 2012.

194. Member Feese sustained serious injuries when a suicide bomber crashed a vehicle into the UN headquarters building in Abuja on 26th August 2011. She was flown to the UK for treatment and Yasmin regularly visited her. We found a letter

addressed to President Jonathan in my daughter's laptop complaining about the event and Nigeria's healthcare system as her response to the incident.

195. "In Loving Memory of Yasmin El-Rufai" is a touching tribute to my daughter by Dipo Salimonu on the Back Page of *ThisDay*, 2nd December 2011. Available online: http://www.thisdaylive.com/articles/in-loving-memory-of-yasmin-el-rufai/104065/ accessed on 16th February, 2012. Yasmin's friendship with Dipo may have begun when I spoke at TEDxEuston on 5th December 2009 at the University of London. They became very good friends and he remains close to our family.

196. "Yasmin – Gone Too Soon" by Second-Lieutenant Bashir Bala was published in the Weekly Trust of 10th December 2011. The moving tribute is also available online http://weeklytrust.com.ng/index.php?option=com_content& view=article&id=7870:yasmin-gone-too-soon&catid =47: tribute &Itemid=168 accessed 18th March, 2012. Bashir contacted me via Facebook requesting me to attend his graduation from the Royal Military Academy, Sandhurst, UK. I agreed and introduced him to Yasmin to finalise the travel arrangements. She became an elder sister to him and a mentor of sorts. Sadly, she died before the graduation which I attended on the 16th of December, 2011, to honour the promise we both made to be with Bashir on that very important day of his life.

197. As state governor of the old North-Eastern State (now six states of North-East Zone), federal minister of petroleum, head of state and chair of PSTF, Buhari executed his assignments with integrity, singular focus, even-handedness and patriotism.

With Oby Ezekwesili

With Oby and Ngozi in the Executive Council Chambers

With Charles Soludo

With Steve Oronsaye in the Executive Council Chambers

Author, some ministers, Speaker Masari, Yayale Ahmed and former Head of State General Yakubu Gowon at Independence Day party with President Obasanjo

Speaker Masari, President Obasanjo, Gen Azazi, AVM Dike at Remembrance Day parade

Welcoming Governor Goodluck Jonathan to observe the FCT Executive Committee meeting in 2006

Sharing a funny photo with President Obasanjo in the Council Chambers

With Bashir El-Rufai and President Ibrahim Babangida at IBB's residence in Minna

Receiving the Silverbird Man of the Year Award 2006 with Hassan Tukur, Hadiza, Dora Akunyili and Ben Murray Bruce.

With Kofi Annan, Ibrahim Gambari, and G. Gettu commissioning UN Building, Abuja

As Head of the FG delegation to North Korea, with Tijjani Abdullahi, Ambassador Sule Buba and the President of the North Korean Presidium Kim Yong Nam

Nuhu Ribadu, Riva Levinson, Author and Molly McKew while on exile in Washington, DC

At a State Banquet in Paris: (L-R) President Jacques Chirac, President Obasanjo and Mrs Stella Obasanjo (RIP)

Welcoming President Hu Jintao of the Peoples' Republic of China to Abuja.

With Ngozi doing a high-five in the Executive Council Chambers

Appendix 1

OFFICE OF CHIEF OF STAFF TO THE PRESIDENT, COMMANDER-IN-CHIEF
State House
PRESIDENTIAL VILLA, ABUJA.

MEMORANDUM

From: **Chief of Staff to the President** To: **HE. The President**

Ref: **SH/COS/25/37/319** Date: **7th June, 2007**

Subject: **RE: SALE OF FGN HOUSES IN ABUJA – DISPOSAL OF FORMER PRESIDENTIAL GUEST HOUSES ATTACHED TO THE OFFICE OF THE VICE PRESIDENT**

Your Excellency would recall the issue of the three guest houses attached to the office of the Vice President which were sold under the programme of sale of non-essential houses in Abuja. The houses in question were:-

i. No 16 Mambilla Street – sold to the former FCT Minister
ii. No 32 Suleiman Barau Crescent – sold to former Minister of Labour;
iii. No. 12 Yakubu Gowon Crescent – sold to MD of AIPDC.

2. These houses, you would recall, were sold on the basis of an approval granted by former President Obasanjo on 16 May, 2007 as can be seen on the copy of the attached document. The house bought by the former FCT Minister situated at No. 16 Mambilla Street has since been occupied by his family members. Security men were drafted to the houses and I understand that Your Excellency had instructed that the status quo on the 3 houses should remain. In my understanding, that meant that the securitymen should be withdrawn from No. 16 Mambilla Street since the house had already been occupied while the other two houses would continue to be guarded.

3. The letter from the Chairman of the FCT Transition Committee, a copy of which is attached herewith, is reporting that the guards at No 16 Mambilla Street had indeed been withdrawn while the other two houses are still under guard. The Chairman of the FCT Transition Committee is seeking Your Excellency's approval for the removal of the guards from the two houses so that the new buyers can take possession of their houses.

RESTRICTED

Prayer:

The letter is pleading with Your Excellency to direct that the guards from the other two houses be also withdrawn to allow the new owners take possession of the two properties.

Above submitted for Your Excellency's directive please.

MAJ GEN A MOHAMMED (Rtd) CFR, GCON
Chief of Staff to the President, C-in-C

COS
go ahead pls.

RESTRICTED

RESTRICTED

Reference: SH/COS/ 25/37/327

12th June, 2007

The Chairman,
FCT Transition Committee
FCDA Secretariat
Area 11, Garki,
Abuja.

RE: DISPOSAL OF FORMER PRESIDENTIAL GUEST HOUSES ATTACHED TO THE OFFICE OF THE VICE PRESIDENT

I wish to refer to your letter No. FCDA/CES/008/vol.II407 dated 7th June, 2007 and to inform you that your request was put before His Excellency, Mr. President who, I am pleased to say, approved the withdrawal of the guards from the houses in question. I have attached herewith, a copy of a Memo containing Mr. President's approval for the withdrawal of the guards.

2. I wish to, by a copy of this letter, therefore, request the DC PRESCORT to withdraw the guards from Houses;

   i. No. 32 Suleiman Barau Crscent, Asokoro,
   ii. No. 12 Yakubu Gowon Crescent, Asokoro.

3. The DC PRESCORT is to hand over the Houses to the authorities of the FCDA so that they could be given to the new owners immediately. Please ensure that the handover exercise is synchronised properly so that the houses are not vandalised or items in the houses pilfered.

4. Best regards.

MAJ GEN A MOHAMMED (Rtd) CFR, GCON
Chief of Staff to the President, C-in-C

Int. Info:
SSAP (Admin) C-in-C
Int. Action:
DC, PRESCORT

RESTRICTED

Appendix 2

1/11/28

Daga mallam Ahmadu dan mallam Kwasau mallamin Makaranta Jaria, Zuwa ga Babban Baturen gona samaru Mr: Sewensa. Sarp Gaisuwa mai yawa da Ladabi da bari Sirma matabba cki da neman taimako. Bayan haka ina so ka taimaka ka bani aikin shan cotton kana taimakon Jama'a ka taimake ni kamar yadda Allah ya Taimakeka. Domin In sanadda ka Ubana ya Mutu maraya ne ni nasan kana taimakon ma uba balle Maraya Allah ya dade da Ranka Amin

Wosalomu

Mr: Sewensa

1st November 1928

Application from Mallam Ahmadu son of Mallam Kwasau, one-time Qur'anic school teacher in Zaria to Mr. Sawensa (Swanson) the Senior Agricultural Officer, Samaru. I am writing this letter to convey my respectful greetings to you, Sir, and seek for your assistance. I need you to consider giving me a veterinary-related job. I am aware that you are a considerate public officer and always helpful to others. I therefore appeal that you assist me in the same way God has Blessed you. I am particularly in need of this job because I am an orphan with fatherly responsibilities. God Bless you, Sir. Best regards, Mr. Sewensa (Swanson)

Appendix 3

The Permanent Secretary,

REQUEST FOR ADVANCE TO PAY SPECIAL ASSISTANTS TO THE MINISTER, FCT

Please refer to the Minister's minutes on page 2.

2. The two Special Assistants to the Minister, Aishatu F. Kolo and Dr. Abdu Mukhtar resumed duty in the Ministry of FCT on 17th July, 2003 but since then, they have not been paid for services rendered by way of salaries or allowances.

3. You may wish to note that under their terms and condition of engagement, they were to draw their remunerations from the World Bank Loan Facility, under <u>Economic Management Capacity Building Credit Scheme</u> which does not exist with FCT, as previously done in Bureau of Public Enterprises.

4. Under the arrangement the officers receive the following:

   (1) **Dr. Abdu Mukhtar - $437 daily**
   (2) **Aishatu F. Kolo - $412.91 daily.**

5. Accordingly, the officers have worked for a total number of 156 (one hundred and fifty six) days without pay.

6. In view of the above, You may wish to consider the granting of an advance to the officers in order to alleviate their problems which will be reimbursed by the Federal Ministry of Finance:

   (a) Dr. Abdu Mukhtar - $437 x N151 x 156 days = N10,293,922.00
   (b) Aishetu F. Kolo - $412 x N151 x 156 days = N9,726,600.00
       Grand Total   = **N20,020,522.00**

7. Submitted for your kind consideration and approval, please.

M.S. HAMIDU
FCT, Chief of Protocol

3rd December, 2003.

clause in the voucher.

3. Comply urgently 4/12/03 BJPS
& You will tax accordingly.

DA
4.12.03.

DD (Aud)
Pending the determination of their engagements in their entirety, especially as to whether they are on Secondment or on Consultancy, process payments, based on:—
(i) Payments are recoverable from the Fed. Min. of Finance.
(ii) PAYE / Taxes as applicable to Consultants/ Seconded officers will be applied accordingly.

DA
11.12.03.

Appendix 4

BUREAU OF PUBLIC ENTERPRISES

Weekly Briefing on the Privatisation and Commercialisation Programme

Prepared for:

President Olusegun Obasanjo, GCFR
Cc: Vice President Atiku Abubakar, GCON

15th JUNE 2001

| A. **FRONT BURNERS** | **COMMENT** |

1. African Petroleum (AP)

Following BPE's commissioning of a corporate governance audit of the affairs of AP, it was discovered that the company:

(i). made unauthorized borrowings of **₦11.75 billion** through the issuance of Commercial Papers and Bankers Acceptances and obtained other bank loans without following due process;
(ii). purchased and sold assets without providing adequate details of sale proceeds and the identity of the buyers;
(iii). failed to reconcile huge debts owed to NNPC estimated at between **₦4 - ₦10 billion**; and
(iv). is alleged to have been involved in insider trading, diverting revenues from bunkering and marine activities, and other general abuses.

The core investors claim that not only were these issues not disclosed, they were actively concealed from them during their pre-sale due diligence on the company.

In order to establish the legitimacy of their claim, BPE held meetings and discussions with the core investors, Mr. Umar Abba Gana (the former Managing Director of AP), the issuing house which supervised the due diligence exercise and other relevant parties.

As a result of the meetings, which are still ongoing, it has been established that because record keeping and financial management in the company was extremely poor, a substantial level of reconciliation of accounts is still required before final conclusions can be drawn. For example, none of the parties can agree on the money owed to NNPC, the banks and other creditors. Accordingly, the parties have been asked to provide more concrete evidence of their respective claims and rebuttals and circulate reports with a view to finally resolving the issue at the next meeting to be held on 12th July, 2001.

2. NITEL

2.1 Financial Restructuring

The Ministry of Communications has with the consent of Mr.President constituted a five-man committee, chaired by DG BPE and comprised of representatives from BPE, NITEL and the Ministry, to further explore financing possibilities and to restructure NITEL's finances. The committee has been charged with:

(i). renegotiating the existing GSM loan (aiming for a lower interest rate/longer maturity date)
(ii). renegotiating the terms and pricing for the GSM and transmission network expansion
(iii). seeking long term vendor financing for the GSM rollout and transmission network expansion

(iv). exploring other financing sources including trade finance and leasing.

The committee has been meeting regularly and is in the process of determining long-term vendor financing options for the GSM rollout. Following the solicitation of bids from various equipment suppliers, the committee has commenced the evaluation of these bids and expects to conclude the process in the next few days.

2.2 Tariff Increase

Mr. President should note that NCC has made public statements critical of the decision to increase NITEL's local and trunk call tariffs. However, under the terms of current governing legislation, NCC does not have the power to regulate NITEL and should not be seen to be making comments contrary to agreed government policy. The House of Representatives and Senate Committees on Communications are taking similar uncooperative positions. Accordingly, we pray that NCC and the National Assembly Committees be brought to order and be asked to support the government's position on this matter with a view to minimizing conflicting signals that will adversely affect the image of our country.

2.3 Privatisation

Only one Expression of Interest (EOI) was received for the purchase of NITEL by the submission deadline of 5pm, Monday 11th June. The submission is from a consortium comprising Orascom and United Telesys with Hakeem Belo-Osagie as the local partner. The privatisation advisers have assured us that more EOIs, from MSI, China Telecom, Korea Telecom and China Mobile will be submitted in the next week and that others may materialise in view of the three week extension. It is becoming clear that the weakness in the global telecoms market, together with the lingering nervousness on the part of international investors in investing in Nigeria remain as disincentives to many potential bidders. However, BPE will be pursuing a more aggressive marketing strategy in the next two weeks with a view to generating a greater degree of interest. Other issues which may serve to hamper swift progress in the transaction and require constant monitoring:

(i). delay in completion of the financial audit
(ii). difficulty in identifying and obtaining Certificates of Occupancy for many of NITEL's properties
(iii). management of the unfunded pension liability of ₦43 billion
(iv). treatment of ₦40 billion state and federal tax liability
(v). retrenchment/redundancy issues

3. Nigerian Aviation Handling Company Limited (NAHCO)

Following an audience granted the Board of NAHCO on May 25th, 2001, Mr. President requested that the foreign airline shareholders increase their equity holding in the company to 51% in recognition of their right to exercise their pre-emptive rights as granted in the Memorandum and Articles of Association of the company. Mr. President was also reported to

Appendix 5

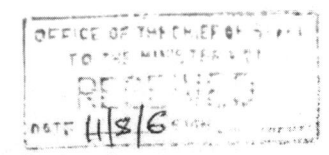

SENATOR A. D. SODANGI

DANMALIKIN NASARAWA & JARMAN LERE
NASARAWA WEST SENATORIAL DISTRICT, FEDERAL REPUBLIC OF NIGERIA
National Assembly Complex, Three Arms Zone, PMB 141, Garki - Abuja.
Tel: 09-2340646

NASS/S/CIA/758   11TH August, 2006

The Honourable Minister
Federal Capital Territory
Abuja

Attention: Alhaji Balarebe
Chief of General Staff to the
Honourable Minister

REQUEST FOR RE-ALLOCATION OF PLOTS

I have the directive of the Distinguished Senator A. D. Sodangi to request your kind consideration re-allocating plots to him. This request is necessitated by the fact that:-

I. The Distinguished Senator was hitherto allocated some parcels of land by the FCT authorities and he is addition bought over some other parcels from other allotees (see attached copies of the letters of allocation and purchase) and he converted same into a Law Firm.

But because of the irregularities in the allocations of the parcels of land to him and those he purchased from other allottees, the structures he put on these parcels of land have been demolished.

II. It is in the light of the foregoing, that the Distinguished Senator is now requesting the Honourable Minister's kind consideration for re-allocation of parcels of land.

Your favourable consideration of this request would be most appreciated by the Distinguished Senator.

Please accept the assurances of the Distinguished Senator A. D. Sodangi's warmest regards.

Abdulkarim A. Mohammed
Senior Legislative Aide to the Senator

CONSTITUENCY OFFICE: NO.1, YUSUF SODANGI ROAD, NASARAWA L.G.A., NASARAWA STATE. Tel: 047-66119

FEDERAL REPUBLIC OF NIGERIA
THE SENATE
COMMITTEE ON FEDERAL CAPITAL TERRITORY
National Assembly Complex,
Three-Arms Zone, P.M.B. 141, Abuja-Nigeria

NASS/S/CFCT/SECT/11   March 28, 2008

Dr. Aliyu Modibbo Umar,
Honourable Minister,
Federal Capital Territory,
Area 11, Garki,
Abuja.

ATTENTION: Alh. Umar Abbas
Director Special Duties on
Sale of FGN Houses

RE: REQUEST FOR ALLOCATIONS OF FEDERAL GOVERNMENT HOUSES: FINAL WALK-IN-SALE

The Committee hereby place on record its appreciation to Your Excellency on the approval granted for the allocation of the Federal Government Houses to Distinguished Members of the Committee on FCT and the Leadership of the Senate, Thursday, 27th March 2008.

However, the Committee wishes to register unreservedly its displeasure at the categories of houses allocated to Distinguished Senators.

The Honourable Minister would recall that while all Members of the House Committee on FCT including their Staff were allocated three (3) Bedroom Flats at choice areas, Distinguished Members of this Committee were allocated Two (2) Bedroom Flats most of which are situated at obscure locations and in most cases in dilapidated high-rise buildings.

The Committee therefore desires that its Members be accorded same treatment as their counterparts in the House of Representatives, as they deserve nothing less.

While we continue to count on Your Excellency's understanding and co-operation, please accept the assurances of the Committee's highest regards.

SENATOR ABUBAKAR D. SODANGI
Chairman,
Senate Committee on FCT.

S/N	FIRST	MIDDLE	LAST	HOUSE NO8	STREET NAME	DISTRICT	OMV	DESCRIPTION
1	ABUBAKAR	D	SODANGI	Block 651 Flat 1	Ado-Ekiti Close (xxx QTRS)	GARKI	N6,200,000.00	flat
2	ANTHONY	O	AGBO	Block 2 Flat 17	MATADI STREET	WUSE	3,750,000.00	flat
3	BASSEY		EWA-HENSHAW	Block 2 Flat 5	MATADI STREET	WUSE	3,750,000.00	flat
4	SMART		ADEYEMI	BLOCK 7 FLAT 18	SASSANDRA STREET	WUSE	4,000,000.00	flat
5	GARBA	ADAMU	TALBA	Block 3 Flat 11	MATADI STREET	WUSE	3,750,000.00	flat
6	CALEB		ZAGI	BLOCK 559(40) FLAT 13	Agric Qtrs, Zone 4	WUSE	3,750,000.00	flat
7	AUDU	IDRIS	UMAR	BLOCK 4(321) FLAT 9	TAMALE STREET	WUSE	3,750,000.00	flat
8	HEINEKEN		LOKPOBIRI	BLOCK 4(321) FLAT 17	TAMALE STREET	WUSE	3,750,000.00	flat
9	SOLA		AKINYEDE	Block 1(A) Flat 14	Mastana Street	WUSE	2,600,000.00	flat
10	ADEFEMI		KOLA	Block 363(36) Flat 13	Agric Qtrs, Zone 4	WUSE	3,750,000.00	flat
11	LAWAL		ADEGBITE	Block 363(36) Flat 16	Agric Qtrs, Zone 4	WUSE	3,750,000.00	flat
12	MOHAMMED	D	ZUBAIRU	Block 364 Flat 15	Agric Qtrs, Zone 4	WUSE	3,750,000.00	flat

Original Copies of the above listed items have been collected by Hon. Kalypsoo A.
[signature]
24/03/08

ATTENTION: Alh. Umar Abbas
Director Special Duties on
Sale of FGN Houses

REQUEST FOR ALLOCATION OF FEDERAL GOVERNMENT HOUSES: 2ND WALK-IN-SALE

A. SENATE COMMITTEE MEMBERS ON FCT

Request for Allocation:

S/N	Description	House No.	Street	Location/District
1.	Sen. Abubakar D. Sodangi			
2.	Sen. Anthony O. Agbo			
3.	Sen. Bassey Ewa-Henshaw			
4.	Sen. Smart Adeyemi			
5.	Sen. Garba Adamu Talba			
6.	Sen. Caleb Zagi			
7.	Sen. Audu Idris Umar			
8.	Sen. Heineken Lokpobiri			
9.	Sen. Sola Akinyede			
10.	Sen. Adefemi Kila			

B. **COMMITTEE SECRETARIAT:**

   (i) *Three Bedroom Flat Allocation:*

S/N	Description	House No.	Street	Location/District
1.	Lawal Adegbite Clerk, Committee on FCT			
2.	Ben Efeturi			
3.	Olufemi Folajin			

already keg a knee ✶

   (ii) *Two Bedrooms Flat Allocation:*

S/N	Name	House No.	Street	Location/District
1.	Godfrey Azumi			
2.	Pauline Mamman (Mrs)			
3.	Gloria Adamgbe (Ms)			
4.	Roseline Dikko			
5.	Habib Umar			
6.	Rabiu Matazu			
7.	Rose Kumbut			
8.	Moshood A. Hussaini			
9.	Chioma J. Ihenacho			
10.	Abraham A. Kamlah			

C. **OFFICE OF THE SENATE COMMITTEE CHAIRMAN ON FCT:** Senator Abubakar D. Sodangi

(i) *Three Bedroom Flat Allocation:*

S/N	Name	House No.	Street	Location/District
1.	Falaludeen S. Mohammed			
2.	Yusuf U. Sabo			
3.	Shamsudeen Abubakar			
4.	Abdullahi S. Abubakar			

(ii) *Two Bedroom Flat Allocation:* Senator Abubakar D. Sodangi

S/N	Description	House No.	Street	Location/District
1.	Barr. Mohammed D. Zubairu			
2.	Fadila S. Mohammed			
3.	Salisu M. Yusuf			
4.	Yusuf Usman			

(iii) *One Bedroom Flat Allocation*: Senator Abubakar D. Sodangi

S/N	Description	House No.	Street	Location/District
1.	Ibrahim M. Abdullahi			
2.	Suleiman Isah			
3.	Abubakar M. Yusuf			
4.	Jibrin S. Mohammed			

D. VICE CHAIRMAN COMMITTEE ON FCT : Senator Anthony O Agbo
Two Bedroom Flat Allocation:

S/N	Description	House No.	Street	Location/District
1.	Mohammed S. Lawal			

550

E. THE SENATE PRESIDENT : Senator David A. B. Mark, GCON

(i) *Three Bedroom Flat Allocation:*

S/N	Name	House No.	Street	Location/District
1.	Hon. Agbo Ogah			
2.	Sen. Emmanuel Okpede			
3.	Igoche Mark			

(ii) *Two Bedroom Flat Allocation:* Senator David A. B. Mark, GCON

S/N	Description	House No.	Street	Location/District
1.	Mrs. E. O. Adigun			
2.	Mr. Kola Ologbondiyan			

F. **THE DEPUTY SENATE PRESIDENT**: Senator Ike Ekweremadu, CFR

(i) *Three Bedroom Flat Allocation:*

S/N	Name	House No.	Street	Location/District
1.	Mrs. Nwanneka Ekweremadu			

(ii) *Two Bedroom Flat Allocation:* Senator Ike Ekweremadu, CFR

S/N	Name	House No.	Street	Location/District
1.	Benjamin Ogugua			
2.	Jonathan Ivoke			

G. **SENATE LEADER AND ALL OTHER PRINCIPAL OFFICERS OF THE SENATE**

(ii) *Two Bedroom Flat Allocation:*

S/N	Name	House No.	Street	Location/District
1.	Sen. Teslim K. Folarin			
2.	Sen. Mahmud K. Bello			
3.	Sen. Victor Ndoma-Egba			
4.	Sen. Mohammed Mana			
5.	Sen. Maina Ma'aji Lawan			
6.	Sen. Ahmad Rufai Sani			
7.	Sen. Adeleke O. Mamora			
8.	Sen. Kabiru I. Gaya			

NASS/S/CFCT/SECT/01/127   July 30, 2008

Dr. Aliyu Modibbo Umar,
Honourable Minister,
Federal Capital Territory Administration,
Area 11, Garki,
Abuja.

RE: REQUEST FOR ALLOCATION OF FEDERAL GOVERNMENT HOUSES: RETURN OF OFFER LETTERS

I am directed to convey the Committee's gratitude and appreciation for Your Excellency's magnanimous approval of the allocation of Federal Government Houses to Distinguished Members of the Committee.

Your Excellency may however wish to recollect the scenario which took place at the Public hearing in respect of the Houses during which the Distinguished Members of the Committee denied knowledge of the request and consequently declined the offer while directing the Committee Secretariat to return the allocations accordingly.

Consequently, attached hereto are the returned offer letters in respect of Distinguished Members of the Committee:

(1) Senator Abubakar D. Sodangi — Chairman

(2) Senator Anthony O. Agbo — Vice Chairman

(3) Senator Bassey Ewa-Henshaw — Member

(4) Senator Caleb Zagi — Member

(5) Senator Heineken Lokpobiri — Member

(6) Senator Smart Adeyemi — Member

(7) Senator Adefemi Kila — Member

(8) Senator Sola Akinyede — Member

(9) Senator Adamu Garba Talba — Member

(10) Senator Audu Idris Umar — Member

While counting on your continued understanding and co-operation, please accept the assurances of the Committee's highest regards for your esteemed Office.

Alh. Lawal A. Duduyemi
Deputy Director
Clerk, Committee on FCT
For Chairman

Appendix 6

EC CONCLUSIONS

THIS DOCUMENT IS THE PROPERTY OF THE FEDERAL EXECUTIVE COUNCIL

<u>**SECRET**</u>

<u>**EC(2007)19TH MEETING**</u>   **COPY NO.** _____

FEDERAL EXECUTIVE COUNCIL

CONCLUSIONS of the Meeting of the Federal Executive Council held at the Aso Rock Council Chamber, Presidential Villa, Abuja, on **WEDNESDAY, 23RD MAY, 2007**

Present

OLUSEGUN OBASANJO, GCFR
President of the Federal Republic of Nigeria.
(Chairman)

Chief BAYO OJO, SAN, Attorney-General of the Federation and Minister of Justice.	Mallam ADAMU BELLO, FCIB, CFR, OFR, Minister of Agriculture and Water Resources.
Otunba BAMIDELE F. DADA, Minister of State for Agriculture and Water Resources (1).	Dr. (Mrs.) GRACE O. OGWUCHE, Minister of State for Agriculture and Water Resources (2).
Dr. ALIYU MODIBBO UMAR, Minister of Commerce and Industry.	Amb. FIDELIS N. TAPGUN, Minister of State for Commerce and Industry.
Prof. A. B. BORISHADE, CFR Minister of Culture, Tourism and National Orientation.	Prof. IVARA EJEMOT ESU, OFR, Minister of State for Culture, Tourism and National Orientation.
Amb. THOMAS I. AGUIYI-IRONSI, Minister of Defence.	Arc. MIKE O. ONELEMEMEN, Minister of State for Defence.
Dr. SAYYADI ABBA RUMA, Minister of Education.	Dr. ADEWUMI ABITOYE, Minister of State for Education.
Dr. EDMUND M. DAUKORU, Minister of Energy.	Hon. AHMED ABDULHAMID, Minister of State for Energy.
Chief (Mrs.) HELEN U. ESUENE, Minister of Environment, Housing and Urban Development.	Alhaji IKRA ALIYU BILBIS, Minister of State for Environment, Housing and Urban Development.

EC CONCLUSIONS

Mallam NASIR EL'RUFAI, OFR,
 Minister of Federal Capital
 Territory.

Mrs. NENADI E. USMAN,
 Minister of Finance.

Prof. U. JOY OGWU,
 Minister of Foreign Affairs.

Sen. LAWAN GANA GUBA,
 Minister of State for Foreign
 Affairs (2).

Arc. HALIMA TAYO ALAO,
 Minister of State for Health.

Engr. (Dr.) OBAFEMI ANIBABA,
 Minister of State for
 Information and Communications.

Alaowei BRODERICK C. BOZIMO,
 Minister of State for Interior.

Alhaji BALA M. BORODO,
 Minister of Mines and Steel
 Development.

Prof. TURNER T. ISOUN, CFR
 Minister of Science and
 Technology.

Chief CORNELIUS O. ADEBAYO,
 Minister of Transportation.

Mallam HABIBU MUHAMMAD ALIYU,
 Minister of State for
 Transportation (2).

Chief DESMOND AKAWOR,
 Minister of State for Federal
 Capital Territory.

Engr. ELIAS NWALEM MBAM,
 Minister of State for Finance.

Mallam ABUBAKAR A. TANKO,
 Minister of State for Foreign
 Affairs (1).

Prof. EYITAYO LAMBO,
 Minister of Health.

Mr. FRANK NWEKE (Jnr.),
 Minister of Information and
 Communications.

Amb. OLUYEMI ADENIJI, CON,
 Minister of Interior.

Dr. HASSAN MUHAMMAD LAWAL
 Minister of Labour.

Sen. ABDALLAH M. WALI,
 Minister/Deputy Chairman,
 National Planning Commission.

Hon. BALA BAWA KA'OJE,
 Minister/Chairman,
 National Sports Commission.

Chief FEMI FANI-KAYODE,
 Minister of State for
 Transportation (1).

Mrs. INNA MARYAM CIROMA,
 Minister of Women Affairs and
 Social Development.

Chief (Mrs.) SALOME A. JANKADA,
Minister of Youth Development.

EC CONCLUSIONS

EC CONCLUSIONS
Secretariat

Secretary to Council	-	Chief U. J. Ekaette, CFR, mni
Deputy Secretary	-	Amb. Joe Keshi
Assistants	-	Mr. Charles Bonat
	-	Mr. M. O. Ighile
	-	Mrs. A. W. Ediae, fwc
	-	Mr. M. G. Omotosho
	-	Mr. F. F. Ogunshakin
	-	Mr. S. B. Ageloye
	-	Dr. J. O. Magbadelo
	-	Mr. B. E. Bassey
	-	Mr. Nura Abdu
	-	Alhaji Haruna Bello
	-	Mrs. V. A. Ogbulafor
	-	Alhaji B. G. Bukar
	-	Mr. Pius Ogunro

In Attendance

Head of the Civil Service of the Federation,
The Presidency
Abuja.

Chief of Staff to the President,
Presidential Villa,
Abuja.

National Security Adviser,
The Presidency,
Abuja.

Special Adviser to the President/
Head, BMPIU,
Presidential Villa,
Abuja.

Senior Special Assistant to the President on Media,
Presidential Villa,
Abuja.

Senior Special Assistant to the President on Millennium Development Goals.
The Presidency,
Abuja.

Permanent Secretary,
State House,
Abuja.

Permanent Secretary,
Head of the Civil Service of the Federation,
The Presidency,
Abuja.

Permanent Secretary,
General Service Office,
Office of the Secretary to the Government of the Federation,
Abuja.

Solicitor-General of the Federation and Permanent Secretary,
Ministry of Justice,
Abuja.

EC CONCLUSIONS

EC CONCLUSIONS

Permanent Secretary,
Ministry of Interior,
Abuja.

Permanent Secretary,
Ministry of Mines and Steel Development,
Abuja.

Permanent Secretary,
Ministry of Science and Technology,
Abuja.

Permanent Secretary,
Public Service Office,
Office of the Head of Civil Service of the Federation,
Abuja.

Permanent Secretary,
Police Service Commission,
Abuja.

Permanent Secretary,
Special Projects,
The Presidency,
Abuja.

Permanent Secretary,
Ministry of Agriculture and Water Resources,
Abuja.

Permanent Secretary,
Ministry of Commerce and Industry,
Abuja.

Permanent Secretary,
Water Section,
Ministry of Agriculture and Water Resources,
Abuja.

Permanent Secretary,
Service Welfare Office,
Office of Head of the Civil Service of the Federation,
The Presidency,
Abuja.

Permanent Secretary,
Ministry of Labour,
Abuja.

Permanent Secretary,
Management Services Office,
Office of the Head of the Civil Service of the Federation,
Abuja.

Permanent Secretary,
National Sports Commission,
Abuja.

Permanent Secretary,
Civil Service Commission,
Abuja.

Permanent Secretary,
Ministry of Women Affairs,
Abuja.

Permanent Secretary,
Ministry of Youth Development,
Abuja.

Permanent Secretary,
Ministry of Defence,
Abuja.

Permanent Secretary,
Ecological Funds Office,
Office of the Secretary to the Government of the Federation,
Abuja.

EC CONCLUSIONS

EC CONCLUSIONS

Permanent Secretary,
 Ministry of Education,
 Abuja.

Chairman,
 Federal Inland Revenue Services,
 Abuja.

Permanent Secretary,
 Economic Affairs,
 The Presidency,
 Abuja.

Permanent Secretary,
 Ministry of Environment,
 Housing and Urban Development,
 Abuja.

Permanent Secretary,
 Ministry of Finance,
 Abuja.

Permanent Secretary,
 Ministry of Foreign Affairs,
 Abuja.

Permanent Secretary,
 Ministry of Health,
 Abuja.

Permanent Secretary,
 Ministry of Information and Communications,
 Abuja.

Permanent Secretary,
 Special Duties,
 Office of the Secretary to the Government of the Federation,
 Abuja.

Permanent Secretary,
 Special Services Office,
 Office of the Secretary to the Government of the Federation,
 Abuja.

Permanent Secretary,
 Aviation Reforms,
 Ministry of Transportation,
 Abuja.

Permanent Secretary,
 Ministry of Transportation,
 Abuja.

Permanent Secretary,
 Revenue Mobilization, Allocation and Fiscal Commission,
 Abuja.

Permanent Secretary,
 Political Affairs Office,
 Office of the Secretary to the Government of the Federation,
 Abuja.

Special Assistant to the President on Policy and Programme Monitoring,
 Presidential Villa,
 Abuja.

Special Assistant to the President on Presidential Matters,
 Presidential Villa,
 Abuja.

EC CONCLUSIONS

EC CONCLUSIONS

Accountant-General of the
　Federation,
　Ministry of Finance,
　Abuja.

Chairman,
　Board of National Hospital,
　Abuja.

Executive Secretary,
　National Planning Commission,
　Abuja.

Director-General,
　Small and Medium Enterprises
　Development Agency of
　Nigeria,
　The Presidency,
　Abuja.

Director-General,
　National Air Space Research and
　Development Agency,
　Abuja.

Acting Auditor-General of the
　Federation,
　Ministry of Finance,
　Abuja.

Special Assistant to the Chief of Staff
　to the President,
　Presidential Villa,
　Abuja.

Appendix 7

LIST OF SOME BENEFICIARIES OF PLOTS REVOKED AND RE-ALLOCATED BASED ON THE FALSE "FUNCTUS OFFICIO" CONCLUSION

File No.	Name	Plot No.	District	Size (m2)	Land Use	Allocation Date	Position	Role?
NS 60098	Abubakar Danso Sodangi	1778	Guzape	1981	Residential	8/9/2008	Senator	Co-Chair
AN 65513	Ikechukwu Obiora	1729	Guzape	833	Residential	24/09/2008	Senator	Co-Chair
EB 60037	Anthony Oduma Agbo	1777	Guzape	1786	Residential	24/09/2008	Senator	Vice Chai
CR 60069	Bassey Ewa Henshaw	1676	Guzape	2011	Residential	8/9/2008	Senator	Member
BY 60047	Heineken Lokpobiri	1708	Guzape	1240	Residential	8/9/2008	Senator	Member
EK 60073	Adefemi Kila	1689	Guzape	1588	Residential	8/9/2008	Senator	Member
YB 60034	Adamu Garba Talba	1709	Guzape	1339	Residential	5/9/2008	Senator	Member
KD 60230	Caleb Zagi	1737	Guzape	1231	Residential	8/9/2008	Senator	Member
KG 60400	Smart Adeyemi	1759	Guzape	1329	Residential	25/09/2008	Senator	Member
BN 60178	David Alechenu Mark	1923	Maitama	2294	Residential	3/9/2008	Senator	Prin Offr
AN 65482	Ike Ekweremadu	2477	Asokoro	1867	Residential	3/9/2008	Senator	Prin Offr
AN 65482	Ike Ekweremadu	1474	Mabushi	1725	Residential	25/9/2008	Senator	Prin Offr
OY 60118	Teslim Kolawole Folarin	953	Katampe Ext	1656	Residential	5/9/2008	Senator	Prin Offr
CR 60070	Victor Ndoma-Egba	1414	Katampe Ext	1243	Residential	5/9/2008	Senator	Prin Offr
KT 60152	Mahmud Kanti Bello	1779	Guzape	2002	Residential	8/9/2008	Senator	Prin Offr
AB 60084	Vincent Eze Ogbulafor	1683	Guzape	2994	Residential	5/9/2008	PDP Chairman	
KB 60069	Bello Halliru Mohammed	1383	Katampe Ext	2609	Residential	13/10/2008	PDP Chieftain	
KN 60231	Abdullahi Sarki Mukhtar	1922	Maitama	2457	Residential	3/9/2008	NSA/Cabinet	FEC
DT 60021	Mustapha J. Onoyiveta	1722	Guzape	1450	Residential	10/9/2008	ADC to Yar'Adua	
BA 60021	Yusuf Mohammed Tilde	1615	Guzape	1320	Residential	19/9/2008	CSO to Yar'Adua	
PL 60144	Inuwa Auwal Baba	1669	Guzape	1886	Residential	19/9/2008	Special Assistant	to Yar'Adua
KT 60174	Mustapha Bala Batsari	831	Jabi	2197	Residential	3/9/2008	Special Assistant	to Yar'Adua
BY 60000	Owoye Andrew Azazi	1768	Guzape	1704	Residential	5/9/2008	General	Army
RV 60018	Mike Mbama Okiro	1925	Maitama	1966	Residential	29/8/2008	Insp General	Police
BN 60219	Farida Mzamber Waziri	1460	Mabushi	2336	Residential	24/9/2008	EFCC Chairman	Investigatic
CR 60088	John Ogar Odey	1390	Katampe Ext	1446	Residential	9/9/2008	Minister	FEC
AD 60186	Aliyu Idi Hong	1758	Guzape	1804	Residential	5/9/2008	Minister	FEC
GO 60135	Aishatu Jibril Dukku	1681	Guzape	1892	Residential	5/9/2008	Minister	FEC
OS 21346	Akinlabi Olasunkanmi	1735	Guzape	1322	Residential	5/9/2008	Minister	FEC
AN 24842	Dora Nkem Akunyili	1684	Guzape	1736	Residential	5/9/2008	Minister	FEC
EB 60025	Igwe Aja-Nwachukwu	1678	Guzape	1904	Residential	5/9/2008	Minister	FEC
OD 60015	Adetokunbo Kayode	1733	Guzape	1947	Residential	5/9/2008	Minister	FEC
LA 60151	Ademola Rasaq Seriki	1613	Guzape	1232	Residential	12/9/2008	Minister	FEC
OY 60134	Aderemi Waheed Babalola	512	Katampe Ext	2626	Residential	12/9/2008	Minister	FEC
PL 60147	Ibrahim Dasuki Nakande	404	Karmo	1407	Residential	19/9/2008	Minister	FEC
EK 60014	Emmanuel Oltunde Odusina	1306	Katampe Ext	1215	Residential	13/10/2008	Minister	FEC
KW 60137	Halima Tayo Alao	1780	Guzape	1828	Residential	13/10/2008	Minister	FEC
IM 60373	Charles C. Ugwuh	1613	Guzape	1436	Residential	13/10/2008	Minister	FEC
BY 60036	Godsday Peter Orubebe	1736	Guzape	1224	Residential	7/10/2008	Minister	FEC
KN 60241	Shamsudeen Usman	15	Katampe Ext	2939	Residential	5/9/2008	Minister	FEC
BA 60070	Mahmud Yayale Ahmed	3386	Asokoro	1756	Residential	9/9/2008	Minister	FEC
DT 21917	Joseph Chiedu Keshi	1614	Guzape	1304	Residential	10/9/2008	Perm Sec	FEC
MISC 102027	Ferodox Ventures Limited	3457	Maitama	3153	Residential	24/9/2008	Associated	Company
MISC 102026	Promodutch Investment Ltd	5030	Maitama	5274	Residential	24/9/2008	Associated	Company
MISC 101907	Fortrade Global Services	1459	Mabushi	1711	Residential	24/9/2009	Associated	Company
OS 60187	Reuben Adeleye Abati	2174	Katampe	1546	Residential	24/9/2008	Columnist	Media
YB 60047	Garba Deen Mohammed	1282	Katampe	1442	Residential	24/9/2008	Columnist	Media
KT 60178	Ibrahim Mohammed Sheme	1095	Katampe	1005	Residential	24/9/2008	Columnist	Media

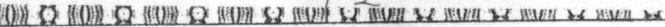

FEDERAL REPUBLIC OF NIGERIA
FEDERAL CAPITAL TERRITORY, ABUJA
OFFER OF STATUTORY RIGHT OF OCCUPANCY

Name: MAHMUD KANTI BELLO
Address: 6 JIM NWOBODO STREET, GUDU, ABUJA, FCT, NIGERIA
New File Number: KT 60152
Old File Number: -
R-of-O Date: 08/09/2008

I am hereby directed to convey the approval of the Minister of the Federal Capital Territory of the grant of a Right of Occupancy in respect of Plot No.: 1779 having an area of approximately 2002.05m² in Cadastral Zone A09 of GUZAPE on the following terms and conditions:

(i) Premium:	₦	2,000.00/m²
(ii) Rent Per Annum:	₦	15.00/m²
(iii) Improvement Value:		NOT LESS THAN FIVE MILLION NAIRA
(iv) Purpose:		RESIDENTIAL (PRIV. RESIDENTIAL)
(v) Lease Term:		99 YEARS
(vi) Rent Revision:		EVERY FIVE YEARS

(2) Furthermore, the following conditions shall, in addition to other conditions, be included in the Certificate of Occupancy evidencing the grant of this Right of Occupancy:

  (i) Within two years from the date of the commencement of this Right of Occupancy to erect and complete on said plot the buildings or other works specified in the detailed plans approved by the Federal Capital Development Authority or any other Agency empowered to do so.

  (ii) Not to erect or build or permit to be erected or built on the said plot any buildings other than those permitted to be erected by virtue of the Certificate of Occupancy nor make or permit to be made additions or alterations to the said buildings to be erected or buildings already erected on the plot except in accordance with the plans and specifications approved by the Federal Capital Development Authority or any other Agency empowered to do so.

  (iii) Not to alienate the Right of Occupancy hereby granted or any part thereof by sale, assignment, mortgage, transfer of possession, sub-lease or bequest, or otherwise howsoever without the prior consent of the Minister first had and obtained.

  (iv) The Minister or any public officer duly authorized by the Minister in his behalf, shall have the power to enter upon and inspect the land comprised in any statutory Right of Occupancy or any improvements effected thereon, at any reasonable hours during the day and the occupier shall permit and give free access to the Minister or any such officer to enter and so inspect.

(3) This Right of Occupancy shall commence on the date of acceptance as signified by you in writing and should be within two months from the date of this letter.

(4) You would also be required to pay other fees and charges at a rate to be determined for the survey, preparation, and execution of the Certificate of Occupancy, and building plan approvals.

Yours faithfully,

for: Minister Federal Capital Territory

ABUJA GEOGRAPHIC INFORMATION SYSTEMS (AGIS), 4 PEACE DRIVE, CENTRAL AREA, ABUJA
TELEPHONES: 09-671 6100 09-671 6200, 09-671 6300, 09-671 6400. http://www.abujagis.com, info@abujagis.com

FEDERAL REPUBLIC OF NIGERIA
FEDERAL CAPITAL TERRITORY, ABUJA
OFFER OF STATUTORY RIGHT OF OCCUPANCY

Name: BASSEY EWA HENSHAW
Address: 388, ASARI ESO LANE, CALABAR, CROSS RIVER STATE, NIGERIA
New File Number: CR 60069
Old File Number: -
R-of-O Date: 08/09/2008

I am hereby directed to convey the approval of the Minister of the Federal Capital Territory of the grant of a Right of Occupancy in respect of Plot No.: 1676 having an area of approximately 2010.68m^2 in Cadastral Zone A09 of GUZAPE on the following terms and conditions:

(i) Premium:	₦	2,000.00/m^2
(ii) Rent Per Annum:	₦	15.00/m^2
(iii) Improvement Value:		NOT LESS THAN FIVE MILLION NAIRA
(iv) Purpose:		RESIDENTIAL (PRIV. RESIDENTIAL)
(v) Lease Term:		99 YEARS
(vi) Rent Revision:		EVERY FIVE YEARS

(2) Furthermore, the following conditions shall, in addition to other conditions, be included in the Certificate of Occupancy evidencing the grant of this Right of Occupancy:

   (i) Within two years from the date of the commencement of this Right of Occupancy to erect and complete on said plot the buildings or other works specified in the detailed plans approved by the Federal Capital Development Authority or any other Agency empowered to do so.

   (ii) Not to erect or build or permit to be erected or built on the said plot any buildings other than those permitted to be erected by virtue of the Certificate of Occupancy nor make or permit to be made additions or alterations to the said buildings to be erected or buildings already erected on the plot except in accordance with the plans and specifications approved by the Federal Capital Development Authority or any other Agency empowered to do so.

   (iii) Not to alienate the Right of Occupancy hereby granted or any part thereof by sale, assignment, mortgage, transfer of possession, sub-lease or bequest, or otherwise howsoever without the prior consent of the Minister first had and obtained.

   (iv) The Minister or any public officer duly authorized by the Minister in his behalf, shall have the power to enter upon and inspect the land comprised in any statutory Right of Occupancy or any improvements effected thereon, at any reasonable hours during the day and the occupier shall permit and give free access to the Minister or any such officer to enter and so inspect.

(3) This Right of Occupancy shall commence on the date of acceptance as signified by you in writing and should be within two months from the date of this letter.

(4) You would also be required to pay other fees and charges at a rate to be determined for the survey, preparation, and execution of the Certificate of Occupancy, and building plan approvals.

Yours faithfully,

for: Minister Federal Capital Territory

ABUJA GEOGRAPHIC INFORMATION SYSTEMS (AGIS), 4 PEACE DRIVE, CENTRAL AREA, ABUJA
TELEPHONES: 09-671 6100 09-671 6200, 09-671 6300, 09-671 6400. http://www.abujagis.com, info@abujagis.com

FEDERAL REPUBLIC OF NIGERIA
FEDERAL CAPITAL TERRITORY, ABUJA
OFFER OF STATUTORY RIGHT OF OCCUPANCY

Name: HEINEKEN LOKPOBIRI
Address: C/O 09 NEW SENATE WING NASS THREE ARMS ZONE, ABUJA, FCT, NIGERIA
New File Number: BY 60047
Old File Number: -
R-of-O Date: 08/09/2008

I am hereby directed to convey the approval of the Minister of the Federal Capital Territory of the grant of a Right of Occupancy in respect of Plot No.: 1708 having an area of approximately 1240.29m² in Cadastral Zone A09 of GUZAPE on the following terms and conditions:

(i)	Premium:	₦ 2,000.00/m²
(ii)	Rent Per Annum:	₦ 15.00/m²
(iii)	Improvement Value:	NOT LESS THAN FIVE MILLION NAIRA
(iv)	Purpose:	RESIDENTIAL (PRIV. RESIDENTIAL)
(v)	Lease Term:	99 YEARS
(vi)	Rent Revision:	EVERY FIVE YEARS

(2) Furthermore, the following conditions shall, in addition to other conditions, be included in the Certificate of Occupancy evidencing the grant of this Right of Occupancy:

(i) Within two years from the date of the commencement of this Right of Occupancy to erect and complete on said plot the buildings or other works specified in the detailed plans approved by the Federal Capital Development Authority or any other Agency empowered to do so.

(ii) Not to erect or build or permit to be erected or built on the said plot any buildings other than those permitted to be erected by virtue of the Certificate of Occupancy nor make or permit to be made additions or alterations to the said buildings to be erected or buildings already erected on the plot except in accordance with the plans and specifications approved by the Federal Capital Development Authority or any other Agency empowered to do so.

(iii) Not to alienate the Right of Occupancy hereby granted or any part thereof by sale, assignment, mortgage, transfer of possession, sub-lease or bequest, or otherwise howsoever without the prior consent of the Minister first had and obtained.

(iv) The Minister or any public officer duly authorized by the Minister in his behalf, shall have the power to enter upon and inspect the land comprised in any statutory Right of Occupancy or any improvements effected thereon, at any reasonable hours during the day and the occupier shall permit and give free access to the Minister or any such officer to enter and so inspect.

(3) This Right of Occupancy shall commence on the date of acceptance as signified by you in writing and should be within two months from the date of this letter.

(4) You would also be required to pay other fees and charges at a rate to be determined for the survey, preparation, and execution of the Certificate of Occupancy, and building plan approvals.

Yours faithfully,

for: Minister Federal Capital Territory

ABUJA GEOGRAPHIC INFORMATION SYSTEMS (AGIS), 4 PEACE DRIVE, CENTRAL AREA, ABUJA
TELEPHONES: 09-671 6100 09-671 6200, 09-671 6300, 09-671 6400. http://www.abujagis.com, info@abujagis.com

FEDERAL REPUBLIC OF NIGERIA
FEDERAL CAPITAL TERRITORY, ABUJA
OFFER OF STATUTORY RIGHT OF OCCUPANCY

Name: ADEFEMI KILA
Address: 1 OMONIJO STREET, EFON-ALAYE, EKITI STATE, NIGERIA
New File Number: EK 60073
Old File Number: -
R-of-O Date: 08/09/2008

I am hereby directed to convey the approval of the Minister of the Federal Capital Territory of the grant of a Right of Occupancy in respect of Plot No.: 1689 having an area of approximately 1587.51m^2 in Cadastral Zone A09 of GUZAPE on the following terms and conditions:

(i)	Premium:	₦ 2,000.00/m^2
(ii)	Rent Per Annum:	₦ 15.00/m^2
(iii)	Improvement Value:	NOT LESS THAN FIVE MILLION NAIRA
(iv)	Purpose:	RESIDENTIAL (PRIV. RESIDENTIAL)
(v)	Lease Term:	99 YEARS
(vi)	Rent Revision:	EVERY FIVE YEARS

(2) Furthermore, the following conditions shall, in addition to other conditions, be included in the Certificate of Occupancy evidencing the grant of this Right of Occupancy:

  (i) Within two years from the date of the commencement of this Right of Occupancy to erect and complete on said plot the buildings or other works specified in the detailed plans approved by the Federal Capital Development Authority or any other Agency empowered to do so.

  (ii) Not to erect or build or permit to be erected or built on the said plot any buildings other than those permitted to be erected by virtue of the Certificate of Occupancy nor make or permit to be made additions or alterations to the said buildings to be erected or buildings already erected on the plot except in accordance with the plans and specifications approved by the Federal Capital Development Authority or any other Agency empowered to do so.

  (iii) Not to alienate the Right of Occupancy hereby granted or any part thereof by sale, assignment, mortgage, transfer of possession, sub-lease or bequest, or otherwise howsoever without the prior consent of the Minister first had and obtained.

  (iv) The Minister or any public officer duly authorized by the Minister in his behalf, shall have the power to enter upon and inspect the land comprised in any statutory Right of Occupancy or any improvements effected thereon, at any reasonable hours during the day and the occupier shall permit and give free access to the Minister or any such officer to enter and so inspect.

(3) This Right of Occupancy shall commence on the date of acceptance as signified by you in writing and should be within two months from the date of this letter.

(4) You would also be required to pay other fees and charges at a rate to be determined for the survey, preparation, and execution of the Certificate of Occupancy, and building plan approvals.

Yours faithfully,

for: Minister Federal Capital Territory

ABUJA GEOGRAPHIC INFORMATION SYSTEMS (AGIS), 4 PEACE DRIVE, CENTRAL AREA, ABUJA
TELEPHONES: 09-671 6100 09-671 6200, 09-671 6300, 09-671 6400, http://www.abujagis.com, info@abujagis.com

FEDERAL REPUBLIC OF NIGERIA
FEDERAL CAPITAL TERRITORY, ABUJA
OFFER OF STATUTORY RIGHT OF OCCUPANCY

Name: CALEB ZAGI
Address: C/O BLOCK 72 LEGISLATIVE QUARTERS, GUDU, ABUJA, FCT, NIGERIA
New File Number: KD 60230
Old File Number: -
R-of-O Date: 08/09/2008

I am hereby directed to convey the approval of the Minister of the Federal Capital Territory of the grant of a Right of Occupancy in respect of Plot No.: 1737 having an area of approximately 1230.72m² in Cadastral Zone A09 of GUZAPE on the following terms and conditions:

(i) Premium:	₦	2,000.00/m²
(ii) Rent Per Annum:	₦	15.00/m²
(iii) Improvement Value:		NOT LESS THAN FIVE MILLION NAIRA
(iv) Purpose:		RESIDENTIAL (PRIV. RESIDENTIAL)
(v) Lease Term:		99 YEARS
(vi) Rent Revision:		EVERY FIVE YEARS

(2) Furthermore, the following conditions shall, in addition to other conditions, be included in the Certificate of Occupancy evidencing the grant of this Right of Occupancy:

  (i) Within two years from the date of the commencement of this Right of Occupancy to erect and complete on said plot the buildings or other works specified in the detailed plans approved by the Federal Capital Development Authority or any other Agency empowered to do so.

  (ii) Not to erect or build or permit to be erected or built on the said plot any buildings other than those permitted to be erected by virtue of the Certificate of Occupancy nor make or permit to be made additions or alterations to the said buildings to be erected or buildings already erected on the plot except in accordance with the plans and specifications approved by the Federal Capital Development Authority or any other Agency empowered to do so.

  (iii) Not to alienate the Right of Occupancy hereby granted or any part thereof by sale, assignment, mortgage, transfer of possession, sub-lease or bequest, or otherwise howsoever without the prior consent of the Minister first had and obtained.

  (iv) The Minister or any public officer duly authorized by the Minister in his behalf, shall have the power to enter upon and inspect the land comprised in any statutory Right of Occupancy or any improvements effected thereon, at any reasonable hours during the day and the occupier shall permit and give free access to the Minister or any such officer to enter and so inspect.

(3) This Right of Occupancy shall commence on the date of acceptance as signified by you in writing and should be within two months from the date of this letter.

(4) You would also be required to pay other fees and charges at a rate to be determined for the survey, preparation, and execution of the Certificate of Occupancy, and building plan approvals.

Yours faithfully,

for: Minister Federal Capital Territory

ABUJA GEOGRAPHIC INFORMATION SYSTEMS (AGIS), 4 PEACE DRIVE, CENTRAL AREA, ABUJA
TELEPHONES: 09-671 6100 09-671 6200, 09-671 6300, 09-671 6400. http://www.abujagis.com, info@abujagis.com

FEDERAL REPUBLIC OF NIGERIA
FEDERAL CAPITAL TERRITORY, ABUJA
OFFER OF STATUTORY RIGHT OF OCCUPANCY

Name: OBIORA CHUKWUKADIBIA AGHAEGBUNA
Address: BLOCK 55, ACCRA STREET, WUSE ZONE 5, ABUJA, FCT, NIGERIA
New File Number: AN 65513
Old File Number: -
R-of-O Date: 24/09/2008

I am hereby directed to convey the approval of the Minister of the Federal Capital Territory of the grant of a Right of Occupancy in respect of Plot No.:   1729   having an area of approximately   833.38m² in Cadastral Zone A09 of   GUZAPE   on the following terms and conditions:

(i)	Premium:	₦ 2,000.00/m²
(ii)	Rent Per Annum:	₦ 15.00/m²
(iii)	Improvement Value:	NOT LESS THAN FIVE MILLION NAIRA
(iv)	Purpose:	RESIDENTIAL (PRIV. RESIDENTIAL)
(v)	Lease Term:	99 YEARS
(vi)	Rent Revision:	EVERY FIVE YEARS

(2) Furthermore, the following conditions shall, in addition to other conditions, be included in the Certificate of Occupancy evidencing the grant of this Right of Occupancy:

  (i) Within two years from the date of the commencement of this Right of Occupancy to erect and complete on said plot the buildings or other works specified in the detailed plans approved by the Federal Capital Development Authority or any other Agency empowered to do so.

  (ii) Not to erect or build or permit to be erected or built on the said plot any buildings other than those permitted to be erected by virtue of the Certificate of Occupancy nor make or permit to be made additions or alterations to the said buildings to be erected or buildings already erected on the plot except in accordance with the plans and specifications approved by the Federal Capital Development Authority or any other Agency empowered to do so.

  (iii) Not to alienate the Right of Occupancy hereby granted or any part thereof by sale, assignment, mortgage, transfer of possession, sub-lease or bequest, or otherwise howsoever without the prior consent of the Minister first had and obtained.

  (iv) The Minister or any public officer duly authorized by the Minister in his behalf, shall have the power to enter upon and inspect the land comprised in any statutory Right of Occupancy or any improvements effected thereon, at any reasonable hours during the day and the occupier shall permit and give free access to the Minister or any such officer to enter and so inspect.

(3) This Right of Occupancy shall commence on the date of acceptance as signified by you in writing and should be within two months from the date of this letter.

(4) You would also be required to pay other fees and charges at a rate to be determined for the survey, preparation, and execution of the Certificate of Occupancy, and building plan approvals.

Yours faithfully,

_____
for: Minister Federal Capital Territory

ABUJA GEOGRAPHIC INFORMATION SYSTEMS (AGIS) 4 PEACE DRIVE, CENTRAL AREA, ABUJA

FEDERAL REPUBLIC OF NIGERIA
FEDERAL CAPITAL TERRITORY, ABUJA
OFFER OF STATUTORY RIGHT OF OCCUPANCY

Name: ANTHONY ODUMA AGBO
Address: PLOT 68A ONWE ROAD, ABAKALIKI, EBONYI STATE, NIGERIA
New File Number: EB 60037
Old File Number: -
R-of-O Date: 24/09/2008

I am hereby directed to convey the approval of the Minister of the Federal Capital Territory of the grant of a Right of Occupancy in respect of Plot No.: **1777** having an area of approximately **1785.71m²** in Cadastral Zone **A09** of **GUZAPE** on the following terms and conditions:

(i) Premium:	₦	2,000.00/m²
(ii) Rent Per Annum:	₦	15.00/m²
(iii) Improvement Value:		NOT LESS THAN FIVE MILLION NAIRA
(iv) Purpose:		RESIDENTIAL (PRIV. RESIDENTIAL)
(v) Lease Term:		99 YEARS
(vi) Rent Revision:		EVERY FIVE YEARS

(2) Furthermore, the following conditions shall, in addition to other conditions, be included in the Certificate of Occupancy evidencing the grant of this Right of Occupancy:

  (i) Within two years from the date of the commencement of this Right of Occupancy to erect and complete on said plot the buildings or other works specified in the detailed plans approved by the Federal Capital Development Authority or any other Agency empowered to do so.

  (ii) Not to erect or build or permit to be erected or built on the said plot any buildings other than those permitted to be erected by virtue of the Certificate of Occupancy nor make or permit to be made additions or alterations to the said buildings to be erected or buildings already erected on the plot except in accordance with the plans and specifications approved by the Federal Capital Development Authority or any other Agency empowered to do so.

  (iii) Not to alienate the Right of Occupancy hereby granted or any part thereof by sale, assignment, mortgage, transfer of possession, sub-lease or bequest, or otherwise howsoever without the prior consent of the Minister first had and obtained.

  (iv) The Minister or any public officer duly authorized by the Minister in his behalf, shall have the power to enter upon and inspect the land comprised in any statutory Right of Occupancy or any improvements effected thereon, at any reasonable hours during the day and the occupier shall permit and give free access to the Minister or any such officer to enter and so inspect.

(3) This Right of Occupancy shall commence on the date of acceptance as signified by you in writing and should be within two months from the date of this letter.

(4) You would also be required to pay other fees and charges at a rate to be determined for the survey, preparation, and execution of the Certificate of Occupancy, and building plan approvals.

Yours faithfully,

_____
for: Minister Federal Capital Territory

FEDERAL REPUBLIC OF NIGERIA
FEDERAL CAPITAL TERRITORY, ABUJA
OFFER OF STATUTORY RIGHT OF OCCUPANCY

Name: SMART ADEYEMI
Address: 9A ABDULKADIR ROAD, ILORIN, KWARA STATE, NIGERIA
New File Number: KG 60400
Old File Number: -
R-of-O Date: 25/09/2008

I am hereby directed to convey the approval of the Minister of the Federal Capital Territory of the grant of a Right of Occupancy in respect of Plot No.: 1759 having an area of approximately 1328.60m^2 in Cadastral Zone A09 of GUZAPE on the following terms and conditions:

(i) Premium: ₦ 2,000.00/m^2
(ii) Rent Per Annum: ₦ 15.00/m^2
(iii) Improvement Value: NOT LESS THAN FIVE MILLION NAIRA
(iv) Purpose: RESIDENTIAL (PRIV. RESIDENTIAL)
(v) Lease Term: 99 YEARS
(vi) Rent Revision: EVERY FIVE YEARS

(2) Furthermore, the following conditions shall, in addition to other conditions, be included in the Certificate of Occupancy evidencing the grant of this Right of Occupancy:

  (i) Within two years from the date of the commencement of this Right of Occupancy to erect and complete on said plot the buildings or other works specified in the detailed plans approved by the Federal Capital Development Authority or any other Agency empowered to do so.

  (ii) Not to erect or build or permit to be erected or built on the said plot any buildings other than those permitted to be erected by virtue of the Certificate of Occupancy nor make or permit to be made additions or alterations to the said buildings to be erected or buildings already erected on the plot except in accordance with the plans and specifications approved by the Federal Capital Development Authority or any other Agency empowered to do so.

  (iii) Not to alienate the Right of Occupancy hereby granted or any part thereof by sale, assignment, mortgage, transfer of possession, sub-lease or bequest, or otherwise howsoever without the prior consent of the Minister first had and obtained.

  (iv) The Minister or any public officer duly authorized by the Minister in his behalf, shall have the power to enter upon and inspect the land comprised in any statutory Right of Occupancy or any improvements effected thereon, at any reasonable hours during the day and the occupier shall permit and give free access to the Minister or any such officer to enter and so inspect.

(3) This Right of Occupancy shall commence on the date of acceptance as signified by you in writing and should be within two months from the date of this letter.

(4) You would also be required to pay other fees and charges at a rate to be determined for the survey, preparation, and execution of the Certificate of Occupancy, and building plan approvals.

Yours faithfully,

for: Minister Federal Capital Territory

Appendix 8

THIS DOCUMENT IS THE PROPERTY OF THE FCT EXECUTIVE COMMITTEE

SECRET:
FCT EC (07) 18TH MEETING   COPY NO:............

FCT EXECUTIVE COMMITTEE

**Conclusions of Meeting of the FCT Executive Committee
Held in the Conference Hall of the Minister FCT on 22nd May, 2007 at 9.00 a.m.**

PRESENT:

Mal. Nasir Ahmad el-Rufai, OFR
Chairman

Chief Desmond Akawor Hon. Minister of State FCT	Mohammed Sani Alhassan Executive Secretary FCDA
Balarabe A. Lawal Chief of Staff to the Minister, FCT	Bolanle A. Onagoruwa Secretary Education Secretariat
Dr. Auwalu Anwar Secretary Health Secretariat	Amina B. Zakari Secretary Social Dev. Secretariat
Dr. A. O. Odunmbaku-Wilson Secretary Transportation Secretariat	A. Buhari Dikko Administrator Satellite Towns Dev. Agency
Tijjani M. Abdullahi Group Managing Director Abuja Investment Co. Limited	Jummai A. Kwanashie Managing Director, Abuja Metropolitan Mgt. Agency
Ibrahim Habu Sule Director Treasury, FCT	

H. S. Oloja
Director Legal Services/
Secretary, FCT EXCO

IN ATTENDANCE:

Hadiza Abdullahi
Director Establishment &
Training, FCT

Yusuf Tsaiyabu
Director Audit, FCT

B. G. Mainassara
Rep. Director, Abuja Geographic
Information Systems

Dr. Abdu Mukhtar
Senior Special Assistant
Economic Matters

Martins Akumazi
Senior Special Assistant
Project Monitoring

Amina Salihu
Senior Special Assistant
Information & Strategy

Hauwa Yabani,
Special Assistant I
to the Minister, FCT.

Hadiza Usman,
Special Assistant II
to the Minister, FCT.

SECRETARIAT:

Peter T. Manjuk
Asma'u Mukhtar
Ahmed Ismaila
Harisu Umar

(b) He further informed members that the date of the briefing had been tentatively fixed for Sunday 27th May, 2007.

18.2 **TRANSITIONAL FCT ADMINISTRATION**:
(a) The Chairman informed EXCO that Mr. President had approved a transitional administration in the FCT pending the appointment of the next Minister to avoid a vacuum.

(b) He then explained that the Committee would be headed by the Executive Secretary, FCDA while the Chief of Staff and the Secretaries of the Mandate Secretariats would remain in office in the interim.

(c) The Minister further informed EXCO that the Ad-Hoc Committee on Sale of Government Houses would also be in place to conclude the programme and submit their report before winding up.

18.3 **PRIME SOIL**:
The Secretary, Agriculture informed the EXCO that land had been allocated to Prime Soil, who had taken possession of same.

18.4 **MESSAGE OF GRATITUDE**:
(a) Mr. Minister thanked the members of the EXCO and all those that worked with him towards achieving the Abuja dream and stated that it was team work that made things work. He further stated that he had learnt a lot from the experience he acquired in the management of the FCT.

(b) The Minister of State, FCT, Executive Secretary, FCDA and the Secretary, FCT EXCO responded on behalf of the EXCO and thanked Mr. Minister for the qualitative leadership he rendered towards making Abuja an enviable place to be.

19. **CLOSING**:
In the absence of any other business, the meeting adjourned with a prayer at 11.45 a.m. to reconvene on Tuesday 29th May, 2007 at 09.00 a.m. at the same venue.

The Secretariat,
FCT Executive Committee,
Abuja.

22nd May, 2007

Appendix 9

Extraordinary

Federal Republic of Nigeria Official Gazette

| No. 82 | Lagos - 15th August, 2005 | Vol. 92 |

Government Notice No. 155

The following are published as Supplement to this *Gazette* :

S. I. No.	Short Title	Page
15	Child Right Act (Transfer of Certain Statutory Functions) Order	B159
	Approved Guidelines for the Sale of Federal Government Houses in the Federal Capital Territory to Career Civil Servants	462 - 464
	Approved Guidelines for the Sale of Federal Government Houses in the Federal Capital Territory to the General Public and Political Office Holders	483 - 486
	Extract from Conclusions of the Meeting of the Federal Executive Council	486 - 487

Printed and Published by The Federal Government Press, Lagos, Nigeria.
FGP 266/112005/650 (OL 73)
Annual Subscription from 1st January, 2005 is Local : ₦15,000.00 Overseas : ₦21,500.00 [Surface Mail] ₦24,500.00 [Second Class Air Mail]. Present issue ₦350.00 per copy. Subscribers who wish to obtain *Gazette* after 1st January should apply to the Federal Government Printer, Lagos for amended Subscriptions.

CHILD RIGHT (TRANSFER OF CERTAIN STATUTORY FUNCTIONS) ORDER

Under section 2

Commencement date : 13*th September*, 2005.

Exercise of the powers.

In exercise of the powers conferred on me by section 315(2) of the Constitution of the Federal Repubic of Nigeria 1999 and section 2(1) (*a*) (*b*) of the Minister's Statutory Powers and Duties (Miscellaneous Provisions) Act Cap. 228 Laws of the Federation of Nigeria 1990 and all other powers enabling me in that behalf I, Olusegun Obasanjo President of the Federal Republic of Nigeria hereby make the following Order :

Transfer of Certain Statutory Function.

The functions conferred on the Minister charged with the responsibility for matters relating to children under the Child's Right Act 2003 with respect to the powers to make Regulations is hereby transferred to the Minister Federal Capital Territory.

The Minister Federal Capital Territory shall exercise the functions herein transferred only in respect of making Regulations to ensure the effective implementation of the provisions of the Child's Rights Acts as it affects the Federal Capital Territory.

Short Title.

This Order may be cited as the Child Rights (Transfer of Certain Statutory Functions) Order.

MADE AT ABUJA this 7TH DAY of SEPTEMBER, 2005.

Signed
OLUSEGUN OBASANJO GCFR
President of the Federal Republic of Nigeria

FEDERAL CAPITAL TERRITORY ADMINISTRATION
(OFFICE OF THE PRESIDENT OF THE FEDERAL REPUBLIC OF NIGERIA)

CONSTITUTION OF THE FEDERAL REPUBLIC OF NIGERIA 1999
FEDERAL CAPITAL TERRITORY ACT CAP. F6, LFN 2004
PUBLIC NOTICE No. 1

APPROVED GUIDELINES FOR THE SALE OF FEDERAL GOVERNMENT HOUSES IN THE FCT TO CAREER PUBLIC SERVANTS

Preamble

1. The Federal Executive Council has approved guidelines for the sale of ALL RESIDENTIAL FACILITIES (houses, flats, etc.) built, acquired or otherwise owned by the Federal Government and ALL its ministries, departments and agencies except those listed in paragraph 4 below.

2. Towards this end, Mortgage Financing (at competitive rates and tenors) is being arranged through the Federal Mortgage Bank of Nigeria for the acquisition of all properties to be sold. Public Servants in particular are expressly advised to contact their Bankers and/or any Primary Mortgage Institution for additional information.

3. The guidelines issued hereunder are applicable to the sale of houses to ALL public officers that are not political office holders—appointed or elected within the express or implied meaning and intention of the Constitution of the Federal Republic of Nigeria, 1999.

Exemptions

4. The following residential facilities owned by the Federal Government of Nigeria will not be sold for constitutional, statutory or administrative reasons, and are accordingly exempted from the sale programme, that is the residences occupied by :

(*a*) President of the Federal Republic of Nigeria ;

(*b*) Vice-President of the Federal Republic of Nigeria ;

(*c*) Senate President ;

(*d*) Speaker of the House of Representatives ;

(*e*) Deputy Senate President ;

(*f*) Deputy Speaker of the House of Representatives ;

(*g*) Chief Justice of Nigeria ;

(*h*) Minister of the Federal Capital Territory ;

(*i*) Presidential Guest Houses and Safe Houses of the Intelligence Community ;

(*j*) Houses within the Security Zone of the State House ;

(*k*) Justices of the Supreme Court, Court of Appeal, Federal High Court, and High Court of the FCT ;

(*l*) Barracks of the Military, Police, Para-Military and approved uniformed services ; and

(*m*) Institutional residences within schools, hospitals, power plants, dams and universities, etc.

Valuation and Pricing of Houses

5. The valuation of the houses will be based on current replacement cost of the building as determined by FCDA or its appointed professional valuers ; excluding the cost of land and infrastructure.

Conditions of Sale

6. The houses will be sold on "as is, where is" basis at the evaluated price with the current occupants having the first right of refusal to purchase within thirty days of offer. The said right to purchase is neither transferable, assignable nor alienable in any way or form.

7. Strict compliance with development control standards must be adhered to by all purchasers ; no additional structures will be allowed without written approval of the Development Control Department of the FCDA.

8. Sale of houses will be advertised and application fees of ₦10,000.00 (Ten thousand Naira only) must accompany each FREE application form, payable at designated banks. The banks will remit all proceeds to a dedicated account in the name of the Federal Government of Nigeria with the Central Bank of Nigeria.

9. All houses whose rights to purchase are not exercised will be sold in an open Auction whereby all Nigerian citizens shall be given equal opportunity. A simple Auction System by way of competitive bidding shall be employed. All bids must be submitted with a bid bond by way of bank draft from a first class bank equal to ten percent of bid value. All bids without a bid bond stand disqualified. The highest bidder shall be automatically declared the winner, along with the second highest bidder as the reserve bidder; with the bid bond being retained and treated as non-refundable 10 percent deposit. All other bid bonds shall be returned to unsuccessful bidder(s).

10. Each and every public servant shall be entitled to purchase only one residential unit whilst any and all allocated or occupying government houses in Lagos are specifically excluded from purchasing houses in the Federal Capital Territory.

Uncompleted Residential Facilities

11. Uncompleted houses will be sold under the same Guidelines on "as is, where is" basis. No government funds shall be utilised to complete, renovate or repair any residential facilities. No allocation or allotment of an uncompleted building or part thereof shall be recognized. All uncompleted houses shall be sold to the general public via an open auction as in (9) above.

Payment Terms and Conditions

12. All purchasers must complete Application Forms with receipt of payment of ₦10,000 in favour of the Federal Capital Territory Administration, along with the following :

*Letter of initial employment into the Public Service of the Federation,

*Letter of last appointment /promotion in the Public Service of the Federation,

*Letter of allocation of quarters by an Appropriate Authority,

*4 No. high resolution colour Passport Photographs, and

*Proof of Last 6 (Six) Months Rent Deduction.

13. 25 percent of purchase price (including non-refundable deposit of 10 percent), up to a maximum of ₦5 million (National Housing Fund lending limit), must be paid to the Federal Government of Nigeria within 90 days.

14. Balance of 75 percent must be paid by all purchasers within an additional 90 days ; thus, all purchasers must effect full payment within 180 days of contract.

15. The transaction shall be concluded within 210 days of an offer to the allottee, occupant or successful bidder as applicable.

16. Each purchaser will be given custody of the original C-of-O issued by the FCT with his/her picture scanned thereon, unless paragraph 17 below applies.

17. Lender(s) will have immediate custody of original C-of-O with Minister's consent and legal mortgage executed in their favour by the FCT Administration.

18. All transaction charges shall be for the account of the purchaser.

19. In the event that a purchaser fails to comply with the payment terms, part of the initial deposit (being 10 percent of the purchase price) will be forfeited to the Federal Government, the contract of sale shall be rendered null and void, and the house declared unsold. Paragraph 9 of the Guidelines will thereafter apply.

20. In the case of houses offered to public servants in occupation, failure to accept offer and/or comply with the payment terms will lead to immediate eviction and the forfeiture of deposit (if applicable), and the application of paragraph 9 above.

Application Forms

21. Application Forms will be available throughout the FCT, in all Ministries, Departments and Agencies, Bank Branches, Post Offices, and Agencies of the Federal Capital Territory Administration as from April 1, 2005.

22. The Application Forms are FREE and downloadable on the Internet on www.abujagis.com or www.fmf.gov.ng.

23. Applicants must provide all information requested for in the Application Form to avoid delays in processing, or rejection of offer to purchase the residential facilities they occupy.

ABUJA, NIGERIA, 1ST APRIL, 2005.

Appendix 10

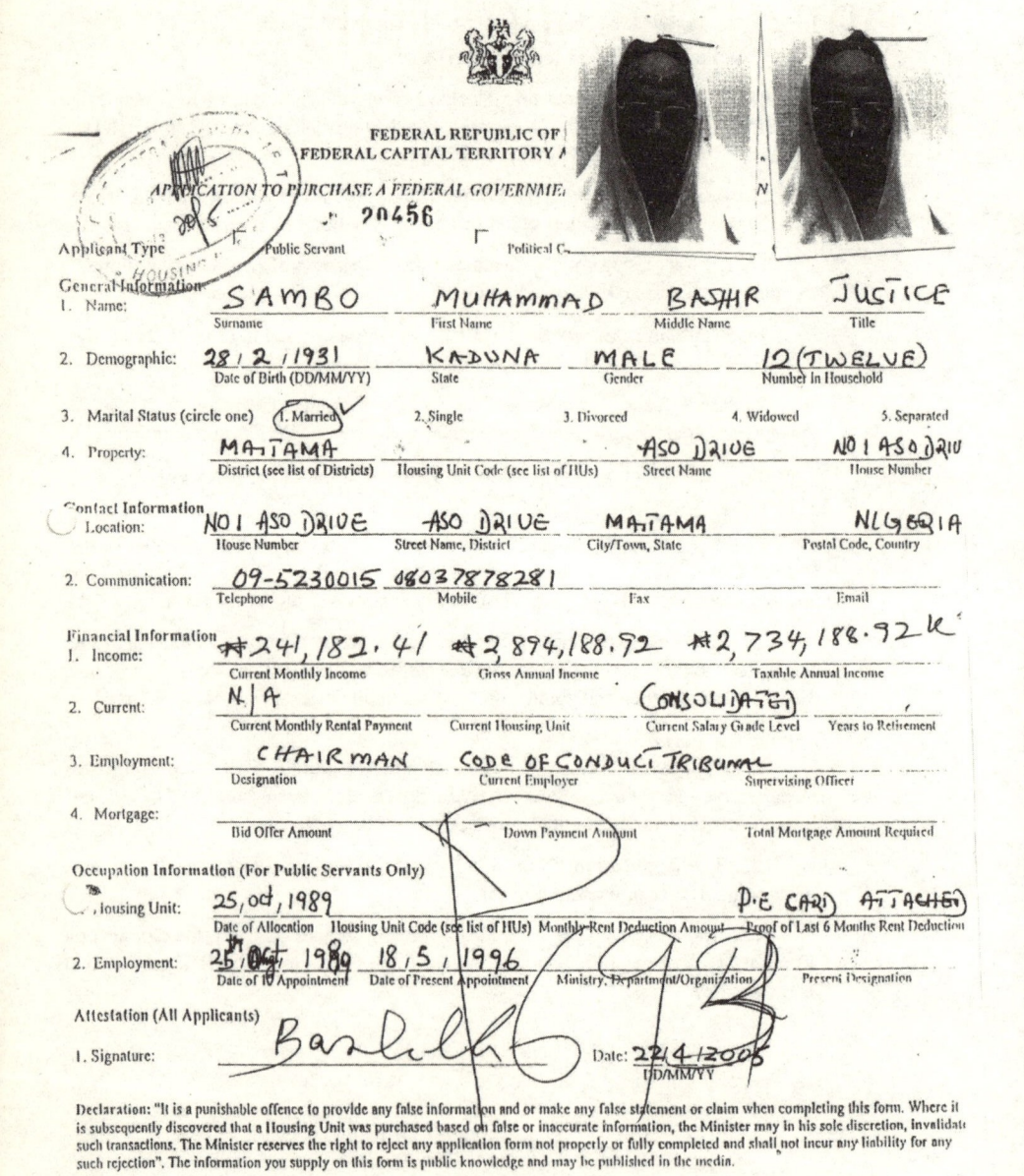

FEDERAL REPUBLIC OF [NIGERIA]
FEDERAL CAPITAL TERRITORY A[DMINISTRATION]

APPLICATION TO PURCHASE A FEDERAL GOVERNME[NT HOUSE]

No. 20456

Applicant Type: Public Servant / Political C[lass]

General Information

1. **Name:** SAMBO (Surname) | MUHAMMAD (First Name) | BASHIR (Middle Name) | JUSTICE (Title)

2. **Demographic:** 28/2/1931 (Date of Birth DD/MM/YY) | KADUNA (State) | MALE (Gender) | 12 (TWELVE) (Number in Household)

3. **Marital Status (circle one):** (1. Married) ✓   2. Single   3. Divorced   4. Widowed   5. Separated

4. **Property:** MAITAMA (District) | (Housing Unit Code) | ASO DRIVE (Street Name) | NO 1 ASO DRIVE (House Number)

Contact Information

1. **Location:** NO 1 ASO DRIVE (House Number) | ASO DRIVE (Street Name, District) | MAITAMA (City/Town, State) | NIGERIA (Postal Code, Country)

2. **Communication:** 09-5230015 (Telephone) | 08037878281 (Mobile) | (Fax) | (Email)

Financial Information

1. **Income:** ₦241,182.41 (Current Monthly Income) | ₦2,894,188.92 (Gross Annual Income) | ₦2,734,188.92k (Taxable Annual Income)

2. **Current:** N/A (Current Monthly Rental Payment) | (Current Housing Unit) | CONSOLIDATED (Current Salary Grade Level) | (Years to Retirement)

3. **Employment:** CHAIRMAN (Designation) | CODE OF CONDUCT TRIBUNAL (Current Employer) | (Supervising Officer)

4. **Mortgage:** (Bid Offer Amount) | (Down Payment Amount) | (Total Mortgage Amount Required)

Occupation Information (For Public Servants Only)

1. **Housing Unit:** 25/Oct/1989 (Date of Allocation) | (Housing Unit Code) | (Monthly Rent Deduction Amount) | P.E CARD ATTACHED (Proof of Last 6 Months Rent Deduction)

2. **Employment:** 25th Oct 1989 (Date of 1st Appointment) | 18/5/1996 (Date of Present Appointment) | (Ministry/Department/Organization) | (Present Designation)

Attestation (All Applicants)

1. **Signature:** Bashir (signed) | **Date:** 22/4/2006 (DD/MM/YY)

Declaration: "It is a punishable offence to provide any false information and or make any false statement or claim when completing this form. Where it is subsequently discovered that a Housing Unit was purchased based on false or inaccurate information, the Minister may in his sole discretion, invalidate such transactions. The Minister reserves the right to reject any application form not properly or fully completed and shall not incur any liability for any such rejection". The information you supply on this form is public knowledge and may be published in the media.

Completed forms should be returned to
Ad-Hoc Committee on Disposal of FG Houses in Abuja at Room 109, Minister's Block, FCDA Secretariat, Kapital Road, Area 11, PMB 24, Garki, Abuja, Nigeria

Tel: 09-6722300, 09-6722400, 09-6722500 Fax: 09-3143859, 09-3141059 Email: FGHouseSale@abujagis.com

CODE OF CONDUCT TRIBUNAL
THE PRESIDENCY
FEDERAL SECRETARIAT COMPLEX
SHEHU SHAGARI WAY, MAITAMA

P.M.B. 149 ABUJA
09-5230015
Telephone: 09-5230012

Ref. No. FCDA/CCT/12/S/1/1/0

Date: 8th Sept. 20 05

The Hon. Minister
Ministry of the Federal Capital Territory,
Abuja.

Attention: Adhoc Committee on Sales
Of Government Houses in Abuja,
Room 109, Garki,
Abuja.

RE: INVITATION TO BID AUCTION OF FEDERAL GOVERNMENT HOUSES IN THE FEDERAL CAPITAL TERRITORY

I am directed to inform you that the attention of the Code of Conduct Tribunal has been drawn in respect of the advertisement of Thisday edition of Friday, September 2nd, 2005. In the advert, the official residences of Hon. Justice Bashir Sambo (OFR) and that of a Member of the Tribunal, Professor P.A.O Oluyede (OON) namely: House No1 Aso Drive, Maitama and House No2, Jomo Kenyeta Street, Asokoro were listed for bidding process to the general public.

2. I am further directed to inform you that the Chairman and Members of the Tribunal are not political office holders but judicial officers. It was probably an error to have placed them as Political appointees, which directly placed their respective houses for public bidding.

3. The 1999 Constitution of the Federal Republic of Nigeria, part 15 sections 2 and 3 provides interalia:-

   a. The Chairman shall be a person who held or is qualified to hold office as a Judge of a Superior Court of Record in Nigeria and shall receive such remuneration as may be prescribed by law;

   b. The Chairman and Members of the Code of Conduct Tribunal shall be appointed by the President in accordance with the recommendation of the National Judicial Council.

4. The purpose of this letter is to appeal to the Honourable [reconsider the sale of their houses through public bidding since the and Members of the Tribunal are not Political office holders but Judici Please, find enclosed photocopies of proof of payments of application Thousand Naira and other necessary documents.

5. Thank you for your kind consideration please.

M.N. Basey Akpan (Mrs)
(Secretary to the Tribunal)
For: Hon. Chairman

FEDERAL CAPITAL TERRITORY ADMINISTRATION
OFFICE OF THE MINISTER

FCDA Secretariat, Kapital Road, Area 11, PMB 24, Garki, Abuja, Nigeria
Tel: (09) 314 1295, 314 2371
Fax: (09) 314 3859

5th October, 2005

JUSTICE MUHAMMMAD BASHIR SAMBO
HOUSE NO. 1
ASO DRIVE
MAITAMA, ABUJA, FCT

Dear JUSTICE SAMBO,

LETTER OF OFFER TO MATCH WINNING BID

We refer to your Application to Purchase the property owned by the Federal Government of Nigeria situate at HOUSE NO. 1 ASO DRIVE MAITAMA, ABUJA, FCT and more particularly described in "Schedule A" hereto, together with all appurtenances, rights, rights of way, easements, reversionary rights and privileges related thereto ("the Property") and, in accordance with the published Approved Guidelines in respect of your position as a Political Appointee, are pleased to offer you the right to match the winning bid received on the Property as herein indicated.

This Letter shall constitute the Terms of Offer from the Federal Capital Development Authority ("FCDA") on behalf of the Federal Government of Nigeria ("the Lessor") and upon execution, the Acceptance by you (the "Lessee") to match the winning bid received on the property, and purchase the Property from the Lessor, on such terms and conditions as are more particularly set forth below:

1. The Lessee shall signify acceptance of this Letter and the Terms contained herein, by the execution of same, the enclosure of the executed duplicate copy, and a bank draft in the sum of N 6525200(Six million five hundred and twenty five thousand two hundred Naira only), representing 10% of the

obtaining all such approvals and licenses as are necessary, facility management, insurance, taxation, charges, utilities, safety, maintenance, public use and liability and such other necessary incidentals;

c. (s)he shall abide by all relevant planning, environmental, health and safety laws, rules and regulations, including but not limited to all conditions, which may from time to time be required and or stipulated by the FCDA or other Municipal Administration; and

d. (s)he shall adhere strictly to development control standards and use his/her best and reasonable endeavors to ensure that no additional structures are erected without the written approval of the Development Control Department of the FCDA.

6. The Lessee hereby agrees and understands that time is of the essence in the performance of each of the conditions aforementioned, which conditions constitute valid and binding obligations enforceable according to the terms set out.

7. This Letter, and the obligations therein contained, shall be governed and construed by and in accordance with the Laws of the Federal Republic of Nigeria.

Kindly indicate your acceptance of this offer by, executing this Letter (and enclosing a duplicate), dating same in the space provided therefor, and returning same along with the non-refundable deposit to the Ad-Hoc Committee on the Sale of FGN Houses, Room 109, Minister's Block, FCDA Secretariat, Area 11-Garki, at which time the Offer and Acceptance become a binding agreement, in commitment to the fulfillment of the conditions precedent.

The Offer shall be deemed to have been withdrawn at the close of business on the Fourteenth (14th) day following the date hereof, unless prior thereto, the Lessor shall have received a written, valid Acceptance, in satisfaction of all conditions precedent, from the Lessee.

Upon Acceptance, by the execution of this Letter of Offer and the return of its duplicate copy, the respective heirs and successors-in-title of the Lessor and the Lessee shall become bound by the terms and conditions of this Agreement.

In the event that this Letter of Offer is not accepted prior to it being withdrawn, the occupant of the property to which it is addressed must vacate within 30 (thirty) days thereof. It must be emphasized that time is of the essence for the acceptance of the Letter or vacation of the Property, as no extension whatsoever shall be granted.

purchase price specified in Clause 3 below, being a non-refundable deposit for the purchase of the Property, within a period of Fourteen (14) days from the date hereof.

2. At the Closing Date as hereinafter defined under Clause 5(a) the Lessee shall purchase the Property, subject to any conditions contained in a Deed of Lease or imposed by any law.

3. The purchase price of the Property shall be N 65252000(Sixty five million two hundred and fifty two thousand Naira only) payable in no more than three (including the initial non-refundable payment in Clause 1 above) installments, each by bank draft as follows:

    a. the payment of a sum not less than 10% of the said purchase price, within Ninety (90) days of the initial payment under Clause 1 above; and

    b. the full and final payment of the balance of the purchase price due, within a period of Ninety (90) days of the payment made under (a) above.

    c. The Lessor shall not grant any extension of the timelines stated herein.

    PROVIDED HOWEVER THAT the Lessee shall be at liberty to make any of the aforementioned payments, including the full and final payment at any time before the Closing date, and in that instance, may make the full payment in one (1) or two (2) installments.

4. In the event of the Lessee failing to comply with the payment terms outlined in (1) and (3) above, this transaction shall be avoided and the Lessee shall forfeit to the Lessor, the initial deposit of 10% and in addition thereto, (s)he shall be responsible for the payment of all costs and charges associated with the transaction.

5. The Lessee's acceptance of this Letter shall constitute an undertaking on his/her part that:

    a. (s)he shall pay the full purchase price, as stipulated in (3) above, being the highest bid on the Property, within a total period of One Hundred and Ninety-four (194) days of this Letter, being the "Closing Date", and in accordance with the timelines stipulated in (1) and (3) above;

    b. where pertinent and at the Closing Date, all common areas and shared facilities (such as in premises of estates, block of flats, terrace houses, etc.) shall be the joint responsibility of the bona fide co-purchasers for value, for purposes including, without limitation, cooperation for

Schedule A

All that Property known as a Duplex situated at HOUSE NO. 1 ASO DRIVE, MAITAMA ABUJA, FCT including and not limited to the party walls, roofs, plumbing and electrical, sewage and other systems, together with all appurtenances, rights, rights of way, easements, reversionary rights and privileges related thereto.

Signature: _____

Nasir Ahmad el-Rufa'i, OFR
Minister of the Federal Capital Territory

Accepted by the within named Lessee

Name: JUSTICE MUHAMMAD BASHIR SAMBO

Signature: _____

Occupation: CHAIRMAN CODE OF CONDUCT TRIBUNAL

Date: 7th OCTOBER, 2005

In the Presence of:

Name: M. M. Ahmed

Date: 7TH OCTOBER, 2005

Signature: _____

CODE OF CONDUCT TRIBUNAL
THE PRESIDENCY
FEDERAL SECRETARIAT COMPLEX
SHEHU SHAGARI WAY, MAITAMA

P.M.B. 149, ABUJA

Telepone:...........

CCT/HQ/CO/ii/605
Ref. No................
Date: 5th Oct., 2005

Mallam Ahmed El-Rufai
Hon. Minister, F.C.T,
Abuja.

AUCTION OF THE HOUSES OF HON. JUSTICE BASHIR SAMBO CHAIRMAN AND PROF. P.A.O. OLUYEDE MEMBER CODE OF CONDUCT TRIBUNAL

I am the Chairman and Prof. Oluyede is a Member of the Code of Conduct Tribunal whose official houses or places of residence have been slated for auction under the ongoing dispensation. A letter dated 08/09/2005 has been written to you but in fact marked for the attention of the Committee on Sales of Government Houses in Abuja. You might, therefore, not have seen it.

2. In the said letter the point was made that both of us concerned are Judicial Officers and not Political Officers. A copy of the letter is attached.

3. An additional reason why the Chairman and Member of the Tribunal should be treated in the sale of their houses is that like civil servants they are given tenure of office by both the 1999 Constitution and enabling Act, the Code of Conduct Bureau and Tribunal Act (Cap 56 of 1990) so that they can stay in office for 15 years or more. The affected Chairman or Member will be

"entitled to pension for life at a rate equivalent to his last annual salary in addition to other retirement benefits to which he may be entitled".

4. Permit us to add that despite the selfless service we have been doing for donkey years; indeed we have decided more than 3,000 cases none of which has been reversed by the Court of Appeal, neither of us has a house of his own here in Abuja. Therefore the only place each of us has lived for about 10 to 15 years ought not to be taken from us by placing prohibitive prices on them via competitive bidding. Our prayer as honest, transparent and hard working elder statesmen of Nigeria is that our houses should be sold to us under the same conditions, terms and prices as those of the civil servants occupying equivalent houses.

5. In conclusion, it should be noted that whether the houses are sold to us under favourable terms or not, according to the terms of our appointments as judicial officers at the time we were employed the Government is bound to provide us with accommodation.

6. We fervently believe that our appeal will be favourably considered and granted by this listening and responsive Administration.

(Hon. Justice Bashir Sambo, OFR)
Chairman

CC: His Excellency,
Chief Olusegun Obasanjo (GCFR)
President,
Federal Republic of Nigeria,
State House,
ABUJA.

CODE OF CONDUCT TRIBUNAL
THE PRESIDENCY
FEDERAL SECRETARIAT COMPLEX
SHEHU SHAGARI WAY, MAITAMA

P.M.B. 149, ABUJA
09-5230013, 15
Telepone:..............................

CCT/HQ/CO/II/621
Ref. No..................................
Date: 7th Oct., 05 20........

Chairman,
Ad-Hoc Committee
Sale of Government of Government Houses
FCDA, Area II
Abuja

INTRODUCTION: MR. KOLO ALIYU OF FCDA

I hereby authorize the above-named who is a staff of FCDA to pay the 10% of the offer price for my house, No. 1 Aso Drive, Maitama, Abuja.

2. Thanks.

(Hon. Justice Bashir Sambo, OFR)
Chairman

FEDERAL CAPITAL DEVELOPMENT AUTHORITY

P. M. B. ABUJA
IDENTITY CARD

No. ....

The Bearer of this card
Mr/Mrs/Miss... **KOLO ALIYU**
Department: **ENGINEERING SERVICES**
Designation........ **H. E. OFFICER**

Whose signature and Photograph appear herein is a staff of Federal Capital Development Authority P. M. B 24, Abuja.

For the Hon. Minister
Federal Capital Territory
Date of Issues: **15 - 09 - 2004**

IF THIS CARD IS FOUND PLEASE RETURN TO THE ABOVE ADDRESS

OFFICE OF THE SECRETARY TO THE GOVERNMENT OF THE FEDERATION
PERMANENT SECRETARY (GENERAL SERVICES OFFICE)

☎: 09 - 5232386
Fax: 09 - 5232243

The Presidency,
Federal Secretariat Complex Phase 1
Shehu Shagari Way, Abuja.

Ref. No. 59700/T.9/215

3rd April, 2006

The Chairman,
Code of Conduct Tribunal,
Federal Secretariat Complex, Phase I,
Shehu Shagari Way,
Abuja.

RE: REQUEST FOR RESIDENTIAL ACCOMMODATION: CHAIRMAN, CODE OF CONDUCT TRIBUNAL (CCT), JUSTICE C. A. R. MOMOH

I am directed to refer to your letter Reference No. CCT/HQ/79/S/V/500 dated 6th March, 2006 on the above subject and to remark that the Federal Executive Council at its 9th Meeting held on 2nd March, 2005 approved the exemption of the Government residential quarters occupied by Judicial officers from the sale exercise under the monetization policy. The Chairman, Code of Conduct Tribunal, whose appointment was approved by Mr. President on the recommendation of National Judicial Council in line with paragraph 15, sub-paragraph 3 of Part I of the Fifth Schedule to the 1999 Constitution of the Federal Republic of Nigeria, is treated as a Judicial Officer whose residential requirement is treated as approved by the Federal Executive Council.

2. In view of the above, I am to say that former House No. 1, Aso Drive, Maitama (now re-numbered as No. 23) which was occupied by the former Chairman of the CCT remains the official residence of the newly appointed Chairman.

3. Please, accept the warm regards of the Secretary to the Government of the Federation.

Dr. B. K. Kaigama, OON, FIPA
Permanent Secretary (GSO)
for: Secretary to the Government of the Federation

Hon. Justice Bashir Sambo OFR

☎:062 - 249740, 310332, Kaduna ☎ 069 333073, 334432 ?q/..
☎:09-5230384, 5237006 Abuja ☎ 08037878281

Date: **4TH APRIL, 2006**

Secretary to the Government of the Federation,
Office of the Secretary to the Government
Of the Federation,
The Presidency,
Federal Secretariat Complex,
Phase 1,
Shehu Shagari Way,
Maitama,
Abuja.

Attention of Permanent Secretary (General Services Office)

RE: REQUEST FOR RESIDENTIAL ACCOMMODATION, CHAIRMAN, CODE OF CONDUCT TRIBUNAL (CCT)

I wish to refer to your letter No. 597001/T.9/215 dated 3rd April, 2006 written to the Hon. Chairman, Code of Conduct Tribunal and copied to myself the former Hon. Chairman.

2.   This wrong decision taken against the sale of the house to me was as a result of the entrenched hatred and maltreatment I have been receiving from the Hon. Minister in the Presidency in charge of Federal Capital Territory, Mallam Nasir El-Rufai for no crime committed by me against him or any one else. I only decide to appeal to Almighty Allah to intervene in this matter of hatred and maltreatment, which I have been receiving from Mallam Nasir El-Rufai.

3.   This decision is wrong for two reasons:
(i) First, it is not stated any where in the Constitution or any law that the Hon. Chairman and members of the Code of Conduct Tribunal are **"JUDICIAL OFFICERS"**. In the 1999 Constitution, Part iv. Interpretation Citation And Commencement, Section 318 " JUDICIAL OFFICE" means the office of Chief Justice of Nigeria or a Justice of the Supreme Court, the president or Justice of the Court of Appeal, the office of the Chief Judge or Judge of the High Court of the Federal Capital Territory, Abuja, the office of the Chief Judge of a State and Judge of the High Court of a State, a

Grand Kadi or Kadi of the Sharia Court of Appeal of the Federal Capital Territory, Abuja, a President or Judge of the Customary Court of Appeal of the Federal Capital Territory, Abuja, a Grand Kadi or Kadi of the Sharia Court of Appeal of a State; and a reference to a "Judicial officer" is a reference to the holder of any such office.

4. And so constitutionally and legally the offices of the Hon. Chairman and Members of the Code of Conduct Tribunal are not Judicial officers as they do not belong to the Judicial officers given by the 1999 constitution until the 1999 constitution is amended to include such offices. While I was the Chairman of the Code of Conduct Tribunal we tried to have the constitution amended to make the offices as Judicial ones but no such amendment has taken place yet. It is therefore wrong to misguide the Federal Executive Council to regard such offices as Judicial offices simply because Mallam El-Rufai hates me and does not want the house to be sold to me.

(ii) Second, the house has been offered to me to buy and I acceded the offer and I have even paid 20% and preparing to pay the remaining 80% for which I have even sought the assistance of Mr. President though without any response from him. There is now a signed agreement of Sale between the Government and myself and, if this Government is our (people) government representing our individual and collective interest, it can not back Mallam Nasir El-Rufai against me in this matter.

5. The right thing to be done for the Hon. Chairman, Code of Conduct Tribunal is to allocate to her another house but not the house which has already been sold to me after serving the Nation in various capacities for many years. I understand that Mr President has kindly reduced 10% of the amounts offered and I sincerely hope that I shall benefit from such gracious action of Mr. President.

(Hon. Justice Bashir Sambo OFR)

cc: The Hon. Chairman
Code of Conduct Tribunal

(Hon. Justice Bashir Sambo OFR)

CODE OF CONDUCT TRIBUNAL
THE PRESIDENCY
FEDERAL SECRETARIAT COMPLEX
SHEHU SHAGARI WAY, MAITAMA

P.M.B. 149, ABUJA

Telepone: ....

Ref. No ....

Date: 7/4/06

From: Justice C.A.R. Momoh
(Chair CCT)

To: Hon Minister FCT

[stamp: 11 APR 2006]

I am taken aback & indeed surprised at the contents of the enclosed letter. I am sure the office of the S.G.F must have alerted you on it. Please let us see Mr President over this and related matters I met on ground on assumption of office at the Tribunal.

My Tel. Nos are:
08027768990; 08036324488
08055105066, 095230015...

Copy of the letter of appointment to see Mr President is enclosed pl As suggested last Friday, we

FEDERAL CAPITAL TERRITORY ADMINISTRATION
OFFICE OF THE MINISTER

FCDA Secretariat, Kapital Road, Area 11, PMB 24, Garki, Abuja Nigeria
Tel: (09) 314 1295, 314 2371
Fax: (09) 314 3859

11th April 2006

Justice Mohammed Bashir Sambo (Rtd),
House No. 1, Aso Drive
Maitama

WITHDRAWAL OF OFFER LETTER

Further to the offer letter earlier granted to you to purchase your official residence at House No. 1 Aso Drive, Maitama, we write to inform you that the house is found to fall within the designated essential houses exempted to be sold by the Federal Government. Consequently, the offer is therefore withdrawn and the house is now reverted to the pool of essential houses.

In view of this, a refund of the 10% paid by you is being processed and we highly regret any inconveniences the withdrawal might have caused you. However, we wish to state that you are equally entitled to express your interest to purchase any other non-essential house through the forthcoming public bidding process. We shall also be willing to assist by way of advice whenever contacted.

Thank you,

Abbas Umar
For: Ad-hoc Committee on the Sale Of FGN Houses

RESTRICTED

STATE HOUSE,
ABUJA,
NIGERIA.

Reference: PRES/83

April 27, 2006

The Hon. Minister,
Ministry of Federal Capital Territory,
Area 11, Garki,
Abuja.

Dear Sir,

RE: APPLICATION FOR PRIVATE AUDIENCE WITH MR. PRESIDENT

Reference:
A.   Letter dated 13th April 2006 by Hon. Justice Bashir Sambo on the above subject matter.

   I am directed to forward Reference A to you and to draw your kind attention to Mr. President's directive.

2.   Humbly submitted for your further action, Sir.

Taiwo Ojo
Special Assistant to the President

Enclosures:
1.   Copy of Reference A.

Copy to:

Internal Information
- COS – President   -   for your kind attention, Sir
- PS – President

External Information:
- SGF

Hon. Justice Bashir Sambo OFR

☎:062 - 2.9740, 310352, Kaduna ☎ 069-333073, 334432, Zaria
☎:09-5230384, 5237006 Abuja ☎:08037878281

Date: 13TH April, 2006

Your Excellency,
Chief Olusegun Obasanjo, GCFR,
President Commander-In-Chief of the Armed
Forces of the Federal Republic of Nigeria,
Aso Villa, Abuja.

Your Excellency,

RE: APPLICATION FOR PRIVATE AUDIENCE WITH MR PRESIDENT

I wish to apply for an urgent private audience with your Excellency regarding the personal problems I have been encountering with Hon. Minister Mallam Nasir Ahmed El-Rufai for Your Excellency's intervention.

(HON. JUSTICE BASHIR SAMBO, OFR)

Y.E.
This is for your info sir.

OFFICE OF THE C IN-C
2 6 APR 2006
RECEIVED

Minister of FCT,
Please speak
OO
27/04/06

Hon. Justice Bashir Sambo OFR

☎:062 - 249740, 310332, Kaduna ☎:069-333073, 334432 Zaria
☎:09-5230384, 5237006 Abuja ☎:08037878281

18th April, 2006
Date:_____

Mallam Nasir Ahmed El-Rufai,
The Hon. Minister,
Federal Capital Administration
Office of the Minister,
Abuja.

(For the Attention of M. Abbas Umar
Ad-hoc Committee On Sale of FGN Houses)

WITHDRAWAL OF OFFER LETTER

I wish to refer to your letter of 11th April, 2006 signed by Abbas Umar a copy is attached here for easy reference and state that I have rejected the withdrawal which has no true and genuine reason to back it up. It is very clear the way you have been treating me on the sale of or withdrawal of the sale of this house to me has nothing to do with the decision of the Federal Executive Council or a directive of Mr. President. I say so because the way you have been treating me and may be others too looks as if you administer what the Federal Government has appointed you to administer as **YOUR PERSONAL PROPERTY.**

2. I believe that the officer whom you directed to write me a letter of withdrawal of the sale may not be aware of the fact that the Secretary to the Government of the Federation has written to the present Hon. Chairman of the Code of Conduct Tribunal and copied me on the same issue which I replied and sent you a copy which you might not care to read as you never read anything I wrote you and you never accept to receive me whenever I express the desire to see you for a discussion.

3. In the circumstances I cannot accept the withdrawal of the offer for the following reasons:

(i) The house under any circumstances can not be counted as one of the essential houses as directed by the Federal Executive

Council. You put the house in the bidding list of houses knowing fully well I am occupying it. It was after the bid that I was offered to buy the house with your reluctance. If you respect our laws and constitution, you will find out that the Offices of the Chairman and Members of the Code of Conduct Tribunal are not judicial offices. You can check sections 6(5) and 318 of the 1999 Constitution together with Enrolment Of Certain Political Public And Judicial Office Holders (Salaries And Allowances, ETC) ACT 2002 SCHEDULE PART I AND PART II and the Government has never recognized the offices as Judicial offices but a parastatal and that is why the Code of Conduct Tribunal is under the Executive arm of Government as a parastatal. While I was the Chairman of the Code of Conduct Tribunal I tried to have the Constitution amended so that the offices can become judicial offices and that trial is yet to succeed and it is only after the amendment of the Constitution that the offices of the Chairman and Members shall be judicial offices.

(ii) The house was put on bid and offered to me to buy; I accepted the offer and paid 20% <u>not</u> 10% as your letter mentioned. By this acceptance of mine of the offer made to me by the Government and payments made the house has legally become mine and the Government has no power to unilaterally withdraw the offer. <u>As a matter of fact I have already sold the house in order to get the money to pay the remaining 80% as others have done.</u>

4. If it is the wish of the present Chairman of the Code of Conduct Tribunal to be allocated a house instead of being given her salary to rent a house, you should do so.

(Justice Muhammad Bashir Sambo, OFR)

CODE OF CONDUCT TRIBUNAL
THE PRESIDENCY
FEDERAL SECRETARIAT COMPLEX
SHEHU SHAGARI WAY, MAITAMA

P.M.B. 149, ABUJA

Telepone:..................................

Ref. No. FCDA/CCT/12/S/1/182

Date: 27th April, 06

The Hon. Minister,
Ministry of Federal Capital Territory,
Area II,
Abuja.

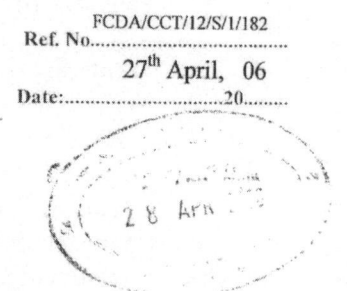

HOTEL ACCOMMODATION FOR
HON. JUSTICE CONSTANCE A. R. MOMOH

I am directed to refer to the discussion of the Hon. Minister with the Chairman, Code of Conduct Tribunal of 31st March, 2006 in respect of residential accommodation for the Chairman who noted your concern and cooperation to assist in the settlement of part of the hotel accommodation pending the determination of offer of a residence.

2. On assumption of office, 28th February, 2006, Hon. Justice Constance A.R. Momoh was checked into Peniel Apartments Wuse II, Abuja where she is presently accommodated. Please find attached the tariff and related information.

3. It would be appreciated if the Hon. Minister would settle the bills up to the end of June, 2006 when the residential accommodation for the Hon. Chairman would be, hopefully, in place.

4. I am also to convey the Chairman's gratitude to the Hon. Minister for the prompt attention given to the accommodation issue as well as be reminded of the promise for quick intervention on the matter.

M. Nkese Bassey Akpan (Mrs)
Secretary CCT
For: Hon. Chairman

**STATE HOUSE,
ABUJA,
NIGERIA.**

Reference: SH/COS/ 25/37/1090   23rd May, 2006.

His Lordship,
Hon. Justice Mohammed Lawal Uwais, GCON,
Chief Justice of Nigeria,
Supreme Court Complex,
Three Arms Zone,
Abuja.

Chief Bayo Ojo, SAN,
Attorney-General of the Federation and
Honourable Minister of Justice,
Federal Ministry of Justice,
Federal Secretariat Complex,
Shehu Shagari Way,
Abuja.

REQUEST FOR LEGAL OPINION ON THE STATUS OF CODE OF CONDUCT TRIBUNAL

Vide the attached letter dated 18th May, 2006 Hon. Justice Mohammed Bashir Sambo OFR complained to His Excellency the President over the withdrawal of the offer for the sale of his official residence by the Minister of the Federal Capital Territory (FCT) after acceptance and full payment of the offered price.

2. Justice Sambo disclosed that the reason given by the Minister FCT for the withdrawal of the offer is that **as Chairman of the Code of Conduct Tribunal at the material time, he was considered as a judicial officer** hence excluded from Federal

Government Monetisations Policy concerning Sale of Government Houses.

3. On his part, Justice Sambo has insisted that **although the Code of Conduct Tribunal is a court, its judges are however not considered as judicial officers.** This contention he said, is supported by the fact that **judges of the Code of Conduct Tribunal are not among persons listed as judicial officers under Section 318-(5) & (6) of the 1999 Constitution and "the certain political and judicial office holders (salaries and allowances, etc) Act, 2002".** This he said, explains why the Code of Conduct Tribunal is placed under the supervision of the Presidency instead of the Judiciary".

4. Having regard to the foregoing and given the fact that the Minister, FCT has insisted that judges of the Code of Conduct Tribunal are judicial officers, **it is considered necessary to seek for your opinion on the issue** to enable me advise Mr. President appropriately.

5. While urging you to treat the matter with utmost urgency, accept the assurances of my highest regards and best wishes, please.

Maj Gen A Mohammed CFR, GCON
Chief of Staff to the President.

CC:
SAP (Admin) C-in-C
Honourable Minister, FCT,
Hon. Justice Bashir Sambo, OFR

ATTORNEY-GENERAL OF THE FEDERATION AND MINISTER OF JUSTICE

P. M. B 192
Telegrams: Solicitor
Telephone: 09-5235194
Telefax: 09-5235208

Federal Ministry of Justice
10th Floor, Federal Secretariat
Shehu Shagari Way,
Maitama, Abuja, FCT
Nigeria.

HAGF/SGF/2006/Vol.1

16th June, 2006

Secretary to Government of
   the Federation,
Office of the Secretary to the
   Government of the Federation,
Federal Secretariat, Phase I,
Abuja.

RE: RESIDENTIAL ACCOMMODATION OF HONOURABLE JUSTICE BASHIR SAMBO, OFR

Your letter ref. no. SGF.19/S.24/T1/249 of May 12, 2006 on the above subject matter refers.

2. After a careful perusal of the facts and the applicable law, I am of the considered view that Justice Sambo is a judicial officer and is therefore exempted from purchasing his quarters under the monetization policy of the Government.

3. The relevant provisions of the fifth schedule to the 1999 Constitution of the Federal Republic of Nigeria are quite instructive in this regard.

4. It is of no consequence that Section 6(5) and 318 of the said Constitution on judicial power, Interpretation, Citation and Commencement does not include the Honourable Chairman in its definition. The spirit and intention of the law is quite clear.

5. On the issue that there is a subsisting agreement based on the offer of the MFCTA and his acceptance and payment of 20% initial deposit, this too would be of no consequence since the agreement was premised on a wrong assumption that he was entitled. Having established that his Lordship is not entitled to purchase the property in the first instance, the agreement is void ab initio and is not enforceable in law.

OFFICE OF THE HON. ATTORNEY-GENERAL OF THE FEDERATION

6. In the above premise, I would advise that his Lordship be offered an alternative property from the list of the other properties still available for sale by the MFCTA, to enable his Lordship have a peaceful retirement.

7. Please accept the assurances of my warm regards and high esteem.

Chief Bayo Ojo, SAN,
Hon. Attorney-General of the Federation and
Minister of Justice

Cc:

✓ **Mr. Nasir El Rufai**
Minister,
Federal Capital Territory Administration, Abuja.

SA_EM

Pls. effect the ejection of Justice Bah Sambo immediately. He can bid any house on offer.

07-07-06

FEDERAL CAPITAL TERRITORY ADMINISTRATION
OFFICE OF THE MINISTER

FCDA Secretariat, Kapital Road, Area 11, PMB 24, Garki, Abuja, Nigeria
Tel: (09) 314 1295, 314 2371
Fax: (09) 314 3859
www.fct.gov.ng

MM/FCT/MO/126/M010

21 September 2006

The Chairman,
Code of Conduct Tribunal,
Abuja.

My Lord Chairman,

RE: SALE OF FGN HOUSES IN ABUJA: OFFER OF "RIGHT TO MATCH" ON ALTERNATIVE HOUSE TO THE "ESSENTIAL HOUSE" YOU CURRENTLY OCCUPY

You may please recall that the Federal Executive Council (FEC) mandated the Federal Capital Territory Administration (FCTA) to implement the sale of FGN non-essential residential housing units in Abuja under specific Guidelines.

2. These Approved Guidelines, vis-à-vis Political Office Holders (POH), grant that all houses occupied by political office holders will be sold in an Open Public Auction whereby all Nigerian citizens shall be given equal opportunity. Furthermore, the highest qualifying bid price will then be offered to the political office holder in occupation to exercise the "right to match" (RTM) by effecting a 10% non-refundable deposit within fourteen days of the Offer.

3. However, occupants of "essential" FGN houses in Abuja were automatically disqualified from benefiting from the RTM as the houses they occupy are reserved from the Sale.

4. Subsequently, the Sale Committee made an appeal and obtained Mr. President's gracious approval that the Ad-hoc Committee on the Sale of FGN Houses in Abuja grant affected occupants of "essential" houses the opportunity to exercise the RTM on alternative houses.

5. Accordingly, the Honourable Members of the Tribunal are invited to please fill the attached Expression of Interest (EoI) forms, identifying any available official Guest House attached to their offices, and return them to the Sale Secretariat located at Room 109, Minister's Block, FCT Secretariat, Area 11, Garki, Abuja within one week of this letter for consideration for an Offer Note, kindly state your current residence under "contact details".

Please accept the assurances of my highest esteem

Nasir Ahmad el-Rufa'i, OFR
Minister of the Federal Capital Territory

Appendix 11

PRESIDENT,
FEDERAL REPUBLIC OF NIGERIA

PRES/134
31 August 2004.

Distinguished Senator Adolf Wabara,
President of the Senate,
Senate Chambers,
National Assembly Complex,
Three-Arms Zone,
Asokoro - Abuja.

Dear President of the Senate,

On noticing the alleged wrong deployment of language of the Minister of Federal Capital Territory on a member or members of the Senate of the Federal Republic, I asked the Honourable Minister to give me an explanation in writing.

I note with some concern the Minister's explanation which seemed to touch on action and reaction between a Distinguished Senator and the Honourable Minister.

But be that as it may, I have cautioned the Minister on the use of language in public about any member of the Federal Legislature no matter how seemingly provoked.

Everything should be done to maintain the very cordial and amicable relationship now existing between the Executive and the Legislature. Therefore, if any offence has been caused, I apologise on behalf of the Minister and I hope that words amounting to alleged threat or blackmail will cease to emanate from Distinguished and Honourable Members of the National Assembly.

Please accept, Mr. Senate President, the assurances of my highest consideration.

Yours sincerely,

OLUSEGUN OBASANJO

Copy: H.E. Vice President Atiku Abubakar

        Honorable Minister of FCT

Appendix 12

MINISTRY OF FOREIGN AFFAIRS
OFFICE OF THE PERMANENT SECRETARY
ABUJA

P.M.B 130, Garki
Telephone 5230210
Telefax: 5230394

Ref. No.: PSO/S.38

Date: 29th Sept., 2009

The Director-General
National Intelligence Agency
Garki, Abuja

WITHDRAWAL OF CONSULAR ASSISTANCE TO MALLAM HUHU RIBADU AND MALLAM EL-RUFAI

I write to acknowledge receipt of your letter Ref. No. Sr.28/Vol.13 dated 15th September, 2009 on the above subject and to attach herewith a copy of the action taken in compliance with your letter mentioned above. However, having implemented the content of your letter under reference, I am directed to raise some concerns of the Ministry of Foreign Affairs, whose advice on the issue would have been useful in the first instance.

2. The decision not to renew the former Minister's passport may unwittingly portray the Federal Government in bad light within the international community as a government that is too sensitive to criticism.

3. The decision could engender more sympathy for him, which he could utilise to greater advantage especially if he opts to pursue the matter in court. That sympathy could also, as in the past, lead to some sympathetic country granting him temporary travelling documents which will in the end defeat our purpose and render our action irrelevant. Equally, is the view that the criticism of the Government could increase resulting in an unnecessary distraction that Government could do without at the moment.

4. The best antidote to the Mallam El-Rufai menace is to generally ignore him, monitor his movement and where necessary respond without delay to some of his most stringent comments. It's our silence and

inability to respond promptly, extensively and effectively to his numerous comments since he left Nigeria that has hurt us most than the things he has said. As it is said in Washington, "a story not denied within 24 hours, is believed to be true", hence the White House information managers are on duty 24 hours and they do not fight shy of taking on the Government's opponent all the time.

5. The essence of this letter therefore is not only to inform you of the implementation of your letter, but to hope that based on the above, you may wish to reconsider the issue, which I have no doubt would show the maturity of the Federal Government.

Amb. Joe Keshi, OON, FPA
Permanent Secretary

CONFIDENTIAL

Appendix 13

TRANSLATION OF APPENDIX 13

Katsina, 26th June 1953

Mallam Ahmadu Rufai,
Fraternal greetings! I received your letter today and I am distressed to learn that your (farming) bull died and you are yet to get a replacement. This is terrible news indeed. I pray for God to put an end to such disasters, Amen. I believe the authorities will assist you since the cattle disease seems to have ravaged many farmers (like you) this year. I hope that there are other bulls available in the (government) flock that could serve as suitable replacements. Indeed, I am saddened by this news, and pray for God to continue to protect you.

I am settling down in my new job, Alhamdulillah (Thanks be to Allah). My mind is more at ease, and all I am praying for is good health. I am grateful for your prayers as I know that you will continue to pray for me. I look forward to seeing you next time I am on tour (around your village).

Please extend my greetings to Abu Tafinta, and ask whether my letters have been delivered to him. My regards to Mr. John Carpenter, Nanadada Bawa and your supervisor if he is still around.

May Allah spare our lives to meet up soon, Amin.

Your student,

Musa Yar'Adua
Assistant Development Secretary

Katsina

Appendix 14

November 19, 2012

Charles T. Okah
Single Cell Block
Kuje Prison
Abuja, Nigeria.

His Eminence
Cardinal Olubunmi Okogie
c/o Catholic Church Secretariat
Lagos, Nigeria.

Your Eminence:

October 1 2010 Bomb Blast Setup and Government Double Standard

Greetings in the name of our Lord Jesus Christ, and I hope this letter meets you well. The reasons I choose to direct this letter to you are that I am a Catholic and you are an old boy of my alma mater, St. Gregory's College, Lagos.

I write from Kuje Prison Abuja where two other Catholics and I have been languishing in solitary confinement for 2 years on trumped-up charges relating to the October 1, 2010 bomb attack claimed by the Movement for the Emancipation of the Niger Delta (MEND).

My name is Charles Tonbra Okah, aka Billy Bones. On October 16, 2010 my residence in Apapa GRA was invaded by operatives of the State Security Services on the warrant that I was the suspected spokesman for MEND using the pseudonym "Jomo Gbomo." My eldest son, visiting from the United States where he attends the University of Kansas (KU) was also arrested.

At the SSS Headquarters Abuja where we were flown to blindfolded with our legs and hands bound, my 'cooperation' was solicited for something completely different to my surprise. My captors threw me a lifeline; offering me our freedom and a lucrative contract in exchange for false testimony against my younger brother Henry, who is resident in South Africa. I was to write a false statement claiming to have been told by Henry about the bomb plot and naming the following persons as his conspirators: Former Head of State, General Ibrahim Babangida, Chief Raymond Dokpesi, Mallam Nasir El Rufai, Chief Timipre Sylva, and Dr. Emmanuel Uduaghan. I bluntly refused.

To maintain pressure on me, I was told that my son would be implicated in the bomb matter, my containers of legitimate imports then at the Tin Can Port would be impounded and my business destroyed. I still did not budge, tossing their lifeline back with royal disdain.

When they realized I was not going to connive in their scheme, they became formal and reverted to the main reason for my arrest. I was asked for the MEND password which I told them I did not know. They bound me in a chair, took off my trousers and clamped a device to my penis. My legs were then put inside a basin of water. The device when turned on passed a high voltage of electricity to my body and I lost consciousness. This was on Monday October 18 at about 6pm. When I regained consciousness, I discovered I was at the National Hospital emergency room. I remember the doctors asking why I had trauma marks on my chest where the SSS doctor performed Cardio Pulmonary Resuscitation (CPR). The SSS operatives were evasive in answering questions at the hospital. That night I was released and taken to rest for the night at the State House Clinic. That was the last time a torture was carried out on me.

My son was eventually released after Mr. Femi Falana visited in the company of my wife after a month of being denied access to a lawyer. However, my containers have been impounded up to date and my bank account frozen.

The SSS stopped asking about the MEND password after Jomo Gbomo made another statement while I was in their custody but refused to still let me go because I did not cooperate earlier with them. Meanwhile in the ongoing trial in South Africa, Henry is accused of being the same Jomo Gbomo by the same people who say I am JG.

Double Standard in Kuje Prison:

On December 24, 2010 we were remanded in Kuje prison as a result of our application to be removed from the SSS detention cell. Unknown to us, the SSS passed instructions from "above" to the prison authorities to carry out "special treatment" in order to stampede us into a trial towards conviction. For 2 years we have been locked up in solitary confinement, are not allowed to exercise or get sunlight outside and are forced to sleep on the floor when bunk beds are available. Even a court order by Justice Gabriel Kolawole to the prison for a change in our confinement style was ignored after it was superseded by an 'order from above."

In late 2011, while locked up inside our cell block, prison officials clothed in protective apparel, face masks and gloves carried out fumigation without opening us to wait outside. Our protests fell on deaf ears and by the time they were finished we were in distress. The Youth Corper doctor on call tried her best within her limits to the emergency she was confronted with. The poisonous gas and barbaric action reminiscent of the Nazi concentration camp infamous gas chambers, eventually led to the death of one Francis Osuwo, aka Gboko, also roped into this case by the SSS and a man I have never met before. Interestingly, the four persons in detention were strangers to each other except for one Obi Nwabueze who is a family friend and close associate of Henry.

The fumigant whose chemical constituent were never relayed to us have affected my neurological system and I have been on a daily prescription of strong neurological medication prescribed by a neurologist of the National Hospital, Professor Bwala.

While the Boko Haram suspects at Kuje prison are allowed to worship in the prison mosque, we have never set foot in the prison chapel. They are also enjoying privileges such as cable television, radio, liberty to move within the prison walls, bunk beds to sleep on and phone calls to their families. We are denied all of the above.
When I asked the current Controller of FCT Command the reason for the disparity, he said "the fear of Boko Haram is the beginning of wisdom." He further said the Moslem community was concerned about their welfare in custody.

Double Standard in the Court:

Even in the Courts where justice is supposed to be blind, the double standard is glaring. While Senator Ndume, accused of being a financier to Boko Haram was given bail by the same Judge presiding over our case, we have been denied bail.

I understand that this Senator was permitted by the same court to travel on his religious obligation to Mecca for the lesser Hajj while we are refused from attending mass in a chapel less than 50 meters from our cell block.

The court is willing to permit the Senator approval to travel abroad for his medical check if he can provide proof that such check up is not done locally. Meanwhile, I have been denied my application to go on a compulsory checkup which in my case is mandatory for a kidney donor, having donated my left kidney to my mother 30 years ago.

Our cases have been adjourned repeatedly for cruelly long durations. The last time I appeared in court was

March 2012 and the next adjourned date is January 31. 2013, that is if that date will not be shifted again under a flimsy excuse.

All we ask is for a free and fair justice from an independent Judiciary that should release us instead of holding us as scapegoats over an obvious power show. While this government continues holding us hostage, our families are becoming destitute.

Our rights to freely worship as Catholics is being infringed by the state who have more respect for Islam when all religions should be treated equally.

Double Standards in the Polity:

The National Security Adviser, Col Sambo Dasuki (rtd.) was quoted as saying that the government of President Goodluck Jonathan has the phone numbers of suspected Boko Haram sponsors. Later the Inspector General of Police said certain individuals had been put on a "watch list" as suspected Boko Haram sponsors.

Now the big question is why did the government not simply have our phone numbers and put us also on its 'watch list" while we move about freely? They did not hesitate to arrest us, clamp us on trumped-up charges and detain us on flimsy excuses. They did not merely talk, they took action even in South Africa where my brother was arrested since 2010. Is there a better word to describe this other than hypocrisy?

The same government eager to negotiate with Boko Haram who claimed responsibility for over 100 attacks where Catholics have suffered the brunt, have refused to negotiate with MEND and continue to delude themselves that all is well.

Why would this government expect Boko Haram to unmask it leaders and negotiate when they can see that perceived leaders and supporters of MEND are being persecuted and jailed?

I welcome a fact-finding visit from the Church in the company of credible Human Rights groups to verify our allegations.

On the two occasions Kuje Prison was visited by the Bishop of Abuja during the Christmas of 2010 and 2011, he was surreptitiously steered away from where were we are held hostage and I believe he has no idea of what is going in inside Kuje prison.

Our prayers is that leaders of our Churches will be more sensitive and proactive in politics of the land that touches the lifes of their followers and not leave delicate issues solely in the hands of corrupt and selfish politicians, and majority of the population rid of a "Potiphar" mentality who believe lies when told by SSS.

May God save our beloved country.

Yours Sincerely,

Charles T. Okah

CC: Pope Benedict, Vatican, Rome
Catholic Bishop of Abuja Diocese, Abuja FCT

"I.was.sick.and in prison, and you visited me."
-Mathew 25. 35, 36

INDEX

Abacha Sani, 51-52, 55, 58, 71, 74, 273
Abba Gana, Mohammed, 245, 257
Abba, Sarki, 464
Abba, Yahaya, 276
Abdu, Mohammed Sani 24
Abdul, Captain 93-97
Abdullahi, Hamza, 287
Abdullahi, Hadiza, 216
Abdullahi, Tijjani Mohammed, 76, 100, 110, 128, 139, 265,422, 434, 441, 456-457, 473
Abiodun-Wright, Modupe, 74, 113
Abiola, Kola, 108
Abiola, M.K.O., 59
Abubakar Abdulsalami, 52-55, 58-59, 64-65, 68,146, 395, 448
Abubakar, Atiku, 62, 67-75, 79, 85, 93-94, 96-97,
100-101, 103-104,107-109, 112, 122, 124, 129, 132,135, 138-140, 142-152, 160,163, 170, 173-174, 176, 198,227-229, 232, 234-235,282, 291, 294-297, 304-305, 308, 314-315, 319, 323, 330-335, 337-350, 352-368, 370-371, 374-377, 381, 389-391, 416-418, 424, 454, 463, 479
Abubakar, Shehu Iya, 422
Abubakar, Fati, 59
Abuja
- Board of Internal Revenue Bill,262
- Enterprise Agency, 311
- Environmental Protection Broad, 243
- Geographic Information System, 244, 252, 254
- Investment Company 285
- Municipal Area Council (AMAC) 286-287

Adam, Baba, 431
Adamu, Adamu, 211
Adamu, Bala, 134
Adamu, Haroun, 67
Adebayo, Niyi 454
Adegoroye, Goke 322
Adekeye, Muyiwa 450
Adeniyi, Segun 404-405, 474
Adenuga, Mike 104, 108-116, 235, 364
Adeola, Fola 173, 445
Adesokan, Abdulkareem, 98
Adetona, Oba Sikiru, 109
Adeyemi, Smart 257
Afenifere Renewal Group, (ARG), 422
African
- Capacity Development Foundation, 306
- University of Science and Technology, 305
- Institute for Applied Economics (AIAE), 187

Agabi, Kanu, 160
Agagu, Olusegun 117-118
Agbaje, Jimi, 422, 434-435, 445- 446
Agbakoba, Olisa 408
Agha, Kingsley 141, 214
Ago, Usman Sabo, 240
Agricultural show, 6
Agunloye, Olu, 100
Agusto, Bode, 173

615

Index

Ahmed, Ajuji, 53, 85
Ahmed, Yayale 259, 314, 322
Aigbogun, Moses 25
Ajanah, Maimuna 290
Ajanlekoko, Segun 37
Ajose-Adeogun, Mobolaji 290
Akagu-Jones, Peter 53, 202
Akerele, Toyosi 477
Akindele, Bode 122
Akinola, Peter 211
Akinrinade, Alani 429
Akiolu, Rilwan, 464
Akunyili, Dora 368, 404
Alghazali, Kalli 422, 434, 441
Alhassan, Ahmed, 25
Ali Amadu, 206, 295-296, 338, 341, 347, 349, 352,417
Ali, Mamman 78
Aliero, Adamu Mohammed 427, 259
Aliyu, Ibrahim 52-53, 55-58, 62, 65, 69
Aliyu, Babangida 281, 305, 448
Aliyu, Farouk Adamu 338
Allison, Ayida Panel, 324
Aluko, Yele, 445
Amadi, Sam, 441
Amalgamated Neighborhood and Corner Shop Owners Association, 285
Ameh, Sylva, 320
American Constitution, 338
Aminchi, Garba, 428
Aminu, Jibril 139
Amsterdam, Robert, 401
Amuchie, Success O. 250
Anenih, Tony 185, 338-339, 341, 343-344, 346, 348-349, 352, 358
Ama, Oka Kama 19
Anohu, Chinelo,78, 432- 433
Anwar, Auwalu 426
Anya, Anya O. 173
Anyim, Pius Anyim 245
Aondoakaa, Mike 402, 427, 461,

Area Boy Phenomenon, 483
Area Councils, 244
Arikawe, Akin, 170
Asemota, Solomon 438
Asika, Ajie Ukpabi 118
Asiodu, Philip 67
Askins, M.R. 30
Ayuba, John 76
Audu, Julius O, 10
Audu, Musa, 249-250
Aulakh, Ravi, 77
Awara, Kenneth 126
Awoniyi, Sunday 150
Azazi, Andrew Owoye 473-474
Aziz, Haruna Zego 80
Azodo, Edwin, 5

Baba, Ali 433
Baba ,Sabiu 24
Baba, Inuwa 427
Baba-Ahmed, Mouftah 47
Babafemi, Femi 399
Babalola, Lanre 78
Babangida, Ibrahim Badamasi 35, 41, 59, 109, 146-149, 331, 448-449, 463
Bai, Bello Kofar 15
Bai, Halilu Kofar 15
Bakare, Tunde, 428-429, 431-435, 438, 439, 443-447, 456-457, 459, 462-463, 465-466, 469, 471-472, 477
Baker S.V, 15, 17
Bala , Bashir 478
Balarabe Musa, Abdulkadir, 429
Balogun, Tafa, 165-167
Bamalli, Ibrahim Sidi 451
Barewa
 - College Days, 14-16
 - Old Boys Association (BOBA), 46
Bashir, Sambo Sago 272-276
Bathily, Abdoulaye, 426
Bathily, Naye, 426

Index 617

Beggar deportation and rehabilitation, 319
Bello, Adamu 453
Bello, Eniola 141
Bello, Mukhtar 18
Bello, Sir Ahmadu (Sardauna of Sokoto) 6-8
Bello-Osagie, Hakeem 119-120, 374, 398, 442, 445
Ben-Okagbue, Roz 78
Bilateral Air Services Agreements (BASAs), 118-119
Bilbis Ikra, Aliyu 259
Birdsall, Nancy 420
Blair, Tony 144, 189,389
Brown, Gordon 177, 189
Bruce, Ben 438
Bugaje, Usman 68, 70, 96, 146, 148-149, 235, 332, 338, 342, 346, 351, 445
Buhari, Muhammadu 39, 64, 193, 335-338, 351, 448, 450, 454, 457-459, 463-466, 471, 479
Bureau of Public Enterprises (BPE), 47, 68-71, 73-77, 79-81, 83, 85-87, 89, 91-95, 98-100, 102-107, 109-110, 112-117, 119-122, 124, 128-129, 131-135,139-140, 145, 152, 156,158-166, 169-170, 173, 183-184, 188, 194, 220, 227, 232, 291, 313, 325, 386, 392, 485
Bureau of Public Service Reforms (BPSR), 322, 324
Byer, Trevor, 79, 82, 98

Campaign for Democracy (CD), 429
Canadian International Development Agency, 189
Cardoso, Yemi, 81
Carter, Jimmy, 389
Centre for Global Development (CGD), 425, 442
Certificate of Occupancy, 240,244-245, 252, 272, 280, 286, 292
Chalker, Baroness Lynda, 171, 188, 356
Challenges Abuja Faced in 2003, 280-281
Change Nigeria Project, (CNP), 420
Charles De Gaulle, 389
Chidoka, Osita, 361, 417
Chife, Aloy, 432, 436
Chikelu, Sonia, 224-225
Chikwe Kema, 118-120, 220
Child Rights Act, 225-226
Chirac, President, 148-149, 296
Christian Association of Nigeria, 210
Chukwumerije, Uche, 344
Ciroma Adamu, 67, 149, 170, 451
Ciroma, Liman, 149
Civil
 – Liberties Organisation, 408
 – Service Reform Decree. No., 43, 1988, 323
Clark, Paul, 235
Clinton, Bill, 144, 390
Code of Conduct Tribunal (CCT), 273, 275,438
Cole, Hadiza, 202
Collier, Paul, 420
Constitutional
 – amendment, 330-331, 333-334, 338, 344, 346, 352
 – immunity, 340
Contract sanctity, 84
Counter-coup, 1966, 7
CPC, 430, 435,441, 446-451, 454, 457-458, 462-465, 467, 471,476
Cultural Revolution, 491
Current Replacement cost Method, 268

Dabo, Abba 107
Dada, Bamidele 233
Dakingari, Saidu 424
Danfodio, Usman 8

Dangote, Aliko 152-153, 364, 371
Daniel, Gbenga 459
Danjuma, T.Y. 152, 279, 303, 467
Dansadau, Saidu, 344
Dantata, Ahmen 34
Dappa Biriye, Harold, 7
Dariye, Joshua 151
Dasuki, Ahmed 445
Dasuki, Ibrahim 84
Debt Management Office, 170
Democracy Day, 59
Department for International Development (DFID), 78, 310
 - grants, 79
Design Cost Associates (Project Management), 35
Destitution management programme, 319
Demographic explosion, 278
Dije Hajiya, 5
Dikko, Buhari, 304
Dikko Hassan, 19
Dikko Husaini, 18, 47-48, 456
Dikko, Umaru, 335
Dokpesi, Raymond, 440
Dorgu, Charles, 302
Douglas, Oronto, 468
Due Process, 182-187
 - Reforms, 172
Duke, Donald, 430, 445
Duru, Nze Chidi 79-80

Economic
 - and Financial Crimes Commission (EFCC), 152, 156, 158-169, 182, 193, 222, 233, 242, 245, 249-250, 339, 359, 367, 378-380, 382, 399, 401-402, 412, 418 437-438
 - Reform, 238
   - Agenda, 271
   - programme, 157, 177, 189, 263, 313
 - team, 155
 - stabilisation, 157
Ediebvie, David, 427
Edigheji, Omano, 455
Edun, Wale, 81
Edu, Yomi, 235

Education
 - Management Information System (EMIS) 310
 - Sector Plan, (ESP), 310
 - Tax Fund, 309
Ekpenyong, Ita 16, 470, 472-473
Ekpo, Eyo 78
Ekwueme, Alex 448-449
Electric Power
 - Policy, 98
 - Sector Reform Bill (EPSP), 98-99
 - Sector Steering Committee (EPIC), 98
El-Rufai
 - as
   - Director General of Bureau of Public Enterprises (BPE), 68-71
   - Minister of FCT, 139
   - President, Quantity Surveying Student Association, 21
 - At
   - Barewa College, 14-16
   - Daudawa Primary School, 10
   - FCT, 199-206
   - George Wimpey, 25-31
   - Harvard Business School (HBS), 129, 131
   - Islamic School, 10
   - Local Education Authority Primary School, Kano, 10

- New Nigeria
Construction Company,
33
- birth of, 1
  - early career thoughts, 20
  - early days in private practice, 36-38
  - National Youth Service Corps Year, 24-31
El-Rufai & Partners (Chartered Quantity Surveyors), 35, 69, 74-51, 115, 124-125, 135, 370, 476
El-Rufai, Ahmed 42
El-Rufai, Aisha Garba Haliru 455
El-Rufai, Asia Mohammed 69, 74
El-Rufai, Aziza 42, 44
El-Rufai, Bashir (Jr), 42
El-Rufai, Bashir Ahmad 5-6, 9-11, 15, 45, 52, 65,
El-Rufai, Bilqis 42
El-Rufai, Hadiza 39, 41, 74, 387, 478
El-Rufai, Hamza 42
El-Rufai, Ibrahim 42
El-Rufai, Mohammed Bello 42, 44, 49, 387, 396, 432, 442
El-Rufai, Mustapha 42
El-Rufai, Ramla 42, 44
El-Rufai, Yasmin, 41-42, 44, 69, 415, 434-436,442-443, 472, 477-479
El-Rufai, Zulkiflu, 42
Engaging Ex-president, 333-338
Eno, Augustine, 19
Environment Seven
 - (E7) Nigeria Limited, 34
 - Chicago, USA, 34
Enwerem, Evans 245
Eriobuna, Nnamdi 98-99, 101
Ethnic minorities, 7
Euro crisis, 61
Ezeife, Chukumama 245
Ezekwesili, Chinedu 478
Ezekwesili, Oby 65, 143, 156, 167-169, 171, 174-175,177-179,181- 191, 193, 195, 233, 368, 387, 398, 407, 416-417, 445-446, 457, 478

Fagge, Sheikh Mamman 14
Falana, Femi 421, 429
Famakinwa, Dipo 434
Fani Kayode, Femi 368, 417, 429, 478
Fashakin, Rotimi 468
Fashawe, Otunba 234-235
Fashola, Babatunde Raji 24,432,445, 454
Fatima (Umma)Ibrahim 4
Federal Capital Development Authority (FCDA), 95, 211, 215-216, 217, 227, 230, 237, 255, 279, 293
Federal
 - Capital Territory
 - Act, 242
 - Action Committee on AIDs (FACA), 311
 - Committee in Street Naming and House Numbering, 267
 - Decree, 279
 - FCT's Abuja Mass Transit Company (RED),307
 - Character, 74, 321
  - Principles, 150
 - Civil Service Commission (FCSC), 315, 327
 - Housing Authority (FHA), 243
 - Mortgage Bank of Nigeria (FMBN), 268, 270
 - Teachers Scheme, 309
Feese, member 477
Feiba, Owen, 278
Fika, Adamu 327, 338
Financial Action Task Force (FATF), 159, 165
Folawiyo, Tunde 81
Ford Foundation, 391

Frazer, Jendayi 382, 425
Functus Officio The Great Land Grab, 257-260
Fundamentalist ideology and beliefs, 9
Furo Bello Dauda, 31

Gabam, Shehu 478-479
Gadzama, Afakirya 16, 46, 383
Galadima, Buba 463
Gana, Jerry 430
Gana, Umar Abba 106
Gandi, Sule Yar 344
Gandonu, Ajato, 279
Gaon, Nessim 84-85
Garba, Bature Shehu 75
Gbadamos, Rasheed 55-56
Gbajabiamila, Femi 338
Geographical Information System, 251
Gidado, Hamza 5
Gimba, Abubakar 53-54
Giwa, Shehu Lawal 37
Goje, Danjuma 83, 445
Good Governance Group (3G)
 - formation of, 422, 425
Gowon, Yakubu 17, 46, 110, 278
Grampton, E.P.T., 17
Grampton, George Audu, 17
Gross Revenues from Sale of House, 269-270
GSM network, 122-123
Gumi, Sheikh Abubakar Mahmud, 8-9
Gummi, Lawal Hassan, 202
Gusau, Aliyu Mohammed 146, 436, 438, 448, 463
Gwandu, Sani 7
Gwandu, Ahmadu 7

Hallett, Deborah Hughes 398
Hamidu, Sagir 199
Hamma, Sule Yahaya 447, 463
Hamza, Yahaya 14-15, 20, 45-47, 144

Haruna, Mohammed 439
Haruna, Boni 151
Harvard Business School, 46.129,131
Hehir, Brian 388
Hino Hiroyuki, 60
HIV/AIDS Control Programmes, 211
Hobgood, Tom, 77
Honourary Presidential Advisory Council on Investments (HPACI), 356
Human Capital Development, 308-311

Ibe, Frances Charity 224,226
Ibn Na'Allah, Bala 338
Ibori, James 151, 177, 366-367, 371, 427, 461
Ibrahim, Bashir Yusuf 76, 173, 219, 235, 474
Ibrahim, Bukar Abba 454
Ibrahim, Danjuma 221, 223
Ibrahim, Isyaku 150
Ibrahim, Jimoh 107
Ibrahim, Toyin (Youth Corps Member), 163
Icha, Greg 34
ICPC - Independent Corruption Practices Commission, 168-169
Idris, Gidado 53
Idris, Akilu 211
Gudado 53
IFC, 119
Igbinedion, Lucky 151, 245
Ige Bola 82-83,113
Ighodalo, Asue 143,173, 183-184, 240, 445, 473
Igweh, J.U.108-109, 290-294
Ikimi, Tom 443
Illegal Land Conversions in Kubwa, 287-289
International Planning Associates, 279
Imam, Kashim Ibrahim 226-227, 230

Imam, Shehu Inuwa 427
Imoehe, Ambassador 407, 411
Imoke, Liyel 417
Independent National Electoral Commission (INEC), 366, 435, 447, 458, 461-462, 465
Indigeneship rights, 303
Indigenization programme, 391
Ingawa, Abba Bello, 18-19, 35, 47-49
Institute of Quantity Surveyors (IQS), 27
Integrated Payroll and personnel Information System, 326
Intercellular Nigeria Limited, 6, 52, 68
International
  - Monetary Fund (IMF), 53, 59-62, 148, 179, 189, 426
  - staff Monitored programme (SMP), 60
  - type structural adjustment programme, 36
  - Planning Associates (IPA), 206
Iro, Ismail 240, 438
Isaiah, Sam Nda 408, 434, 437-438, 448
Isiadinso, Ezogu 37
Islamic
  - jurisprudence, 9, 11
  - law of inheritance, 5
Isma, Muhammad Musa, 278
Iwuagwu, Amah 53, 62, 68, 138, 169
Iya, Shehu 66

Jae, Saidu Abdu 14
Jakande, Lateef 454
Jama'at Nasril Islam, 9, 210, 273
Jefferson, Williams 232, 234
Jega, Attahiru 462
Jeter, Howard 128-129
Jibrin, Altine 245, 438
Jimoh, Abdulkadir 438

Jonathan, Goodluck 16, 57, 356, 427, 433, 437, 439-445, 448, 451-455, 458, 465, 467-470, 473-475, 479
Jones, Peter Akagu 426

Kaita, Muntari Abdu 15
Kalgo, Sani, 281
Kalu, Orji Uzor 151
Kamba, Muhammadu 244-245
Kanu, Ndubuisi 429
Kapoor, Anil 98
Kawu, Abdulkadir, 37
Kekere-Ekun, Akin 93, 102-103, 173
Khodorkovsky, Mikhail 401
Kidnapping problem 483
Kingibe, Babagana 417
Kingsmill, William 128
Kirfi, Bello 314
Kissinger, Henry 389
Kohl, Helmut 148-149
Kolawole, Simon 434
Kolo, Aishetu Fatima 78, 202
Komolafe, Kayode 421
Kubwa
  - Resettlement Project, 250
  - Residents Association (KUREWA), 288
Kumo, Suleiman 338
Kupolokun, Funsho 156
Kuruduma/kpaduma/Apo Tafyi Layouts, 286-287
Kwasau, Muhammadu 4
Kyari, Abba 450

Labour Party (LP), 430, 435, 446, 448, 459
Land
  - Administration system, 240
  - Allocation Organisations, 243
  - Information System, 241, 244
  - Reforms, 238-262
  - Use Act, 242, 246

- use regulations, 280
Lanti, 7
Law
- Administration in 2003, 246-253
- Allocation Criteria, 246-248
- Information System (LIS,) 251
Lawal, Balarabe Abbas 422, 434, 440-442, 451, 456, 473
Lawal, Hassan Mohammed 259
Lawal, Jimi 224-225, 265,432, 434, 437, 443, 445-446, 456-457
Lawan, Maina Ma'aji 245
Leautier, Frannie 306
Lega Basis for Law Reforms, 252-253
Lemu, Sheikh Ahmed 211
Levinson, Riva 401, 421
Liadi, Salisu 75
Liman, Widi 199, 214
London Club debts, 180
Low Income Countries Under Stress (LICUS). 173
Lukman, Salihu 422, 434, 441,446

Mabogunje, Akin, 303
Maccido, Muhammadu 334
Maduekwe, Ojo 52, 220, 338, 349, 352, 417
Mahdi, Abubakar 245
Mahmood, Aminu 19
Mahmood, Ibrahim 34
Maikudi, Sani 15, 18-20, 33, 46, 47-48, 369-370, 434
Mairami, Muhammed 211
Makinde, Bankole 210, 211
Mankiewicz, Frank 235
Mantu, Ibrahim 133-134, 135-141, 143-144, 199, 338, 341
Martins, Kola, 285
Martins, Pedro, 279
Mark, David 344, 346
Masari, Aminu 332, 341, 349-350, 422, 429, 440-442, 446-447, 451,
Massachusetts Institute of Technology (M.I.T), 46
Masters, Carl 364
Mbeki, Thabo 108
Mckenna, CMS Cameron 98
Militancy in Niger Delta, 483
Military
- coup, 1966, 7
- Rule, 63
Mimiko, Olusegun 430
Mitterrand, President 148
Modibbo, Aliyu 257-259, 373, 377-379, 478
Mohammed, Abdullahi 175, 259, 346, 398
Mohammed, Bello Haliru 427
Mohammed, Dantata 53
Mohammed, Lai 436
Mohammed, Murtala 17, 46, 279, 484
Mohammed, Naja'atu 422, 434
Mohammed, Sheikh Musa 211
Mohammed, Waziri 153
Momoh, Tony 463, 476
Moneke, Godson 37
Monetization of Fringe Benefits, 325
Money
- Laundering
- Act, 159
- Law Enforcement, 191
Morgan Commission, 324
Moss, Todd 425
Muazu Usman, 19
Muhammad, Ahmad Rufai 3-5
Mukhtar, Abdu 163
Mukhtar, Abdulahii Sarki 259
Mukhtar Mansur 24, 53, 76, 169-170
Mukhtar, Abdu 78, 202, 266
Mukhtar, Abdullahi Sarki 233, 407, 427, 429
Mukhtar, Sarki 409
Mukoshy, Ibrahim 211

Mustapha, A.U. 474, 476
Mustapha, Abdul-Hakeem, 382
Mutallab, Umar Farouk 431

Na'Abba, Ghali Umar 100
Narula, Rajneesh 17
Nasko, Gado, 284, 288
National
- Council on Privatization, 68, 87, 100
- Economic Empowerment and Development Strategy (NEEDS), 157, 189-190, 313-314
- Intelligence Agency (NIA), 406-407, 411
- Mosque, 211
- Office of Industrial Property (now NOTAP), 85
- Population Commission, 366
- Salaries and Wages Commission, 77
- Telecommunications Policy, 121
- Unity Line (Green), 307
NCP, 75, 80, 110, 122
- code of conduct, 107
Ndanusa, Umaru 93
Ndayako, Umaru Sanda 150
NDIC, 73
Negroponte, Nicholas, 309
Nelson Mandela Institute, 305-306
NERA of South Africa, 98
New Nigeria
- Construction Company, 33
- Development Company (NNDC), 46-47, 75
New York Stock Exchange, 125
Nicon Insurance Corporations, 85
NIDB (now Bank of Industry), 55
Nigerian National Petroleum Corporation (NNPC), 101, 106-107, 156, 364

Nigeria
- Communication Commission (NCC), 79
- Telecommunications Limited (NITEL), 120-129
Nigerian
- Civil War, 7, 12, 28, 64
- Institute of Quantity Surveyors (NIQs), 21, 37
- Investment Promotion Commission (NIPC), 171
Njiddah, Ibrahim Shehu 73, 93, 159
Nnamani Ken, 332, 341, 344, 348-349, 352, 422, 440-442, 429, 446
Nnanna, Joe 156
Northern Political Leaders Forum, 451, 454
Nwuba, Nnamdi 19
Nwabuikwu, Paul 180
Nweke, Frank 235
Nwosisi, Alex 37
Nyako, Abdullahi 68-69
Nye, Joe 389

Obaigbena, Nduka 146, 148-149, 438, 473-474
Obasanjo Presidential Library, 364
Obasanjo, Iyabo 368
Obasanjo, Olusegun 27-28, 57, 62-70, 79, 82-83, 87, 97, 100-101, 103-105, 107-109, 116-120, 122, 124-128, 132-134, 136-137, 139-140, 142, 144-145, 147-153, 155, 157, 160, 167, 169, 170-171, 173-175, 177-183, 185-190 195, 197-198, 206, 208- 209, 212, 220, 229, 235, 241, 245-246, 250, 252-253, 256, 259, 265, 278-280, 282, 288, 319, 323, 330-340, 342-368, 370-372, 374, 376-377, 381, 389-391, 416-418, 431, 435, 438, 441, 450-455, 458-461, 467, 473, 475, 487
Obaseki, Gaius 389

Obiora Ikechukwu 257
Obozuwa, Somi 477
Ocha, Sadiq 104
Odidi, Isa 420, 434
Odumakin, Yinka 422, 428, 430, 432, 434, 443, 445-447, 468
Offor, Emeka 100
Ogan, O.K., 279
Ogbeh, Audu 132, 197-198
Ogbeha, Tunde 344
Ogundamisi, Kayode 472
Ogunlewe, Adeseye 207
Ogunmola, Olu, 282
Ogunsakin, Tunde 399
Ogwuma, Paul 55
Ohakim, Ikedi 448-449
Ojo, Bayo 233, 274, 417
Ojo, Mr. 110
Ojudu, Babafemi 421- 422, 432, 435
Ojukwu, Stella 387
Okagbue, Roz Ben 429, 432
Okechukwu, Osita 429
Okei-Odumakin, Joe 429
Okereke-Onyieri, Felix 37
Okilo, Melford 7
Okocha, Peter 101, 104-105, 107
Okonjo-Iweala, Ngozi 138, 143, 155, 169-176-184, 187-190, 192-195, 368, 387, 416, 421, 445-446, 457, 459, 478
Okoye, Festus 429
Okoye, William 210-211
Okpa-Obaji 75
Olaja, Martins 140-141
Olojede, Amma Ogan 443-444
Olojede, Dele 362, 424, 436, 443-444, 473, 492
Olowolafe, Tunji 432
Omakwu, Sarah 21
Omar, Aliyu 24, 28-29
Omokri, Reno 468
Omolewa, Lucky 298
Onagoruwa, Bola 114, 225-226

Onaiyekan, Archbishop 211
Onoyiveta, Mustapha 427
Onwuanibe, Angela 387, 478
Onyeagocha, Uche 434-435
Onyia, Ejike 93
Open Market Value (OMV), 268-269, 274
 - Approach, 268
Orire, Murtala 210-211
Oronsaye, Steve 67, 69, 126-127, 156, 170-171, 324, 458
Orubebe, Godsday 439, 451-453
Oshiomole, Adams 93
Oshun, Olawale 434-435, 445-446
Oshuntokun, Akin 458
Osibodu, Funke 131
Osomo, Mobolaji 265
Osuji Charles, 110-114, 140
Osunbor, Oserhiemen, 348
Osuntoki, Akin 131
Osuntokun, Akin, 434-435
Otedola, Femi, 107
Othman, Idris, 216, 434, 456, 473
Otto von Bismarek, 389
Owete, O.W.E., 37
Oyebode, Gbenga, 81
Oyedele, Ife, 463
Ozigi, Albert, 297

Paris Club, 177
 - Debt relief, 61, 170-171, 189, 195
Pay Reform and Medium Term Pay Policy, 325
Penal code, 8
Peoples Democratic Party (PDP), 147, 149, 151, 194, 198, 235, 291, 295-296, 315, 338, 341 416-417, 427, 433, 440-442, 445-447, 449, 451-454, 457, 461-466
PDP Reform Forum, 440
Peter, Segun, 322
Peterside, Atedo, 445
Petroleum

- (Special) Trust Fund (PTF), 64, 67
- Technology Development Fund (PTDF), 232, 234-235

Phido, Tony, 170
Philips, Dotun, 324
Piercy, Jan, 187
Pilot Mortgage System, 270-271
Pioneers of Abuja, 279-280
Poisonous politics, 6
Police Service Commission, 429
Political
- parties, 52,58, 456
- Platform, 194
- realm, 7
- successors, 7

Politics and Ethics of Statecraft, 388-390
Power
- Purchase Agreement (PPA), 82
- Sector reform programme, 79, 82, 99

Presidential
- election, 58
- International Advisory Council, 171

Privatisation
- programme, 87, 188
- and Commercialisation
- Act, 163
- programme, 67,92
- Council, 67, 75, 77, 97, 111-112, 103 104, 122, 363
- decree, 68
- programme, 61, 68, 77, 129

Programme Implementation and Monitoring
  Committee (PIMCO), 53-55, 58-60, 62, 67, 76, 85, 169

Proquest Consultants (Procurement Advisory), 35
Public
- sector reform, 63, 157
- Service Reform, 320, 322
- programme, 314

Team (PSRT), 316, 324-326
- creation of, 321-0322
- Service Rules and Financial Regulations

Quadri, Yinka, 434

Raux-Cassin, Dominique, 294
Reform programmes, 60
Religious
- Anarchism of Boko Haram, 483
- war-Jihad, 8

Resettlement of Original Inhabitants, 303-305
Review and update of, 326
Ribadu Nuhu, 107,156, 158-169, 193-194, 196, 221, 235, 335, 344, 346, 354, 357-364, 368, 371, 375, 411, 417-420, 422, 424, 429-430, 435-436, 438, 442-446, 456, 471, 478
Roosevelt, Theodore, 487
Royal Institution of Chartered Surveyors (RICS), 27, 35
Rufai Ali, 380
Ruma Sayyadi Abba, 259, 427

Sachs, Jeffrey, 62, 156, 183, 186
Sale Process of Government Houses in Abuja, 269
Salimonu, Dipo, 478
Sall Khalifa, 425-427
Sambo Bashir, 210-211, 272-276
Sambo, Namadi, 439-440, 466
Sanda, Umaru, 14
Sanders, Robin, 428, 466
Sani, Hadiza Dagabana, 163
Sani, Shehu, 429
Sani, Uba, 146, 429, 471
Sarai, Boko, 341
Saraki Bukola, 371, 424, 427
Sarkin Maska Shehu, 7

Satellite Towns Development Agency (STDA), 312, 304-305
Save Nigeria Group (SNG), 428, 438, 448
Securities and Exchange Commission (SEC), 106
Sekibo, Abiye, 441
Shagari, Shehu, 334-336
Shagaya, John, 430
Sharia Law, 8
Sheikh Sabah College (Sardauna Memorial College), 9
Shuaibu Kabir, 479
Shuaibu, Lawali, 166, 344
Smith, Craig, 235
Social Democratic Mega Party (SDMP), 446
Sodangi, Abubakar Danso, 379
Sodango Senator, 257-258
Sokoto caliphate, 8
Solarin, Tai, 278
Soleye, Tunde, 53, 59
Soludo, Charles Chukwuma, 156, 169, 187-193, 195
Sonic Global Company (Yellow), 307
Soyinka, Wole, 430
State Security Service (SSS), 16, 222-223
Stephen Matthew, 19
Stock exchange, 74, 101, 363
Street naming and house numbering scheme, 284
Structural Adjustment Programme, (SAP), 36, 323
Success, Amuchie, 244-245
Sudan Telecom, 6

Tafida, Dalhatu Sarki, 133, 338, 407, 409, 412
Tariqah sects, 14
Task Force on Master Plan Enforcement, 282-283
TCPC, 47
Tenure elongation, 329
Test of Leadership, 485-487
Thatcher, Margaret, 101
Theory of Second Coming, 390-393
Third term project, 57, 331, 338, 346-347, 351, 356, 417
 – initiation of 339-346
Tilde, Yusuf, 427
Tinubu Bola, 81-82, 63, 425, 429, 442, 457
Tinubu, Wale, 81
Tostevin, Mattew, 433
Transparency International., 145, 391, 183-184
Tsaiyabu, Yusuf, 320
Tsiga, Ismaila, 9
Tudor Davis Commission, 323
Tukur Hassan, 439, 452
Dr. Tukur Mahmud, 335, 338, 450
Uba, Andy, 339, 349, 352, 356, 371
Udoji, Jerome,. 324
Udoma Udo Udoma, 445
UK Property Services Agent, 40
Ukpo, Anthony, 53
Umar Baba Kura, 257
Umar, Abdullahi Idris, 99
Umar, Abubakar Dangiwa, 429
Umar, Ahmed, 406
Umar, Dangiwa, 429
Un-issued Letters of Offer (R of O), 253-254
Uranta, Tony, 439
Usman Ismaila, 55-57, 60
Usman, Hassan Musa, 78, 123
Usman, Nemadi, 138, 175-176, 178-180
Usman, Shamsuddeen, 55
Usman, Yusuf Bala, '19
Utomi, Pat, 445-446, 454
Uwais, Mohammed Lawal, 58, 202, 275

Valuation of the Properties for Sale, 267-269
Verr, Bernard, 47, 73-74

Wabara, Adolphus, 199
Wade, Abdoulaye, 425-427
Wali, Salahu Naibi, 19
Wallis, William, 470
Wanka, Ado, 131
Washington Consensus, 61
Water supply (in Abuja), 226-232
Waziri, Adamu Maina, 307, 422, 429, 442, 447
Waziri, Farida, 379, 399-401, 418, 453, 479
Weidenfeld, Ed, 235
Western education, 2, 8
Whitaker, Rosa, 398
Whitman, Hans, 278
Wilson, Woodrow, 389
Wolfensohn, James, 170-173
World
- Bank Young Professional Programme, 78
- Computer Exchange Programme, 309
Wsa, Andy, 185-186

Yabani, Hauwa, 306
Yadudu Auwalu, 56

Yahaya, Lai, 78
Yahaya, Sulayman, 234
Yakassai, Ibrahim Adamu, 19
Yakowa, Patrick, 451
Yakubu Musa, 56
Yakubu Tanimu, 271, 306, 357, 371, 373, 376, 401, 427
Yakubu, Suraj, 171
Yar' Adua Turai, 424, 427, 431, 434, 438, 479
Yar'Adua, Umaru Musa, 15, 18, 46, 57, 248, 257, 354-360, 362, 364, 367-377, 378-381, 387-388, 395, 399-405, 407-410, 413-415, 417, 419-421, 423-424, 427, 430, 433, 437, 439, 442, 461
Yari, Abdullahi, 123
Yesufu, Aljahi, 53
Yew, Lee Kuan, 197, 355
Young Andrew, 83
Yuguda, Isa, 424
Yusuf Luka, 46
Yusuf, Yahaya, 289
Zakari, Amina Bala, 426
Zayyad, Hamza, 45-47, 75, 92
Ziaoping, Deng, 491
Zoning, 150
Zwingina, Jonathan, 98, 133-139, 141-144, 199, 245